History of Economic Thought

Third Edition

Harry Landreth
Centre College

David C. Colander
Middlebury College

Houghton Mifflin Company Boston Toronto
Geneva, Illinois   Palo Alto   Princeton, New Jersey

Sponsoring editor: *Denise Clinton*
Development editor: *Kelly Faughnan*
Associate project editor: *Susan Merrifield*
Associate production/design coordinator: *Jennifer Waddell*
Senior manufacturing coordinator: *Priscilla Bailey*
Marketing manager: *Robert D. Wolcott*

Cover design: Judy Arisman; cover image: Ricardo—University College Library, ms. Angl. 11/26, David Ricardo to Hutches Trowers, 12 Nov 1819; Keynes and Marshall—Marshall Library, University of Cambridge; Smith—Edinburgh University Library; Marx—*Karl Marx Frederick Engels Collected Works,* Volume 1, compiled by the Institute of Marxism-Leninism, Moscow

Part opener credits:

Part I: Aristotle and St. Thomas Aquinas: The Bettmann Archive; William Petty and François Quesnay: Historical Collections, Baker Library, Graduate School of Business Administration, Harvard University

Part II: Adam Smith, David Ricardo, and John Stuart Mill: Historical Collections, Baker Library, Graduate School of Business Administration, Harvard University; Karl Marx: courtesy of German Information Center

Part III: William Stanley Jevons: Stock Montage; Carl Menger and Alfred Marshall: Historical Collections, Baker Library, Graduate School of Business Administration, Harvard University; Léon Walras: Université de Lausanne, Switzerland

Part IV: Thorstein Bunde Veblen: Brown Brothers; John R. Commons: State Historical Society of Wisconsin; Joseph Alois Schumpeter: The Bettmann Archive; Ludwig von Mises: photo by Bettina Bien Greaves, courtesy of Foundation for Economic Education, Irvington, N.Y.

Part V: Irving Fisher: The Bettmann Archive; John Maynard Keynes: courtesy of Dr. Milo Keynes; Paul Samuelson: courtesy of Paul Samuelson; Milton Friedman: photograph by Bachrach

Chapters 5, 12, and 16: Excerpts from *The General Theory of Employment, Interest, and Money* by John Keynes are reprinted by permission of Harcourt Brace Jovanovich, Inc.

Printed in the U.S.A.

Library of Congress Catalog Card Number: 93-78675
ISBN: 0-395-66858-1

123456789-AM-97 96 95 94 93

For Donna and Patrice

Contents

P A R T

II Classical Economic Thought, Malthus, and Marx   60

CHAPTER 4 Adam Smith   67

CHAPTER 6   J. S. Mill and the Decline of Classical Economics   144

CHAPTER 7 Karl Marx   **174**

P A R T

III   Neoclassical Economic Thought   210

CHAPTER 8   Jevons, Menger, and Austrian Foundations of Marginal Analysis   213

CHAPTER **9** **The Transition to Neoclassical Economics: Marginal Analysis Extended**   **235**

CHAPTER **10** **Walras and General Equilibrium Theory**   **266**

CHAPTER 11 **Alfred Marshall and Neoclassical Economics**   **285**

PART

IV **Heterodox Economic Thought**   **318**

CHAPTER 14 The Development of Modern Heterodox Economic Thought   **380**

Preface

Economic ideas are important. But, too often in the teaching of modern economics, emphasis on techniques overwhelms ideas. We find that sad. Ideally economics courses would eschew the teaching of techniques for its own sake, but mathematical economics has become too deeply ingrained into the economics curriculum to allow that to happen in the near future. Concerned economics departments must, therefore, resort to a second best solution, namely provision of a course in the history of economic thought.

We have written this book not for the scholar but for the student. Hence we've tried to strike a balance between oversimplification and extreme complexity, and to cover important issues in an intellectually satisfying manner while remaining clear and interesting to the undergraduate. And since most students justifiably seek relevance, we structure the book to demonstrate how uniquely relevant the history of economic thought really is to our discipline. Students should benefit enormously from the insights and historical contexts this text provides as a backdrop to the material they encounter in other courses.

In our discussion of modern theory, we do not rehash the content of standard economic courses, but instead provide interpretations of recent theory grounded in the knowledge of past literature. History-of-thought books without any assessment of the place and significance of past writers have voids where their hearts should be. We leave it to the reader to weigh our assessments, however, and students should expect differences between their teachers' assessments and ours.

Similarities to the Second Edition

The core of this book is the same as the last edition. As in the last edition, we not only discuss methodology in an introductory chapter but also integrate it into each subsequent section. We explicitly examine the scope of economics as it has been viewed by major economists and schools and cover not only pre-1900 heterodox economic ideas, but modern non-mainstream theory as well. This book discusses the development of the scope, method, and content of economics from about 1200 to the present, examining each writer or group of writers from several different vantage points. It treats particular theoretical contributions in some detail so that the internal workings of given theoretical structures may be articulated. We also discuss the broad policy implications of theories and their impact on subsequent developments in theory and policy. Almost no mathematical notation is used, and the number of graphs is deliberately limited.

Changes from the Second Edition

The first change is on the title page; the title of this book is now the history of economic thought rather than the history of economic theory. Usage now seems to indicate that "history of economic theory" suggests a narrowly focused book dealing with how past ideas have contributed to the content of mainstream orthodox economic theory. Our previous editions have explicitly indicated, however, that we felt it important to present heterodox as well as orthodox economic ideas. Thus, our change in title to "thought" rather than "theory" does not represent a change in content but a change in terminology to conform to nuances of current usage.

Besides the change in title there are substantial differences from the last edition. First, we now divide the book into five parts, preclassical, classical, neoclassical, heterodox, and recent economic thought, covering major groupings of writers in each section. We provide a brief introduction for each part to make it easier for the student to follow the broad evolution of schools of thought. Second, we reorganized a number of chapters to respond to very useful reviewer comments. For example, we now have two chapters on preclassical economic theory and expanded coverage of mercantilist thinkers. The chapter on the emergence of marginal analysis was divided into two, to allow for expanded treatment of Jevons and Menger and an entire chapter on Walras' contributions to general equilibrium theory.

The third and most substantial change is the addition of three new chapters: Chapter 12, on early critics of neoclassical economics, which includes extensive coverage of institutionalists and the historical school; Chapter 13, on economic thinking about socialism and capitalism; and Chapter 17, on the history of econometrics and empirical methods, which reflects recent interesting work. We included Chapter 13, because we felt that with current developments in the former Soviet Union, a reflective chapter on thinking about economic systems would be helpful to the students. Chapters 12 and 13 together with the chapter on recent heterodox thought comprise, moreover, an entire section on heterodox economics. These new chapters, and the reorganized framework within which they are presented, should add significantly to the book.

A fourth change is a slight decrease in and simplification of the coverage of modern economic thought stemming out of difficulties many professors have in covering so much material in a single term. We fully understand the difficulty; we too have often run out of time in teaching a comprehensive course. We believe that these chapters in Part V are useful, however, even if they are not covered in class, but are simply read by students. They are written so students can read, rather than be taught them, since they do not focus on technical issues covered in other classes, but instead provide interpretative materials that complement other classes.

That is why we call Part V, Recent Economic Thought: Understanding the Present Through the Past.

A fifth change lies in our description of economic policy. Since economic thought is the basis for economic policy, we have emphasized how economists and policy-makers take economic theory and a particular set of goals and derive from them recommendations for economic policy. Taking the standard dichotomy between positive and normative economics, we suggest that the art of economics, an application of the best economic theory to the given normative goal, involves analytical skills often overlooked by economists, who tend to focus instead on abstract theory. Adam Smith was a master at the art of economics, deriving policy recommendations always in the context of the institutions of his time. The distinctions between the science of economics, normative goals, and the art of economics, presented in Chapter 1, provides a theme carried forward wherever appropriate throughout the remainder of the book.

A sixth change in the book concerns pedagogy. At the beginning of each chapter where several theorists are covered, we list the important writers, their principle contributions to economic literature, and the date of their publication. At the end of each chapter we have added questions for review, discussion, and research. One of these questions in relevant chapters is a "back to the original sources" question. Its purpose is to send the student to the library examining original sources. Even if they only skim the sources, it is a step in the right direction. As in the last edition, a bibliography of suggested readings follows each chapter. We have carefully selected a few readings in both secondary and original sources rather than dazzle the student with a long list.

People to Thank

This book, like most books, has relied on many important contributions from others besides the authors. Helen Reiff was a key person from start to finish. Our students, colleagues, and the academic administrations at Centre and Middlebury indirectly helped much by providing an intellectually stimulating environment. Others we want to thank for their valuable advice and critical insights are:

William Allen, University of California, Los Angeles
Cecily Armstrong, Centre College
Bradley Bateman, Grinnell College
John Bethune, Bellarmine College
Stanley R. Campbell, Centre College
A. W. Coats, Duke University and University of Nottingham
Steve Cunningham, University of Connecticut
Richard Du Boff, Bryn Mawr College
Louis Falkson, Cornell University
John Farris, Centre College
Peter Garlick, SUNY College at New Paltz
Mary Beth Garriott, Centre College

Robert E. Glass, Centre College
Daniel Hammond, Wake Forest University
Suzanne Helburn, University of Colorado at Denver
Bruce Johnson, Centre College
Connie Klimke, Centre College
Mark Knell, Middlebury College
S. Todd Lowry, Washington and Lee University
David McFarland, University of North Carolina at Chapel Hill
Judy Nystrom, Centre College
Dianne Pasick, Centre College
Sandra Peart, Baldwin Wallace College
Joseph Persky, University of Illinois
Sunder Rameswamy, Middlebury College
Donald A. Walker, Indiana University of Pennsylvania
Phanindra V. Wannava, Middlebury College
Harold Wolozin, University of Massachusetts, Boston
Nancy Wulwick, Old Dominion College

We are indebted to the many professionals at Houghton Mifflin Company who have contributed considerably to the final product. In particular we want to thank Denise Clinton, sponsoring editor; Kelly Faughnan, development editor; Susan Merrifield, associate project editor; and Rosemary Winfield, senior project editor, for their expert assistance in every phase of the book's production.

Our greatest debts, however, are to Donna Landreth and Patrice Colander to whom this book is dedicated.

H. L.
D. C.

 **Introduction**

"The beginnings and endings of all human undertakings are untidy . . ."

—John Galsworthy

The aim of this work is to chart the development of economics through the ages, demonstrating primarily how past mainstream thought has contributed to the scope and content of modern economics, but also discussing deviations from orthodoxy that have helped to shape contemporary economic thought. The book considers major methodological issues, explains the relationships between the development of a theory and the prevailing economic conditions, and examines the internal working of theories that provide particularly useful insights. It also explains the significance of particular ideas to the development of theory and the broader implications of theory for the formulation of economic and social policy.

In doing so it recognizes that economic thought consists of both a vision and a formal theory. The vision is the broad perception with which individuals look at the world. The theory comprises the specific models that capture the vision. To understand the thought of individual economists, one must understand both their vision and their model.

THE CENTRAL FOCUS OF MODERN ECONOMIC THOUGHT

Economics is a social science. It examines the problems that societies face because individuals desire to consume more goods and services than are available, which creates a problem of relative scarcity. Wants are generally unlimited and apparently insatiable, whereas resources (which are often subdivided into land, labor, capital, and entrepreneurship) are limited. To meet the problem of scarcity, a social

mechanism is required for allocating limited resources among unlimited alternatives. One aspect of the process involves restricting individual wants and increasing willingness to supply resources.

Historically, four mechanisms have been used to mediate the problem of
scarcity. The oldest is brute force, which existed in some early societies and is still
used today (Somalia and Bosnia provide examples from the early 1990s). Next
comes tradition, which gives major emphasis to past ways of allocating resources.
With civilization came another societal mechanism for resource allocation:
namely, authority in the institutions of government and church. A recent resource-
allocating social institution is the market, which developed over time and became
a primary allocator in Western Europe as feudalism waned and industrial market-
oriented societies developed. These mechanisms are not mutually exclusive, nor
has their use by societies been linear. Modern market societies use force, tradition,
and authority as well as markets. Similarly, in the early 1900s a number of societies
moved toward central planning, which involved governmental control of allocation. More recently, these societies have moved more toward markets and brute
force.

Modern economic theory examines the ways in which contemporary societies
cope with the problems that flow from relative scarcity. It focuses largely on
market processes, which have replaced the church, tradition, and the state as the
primary resource-allocating mechanism. The movement from tradition-state-
church economies to market economies has not been linear, with all societies in
the world participating. Some areas, almost entire continents, are still locked
in economic activity dominated by the past. Some societies have turned from
premarket feudal economies to modern command economies in which the
state allocates resources. In Eastern Europe one finds movements, whose outcomes are unknown, that are turning from command economies toward market
orientation.

To say that the market is the primary allocation mechanism is not to say that
it is the only mechanism. In modern market societies in Europe and North
America, market allocation is continually being influenced by social and political
forces.

Modern economic theory is still trying to come to grips with the interrelationships between economic, social, and political forces. It has focused on how market
forces operate, concentrating on how markets allocate scarce resources and on the
forces that determine the level and growth of economic output. But economic
thought goes beyond such questions. Our study of the antecedents of modern
economic theory starts before markets were highly developed. Beginning with this
earlier period enables us to see approaches to the broader questions. As you will
see, many of the questions raised by early premarket writers addressed broader
philosophical and ethical issues that help provide perspective for modern economic thought.

Regardless of what mechanism society uses to allocate resources, the harsh
reality of scarcity requires that some wants remain unmet; thus, issues of equity,

justice, and fairness are embedded in the problem of scarcity. Resource allocation mechanisms determine who gets, and who does not get, resources.

DIVISIONS OF MODERN ECONOMIC THEORY

In modern economic thought the problems associated with relative scarcity are commonly divided into micro- and macroeconomics. Microeconomics considers questions of allocation and distribution. Macroeconomics considers questions of stability and growth. The allocation problem (what to produce and how to produce) and the distribution problem (how real income is divided among the members of a society) generally fall under *microeconomic theory.* Microeconomic theory begins with an analysis of an individual and builds up to an analysis of society. The major theoretical tools of modern microeconomic analysis are demand and supply, which are applied at the level of the household, firm, and industry. A primary purpose of microeconomic theory is to explain the forces that determine relative prices, which economists believe are the essential forces in allocating resources and distributing income.

The other approach used in modern economics is *macroeconomic theory.* It begins with analysis of society as a whole and works downward to the individual. Macroeconomics has focused on the stability and growth of an economy, utilizing aggregate variables for the entire economy: the level of income and employment, the general level of prices, and the rate of economic growth.

Modern *orthodox economic theory* consists of a body of knowledge contained in both micro- and macroeconomics. A history of economic thought must examine the development of concepts and tools that culminated in this body of knowledge.

Although mainstream modern economics focuses on the use of markets to cope with the problems associated with relative scarcity, there have always been economists who are interested in different aspects of society. A number of these writers are concerned with broader philosophical issues; often their writings do not fall neatly into any single field of study. Some writers straddle disciplines within the social sciences—between economics and political science, for example; others lie between the social sciences and the humanities.

OUR APPROACH TO THE HISTORY OF THOUGHT

Many of the problems confronting a historian of economic thought are faced by all historians. A history of economic thought must be selective; otherwise it would overwhelm the reader and serve little purpose. Selection requires interpretation; therefore, hidden in the selection process are the historian's biases, prejudices, and value system. One of our biases is a love of controversy; we find controversy more interesting than agreement. Another is a "let 1,000 flowers bloom" approach to life: you never know what beauty might come from a small seed. These biases are reflected in the book and make it slightly different from others.

A Sociology of Knowledge—A Theory of Theory

Can one formulate a theory to explain the development of economic theory—a sociology of knowledge for economics? How does economic theory arise? There are two approaches to answering this question: the *relativist approach* and the *absolutist approach*.

Relativist historians concern themselves (1) with the historical, economic, sociological, and political forces that brought men and women to examine certain economic questions and (2) with the ways in which these forces shape the content of emerging theory. They hold that history plays a part in the development of every economic theory. A relativist would emphasize, for example, the relationships between the emergence and content of classical economics and the industrialization of England, between Ricardian economics and the conflict between English landlords and businessmen, and between Keynesian economics and the Great Depression of the 1930s.

Absolutist writers (in this context named Whigs by some) stress internal forces, such as the increasing professionalism in economics, to account for the development of economic theory. The absolutists claim that the progress of theory does not merely reflect historical circumstances but depends on the discovery and explanation of unsolved problems or paradoxes by trained professionals reacting to intellectual developments within the profession. According to this view, it is possible to rank theories absolutely according to their worth; the most recent theory is likely to contain less error and be closer to the truth than previous theories.

Prior to the 1950s the most influential historians of economic theory took a relativist position. Beginning in the 1950s the absolutist position was forcefully stated, which provoked discussion of these issues among historians of economic thought.

In our view, neither the absolutist nor the relativist position is convincing in and of itself. A more fruitful approach is to view the history of economic thought as a dynamic process of interaction between forces external and internal to the discipline that bring about new theoretical developments. In some cases these developments are better explained as proceeding from an intellectual reaction within the profession, but in others an examination of the economic and political issues of the times will give a better insight. In a number of cases the mixture of forces bringing about new developments is so complex that it is difficult to explain satisfactorily the emergence of theory by emphasizing either absolutist or relativist causes.

Orthodox and Heterodox Economists

A desire to use an understanding of the past to better comprehend the present does not mean that one follows a Whig approach to history—that all economic thought is a progression of ideas toward the grand finale of present-day thought. Far from it. Although there is some progression, there is also some regression; and in reading earlier thinkers, we are often impressed with the depth of their understanding, which at times seems to transcend modern thought. This view reflects our "let 1,000 flowers bloom" bias.

In this book we go beyond the mainstream thinking of a period and view the diversity of thought within the profession. Thus, the more important and interesting proponents of *heterodox economic theory,* past and present, appear along with the major orthodox thinkers. Included with the modern heterodox schools are the Austrians, institutionalists, post-Keynesians, and radicals, each of which shares some history with the mainstream but differs in its perception of which previous economists deserve to be remembered and which forgotten.

We believe that studying the history of thought gives us a much better understanding of these modern heterodox economists. It shows their history and demonstrates that they are not simply malcontents but are the carriers of traditions that the modern mainstream has lost. For example, heterodox economists have often ventured beyond the boundaries of orthodox economic theory into a no man's land among economics, sociology, anthropology, psychology, political science, history, and ethics. Modern economics is only now beginning to see the need to do that.

One way to understand the issues separating orthodox and heterodox writers is by examining the questions they were trying to answer. Whereas modern orthodox theorists have largely focused on the four problems of allocation, distribution, stability, and growth, heterodox economists have studied forces that produce changes in the society and economy. Whereas orthodox writers have taken as given (something they are not interested in explaining) the specific social, political, and economic institutions and have studied economic behavior in the context of these institutions, heterodox writers have focused on the forces leading to the development of these institutions. Often what orthodox writers take as given, heterodox writers try to explain; what heterodox writers take as given, orthodox economists try to explain. Thus, the differences between heterodox and orthodox economists are often differences in focus, not diametrically opposed theories.

The Problems of Presenting Diversity

Presenting the diversity of thought included in this text poses a number of problems. The history of the economic thought that has helped to shape current economics is a multidimensional history composed of many interwoven strands, like the electrical wires in the wiring harness of a car. Separating those strands by source and effect is about as difficult as finding an electrical malfunction somewhere in the harness. In order to condense the contributions of like-minded writers, we have grouped them into schools. But this causes problems. We hesitate, for example, to summarize some 250 years of economic theory from 1500 to 1750 under the general term of *mercantilism;* time and space oblige us to do so. We must stress, however, that to truly know the history of economic thought one must read the original texts. We hope merely to whet your appetite for the works of the many creative minds to which this work introduces you.*

Where the diversity of a school is too great to allow us to discuss all its members, we have selected one or more members as representative, realizing nevertheless that no single writer's views are likely to correspond exactly to the views imputed to the school. In selecting such representative authors, we emphasize those who most influenced subsequent thought rather than those who originated economic ideas. We do so for two reasons. First, it is very difficult to separate the original contributions of economic writers from those of their predecessors. Second, it often happens that the actual originators of ideas have little influence on subsequent thinking because their contemporaries ignore or reject their contributions.

Two examples illustrate this point. Richard Cantillon's (c. 1680–1734) *Essai sur la nature du commerce en général,* written between 1730 and 1734, was not published until 1755. What little influence it had was limited almost exclusively to Western Europe and chiefly to France, where it circulated before publication. But this book anticipates both Adam Smith's *Wealth of Nations* (1776) and the notion of an interrelated economy developed in François Quesnay's *Tableau économique* (1758). Though Quesnay and Smith may well have been influenced by Cantillon, he was ignored by the majority of his contemporaries. It was not until W. S. Jevons rediscovered Cantillon's work in 1881 that Cantillon received the recognition he deserved for his seminal contributions. An entire chapter could be devoted to each of these thinkers, but as a result of space constraints, we devote a separate chapter only to Smith because his work had the greatest influence on subsequent thought.

The case of H. H. Gossen provides a similar example. In the early 1870s three independently published books appeared, asserting that classical economists had erred in explaining the forces determining relative prices by exclusively emphasizing supply. The three works, all of which maintained that relative prices were better explained by the forces of marginal utility, or demand, were *Theory of Political Economy* (1871), by W. S. Jevons (1835–1882); *Grundsätze de Volfwirtschaftslehre* (1871), by Carl Menger (1840–1921); and *Éléments d' économique politique pure* (1874), by Léon Walras (1834–1910). Jevons, in the second edition of *Theory of Political Economy* (1879), reported that he had become aware of a book by H. H. Gossen published in 1854 that completely anticipated his own. But even though Gossen's work clearly antedated that of Jevons, Menger, and Walras, Gossen did not influence subsequent theory as they later did; therefore, he is not included in our discussions of marginal utility.

Once we have chosen a representative writer, we must further decide which of that writer's works will provide the basis of our discussion. Thomas R. Malthus (1776–1834), for example, is best known for his population theory; although he was not its originator, his presentation of the theory so influenced subsequent

---

* To encourage you to look at original sources, one end-of-chapter question is a "library research" question in which you are asked to find a bibliographical reference for an absent-minded professor.

thinking that the doctrine is known as the Malthusian theory. His *Essay on Population* was so popular, in fact, that it went through seven editions. Which should we use? Since the first and second editions differ significantly from each other, whereas the rest essentially follow the second, we have chosen to study both the first and second editions so as to cover adequately both the population theory and the influence of Malthus on the development of economic methodology. Similarly, whereas J. M. Keynes's *General Theory* (1936) secures the author a place in the history of theory, his views developed and changed both before and after its publication, so it is sometimes difficult to pin down the "real" Keynes. Inconsistencies in the presentation of such complex authors in this text do not indicate inaccuracies as much as they reflect the depth and vigor of the authors' thought, some of which is lost in condensation. Such inconsistencies should be viewed as invitations to study the original works.

ECONOMICS AS A PROFESSION

In his classic work *History of Economic Analysis* Joseph Schumpeter wrote that "the first discovery of a science is the discovery of itself." If one accepts that view, the science of economics is rather young, since the professionalization of economics has occurred only within the last one hundred years. Even if we take a broader view and consider economics as an intellectual discipline, it is still relatively young. Before 1500 no groups were concerned exclusively with understanding economies. Between 1500 and 1750, however, the quantity of economic literature increased significantly in Western Europe. The early writers were mostly businessmen who were interested in questions of economic policy and who wrote tracts or pamphlets on particular issues, rather than treatises that attempted to codify economic knowledge. A body of economic knowledge did begin to evolve during the last one hundred years of the period, from 1650 to 1750, when economics as an intellectual discipline emerged. Like most infants, it was at first somewhat ill-proportioned.

Adam Smith, a prodigious scholar who was trained in moral philosophy, took the inchoate economic literature generated between 1650 and 1750 and fashioned it into an intellectual discipline he named *political economy* in his book *Wealth of Nations* (1776). For about the next one hundred years, there was no clear-cut profession of economics, no group concerned exclusively with analyzing economic activity. Books such as Smith's, written to codify the existing state of knowledge of political economy, appeared with increasing frequency, but their authors were usually businessmen or academics who had developed an interest in economic issues. The period from 1776 to 1876 witnessed an increasing professionalization of the discipline of political economy, as its study moved farther away from men of affairs and into academia.

By 1900 political economy had a new name, *economics,* and was being offered as a course of study in both American and European universities. As economics became professionalized, those claiming to be economists had to receive graduate training; centers for its study grew up in England as well as in Germany, where many Americans went to study graduate economics. Thereafter, many public and private colleges in the United States began to expand their undergraduate offerings in economics and to initiate graduate programs.

The Great Depression of the 1930s and the increasing involvement of government in economic activity spurred interest in economic education. At the same time, religious persecution by the Nazis and the threatening war in Europe were bringing large numbers of academics from all disciplines to the United States. The center for graduate economic education shifted during this period from Western Europe to the United States, where many of the world's economists now receive their education. By the 1930s most Ph.D. economists were employed by academic institutions, where their concerns were with teaching and advancing the understanding of the economy rather than with practical policy and business.

These historical events, which transferred the concerns of economics from practical policy and business affairs to analysis of the operation of an economy, have significantly influenced the development of economic theory. The pre-Smithian political economists, who were businessmen with considerable practical knowledge of the institutions and operation of the economy, came to be replaced by academics, who by nature and training were oriented toward more abstract, theoretical issues.

THE SPREAD OF ECONOMIC IDEAS

In 1650 there were no economists, but today they seem to be everywhere—in the newspapers, on television, in government and industry. Yet the university is the center for much of the research activity that extends the boundaries of economic knowledge. The current state and direction of economic thinking are a result of research conducted at universities and research agencies. Research is presented to the profession in seminars and working papers until it becomes sufficiently refined to be published, usually as an article in a journal attached to a professional organization or a graduate economics department. Many seminal ideas flow from research done as Ph.D. dissertations, and many refinements and extensions of seminal ideas are brought about by Ph.D. candidates working under giants in the profession.

Once out of graduate school, academic economists experience the market firsthand. "Publish or perish" rules the cruel competitive world faced by each potential full professor at major graduate and many undergraduate schools. Because the top schools turn out many more Ph.D.s than are required for the staffing of their own departments, the probability is high that a given graduate from these schools will find employment in the lower-ranked schools or in industry or government.

Because graduate school is so important in determining an economist's mindset, and because publishing is so important to an economist's success, the content of graduate courses in economics and the decisions of editors of economics journals greatly influence the direction of economic thinking. Such program and editorial decisions of mainstream economics departments and journals reflect the collective judgment of prevailing orthodox professional opinion. Of course, there are some economics departments and journals that do reflect heterodox views. The continuing appearance of new journals and divergent curricula reflects the lack of agreement in the profession on the correctness of prevailing opinion.

An open competition of thinkers and researchers in pursuit of knowledge should lead to progressive research programs and the rejection of incorrect ideas. But economics is a social science closely linked to ethical issues that have no easy answers. Each economist works within a broader social milieu permeated by normative attitudes that are difficult to expel from research and difficult even to discern. Because of these difficulties, the choice of an appropriate methodology by economists is crucial to the advancement of economic knowledge. Before we proceed to our examination of the flow of economic ideas over time, it is therefore appropriate that we trace the development of contemporary views on methodology.

METHODOLOGICAL ISSUES

In thinking about what economists do, one is naturally led to ask, "What do economists know and how do they know that they know it?" Such questions belong broadly to *epistemology,* the study of human knowledge; in the philosophy of science they are included in the subject of "methodology." Because certain methodological terms will appear throughout this book and because methodology significantly influences what economists do, we will briefly consider the evolution of methodological thinking and its influence on economic thought.

It is sometimes said that discussions of methodology should be left to the grand old men in the profession who are ready for retirement. Quite the contrary. Before you can begin to study economic issues, you must decide what you will study and what approach you will take—you must make methodological decisions. Once you have embarked on a course of action, you often become too involved in it to change your *modus operandi.* (In economic jargon, your investment in specific human capital ties you in.) Thus, methodological questions are more relevant to young than to old economists.

Enlisting young economists for methodological studies cannot, however, be undertaken without certain caveats: forays into the methodological netherworld are made at one's own peril. The study of methodology is addictive; it lulls you into thinking about what you are doing rather than doing it. Methodological questions are awash with complications, and the neophyte may miss subtle points that could totally invalidate his or her insights. Nonetheless, musing over abstract ideas with the understanding that the insights thus gained are not the final word is important. Having given these warnings and admitting the impossibility of going deeply into methodology, we present in the next few pages a superencapsulated survey of methodological issues that have arisen in the philosophy of science from the ancient Greeks to modern-day thinkers.

Economics as an Art and as a Science

Perhaps the most important distinctions in economic thought are between *the art of economics, positive economics,* and *normative economics.* Positive economics concerns the forces that govern economic activity. It asks such questions as: How does the economy work? What are the forces that determine the distribution of income? The sole purpose of these inquiries is to obtain understanding for the sake of understanding. Normative judgments should enter into the analysis as little as possible. Normative economics explicitly concerns questions of what should be. It is the philosophical branch of economics that integrates economics with ethics.

The art of economics concerns questions of policy. It relates the science of economics to normative economics and asks questions such as: If these are one's normative goals, and if this is the way the economy works, then how can one best achieve these goals?

The distinction is important because positive economics and the art of economics have quite different methodologies. The methodology of positive economics is formal and abstract; it tries to separate economic forces from political and social forces. The methodology of the art of economics is more complex because it concerns policy and must address interrelationships among politics, social forces, and economic forces. In it one must add back all the dimensions of a problem that one abstracted from in positive economics.

Whether positive economics or the art of economics should be the primary focus of economics has prompted unending debate in the history of economic thought. The German historical school and the English Marshallian school have advocated that primary attention be given to the art of economics. They draw strength in this advocacy from the work of Adam Smith. Modern orthodox economists focus on positive economics and find support for this position in the writings of David Ricardo. Consistent with that view, most of modern methodological writing has centered on positive economics; and our methodological discussion in the next section will follow that focus. We will, however, return to the many interesting issues surrounding the art of economics when we examine the economic policies put forward by various economists.

The Importance of Empirical Verification

How we go about answering the questions "What do we know?" and "How do we know that what we know is right?" depends on the answer to the question "Is there an ultimate truth that scientists are in the process of revealing (an absolutist view), or is there no underlying truth (a relativist position)?" If there is ultimate truth, how do we find it? If there is none, are some propositions more truthful than others? Methodologists past and present have failed to reach consensus on these problems but have generated an enormous amount of material on the subject. Believing that an ultimate truth exists leaves one with the problem of deciding when one has discovered it.

The means by which the growing scientific world strove to discover the truth involved trained empirical observation as exemplified in the scientific method. This entailed the integration of reason with empirical observation. Being a subject far too complicated for us to elaborate, verification is discussed in detail in the writings of Kant, Hume, Descartes, and other seventeenth- and eighteenth-century philosophers. We will simply define two terms that are essential to the discussion, *inductive* and *deductive*. Inductive reasoning is empirical, proceeding from sensory perceptions to general concepts; deductive reasoning (logic) applies certain clear and distinct general ideas to particular instances. Because most philosophers believe that knowledge derives from a mix of these, the debate usually centers on the nature of the optimal mix.

The Rise of Logical Positivism

The methodology of science moved into the twentieth century with the development of logical positivism, which provided the scientific method with philosophical foundations. It established a working methodology expressing the empirical and nonempirical, or rational, aspects we have just discussed. *Logical positivism* linked with deductive reasoning a positivist desire to let the facts speak for themselves. It originated with a group known as the Vienna Circle, which attempted to formalize the methods of scientists by describing the methods scientists actually followed.

The logical positivists argued that scientists develop a deductive structure (a logical theory) that leads to empirically testable propositions. A deductive theory is true, however, only after it has been empirically tested and verified. The role of the scientist, they said, is to develop these logical theories and then to test them. Although there was debate among the logical positivists as to what constituted truth, all concurred that it would be discovered through empirical observation.

Logical positivism reigned in the philosophy of science only from the 1920s through the 1930s, but its influence in economics continued much longer. It was logical positivism that led to the distinction between normative and positive economics in most introductory textbooks, which describe economics as a positive science whose goal is to devise theories that can be empirically validated. Normative discussions were purged from economics as unscientific.

From Logical Positivism to Falsificationism

Logical positivism represented a culmination of the belief that the purpose of science is to establish "truth." The methodology of science has since progressively removed itself from that view. The first departure resulted from a concern about the "verification" aspect of logical positivist theory. This concern is best expressed in the writings of Karl Popper, who argued in the 1930s that empirical tests do not establish the truth of a theory, only its falsity—which is why Popper's approach is sometimes called *falsificationism*. According to Popper, it is never possible to "verify" a theory, since one cannot perform all possible tests of the theory. For example, assume that a theory predicts that when the money supply increases, prices will increase by an equal percentage. Then assume that in an appropriate experiment the predicted result does in fact occur. According to Popper, this indicates only that the theory has not yet been proved false; it may or may not be true, since in the next experiment, it may produce a result that is not consistent with the theory's prediction.

Popper asserts, therefore, that the goal of science should be to develop theories with empirically testable hypotheses and then to try to falsify them, discarding those that prove false. The progression of science, according to Popper, depends upon the continuing falsification of theories. The reigning theory will be the one that explains the widest range of empirical observations and that has not yet been falsified.

From Falsificationism to Paradigms

It would be nice if methodological problems could be resolved as neatly as Popper's approach suggests, but methodological debates are anything but neat. More recent developments have moved methodology progressively away from such neat distinctions. The modern rejection of Popper's theory is not without grounds: falsificationism has several serious problems. First, empirical predictions of some theories cannot be tested because the technology to test them does not exist. What should one do with such theories? Second, it is difficult to determine when a theory has or has not been falsified. For example, if an empirical test does not produce the expected results, the researcher can and often does attribute the failure to shortcomings in the testing procedure or to some exogenous factor. Therefore, one negative empirical test often will not invalidate the theory.

A third problem arises from the mindset of researchers who may fail to test the implications of an established theory, assuming them to be true. Such a mindset can block the path to acceptance of new and possibly more tenable theories.

Partly in response to these problems, Thomas Kuhn, in *The Structure of Scientific Revolutions* (1962), marshaled methodology away from logical positivism by introducing the concept of the *paradigm* into the debate. A paradigm, as Kuhn uses the word, is a given approach and body of knowledge built into researchers' analyses that conforms to the accepted textbook presentation of mainstream scientific thought at any given time. Kuhn argued that most scientific work is *normal science;* in which researchers try to solve puzzles posed within the framework of the existing paradigm. This work often leads to the discovery of anomalies the paradigm fails to account for, but the existence of such anomalies is not sufficient to overthrow the reigning paradigm: only an alternative paradigm better able to deal with the anomalies can do so. Once such a superior paradigm develops, a scientific revolution becomes possible. In *revolutionary science,* first the existing paradigm is rejected by part of the scientific community, and then the old and the new paradigms begin to compete and communication between researchers in the opposing camps becomes difficult. Ultimately, if the revolution is successful, new questions will be posed within the new framework and a new normal science will develop.

Whereas in Popper's view "truth" (or the closest we can get to truth) will win out, in Kuhn's view a superior theory might exist but not be adopted because of the inertia favoring the existing paradigm. Hence the reigning theory is not necessarily the best.

Those who disagreed with mainstream theory quickly adopted Kuhn's analysis, because it suggested that the paradigm they preferred might prove to be superior to, and thus able to supplant, the mainstream view. Moreover, Kuhn's work suggested that changes occur by revolutions; it offered hope that change, when it came, would come quickly. Although Kuhn focused on the natural sciences, he had a significant influence on the social sciences, such as economics. Methodological discussions throughout the 1970s and 1980s were peppered with the term *paradigm.*

From Paradigms to Research Programs

The view that the existing theory might not embody the truth was extended by Imre Lakatos during the late 1960s and 1970s. He tried to grasp and articulate the procedures good scientists were actually following; he observed that scientists are engaged in the development of competing research programs, each of which involves analyzing and attempting to falsify a set of data but also involves unquestionably accepting a set of hard-core logical postulates. Each study derives a set of peripheral implications from the hard core and then attempts to falsify them. Falsification of a single peripheral implication will not require rejection of the theory but will occasion a reconsideration of the logical structure and, perhaps, an ad hoc adjustment. Only if "sufficient" peripheral implications are falsified will the hard-core assumptions be reconsidered. Lakatos called research programs *progressive* if the process of falsifying the peripheral implications was proceeding, *degenerative* if it was not. Lakatos's work has two significant features: (1) it recognizes the complexity of the process whereby a theory is falsified; and (2) whereas earlier analyses required that one theory predominate, Lakatos provides for the simultaneous existence of multiple workable theories whose relative merits are not easily discernible.

From Research Programs to Sociological and Rhetorical Approaches to Method

The developments we have just outlined, in one way move progressively away from logical positivism, but in another way are refinements of it that recognize the limitations of empirical testing. A much more radical departure from previous methodology can be found in Paul Feyerabend's *Against Method: An Outline of an Anarchistic Theory of Knowledge* (1975). Feyerabend argues that the acceptance of any method limits creativity in problem solving and that the best science is therefore to be confined to no method—in other words, anything goes. Though his radical argument at first seems crazy, he has provided some new perspectives on knowledge that throw light on the rhetorical and sociological approaches that have influenced recent developments in the methodology of economics. Whereas earlier approaches acknowledged the difficulty of discovering truth, they did not question the Platonic vision of truth as absolute. The rhetorical and sociological approaches do just that. Since they refuse to assume the existence of an ultimate and inviolable truth, they search out other reasons to explain why people believe what they believe.

The *rhetorical approach* to methodology emphasizes the persuasiveness of language, contending that a theory may be accepted not because it is inherently true but because its advocates succeed in convincing others of its value by means of their superior rhetoric. The *sociological approach* examines the social and institutional constraints influencing the acceptability of a theory. Funding, jobs, and control of the journals may determine which theory is accepted as much as the theory's ability to accurately explain phenomena. Those who adhere to the sociological approach contend that most researchers are interested less in whether the theories they advance are correct than in whether they are publishable. What these two theories most notably share is a skepticism about one's ability to discover truth, even whether truth exists at all. According to these approaches, a theory has not necessarily evolved because it is the closest to the truth but because of a variety of other reasons, of which truth—if it exists—is only one.

Postrhetorical Methodology

Where does this leave us with respect to methodology? In a somewhat muddled state, but being muddled is not unusual for methodology. Following the progress of epistemology through the past few decades, we have seen the answers to questions about how and what we know become progressively vaguer until methodology is all but annihilated: the most persuasive researchers win out regardless of the value of their work. Fortunately, however, we need not accept such a view as total reality. Although such extreme viewpoints provide interesting insights, they clearly need to be tempered by common sense. Even admitting the social and rhetorical influences on the direction of science, one need not accept that Feyerabend's "anything goes" attitude necessarily follows. Methodology, moreover, is not going to end here. A *postrhetorical methodology* will probably combine insights such as Feyerabend's with more workable approaches.

Although researchers may never know with certainty whether a given theory is true or false, they must accept the most promising ideas as tentatively true working hypotheses. They may revert to certain elements of logical positivist and falsificationist methodology to do this. They may even accept all the arguments of the rhetorical and sociological schools and still behave as they always have toward the truth or falsity of their research. The difference will be in perspective:

postrhetorical economists will be more skeptical of their knowledge, less likely to dismiss an argument as false before they have closely considered it, and more likely to "let 1,000 flowers bloom." A postrhetorical economist will scrutinize the incentives of researchers to study particular theories and will view with skepticism the results of studies that coincide with the researcher's own interests or preconceived beliefs. Finally, a postrhetorical economist will be much more likely to follow Bayesian, rather than classical, statistics than would a logical positivist or a falsificationist.

Bayesians believe one can discover higher or lower degrees of truth in statements, but not ultimate truth. The Bayesian influence will engender a reinterpretation of classical statistical tests, rendering them less exact, less persuasive, and not independently representative of a specific confidence level. In the methodology of the future, information about the researcher as well as the research will probably be a necessary component of statistical reporting.

For both the Bayesian and the rhetorical economists, understanding ultimately rests on faith. Having said that, let us proceed with the search for understanding; in that search, too skeptical a mindset stymies creativity. Thus, rhetorical methodology should provide only a metamethodology that, once accepted, little affects the day-to-day work of economists. They do what they do.

Methodological Conclusions

Methodological arguments in economics have generally lagged far behind those in epistemology and the philosophy of science. According to most economics textbooks, the reigning methodology in economics is still logical positivism, which was long ago declared dead in other fields as well as in the methodologically oriented economics journals. But occasionally the economics profession goes through a methodological spasm, looking inward and asking, "Is this what we should be doing?" It never fully answers but goes on as before, though equipped with slightly updated methodological views. Even though methodology is seldom discussed, ultimately it is methodology that accounts for many of the differences among economists. Formalists are more likely to use a logical positivist or falsificationist methodology and believe in an absolutist approach; nonformalists are more likely to use a sociological or rhetorical approach and believe in a relativist approach.

BENEFITS TO BE GAINED FROM THE STUDY OF THE HISTORY OF ECONOMIC THOUGHT

A primary reason for studying the history of economic thought is to become a better economist. With few exceptions, the important economists of past and present have been well acquainted with the theoretical history of their discipline. Reading the history of economic thought strengthens theoretical and logical skills by providing opportunities to relate assumptions to conclusions: one learns to work through the logic of systems that are different from one's own. Social scientists also need to be aware of their methodologies. An effective means of achieving this awareness is to study historical controversies—such as those between deductive and inductive approaches, or between the advocates of rigorous abstract theoretical models and advocates of a more historical, descriptive approach—and to note the gains and losses to be realized by each methodology.

The history of economic theory can also teach us humility. When we see great minds make important theoretical errors or fail to examine or pursue what appear from historical hindsight to be obvious paths, we realize that our own theoretical paradigms may be faulty in ways that are difficult for us to perceive, because we are blinded by our preconceptions. Ernest Hemingway once said that it is counterproductive for a writer to live in New York City, where the writers are like earthworms living in a jar. Our culture, with its sometimes narrow values and preconceptions, can be seen as the jar in which we live. Although it is difficult to get outside the jar and view our society and its economy with perfect objectivity, a study of the development of economic theory can make us more aware of the importance of trying to do so and less willing to accept current theory uncritically.

Yet another reason for studying old ideas is to foster new ones. Study of past economic theory is often the source of inspiration for a new idea. Theories sometimes get lost in the past and are not carried forward to the future, or they may become linked to specific applications. A good example of this is the development around 1815 of the concept of diminishing returns and rent. Until about 1890, when their applicability to factors of production was finally recognized, returns and rent were applied only to land. Also, fruitful ideas may be discarded along with an outworn or otherwise objectionable ideology to which they are linked. Orthodox theory largely ignored the work of Marx until the Great Depression of the 1930s necessitated a search through past economic theory for an explanation of the causes of depression in a capitalist system.

With this background, we shall proceed to a study of the history of economic thought, tracing the emergence of modern orthodox economics while still taking into account the deviations from orthodoxy that have helped to shape the content of present-day economics. In addition to the scope and content of theory, we shall note major methodological issues and the relationships between the development of a theory and the economic conditions at the time of its development. Where the internal workings of particular theories provide insights, we shall explain them. From time to time we shall indicate the general significance of particular ideas in the development of theory and the broader implications of theory as a basis for the formulation of economic and social policy.

Key Terms

microeconomic theory	relativist approach
macroeconomic theory	absolutist approach
orthodox economic theory	heterodox economic theory

political economy
epistemology
the art of economics
positive economics
normative economics
inductive reasoning
deductive reasoning
logical positivism
falsificationism

paradigm
normal science
revolutionary science
progressive
degenerative
rhetorical approach
sociological approach
postrhetorical methodology
Bayesians

Questions for Review and Discussion

1. Historically, four mechanisms have been used to mediate the problem of scarcity. What are these four methods? Do they all fall under the purview of economics?
2. Is the division of economics into micro- and macroeconomics a natural division? Which should one study first? Why?
3. Some people argue that one should study the history of thought because it is interesting in its own right. Others argue that it should be studied because it sheds light on the present. Which of these arguments is correct? Are they incompatible?
4. Why is it important to study some of the ideas of heterodox economists as well as those of orthodox theorists? (This is a good question to answer again after you have read all the chapters.)
5. The authors of this book admit having a bias toward interest in the history of thought as a means to gain better understanding of recent thought. How might that have influenced their treatment of H. H. Gossen?
6. Histories of ideas must be selective. Write an essay about some of the issues of selection that must be faced by people writing a history of economic thought.
7. Write an essay in which you distinguish between positive economics, normative economics, and economics as an art.
8. Trace the methodology used by economists during the twentieth century.
9. Would a person who believes in paradigms be likely to believe in falsificationism as well?
10. What are some of the benefits to be gained by studying the history of economic thought?

Suggested Readings

Blaug, Mark. *Economic Theory in Retrospect.* Cambridge: Cambridge University Press, 1985.
————. *The Methodology of Economics.* Cambridge: Cambridge University Press, 1978.

Boland, Lawrence A. *The Foundations of Economic Method*. London: George Allen and Unwin, 1982.

Caldwell, Bruce. *Beyond Positivism: Economic Methodology in the Twentieth Century*. London: George Allen and Unwin, 1982.

Coats, A. W., ed. *Methodological Controversies in Economics: Historical Essays in Honor of T. W. Hutchison*. Greenwich, Conn.: JAI Press, 1983.

Feyerabend, Paul. *Against Method: An Outline of an Anarchistic Theory of Knowledge*. London: New Left Books, 1975.

Hausman, Daniel. *The Inexact and Separate Science of Economics*. Cambridge: Cambridge University Press, 1992.

Hutchison, T. W. *Knowledge and Ignorance in Economics*. Oxford: Basil Blackwell, 1977.

Kuhn, Thomas S. *The Structure of Scientific Revolutions*. 2nd ed., enlarged. Chicago: University of Chicago Press, 1970.

Lakatos, Imre. *The Methodology of Scientific Research Programmes: Philosophical Papers*. Vol. 1. Cambridge: Cambridge University Press, 1978.

Latsis, S. J. *Method and Appraisal in Economics*. Cambridge: Cambridge University Press, 1976.

McCloskey, Donald N. *The Rhetoric of Economics*. Madison, Wis.: The University of Wisconsin Press, 1985.

Popper, Karl R. *The Logic of Scientific Discovery* (1934). New York: Basic Books, 1959.

Preclassical Economics

"Where do we start?" asked the Red Queen.
"Start at the beginning," answered the Dodo.

—Lewis Carroll

Clockwise from top left: Aristotle, St. Thomas Aquinas, William Petty, François Quesnay

Although economic activity has characterized human culture since the dawn of civilization, there was little formal analysis of that activity until merchant capitalism developed in Western Europe during the fifteenth century. At that time the chiefly agrarian European societies began increasingly to trade among themselves, setting the stage for the birth of economics as a social study. The economic studies of this time were not systematic: economic theory evolved piecemeal from individual intellectual responses to contemporary problems. No grand analytical systems appeared. It was not until the mid-eighteenth century, with the emergence of "classical economics" under Adam Smith, that economics made significant movement toward the status of a full-blown social science.

Given this reality, our study of the history of economic ideas could begin with classical economics. But there are other approaches. For example, we could begin around 1200, when the possibilities of economic analysis were first being recognized. Another approach would be to start with writers of the Middle Ages. Yet another would be to take account of the fact that possibly the most significant development in the social sciences has been the realization that it is possible to examine aspects of society analytically. The notion that social structures could be analyzed just as the physical universe could, was centuries in its making and even dates back to ancient Greek thought. Although the Greek philosophers did not recognize that the economy was capable of being analyzed (as they clearly did the political aspects of society), nevertheless their analysis of what were essentially premarket societies gave later thinkers a foundation that made their task easier. The foundations argument suggests yet another alternative. Earlier societies often passed on their writings in the form of religious tomes; thus, one could begin an analysis of economic ideas with the earliest recorded history.

Faced with these alternatives, we have decided to begin with the development of Greek thought and then to consider the writings of the scholastics, the mercantilists, and the physiocrats, but to keep our consideration of these writings short. Thus, Part I is shorter than other sections but long enough to give a sense of the importance of the earlier writings.

An important reason for examining the preclassical and premercantile ideas of the Greeks and the medieval schoolmen is to gain insight into some of the more philosophical-ethical issues of relative scarcity. A fundamental tenet of modern orthodox theory is that more goods are better than fewer goods, and prevailing patterns of activity in modern societies lend strong confirmation to this tenet. Early religious, Greek, and scholastic thinkers did not begin with this premise, and the questions they raised about economic versus non-economic goals of the individual and society are eternal. The theme that there is more to life than material goods has been addressed by various heterodox economic writers throughout the history of economics.

In Chapter 3 we consider economic thinking from the 1500s to the mid-1700s. During this period the first of what might be called a school of economic thought, mercantilism, developed. The mercantilist school believed that the wealth of a nation and the amount of gold in a country were closely related, and it found a major role for the state in seeing that the economy functioned well. Mercantilist thought reigned from the sixteenth century to the mid-1700s.

Around the middle of the 1600s, however, economic thinking began to change; liberalism was in its infancy, and the seeds of both political and economic revolution were beginning to sprout. An important group of French writers developed; they have become known as the physiocrats. The most important of these was François Ques-

ney (1694–1774), a physician to Louis XV who developed an analytical system that regarded the economy as a circular flow in which natural law, rather than the government, controlled the economy. It was the physiocrats who developed the concept of *laissez faire, laissez passer* ("let it be, let it go"); their views were direct precursors of classical economic views.

Besides the physiocrats, there were other interesting preclassicals. William Petty (1623–1687) was first to suggest the importance of measuring economic phenomena. In a series of wonderfully satirical poems and other writings, Bernard Mandeville (c. 1670–1733) ridiculed aspects of the sentimental moralists and argued that self-interest guided by government intervention leads to social benefit. Richard Cantillon (c. 1680–1734) did not influence the development of thought, but in terms of the logic of his ideas he has been called by some a cofounder of the classical school. We also examine David Hume (1711–1776), who in a number of essays made significant contributions to theoretical economics.

In thinking about these preclassical writers, it is important to keep in mind two points. First, they addressed limited aspects of the economy and did not articulate their analysis into a comprehensive economic system. These writers had enormous mental acuity but were simply not searching for grand theories; later, once the physiocrats and liberal mercantilists began to envision a more comprehensive system, they had to resolve complex analytical problems before they could even begin to synthesize past analysis into an integral body of economic theory. Second, the changes in economic thinking that occurred over the centuries were, in part, responses to the changing economic organization of society. In England, for example, scholastic economic thought derived from feudalism, and mercantilist theory from merchant capitalism. The classical laissez faire ideas that appear in the writings of the liberal mercantilists were likewise associated with the beginnings of producer capitalism. Thus, although this is a book on the history of economic thought, a knowledge of economic history adds important dimensions to our understanding of economic thought.

2 Early Preclassical Economic Thought

"The birth of economic analysis in the West was the result of a union of two elements in Hellenic thought. One of these was the ability to reason about social relationships in a generalized or abstract form. The second was reflection on living in a sophisticated economic environment created during an upsurge of export-led growth."

—Barry Gordon

IMPORTANT WRITERS

HESIOD	*Works and Days* c. 800 BC
XENOPHON	*Ways and Means to Increase the Revenues of Athens* c. 355 BC
PLATO	*The Republic* c. 400 BC
ARISTOTLE	*Politics* c. 310 BC
ST. THOMAS AQUINAS	*Summa Theologica* c. 1273

Classical economics is dated with the publication in 1776 of Adam Smith's *Wealth of Nations*. That, of course, is only a rough date; as we will see in the next chapter, the ideas in *Wealth of Nations* were being developed during the two hundred years before 1776. We divide the prior period into two parts: an early preclassical period from about 800 BC to 1500, and a preclassical era from 1500 to 1776. In this chapter we deal with the early preclassical period. Because the early preclassical period spans 2,300 years, roughly twelve times the two hundred or so years that have passed since 1776, enormous selectivity is necessary. In making our selections we have relied on the work of scholars such as Barry Gordon, Odd Langholm, S. Todd Lowry, and Stephan Worland, who in the past thirty years have made important contributions to understanding this period.

We divide the early *preclassical period* into two subperiods: Greek thought, in which we focus on the work of Hesiod (c. 800 BC), Xenophon (c. 430–355 BC), and Aristotle (384–322 BC); and economic thought of the scholastic period, in which we focus on the writings of St. Thomas Aquinas (1225–1274).

SOME BROAD GENERALIZATIONS

Modern economic theory finds the source of all economic problems in relative scarcity. Scarcity is a result of our desire to consume more goods and services than our society can produce. Modern economies are market economies; thus, modern economic theory focuses on how markets help to mediate the problems of scarcity and gives much less attention to the use of force, authority, and tradition. The early preclassical thinkers reflected on aspects of their economic lives but gave greatest attention to nonmarket-allocating mechanisms. Unlike modern economists, who are especially concerned with the efficiency of resource allocation, the early preclassical thinkers considered the consequences of various types of economic activities for the quality and justice of life.

Although there was a growth of market activities, as well as a growth in the size of cities, increasing improvements in transportation, and improved and more efficient methods of producing goods in the 2,300 years spanning the Greek period to the end of scholasticism, the fundamental economic structure of society did not change significantly during this time. People were not market dependent on others to produce the goods they consumed but were for the most part self-sufficient. Thus, early preclassical writers were not interested in markets because of their relative unimportance in the daily activities of people. One of the most significant differences between early preclassical and modern orthodox economic thought concerns the mechanism for resource allocation. In a premarket setting, thinkers focused on the use of authority as an allocator of resources.

The early writers had little notion of the meaning and implications of scarcity and how markets coordinated individual activities. This observation does not denigrate the accomplishments of these intellectuals, for it was a long and tortuous road to recognizing the meaning and implications of scarcity and realizing that an economy existed that was capable of analysis. Historians of economic ideas acknowledge that the early writers identified a number of concepts and tools that enabled later writers to understand the developing market economy.

Two important themes emerge from early preclassical doctrine. One concerns the level of inquiry appropriate for analyzing society. These writers believed that it was inappropriate to separate any particular activity—economic, for example—from all other activities. The very ability to make such abstract separation represents part of the intellectual apparatus necessary for the "birth" of economics and the other social sciences. It is ironic that although the Greek writers and St. Thomas Aquinas rejected the artificial separation of activities, in their development of abstract reasoning they gave the social sciences a significant and prerequisite building block.

A second theme is the focus on broad philosophical issues, giving particular attention to questions of fairness, justice, and equity. The preclassical writers examined exchange and price with the purpose of evaluating their fairness, justice, and equity. Such concern makes sense in a premarket society. The two themes, the illegitimacy of abstraction and the focus on equity, can be found within a good deal of heterodox economic writing from the eighteenth century to the present.

GREEK THOUGHT

One might think that Greek economic thought has been thoroughly explored and that full agreement among scholars on the relative importance of various writers has been reached, but that is not the case. For example, recent scholarship by S. Todd Lowry, listed in the *Suggested Readings,* has found seminal contributions to modern economic analysis by the Greek writer Protagoras. Should he be included? We decided to await confirmation of these conclusions by our colleagues before including Protagoras in our examination. Instead, we begin our analysis with Hesiod and Xenophon.

Hesiod and Xenophon

The ideas of Hesiod were orally presented during the eighth century BC. The most important work attributed to Hesiod is an accounting of the birth of the gods, *Theogony.* According to Hesiod, scarcity does not arise from a human condition concerning limited resources and unlimited desires; rather, it was one of the evils released when Pandora opened the Box. Hesiod's economic ideas are presented in *Works and Days,* in which he initiates a pursuit of economic questions that continued for two centuries. Being a farmer, Hesiod was interested in efficiency. Economists use the concept of *efficiency* in a number of contexts in which it is measured as a ratio of outputs to inputs. Maximum efficiency is seen as achieving the largest possible output with a given input. The units of measurement of outputs and inputs can be stated in physical terms (e.g., bushels of wheat per acre) or in monetary units (e.g., dollars of output or input). Of course, one can take a different perspective and measure efficiency not in terms of productivity but in terms of costs (e.g., cost per acre of a bushel of wheat, or the dollar cost of a unit of output). Maximizing efficiency can be expressed as maximizing output or minimizing costs.

It is to be expected that most farmers and producers would be interested in efficiency; indeed, much of the writing about efficiency during the early preclassical period concerned the level of the producer and household. A much more subtle and complex set of issues is encountered when one begins to examine questions of efficiency at the level of the economy. At this level one can no longer measure productivity or costs in physical terms, and economists have turned to monetary measures even though they are not fully satisfactory.

The early writers were not interested in efficiency at the level of society because they had no real insight into the concept of scarcity, its implications, and an economy. The word *economics* comes from the Greek language and was used by Xenophon as the title of his book *Oeconomicus*. As the term was first used in Greek, it refers to efficient management at the level of the producer and/or the household. Hesiod, Xenophon, and other early writers were pursuing a set of problems relating to efficiency at the level of the producer and household, that had to be tackled before much more difficult and less obvious issues of efficiency for an entire economy could be dealt with. It is interesting that economics as a discipline was quite well developed before a full and complete understanding of efficiency at the level of the firm and household was established, at the end of the nineteenth century, with the use of marginal analysis and differential calculus.

Xenophon, writing some four hundred years after Hesiod, took the concepts of efficient management much farther than Hesiod and applied them at the level of the household, the producer, the military, and the public administrator. This brought him insights into how efficiency can be improved by practicing a division of labor. Attention to the division of labor was continued by other Greek writers, including Aristotle, and, later, by the scholastics. We will see that at the level of the economy and society, Adam Smith gave special recognition to this influence on the wealth of a nation.

Aristotle

Aristotle is important not only for his contributions to philosophical thinking but for the impact he had on economic ideas during the period of scholasticism. It was to Aristotle's views that St. Thomas Aquinas and other churchmen reacted in the period 1300 to 1500.

Democritus (c. 460–c. 370 BC) had not only argued for a division of labor but advocated the private ownership of property as an incentive that would lead to greater economic activity. Aristotle's teacher, Plato, had argued that the ruling class of his ideal society, the soldiers and philosophers, should not possess *private property* but should hold *communal property,* to avoid conflicts over property that might divert their attention from more important issues. However, Aristotle believed that private property served a useful function in society and that no regulations should be made to limit the amount of property in private hands. His apparent inconsistency in condemning the pursuit of economic gain while endorsing the right to private property troubled moral philosophers until the sixteenth century.

Aristotle's main contributions to economic thinking concerned the exchange of commodities and the use of money in this exchange. People's needs, he said, are moderate, but people's desires are limitless. Hence the production of commodities to satisfy *needs* was right and natural, whereas the production of goods in an attempt to satisfy unlimited *desires* was unnatural. Aristotle conceded that when goods are produced to be sold in a market, it can be difficult to determine if this activity is satisfying needs or inordinate desires; but he assumed that if a market exchange is in the form of barter, it is made to satisfy natural needs and no

Needs and Wants

Today's mainstream economist does not distinguish between human needs and desires, especially in a society in which the household or family unit is no longer self-sufficient. Households today not only produce few of the *goods* they consume, they even buy many *services* in the market. As specialization and division of labor evolved and economic exchange began, a medium of exchange—money—became essential. According to modern orthodox theorists, distinguishing between needs and wants in a market economy is objectively impossible. They feel that Aristotle's precepts should be viewed as guidelines relevant to his times but not to ours, because they are inconsistent with present economic realities. Modern orthodox economists believe that ultimately it should be left to the individual to determine whether he or she is acting virtuously in producing and exchanging goods. But many heterodox groups, the institutionalists and Marxists, for example, disagree with this position. They contend that it is impossible for mainstream economists to avoid making value judgments and that not separating needs and wants involves a value judgment. They argue, in accord with Aristotle, that needs can and must be distinguished from wants.

economic gain is intended. Exchange using the medium of money, however, suggests that the objective is monetary gain, which Aristotle condemned.

Aristotle agreed with Plato and most other Greek thinkers on the necessity of viewing economic activity in a broader context and not compartmentalizing inquiry. One of the interesting points Aristotle made is that the problem of scarcity can be addressed by reducing consumption, by changing human attitudes. This is a powerful idea for the various utopians and socialists who hope to end societal conflicts by eliminating the conflicts that are inherent in scarcity.

SCHOLASTICISM

The Feudal Foundation of Scholastic Thought

Scholastic economic doctrine is best understood in the context of its time, extending from before the fall of the Roman Empire to the beginnings of mercantilism in Western Europe. We shall discuss some of the chief characteristics of medieval society that bear on the nature and significance of *scholasticism*.[1] The kind of economic activity we see today in the industrialized areas of the world did not exist to any significant degree during the Middle Ages. In particular, although the production of goods for sale in a market increased throughout the period, it did not play a dominant role in everyday life. The *feudal economy* consisted of

[1] The best short historical analysis of this period can be found in Henri Pirenne, *Economic and Social History of Medieval Europe,* trans. I. E. Clegg (New York: Harcourt Brace, 1937).

subsistence agriculture in a society bound together not by a market but by tradition, custom, and authority; the society was divided into four groups: serfs, landlords, royalty, and the church. All land was fundamentally owned by the Roman Catholic church and the king. Use of the land owned by the king was given to the lords or noblemen, who in exchange had certain obligations to the central authority. These obligations, based not on contracts (as in the modern market economy), but on tradition and custom, consisted of supplying services and goods. The right of land use, with its corresponding obligations, was passed by birthright from father to son. Since the secular central authority was never very strong during the Middle Ages, the lord was, for the most part, master of his domain. The relationship between lord and serf was also dictated by custom, tradition, and authority. The serf was tied to the land by tradition and paid the lord for use of the land with labor, crops, and sometimes money. In return, the lord protected the serf from outsiders during times of war. Each manor or estate was a virtually complete economic and political unit. It usually had its own church, built by the lord and partly managed under the influence of the lord, since he nominated the pastor. As the largest landholder in Western Europe, the church had significant secular influence. In general its estates were better managed than those of the feudal lords, partly because the churchmen were the only class proficient in reading and writing.

Most individuals accepted their place in feudal society without much question. There were scattered examples of serfs revolting against their lords, but these were unusual occurrences. All land belonged to God, who had put it in the custody either of a man who was king by divine right or of the church. Not to accept the authority of one's superiors was to oppose the will of God, who had given them authority, and to endanger one's salvation in the next life. In such a system land, labor, and capital were not commodities bought and sold in a market as they are today, and there was very little production of goods for sale in the market.

Although there were strong elements in the feudal society that reinforced tradition and were hostile to change, other factors began to erode feudalism's foundations. Most economic historians regard changing technology as the major cause of the decline of feudalism. Changes in agricultural technology had disruptive influences on the manor. Manufacturing began, which was based on the replacement of man and animal power by mechanical power from water and wind. Thus, in the course of the Middle Ages and especially during the five hundred years prior to 1450, society was transformed.

The scholastic writers were educated monks who tried to provide religious guidelines to be applied to secular activities. Their aim was not so much to analyze what little economic activity was taking place as to prescribe rules of economic conduct compatible with religious dogma. The most important of the scholastic writers was St. Thomas Aquinas.

St. Thomas Aquinas

Although the scholastics, in attempting to adapt to the nascent economic changes of their times, produced a somewhat diverse body of economic ideas, they essentially addressed the same core of economic issues: the institution of private property and the concepts of just price and usury. With minor qualifications, it is reasonable to characterize and summarize this literature as a struggle to reconcile the religious teachings of the church with the slowly increasing economic activity of the time. Scholastic writing represents a gradual acceptance of certain aspects of economic activity as compatible with religious doctrine, achieved by subtle modifications of that doctrine to fit the economic conditions. The significance of St. Thomas Aquinas's ideas lies in his fusion of religious teaching with the writings of Aristotle, which provided scholastic economic doctrine with much of its content.

In attempting to reconcile religious doctrine with the institution of private property and with economic activity, Aquinas had to reckon with numerous biblical statements condemning private property, wealth, and the pursuit of economic gain. Based upon the New Testament, early Christian thought held that communal property accorded with natural law and that privately held property fell short of this ideal. Thus, early Christian society, modeled on the lives of Jesus Christ and his apostles, was communal. But the early scholastic writers had long struggled to establish that some ownership of private property by laymen was not incompatible with religious teaching. In the thirteenth century, after Aristotle's writings had been reintroduced into Western Europe, Thomas Aquinas, adapting Aristotelian thought to his own writing, was able to argue convincingly that private property is not contrary to natural law. Although he conceded that under natural law all property is communal, he maintained that the growth of private property is an addition, not a contradiction, to natural law. Aquinas argued that to be naked was in accordance with natural law and that clothing was an addition to natural law and devised for the benefit of man. The same reasoning applied to private property.

> We might say that for man to be naked is of the natural law, because nature did not give him clothes, but art invented them. In this sense, the possession of all things . . . [is] said to be of the natural law, because, namely, the distinction of possession . . . [was] not brought in by nature, but devised by human reason for the benefit of human life.[2]

Again following Aristotle, Aquinas approved the regulation of private property by the state and accepted an unequal distribution of private property. However, in the spirit of Plato, he still advocated poverty and communal living as the ideal for those of deep religious commitment, because the communal life enabled them to devote the greatest part of their energies to religious activities.

Aquinas and other scholastics were also concerned with another aspect of greater economic activity, the price of goods. Unlike modern economists, they were not trying to analyze the formation of prices in an economy or to understand the role that prices play in the allocation of scarce resources. They focused on the ethical aspect of prices, raising issues of equity and justice. Did religious doctrine

---

[2] Quoted from *Summa Theologica*, I-II, Q. 94, Art. 5, by Richard Schlalter, *Private Property* (New Brunswick, N.J.: Rutgers University Press, 1951), p. 47.

The Relevance of Scholasticism

The ethical issues raised by the medieval school remain relevant today. From the broadest perspective, we still ask ourselves what constitutes "the good life" and by what criteria we are to evaluate the quality of our experiences and activities as human beings. Relationships with family and friends, good deeds, and high ideals are non-economic aspects of our lives that may or may not be considered in the context of a particular religious doctrine. The medieval church was concerned that increasing economic activity would turn the minds and hearts of humans from religious and ethical concerns and toward materialism.

The post–World War II period in the United States has seen several shifts in attitudes about economic and noneconomic motivation, especially in the beliefs of young adults. During the immediate postwar period, in the aftermath of the war and the Great Depression, young adults placed high priority on economic values. By the 1960s, however, many young people began to censor the older generation's concern with economic values. A societywide "generation gap" ensued, with leaders of youth admonishing young people to trust no one over age thirty. In the 1980s the pendulum swung again and young adults readopted the economic values of the postwar period. Business schools became the fastest-growing divisions in many universities.

The scholastics' concern with justice or lack of justice in the price system is applicable to the current social and economic system. Public utility regulation represents an attempt by society, through government, to guarantee the fairness of telephone, electric, and water usage rates. Regulatory commissions generally try to set prices that are "just" in that they are limited to the costs of producing those services, including the costs of providing capital to the firms that provide them.

As interest rates fell during the late 1980s and early 1990s, a number of consumer advocates became concerned about the fixed interest rates charged by issuers of consumer credit cards. Mortgage interest rates, business borrowing interest rates, and interest rate returns on government and business debt all declined considerably, but interest rates charged by credit card issuers remained fixed at about 18 percent. Most of the discussion of these issues was framed in ethical terms. Two other examples that illustrate how ethical considerations may outweigh economic concerns are (1) farm programs that permit farmers to borrow at lower interest costs than other businesses and (2) loan programs that are available to students and minority-owned businesses.

forbid merchants to sell goods for more than they paid for them? Were making profits and taking interest sinful acts? In discussing these issues, Aquinas combined religious thinking with Aristotle's views. When exchanges take place in the market to meet the needs of the trading parties (using Aristotle's conception of need), Aquinas concluded no ethical issues are involved. But when individuals produce for the market in anticipation of gain, they are acting virtuously only if their motives are charitable and their prices are just. If the merchant intends to use any profits for self-support, for charity, or to contribute to the public well-being, and if his prices are just, so that both the buyer and the seller benefit, the merchant has acted rightly.

Historians of economic theory differ in their interpretations of the scholastic notion of *just price*. Some hold that the scholastics, including Aquinas, considered a just price to be an equivalent in terms of labor cost. Others say that it is an equivalent in terms of utility, and still others regard it as an equivalent in terms of total cost of production. Thus, the scholastic concept of just price is seen alternatively as a forerunner of the Ricardian-Marxian labor theory of value, the marginal utility position, and the notion implicit in classical-neoclassical theory that competitive markets yield ideal just prices. Another widely held view regards the scholastic notion of just price as an integral part of the set of social and economic forces that maintained the hierarchy of feudalism. If all prices in the market were just prices, this view holds, no one would be able to change his or her social status by means of economic activity. The lack of economic analysis in scholasticism makes it difficult to judge exactly what was meant by "just price." Our interpretation is that for scholasticism in general and Aquinas in particular, just price meant simply the prevailing market price. If this is correct, however, since the scholastics had no theory with which to explain the forces that determine market price, no useful conclusion can be reached regarding the economic or even the ethical content of the concept of just price.

A corollary to the concept of just price was the scholastic notion of *usury*. The church's views on just price and morality in economic behavior were, for the most part, general enough not to impinge on the growing economy. But its views on usury were specific and consequential enough to create conflict between the church and the emerging business community. The meaning of the term *usury* has changed since the time of scholasticism. As used today, it denotes charging an *excessive* rate of interest; but in scholastic doctrine it conveys the biblical and Aristotelian sense of *any* taking of interest. Scholastic usury doctrine was itself derived largely from the Bible and the writings of Aristotle. The biblical condemnation of usury rose from the danger that the strong would take advantage of the weak. Moreover, Aristotle had argued that the taking of interest on loans was unnatural, since money is barren. The scholastic view gradually moderated from a fairly strict prohibition of interest early in the period to its acceptance—at least for business purposes—later.

St. Thomas Aquinas was a very complex and interesting thinker. On the one hand, he held back economic thinking by emphasizing ethical issues and focusing on moral philosophy; on the other hand, he advanced economics and all the social sciences by his use of abstract thinking. Stephan Worland points to the use of abstraction in St. Thomas Aquinas:

[He] largely disregards the institutional framework through which economic activity takes place and treats such activity simply as the conduct of private individuals. . . . Concentrating on questions of fundamental principle, he confines his economic investigation to a relatively high level of abstraction. . . . His conception of an economic system is that of a number of undifferentiated members of the human species held together by those basic institutions—private property, division of labor, exchange—which are "natural" to man.[3]

SUMMARY

Greek and scholastic thinkers did not pursue economics as a separate discipline; they were interested in much broader, more philosophical, issues. When they turned to analyze economic activity, it was not a market system they found. Therefore, they concentrated not on the nature and meaning of a price system but on ethical questions concerning fairness, justice, and equity. However, their insights into certain economic phenomena were used by later writers.

The Greek thinkers, particularly Hesiod and Xenophon, studied the administration of resources at the level of the household and producer and forged ideas about efficiency and its relationship to an appropriate division of labor. Aristotle and other Greeks examined the role of private property and incentives. In his discussion of needs and wants, Aristotle raised timeless concerns about the purpose of life, concerns that became the focal point of later examination by the scholastics.

Scholastic doctrine did not attempt to analyze the economy but to set religious standards by which to judge economic conduct. In a society with very little economic activity, in which land, labor, and capital were not traded in markets, and in which custom, tradition, and authority played important roles, there seemed—at least to the educated churchmen—to be a "higher good" than economic goods. However, the disruptive consequences of changing technology were slowly upsetting the feudal order, and economic life posed an ever greater challenge to spiritual life.

By the middle of the fifteenth century, scholastic notions of the virtuous life were out of step with prevailing economic practice, and the ethical judgments of the church seemed inappropriate to the developing economies of Western Europe. Nevertheless, scholastic doctrine did provide insights into the operation of the growing market economy and helped to form a base for the development of a more analytical approach.

A number of things had to happen before the market economy could fully develop and release the tremendous flood of goods inherent in the natural resources available for use and the knowledge and technology available for their exploitation. One of the most crucial changes was a great transformation of the institutional structure of Western Europe. Freedom was the key element in this change: freedom from the cold hand of tradition that stifled change, freedom from the ideology of religious teaching that viewed economic activity with disfavor, freedom from the political and economic power of the church that resisted the

[3] S. T. Worland, *Scholasticism and Welfare Economics* (Notre Dame, Ind.: University of Notre Dame Press, 1967), pp. 8–9. This passage is approvingly quoted by Barry Gordon on p. 155 of his *Economic Analysis Before Adam Smith.*

rise of new economic interests, and freedom from government that created and supported monopoly and engaged in other activities retarding economic advancement. Viewed over time, scholastic doctrine represents a slow retreat to a greater acceptance of economic pursuits. Freeing the economy from the church had to take place at an intellectual level as well as at a practical level.

Key Terms

preclassical period
efficiency
private property
communal property
needs

desires
scholasticism
feudal economy
just price
usury

Questions for Review and Discussion

1. What is the meaning of the assertion that neither the Greeks nor the scholastics understood the full meaning and implications of scarcity?
2. Explain the difference between the use of tradition, authority, and a market system as allocators of scarce resources.
3. Do you think it is appropriate to isolate the economic, political, sociological, and psychological facets of society from the total society?
4. What aspects of efficiency concerned some of the Greek thinkers?
5. What were Aristotle's views on the appropriateness of economic activity?
6. Use Aristotle's distinction between needs and wants to evaluate your own consumption patterns.
7. How does a feudal society differ from a market society?
8. Contrast and compare Plato, Aristotle, and St. Thomas Aquinas on the desirability of private property.
9. Explain the concept of just price and write an essay on the difficulties of objectively determining a just price.
10. Explain the evolving concept of usury and show how this idea is still used in our society.
11. You have just found a job as a research assistant to an absent-minded professor. She wants to quote the following passage from Aquinas but has lost the bibliographic citation. Your first assignment is to find the passage.

> To take usury for money lent is unjust in itself because this is to sell what does not exist, and this evidently leads to inequality which is contrary to justice.

Suggested Readings

Dempsey, Bernard W. "Just Price in a Functional Economy." *American Economic Review,* 25 (1935).

De Roover, Raymond. "The Concept of Just Price: Economic Theory and Policy." *Journal of Economic History,* 28 (December 1958).

Gordon, Barry. *Economic Analysis Before Adam Smith.* New York: Barnes and Noble, 1975.

————— . *The Economic Problem in Biblical and Patristic Thought.* Leiden: E. J. Brill, 1989.

Hollander, Samuel. "On the Interpretation of Just Price." *Kyklos,* 18 (1965).

Langholm, Odd. *Price and Value in the Aristotelian Tradition.* Bergen, Norway: Universitetsforlaget, 1979.

Lowry, S. Todd. *The Archaeology of Economic Ideas.* Durham, N.C.: Duke University Press, 1987.

Pirenne, Henri. *Economic and Social History of Medieval Europe.* New York: Harcourt Brace, 1937.

Viner, Jacob. "Religious Thought and Economic Society." *History of Political Economy,* 10 (Spring 1978).

Worland, Stephan T. *Scholasticism and Welfare Economics.* Notre Dame, Ind.: University of Notre Dame Press, 1967.

————— . "Justium Pretium: One More Round in an Endless Series." *History of Political Economy,* 9 (Winter 1977).

————— . Review of Langholm's book cited above. *History of Political Economy,* 12 (Winter 1980).

3 Mercantilism, Physiocracy, and Other Precursors of Classical Economic Thought

"For it is remarkable that the inventors had none of that detached objectivity that goes by the name of 'scientific attitude.'"

—William Letwin

IMPORTANT THINKERS

THOMAS MUN	*England's Treasure by Forraign Trade* 1664
ISAAC NEWTON	*Principia Mathematica* 1687
WILLIAM PETTY	*Political Arithmetic* 1690
BERNARD MANDEVILLE	*The Fable of the Bees* 1714
DAVID HUME	*Political Discourses* 1752
RICHARD CANTILLON	*Essay on the Nature of Commerce in General* 1755
FRANÇOIS QUESNAY	*Tableau Économique* 1758

The 150-year period from 1600 to 1750 was characterized by an increase in economic activity. Feudalism, with its economically, socially, and politically self-sufficient manor, was giving way to increasing trade, the growth of cities outside the manor, and the growth of the nation-state. Individual activity was less controlled by the custom and tradition of the feudal society and by the authority of the church. Production of goods for the market became more important; and land, labor, and capital began to be bought and sold in markets. This laid the groundwork for the Industrial Revolution.

During this period economic thinking developed from a simple application of ideas about individuals, households, and producers to a more complicated view of the economy as a system with laws and interrelationships of its own. We divide our consideration of this period into three main headings: mercantilism, precursors of classical economic thought, and physiocracy.

MERCANTILISM

Mercantilism is the name given to some 250 years of economic literature and practice between 1500 and 1750. Although mercantilist literature was produced in all the developing economies of Western Europe, the most significant contributions were made by the English and the French.

Whereas the economic literature of scholasticism was written by medieval monks, the economic theory of mercantilism was the work of merchant businessmen. The literature they produced was closely connected to questions of economic policy and was usually related to a particular interest the merchant-writer was trying to promote. For this reason there was often considerable skepticism regarding the analytical merits of particular arguments and the validity of their conclusions. Few authors could claim to be sufficiently detached from the issues to render objective analysis. Yet throughout the mercantilistic period, both the quantity and the quality of economic literature grew. From 1650 to 1750 the mercantilistic literature was of distinctively higher quality, and scattered throughout it are nearly all the analytical concepts on which Adam Smith based his *Wealth of Nations,* which was published in 1776.

Every Man His Own Economist

The age of mercantilism has been characterized as a time when every person was his own economist. Diverse views appeared from the various writers between 1500 and 1750, so it is difficult to generalize about the resulting literature. Furthermore, each writer tended to concentrate on one topic, and no single writer was able to synthesize these contributions impressively enough to influence the subsequent development of economic theory. Perhaps this was because economics as an intellectual discipline had not yet found a home in the university; rather, it was largely studied by men of affairs who wrote pamphlets about the particular economic problems that concerned them.

Power and Wealth

Mercantilism can best be understood as an intellectual reaction to problems of the times. In this period of the decline of the manor and the rise of the nation-state, the mercantilists tried to determine the best policies for promoting the power and wealth of the nation. Just as Machiavelli, the Italian statesman, political theorist, and author of *The Prince* (1513), had advised rulers about expedient political policies, the mercantilists advised them about the economic policies that would

best consolidate and increase the power and prosperity of the developing economies.

The mercantilists proceeded on the assumption that the total wealth of the world
was fixed. Using the same assumption, the scholastics had reasoned that when
trade took place between individuals, the gain of one was necessarily the loss of
another. The mercantilists applied this reasoning to trade between nations, concluding that any increase in the wealth and economic power of one nation occurred
at the expense of others. Thus, the mercantilists emphasized international trade as
a means of increasing the wealth and power of a nation and, in particular, focused
on the balance of trade between nations.

The goal of economic activity, according to most mercantilists, was production—not consumption, as classical economics would later have it. For the
mercantilists the wealth of the nation was not defined in terms of the sum of
individual wealth. They advocated increasing the nation's wealth by simultaneously encouraging production, increasing exports, and holding down domestic
consumption. Thus, the wealth of the nation was based on the poverty of the many.
Although the mercantilists laid great stress on production, a plentiful supply of
goods within a country was considered undesirable. High levels of production
would permit increased exports, and through trade the nation's wealth and power
could be increased. The mercantilists advocated low wages in order to give the
domestic economy competitive advantages in international trade and because they
believed that wage levels above a subsistence level would result in a reduced labor
effort. Higher wages would cause laborers to work fewer hours per year; thus,
national output would fall. Poverty for the individual, therefore, benefits the nation
when the goal of economic activity is defined in terms of national output and not
in terms of national consumption.

Balance of Trade

According to mercantilistic thinking, a country should encourage exports and
discourage imports by means of tariffs, quotas, subsidies, taxes, and the like, in
order to achieve a so-called favorable balance of trade. Production should be
stimulated by governmental interference in the domestic economy and by the
regulation of foreign trade. Protective duties should be placed on manufactured
goods from abroad; and the importation of cheap raw materials, to be used in
manufacturing goods for export, should be encouraged.

Historians of economic thought disagree over the nature and significance of the
balance of trade doctrine in mercantilist literature. It is clear, however, that many
early mercantilists, who defined the wealth of a nation not in terms of its
production or consumption of goods but in terms of its holdings of precious metals,
argued for a favorable balance of trade because it would produce a flow of precious
metals into the domestic economy to settle the trade balance.

The first mercantilists argued that a favorable balance of trade should be struck
with each nation. A number of subsequent writers, however, argued that only the
overall balance of trade with all nations was significant. Thus, England might have

an unfavorable balance of trade with India, but because it could import from India cheap raw materials that could be used to manufacture goods in England for export, it might well have a favorable overall trade balance when all nations were taken into account.

A related issue concerned the export of precious metals or bullion. The early mercantilists recommended that the export of bullion be strictly prohibited. Later writers suggested that exporting bullion might lead to an improvement in overall trade balances if the bullion were used to purchase raw materials for export goods. The mercantilists' persistent advocacy of a favorable balance of trade raises some perplexing questions, which are best handled by examining the mercantilists' views about money.

Money and Mercantilism

Adam Smith devoted nearly two hundred pages of *Wealth of Nations* to a harsh and only partly justifiable criticism of mercantilistic theory and practice, particularly its equating of the wealth of a nation with the stock of precious metals internally held. Early mercantilists were very impressed with the significance of the tremendous flow of precious metals into Europe, particularly into Spain, from the New World. However, later mercantilists did not subscribe to this view and were able to develop useful analytical insights into the role of money in an economy. For example, the relationship between the quantity of money and the general level of prices was recognized as early as 1569 by the Frenchman Jean Bodin. He offered five reasons for the rise in the general level of prices in Western Europe during the sixteenth century, the most important of which was the increase in the quantity of gold and silver there resulting from the discovery of the New World. By the end of the seventeenth century, John Locke was able to analyze the role of money with even greater sophistication, demonstrating that the level of economic activity in an economy depends upon the quantity of money and its velocity. In the middle of the eighteenth century, David Hume presented a reasonably complete description of the interrelationships among a country's balance of trade, the quantity of money, and the general level of prices. In international trade theory this has become known as the *price specie–flow mechanism*. Hume pointed out that it would be impossible for an economy to maintain a favorable balance of trade continuously. A favorable balance of trade would lead to an increase in the quantity of gold and silver (specie) within an economy. An increase in the quantity of money would lead to a rise in the level of prices in the economy with the favorable balance of trade. If one country has a favorable balance of trade, some other country or countries must be having an unfavorable balance with a loss of gold or silver and a subsequent fall in the general level of prices. Exports will decrease and imports will increase for the economy with the initial favorable trade balance because of prices that are relatively higher than those of other economies. The opposite tendencies will prevail in an economy with the initial unfavorable balance. This process will ultimately lead to a self-correction of the trade balances.

These developments occurred later, however, because in the early 1500s there was little comprehension of the consequences of trade balances between nations and almost no understanding of the consequences of increases in the money supply. By the middle of the eighteenth century, considerable analytical progress had been made in understanding these issues. Until that time there was a fairly steady increase of analytical insight into the operation of a market economy. The period from 1660 to 1776 was marked by particularly noteworthy development.

A central feature of mercantilist literature is its conviction that *monetary factors,* rather than real factors, are the chief determinants of economic activity and growth. Mercantilists maintained that an adequate supply of money is particularly essential to the growth of trade, both domestic and international. Changes in the quantity of money, they believed, generate changes in the level of real output—in yards of cloth and bushels of grain.

All this would change with the advent of Adam Smith and classical economics, which would contend that the level of economic activity and its rate of growth depend upon a number of *real factors:* the quantity of labor, natural resources, capital goods, and the institutional structure. Any changes in the quantity of money, classical economists averred, would influence the level of neither output nor growth but only the general level of prices.

Modern Analysis of Mercantilism

Evaluating past writers raises a number of difficult but interesting issues. There are always differences of opinion about what particular writers really meant by what they said. Imprecise language can make interpretation difficult. When J. M. Keynes discussed the mercantilists in a section of his *General Theory* titled "Notes on Mercantilism," he credited them with having insight into an acceptable policy by which to stimulate economic development. But Adam Smith, other classicals, and the orthodox line of economic thinkers from 1776 until the time of Keynes found little of merit in much of the mercantilist literature. This divergence of opinion is understandable, though, when we compare some aspects of classical and Keynesian thought. Because Smith and other classical economists stressed the *real* forces that determine the level of output, their theories focused almost exclusively on the side of supply. However, Keynes, because he emphasized the role of aggregate demand, enlarging on actual mercantilist thought, found some common bonds between his theory and that of the mercantilists. He was sympathetic to their underconsumptionist views and declared sound their belief that increases in the quantity of money would increase output. The mercantilists, Keynes said, held that a favorable balance of trade would increase domestic spending and thereby raise the level of income and employment.

Another problematical aspect of evaluating the contributions of past writers lies in the need to assess their intellectual achievement. Should this judgment be based wholly on modern standards or should it be kept strictly in the context of the analytical apparatus of their times? Even though most historians of ideas take a position between these polar views, a good deal of controversy as to the relative merits of past economists still results.[1]

Another attitude toward mercantilism deserves mention. Some assessments of mercantilism have scrutinized not the ideas of its proponents but their motivations. The mercantilists, in the jargon of modern economics, were "rent-seekers." They were driven by profit motives to use government to gain economic privilege for themselves. They were generally merchants who favored government granting of monopolies that would enable the merchant-monopolists to charge higher prices than would have been possible without monopoly privileges.

Theoretical Contributions of the Mercantilists

The study of mercantilism by historians of economic theory demonstrates that from about 1660 to 1776 the quantity and quality of economic analysis increased. The improvement in the quality of economic analysis during the later part of the mercantilistic era was so pronounced that the period has been characterized as a transitional time containing the origins of scientific economics.

Possibly the most significant accomplishment of the later mercantilists was the explicit recognition of the possibility of analyzing the economy. This development represented a transfer to the social sciences of attitudes then prevalent in the physical sciences. It reached its full fruition after the time of Isaac Newton (1642–1727), and its impact is still felt today. The substitution of cause-and-effect analysis for the moral analysis of the scholastics does not represent a clear break with the past, however, because logical analysis was used by some of the scholastics and moralizing still exists in modern economic literature. But the view that the laws of the economy could be discovered by the same methods that revealed the laws of physics was an important step toward subsequent developments in economic theory.

Many mercantilists saw a highly mechanical causality in the economy, believing that if one understood the rules of causality, one could control the economy. It followed that legislation, if wisely enacted, could positively influence the course of economic events and that economic analysis would indicate what forms of government intervention would effect a given end. Mercantilists realized, however, that government interference must not be haphazard nor complicate basic economic truths such as the law of supply and demand. Some correctly deduced, for example, that price ceilings set below equilibrium prices lead to excess demand and shortages. The later mercantilists frequently applied the concepts of economic man and profit motive in stimulating economic activity. Governments, they said,

---

[1] For a provocative exchange on the mercantilists, see William R. Allen, "Modern Defenders of Mercantilistic Theory," *History of Political Economy,* 2 (Fall 1970); A. W. Coats, "The Interpretation of Mercantilist Economics: Some Historiographical Problems," *History of Political Economy,* 5 (Fall 1973); and William R. Allen, "Rearguard Response," *History of Political Economy,* 5 (Fall 1973).

cannot change the basic nature of human beings, particularly their egoistic drives. The politician takes these factors as given, in attempting to create a set of laws and institutions that will channel these drives so as to increase the power and prosperity of the nation.

As we will see, many of the later mercantilists became aware of the serious analytical errors of their predecessors. They recognized, for example, that specie is not a measure of the wealth of a nation, that all nations could not have a favorable balance of trade, that no one country could maintain a favorable balance of trade over the long run, that trade can be mutually beneficial to nations, and that advantages will accrue to nations that practice specialization and division of labor. An increasing number of writers recommended a reduction in the amount of government intervention. Thus, the literature included statements of incipient classical liberalism.

Yet none of the preclassical writers was able to present an integrated view of the operation of a market economy—the manner in which prices are formed and scarce resources are allocated. This failure of the mercantilists to reach the understanding eventually achieved by Adam Smith and subsequent classical economists may be attributable to one important difference between classical and mercantilistic theory. The mercantilists believed there was a basic conflict between private interests and the public welfare. Therefore, they considered it necessary for government to channel private self-interest into public benefits. Classical economists, on the other hand, find a basic harmony in the system and see public good as flowing naturally from individual self-interest. Even the later mercantilists who advocated laissez faire policies lacked sufficient insight into the operation of the market to make an adequate argument to support them. Still, the writings of the later mercantilists were used by Smith to develop his analysis.

INFLUENTIAL PRECURSORS OF CLASSICAL THOUGHT

Ideas don't generally come out of thin air; instead, the germs of an idea are often in the air long before they become a central idea of a period. During the mercantilist period, the ideas that would become the focus of the classical school were germinated. They were formulated in various ways. Initially they were rejected by the majority of writers in the period as outrageous; then they were accepted by a few, then by a few more, until finally the mercantilist period ended and the formerly outrageous ideas became the central ideas of the classical period. Thus, the ideas attributed to Adam Smith could take hold—largely due to the earlier heterodox writers who dissented from the mercantilist mainstream.

To give a flavor of the diversity and quality of English writers during the period from 1500 to 1750, we will briefly examine several thinkers: Thomas Mun, William Petty, Bernard Mandeville, David Hume, and Richard Cantillon.

Thomas Mun

Book IV of Adam Smith's *Wealth of Nations* (1776) is largely a refutation of mercantilistic theory and policy; in it Smith quoted Mun as a leading mercantilist. Mun (1571–1641) was a director of the East India Company, which had been criticized for two things that some writers found undesirable: (1) England imported more from India than it exported, and (2) England sent precious metals to India to pay for imports. Mun represents a typical mercantilist—a proponent of governmental policies that benefited a particular business interest. Mun's first book, *A Discourse of Trade from England Unto the East Indies,* was published in 1621; it defended the Company from these charges in a partisan manner. He produced a second book, *England's Treasure by Forraign Trade,* in 1628, which was published posthumously in 1664 by his son. The book had several editions, and its popularity was evidently the reason why Smith chose it for rebuttal. It is often said that Mun's 1664 book is the classic of English mercantilistic literature.

American students are indirectly informed about mercantilistic theory and practice because of their awareness of the history of the American colonies. English policy was designed to keep the colonies a raw material–exporting economy dependent on England for manufactured goods.

Mun asserted in the title of his book that England's treasure was gained by foreign trade. His thinking is typically mercantilistic in that he confused the wealth of a nation with its stock of precious metals and therefore argued for a favorable balance of trade and an inflow of gold and silver to settle the trade balance. He believed that government should regulate foreign trade to achieve a favorable balance, encourage importation of cheap raw materials, encourage exportation of manufactured goods, enact protective tariffs on imported manufactured goods, and take other measures to increase population and keep wages low and competitive.

Mun presented these mercantilistic ideas but refuted some of the cruder mercantilistic notions that embodied criticisms of the East India Company. He pointed out that even though a favorable balance of trade with all nations was desirable and an outflow of precious metals to all nations was undesirable, the unfavorable balance and export of precious metals to India was beneficial to England in that such practices enlarged its trade balances with all nations and, thereby, its inflow of gold and silver. By the time the last edition of Mun's famous book was published in 1755, many of the more perceptive mercantilists were seeing the serious errors of the mercantilistic paradigm. These *liberal mercantilists* were beginning to articulate the intellectual foundation for Smith's *Wealth of Nations.*

William Petty

William Petty (1623–1687) published one work during his lifetime (in 1662), but in the ten years following his death four others were printed. We term these "works," for they were more tracts than books, lacking coherent organizational structure. Petty was a brilliant thinker who rose from poverty as a weaver's son to master Latin, Greek, French, arithmetic, geometry, and navigation by the time he was fifteen years old. He ended life as a wealthy man after spending time as a sailor, physician (he studied anatomy in Paris with Hobbes), inventor, surveyor, and—most important—the first economic writer to advocate the measurement of economic variables. His economic writings were not general treatises; they were the result of his practical interests in matters such as taxation, politics, money, and measurement.

Petty's *Political Arithmetic* was written in 1676 but not published until 1690. He seemed conscious that he was breaking new ground by discussing the methodology of political arithmetic.

> The method I take to do this is not yet very usual. For instead of using only comparative and superlative words and intellectual arguments, I have taken the course ... to express myself in terms of number, weight, or measure; to use only arguments of sense, and to consider only such causes as have visible foundations in nature.[2]

Petty was influenced by broad philosophical movements that took place before and during his lifetime. Aristotle and the scholastics developed their arguments almost exclusively with words; but Descartes, Hobbes, and Bacon brought induction, empiricism, and mathematics to the attention of the intellectual community.

Petty apparently was the first to be self-conscious in his advocacy of the use of what we would call statistical techniques to measure social phenomena. He tried to measure population, national income, exports, imports, and the capital stock of a nation. His methods were crude almost beyond belief, which led Adam Smith to indicate that he had little use for political arithmetic.

A fairly typical mercantilist in his analysis and policy conclusions, Petty does represent the beginning of an aspect of economics and the social sciences whose full conclusion has yet to play out. In Chapter 1 we examined some of the methodological issues in economics; one of the most crucial concerns was the mechanisms used in an attempt to establish fundamental principles. One of the strongest traditions in economics has been a literary methodology whereby problems are explored and theories are developed by the use of language. Testing of hypotheses was done by appealing to present circumstances or to history, and the use of statistics was minimal until the end of the nineteenth century. Petty's seminal insight to express ideas in terms of numbers, weight, and measure and to accept only arguments that have visible foundations in nature represents the cornerstone of modern thinking in economics. His early use of statistics was crude, but the methodological position he represents has a lineage from the empirical inductionism of his time to the modern application of econometrics that is prevalent in contemporary economics journals. We will return to these issues of measurement and establishment of the principles of economics in Part V, Understanding the Present Through the Past.

[2] Sir William Petty, *The Economic Writings,* 2 vols., ed. C. H. Hull (London: Cambridge University Press, 1899), I, 244.

Bernard Mandeville

Whereas many of the mercantilists were staid businessmen who wrote dry treatises of advocacy, Bernard Mandeville (c. 1670–1733) used playful language and thought in an allegorical poem to convey his message. His *Fable of the Bees; Or, Private Vices, Publick Benefits* (1714) not only provoked his contemporaries but has continued to be of interest to students of literature, philosophy, psychology, and economics. Keynes approvingly fills two pages of the *General Theory* with quotations from Mandeville.[3]

Mandeville's satirical poem was an attack on the so-called *sentimental moralists,* whose appellation indicates their belief that morality is not made of purely rational principles. In their view morality consists of emotions or sentiments as well as human reason. The first important sentimental moralist was Anthony Ashley Cooper, the third Earl of Shaftesbury, who agreed with Rousseau in maintaining the natural goodness of humankind. Shaftesbury was a significant influence on Francis Hutcheson, who was a teacher of Adam Smith.

Shaftesbury's optimism concerning the innate goodness of human beings was in sharp contrast to *Puritanism* and *Hobbism.* The rational, selfish drives of human beings worked toward the social good because moral sentiment tempered egoism and permitted an understanding of the difference between right and wrong and of how to chose the right way. Mandeville argued that selfishness was a moral vice but that social good could result from selfish acts if these actions were properly channeled by the government. As a mercantilist Mandeville had no concept of a natural harmony, which was an essential ingredient in Adam Smith's advocacy of laissez faire. He found the world to be wicked but maintained that "private vices by the dexterous management of a skillful politician might be turned into public benefits."[4]

Mercantilistic beliefs incorporated a fear of goods, a concern with overproduction and underconsumption. Individual saving was undesirable because it led to lower consumption, lower output, and lower employment. But for many, then and now, saving is a virtue and spending a vice. In his poem Mandeville took great delight in poking fun at the sentimental moralists. He postulated a beehive in which economic activity is driven by private vices.

> The Root of Evil, Avarice,
> That dam'd ill-natur'd baneful Vice,
> Was Slave to Prodigality,
> That noble Sin; whilst Luxury
> Employ'd a Million Poor,
> And Odious Pride a Million more:
> Envy it self, and Vanity,
> Were Ministers of Industry;

[3] John Maynard Keynes, *The General Theory of Employment, Interest and Money* (New York: Harcourt, Brace, and Company, 1936), pp. 358–362.
[4] Bernard Mandeville, *A Letter to Dion* (Los Angeles: The Augustan Reprint Society, 1953), p. 37.

> Their darling Folly, Fickleness,
> In Diet, Furniture and Dress,
> That strange ridic'lous Vice, was made
> The very Wheel that turn'd the Trade.[5]

Mandeville then suggested that the moralists persuade the bees to behave virtuously, replacing the private vices of prodigality, pride, and vanity (which brought about much consumption spending) with the usual virtues. To Mandeville the end result of private virtue is economic depression.

He was a pure mercantilist in his insistence that government regulate foreign trade to ensure that exports always exceed imports. The mercantilist view toward labor is in sharp contrast to that of the classicals; Mandeville's position on labor is particularly clear and, from a modern view, alarming. Because the goal of society is production—not consumption, as advocated by the classicals—Mandeville advocated a large population and child labor, and he condemned idleness. A large population with high labor-force-participation rates results in low wages, which gives the nation a competitive advantage in exports and international trade. Low wages also ensure an adequate supply of labor, for Mandeville saw a *downward-sloping labor supply curve.* Higher wages reduce labor supply, in Mandeville's view.

Mandeville and Smith make interesting contrasts between mercantilism and classical liberalism.

> *Mandeville:* I have laid down as Maxims never to be departed from, that the Poor should be kept strictly to Work, and that it was Prudence to relieve their Wants, but Folly to cure them; that Agriculture and Fishery should be promoted in all their Branches in order to render Provisions, and consequently Labour cheap.[6]

> *Mandeville:* [W]ealth consists of a Multitude of laborious poor.[7]

> *Smith:* The liberal reward of labour, therefore, as it is the effect of increasing wealth, so it is the cause of increasing population. To complain of it is to lament over the necessary effect and cause of the greatest public prosperity. The liberal reward of labour, as it encourages the propagation, so it increases the industry of the common people. The wages of labour are the encouragement of industry, which like every other human quality, improves in proportion to the encouragement it receives.[8]

---

[5] Bernard Mandeville, *The Fable of the Bees,* ed. F. B. Kaye (2 vols; Cambridge: Oxford University Press, 1924), I, p. 25.

[6] *Ibid.,* pp. 248–249.

[7] *Ibid.,* p. 287.

[8] Adam Smith, *Wealth of Nations,* ed. E. Cannan (New York: The Modern Library, 1937), p. 81.

One of Mandeville's major points is that one should accept men and women as they are and not try to moralize about what they should be. It is the role of government to take imperfect humankind, full of vice, and by rules and regulations channel its activities toward the social good. However, the mercantilists' social good (in which wealth consists of multitudes of laborious poor) is quite different from the classicals' social good. One might compare the message of the mercantilists with practice in the former Soviet Union, where the focus was on power for the state and production of goods with little concern for increasing the consumption of the masses.

David Hume

Economics suffered by the failure of David Hume (1711–1776) to devote more of his brilliance and analytical abilities to questions of economics; but our loss has been the gain of philosophy, politics, and history. Hume was a close personal friend of Adam Smith; their joint intellectual output is awesome in terms of its impact on following generations.

Like many of his contemporaries, Hume could be called a liberal mercantilist; he had one foot in mercantilism but with the other stepped forward into classical political economy. Hume took the insights of John Locke on the consequences of a change in the money supply and developed the *price specie–flow mechanism* discussed in the previous section on money and mercantilism. The ability to have continuing favorable balances of trade, which were advocated by many mercantilists, was shown by Hume's argument to be an impossibility. The mercantilists paid little attention to Hume on this score, and it is interesting that Adam Smith did not use Hume's argument in his long and strongly worded condemnation of mercantilistic theory.

Hume's basis in mercantilism is represented by his views on the consequences of a gradual increase in the money supply on the level of real output and employment. The mercantilists had argued that changes in the money supply could increase real output. The classicals maintained that real output depended not on the quantity of money but on real forces: labor supply, natural resources, capital goods, and the institutional structure. Changes in the money supply would change only the general level of prices. Hume believed that although the absolute level of money in a nation would not influence real output, a gradual increase in the money supply would lead to an increase in output.

Two other, much broader, ideas put forth by Hume are worthy of mention. One may be particularly relevant to the present, when many countries in Eastern Europe and the former Soviet Union are restructuring their societies and economies. Hume searched for a connection between economic freedom—the freedom to sell one's resources, labor or nonlabor, when, where, and at what price one chooses; the freedom to produce and sell the fruits of one's activities; and the freedom to buy outputs or inputs without constraint by outside forces—and political liberty. Hume maintained that the growth of economic freedom went hand in hand with the growth of political freedom.

Finally, Hume was a precursor of the distinction made later by Nassau Senior, John Neville Keynes, and Lionel Robbins concerning the difference between positive and normative statements. That what ought to be (normative statements) cannot be derived from what is (positive statements) is called *Hume's Dictum*.

Richard Cantillon

Richard Cantillon (c. 1680–1734) was an unusual figure in the history of economic ideas. His birth date and place of birth are not completely certain, but the consensus is that he was born between 1680 and 1690 in Ireland. He lived most of his life in Paris and was successful in amassing a fortune as a banker. His one book was evidently written around 1730 and was widely read in both France and England by intellectuals who were interested in economics. He died in England in 1734; his book was not published until 1755.

What is unique about Cantillon is that his book was unusually sophisticated and advanced in its understanding of economic questions, yet it was not given much attention in England after the publication of Adam Smith's *Wealth of Nations* in 1776. In 1881 William Stanley Jevons rediscovered Cantillon's book and heaped praise on it, describing it as "the first systematic treatment in political economy" and "the cradle of political economy."

What is Cantillon's place in the history of economic thought? He evidently had little subsequent influence on writers, although his book was read by the physiocrats and cited by Smith in his *Wealth of Nations*. Even though it is a brilliant and insightful work, its only important influence that can be traced is on the physiocrat François Quesnay. Cantillon himself acknowledged the influence of John Locke, for his theory of money, and William Petty, for his emphasis on the importance of measuring economic phenomena. Cantillon was part mercantilist (mostly in his views on foreign trade), part physiocrat (in his emphasis on the primary role of agriculture in the economy), and part physiocrat-classical (in his vision of the interrelatedness of the various sectors of the economy). Unlike Petty, who produced works of a practical nature exploring various topics in economics, Cantillon was modern in that (1) he started with the goal of establishing basic principles of economics through the process of reasoning, and, more important, (2) he wanted to collect data to use in the process of verifying his principles. Unfortunately, his statistical work is lost.

Cantillon's seminal vision, which was to a lesser extent possessed by some of the physiocrats and liberal mercantilists, was of a market system that coordinated the activities of producers and consumers through the medium of individual self-interest. The key actors in this self-regulating system were entrepreneurs who, in their pursuit of profit, produced social results that were superior to ones that could be produced by government interference. Given competitive markets in which entrepreneurs pursue customers in final goods markets and compete with one another in factor markets, Cantillon was able to point to the adjustment processes as demands, costs, technology, and other factors change. He did not

The Servant Did It

This book for the most part shies away from discussing the personal lives of economists. The reason is twofold: (1) information about their personal lives is often not directly relevant to their ideas and their contributions; and (2) their personal lives are often so interesting and entertaining (economists, after all, are extraordinarily interesting people) that to present them would tend to distract you from their ideas and contributions.

Still, for Richard Cantillon, we will make a slight exception, at least in regard to his death. For Cantillon did not die a natural death; he was murdered.

The likely murderer was a servant whom he had dismissed ten days earlier. At the time of his murder, his house was also set ablaze, destroying who knows what of his other contributions. Because of this, he remains known to us as an Irishman with a Spanish name who wrote a book extremely advanced for the 1730s, in either French or English, that was not published for twenty years and that influenced Smith and the physiocrats. It is possible that Cantillon, had he not been murdered by a servant he had fired, not Smith, would be known as the father of modern economics.

make the plea for laissez faire with the force of Smith, which may account for his neglected recognition.

He tended always to treat any element of the economy as part of an integrated structure; for example, population changes were endogenous to his system, not exogenous. His explanation of the forces that determine prices was surprisingly modern in that he distinguished between market prices, determined by short-run factors, and what he called intrinsic value, long-run equilibrium prices. He was able to apply his analysis of prices and markets to international trade and view the adjustment processes that take place there.

Some of his most accomplished technical analysis was not in microeconomics but in the macroeconomic aspects of changes in the supply of money on prices and production. He divided the economy into sectors and analyzed the flow of income between them; although he did not explicitly formulate an economic table to represent these flows, he clearly influenced Quesnay, who did. Cantillon acknowledged his debt to John Locke and his early statement of the *quantity theory of money*, but Cantillon was able to see subtleties in Locke's analysis that escaped Smith and his contemporaries. The consequences of an increase in the quantity of money were not simply macro effects on output or prices. In an early examination of the micro foundations of macroeconomics, Cantillon saw that the points at which the new funds entered the economy would influence their impact. Accordingly, the general level of prices could change, but relative prices could also change with subsequent impacts on the various sectors of the economy.

As we suggested in the closing pages of Chapter 1, historians of economic thought must make choices about how much attention to give to various economists. Our criteria assign great weight to the impact of a given writer on the subsequent development of economic ideas, not to the creativeness or brilliance of a given thinker. If our criteria emphasized who said it first or who said it best, Cantillon would have a place alongside Smith as a founder of political economy.

PHYSIOCRACY

Adam Smith was influenced during his travel in France by a group of French writers who have become known as the physiocrats. They perceived the interrelatedness of the sectors of the economy and analyzed the working of nonregulated markets.

Although mercantilism was much in evidence in eighteenth-century France, a new but short-lived movement called *physiocracy* began there around 1750. Because it provided significant analytical insights into the economy, its influence on subsequent economic thought was considerable. Scholars of economic ideas often arbitrarily group men of divergent ideas into a school of thought, usually on the basis of a single similarity. However, the writings of the physiocratic school express remarkably consistent views on all major points. There are three reasons for this. (1) Physiocracy developed exclusively in France. (2) The ideas of the physiocrats were presented over a relatively short period of time, from about 1750 to 1780. (It has been said that no one was aware of physiocratic ideas before 1750, and after 1780 only a few economists had heard of them.) (3) Physiocracy had an acknowledged intellectual leader, François Quesnay (1694–1774), whose ideas were accepted virtually without question by his fellow physiocrats. Their own writings were mainly designed to convince others of the merit of Quesnay's economics.

Natural Law

The physiocrats, like the later English mercantilists, developed their economic theories in order to formulate correct economic policies. Both groups believed that the correct formulation of economic policy presupposed a correct understanding of the economy. Economic theory was therefore a prerequisite of economic policy. The physiocrats' unique idea was of the role of *natural law* in the formulation of policy. They maintained that natural laws governed the operation of the economy and that although these laws were independent of human will, humans could objectively discover them—as they could the laws of the natural sciences. This idea contributed significantly to the development of economics and the social sciences.

The Interrelatedness of an Economy

Even though physiocratic theory was deficient in logical consistency and detail, the physiocrats did determine the necessity of building theoretical models by isolating key economic variables for study and analysis. Using this process, they achieved significant insights into the interdependence of the various sectors of the economy on the levels of both macro- and microeconomic analysis.

The major concern of the physiocrats was with the macroeconomic process of development. They recognized that France was lagging behind England in applying new agricultural techniques. Some areas of northern France were introducing advanced techniques, but most of France was maintaining its old ways; thus, the country was developing unevenly. To cope with this problem, the physiocrats, like the English and French mercantilists, wished to discover the nature and causes of the wealth of nations and the policies that would best promote economic growth. French mercantilism had been even more thoroughgoing in its regulation of domestic and foreign economic activity than its British counterpart, and physiocracy was an intellectual reaction to this regulation. The physiocrats focused not on money but on the real forces leading to economic development. In reaction to the mercantilistic notion that wealth was created by the process of exchange, they studied the creation of physical value and concluded that the origin of wealth was in agriculture, or nature.

In the economy of their time, more goods were produced than were needed to pay the real costs to society of producing those goods. Therefore, a surplus was generated. Their search for the origin and size of this surplus led them to the idea of the *net product*. The agricultural production process provides a good example of a net product. After the various factors of production—seed, labor, machinery, and the like—are paid for, the annual harvest leaves an excess that the physiocrats regarded as resulting from the productivity of nature. Labor, according to them, could produce only enough goods to pay the costs of labor, and the same held true for the other factors of production with the exception of land. Therefore, production from land created the surplus that the physiocrats called the net product. Manufacturing and other nonagricultural economic activities were considered "sterile," because they created no net product. The belief that only agricultural production was capable of returning to society an output greater than the social costs of that output may seem quaint today, but it may be explained by the fact that the physiocrats focused on physical productivity rather than value productivity. However, because large-scale industry had not yet developed in France in the middle of the eighteenth century, the productivity of industry was not apparent in the economy of the physiocrats. The small employer with only a few employees did not seem to be making any surplus, and his standard of living was not significantly different from that of his employees. Having established that the origin of the net product was in land, the physiocrats concluded that land rent was the measure of the society's net product.

Figure 3.1 (on page 52) shows the original *Tableau Économique*. Figure 3.2 (on page 53) is a simplification that shows the essence of the physiocratic analysis. It shows three sectors of society: farmers, landowners, and artisans and servants. There is no foreign sector, government sector, or manufacturing sector above the artisan level. The physiocratic analysis began with a net product at the beginning of the economic period of 2,000 livres held by landowners (the livre was the French

Figure 3.1   Tableau Économique

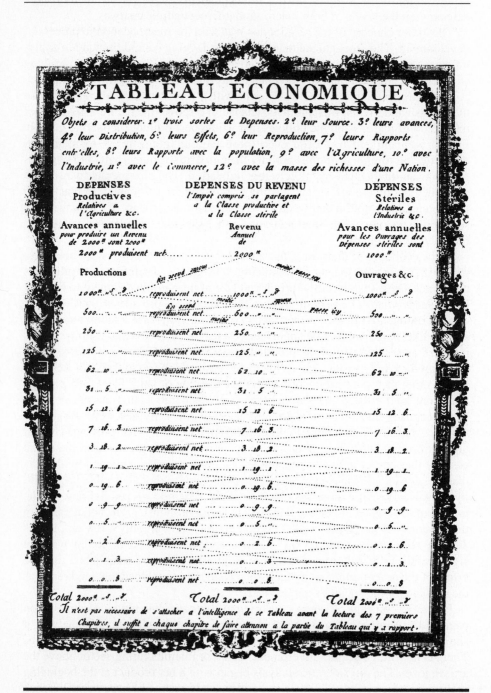

Figure 3.2   Quesnay's Tableau Économique

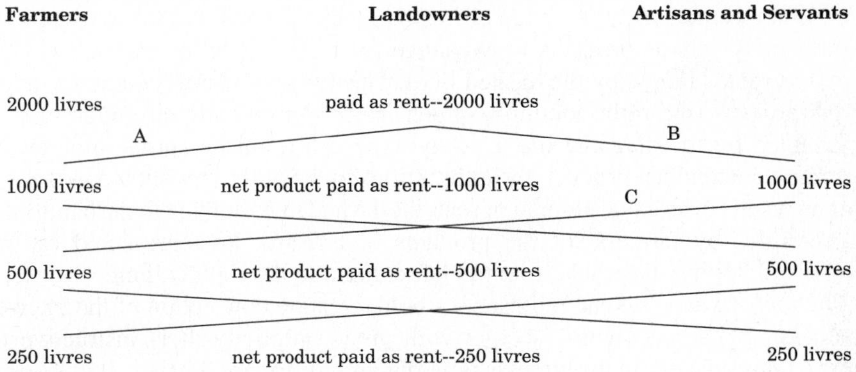

Farmers	Landowners	Artisans and Servants

2000 livres   paid as rent--2000 livres

      A   B

1000 livres   net product paid as rent--1000 livres   1000 livres

                                              C

500 livres   net product paid as rent--500 livres   500 livres

250 livres   net product paid as rent--250 livres   250 livres

monetary unit before the franc). This net product was paid to the landowner as rent from economic activity in the previous period. The physiocrats assumed that only land could produce an output greater than its cost of production; in the *tableau* this productivity was assumed to be 100 percent. Activities of artisans, for example, result in products produced, and the payments to factors of production equal the value of the goods produced. For land alone, output is greater than factors consumed; in the *tableau* 2,000 livres invested in agricultural production result in a net product of 2,000 livres, which the landowners receive as rent.

Starting at the top center of the *tableau,* the landowners spend last year's net product of 2,000 livres by buying 1,000 livres of goods from artisans and 1,000

Figure 3.3   Quesnay's Table Translated as a Circular Flow Diagram

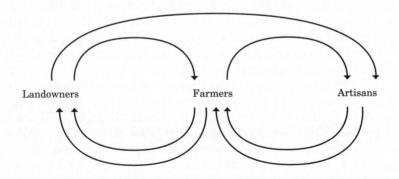

livres of agricultural goods from farmers (this is represented by the diagonal lines *A* and *B* from the center [landowner] column of the *tableau,* descending toward the columns representing the farmers and artisans). The 1,000 livres spent in the farm sector generates 2,000 livres of income, half of which (1,000 livres) flows to the landowners as products in exchange for their purchases and half (1,000 livres) as rents (shown by the dashed line). The 1,000 livres of income received by the artisans (the right column) is spent partly on agricultural goods: this is represented by the diagonal line *C*. Any expenditure in the agricultural sector generates an equal net product, by assumption; so the 500 livres shown in the left column results in an equal amount of rent, the dashed line, flowing to the landlords. Expenditures by farmers for the products of artisans are represented by the downward-sloping diagonals from the left column to the right column.

The *tableau économique* represents a bold, creative conception of the interrelatedness of macroeconomic sectors with great simplicity. It is instructive to interpret this concept in the circular flow diagram of Figure 3.3.

Farmers are placed at the center of the circular flow, because (according to the physiocrats) land is the only factor producing a net product. Income-flows between the macro sectors are represented by the clockwise arrows. Landowners receive income from farmers in the form of rent and spend it for goods produced by farmers and artisans. The artisans receive income from landowners and farmers and spend it on goods supplied by farmers. Flows within a macro sector are crucial only for farmers because they alone produce a net product. These intrasector flows are not indicated in Figure 3.3.

The physiocrats' vision of the interrelatedness of the economy was macro in its conception and orientation. They made few efforts to develop a theory of the interrelatedness of an economy in a micro sense, as did Adam Smith. Circular flow diagrams of the connections between households and firms are commonly used in introductory economics courses to give insights into the relationships between factor and final goods market and the role of markets in allocating resources. In Chapter 10 we use a circular flow diagram in Figure 10.2 to illustrate a general equilibrium approach to understanding the interrelatedness of micro sectors of an economy.

The physiocrats considered their crowning theoretical achievement to be Quesnay's "economic table." It gave a crude representation of (1) the flow of money incomes between the various sectors of the economy, and (2) the creation and annual circulation of the net product throughout the economy. Quesnay's table represents a major methodological advance in the development of economics—a grand attempt to analyze raw reality by means of abstraction.

The physiocrats not only theorized about the relationships between various sectors of the economy but also attempted to quantify their size. On this level physiocracy anticipated Nobel Prize–winning Wassily Leontief's celebrated input-output table and the work of the specialized group of quantitative economists known as econometricians. The economic table demonstrates awareness of the interdependence of the various sectors of the economy. Some of the later mercantilists also became aware of this interdependence, and their combined influence was the basis for Adam Smith's attempt at a more complete description of the workings of a market economy.

Physiocratic Economic Policy

The physiocrats' contributions to micro theory were not as significant as their contributions to macro theory. They believed that the basic motivation for the economic activities of human beings was the desire to maximize gain. Prices were formed in the market by economic activity; and the formation of these prices could be studied, because it was governed by natural laws independent of human will. Although the physiocrats did not develop a coherent theory of prices, they concluded that free competition led to the best price and that society would benefit if individuals followed their self-interest. Furthermore, believing that the only source of a net product was agriculture, they concluded that the burden of taxes would ultimately rest on land. A tax on labor, for example, would be shifted to land, because competition had already ensured that the wage of labor was at a subsistence level. Perhaps most important, they began to be aware of the function of prices in integrating the activities of the various factors in the economy. Like the more perceptive mercantilists, they recognized that an individual who appears to be working independently in a market economy is actually working for others and that these independent activities are integrated by the price system. Their micro analysis tended to lack detail. For example, they offered no detailed argument that free competition would result in an optimum allocation of resources. But they did have some notion of the nature and function of relative price, a notion subsequently used by Adam Smith.

Because the physiocrats believed that a natural order existed that was superior to any possible human design, they conceived of the economy as largely self-regulating and thus rejected the controls imposed by the mercantilist system. The proper role of government was to follow a policy of *laissez faire*—to leave things alone. In the hands of Adam Smith and subsequent economists, this idea was of tremendous importance in shaping the ideology of Western civilization. Certain English writers were also advocating nonintervention as a general policy at the time, and they, too, influenced Smith.

The physiocrats maintained that the primary obstacles to economic growth proceeded from the mercantilist policies regulating domestic and foreign trade. They objected particularly to the tax system of the mercantilists and advocated that a single tax be levied on land. Of course, according to their theory, all taxes would ultimately fall on land anyway, but only after causing much friction in the economic system.

The most unfortunate of the many governmental regulations, according to the physiocrats, was the prohibition on the export of French grain. It kept down the price of grain in France, they said, and was therefore an obstacle to agricultural development. Because the physiocrats did not foresee the development of manufacturing, they concluded that a laissez faire policy would produce tremendous growth in French agriculture as the small-scale agriculture of the feudal economy was replaced by large-scale agriculture. Thus, the wealth and power of the French economy would be increased. The mercantilists had, in effect, found the source of the net product to be exchange—particularly exchange in the form of international trade—and therefore advocated policies designed to foster a favorable trade balance. The physiocrats, who considered the source of the net product to be agriculture, maintained that laissez faire would lead to increased agricultural production and ultimately to greater economic growth.

SUMMARY

The mercantilists and the physiocrats made useful contributions to economic theory, the most important of which was their recognition that the economy could be formally studied. At the same time, these writers developed an abstract technique by which to discover the laws that regulated the economy. They were the first model builders in economics; because economic theory is based on the abstract, model-building process, it is reasonable to regard the mercantilists and the physiocrats as the first economic theorists.

The mercantilists achieved the first tentative insights into the role of money in determining the general level of prices and into the effects of foreign trade balances on domestic economic activity. The most significant contribution of the physiocrats was their concept of the interrelatedness of the various sectors of an economy.

The mercantilists and the scholastics perceived a fundamental conflict in the economy, viewing exchange as a process in which one party gains at the expense of another. Therefore, both advocated intervention into the economy by either government or church. The physiocrats, on the other hand, perceived the working-out of the conflicts inherent in relative scarcity as basically harmonious. They called not for intervention into the economy but for laissez faire, and thus were an important influence on Adam Smith and the subsequent development of economic policy. Some English writers of this period do not fit neatly into either the mercantilist or the classical camp. It was they who rejected the cruder mercantilist ideas of inherent conflict in exchange, who disproved the necessity of always maintaining a favorable balance of trade, and who saw how markets work to coordinate individual economic activities. These liberal mercantilists and the physiocrats gave Adam Smith the tools to build the house of political economy.

Although we have painted with a broad brush the ideas of the mercantilists and physiocrats, we have also studied particular writers. William Petty, who was essentially a mercantilist, was significant in that he represents a first attempt to ground economics in empirical observation. Smith's rejection of political arithmetic and the problems of obtaining reasonably accurate data delayed the movement toward quantification for nearly one hundred years. Cantillon was a creative analytical thinker who made important inroads in understanding the functioning of a market system and who followed Petty's desire to quantify economic reasoning. Unfortunately, Cantillon had little influence on the subsequent development of economic thought. Mandeville, a mercantilist, was a good representative of an underconsumptionist and a biting critic of the line of sentimental moralists (Shaftesbury, Hutcheson, Smith).

Adam Smith's close friend David Hume was the other towering intellect of the second half of the 'eighteenth century; his occasional focus on the field of economics produced important contributions to economic thinking. Although Hume was never able to free himself completely from mercantilist ideas, he did refute a good many crude mercantilist notions about maintaining favorable balances of trade: his analysis showed that a given trade balance would lead to changes in prices, exports and imports, and, finally, a reversal of the given trade balance. The death of mercantilism as an acceptable idea, but not as a set of policies used to gain advantage, is probably no better summed up than by David Hume's declaration "I shall therefore venture to acknowledge, that not only as a man, but as a British subject I pray for the flourishing commerce of Germany, Spain, Italy, and even France itself."[9]

Before Smith published his famous book, a number of writers had significant insights into the workings of an economic system and the flawed policies of the mercantilists and physiocrats. But none were able to put it all together in a way that caught the attention of their contemporaries. This was to be Adam Smith's role, to which we turn in the first chapter of Part II. He became the father of political economy and the first great figure in the line of orthodox economists.

Key Terms

mercantilism	laissez faire
balance of trade	downward-sloping labor supply curve
price specie–flow mechanism	Hume's Dictum
monetary factors	quantity theory of money
real factors	physiocracy
liberal mercantilist	natural law
sentimental moralists	net product
Puritanism	*tableau économique*
Hobbism	

Questions for Review, Discussion, and Research

1. Explain the economic ideas of the mercantilists.
2. Some writers are neither mercantilist or classical but somewhere in between. Write an essay explaining the notion of a liberal mercantilist and illustrate by example.
3. Explain the economic ideas of the physiocrats.

[9] David Hume, "Of the Jealousy of Trade," *The Philosophical Works,* ed. T. H. Green and T. H. Grouse (4 vols.; Darmstadt, Germany: Sienta Verlag Aalen, 1964), III, 348.

4. The assumption that total wealth in the world is fixed had important consequences for the analysis of both the mercantilists and the scholastics. Explain.
5. Explain why the goal of a society, production or consumption, has important implications for analysis and policy.
6. Write an essay explaining the economic policies of the mercantilists and relate this to your knowledge of the American colonies and English rule.
7. Contrast and compare the mercantilist and scholastic approaches to analyzing an economy.
8. Write an essay on the pros and cons of an advocacy group's (e.g., the mercantilists) producing an objective analysis of an economy.
9. Explain how the use of statistical data might be crucial in establishing knowledge in any scientific discipline.
10. Write an essay on the importance to the development of economic thought of the recognition of the interrelatedness of economic activity and how a price system coordinates individual activities.
11. That absent-minded professor has another job for you. She knows that somewhere in Mun's writing, he essentially stated that countries should run trade surpluses, but she does not quite remember where. Your assignment is to find the selection and the complete bibliographic citation for it.

Suggested Readings

Allen, W. R. "Modern Defenders of Mercantilist Theory." *History of Political Economy,* 2 (Fall 1970). See also Allen's "Rearguard Response." *History of Political Economy,* 5 (Fall 1973).

Bowley, Marian. *Studies in the History of Economic Theory Before 1870.* London: Macmillan, 1973.

Coats, A. W. "The Interpretation of Mercantilist Economics: Some Historiographical Problems." *History of Political Economy,* 5 (Fall 1973).

Ekelund, Robert B., and Robert D. Tollison. *Mercantilism as a Rent-Seeking Society.* College Station: Texas A&M University Press, 1981.

Furniss, Edgar S. *The Position of the Laborer in a System of Nationalism.* New York: A. M. Kelley, 1965.

Gide, Charles, and Charles Rist. "The Physiocrats." Chapter 1 in *A History of Economic Doctrines.* Boston: D. C. Heath, 1948.

Grampp, William D. *Economic Liberalism.* 2 vols. New York: Random House, 1965.

Groenewegen, Peter. "Turgot's Place in the History of Economic Thought: A Bicentenary Estimate." *History of Political Economy,* 15 (Winter 1983).

Heckscher, Eli F. *Mercantilism.* 2 vols. London: George Allen and Unwin, 1935.

Landreth, Harry. "The Economic Thought of Bernard Mandeville." *History of Political Economy,* 7 (Summer 1975). Reprinted in *Pre-Classical Economists.* Vol. III. Ed. Mark Blaug. Brookfield, Vt.: Edward Elgar, 1991.

Letwin, William. *The Origins of Scientific Economics.* London: Methuen, 1963.

Meek, Ronald L. *The Economics of Physiocracy.* London: George Allen and Unwin, 1962.

Myers, M. L. "Philosophical Anticipations of Laissez-Faire." *History of Political Economy,* 4 (Spring 1972).

Phillips, Almarin. "The Tableau Economique as a Simple Leontief Model." *Quarterly Journal of Economics,* 69 (1955).

Polanyi, Karl. *The Great Transformation.* New York: Farrar and Rinehart, 1944.

Spengler, Joseph J. "Mercantilistic and Physiocratic Growth Theory." In *Theories of Economic Growth.* Ed. Bert F. Hoselitz. Glencoe, Ill.: Free Press, 1960.

Spengler, Joseph J., and William R. Allen. *Essays in Economic Thought.* Chapters 1–9. Chicago: Rand McNally, 1960.

Taylor, Overton H. "Economics and the Idea of Natural Laws" and "Economics and the Idea of Jus Naturale." In *Economics and Liberalism.* Cambridge, Mass.: Harvard University Press, 1965.

Vickers, Douglas. *Studies in the Theory of Money 1690–1776.* Philadelphia: Chilton, 1959.

Viner, Jacob. "Power versus Plenty as Objectives of Foreign Policy in the Seventeenth and Eighteenth Centuries." In *The Long View and the Short.* Glencoe, Ill.: Free Press, 1958.

————. *Studies in the Theory of International Trade.* New York: Harper, 1937.

PART

II

Classical Economic Thought, Malthus, and Marx

Clockwise from top left: Adam Smith, David Ricardo, John Stuart Mill, Karl Marx

IMPORTANT WRITERS

ADAM SMITH	*Wealth of Nations* 1776
THOMAS ROBERT MALTHUS	*An Essay on the Principle of Population* 1798
DAVID RICARDO	*On the Principles of Political Economy and Taxation* 1817
NASSAU SENIOR	*An Outline of the Science of Political Economy* 1836
JOHN STUART MILL	*Principles of Political Economy* 1848
KARL MARX	*Capital,* Volume I, 1867

THE CLASSICAL PERIOD, 1776–1890

Classical economics covers more than one hundred years of economic thought and was almost exclusively British in its orientation and major contributors. The three major treatises of the classical period were *Inquiry into the Nature and Causes of the Wealth of Nations* (1776) by Adam Smith (1723–1790), *On the Principles of Political Economy and Taxation* (1817) by David Ricardo (1772–1823), and *Principles of Political Economy* (1848) by John Stuart Mill (1806–1873). In addition, a number of minor anticipations of neoclassical theory appeared shortly after the publication of Ricardo's book. John Stuart Mill represents the end of the classical period, but we will see later that he was uncomfortable with some of the classical dogma. Smith, Ricardo, and J. S. Mill ruled economic thought from 1776 until the final part of the nineteenth century: Smith from 1776 until nearly 1820, Ricardo from roughly 1820 until the 1850s, and J. S. Mill from the 1850s until the 1890s.

Two other seminal thinkers, though in some ways classical, were in a more fundamental sense outside the classical school. The population theory of Thomas Malthus (1766–1834) accords with classical theory, but Malthus deviated significantly from the orthodox classical tradition in his analysis of certain macro aspects of the economy and in his defense of the role and significance of the landowning class. Malthus's population theory will be included in the discussion of classical economics, but we shall examine separately the famous debate between Malthus and Ricardo concerning the ability of the economy to automatically achieve full employment of resources. Karl Marx (1818–1883) drew some elements from classical economics, added a different perspective and some new analytical concepts, and reached conclusions that were diametrically opposed to classical theory and policy.

We have observed in the writings of the later mercantilists, and especially those of the physiocrats a growing recognition of the interdependence of the elements of the economic system. Yet prior to 1776 no writer had been able to synthesize the important contributions of mercantilism and physiocracy into a single coherent system. Such was the state of economic thinking when a Scottish moral philosopher, Adam Smith became interested in political economy.

Classical Economics, Malthus, and Marx

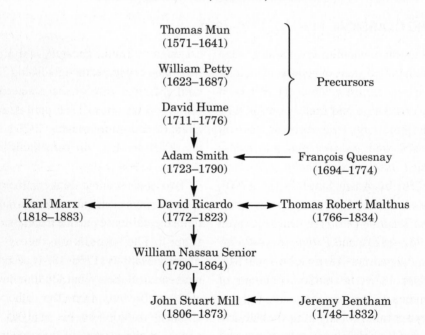

Arrows indicate direction of influence

CLASSICAL POLITICAL ECONOMY

The economic ideas of the scholastics, physiocrats, and mercantilists contained the seeds of concepts that were eventually articulated into a more or less unified system by the classical economists. A number of characteristics link these individuals and distinguish them from previous and subsequent economic writers. Their most significant departure from mercantilist thought was their favorable attitude toward the results that flow from the natural working of economic forces. The classical vision of a mostly harmonious economic system contrasts sharply with the mercantilist and scholastic beliefs that the market is characterized by disharmonies calling for restraints or intervention. This sanguine vision of the operation of markets, with its various aspects and ramifications, is one of the chief traits of classical thought.

The view that markets automatically provide harmonious solutions to the conflicts flowing from relative scarcity was first significantly advanced by the physiocrats of France. Assuming such harmony, according to the physiocrats, it followed that the government should adopt a general policy of noninterference in the economy—a policy of laissez faire. Whereas the scholastics considered it appropriate for the church to adjudicate the morality of economic activities and the mercantilists advocated government intervention, the classicals, like the physiocrats, favored free, unregulated markets and maximum individual freedom. They were sure that freedom and liberty were good in and of themselves. But freedom, particularly economic freedom, also provided a means by which the economy could function most efficiently. Individuals and businesses, they averred, should be free to trade without government interference. The classicals, moreover, perceived political and economic freedom to be inseparably bound; the two cross-fertilized each other.

Although the primary vision of the classicals was one of a harmonious working-out of the economic process, they were very much aware of conflicts in society, particularly between the landlords and those advocating and benefiting from economic growth and change. The long-run tendencies of capitalism as seen by both Smith and Ricardo led to such dissonant results that economics came to be called the dismal science. Malthus had raised the specter of overpopulation and questioned the self-equilibrating nature of the economy. Thus, the seeds of both modern orthodox and heterodox visions can be seen in the classicals.

Since the development and full flowering of classical thinking in the century between 1776 and the 1870s, one can trace two broad developments relating to the concept of harmony in the economic system. On the one hand, main-stream orthodox economic thinking, although continuing to accept the basic premise of a harmoniously operating economic system, has slowly but steadily weakened its stance by increasingly advocating political rather than market responses to economic problems. On the other hand, some heterodox economic ideas have denied the harmony accepted by classical economics and find in the system such fundamental conflicts that resolution would require major changes in the institutional structure. Marxian thought provides the most significant example of economic thinking that views the economic system as replete with conflict not resolvable by market forces.

A second characteristic of the classical school is its concern for economic growth. Being essentially macro-oriented—though in a very different sense from that of modern macroeconomists—the classical economists sought to discover the forces that determine the rate of economic growth. Like those who study the less developed economies of today, the classicals had a much broader frame of reference than modern macroeconomists. They were concerned not only with the economic forces that determined growth but also with cultural, political, sociological, and historical factors. The main focus for Keynesians is on the forces that determine the level of economic activity, given these broader factors. They

consider whether an economy is operating at less than full employment of its resources at a point in time. The classicals, having concluded that economies would tend to operate at a full utilization of their resources, were not interested in this question.

Their concern for growth led the classical economists to a study of markets, and the price system as an allocator of resources. The classicals studied the formation of relative prices and markets in order to understand their impact on economic growth. The classicals were very much interested in the forces changing the distribution of income over time and, therefore, in the causes of changes in relative prices over time. With their concern for growth, the classicals continued in the tradition of the mercantilists. Neoclassical economics or modern microeconomics also examines the functioning of markets and the price system, but from a significantly different perspective. Neoclassical theory studies markets in a comparative static framework in order to throw light on the problems of what determines relative prices, what kinds and quantities of consumer goods are produced, what kinds and scale of economic enterprises are used, and how the personal and functional distributions of income are determined. It was not until the 1870s that nascent neoclassical economic theory directed the attention of economists away from growth and almost exclusively toward micro-economic questions of allocating scarce resources among alternative uses.

A final unifying characteristic of classical economics represents another notable departure from mercantilist thinking. Even though the mercantilists' theoretical structure was weak, they trusted their ability to understand the operation of the economy. Once they believed they had gained that knowledge, they considered it appropriate to attempt to remedy any defects they discerned in the functioning of the economy, either by changing the institutional structure or by allowing government to intervene. The mercantilists liked to compare themselves to a doctor with a patient: they had remedies for the malfunctioning economy, and those usually entailed government intervention. This certainty of knowledge on the part of the mercantilists contrasts starkly with the skepticism of Adam Smith, who questioned the wisdom (not to mention the expertise) of the politician who dared to substitute his judgments for those of the market.

MARX'S POLITICAL ECONOMY

Karl Marx was a student of the history of economic ideas. Like all great theorists, he borrowed from past writers; the most important economist who influenced Marx was Ricardo. Several classical interests became incorporated into Marx's analysis of capitalism. Although the classicals found in the economy a basic harmony that led them to advocate a governmental policy of laissez faire, they also found a number of conflicts. One was the conflict between landlords and capitalists; Marx pointed to the economic clash between capitalists and laborers. The classicals' labor theory of value was adapted by Marx to support his view that labor was exploited by the capitalists.

Classical economic theory, unlike neoclassical theory, was dynamic in its interests and structure. Adam Smith had focused on economic growth, and David Ricardo was interested in long-run changes in the distribution of income that would take place under capitalism. Marx's economic analysis is a part of a broader interest in the forces causing historical change, but some of the same dynamic questions that engaged the classicals also interested Marx: What will happen to the distribution of income over time? What course will the rate of profit take over time? What are the prospects for the level of well-being of the masses?

Marx, like Ricardo, was intrigued by the theoretical problems of a labor theory of value. Both men also had an interest in the labor theory of value, but not as a theory to explain what determined relative prices at a point in time nor to throw light on the problem of efficiently allocating scarce resources among alternative uses. Marx wanted to show how exploitation was embedded in a system in which labor did not own the means of production; Ricardo used the labor theory of value to explain changes in the distribution of income over time.

There is another important sense in which Marx borrowed from classical economics. The significant actors for the classicals were the capitalists, land-lords, and laborers. Classical theory is, in a sense, an analysis of the economic functions and future of these classes. The classicals and Marx both regarded the dynamic element in society as a result of the activities of the capitalist class.

Differences between the classicals and Marx are more significant than similarities, and the most important divergence was apparent in their clashing ideological perspectives. The classicals found that the profit motive of the capitalists led to an efficient allocation of capital in the economy and to saving, which promoted growth and wealth. Marx saw the activities of the capitalists as ultimately harmful to the proletariat and the society. Classical economics was an ode to capitalism; Marx wrote an ode on the faults of capitalism.

4 Adam Smith

> *"Adam Smith occupies so central a place in the history of Political Economy that the prudent mariner hesitates to embark on so vast an ocean."*
>
> —Alexander Gray

ADAM SMITH AND CLASSICAL ECONOMICS

The work of Adam Smith (1723–1790) was a watershed in the development of economic ideas. Though Smith was the first of the group of writers known as classical economists, the end of English mercantilism and the beginning of classicism occurred over a considerable period of time. The last stages of an intellectual era always produce thinkers who deviate from the accepted doctrine. Thus, anticipations of classical liberalism occurred in economic literature a century before the publication of Smith's *Wealth of Nations.*

Adam Smith was typical of early economic writers in that he was not exclusively an economist. He was an academic, which allowed him a degree of detachment and objectivity that was lacking in the mercantilist writers, who were generally businessmen. As a professor in Glasgow giving a series of courses that encompassed what we now call the social sciences and humanities, he was basically interested in moral philosophy, which colored a good part of his economics. He had read extensively in the previous literature of the social sciences and humanities and was able to synthesize it into a single work. Smith was not a narrowly technical theoretician but a careful scholar who had a grand vision of the interrelatedness of the society. Although we pay particular attention to his vision of the interrelatedness of the economy, Smith dealt with the important connections across many areas of society—what today are studied by economists, political scientists, sociologists, and philosophers—particularly issues of ethics. He saw, for example, important connections between economic and political freedom, between private property rights and a just state, and between individuals motivated partly by self-interest and partly by concern for the consequences of their actions on others.

Smith was influenced by his teacher, Francis Hutcheson (1694–1746), and by David Hume (1711–1776). Smith shared Hutcheson's strong disapproval of the ideas of Bernard Mandeville (c. 1670–1733), whose satirical style had given his presentation of the mercantilist position wide currency. Mandeville and Smith started with the same assumption regarding the egoistical nature of humans but reached opposite conclusions. Mandeville maintained that the pursuit of individual self-interest would generate many undesirable social and economic consequences, and therefore he built a case for government intervention in the economy.

Smith has often been called the father of economics. Although each of the precursors of classical economics saw bits and pieces of the puzzle, none had been able to integrate into a single volume an overall vision of the forces determining the *wealth of nations,* of the appropriate policies to foster economic growth and development, and of the way in which millions of economic decisions are effectively coordinated by market forces.

Smith's major book is titled *An Inquiry into the Nature and Causes of the Wealth of Nations*[1] (1776). Two other important sources of his ideas are his earlier book, *The Theory of Moral Sentiments*[2] (1759), and the lectures he gave at the University of Glasgow. Unfortunately, Smith's own copies of his lectures were destroyed, and it was not until 1895 that a manuscript was discovered containing a copy of notes taken in 1763 by one of his students. These have been published as *Lectures on Justice, Police, Revenue, and Arms.*[3]

Smith's conception of the scope of economics followed that of the English mercantilists. He was interested in explaining the nature and causes of the wealth of nations. Modern economists would describe Smith as a macro theorist interested in the forces determining economic growth. But the forces that Smith examined were broader than those studied in modern economics, and he filled in his economic model with political, sociological, and historical material. He gave some attention to the determination of relative prices—included today in microeconomic theory—but his main interest was in economic development and policies to promote economic growth.

However, because Smith concluded that an economy would always employ its resources fully in production, he left untouched an important problem of macroeconomics: given the productive capacity of an economy, what forces determine the levels of income and employment?

---

[1] Adam Smith, *An Inquiry into the Nature and Causes of the Wealth of Nations,* edited with an introduction, notes, marginal summary, and enlarged index by Edwin Cannan, with an introduction by Max Lerner (New York: Modern Library, 1937).

[2] Adam Smith, *The Theory of Moral Sentiments* (New York: A. M. Kelley, 1966).

[3] Adam Smith, *Lectures on Justice, Police, Revenue, and Arms,* reported by a student in 1763, edited with an introduction and notes by Edwin Cannan, Reprints of Economic Classics (New York: A. M. Kelley, 1964).

Protestantism and Capitalism: A Causal Connection?

One aspect of the rise of the new industrial order has been the subject of frequent debate. According to R. H. Tawney, in *Religion and the Rise of Capitalism* (1926), and Max Weber, in *The Protestant Ethic and the Spirit of Capitalism* (translated, 1930), the Reformation and the rise of the Protestant ethic did much to promote the Industrial Revolution and the emergence of capitalism. We have already seen that Catholic teaching, with its roots in Aristotle, was inimical to the growth of the new industrial order. The teachings of John Calvin (1509–1564) and his followers, however, were compatible with economic activity; and the Weber-Tawney thesis is that they contributed directly to the rise of the capitalist system. Weber and Tawney have been criticized by many writers, but both were careful scholars who recognized the tremendous difficulties in assigning a sequence of causal relations among religious ideas, economic action, and economic institutions. They were aware, for instance, that causality can also run from economic institutions to religious ideas,

and that the Industrial Revolution and the development of capitalism might equally well account for the development and acceptance of the *Protestant ethic.* On balance, however, they concluded that changing religious thought effected the profound change in the structure of the society, rather than the other way around.

Scholastic dogma had maintained that success in economic activity as manifested in individual wealth was a strong indication of sinful behavior— charging excessive prices, lending at high rates of interest, devoting too much attention to the pursuit of gain and too little to the search for salvation. According to the Protestant ethic, economic success bespoke predestination for eternal salvation. The Protestants also believed that hard work was good for the soul and that conspicuous consumption was to be avoided. The religious views stressing the virtues of work and saving have been regarded as major factors in promoting the emergence of modern economic society.

Smith's methodology, which entailed combining deductive theory with historical description, is also worth noting. His theoretical models lack elegance and rigor, but his description of the interrelationships within and the workings of the economy, and his ability to weave historical examples into his analysis, are unparalleled. A modern mathematical economist could condense the fundamental propositions contained in the nine hundred pages of *Wealth of Nations* into a short pamphlet. In fact, Ricardo, who possessed some theoretical skill but did not use mathematical notation, was able to cover more theoretical ground in a book less than half the length of Smith's.

SMITH'S ANALYSIS OF MARKETS AND POLICY CONCLUSIONS

There are two possible approaches to the writings of Adam Smith. One is to examine the overall theoretical structure and the policy implications that are either inherent in the theoretical system or stated explicitly by Smith. Another is to examine the theoretical structure in detail to evaluate its internal consistency or lack thereof. We will use the first approach before examining the internal workings of the system, because Smith's importance in the history of economic thought is a result of (1) his broad understanding of the interconnectedness of the economy, and (2) his influence on economic policy. Smith is still read today for these insights, not for his contributions to the technical part of economic theory. Our first tasks, therefore, will be to take a broad view of Smith's theoretical structure and to examine the policy conclusions that flow from a more detailed economic analysis. Smith's great strength as an economist lay in his vision (1) of the interdependence of the segments of the economy, and (2) of the policies to be followed to promote the wealth of a nation. On close examination his theory will be found to contain many flaws and contradictions, but his impact on subsequent economic thinking with respect to policy has been equaled by few. He was not an economist in the narrow sense of the word, but rather a philosopher who pointed the way toward economic development and affluence.

Contextual Economic Policy

Adam Smith's methodological approach shaped both his analysis of the economy and his determinations concerning government policy. More abstract methodologists base their arguments on reasonably tight theoretical structures. An abstract theorist might conclude, for example, that markets without government intervention result in an optimum allocation of resources because, in the long run under competitive markets, firms produce at the lowest possible average cost. Another abstract theorist may argue against markets and for government intervention, using theoretical constructs such as those dealing with externalities or third-party effects. In short, the more theoretical economists judge whether markets work or fail on the basis of abstract arguments separated from historical or institutional context. Adam Smith's argument for *laissez faire* is, of course, based in part upon a theoretical model of how markets produce certain results. But significantly, his arguments are more than just theoretical; they are contextual—that is, they are based on his observations of the existing historical and institutional circumstances. Smith's laissez faire advocacy is rooted in a methodological approach that asks this question: does experience show that government intervention will produce better results than will the unimpeded workings of markets? Smith conceded that markets often fail to produce ideal social results, but realism convinced him that the results of government intervention were less acceptable than those flowing from free markets. Hence Smith advocated laissez faire not because he believed markets to be perfect but because in the context of history and the institutional structure of the England of his time, markets usually produced better results than did government intervention.

In Chapter 1 we revealed and illustrated the concepts of the art of economics, the science of economics, and normative economics. The science of economics concerns positive, matter-of-fact relationships between economic variables—often expressed as what is. Normative economics involves questions of what should be—often expressed as what ought to be. The art of economics is policy-oriented. It takes our knowledge of how things are (the science of economics) and our goals (normative economics), and it makes recommendations on the best ways to achieve our goals given our understanding of the science of economics *and* our comprehension of how policies are put into operation through government actions.

Adam Smith's particular proclivities were not those of an abstract theorist. Instead, he was a policy formulator par excellence; his broad knowledge of history and how people behave in practice, if not in theory, led him to be a master of the art of economics. *Contextual economic policy,* then, is just another way of expressing the idea of the art of economics.

Later economic thinkers varied in their approach. Ricardo's advocacy of laissez faire was noncontextual in accordance with his abstract, ahistorical methodology. J. S. Mill and Alfred Marshall returned to the Smithian tradition of judiciously trying to blend theory, history, and contemporary institutions in their analyses and policy conclusions. Modern orthodox neoclassical economics, however, has reverted to the Ricardian tradition of abstract theorizing with less focus on contextual policy advocacy.

Currently, mainstream economics gives the art of economics less attention than in the past. However, there appear to be some modern developments in economics that have the potential to resurrect the art of economics. A number of economists and political scientists are examining how governments and governmental policies actually work. One unintended result of the work of these modern public-choice theorists may be a renewed interest in contextual economic policy—the art of economics.

Natural Order, Harmony, and Laissez Faire

The economics of Adam Smith and the mercantilists share certain basic elements. Influenced by developments in the physical sciences, the mercantilists and Smith believed it was possible to discover the laws of the economy by means of hard analysis. Matter-of-fact, cause-and-effect relationships, they believed, could be revealed through scientific investigation. Smith also assumed the same things about human nature as the mercantilists: human beings are rational and calculating and largely driven by economic self-interest.

One difference between Smith's system and that of most mercantilists was his assumption that for the most part competitive markets exist, and that within these markets the factors of production move freely to advance their economic advantage. A second difference was the assumption that a natural process at work in the economy can resolve conflicts more effectively than any arrangements devised by human beings. Smith expressed this beneficent working of market forces in the following passage:

> As every individual, therefore, endeavours as much as he can to employ his capital in the support of domestic industry, and so to direct that industry that its produce may be of the greatest value; every individual necessarily labours to render the annual revenue of the society as great as he can. He generally, indeed, neither

intends to promote the public interest, nor knows how much he is promoting it. By preferring the support of domestic to that of foreign industry, he intends only his own security; and by directing that industry in such a manner as its produce may be of the greatest value, he intends only his own gain, and he is in this, as in many other cases, led by an invisible hand to promote an end which was no part of his intention. Nor is it always the worse for the society that it was no part of it. By pursuing his own interest he frequently promotes that of society more effectually than when he really intends to promote it. I have never known much good done by those who affected to trade for the public good. It is an affectation, indeed, not very common among merchants, and very few words need be employed in dissuading them from it.[4]

The syllogism from which Smith drew his major policy conclusion is very simple. Human beings are rational and calculating and driven by self-interest. If left alone each individual will follow his or her own self-interest, and in promoting self-interest they promote that of society. Government should not interfere in this process and should therefore follow a policy of laissez faire. Throughout his book Smith pointed out how private self-interest will lead to the public good in a nonregulated market economy. The key to understanding how some degree of harmony and good proceed from conflict and self-interest lies in the activities of the capitalist. Smith showed that capitalists are driven not by altruistic motives but by a desire to make profits—it is not as a result of the benevolence of the baker that we get our bread. The capitalist views the market in term of final goods and, in order to increase revenues, produces the commodities people desire. Competition among capitalists will result in these goods' being produced at a cost of production that will return to the producer an amount just sufficient to pay the opportunity costs of the various factors. If profits above a normal rate of return exist in any sector of the economy, firms will enter these industries and force down prices to a cost of production at which no excess profits exist. Capitalists will bid for the various factors of production, offering higher prices for the more productive factors and thereby channeling labor and land into those areas of the economy in which their efficiency is greatest. Consumers direct the economy by their dollar votes in the market; changes in their desires are shown in rising and falling prices—and, consequently, rising and falling profits. Smith concludes that it is wonderful how the market, without planning or governmental direction, leads to the satisfaction of consumer desires at the lowest possible social cost. In the terminology of modern economics, he concludes that an optimum allocation of resources occurs in competitive markets without government intervention.

The Working of Competitive Markets

Smith's most significant contribution to economic theory was his analysis of the working of competitive markets. He was able to specify with greater accuracy than

---

[4] Smith, *Wealth of Nations*, p. 423.

previous writers the mechanism whereby the price resulting from competition would, in the long run, equal the cost of production. In his analysis of price formation and resource allocation, he called short-run prices "market prices" and long-run prices "natural prices." His primary concern was with long-run natural price formation. He saw competition as fundamentally requiring a large number of sellers; a group of resource owners knowledgeable about profits, wages, and rents in the economy; and freedom of movement for resources among industries. Given these conditions, the self-interest of resource owners would lead to long-run natural prices, which would equalize the rate of profits, wages, and rents among the various sectors of the economy. If, for example, the price of a final good is higher than its long-run natural price, then either profits, wages, or rent in this sector of the economy must be higher than their natural return, and adjustments will take place via the movement of resources until the natural price prevails. With competitive markets and an absence of government regulation, the resulting natural prices bring about an optimum allocation of resources in that consumers receive the goods they want at the lowest possible cost and maximum rates of growth are ensured.

Having established the superiority of competitive markets, Smith easily constructed his case against monopoly and government intervention. He recognized the desire of businessmen to monopolize trade by joining forces, and although he was not able to specify what the monopoly price would be, he recognized that monopolists would extract a higher price by restricting output. Note that Smith's advocacy of laissez faire assumes the existence of competitive markets. Various groups in the economy have parroted Smith's denunciation of government intervention while ignoring his precept that a laissez faire policy presupposes the existence of competitive markets.

Smith's argument against government intervention in the economy has political, philosophical, and economic bases. He argued that in general any government interference is undesirable, because it infringes upon the natural rights and liberties of individuals. However, he examined the economic arguments against government intervention much more extensively. He reviewed many of the mercantilist regulations of domestic and foreign trade and showed how they result in an allocation of resources less desirable than that produced by competitive market forces. Smith believed that many of the mercantilist arguments for government intervention, although purporting to promote the social good, were in fact self-serving. The regulation of domestic and foreign commerce benefited not the nation but the merchant. This was not a purely theoretical argument; it came from the context of Smith's personal observation of how governments actually operate. It was Smith practicing the art of economics, looking at the policy of regulation in the context of the institutions of his time. If governments were different, they could promote the social good; but given the way they are, they inevitably do more harm than good. In this sense, the roots of modern public-choice theory extend back to Adam Smith's perception of how merchants use government to enrich themselves.

Smith's great achievement was his brilliant overview of the workings of markets. Though he did not himself fashion his analytical tools, and despite the difficulties and inaccuracies in his analysis of the formation of relative prices, his accomplishment was immense. He supplemented his broad overview of market processes with descriptive and historical material and produced a work that could be read and understood by the educated people of his time. In this manner he was able to exert an influence on economic policy and lend support to the increasingly favored view that the wealth of England would best be promoted by a government policy of laissez faire.

Smith's advocacy of laissez faire must be qualified, however, for he cited several areas in which he believed government intervention, in the context of the historical, political, and institutional structure of his time, was necessary. For example, although he was generally against the regulation of international trade, he made exceptions for tariffs that protected infant industries. Trade regulation was also necessary when national defense might be weakened by a policy of perfectly free international trade. The government was to provide for the national defense, build and maintain roads and schools, administer justice, and keep vital records. It is most significant that Smith qualified his argument for laissez faire by advocating government provision of goods that have great social benefits but

How Does Adam Smith Rank?

Some historians of economic theory have attempted to rank economists according to their technical brilliance— their ability to develop new techniques of economic analysis and their virtuoso performance in applying technique. Judged by this criterion, Adam Smith ranks low. Other historians have attempted to rank past writers by originality. Judged in this way, Smith ranks behind Cantillon, Quesnay, and Turgot. But viewed historically, Smith's abilities and his contribution to the flow of economic ideas represent a much scarcer resource than either originality or technical competence: his role was to take up the best ideas of other men and meld them, not with technique but with judgment and wisdom, into a comprehensive system that not only revealed the essential functioning of the economy but also provided rich insights into policy questions. Smith's system was not an abstract, bare-bones analytical framework of pure economic theory; it

was political economy focused almost exclusively on the question of which policies best promote what today we call economic growth and what Smith called the wealth of nations. Smith was a master at contextual policy-making, first rate at the art of economics.

In advocating a laissez faire policy, Smith was very cautious: his invisible hand works to tie public interests to private interests only when competitive forces exist to channel self-interest to the social good. His exceptions to laissez faire—situations in which he saw the public good as not flowing from competitive markets—are standard fare in modern welfare economics and are sometimes cited in socialist calls for government intervention. No other economist, with the possible exception of J. M. Keynes, has had the impact on economic policy of Adam Smith. Modern economics has added extensive formalization to Smith's vision but little to its inherent insights.

that are not supplied by the private market because supplying them would not be sufficiently profitable. For example, the social benefits of education are very great, but the profits to be realized from the private provision of education are so small that if the market is left alone, less education will be supplied than is socially desirable. (Much of modern welfare economics deals with externalities, third-party or spillover effects, and how these must be considered if maximum social welfare is to be achieved.) The qualifications of the laissez faire maxim are an index of Smith's scholarship and intellectual honesty. They did little, however, to diminish the vigor of his laissez faire creed.

Capital and the Capitalists

Smith contributed several important concepts concerning the role of capital in the process of producing wealth and in economic development. He pointed out, first, that the present wealth of a nation depends upon *capital accumulation,* because this is what determines the division of labor and proportion of the population engaged in productive labor. Second, Smith concluded that capital accumulation also leads to economic development.

> In the midst of all the exactions of government, this capital has been silently and gradually accumulated by private frugality and good conduct of individuals, by their universal, continual, and uninterrupted effort to better their own condition. It is this effort, protected by law and allowed by liberty to exert itself in the manner that is most advantageous, which has maintained the progress of England towards opulence and improvement in almost all former times, and which, it is to be hoped, will do so in all future times.[5]

Third, individual self-interest coupled with the accumulation of capital leads to an optimum allocation of capital among the various industries.

> Every individual is continually exerting himself to find out the most advantageous employment for whatever capital he can command. It is his own advantage, indeed, and not that of society, which he has in view. But the study of his own advantage naturally, or rather necessarily leads him to prefer that employment which is most advantageous to the society.[6]

One aspect of Smith's view of the role of the capitalist and capital accumulation needs further elaboration. It is clear that the capitalist plays the key role in the functioning of the economy. His pursuit of wealth and profits directs the economy to an efficient allocation of resources and to economic growth. The source of capital in a private property economy is savings by individuals. Smith believed that labor could not accumulate capital because the level of wages permitted only the satisfaction of immediate consumption desires. Members of the landowning

[5] *Ibid.,* pp. 328–329.
[6] *Ibid.,* p. 421.

class, he observed, have incomes sufficient to accumulate capital, but they spend them on unproductive labor to satisfy their immense desires for high living. It is the members of the rising industrial class, striving for profits, striving to accumulate capital to increase their wealth through saving and investment, who are the benefactors of society, Smith concluded. An unequal distribution of income in favor of the capitalists is therefore of tremendous social importance. Without an unequal distribution of income, economic growth is not possible, for the whole of the yearly output would be consumed.

The Impact of Smith on Policy

Smith's major policy conclusion is that the government should follow a policy of laissez faire. The impact of this conclusion on economic policy in the industrialized world, especially in the United States, has been immense. It has become the economic ideology of our society, and we attempt to promote this view in the underdeveloped areas of the world. It is possible that no idea and no single writer have had more influence on the development of our economy and society.

Adam Smith's fundamental contribution to economic theory was not a detailed theoretical analysis but a broad overview of the way in which a market economy allocates scarce resources among alternative uses. We shall now examine in greater detail the theoretical aspects of Smith's work. The space we devote to some of the theoretical issues discussed by Smith should not lead students to believe that this was the important part of Smithian economics. Our main purpose in this extended discussion, particularly of the labor theory of value, is to prepare the way for a discussion of the writers who followed Smith, particularly Ricardo and Marx, since Smith's analysis provided a point of departure for subsequent writers.

THE NATURE AND CAUSES OF THE WEALTH OF NATIONS

In the first sentence of *Wealth of Nations,* Smith explained his conception of the nature of the wealth of nations. In so doing he separated his views from those of the mercantilists and physiocrats.

> The annual labour of every nation is the fund which originally supplies it with all the necessaries and conveniences of life which it annually consumes, and which consists always either in the immediate produce of that labour, or in what is purchased with that produce from other nations.[7]

In a number of places throughout *Wealth of Nations,* Smith berated the mercantilists for their concern with the accumulation of bullion and identification of bullion with the wealth of a nation. Smith believed, in fact, that all the mercantilists were confused on this issue. For him wealth was an annual flow of goods and

---

[7] *Ibid.,* p. lvii.

services, not an accumulated fund of precious metals. He also revealed an understanding of a link between exports and imports, perceiving that a fundamental role for exports is to pay for imports. Furthermore, in his opening sentence he implied that the end purpose of economic activity is consumption, a position he developed more fully later in the book and one that further distinguishes his economics from that of the mercantilists, who regarded production as an end in itself. Finally, in emphasizing labor as the source of the wealth of a nation, he differed from the physiocrats, who stressed land.

Smith went on to suggest that the wealth of nations be measured in per capita terms. Today when it is said, for example, that England is wealthier than China, it is understood that the comparison is based not on the total output or income of the two countries but on the per capita income of the population. In essence, Smith's view has been carried forward to the present. In the same paragraph in which Smith stated that consumption is "the sole end and purpose of all production," he rebuked the mercantilists because in their system "the interest of the consumer is almost constantly sacrificed to that of the producer" and because they made "production, and not consumption . . . the ultimate end and object of all industry and commerce."[8]

So much for the nature of the wealth of nations. The rest of Smith's book is concerned with the causes of the wealth of nations, directly or indirectly—sometimes very indirectly. Book I deals with value theory, the division of labor, and the distribution of income; Book II with capital as a cause of the wealth of nations. Book III studies the economic history of several nations in order to illustrate the theories presented earlier. Book IV is a history of economic thought and practice that examines mercantilism and physiocracy. Book V covers what today would be called public finance.

Causes of the Wealth of Nations

Smith held that the wealth of a nation, what we today call the income of a nation, depends upon (1) the productivity of labor, and (2) the proportion of laborers who are usefully or productively employed. Because he assumed that the economy will automatically achieve full employment of its resources, he examined only those forces that determine the capacity of the nation to produce goods and services.

Productivity of labor.   What determines the productivity of the labor force? In Book I Smith stated that the *productivity of labor* depends upon the *division of labor.* It is an observed fact that *specialization and division of labor* increase the productivity of labor. This had been recognized long before the publication of *Wealth of Nations,* but no writer emphasized the principle as Smith did. In our modern economy—even in the academic world—division of labor is widely practiced, with notable influence on productivity. Smith illustrated the advantages

[8] *Ibid.,* p. 625.

of specialization and division of labor by borrowing from past literature an example that measured output per worker in a factory producing straight pins. When each worker performs every operation required to produce a pin, output per worker is very low; but if the production process is divided into a number of separate operations, with each worker specializing in one of these operations, a large increase in output per worker occurs. In Smith's example, when the process is divided into eighteen distinct operations, output per worker increases from twenty pins to forty-eight hundred per day. It is interesting that although Smith recognized the economic benefits of specialization and division of labor, he perceived some serious social costs. One social disadvantage of the division of labor is that workers are given repetitious tasks that soon become monotonous. Human beings become machines tied to a production process and are dehumanized by the simple, repetitive, boring tasks they perform. But Smith had no doubt that human welfare is, on balance, increased by the division of labor.

The division of labor, in turn, depends upon what Smith called the *extent of the market* and the accumulation of capital. The larger the market, the greater the volume that can be sold and the greater the opportunity for division of labor. A limited market, on the other hand, permits only limited division of labor. The division of labor is limited by the accumulation of capital because the production process is time-consuming: there is a time lag between the beginning of production and the final sale of the finished product. In a simple economy in which each household produces all of its own consumption needs and the division of labor is slight, very little capital is required to maintain (feed, clothe, house) the laborers during the production process. As the division of labor is increased, laborers no longer produce goods for their own consumption, and a stock of consumer goods must exist to maintain labor during the time-consuming production process. This stock of goods comes from saving and is, in this context, what Smith called capital. It is a major function of the capitalist to provide the means for bridging the gap between the time when production begins and the time when the final product is sold. Thus, the extent to which production processes requiring division of labor may be used is limited by the amount of capital accumulation available. Smith therefore concluded: "As the accumulation of stock must, in the nature of things, be previous to the division of labour, so labour can be more and more subdivided in proportion only as stock is previously more and more accumulated."[9]

Productive and unproductive labor.   The accumulation of capital, according to Smith, also determines the ratio between the number of laborers who are productively employed and those who are not so employed. Smith's attempt to distinguish between productive and unproductive labor became confused and reflected normative or value judgments on his part. However, it manifests an awareness of the problem of economic growth. Labor employed in producing a vendible commodity is productive labor, Smith held, whereas labor producing a service is unpro-

[9] *Ibid.*, p. 260.

ductive. As an advocate of the changing social and economic order, he postulated that the activities of the capitalists, which resulted in an increased output of real goods, were beneficial to economic growth and development, while the expenditures of the landowners for servants and other intangible goods were wasteful. "A man grows rich by employing a multitude of manufacturers: he grows poor by maintaining a multitude of menial servants."[10] According to Smith, what is true of the individual is true for the nation; thus, for the economy as a whole, the larger the share of the labor force involved in producing tangible real goods, the greater the wealth of the nation. Capital is required to support the productive labor force; therefore, the greater the capital accumulation, the larger the proportion of the total labor force involved in productive labor. "Capitals are increased by parsimony, and diminished by prodigality and misconduct."[11]

This distinction between productive and unproductive labor also affects Smith's view of the role of the government in the economy. Just as the expenditures of the landowning class for servants and other forms of unproductive labor are detrimental to economic development, so is some part of government expenditures. "The sovereign, for example, with all the officers both of justice and war who serve under him, the whole army and navy, are unproductive labourers."[12] Smith insisted that the highest rates of economic growth would be achieved by distributing large incomes to the capitalist class, who save and invest, and low incomes to the landlords, who spend for menial servants and "who leave nothing behind them in return for their consumption."[13] Furthermore, because economic growth is inhibited by government spending for unproductive labor, it is better to have less government and, consequently, lower taxes on the capitalists so that they may accumulate more capital.

Summary of the causes of the wealth of nations.   We began this discussion with this question: what determines the wealth of a nation? Although the opening sentence of Smith's book suggests that the "annual labour of every nation" might be the cause of its wealth, a closer look at his reasoning reveals that it is the accumulation of capital. Examine Figure 4.1 (on page 80), which summarizes in outline form Smith's discussion of what produces wealth.

The immediate determinants of the wealth of nations are the productivity of labor and the proportion of labor that is productive. These two immediate causes of wealth are shown in Figure 4.1 to depend ultimately upon the accumulation of capital—the entire bottom line in the figure.

The result of this chain of reasoning is clear. Capital is the chief determinant of the wealth of nations. Smith stated that the rate of economic growth depends in large measure on the division of the total output of the economy between consumer

[10] *Ibid.,* p. 314.
[11] *Ibid.,* p. 321.
[12] *Ibid.,* p. 315.
[13] *Ibid.,* p. 321.

Figure 4.1   Determinants of the Wealth of a Nation

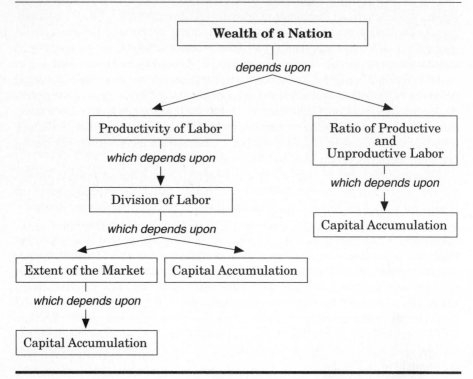

goods and capital accumulation. The larger the proportion of capital accumulation to total output, the greater the rate of economic growth. This conclusion has had an important influence on policy in economies with widely different structures—for example, the United States, the former Soviet Union, China, Japan, and all the underdeveloped countries.

Smith's own summary of this reasoning follows:

> The annual produce of the land and labour of any nation can be increased in its value by no other means, but by increasing either the number of its productive labourers, or the productive powers of those labourers who had before been employed. The number of its productive labourers, it is evident, can never be much increased, but in consequence of an increase of capital, or of the funds destined for maintaining them. The productive powers of the same number of labourers cannot be increased, but in consequence either of some addition and improvement to those machines and instruments which facilitate and abridge labour; or of a more proper division and distribution of employment. In either case an additional capital is almost always required.[14]

[14] *Ibid.,* p. 326.

The Relevance of Adam Smith

The revolutions that brought into being the former Soviet Union and China, the attempts by less developed countries to achieve growth by planned economies, and the dramatic changes taking place in the former Soviet Union have restored the relevance of many questions Adam Smith raised concerning the appropriate mix of private and public sectors. Smith maintained that the primary determinant of growth was capital accumulation. The distribution of the yearly output between capital and consumer goods, according to Smith, determines the rate of growth of national output: the slicing of today's pie determines the size of tomorrow's. Smith's conclusion has never been more assiduously applied than in the former Soviet Union and, more recently, in Japan. But what Smith envisioned was that capital accumulation would take the form of private, not state-owned, property. Recent experience in the United States, which has seen falling rates of capital accumulation, or saving, and consequently slower rates of economic growth, has revived economists' interest in these issues.

Smith's less abstract, more institutional perspective on and approach to economic analysis, within its broad framework of the social sciences and history, is also attracting increasing attention today. The term *political economy* was absent from economic jargon for nearly one hundred years, but a number of economists are now urging a return to the more Smithian breadth of economics the term suggests. Public choice theory, and the new institutional economics, both of whose roots extend back to Adam Smith, have been growth industries in economics.

Generations continue to ask how we should judge those who have the power to impinge upon our national economic destiny—those in high finance, for example, who are changing the face of corporate America through mergers and acquisitions. Should we examine the motives for their activities, or the consequences? Smith responded forcefully to such queries in his time, asserting that consequence of action should be our touchstone for judging the appropriateness of economic activities.

For Adam Smith there was no question that capital accumulation required an institutional framework of free markets and private property. In a system of free markets operating without government direction, a given level of investment spending would be allocated so as to ensure the highest rates of economic growth. In a system of private property, a further requirement for high rates of capital accumulation is an unequal distribution of income.

VALUE THEORY

Certain questions regarding value, or price, that should be kept separate were sometimes confused by early economists. (1) What determines the price of a good? In the language of modern economics, what determines relative prices? (2) What determines the general level of prices? (3) What is the best measure of welfare? The first and third questions are part of modern microeconomics; the second, although it defies the usually simple micro-macro dichotomy, is generally included under the broad umbrella of macroeconomics. Smith did not provide an unambiguous answer to any of these different questions. His treatment of them is in places confusing in this regard because he intermingled his discussion of what determines relative prices with his attempt to discover a measure of changes in welfare over time.

It is not surprising that historians of economic ideas have argued over Smith's true opinion. One group of writers holds that Smith had three theories of relative prices (labor cost, labor command, and cost of production) and a theory explaining the general level of prices. Another group maintains that he settled on a cost of production theory of relative prices, a theory measuring changes in welfare over time, and a theory of the general level of prices. The latter group denies that Smith had a labor theory of relative prices. We believe that Smith experimented with all these theories: a theory of relative prices consisting of labor cost and labor command for a primitive society, and cost of production for an advanced economy; the formulation of an index measuring changes in welfare over time; and a theory explaining the general level of prices. We first consider his theory of relative prices.

Relative Prices

Although Adam Smith explained relative prices as determined by supply or costs of production alone, he did not completely ignore the role of demand. He believed that market, or short-run, prices are determined by both supply and demand. Natural, or long-run equilibrium, prices generally depend upon costs of production, although Smith sometimes stated that natural price depends upon both demand and supply. These inconsistencies provide ample opportunity for historians of economic theory to debate Smith's real meaning.

Smith's analysis of the formation of relative prices in the economy of his time includes two time periods, the short run and the long run; and two broad sectors of the economy, agriculture and manufacturing. During the short-run, or market, period in both manufacturing and agriculture, Smith found downward-sloping demand curves and upward-sloping supply curves: therefore, *market prices* depend upon demand and supply. Smith's analysis of the more complicated "natural price," occurring in the long run, contains some contradictions. For the agricultural sector, *natural price* depends upon supply and demand because the long-run supply curve is upward-sloping, indicating increasing costs. But for the manufacturing sector, the long-run supply curve is at times assumed to be perfectly elastic, representing horizontal or constant costs; and in other parts of the analysis the supply curve is downward-sloping, indicating decreasing costs. In cases of manufacturing, when the long-run supply curve is perfectly elastic, price depends entirely on cost of production; but when it is downward-sloping, natural price depends upon both demand and supply.

There are a number of possible interpretations of Smith's statements with regard to the forces determining natural prices for manufactured goods. One may assume that he was merely inconsistent—possibly because of the long period of time it took him to write *Wealth of Nations*—or that he thought these issues were of minor importance. Another approach is to select one of his manufacturing costs as representative of "the real Adam Smith." It makes little difference which approach is employed, because Smith consistently noted the role of demand in the formation of natural prices and in the allocation of resources among the various sectors of the economy. Nevertheless, regardless of the shape of the long-run supply curve in manufacturing, the major emphasis is on cost of production in the determination of natural prices, an emphasis that is characteristic of Smith and subsequent classical economists.

The scholastics became interested in the question of relative prices because they were concerned with the ethical aspects of exchange, and the mercantilists considered it because they thought wealth was created in the process of exchange. Even though Smith on occasion discussed prices in ethical terms, he had a more important reason for being interested in the factors determining relative prices. Once an economy practices specialization and division of labor, exchange becomes necessary. If exchange takes place in a market such as the one existing at the time Smith wrote, certain obvious problems arise. First, there is the question of a medium of exchange, if exchange is to be on a level higher than barter. The medium used is money, and Smith discussed the role of money as a medium of exchange in Chapter 4 of Book I. Second, there is the question of value, or relative price. To use Smith's language, what principles determine the relative or exchangeable value of goods? He took up this question in Chapters 5, 6, and 7 of Book I. Third, there is the question of how the output of an economy is divided among those engaged in production. Smith considered the distribution of income in the remaining chapters of Book I.

The Meaning of Value

Smith believed that the word value

> has two different meanings, and sometimes expresses the utility of some particular object, and sometimes the power of purchasing other goods which the possession of that object conveys. The one may be called "value in use"; the other, "value in exchange." The things which have the greatest value in use have frequently little or no value in exchange; and on the contrary, those which have the greatest value in exchange have frequently little or no value in use. Nothing is more useful than water: but it will purchase scarce any thing; scarce any thing can be had in exchange for it. A diamond, on the contrary, has scarce any value in use; but a very great quantity of other goods may frequently be had in exchange for it.[15]

According to Smith, *value in exchange* is the power of a commodity to purchase other goods—its price. This is an objective measure expressed in the market. His concept of *value in use* is ambiguous; it resulted in a good part of his difficulties

[15] *Ibid.*, p. 28.

in explaining relative prices. On the one hand, it has ethical connotations and is therefore a return to scholasticism. Smith's own puritanical standards are particularly noticeable in his statement that diamonds have hardly any value in use. On the other hand, value in use is the want-satisfying power of a commodity, the utility received by holding or consuming a good. Several kinds of utility are received when a commodity is consumed: its total utility, its average utility, and its marginal utility. Smith's focus was on total utility—the relationship between marginal utility and value was not understood by economists until one hundred years after Smith wrote—which obscured his understanding of how demand plays its role in price determination. It is clear that the total utility of water is greater than that of diamonds; this is what Smith was referring to when he pointed to the high use value of water as compared to the use value of diamonds. However, because a commodity's marginal utility often decreases as more of it is consumed, it is quite possible that another unit of water would give less marginal utility than another unit of diamonds. The price we are willing to pay for a commodity—the value we place on acquiring another unit—depends not on its total utility but on its marginal utility. Because Smith did not recognize this (nor did economists until the 1870s), he could neither find a satisfactory solution to the *diamond-water paradox* nor see the relationship between use value and exchange value.

Smith's Three Theories of Relative Prices

As we have seen, Smith was somewhat confused about the factors determining relative prices, but it is worth examining some of his views in order to understand certain important conceptual problems encountered by Ricardo and Marx in their attempts to formulate a theory of relative prices, particularly a labor theory of value. We shall confine our examination to his three major theories of relative prices, presenting only brief summaries of his explanations of wages, profits, and rents, for he had several contradictory theories for each of these income categories.

Smith developed three theories of relative prices: (1) a *labor cost theory of value,* (2) a *labor command theory of value,* and (3) a *cost of production theory of value.* He postulated two distinct states of the economy: the *early and rude state,* or *primitive society,* which is defined as an economy in which capital has not been accumulated and land is not appropriated; and an *advanced economy,* in which capital and land are no longer free goods (they have a price greater than zero). For the early and rude state of society, he advanced two explanations of relative prices: a labor cost theory and a labor command theory.

Labor cost theory in a primitive society.

In the early and rude state of society which precedes both the accumulation of stock [i.e., capital] and the appropriation of land, the proportion between the quantities of labour necessary for acquiring different objects seems to be the only circumstance which can afford any rule for exchanging them for one another. If among a nation of hunters, for example, it usually costs twice the labour to kill a beaver which it does to kill a deer, one beaver should naturally exchange for or be worth two deer.[16]

According to Smith's labor cost theory, the exchange value, or price, of a good in an economy in which land and capital are nonexistent, or in which these goods are free, is determined by the quantity of labor required to produce it. This brings us to the first difficulty with a labor cost theory of value. How are we to measure the quantity of labor required to produce a commodity? Suppose that two laborers are working without capital, that land is free, and that in one hour laborer Jones produces one unit of final product and laborer Brown produces two units. Assume that all other things are equal—or, to use the shorthand expression of theory, *ceteris paribus*—so that the only cause of the differences in productivity is the difference in the skills of the workers. Does a unit of output require one hour of labor or two? Smith recognized that the quantity of labor required to produce a good cannot be measured by clock hours, because in addition to time, the ingenuity or skill involved and the hardship or disagreeableness of the task must be taken into account.

At this point Smith encountered a difficulty that all labor cost theories of value have encountered and that has not been successfully solved by subsequent writers. If the quantity of labor is a function of more than one variable, then we must find a means of stating the relative importance of all the variables. Suppose we have the following information about the production of good A and good B:

	Time	Hardship	Ingenuity
Good A	1 hour	X	$2Y$
Good B	2 hours	$2X$	Y

How does one compare the quantity of labor required for good A with that of good B? The units of measuring time are clock hours, but the units of measuring ingenuity and hardship are not given. Though it is not crucial to know these units for the problem at hand, it is essential to be able to measure the differences in the amount of hardship and ingenuity required to produce the two goods. Smith tried to solve this problem of reducing time, hardship, and ingenuity to a common denominator by maintaining that differences in time, hardship, and ingenuity are reflected in the wages paid to labor. If laborer Smith receives wages of $2 per hour and Jones wages of $1 per hour, these wage payments reflect differences in their skill or ingenuity; and if they work in different industries, their wages will also reflect (in part) varying degrees of unpleasantness or hardship.

Smith's suggestion merely restates the problem rather than providing a solution. The purpose of his *value theory* is to explain those forces that determine relative prices, but wages themselves are one of the many prices in an economy that his theory must explain. When he concluded that the wage paid to labor is a measure

[16] *Ibid.*, p. 47.

of the relative amounts of time, hardship, and ingenuity required to produce a commodity, he was begging the question. He was saying that a good has value according to the wages paid to labor, not according to the quantity of labor contained in the good. This is circular reasoning. Smith used one set of prices, namely wages, to explain another set of prices.

To gain further insight into Smith's analysis of the labor cost theory and the determination of prices in a primitive society, let us go hunting with him. If it requires two hours to capture one beaver or two deer, Smith concludes that two deer will be equal to one beaver in the market, or the price of beaver will be twice the price of deer. The reasoning necessary to reach this conclusion and the assumptions on which the model is based are worth examining carefully, for Smith, like many economists, neither gives his reasoning in full nor states explicitly all the assumptions required to reach his conclusions. The price—two deer equal one beaver—is what Smith calls the natural price and what modern theorists would call the long-run equilibrium price. To explain why this is the long-run equilibrium price, let us examine other prices in order to determine if they are disequilibrium prices and to find the direction of movement away from them. Suppose that the demand for beaver increases and a new price emerges in the market: three deer equal one beaver, or 3D = 1B. This represents a rise in the price of beaver and a corresponding fall in the price of deer. This new price Smith calls a market price and modern theorists call a short-run equilibrium price.

With the rise in the price of beaver, the hunters in our primitive society would no longer hunt deer and would spend their time hunting beaver, for the following reason. Deer can be acquired in two ways: directly, by hunting deer; or indirectly, by hunting beaver and trading them for deer in the market. With a price of 3D = 1B, the rational choice is to hunt beaver and trade beaver for deer in the market. The net gain resulting from this method can be calculated. Two deer could be acquired directly by expending two hours of labor in hunting deer. They could be acquired indirectly by hunting two hours for a beaver and trading it in the market for three deer, a net gain of one deer. Assuming that beaver and deer are divisible goods, the advantage of using the market could also be calculated in time. Rather than spend one hour directly hunting deer, the clever hunter spends two thirds of an hour hunting beaver and trades in the market for one deer the one-third beaver acquired by hunting. The net gain is the one-third hour saved for each deer acquired through the market.

The result of this process would be to increase the supply of beaver in the market and to decrease the supply of deer. The price of beaver would then fall, and the price of deer rise. We have established that a price for beaver higher than 1B = 2D is a disequilibrium price and that at any price for beaver higher than 1B = 2D, market forces will operate to lower the price toward the long-run equilibrium price. At a price for beaver below this price of 1B = 2D, the supply of beaver would decrease and their price would rise toward what Smith called the natural price.

There are some important insights to be gained from our examination of the Smithian model of price determination using a labor cost theory in a primitive society. First, Smith assumes that the hunters in this early state are rational, calculating, and driven by motives of economic self-interest. In short, these hunters act as though they are on the floor of a stock or commodity exchange, not like members of a primitive tribe. A cultural anthropologist might take a completely different approach, perhaps considering the influence of habit and custom that could cause a beaver hunter to follow the pursuits of his elders rather than the dictates of the market. (My father shot beaver; therefore, I will shoot beaver.) Second, Smith's model assumes perfect competition: the hunters (firms) in the market are price takers and quantity adjusters who individually have no market power and who form no sort of organization to regulate supply and, consequently, market price. Third, Smith assumes that both beaver and deer can be produced in larger quantities while the average cost per unit of output remains constant; in other words, that supply curves in the long run are horizontal, or perfectly elastic. However, if more beaver are supplied, one might expect that the number of hours necessary to kill a beaver would in fact increase; the supply curve would slope up and to the right.

Under this assumption of constant costs, demand plays no role in determining relative prices in the long run. Changes in demand will reallocate factors of production among industries but will not influence long-run prices. Price depends entirely on cost of production, or supply; if labor is the only cost of production, as in Smith's model, what results is a labor theory of value. However, if the supply curve slopes up and to the right, the industries, in the jargon of micro theory, are increasing-cost industries: price is a function of both demand and supply. Smith's model is comparatively static. His concern is with final long-run equilibrium positions rather than with the intervals between equilibria. It is a "timeless" analysis because it starts with long-run equilibrium, then postulates some disturbance of the equilibrium, and then deduces the new equilibrium price. The time path of the variables in the system is not considered; analytically, the process of adjustment is regarded as instantaneous.

Labor command in a primitive society.   Now that we have worked through the labor cost theory of relative prices for a primitive economy, the labor command theory will be smooth sailing. According to Smith, under the labor command theory the value of a good "to those who possess it, and who want to exchange it for some new productions, is precisely equal to the quantity of labour which it can enable them to purchase or command."[17] Using Smith's example, we find that a beaver will command two hours of labor and a deer one, so their relative price will again be 1B = 2D. Thus, in primitive societies the same prices result whether we use labor cost or labor command theory.

Labor theory in an advanced economy.   Smith's model for an advanced society differs from his primitive economy model in two important respects: capital

[17] *Ibid.*, pp. 30–31.

has been accumulated and land appropriated. They are no longer free goods, and the final price of a good also must include returns to the capitalist as profits and to the landlord as rent. Final prices yield an income made up of the factor payments of wages, profits, and rents. Assume that wages are $3/4$ of the final price and that profits and rents are $1/4$ of the final price for both beaver and deer. What are the exchange ratios, using labor cost and labor command theories?

Because under labor cost, a beaver requires two hours of labor time and a deer one hour, they would exchange at a ratio of 1B = 2D. Labor command is slightly more complicated. Using X as our unknown, or the quantity of labor a beaver can command, we know that $3/4 X = 2$ units of labor, or that $X = 2^2/3$. A beaver would therefore command $2^2/3$ units of labor, of which 2 units would be paid as wages and $2/3$ unit would be paid as profits and rents. Thus, under the assumptions of an advanced economy, the buyer of a beaver would have to offer more units of labor than were required to produce it, because the capitalist and the landlord must be paid, as well as labor. Under these circumstances the quantity of labor the commodity beaver can command exceeds the quantity of labor required to produce it. Using the same reasoning, a deer would command $1^1/3$ units of labor ($3/4 X = 1$, or $X = 1^1/3$).

Once capital has been accumulated and land appropriated, once profits and rents must be paid, labor cost no longer equals labor command. Yet when we examine the *relative* price of beaver and deer—which is the object of any theory of relative prices—we find that the exchange ratio between beaver and deer is the same under either labor cost or labor command ($1:2 = 1^1/3:2^2/3$). It was at this point that Smith perceived some of the real difficulties of a labor theory of relative prices and, unable to solve these problems theoretically, abandoned a labor theory for an advanced model economy in favor of a cost of production theory. Later, Ricardo, with great theoretical skill, would return to the task of trying to work out the difficulties inherent in a labor theory of value for an advanced economy. Before turning to Smith's cost of production theory, we shall examine some further implications of a labor theory.

Our conclusion that in Smith's model relative prices are the same under a labor cost or labor command theory depends on one crucial assumption: that wage payments are the same proportionate part of final price in both the beaver and the deer industries. Is this assumption consistent with the conditions that exist in an advanced economy? If the fertility of land varies, rent is likely to be a different proportionate part of the final price for commodities produced on different grades of land. Similarly, labor-capital ratios are likely to vary from one industry to another, and profit is likely to be a larger part of final prices in capital-intensive industries. Suppose we work through our example using the more reasonable assumption that labor's share of final price differs between the beaver and the deer industries because of differing fertilities of land and differing labor-capital ratios. Assume that labor receives $2/3$ of the final price in the beaver industry and

¾ of the final price in the deer industry. A beaver now commands 3 units of labor ($\frac{2}{3}X = 2$, or $X = 3$), and a deer commands $1\frac{1}{3}$ units of labor ($\frac{3}{4}X = 1$, or $X = 1\frac{1}{3}$). The relative prices, using labor cost and labor command, are no longer the same. Using labor cost, the price ratio is 1B = 2D; under labor command 1B = $2\frac{1}{4}$D. To put this another way,

$$1{:}2 \neq 1\frac{1}{3}{:}3 \;.$$

We will return to these and other difficulties inherent in a labor theory of value when we examine the solutions offered by Ricardo and Marx.

Cost of production theory of relative prices.   Although Smith did not recognize all the difficulties involved in applying a labor theory of value to an advanced economy, he saw enough to reject both the labor cost and the labor command theories and to suggest that for the economy of his time the appropriate theory to explain relative prices was a cost of production theory. In a cost theory the value of a commodity depends on the payments to all the factors of production: land and capital in addition to labor. In Smith's system the term *profits* includes both profits as they are understood today and interest. The total cost of producing a beaver is then equal to wages, profits, and rent, $TC_B = W_B + P_B + R_B$; likewise for a deer, $TC_D = W_D + P_D + R_D$. The relative price for beaver and deer would then be given by the ratio of TC_B/TC_D. Where Smith assumed that average costs do not increase with increases in output, this calculation gives the same relative prices whether total costs or average costs are used. Where Smith assumed that average costs change with output, prices depend upon both demand and supply. However, in his analysis of the determination of long-run natural prices, Smith emphasized supply and cost of production, even when the supply curve was not assumed to be perfectly elastic. Where competition prevails, he maintained, the self-interest of the businessman, laborer, and landlord will result in natural prices that equal cost of production.

Figure 4.2 helps summarize Adam Smith's theories of value and certain difficulties in formulating a labor theory of value. The left side of the figure shows two different economies for which Smith tried to explain relative prices (the primitive and advanced economies). There are three value theories: labor cost and labor command, which are applicable to a primitive economy; and cost of production, which is applicable to an advanced economy. The right side of the figure identifies nuances of a labor theory of value and shows why Smith, Ricardo, and Marx had difficulties in formulating a labor theory of value for an advanced economy. Labor cost and labor command give identical relative prices in a primitive economy. In an advanced economy labor cost is greater than labor command. This causes no problems in devising a theory of relative prices as long as labor cost is the same part of price for all industries (beaver and deer in our

Figure 4.2   Smith's Value Theories

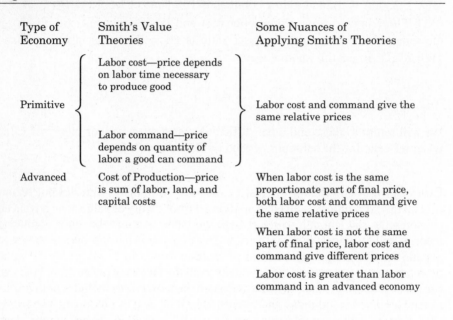

Type of Economy	Smith's Value Theories	Some Nuances of Applying Smith's Theories
Primitive	Labor cost—price depends on labor time necessary to produce good

Labor command—price depends on quantity of labor a good can command | Labor cost and command give the same relative prices |
| Advanced | Cost of Production—price is sum of labor, land, and capital costs | When labor cost is the same proportionate part of final price, both labor cost and command give the same relative prices

When labor cost is not the same part of final price, labor cost and command give different prices

Labor cost is greater than labor command in an advanced economy |

Primitive is defined as economy where land is free and capital does not exist.
Advanced is defined as economy where land and capital are scarce resources.

example)—both labor cost and labor command give the same relative prices. When labor cost is not the same part of price in all industries, labor cost and command give different relative prices. Ricardo, Marx, and legions of other economists have struggled with this problem of a labor theory of value without success. A labor theory of value is not a satisfactory measure of relative prices for a modern economy.

DISTRIBUTION THEORY

The personal distribution of income depends on the prices and quantities of factors of production sold by individuals. Labor is the only factor of production owned by most households, so a household's income generally depends upon the wage rate and the number of hours worked. The amount of property income received by those households that do own property depends on the quantity of capital and land held by the household and the prices of these factors. Because wages, profits, and rents are prices in an economy, their relative values—along with the quantities of labor, capital, and land that individuals bring to the market—determine the distribution of income. Although distribution of income was not of prime concern to Smith, he did offer several different and sometimes contradictory theories of wages, profits, and rents. We shall confine ourselves to mentioning some aspects of his analysis that anticipate later writers and illustrate both his insights and his misunderstandings.

Wages

Smith offered a number of theories to explain wages. In Chapter 8, Book I, he suggested a subsistence theory of wages, a productivity theory, a bargaining theory, a residual claimant theory, and a wages fund theory. Apparently he was not disturbed by the contradictions among these positions, and in other parts of his book he explicitly rejected some of his own propositions. However, two aspects of his discussion of wages deserve further comment.

Smith pointed out that labor is at a disadvantage in the wage-bargaining process. Because there are fewer employers than employees, he said, employers can more easily join together to strengthen their position. Furthermore, the law permits these employer combinations but prohibits employees from forming unions. Parliament has many acts against raising wages, according to Smith, but none against lowering them. Finally, employers have ample resources that make it possible for them to live even if they employ no labor during a strike or lockout. On the other hand, "many workmen could not subsist a week, few could subsist a month, and scarce any a year without employment."[18] In these passages Smith weakened his case for the beneficent working of market forces and appears to have recognized that his assumption of perfectly competitive markets is subject to qualifications.

Wages Fund Doctrine

In his discussion of wages, Smith presented his version of the *wages fund doctrine*, which became an important tool of the classical economists. The doctrine supposes that there is a fixed fund of capital destined to pay wages. Because the production process is time-consuming, it requires previously produced goods that laborers can use for food, clothing, housing, and other things between the start of the process and the final sale. This inventory of goods or capital is termed the wages fund, and its source is the saving, or failure to consume, of the capitalists. Given the size of the labor force and the wages fund, the wage rate is determined as wage rate = wages fund/labor force. Smith did not develop all the theoretical and policy implications of this doctrine. He did, however, suggest that an increase in wage rates will result in increased population and labor supply, so that wages will eventually fall back to the former level, thus anticipating the Malthusian theory of

[18] *Ibid.*, p. 66.

population. We will return in the next chapter to the implications of the wages fund doctrine and its importance in the classical system.

Profits

It is surprising that Smith's discussion of the nature and source of profits is extremely brief. In general, the classical economists made no serious attempts to explain the nature and source of profits until the 1820s, when they responded to socialist criticism of profit. Smith apparently accepted without question the legitimacy of profits as a payment to the capitalist for performing a socially useful function, namely, to provide labor with the necessities of life and with materials and machinery with which to work during the time-consuming production process. According to Smith, labor permits this deduction of profits from its output because it has no materials to work with and no independent means of support. Here, then, profit is composed of two parts: a pure interest return and a return for risk.

Smith's brief and inadequate treatment of profits opened the door to the exploitation theory of profit advanced by Marx:

> The produce of labour constitutes the natural recompence or wages of labour.
> In that original state of things, which precedes both the appropriation of land and the accumulation of stock, the whole produce of labour belongs to the labourer. He has neither landlord nor master to share with him.[19]

Thus, in Smith's primitive economy the laborer received the whole of the product, but in his own time labor had to share the product with the capitalist and the landlord. Smith never explained why profits and rents are deducted from the output of labor, and he thereby exposed his system to attack by any reader who is critical of a private property, capitalist economy. Readers who, like Smith, believe in the basic harmony in the system would probably not even notice this omission.

Rent

Smith suggested at least four theories of rent, all of which contradict one another. The origins of rent are variously held to be (1) demands by the landlord, (2) monopoly, (3) differential advantages, and (4) the bounty of nature. Early in *Wealth of Nations,* rent is regarded as price-determining,[20] whereas later Smith anticipated Ricardo and regarded rent as price-determined.[21] Smith was usually very critical of landlords who "love to reap where they never sowed."[22] He sensed the basic conflict between the interests of the landlords and those of the capitalists, which Ricardo expounded in full. This is another example of Smith's realization that the basic harmony in the economy is subject to some areas of discord.

---

[19] *Ibid.,* p. 64.
[20] *Ibid.,* p. 50.
[21] *Ibid.,* pp. 145–146.
[22] *Ibid.,* p. 49.

The Rate of Profit over Time

Smith believed that the economic growth of a nation depended on the accumulation of capital. Although he paid little attention to the nature and source of profits, he was extremely interested in changes in the rate of profit over time. He predicted that the rate of profit would fall over time for three reasons. (1) *Competition in the labor market*. The accumulation of capital will result in competition among capitalists in the labor market with the result that wages will rise. Smith concluded that the increased wages would bring about a fall in profits. (2) *Competition in the commodity market*. Smith reasoned that as output increased so would competition among producers, with the consequences that commodity prices would fall and profits decline. This implies the possibility of overproduction for the entire economy, which conflicts with Smith's position that overproduction cannot occur. (3) *Competition in the investment market*. Smith apparently believed that there were a limited number of investment opportunities and that increased capital accumulation would therefore lead to falling profits. When he examined what historical information was available on the secular trend of interest rates, the data supported his theoretical conclusions. He did note that some of the colonies (e.g., those in North America) were characterized by both high wages and high profits.

WELFARE AND THE GENERAL LEVEL OF PRICES

We pointed out earlier that Smith's discussion of value theory failed to formulate distinct theories of welfare, relative prices, and the general price level. We now consider his theories of how to measure changes in welfare over time and what factors determine the general level of prices.

Chapter 5, Book I

Historians of economic theory have wrestled with Chapter 5, Book I, of Smith's *Wealth of Nations*, titled "Of the Real and Nominal Price of Commodities, or of Their Price in Labour, and Their Price in Money." We believe that in this chapter Smith tried to answer several questions that, although related, create confusion when they are examined simultaneously. He attempted to discover, first, the factors determining the general level of prices, and second, the best measure of changes in welfare over time. The second question is the more difficult. How are we to define welfare in an unambiguous way so that changes in welfare can be measured? Suppose that an economy produces only one final product, deer. Welfare for the economy could be defined and measured in terms of the quantity of deer consumed. Consumption of larger quantities of deer would represent increased welfare for the society, and smaller quantities would represent decreased welfare or "illfare." The issue becomes more complex when we introduce a second final good, beaver. We can state unequivocally that more of both beaver and deer will increase welfare, and less of both will decrease it. But what if consumption of beaver increases and consumption of deer decreases? The welfare of the people in the society who place a high value on beaver would increase, and the welfare of those who value deer would decrease. Is it possible to define and measure changes in welfare for an economy of two or more products? Smith tried to answer this question.

If welfare is defined as either the total consumption or the output of society, the initial problem to be solved for a multiple-product economy is to find a way to add the output or consumption of the products—for example, beaver and deer. A possible solution to this problem is to convert all commodities to one common measure. If 1B = 2D, then an increase in output of two beaver coupled with a decrease in output of two deer represents an increase in welfare. The new level of output can be said to be one beaver better off, or two deer better off. However, if the relative prices of beaver and deer change as their outputs change, the problem of measuring welfare becomes much more complicated. In an economy of many products, the relative prices of commodities are expressed in a common measure, usually the monetary unit of the government. In theory, and occasionally in practice, this common measure (in the jargon of economics, the *numeraire*) could be any one of the commodities of the economy—for example, cows, corn, or gold. Our economy measures output by adding up the money value of each commodity to obtain a sum we call the gross domestic product. If the gross domestic product increases from one year to the next, can we conclude that welfare has increased?

Measuring changes in output in a multiple-product economy by this means presents difficulties, because the unit of measurement, the yardstick money, is itself variable. The general level of prices changes; therefore, the money value of output may not correctly reflect the true output. Smith considered the possibility of using gold or silver as a common measure, or *numeraire,* but concluded that because the prices of these commodities vary, they are unsatisfactory for this purpose. He then turned to labor but found that the price of labor also varies over time. In the end, the only invariant measure he could find to assess changes in welfare was the disutility of work, because "equal quantities of labour, at all times and places, may be said to be of equal value to the labourer."[23]

Given Smith's conclusion that labor disutility can be used in computing an index of welfare, the problem of measuring changes in welfare is easily solved. We first measure changes in total output in terms of the monetary unit; then we adjust for changes in the general level of prices according to changes in the price of either gold, silver, or corn. By this process we have converted money income and nominal price into real income and real price. To measure changes in welfare, we then compare the amount of labor disutility involved in producing the different outputs. For example, if the money value or output increases 10 percent and the general level of prices as measured by the price of gold also goes up 10 percent, the real value of output remains the same. Welfare increases if the disutility of producing this output decreases. Translated into everyday language, if we could produce the same quantity of output with less labor, we would have more leisure and be better off.

[23] *Ibid.*, p. 33.

Measuring changes in welfare is much more complicated than Smith thought, however, and our discussion cannot touch on all the issues involved. Smith did not discuss how to define or measure the disutility of labor. This appears to be completely subjective. One of his assumptions that was not questioned by orthodox economists until the twentieth century was that more goods are better than fewer, or that increases in output occurring without increases in labor disutility must always result in increased welfare. The various goods that constitute total output are not an issue in his writing. Growth of output is an improvement in welfare even if the enlarged output includes goods of doubtful benefit to the society. Furthermore, Smith and the orthodox economists who followed did not consider the "quality of life" produced by this enlarged output. Little or no attention was given to the costs society might pay in the form of pollution or other harmful externalities for ever-larger outputs.

SUMMARY

Smith's contribution to and influence on economic thought is tremendous. More than any other writer of his time, he saw the central ideas and forces that govern a market economy. However, his work is not without problems. Smith confused himself and generations of economists by failing to elaborate separate theories of, and distinguish clearly among, relative prices, the general level of prices, and changes in welfare. Historians of economic ideas have debated whether Smith propounded a labor theory of value. If this means a labor theory of relative prices, the answer is yes and no. He applied a labor theory of relative prices to a primitive economy, but for a modern economy he held to a cost of production theory. According to Smith, the general level of prices can best be measured by the price of gold, silver, or corn. To explain changes in welfare over time, he formulated a subjective labor-disutility theory. We must conclude that for a modern economy Smith did not accept a labor theory of value to explain relative prices. Once land and capital become economic goods, natural prices will depend mainly on costs of production—namely, wages, profits, and rents.

Smith was primarily interested in questions of economic policy affecting economic growth and development, specifically in determining policies that would best promote the wealth of the nation. His major recommendation was that the government follow a policy of laissez faire; this, he claimed, would effect a maximum rate of growth of per capita income in the economy. His analysis of the workings of markets (what today would be called the micro aspects of the economy) must be viewed within the framework of his concern for economic development. His belief that laissez faire was the most effective policy available was based not primarily on its efficiency in allocating resources but on its beneficial effects on economic growth. His policy positions, for both laissez faire and government intervention, were always contextual. They were based on theoretical arguments combined with his observations of households, firms, politicians, and institutions. Nor was his methodological predilection that of a pure theorist; he also took into consideration political, historical, and institutional factors. This stance extended, moreover, from his analysis to his policy. The mercantilist regulations of domestic and foreign trade had been designed purportedly to increase the wealth of the nation, but Smith concluded that they were misguided and that economic growth was best promoted by the free operation of markets. Smith's policy conclusions flowed not solely from his theoretical structure but in part from his application of the art of economics.

Although Smith was concerned chiefly with questions of economic development, it was in his investigation of the workings of competitive markets that he contributed most significantly to economic theory. In this endeavor he drew from the later mercantilists and the physiocrats and brought together in one book much of the solid analysis of his predecessors. He was able to describe the functioning of competitive markets with greater precision than previous writers. In the details of his theoretical structure, particularly in his attempts to formulate a value theory, he provided a necessary point of departure for Ricardo and other theorists who followed.

Smith was not a pure theorist; rather, he was a political economist who was able to supplement a grand vision of the interrelatedness of the sectors of a market economy with descriptive and historical material and to influence economic policy for at least two hundred years. The pure theorist Ricardo was followed by J. S. Mill, and Mill by Alfred Marshall; both tried to return economics to Adam Smith's contextual analysis and policy. With few exceptions, the methodological position of orthodox economists following Marshall was one of almost exclusive focus on pure abstract theory with little attention to historical and institutional material. In that focus modern mainstream orthodox theory has rejected the Smithian methodology, but it has been kept alive by heterodox economists who rejected his laissez faire policy conclusions.

Generally speaking, the history of economic analysis and policy discloses three major developments following Smith. (1) Microeconomic theorists have tried to fill in the details of Smith's grand vision of how markets work. Part of this activity has been technical, aimed at giving greater precision to Smith's vision; part has attempted to develop areas that Smith failed to treat or to comprehend, including the development of the demand side of price analysis, the formulation of a theory of the economic forces determining the distribution of income, and the analysis of resource allocation in other than perfectly competitive markets. (2) After Smith, macroeconomic analysis received little attention from orthodox theorists until the 1930s, when Keynes returned to one of the mercantilists' concerns and attempted to explain the forces determining the level of income and employment. (3) Smithian economic policy remained virtually intact, despite the grumblings of Marx, Veblen, and others outside the orthodox camp, until the twentieth century, when theoretical developments (welfare economics and some parts of Keynesian theory) and events in the real world (revolutions that replaced some private property economies and severe depressions that shook the remaining ones) led to either rejection or re-examination of Smithian policy.

We turn now to the second great classical economist, David Ricardo. Like Smith, he was primarily interested in questions of macroeconomics; but in the course of developing a theory of distribution, he was instrumental in turning orthodox economics away from macro questions for more than a century.

Key Terms

wealth of nations	value in use
Protestant ethic	diamond-water paradox
laissez faire	labor cost theory of value
contextual economic policy	labor command theory of value
capital accumulation	cost of production theory of value
productivity of labor	early and rude state
division of labor	primitive society
specialization and division of labor	advanced economy
extent of the market	value theory
market price	profits
natural price	wages fund doctrine
value in exchange	numeraire

Questions for Review, Discussion, and Research

1. Contrast and compare Adam Smith's and the mercantilists' views on the nature and causes of the wealth of nations.
2. What do you think is the relationship, if any, between the rise of capitalism in Western Europe and religious beliefs?
3. Explain Adam Smith's analysis of the consequences of self-interest coupled with competitive markets.
4. Contrast and compare Adam Smith and the mercantilists on the proper role of government in the society.
5. Explain how the former Soviet Union was mercantilistic rather than Smithian.
6. List Adam Smith's qualifications of his laissez faire policy (reasons for government intervention in the society) and then give your own views on the proper role of the government in society.
7. The success of Adam Smith is explained by the fact that his theories rationalized the activities of the rising capitalist class. Write an essay that either supports or refutes this statement.
8. Explain Smith's theories of relative prices and the problems of formulating a labor theory of value for an advanced economy.
9. Explain Smith's views of why the rate of profit will fall as capitalism grows older.
10. What do you think is the relationship between a person's well-being and his or her possession and consumption of economic goods? Is it possible for an individual as well as a society to be better off with fewer goods? Does your answer to this question depend upon where you are in the present distribution of income?
11. The absent-minded professor has another job for you. She knows that somewhere in Smith's writing, there is a famous "dogs don't trade" quotation, but

does not quite remember where. Your assignment is to find the selection and the complete bibliographic citation for it.

Suggested Readings

Anspach, Ralph. "The Implications of the *Theory of Moral Sentiments* for Adam Smith's Economic Thought." *History of Political Economy,* 4 (Spring 1972).

Clark, John M., et al. *Adam Smith 1776–1926.* Chicago: University of Chicago Press, 1928.

Hollander, Samuel. *The Economics of Adam Smith.* Toronto: University of Toronto Press, 1973.

Hutchison, T. W. "The Bicentenary of Adam Smith." *Economic Journal,* 86 (September 1976).

Robbins, Lionel. *The Theory of Economic Policy in English Classical Political Economy.* London: Macmillan, 1952.

Robertson, H. M., and W. L. Taylor. "Adam Smith's Approach to the Theory of Value." *Economic Journal,* 67 (June 1957).

Rosenberg, Nathan. "Adam Smith on the Division of Labor: Two Views or One?" *Economica,* 32 (May 1965).

————. "Some Institutional Aspects of the *Wealth of Nations.*" *Journal of Political Economy,* 68 (December 1960).

Samuels, Warren J. *The Classical Theory of Economic Policy.* Cleveland: World, 1966.

Scott, W. R. *Adam Smith as a Student and Professor.* Glasgow: Jackson, 1937.

Skinner, A. S., and Thomas Wilson. *Essays on Adam Smith.* London: Clarendon Press, 1975.

Smith, Adam. *An Inquiry into the Nature and Causes of the Wealth of Nations.* Ed. Edwin Cannan. New York: Modern Library, 1937.

Spengler, Joseph J. "Adam Smith's Theory of Economic Growth." *Southern Economic Journal,* 25-26 (April-July 1959).

Stephenson, Matthew A. "The Paradox of Value: A Suggested Interpretation." *History of Political Economy,* 4 (Spring 1972).

Stigler, G. J. "The Successes and Failures of Professor Smith." *Journal of Political Economy,* 84 (December 1976).

Readings in Original Sources

All readings by Adam Smith are from his *Wealth of Nations.*
Value: Introduction and Plan of Work; Book I, Chapters 1–7.
Wages: Book I, Chapters 8 and 10 (Part I).
Profits: Book I, Chapter 9; Book II, Chapter 4.
Rent: Book II, Introduction and Chapters 1–3, 5.

5 Ricardo and Malthus

"Ricardo's intellectual appeal then and now rested on his remarkable gifts for heroic abstractions."

—Mark Blaug

DAVID RICARDO

A Theorist's Theorist

David Ricardo (1772–1823), a stockbroker turned economist, made significant contributions to a number of areas of economic theory, including methodology, theories of value, international trade, public finance, diminishing returns, and rent. He began his study of economics sometime around 1799, when he was twenty-eight years old, and in 1810 published his first pamphlet, *The High Price of Bullion*. His essays on the Corn Law controversy, published around 1815, established him as one of England's most able economists. His major work, *Principles of Political Economy and Taxation,* published in 1817, soon replaced Adam Smith's *Wealth of Nations* as the accepted book on economic questions. It is the third and final edition of this work, printed as Volume I in the Sraffa and Dobb edition of *Works,* that we shall use for reference.

The quantity of material written about Ricardo and his theories is equaled only by that on Smith, Marx, and Keynes. In 1951 *The Works and Correspondence of David Ricardo* was published in ten volumes under the capable hands of Piero Sraffa and Maurice Dobb. This edition took a good twenty years to produce and is a monument to one of the most gifted of economic theorists. That Ricardo's work continues to attract attention is evidenced by its recent re-examinations by Piero Sraffa, Samuel Hollander, and others.

The Period Between Smith's *Wealth of Nations* and Ricardo's *Principles*

Until the appearance of Ricardo's *Principles of Political Economy and Taxation* in 1817, Adam Smith's *Wealth of Nations,* published in 1776, dominated English economic thought of the period. In the four decades that intervened, no major new economic theory appeared, although several significant contributions to economic analysis were made. Thomas Robert Malthus (1766–1834) published an essay in 1798 and a book in 1803 on population; in 1815 Edward West, Robert Torrens, Malthus, and Ricardo published essays discussing the concept and economic significance of rent. Ideas on both these subjects came to be embodied in classical economics. Because the Malthusian population thesis is essential to an under-standing of certain parts of Ricardian theory, we will consider it first. Then we will discuss and evaluate Ricardo's major contributions to economic thought, including his rent theory. Finally, we will return to Malthus to examine ideas developed in his *Principles of Political Economy* (1820) concerning the ability of the economy to operate automatically at full employment. In one of the liveliest controversies in the development of economic ideas, Malthus and Ricardo hotly debated this issue.

THE MALTHUSIAN POPULATION DOCTRINE

Population Theory as an Intellectual Response to Problems of the Times

The principal thesis of Malthus, that population tends to increase faster than the food supply, was not original with him: it can be found in the writings of others, including Adam Smith and Benjamin Franklin. It was his presentation of the population problem, however, that significantly influenced existing and sub-sequent economic thinking.

Three factors appear to account for the formation of Robert Malthus's theory. The first was the pressure of population on England's food supply. Until about 1790 England had been largely self-sufficient in its food supply, but beginning in that year it became necessary to import food, and prices rose noticeably. A second factor was the perceived increasing poverty of the lower-income classes. England was becoming urbanized as factory production replaced production in the home, and with the growth of the towns the misery of the lower-income class appeared to increase. The third factor, which also occasioned the writing of the first essay on population in 1798, was an argument that developed between Malthus and his father, Daniel. Malthus's father was impressed with the views expressed by the English and French utopian writers William Godwin and Marquis de Condorcet. The basic view of Godwin and Condorcet, which Daniel Malthus accepted, was that the character of an individual is not inherited but is shaped by the environment in which he or she lives. Godwin in particular was disturbed by the hardship, misery, unhappiness, and vice he perceived in the world around him. He concluded that the element primarily responsible was government, and for this reason Godwin is sometimes called the father of philosophical anarchism. Robert Malthus wanted to show that the ideas his father had accepted were incorrect. In particular, he tried to prove in the first edition of his essay on population that poverty and misery were not the result of social and political institutions and that changes in these institutions would not remove the evils of the society. Young Malthus was no match for his father in oral argument, so he decided to present his position in writing. When he showed his essay to friends, they encouraged him to publish it. He did so, anonymously, in 1798.

The Population Thesis

Malthus's basic principle, established in the first edition of his essay, was founded on two assumptions: (1) that food is necessary for the existence of humankind, and (2) that passion between the sexes is necessary and will remain unchanged. He concluded that population tends to grow at a faster rate than the food supply. Malthus contended that human beings, in the absence of checks on population, will tend to increase their numbers geometrically (1,2,4,8,16 . . .) but that the food supply can only increase arithmetically (1,2,3,4,5 . . .). This, he said, is the cause of poverty and misery. In the first edition of his essay, he offered no statistical proof of his assertion on either population or the food supply. Nor did he use the principle of diminishing returns of agriculture to justify his claim that the economy was unable to increase the food supply significantly, although he acknowledged the limitation of the supply of land. Although the principle of *diminishing returns* was first developed by a French economist, Turgot, in 1765, it had to be rediscovered by West, Malthus, Torrens, and Ricardo in 1815, seventeen years after the first edition of Malthus's essay. Malthus's failure to recognize the possibility of technological developments that could solve the population problem also vitiated much of his theory.

He concluded that checks will develop to keep the rate of population growth in line with the rate of growth of the food supply. He examined various checks, which differ in the first and subsequent editions. In the first edition he postulated two types, positive and negative. Positive checks are increases in the death rate as a result of wars, famines, disease, and similar disasters. A negative check is the lowering of the birth rate, which is accomplished by the postponement of marriage. In the first edition of his essay on population, Malthus concluded that the postponement of marriage could only result in vice, misery, and degradation of character, because premarital sexual relations would occur. Changing the institutional structure would therefore not remove the misery and vice from society as long as humans required food and sexual drives were strong. The specter of overpopulation inherent in Malthus's thesis led Thomas Carlyle to name economics the *dismal science*.

This thesis caused considerable controversy and aroused interest in the population problem. Dissatisfied with his initial offering, Malthus published a second edition of his essay (in 1803), which differed from the first in purpose, methodology, argument, and conclusions. He no longer attempted to criticize the views of his father, Godwin, and Condorcet, determining instead to articulate the population problem in as scientific a manner as available data permitted. Whereas the methodology of his first edition was wholly deductive, the second was somewhat inductive and the argument was now supported by statistical data. Thus, the second edition was scientific in method as well as purpose. Most important, the argument and conclusions were changed. In the first edition the checks on population resulted in vice and misery, but in the second edition a new check was introduced: moral restraint, or the postponement of marriage without premarital sexual activities. This new check destroyed Malthus's argument against the utopians, but he was no longer concerned with refuting them. His essay on population went through seven editions with little change after the second. The one generally available today is the seventh.

Malthus's population thesis has several obvious flaws. Like most of his contemporaries, he never seriously discussed the feasibility of controlling population by means of contraception, though many so-called neo-Malthusians in more recent times do advocate contraceptive measures. Malthus, moreover, confused the instinctive desire for sexual relationships with the desire to have children. Although the sexual drive is strong among people of all societies, increasing levels of affluence and education tend to introduce a distinction between sexual desires and the decision to have children. Another difficulty is Malthus's arbitrary assumption that the food supply cannot increase faster than the population. In other words, he failed to consider the possibility that developments in agricultural technology might permit sufficient increases in the supply of food to feed an increased population. But it is unfair to criticize Malthus too severely for this omission, as economists have never developed a theory explaining the rate of technological development and have, therefore, historically underestimated the impact of technology on the economy.

The population thesis of Malthus found an application in classical economic theory and policy. The wages fund doctrine, developed by Smith and extended by Ricardo and his followers, implied that an increase in the real wage of labor would result in increases in population, which would eventually bring the wage rate back to its former level. It was therefore argued that any attempt to improve the economic welfare of the lower-income groups in society would be frustrated by an increase in the size of the population. Thus, although humanitarian feelings might call for social measures to raise the income of the laboring poor, sound economic thinking argued that such efforts would be futile. Attempts to alleviate the economic plight of low-income groups in England by means of legislation began around 1600; they are referred to as the *Poor Laws* by economic historians. Classical economists used the Malthusian population doctrine as an argument against the Poor Laws. The analysis of wage rates they achieved by combining the Malthusian thesis with the wages fund doctrine has been called the iron law of wages.

Economics: The Happy Science

Present interest in the underdeveloped areas of the world and in the problems of controlling the environment in the developed economies has led to a re-examination of the Malthusian population thesis. In the period immediately following World War II, it was generally held that controlling the rate of population growth was of concern only in the underdeveloped economies. Beginning in the 1960s, people expressed concern over the growth of population in developed economies, not because of an inadequate food supply but because of the environmental damage associated with increases in population density in the past. Earth has been compared to a spaceship that may already have more than an optimum number of passengers on board.

Since the 1980s a different sort of apprehension concerning population in the developed countries has been expressed. Some writers are alarmed at the consequences for economic growth and world power of the *declining* birth-

rate in the United States. Unlike the environmentalists, who continue to call for lower growth rates, some economists are advocating increasing U.S. population growth.

One economist, Julian Simon, in his book *People, the Ultimate Resource,* has argued that history is clearly a case of *increasing population and increasing consumption per person.* Both have increased because technological growth has consistently exceeded population growth. Simon argues that this simultaneous increase is no accident. He suggests that technological growth is dependent on people, and that population growth increases the number of people, and hence also increases technological growth.

If this relationship is true, population growth will never be excessive—diminishing returns will continually be outrun by technological growth, and economics is the opposite of dismal science: it is the happy science.

The Malthusian model has had far more extensive repercussions than its originator could ever have imagined. The British naturalists Charles Darwin and A. R. Wallace, who independently formulated what has become known as the Darwinian theory of evolution, both acknowledged Malthus as an important influence on their thinking.

David Ricardo incorporated Mathusian population theory into classical political economy. Before examining in detail Ricardo's theoretical contributions, we need to paint with a broad brush his concept of the scope and method of economics.

RICARDO: METHOD, POLICY, SCOPE

Ricardo's Method

Adam Smith had dealt with questions of political economy in two ways: (1) by using deductive theory to analyze the economy of his time, and (2) by presenting a descriptive, informal narrative of contemporary and historical institutions. Smith's method blended theory with historical descriptive material. Ricardo, on the other hand, represents the pure theorist at work. He abstracted from the economy of his time and built an analysis based on the deductive method. His skill was so great that he is admired by pure theorists today even though his mathematical technique was somewhat clumsy. Though Ricardo's method might give the superficial observer the impression that he was a purely theoretical, impractical economist, Ricardian economics is strongly oriented toward policy. The burning issue of his time was the tariffs on the importation of grain into England and their effect on the distribution of income, and Ricardo was keenly aware of this question. He steadfastly maintained, nevertheless, that theory was a prerequisite to concrete analysis of the policy issues of the real world.

Ricardo and Economic Policy

Ricardo was absorbed by the compelling economic problems of his time: rising grain prices, rising rents, and the more general but extremely important issues that were a result of the changing structure of England's economy—the relative growth of industry and relative decline of agriculture. The changing economic structure had obvious implications for and interconnections with the comparative political power of manufacturing and agricultural interests. One key point at which all these issues converged concerned the policy question of free versus regulated international trade. The landlords wanted protection from foreign agricultural products, and many of the rising industrialists were becoming advocates of free trade, particularly in British industries in which costs were less than on the Continent and/or for which cheaper raw materials could be imported.

Ricardo's approach to policy had significant influences on the development of the manner by which subsequent economists have engaged the making of policy. The way to formulate good policy, using Ricardo as a model, is to abstract from the nonessential and build a highly theoretical model that will reveal the causal relationships between variables. In order to achieve strong theoretical conclusions it may be necessary to abstract from, or to freeze, variables that would significantly influence outcomes when the theoretical model is used as a basis for making economic policy. The difficulty with this Ricardian noncontextual theoretical policy-making is that in the real world of policy-making, these "frozen" givens often become unfrozen and have unintended results.

In Chapter 1 we drew a distinction between positive economics or the science of economics, normative economics, and the art of economics. We saw in Chapter 4 that Adam Smith was rather clumsy in formulating rigorous abstract theories but was a master at the art of economics; his policy recommendations depended on more than merely theoretical conclusions and were made in the context of how the policies were likely to work in practice given the institutional arrangements of his time. In contrast, Ricardo was a very able theoretician whose policy recommendations were noncontextual; they were based on purely theoretical considerations. Ricardo's method (highly abstract) and his approach to policy (noncontextual) ultimately became the path followed by mainstream economic thinking. But Ricardo's abstract method and noncontextual approach to economic policy did not become mainstream until well into the twentieth century, as J. S. Mill and Alfred Marshall were decidedly Smithian, not Ricardian, on these issues. Many heterodox economists, from the German historical school, to the American institutionalists believed that even Mill and Marshall were too abstract and noncontextual.

Two components of Ricardianism remain today: highly abstract theory, which by assumption eliminates so many variables that the final conclusion is indisputable; and noncontextual policy-making based on abstract models. Some would regard this as a dubious heritage from a master theoretician. Others would argue that an important part of the art of economics is being able to abstract from reality and to formulate policy options in a noncontextual framework. A review of the history of economic thought and policy does not give a clear answer to the complex issues surrounding the degree of abstraction and contextual analysis appropriate to understanding the economy and the making of economic policy.

The Scope of Economics According to Ricardo

Ricardo represents a turning point in the conception of the basic task of economics. Whereas Adam Smith had continued the mercantilist concern with the forces determining the wealth of nations, Ricardo maintained that the principal purpose of economics is to determine the laws that regulate the distribution of income among landlords, capitalists, and laborers:

> To determine the laws which regulate this distribution [of income], is the principal problem in Political Economy: much as the science has been improved by the writings of Turgot, Stuart, Smith, Say, Sismondi, and others, they afford very little satisfactory information respecting the natural course of rent, profit, and wages.[1]

Ricardo was preoccupied with what is now called the *functional distribution of income,* the relative shares of yearly output going to labor, land, and capital. In modern national income accounting, national income is defined as the payments to the factors of production at factor prices. When modern theorists analyze the functional distribution of income, they often use the concept of an aggregate production function for the economy. Though studies of the functional distribution of income do not really fit into the conventional macro-micro division of modern economics, they are generally considered to be a part of macro theory.

Ricardo was particularly absorbed by *changes* in the functional distribution of income over time, a part of macroeconomics in his system. He considered this problem in the context of a society made up of three classes: capitalists receiving

[1] David Ricardo, *On the Principles of Political Economy and Taxation,* in *The Works and Correspondence of David Ricardo,* eds. Piero Sraffa and M. H. Dobb, I (Cambridge: Cambridge University Press, 1953), p. 6.

profits and interest, landlords receiving rent, and laborers receiving wages. In order to explain changes in the shares of the capitalist, landlord, and laborer, he found it necessary to develop a theory explaining profits, interest, rent, and wages. Like Smith, Ricardo was obliged to formulate theories at the micro level of the economy (although Ricardo did consider many other macro questions, such as population theory, wages fund doctrine, size of the labor force, general level of prices, and short- and long-run stability of the economy). In particular, his interest in the forces causing a change in the distribution of income over time led him to examine the forces causing changes in relative prices over time. However, he was primarily concerned with the effects of changes in income distribution on the rate of capital accumulation and of economic growth. Thus, it was contrary to his intent that he had the effect of directing subsequent economic investigation toward micro issues rather than macro issues. Nevertheless, his intensive examination of a labor theory of value became the starting point for subsequent attempts to explain the formation of relative prices. On the other hand, Ricardo's victory over Malthus concerning the macro stability of the economy closed this issue to further debate by orthodox theorists for nearly a century.

RICARDO'S MODEL

An Overview

There are three main groups in the Ricardian model: capitalists, laborers, and landlords. The capitalists perform the essential roles in the economic play, because they are the producers, directors, and the most important actors. They perform two essential functions for the economy. First, they contribute to an efficient allocation of resources because they move their capital to the areas of highest return, where, if perfectly competitive markets prevail, consumer demands are met at the lowest possible social cost. Second, they initiate economic growth by saving and investing.

Although Ricardo held to a *labor cost theory* to explain changes in relative prices over time, labor is essentially passive in his model. He used the *wages fund doctrine* and Malthusian population theory to explain the *real wage* of labor: real wages = wages fund/labor force. The wages fund depends upon capital accumulation, and the size of the labor force is governed by the Malthusian population principle. If the wages fund increases as a result of capital accumulation, then real wages will rise in the short run. Increasing real wages will result in an increase in population and, hence, in the labor force. Long-run equilibrium will exist when the labor force has increased sufficiently to return real wages to the cultural subsistence level.

The landlords are mere parasites in the Ricardian system. We will see this more clearly after examining his theory of land rent. For Ricardo, the supply curve for land is perfectly inelastic and the social opportunity cost of land is zero. Landlords receive an income, rent, merely for holding a factor of production without serving any socially useful function. The classical economists were particularly critical of the spending habits of landlords. Instead of saving and accumulating capital—so as to increase the supply of capital goods in the economy—the landlords engage in consumption spending. The classical economists considered the activities of the landowning class to be harmful to the growth and development of the emerging industrial society.

Ricardo's model presents the following relationship between the growth of the wealth of the nation and the three major economic groups. The total output, or gross revenue of the economy, is distributed to the laborers, capitalists, and landlords. The part of total output not used to pay labor its cultural subsistence wage and to replace the capital goods worn out in the production process can be called net revenue or economic surplus: gross revenue – (subsistence wages + depreciation) = net revenue. Net revenue will thus consist of profits, rents, and wages over the subsistence level. In long-run equilibrium, wages will be at a subsistence level and net revenue will equal profits and rents. The workers and landlords will always spend their entire income on consumption, so profits are the only source of saving, or capital accumulation. Using his theory of land rent, Ricardo concluded that a redistribution of income favoring the landlord takes place over time as profits decrease and rents rise, with a consequent reduction in the rate of economic growth.

The Problem of the Times: The Corn Laws

Some of the most interesting economic questions of the early 1800s centered on the consequences of the *Corn Laws,* regulations placing tariffs on the importation of grain (not American Indian corn) into England. Coupled with this interest in the Corn Laws was growing concern over the pressure of population on the food supply. Food prices, rents, and investment in land were rising steadily. The most dramatic index of the growing concern about tariffs, land rents, and food prices is the price of wheat during the period. Edwin Cannan reported the following average prices (shillings per quarter of a ton) in his *History of the Theories of Production and Distribution*:

1770–1779	45 shillings
1780–1789	45 shillings
1790–1799	55 shillings
1800–1809	82 shillings
1810–1813	106 shillings

The highest price was reached during 1801, when wheat was selling for 177 shillings a quarter.[2]

[2] Edwin Cannan, *A History of the Theories of Production and Distribution in English Political Economy,* 3rd ed. (London: D. S. King and Son, 1917), p. 117.

For a full understanding of the Corn Law controversy, it is important to remember that this was the period of the Napoleonic wars. The wars had artificially protected British agriculture from continental grain, and this, coupled with Britain's inability to be agriculturally self-sufficient after 1790, resulted in rising grain prices and rents. When the Treaty of Amiens was signed in 1802, English landlords and farmers were apprehensive about the effects of peace on grain prices, so they went to Parliament to get increased protection. The Corn Laws then in effect had been passed in 1791; they placed a floor on the price of grain at 50 shillings per quarter, which was raised in 1803 to 63 shillings per quarter with very little controversy or discussion of the issues. After a year of peace the war resumed until 1813, when Napoleon was captured, and the question of the proper level of tariffs was again raised in Parliament by the agricultural interests.

The landlords were now asking for a floor of 80 shillings per quarter; this time their request prompted an extensive controversy, during which Ricardo, Malthus, Torrens, and West introduced new economic ideas into the debate. There was much public discussion of these issues, and strong opposition to the agricultural interests developed inside and outside of Parliament. Study commissions were appointed by both houses of Parliament, and in 1814 a celebrated report titled *Parliamentary Reports Respecting Grain and the Corn Laws* was published. As a result of commission hearings, many groups were drawn into the controversy. A common method of reaching the public at this time was to publish pamphlets, and the most significant pamphlets explaining the rising prices of grain and rising rents were those of Ricardo, West, Torrens, and Malthus.

A number of the arguments disturbed Ricardo. One was that higher tariffs would result in lower grain prices. The argument was that higher tariffs would encourage greater investment in British agriculture, and when the resultant increased output or supply came to the market, the price of grain would fall. Ricardo did not agree with these conclusions. Another argument was that the high price of grain was the result of high rents. Rents, under this reasoning, were price-determining. Ricardo disagreed, arguing that rents were price-determined. The fundamental question of the Corn Laws, clearly perceived by Ricardo, concerned the distribution of income. Higher tariffs would shift the distribution of income in favor of the landlords. Because Adam Smith's discussion of the forces determining the distribution of income had not been satisfactory, Ricardo redirected economics toward this question.

Analytical Tools and Assumptions

In his attempt to deal with the many policy issues arising from the Corn Law controversy, Ricardo developed a sophisticated and extensive model, making use of a number of analytical tools and assumptions. Before examining his theories we should become familiar with these tools and assumptions. As listed in Table 5.1, they include: (1) *Labor cost theory.* Changes in relative prices over time are explained by changes in labor cost measured in hours. (2) *Neutral money.* A change in money supply might result in changes in both the absolute level of prices and

Table 5.1   Tools and Assumptions Used by Ricardo

1. labor cost theory	5. full employment
2. neutral money	6. perfect competition
3. fixed coefficients of production	7. economic actors
4. constant returns in manufacturing and diminishing returns in agriculture	8. Malthusian population thesis
	9. wages fund doctrine

in relative prices. Ricardo, however, was interested in changes in relative prices over time other than those caused by changes in the money supply, so he assumed in his model that changes in the money supply would not cause changes in relative prices. (3) *Fixed coefficients of production for labor and capital.* Only one combination of labor and capital inputs can be used to produce a given output. Three cubic yards of dirt can be dug in a day by one person using one spade. To increase output per day, as additional labor is added, additional capital (spades) must be added in a fixed proportion. In other words, the labor-capital ratio is fixed by technological considerations for each type of economic production and does not vary with changing output. (4) *Constant returns in manufacturing and diminishing returns in agriculture.* Supply curves in manufacturing are horizontal, or perfectly elastic (marginal costs are constant as output increases); supply curves in agriculture slope upward (marginal costs increase as output expands). (5) *Full employment.* The economy tends to operate automatically at full employment of its resources in the long run. (6) *Perfect competition.* The market contains many independent producers whose products are homogeneous, and no single seller is able to influence the market price. (7) *Economic actors.* Individuals are rational and calculating in their economic activities. Capitalists strive to achieve the highest rates of profits, workers the highest wages, and landlords the highest rents. The interaction of such a society in perfectly competitive markets will lead to a uniform rate of profits for investments of comparable risk, to uniform levels of wages for laborers of the same skills and training, and to common levels of rent for land of the same fertility. (8) *Malthusian population thesis.* Population tends to increase at a faster rate than the food supply. (9) *Wages fund doctrine.* The wage rate equals the wages fund divided by the size of the labor force.

RICARDO'S THEORY OF LAND RENT

Diminishing Returns

In the process of analyzing the issues raised by the Corn Law controversy, Ricardo, Malthus, West, and Torrens formulated the principle of diminishing returns, which has become an important economic concept. Actually, the principle of diminishing returns appears to have been first discovered by the French economist Turgot in 1765; and although a Scottish economist, Anderson, had envisaged the concept for the extensive margin by 1777, it was rediscovered in 1815.

The principle of diminishing returns states that if one factor of production is steadily increased while the others are held constant, the rate at which the total product increases will eventually diminish. As we have seen, Ricardo assumed that the coefficients of production for labor and capital were fixed by technological considerations, so his examples assume a fixed quantity of land to which doses of capital and labor are added. In these examples he assumed that diminishing returns begin immediately, so that the *marginal product* of the second dose of capital and labor is less than that of the first.

Rent Viewed from the Product Side

Ricardo was primarily interested in explaining the changing amounts of total output received by the landlord and the capitalist in the long run, so it is crucial to his theory to make a clear distinction between rent and profits. Obviously, this distinction is easier to make in theory than in practice. Ricardo recognized that terms used in everyday language are not precise. A farmer pays a landlord a sum for the use of land that in commerce is called a rent; but the payment most likely contains elements of both profits and rents. If land has been improved by fencing, draining, or adding buildings, the so-called rent payment will represent, in part, a return to the landlord for these improvements.

Ricardo maintained that rents exist because of (1) the scarcity of fertile land, and (2) the law of diminishing returns:

> If, then, good land existed in quantity much more abundant than the production
> of food for an increasing population required, or if capital could be indefinitely
> employed without a diminished return on the old land, there could be no rise of
> rent; for rent invariably proceeds from the employment of an additional quantity
> of labour with a proportionally less return.[3]

Ricardo saw rent as a payment to the landlord that equalizes the rate of profits on land of differing fertilities. Figure 5.1 assumes that there are two plots of land and that single doses of capital and labor applied to each will yield a total physical output of 100 bushels of wheat on the better land and 90 bushels on the poorer. In a competitive market, forces would operate to equate the rate of profits on the two grades of land. A farmer working grade B land would be willing to pay the landlord owning grade A land a rent for the use of the land. Any rent less than 10 bushels of wheat for grade A land would result in a higher profit from farming A than from farming B. Thus, the rent on grade A land would be 10, and grade B land would yield no rent.

---

[3] Ricardo, *Principles,* p. 72.

Figure 5.1   Ricardian Rent

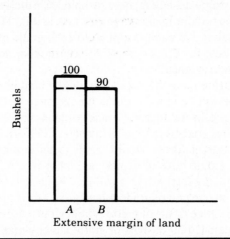

Extensive margin of land

To understand Ricardo's concept of land rent more fully, let us extend our analysis to three grades of land and at the same time introduce the notion of an *intensive margin* and *extensive margin*. Assuming that 3 doses of labor and capital are applied to grade A land, 2 doses to grade B, and 1 dose to grade C, suppose the marginal products of three separate plots of land are as shown in Table 5.2.

The intensive margin describes the effect of successive doses of capital and labor on a given plot of land. If one dose is applied to grade A land, 100 bushels of wheat are produced; if a second dose is applied, total output is 190 bushels and the marginal product of the second dose is 90 bushels; and so on. The intensive margin reflects the principle of diminishing marginal returns, which is assumed to be operative immediately in our example. As the marginal product on grade A land diminishes, it becomes economically feasible to use lands of lower fertility, and grade B land is brought into production. Moving from grade A land to grade B land represents the extensive margin, moving to the hillside after the more fertile

Table 5.2   The Intensive and Extensive Margins (marginal products in bushels)

	Extensive margin →		
	Plot A	Plot B	Plot C
Intensive margin	100	90	80
	90	80	
	80		

valley is cultivated. If there were no diminishing returns in our example, plot B would never be farmed, as plot A's initial marginal product is the largest that can be produced with a single dose of labor and capital. Similarly, plot C would never be used in the absence of diminishing returns on A and B. The marginal products of the last dose of labor and capital applied to each grade of land will be equal; otherwise it would be economically feasible to shift labor and capital to the land with a higher marginal product.

We can now measure the rent on these grades of land in order to get a notion of the Ricardian concept of rent. If rent is the payment to the landlord that will equalize the rate of profits on different grades of land, the rent on grade A land is 30 bushels, the rent on grade B land is 10 bushels, and there is no rent on grade C land. Competitive market forces would result in these rents being paid in the following way. If a single dose of capital and labor is applied to three separate units of grade C land, the total product will be 240 bushels of grain. Three doses of labor and capital on one unit of grade A land yield a total product of 270 bushels $(100 + 90 + 80)$. The price (rent) of grade A land would rise as farmers competed for it until the rent equaled 30 bushels of grain, thereby making the rate of profit on the two grades equal. The same reasoning shows that the rent on grade B would equal 10 bushels $(170 - 160)$. We also can measure rent on a given grade of land by computing the differences between the marginal product of a dose of labor and capital at the intensive margin and the marginal products of earlier, intramarginal doses. For example, rent on grade A land is 30 bushels $[(100 - 80) + (90 - 80)]$, and grade B receives a rent of 10 bushels $(90 - 80)$.

Rent Viewed from the Cost Side

It is instructive to consider rent from the point of view of costs of production rather than of product or output. In our example the marginal returns on grade A land diminished as successive doses of labor and capital were applied. Another way of expressing this result is to say that the marginal costs of producing grain increase as the land is more intensively farmed. *Marginal cost* is defined as the increase in total cost required to produce an incremental amount of final product. Suppose that a dose of capital and labor sells in the market for $100. The marginal cost of producing the one-hundredth bushel of grain on grade A land is then equal to $1.00 (the change in total cost of $100 divided by the change in total product of 100 bushels). As the intensive margin on grade A land is pushed down, the marginal cost of producing grain increases, so that the marginal cost of the one-hundred-ninetieth bushel is $1.11 $(100/90)$ and the marginal cost of the last bushel is $1.25 $(100/80)$. The marginal cost of the last bushel of grain produced on grades B and C land is also equal to $1.25. Brief reflection will show that this must be the case if perfectly competitive markets exist. As more grain is produced on grade A land, marginal costs increase and grade B land (where the marginal cost is lower) will be used. If marginal costs differed for the last units of output on the three grades of land, it would be economically feasible to reduce the total costs of production by shifting labor and capital. In long-run equilibrium, when marginal physical products are equal on the three grades of land, marginal costs at the margin must by definition be equal.

From the cost side, rent can be measured not in bushels of wheat but in money. To compute rent in dollars, we need to find the total revenue from selling grain and the labor and capital costs of producing grain on each grade of land. For grade A land the total revenue is $337.50, which is computed by multiplying the output of 270 bushels times the price of grain of $1.25 per bushel. How did we know the price was $1.25? In competitive markets there can be only one price. If farmer Jones sells grain at a lower price than farmer Smith, Smith will not sell any grain until he lowers his price. Competition between sellers will result in one price in the market, the price that equals the marginal cost of the most inefficiently produced grain. In competitive markets the supply curves of individual firms are their marginal cost curves, and the industry supply curve is the sum of the individual firms' supply curves. We have already concluded that the marginal cost of producing the last unit of grain on each grade of land is $1.25 per bushel, so this is the market price. Ricardo's statement of the principle that price depends upon the marginal cost of the last unit produced by the least efficient producer is as follows:

> The exchangeable value of all commodities, whether they be manufactured, or the produce of the mines, or the produce of land, is always regulated, not by the less quantity of labour that will suffice for their production under circumstances highly favorable, and exclusively enjoyed by those who have peculiar facilities of production; but by the greater quantity of labour necessarily bestowed on their production by those who have no such facilities; by those who continue to produce them under the most unfavorable circumstances; meaning—by the most unfavorable circumstance—the most unfavorable under which the quantity of produce required, renders it necessary to carry on the production.[4]

Total revenue on grade A land, then, is price times the quantity of output, or $337.50 ($1.25 × 270 bushels). Total cost of labor and capital is $300, because three doses of labor and capital were used at a cost of $100 per dose, and rent is the difference between total revenue and cost, or $37.50. Rent on grade B land is $12.50, because total revenue is $212.50 ($1.25 × 170 bushels) and labor and capital costs are $200. Rent on C grade land is zero, because the total revenue of $100 ($1.25 × 80 bushels) is just equal to the cost of one dose of labor and capital.

It was stated earlier that rent was the payment to the landlord that equalized the rate of profit on differing grades of land. Our computation of rent in dollars clarifies this point. Suppose that the $100 cost of a dose of capital and labor in our example consists of $75 of labor cost. If grades A and B land do not receive rent, the rate of profits of the three grades of land will differ. For example, let us compute the dollar return per unit of capital on grade A land, assuming it receives no rent. Total revenue is $337.50, labor costs are $225 ($75 × 3 units of labor), and the residual

[4] *Ibid.*, p. 73.

The Taxation of Land

The Ricardian analysis of rent, with its assertion that the rental income of the landlord was an unearned income, made land rents highly suitable for taxation. We have already noted the physiocrats' conclusion that because land was the only factor in the economy producing a surplus or "net product," all taxes would ultimately be shifted to the landlord. James and J. S. Mill both advocated taxes on land, but the greatest thrust to the notion of taxing land was given by the publication of *Progress and Poverty* by an American, Henry George, in 1879. This curious book has sold more than a million copies and has been translated into several languages.

George was an Easterner who moved to California, where he was impressed by the rising land values as the area became more densely populated. He concluded that the rising price of land and rents resulted from social and economic forces largely unconnected with the activities of the landowners. Because rent was an unearned income, he advocated a tax on land that would completely remove all rents. He maintained that if all land were so taxed, the revenues generated would be sufficient to pay all the costs of government. It was

for this reason that the movement he started came to be called the *single tax movement.*

Ricardo's concept of land rent helps us to understand the economics of George's proposal. If the supply curve of land is perfectly inelastic, then all the return to land is rent. A tax on land would be paid wholly by the landowner, as it would not be possible to shift the burden of the tax to others in the economy. If a tax is placed on land and the net return to the landowner decreases after the tax has been paid, this has no influence, according to George, on the quantity of land supplied. The landowner then has the options of receiving lower yearly income because of the tax or of completely withdrawing his land from the market and receiving no income. He will, of course, prefer less income to no income and will therefore absorb the tax. The amount of the tax can be raised to take away all but the last penny of the landowner's rental income without affecting the quantity of land supplied. Figure 5.2 represents the supply and demand for all land in the Georgian scheme. The entire shaded area of rent would become tax revenues to the government.

left for profits is $112.50, or $37.50 per unit of capital. The dollar returns per unit of capital on grades B and C computed in a similar manner equal $31.25 and $25. In competitive markets this would cause the farmers on grade C land to bid up the price (rent) of grades A and B land. When grade A yielded a rent to the landlord of $37.50 and grade B a rent of $12.50, the advantage of farming grades A and B as against grade C would disappear and the rate of profit per unit of capital would be $25 on all three grades of land.

This simple agricultural model reveals several important points about the concept of rent and the workings of competitive markets: (1) competition among farmers in the market will force the price of grain to the marginal cost of the highest cost unit of output; (2) competition for land will result in rents being paid to the

Figure 5.2   Land Rent

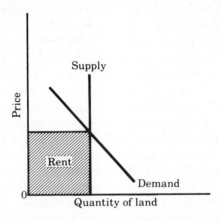

landlords owning the most fertile land; and (3) competition will result in a uniform rate of profit on all grades of land. These same competitive forces play a part in determining prices, rents, and profits even in today's complex economy. Rent is thus price-determined, not price-determining, in Ricardo's scheme. The high price of corn was not determined by high rents; high rents were determined by the high price of corn.

Import restrictions imposed by the Corn Laws could be seen to result in the intensive and extensive margins being pushed down because of the scarcity of fertile land and the principle of diminishing returns. The marginal physical products of added doses of labor and capital would decrease, which is equivalent to saying that marginal costs would increase and, consequently, both grain prices and rents would rise.

A More General View of the Concept of Rent

In his discussion of land rents, Ricardo was dealing with a very powerful tool of economic analysis. He limited his application of the notion of rent to agriculture because he thought that the amount of available land was fixed, with a perfectly inelastic (or vertical) supply curve, and that agriculture was the only sector of the economy to which the principle of diminishing returns pertained. But the concepts of diminishing returns and rent actually have a much broader application: they are the foundations of the marginal productivity theory, which explains the supply side of the forces determining the prices of all factors of production. It was not until the end of the nineteenth century, however, that economists were able to see that Ricardo's concept of land rent was a special case of a general analytical-theoretical principle. A discussion of these issues in detail will have to be postponed until we take up the economics of Alfred Marshall; but we shall now examine a more general concept of rent.

Today most economists would agree with Ricardo that to society as a whole, land rent is not a cost of production and is therefore not price-determining. The quantity of land is approximately fixed; therefore, increases in demand will result in higher prices (rents) with no increase in quantity supplied. To Ricardo, who viewed rent from the level of society as a whole, the opportunity cost of land was zero. From the point of view of any individual member of society, however, land rent is a cost of production and therefore is price-determining. A person who wants to use land in a production process or to use its site value must make a payment to secure and retain the services of land in the face of competition with other possible users. To a farmer rent is price-determining, for he must pay rent to the landlord; and the amount of rent will be equal to the *opportunity cost* of land—that is, to the amount of rent land could earn in alternative uses: if it were planted with a different crop, for example, or subdivided. In short, economists today distinguish between the viewpoints of society as a whole and those of individual members of the society in deciding if a rental payment is price-determined or price-determining.

RICARDO'S VALUE THEORY

Ricardo's theory of value was developed in response to the Corn Law controversy. A number of writers, chiefly Malthus, argued that raising tariffs on the importation of grain would be beneficial to England. Ricardo, however, was in favor of free international trade and against tariffs, which he maintained would be harmful to English economic development. He reasoned that high tariffs would reduce the rate of profits, which in turn would mean a slower rate of capital accumulation. Because the rate of economic growth depended upon the rate of capital accumulation, tariffs would lower the growth rate.

Ricardo found Adam Smith's economic theory unsatisfactory in several ways in dealing with this problem. The cost of production theory of value was being used by protectionists to argue that higher tariffs would not result in lower profits. Ricardo and the protectionists agreed that higher tariffs would result in higher money wages, but a long and bitter debate arose concerning their effect on profits and rent. Both sides agreed that increased tariffs would push down the margin as less fertile lands were utilized and land under cultivation was farmed more intensively. The resulting increase in costs of producing grain would require an increase in money wages in order for workers to maintain a subsistence standard of living, because the cost of grain was a major part of the workers' food budgets. The protectionists argued, using Smith's cost of production theory of value, that higher money wages would not necessarily reduce profits.

Some protectionists also argued that removing or lowering the tariffs on grain would produce falling food prices and money wages, followed eventually by a general fall in all prices, which would lead to depression. Ricardo, therefore, wanted to refute the prevailing cost of production theory of value to establish the benefits to England of removing the tariffs on grain. He also saw that the most important economic consequence of the Corn Laws was their impact on the distribution of income and that the prevailing economic theory had no satisfactory income distribution theory. Thus, he was led to develop an alternative theory of value.

Most theories of value attempt to explain the forces determining relative prices at a given point in time. However, according to Ricardo, the primary problem of a value theory is to explain the economic forces that cause *changes* in relative prices over time. Ricardo attacked the question of value in this way because of his interest in the income distribution consequences of the Corn Laws. So he is not concerned with determining why two deer exchange for one beaver at a point in time, but with what forces cause changes in this ratio over time. If, for example, the price of beaver increases so that 3D = 1B, there is a problem of interpretation. Which is correct to say: that the price of beaver increased, or that the price of deer decreased? Both conclusions are correct, but neither tells us as much as an invariable measure of value would. With an invariable measure of value, we could ascertain whether the price of beaver increased because beaver had become more costly to produce or because deer had become less costly to produce. If there were some commodity whose value was invariant over time, then the true causes of changes in relative prices over time could be discovered.

Ricardo recognized that no such commodity existed; but finding this problem challenging, he expended some effort in trying to formulate a measure of *absolute value* that would be invariant over time. He considered the latter problem in the first edition of the *Principles* and discussed it thoroughly in his last paper, "Absolute Value and Exchangeable Value." (Curiously enough, this paper was lost and not rediscovered until 1943. It had passed from James Mill to John Stuart Mill and then to Mill's heirs. It can be found in Volume IV of Ricardo's *Works*.) But Ricardo was never able to formulate a satisfactory measure of absolute value. We turn, therefore, to Ricardo's primary concern with respect to value: what causes changes in relative prices over time?

Ricardo's Labor Cost Theory of Value

Ricardo began his book with a chapter on value, which starts by clearly distinguishing his views from those of Adam Smith: *"The value of a commodity, or the quantity of any other commodity for which it will exchange, depends on the relative quantity of labour which is necessary for its production, and not on the greater or less compensation which is paid for that labour."*[5] Ricardo italicized the opening sentence because he wanted to stress the fact that he was not caught in the confusion and circular reasoning that had trapped Smith in his formulation of a labor cost theory of relative prices. Smith had solved the problem of measuring

---

[5] *Ibid.*, p. 11.

the quantity of labor necessary to produce a commodity (the skill, hardship, ingenuity question) by concluding that the wages paid to labor were a measure of the necessary labor time. Ricardo saw that this was circular reasoning, so in his opening sentence he explicitly stated that value depends upon the quantity of labor necessary for production, not on the wages paid to labor.

Ricardo then addressed the confusion over value in use and value in exchange that Smith had illustrated in the diamond-water paradox. Unlike Smith, who saw little connection between use value and exchange value, Ricardo holds that use value is essential for the existence of exchange value, though not its measure. In modern terminology he was saying that before a commodity will have a positive price in the market, a demand must exist, but demand is not the measure of price. The price of commodities that yield utility derives from two sources: their scarcity and the quantity of labor required to produce them.

Some commodities, however, have a price determined by their scarcity alone. These are commodities that are not freely reproducible and whose supply, therefore, cannot be increased—in modern phrasing, those that have a perfectly inelastic (or vertical) supply curve, such as rare pictures, books, coins, and wines. He said of these goods that "their value is wholly independent of the quantity of labour originally necessary to produce them, and varies with the varying wealth and inclinations of those who are desirous to possess them.[6] What Ricardo was saying, in effect, is that given a fixed inelastic supply curve, the position of the demand curve will determine price, and the demand curve's position is a function of an individual's preferences and income.

Competitively Produced Goods

Ricardo excluded those scarce, not freely reproducible commodities from his labor theory of value without much concern, because they "form a very small part of the mass of commodities daily exchanged in the market."[7] His value theory therefore applies only to commodities that are freely reproducible and produced in perfectly competitive markets. He assumed that the supply curve of goods produced by the manufacturing sector of the economy is perfectly elastic, which is another way of saying that for manufacturing he assumed constant costs. For agriculture he assumed increasing costs, so supply curves slope up and to the right, exhibiting elasticities greater than zero but less than infinity.

After analyzing Smith's explanations of the determinants of relative prices, Ricardo discarded the labor command and cost of production theories of value in favor of a labor cost theory of value. Whereas Adam Smith had rejected a labor cost theory as applied to an economy in which capital and land received returns, Ricardo maintained that this theory was appropriate to the economy of his own time. In literature that ranks among the most difficult to comprehend in all of economics, Ricardo attempted to prove his labor cost theory of value.

[6] *Ibid.*, p. 12.
[7] *Ibid.*

Difficulties of a Labor Cost Theory of Value

Ricardo encountered some of the problems that had led Smith to abandon the labor cost theory, but he saw clearly difficulties that Smith only vaguely perceived. He wrestled with these theoretical issues, trying in various ways to surmount them. A number of historians of economic ideas (with whom we tend to agree) believe that the labor theory of value received its most mature treatment in the works of Ricardo, that Ricardo developed the theory to its limit, and that Marx added little to our understanding of the theoretical difficulties of developing such a theory. Some even refer to Marx as a minor Ricardian, but because Marx's vast contributions to economics and the social sciences have little connection with his analysis of the problem of relative prices through a labor theory of value, he hardly deserves such an epithet.

Our next task is to indicate Ricardo's solutions to five fundamental problems confronting any theoretician developing a labor theory of value: (1) to measure the quantity of labor, (2) to reflect the fact that labor skills vary, (3) to account for capital goods as a factor influencing prices, (4) to account for land in price determination, and (5) to account for profits in price determination.

A measure of the quantity of labor.   Smith was unwilling to use clock hours, or time, as a measure of the quantity of labor necessary to produce a good because he reasoned that the skill of the laborer and the hardship of the job were also relevant. He argued that skill and hardship were settled by the "higgling and bargaining" in the market, and that the wage rates paid to different laborers would reflect their skills and the hardship of their jobs. Ricardo saw that Smith's logic was faulty and, as we have already observed, stated explicitly in the first sentence of his *Principles* that it is the quantity of labor that determines relative prices, not the wages paid to labor. Ricardo's solution is to measure the quantity of labor by the amount of time involved in producing a good, that is, by clock hours alone.

The differing skills of labor.   Using clock hours as a measure of the quantity of labor embodied in a commodity creates the same problem for Ricardo that Smith was trying to avoid. We call this the skilled-labor problem; it results from the fact that labor is not a homogeneous product, so one hour of labor time may produce different amounts of output. Assume that two laborers are working under the same conditions with the same quantities of land and capital to assist them. If one laborer produces two deer per hour and the other produces one deer per hour, what is the quantity of labor necessary to produce a deer? Ricardo solved this problem by using wages paid to laborers to measure their relative productivities. Thus, the wage of the laborer producing two deer per hour would be twice that of the less productive laborer. Superficially it would appear that Ricardo had involved himself in the same circular reasoning as Smith, for relative wages, which are prices, are used to explain relative prices. However, Ricardo's reasoning is not circular, because he was not attempting to explain relative prices at a point in time but was devising a theory to explain changes in relative prices over time.

He responded to the objection as to circular reasoning by pointing out that if differences in the wages paid to laborers because of differing skills remain constant over time, changes in the prices of final products will not be a result of the wages paid to labor. Thus, if a skilled laborer receives twice the wage of an unskilled laborer today and this ratio remains the same at some future date, any changes in the relative prices of the products produced by these two laborers must be explained by factors other than the wages paid to labor. Ricardo's assumption that wages paid to laborers of differing skills remain constant over time is open to question; but, granted this assumption, his solution of measuring labor in terms of clock hours is not circular reasoning, given the problem he was trying to solve.

Capital goods.   Almost all commodities are produced by the utilization of both labor and capital. What is the influence of capital on the prices of final goods under a labor cost theory? Ricardo solved this problem by identifying capital as merely stored-up labor, labor that has been applied in a previous period. The quantity of labor in a commodity produced by both labor and capital is measured by the quantity of labor immediately applied as well as by the quantity of labor stored in the capital good that is used to produce the final product. If a capital good requires 100 hours of labor for its production and wears out, or depreciates, at the rate of one-hundredth of its cost for each unit it produces, then the total labor required to produce a final good, using this capital good, is the number of hours of labor immediately applied plus 1 hour of labor used up from the capital good.

In modern terminology, when a commodity is produced with labor and capital, the capital depreciates during the production process. If the accountant's depreciation is an accurate measure of the capital destroyed in the production process, it is equivalent to the portion of the labor originally required to produce the capital, which becomes embodied in final goods. Ricardo would therefore handle the capital goods problem by summing the labor immediately or directly applied plus the time equivalent of the depreciation of capital goods during the manufacturing process.

Ricardo's solution to the capital goods problem is not completely satisfactory. If labor has been applied in some past period to produce a capital good, the price of a final good produced by using up this capital good must include an amount necessary to pay the labor directly applied, the indirect labor used to produce the capital good, *and* the interest on the funds paid to the indirect labor, from the time of payment until the final good is sold. To put this in its simplest form, an hour of labor applied to produce a capital good *two* years ago would have a different influence on the price of a final good produced today than would an hour of labor applied *one* year ago. A more accurate solution would be to sum both labor and interest costs from the past, but this would be inconsistent with a theory of value based exclusively on labor.

Land rent. A labor theory of value must also deal with the question of land rent. Adam Smith was unable to develop a labor theory of value once land had become an economic good, which is one reason for his turning to cost of production theory. Suppose that there are two laborers of equal skill working on two plots of land of different fertility. In one year the laborer on the more fertile land will produce more than the laborer on the less fertile land. What, then, is the quantity of labor necessary to produce a bushel of wheat? Ricardo solved this problem through his theory of land rent. For him, the price of a bushel of wheat depends upon the marginal cost of the bushel of wheat produced least efficiently. Price is determined at the margin, and at the margin there is no rent. Rent, as we have seen, is price-determined and not price-determining. The differing rents received by lands of differing fertilities will not, therefore, influence changes in relative prices over time.

Profits. Another difficulty inherent in any labor theory of value is determining the role of profits. If profits were the same proportionate part of the final prices of all commodities, as we saw before in our discussion of Smith's value theories, finished goods would exchange at the same ratios whether a labor cost or labor command theory of value was used. If profits are a different percentage of final price for various commodities, then relative prices or changes in relative prices cannot be correctly measured by labor alone. Casual empiricism indicates that profit is not a constant percentage of the final price of commodities. The amount of profit (defined, according to the Smith-Ricardo tradition, to include what modern economists would call profits and interest) in final sales price may vary for a number of reasons. The amount of capital per unit of final output can be expected to vary from one industry to another. Profit will be a larger element in final prices in industries that are capital-intensive than in industries that are labor-intensive. The rate of turnover of capital will also vary by industry, depending on the proportion between fixed and circulating capital. Industries with a faster rate of capital turnover will produce goods whose ratio of profit to final price is lower than that of goods produced in industries with a slower rate of capital turnover.

After thoroughly examining the problems the existence of profits raises for a labor theory of value, Ricardo concluded that they do not alter his fundamental proposition that changes in relative prices over time depend upon changes in the relative quantities of labor embodied in commodities. His conclusion is that the influence of the rate of profits is not quantitatively important.

Did Ricardo Hold a Labor Theory of Value?

Two aspects of this question have troubled historians of economic ideas: (1) Did Ricardo hold a labor theory of value? (2) Did Ricardo change his mind about the merits of a labor theory of value? Ricardo did not hold a theoretical labor theory of value, because he admitted that changes in the quantity of labor required to produce goods are not the only forces causing changes in relative prices. "Mr. Malthus shows that in fact the exchangeable value of commodities is not *exactly* proportional to the labour which has been employed on them, which I not only admit now, but have never denied."[8] He did, however, feel that changes in the amount of labor necessary to produce goods were quantitatively by far the most crucial element in explaining changes in relative prices.

George Stigler has labeled Ricardo's theory a 93-percent labor theory of value. On the basis of Ricardo's own illustrative figures, 93 percent of variations in relative prices can be explained by changes in the quantity of labor required to produce commodities. Ricardo's view is that even though changes in either the rate of profit or wage rates theoretically will cause changes in relative prices over time, these various changes in prices are quantitatively insignificant. He therefore concluded, "I shall consider all the great variations which take place in the relative value of commodities to be produced by the greater or less quantity of labour which may be required from time to time to produce them."[9]

Prior to the Sraffa edition of Ricardo's *Works,* historians of economic thought generally believed that Ricardo himself was backing away from a labor cost theory of value and moving toward a cost of production theory with costs including profits as well as labor costs. They concluded this largely on the basis of a passage from a letter Ricardo wrote to his friend J. R. McCulloch in 1820, following publication of the second edition of his *Principles* but before the third:

> I sometimes think that if I were to write the chapter on value again which is in
> my book, I should acknowledge that the relative value of commodities was regu-
> lated by two causes instead of by one, namely, by the relative quantity of labour
> necessary to produce the commodities in question, and by the rate of profit for
> the time that the capital remained dormant, and until the commodities were
> brought to market.[10]

On the basis of all the correspondence now published in Ricardo's *Works* and on the content of the third edition of his *Principles,* the editors of Ricardo's *Works* conclude that this one letter to McCulloch represented "no more than a passing mood" and that Ricardo maintained to the end that labor was quantitatively the most important element explaining variations in prices.[11] The validity of a labor cost theory of value is certainly subject to question, but it does seem to be beyond dispute that Ricardo thought it was valid.

Summary of Ricardian Value Theory

It may be helpful to summarize the highlights of Ricardo's value theory. (1) As opposed to Adam Smith, Ricardo held that use value was necessary for the

---

[8] Ricardo, *Notes on Malthus's Principles of Political Economy,* in *Works,* II, p. 66.
[9] *Ibid.,* pp. 36–37.
[10] Ricardo, *Letters, 1819–1821,* in *Works,* VIII, p. 194.
[11] Ricardo, *Principles,* p. xl.

Popularizers of Classical Economics*

One year before Ricardo's *Principles* was published, Jane Marcet (1769–1858), who had been successful with a popular book on chemistry published in 1806, wrote *Conversations on Political Economy* (1816). The book, translated into French, German, Dutch, and Spanish, was not only a financial success but was praised by J. R. McCulloch (1789–1864), an important disciple of Ricardo who published extensively and thereby carried Ricardo's economics to business and professional circles. David Ricardo, Robert Malthus, and J. B. Say also approved of Marcet's rendition of classical theory and encouraged her efforts at popularization. In the twenty-three years after its first edition in 1816, six more editions of Marcet's *Conversations* were published. Marcet followed her success with books for a different audience: *John Hopkins' Notions on Political Economy* (1833) was directed at the working class, and *Rich and Poor* (1851) at children.

Harriet Martineau (1802–1876) became a professional writer out of necessity. Because she was deaf, she was limited in occupational choice. She read of and was encouraged by Marcet's success as a popularizer of political economy and set out to explain classical economics using examples from daily activities. She encountered great difficulties in finding a publisher, but in 1832 the first of her efforts in economics was published as *Illustrations of Political Economy.* Over the next two years some 3,000 pages of *Illustrations* were published in twenty-four stories. This brought fame and fortune to Martineau and the work was translated into several languages.

*This box relies on an unpublished paper by Bette Polkinghorn, "Jane Marcet and Harriet Martineau: Motive, Sales and Reception of Their Contributions to Classical Economic Political Economy." Dr. Polkinghorn is completing a biography of Jane Marcet.

existence of exchange value. (2) His labor theory of value was developed only for freely reproducible goods produced under market conditions of pure competition. (3) His main concern was to explain the economic forces causing changes in relative prices over time. (4) Although changes in market, or short-run, prices may result from a number of demand and supply factors, changes in natural, or long-run, equilibrium, prices are explained by changes in the quantity of labor required to produce commodities. (5) Although certain factors modify these principles, particularly the element of profits, they do not confute the essential conclusion that changes in relative prices are for the most part explained by the quantity of labor required to produce goods.

RICARDIAN DISTRIBUTION THEORY

Now that we have a sense of Ricardo's labor theory of value, his theory of rent, and the Malthusian population doctrine, we can examine three of his major concerns: what determines the functional distribution of income among wages, profits, and rents at a point in time; what will happen to the distribution of income over time as economic development occurs; and what the consequences of the Corn Laws are on the distribution of income and the rate of economic growth. Ricardo could not answer these questions until he had first developed a theory of value and rent.

Distribution Theory

With the aid of a simple graph, we can develop Ricardo's argument about distribution from the Ricardian model by which doses of capital and labor in fixed proportions are added to the fixed quantity of land available to the economy. In Figure 5.3 doses of capital and labor are plotted on the horizontal axis, and the marginal physical products of these doses are measured in bushels of wheat on the vertical axis. The curve *ABHQM* represents these marginal physical products. Let us start with a position of equilibrium by assuming that a certain quantity of capital and labor represented by the distance *OC* is applied to the available land. The marginal product of the last unit of capital and labor applied is represented by the distance *BC,* and the total agricultural output of the model is equal to the area *OABC,* because the total product is the sum of all the marginal products. Ricardo's problem was to determine the division of the total product among wages, profits, and rent. His analysis was ingenious, for he had three variables to determine and

Figure 5.3   The Stationary State

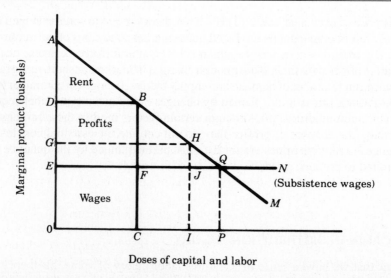

he solved for the various shares by subtraction. For this reason, Ricardo's theory of income distribution is often called a *residual theory*.

First let us determine rent. At the margin, rent falls to zero and any product above the line *BD* would be paid to the landowner. Rent would therefore be equal to the area *DAB*. The subsistence level of wages is given by the Malthusian population theory, and we assume for our example that this wage is the line *EFJQN*. The wage rate is then *FC*, and total wages are the area *OEFC*. When we subtract the wage rate from the marginal product at the margin, profit is *BF* for the last dose of capital and labor, and total profit is equal to the area *EDBF*. We have therefore divided the total output into its three shares of rent (*DAB*), profits (*EDBF*), and wages (*OEFC*). Notice that the level of profits depends upon the marginal product of the last dose of capital and labor, and the level of the real wage at subsistence.

Distribution of Income over Time

A related question of great interest to Ricardo was the changing over time of the relative shares of national income received by capitalists, landlords, and laborers. He found the analysis of Smith and other writers on this subject to be unsatisfactory, so he developed his own theory. Smith predicted a falling rate of profit over time, as a result of competition in the labor, investment, and commodity markets. Ricardo agreed that the rate of profit would fall over time, but he rejected all of Smith's reasons.

Smith's first reason is inconsistent with his own cost of production theory of value. As competition increases in labor markets and wages rise, there is no reason, under the cost of production theory of value, to suppose that profits must fall. Ricardo refuted Smith by using Malthusian population doctrine, arguing that if competition did bid real wages up, increases in population would in the long run increase the size of the labor force and wages would fall back to the former level.

He rejected Smith's second and third reasons for falling profits, competition in the investment and commodity markets, by an argument known as *Say's Law*. Ricardo argued that Smith's second and third explanations of falling profits implied the existence of general overproduction, because competition in investment markets will result in falling profits only if it is not possible to sell at previous prices the increased output that results from new investment. Ricardo maintained that the increased output from new investment could be sold at previous prices; hence the rate of profit would not fall. He used the same argument to refute Smith's third reason for falling profits, pointing out that competition in commodity markets will not result in a fall in the general level of prices. We will examine Say's Law again at the end of this chapter.

In brief, Ricardo asserted that Smith had the right answer—profits would fall—but for the wrong reasons. Ricardo's analysis starts with a young economy and follows it through the following sequence of economic development. The young economy is characterized by a high rate of profit and, because the source of capital accumulation is profits, a high rate of capital accumulation. This capital accumulation bids up wage rates so that real wages rise and, in accordance with the Malthusian population doctrine, the size of the population increases. These increases in population require larger quantities of agricultural food products, so the extensive and intensive margins are pushed down, lands with less and less fertility are brought into production, and land under cultivation is farmed more intensively. As the margin is pushed down, rents rise and profits fall. This is an important theoretical point: Ricardo argued that pushing down the margin causes both a rise in rents and a fall in profits. As profits fall, the rate of capital accumulation decreases; this process continues gradually until the rate of profit is close to zero and capital accumulation ceases. At this point the entire dynamic of the capitalistic system is at a standstill: the rate of profits is approaching zero; there is no capital accumulation and therefore no economic growth; population growth has stopped; wages are at a subsistence level; and rents are high.

One may argue that all Ricardo has shown is that profits must fall in agriculture. But what about manufacturing? Assuming perfectly competitive markets, as the rate of profit falls in agriculture, capital will move to take advantage of higher rates of profit in manufacturing. In long-run equilibrium the rate of profits must be everywhere the same throughout the economy; so as the rate of profit falls in agriculture, it must also fall in manufacturing. Once the dynamic force in the Ricardian model, capital accumulation, is reduced, the entire system is affected, eventually arriving at what has been called the classical stationary state. This dire prediction of classical economics reinforced the view that economics was the dismal science.

We can cover the same analytical ground by using Figure 5.3. As capital accumulation and population growth take place in a growing economy, more and more units of capital and labor are applied to the fixed quantity of land. If the margin is extended so that OI represents the last dose of capital and labor applied, we find that the new, higher level of rent is the area GAH; profits have been reduced to the area $EGHJ$; and the total wage bill is now $OEJI$. As the margin is pushed out further, the level of rent increases until the total product is now comprised exclusively of wages and rents, and profits are zero. This is the stationary state; it is reached when OP doses of capital and labor are applied, rent is EAQ, wages are $OEQP$, and profits are zero.

Back to the Corn Laws

The foregoing analysis of the forces determining the distribution of income and changes in the distribution of income over time reveals some of the economic consequences of the Corn Laws. Protection of British agriculture from foreign competition caused imports of grain to decline and the output of grain in England to increase. As grain output expanded in England, the intensive and extensive margins were pushed out and profits declined as rents increased. Although Ricardo had already concluded that the long-run trend in the economy would bring about this redistribution of income from the capitalists and toward the landlords, he was against the Corn Laws because they would accelerate the process. Because the source of economic growth was capital accumulation by the capitalists, the Corn Laws had the undesirable consequence of slowing down the rate of economic growth and hastening the arrival of the stationary state.

It is interesting to note that although Ricardo bought land and presumably applied his economic analysis to the management of his own investments, when he died his estate was valued at about $100 million at today's prices; as a member of Parliament and as an individual citizen he consistently argued against the economic interests of landlords and for the reduction of tariffs on agricultural goods and for free international trade. He was, in this instance, placing the welfare of the society above his own self-interest as a landowner.

Ricardo developed a second argument against the Corn Laws, namely, that barriers to international trade diminish the welfare of *all* the world economies. To understand this reasoning we must first examine his doctrine of comparative advantage.

COMPARATIVE ADVANTAGE

The tremendous subtlety of Ricardo's mind is evident in his doctrine of *comparative advantage* as applied to international trade. With this argument he strengthened the case for free trade by extending Adam Smith's analysis of the gains to be achieved by the free movement of goods across international boundaries. If nation A could produce a good at a lower cost than nation B, and nation B could produce another good at a lower cost than nation A, both nations would gain by practicing territorial specialization and trading. In the terminology of international trade theory, if one nation has an absolute advantage in the production of one commodity and another nation an absolute advantage in the production of another commodity, each can gain by specializing in the commodity that costs it the least to produce. Historians of economic thought disagree as to the originator of the doctrine of comparative advantage. The principal nominees include Ricardo, Robert Torrens (1780–1864), and James Mill (1773–1836). In any event, it was Ricardo's presentation of it that influenced subsequent economic thinking.

Absolute Advantage

Before proceeding to Ricardo's theory of comparative advantage, let us first take a two-commodity, two-country model and examine international trade when each country has an *absolute advantage* in one of the commodities.

According to the data in Table 5.3, England has an absolute advantage over Portugal in the production of cloth. The data illustrate this advantage from the output side, but this advantage can also be viewed from the cost side. Thus, the cost of producing cloth, measured in labor time, is less in England than in Portugal. Portugal has an absolute advantage in the production of wine. To demonstrate that international trade will take place, it is necessary first to show that both nations

Table 5.3 Output per Unit of Labor

	Wine (gallons)	Cloth (yards)
England	4	2
Portugal	8	1

could gain by trading. If total production of wine and cloth can be increased by specialization, and if international prices or terms of trade for wine and cloth can be reached that benefit both nations, there will be a basis for international trade.

If England transfers a unit of labor from the wine to the cloth industry and Portugal transfers a unit of labor from the cloth to the wine industry, the total output of both wine and cloth is increased while the same total quantity of labor is still applied in both economies. Although the movement of a unit of labor out of the wine industry in England reduces output by 4 gallons, the application of another unit of labor in the wine industry in Portugal increases output by 8 gallons, so that the total world production of wine is now 4 gallons more. Likewise, while cloth output falls by 1 yard in Portugal from the transfer of a unit of labor out of cloth production, the added unit of labor in the English cloth industry increases output by 2 yards, and the total production of cloth thereby increases by 1 yard. Thus, the total output for our two-nation world is larger as a result of transferring labor to the industries having an absolute advantage.

Our next problem is to determine if prices that would benefit both nations can be established by means of international trade. We shall treat prices in barter terms. In England 1 yard of cloth would trade for 2 gallons of wine; the price of cloth is twice the price of wine. The English would be willing to trade cloth for wine if they could receive more than 2 gallons of wine for 1 yard of cloth. In Portugal the internal prices for wine and cloth would be 8 gallons of wine for 1 yard of cloth. If the Portuguese could trade anything less than 8 gallons of wine and receive in exchange 1 yard of cloth, they would do so. We have therefore established that there a series of international prices for wine and cloth that would benefit both nations, and that both would gain from trading at prices between 7.9 gallons of wine for 1 yard of cloth and 2.1 gallons of wine for 1 yard of cloth.

Comparative Advantage

Both Smith and Ricardo recognized the benefits from international specialization and trading when countries have absolute advantages, but what happens when one country is more efficient in the production of all commodities? Let us modify our example by assuming that a threefold increase in productivity occurs in England, resulting in the outputs per unit of labor given in Table 5.4.

Now England is more productive than Portugal in both industries; correspondingly, costs of production measured in labor time are less in England for both goods. The comparative advantage argument demonstrates that with the data in

Table 5.4   Output Per Unit of Labor

	Wine (gallons)	Cloth (yards)
England	12	6
Portugal	8	1

Table 5.4, trade will still be advantageous to both nations. Although England has an absolute advantage in the production of both goods, it is not absolute but comparative advantage that is crucial in determining whether international trade will be beneficial. In this example England has a comparative advantage in the production of cloth and Portugal has a comparative advantage in the production of wine. Comparative advantage is determined by examining the relative productivities within each economy. England's comparative advantage in cloth is demonstrated by the fact that in England each unit of added output of cloth means the loss of 2 units of wine, whereas for Portugal 8 gallons of wine must be given up to obtain another yard of cloth. Portugal's comparative advantage in wine is indicated by the fact that in Portugal the loss of only $\frac{1}{8}$ yard of cloth gains another gallon of wine, whereas England must give up $\frac{1}{2}$ yard of cloth to produce another gallon of wine.

To establish that total world output can be increased by specialization and trade, let us determine the gains and losses that occur if England produces more cloth and less wine, and if Portugal produces less cloth and more wine. Moving a unit of labor from the wine to the cloth industry in England increases the output of cloth by 6 yards and decreases that of wine by 12 gallons. Transferring 2 units of labor in Portugal to the wine industry increases wine output by 16 gallons and decreases cloth output by 2 yards. The net gain from these transfers of labor in the two countries is 4 gallons of wine (16 – 12) and 4 yards of cloth (6 – 2).

It is easy to establish a series of mutually satisfactory prices. When we increased productivity in England in order to illustrate the principle of comparative advantage, we did not affect internal prices in England: the data from either Table 5.3 or Table 5.4 allow us to determine that 2 gallons of wine are worth 1 yard of cloth in England. Both England and Portugal would gain from trading at prices between 7.9 gallons of wine for 1 yard of cloth and 2.1 gallons of wine for 1 yard of cloth.

By means of his comparative advantage doctrine, Ricardo proved that the determining element for gains from international trade is not absolute advantage but comparative advantage. We have shown with the data in Table 5.4 that England can benefit from trade with Portugal, even though England has an absolute advantage in every industry, as long as Portugal has a comparative advantage in one industry. What is important is not the productivity of the English wine industry as compared with the Portuguese, but the opportunity cost of cloth in England as compared with the opportunity cost of cloth in Portugal.

Using the data of Table 5.4 we can construct Table 5.5, which measures the opportunity costs of the two goods in the two nations. Under Ricardo's assumption

Table 5.5   Opportunity Costs

	Wine	Cloth
England	½ yard of cloth	2 gallons of wine
Portugal	⅛ yard of cloth	8 gallons of wine

of full employment, if we are to produce more of any good, the cost will be measured by the quantity of the goods whose output must be reduced as resources are shifted from the contracting to the expanding industry. Our simple two-commodity model allows us to measure opportunity cost in terms of the other good in the economy. The opportunity cost of cloth in England (2 gallons of wine) is less than the opportunity cost of cloth in Portugal (8 gallons of wine), and the opportunity cost of wine in Portugal (⅛ yard of cloth) is less than that in England (½ yard of cloth). Thus, when England produces cloth and trades for the wine that Portugal produces, total world output is larger and both countries gain from trade.

To illustrate the importance for trade of differences in opportunity costs, let us change the data of our previous examples to that of Table 5.6. England now has an absolute advantage in the production of wine and cloth, but a comparative advantage in neither. The opportunity costs within each nation are the same—the opportunity cost of a yard of cloth is 2 gallons of wine and the opportunity cost of a gallon of wine is ½ yard of cloth. In other words, the relative prices of the two goods are the same in each country—2 gallons of wine equal 1 yard of cloth (price of cloth divided by the price of wine equals 2). Where opportunity costs are the same, neither country has a comparative advantage and trade will not be beneficial to either nation.

Although Ricardo established the benefits of trade when opportunity costs differ between nations, he failed to consider another aspect of the problem. What would be the international price of cloth and wine, and how would the gains from trade be divided between countries? In the example Ricardo used, he assumed that the price or exchange ratio between wine and cloth in international trade would settle at a point halfway between the prices most favorable to each nation; thus, the gains from trade would be evenly divided between the two countries. Torrens also considered this issue, but it was J. S. Mill who correctly

Table 5.6   Output per Unit of Labor

	Wine (gallons)	Cloth (yards)
England	12	6
Portugal	8	4

solved the problem by concluding that the terms of trade or international price would depend on the relative strengths of the demand for commodities in the trading nations.

The Ricardian concept of comparative advantage has not only theoretical elegance but important policy implications as well. If we replace the simple two-commodity, two-nation model with a multicommodity, multination world, the principle of comparative advantage indicates that as long as opportunity costs differ among nations, there are gains to be achieved by international trade. The classical case against government intervention in international trade, first forcefully presented by Smith, was considerably extended by Ricardo. By placing impediments to the free flow of goods across international boundaries, the English Corn Laws not only slowed down the rate of economic growth in England by redistributing income away from the capitalists toward the landlord, but they also reduced the welfare of the average citizen in all nations. The fallacy in the prevalent notion that the burden of a tariff is borne by foreigners is exposed by the doctrine of comparative advantage.

The comparative advantage doctrine has even wider and more important implications than for international trade. We have seen that both the scholastics and the mercantilists regarded exchanges or trades between parties as benefiting one at the expense of the other. This was because they implicitly assumed that the total amount of goods was fixed and, therefore, if one party gained another lost. This is also an implicit assumption of some theories that perceive conflict in economic exchanges in which there must be winners and losers.

What Ricardo proved with his theory of comparative advantage is that voluntary trade or exchanges between parties can benefit both, because the increased efficiences that result from specializing in the product in which one has a comparative advantage lead to larger total output. One might approach the importance of this idea with examples from the small town, nation, and international trade. Let us assume that the best lawyer in town is also the best typist. Does she type her own legal work? No; she hires a typist, because even though she has an absolute advantage in both legal work and typing, she receives higher income by spending her time in her area of comparative advantage. And her secretary, who voluntarily agrees to type at a wage much lower than a lawyer's hourly fee, is better off as a result of specializing in his area of comparative advantage. The total amount of output is greater as a result of the practice of comparative advantage; the economic pie is larger. Once this argument is comprehended, applying it between lawyer and typist, New York and California, and England and Portugal is easy.

The mercantilist case for protecting industries from foreign trade was damaged by Smith's absolute advantage principle; it was nearly demolished by the comparative advantage doctrine. More important, the doctrine also shows that even though there are conflicts in society because of relative scarcity, voluntary exchanges between economic actors will lead to larger total output and mutual gains. Fortunately, neither the lawyer nor the typist needs to understand the theory of comparative advantage; it explains how they act, not how they think.

Ricardo and the Art of Economics

In the introductory chapter we pointed to the distinction between positive economics, normative economics, and the art of economics. In Chapter 4 we saw how
Adam Smith was a master at using contextual analysis to develop his economic
policy proposals. Ricardo, who had a more abstract methodology than Smith and
a more noncontextual policy approach, was still very good at the art of economics.
Ricardo was concerned with the consequences of the economic policies that were
protecting British agriculture. Using a labor theory of value and other equally
abstract assumptions, he concluded that the Corn Laws protecting British agriculture would reduce profits and lead to slower rates of capital accumulation and
economic growth. Free trade was good policy according to Ricardo. His model of
comparative advantage was equally abstract and devoid of contextual grounding.
It concluded that freely made voluntary exchanges would increase the size of the
economic pie. Evidently, from the examples of Smith and Ricardo, the art of
economic policy can be mastered by economists with different methodological
proclivities.

STABILITY AND GROWTH IN A CAPITALISTIC ECONOMY

An argument between Ricardo and Malthus over the ability of a capitalist system
to maintain full employment of its resources significantly influenced the development of economic theory. In the literature of economics this argument is known
as the controversy over Say's Law, after the French economist J. B. Say (1776–
1832). Ricardo won the argument; thereafter orthodox economic theory paid little
attention to the issues raised by Say's Law until the 1930s, when J. M. Keynes
developed his macroeconomic theory and at the same time criticized the views of
Ricardo. The essence of Say's Law is that a capitalistic system will automatically
provide full employment of its resources and high rates of economic growth.
Ricardo, James Mill, and J. B. Say favored this position, but Malthus attacked it.
Actually, the argument concerning stability and growth in a capitalist system had
already developed in mercantilist literature, so we will gain perspective by starting
there.

Mercantilist Views of Aggregate Demand

Most of the mercantilists believed that individual thrift and saving were beneficial
to the nation. Some, however, argued that saving caused unemployment and that
greater consumption spending would increase economic activity and thus benefit
the economy. The most forceful advocate of this view was Bernard Mandeville,
who presented his views in an allegorical poem and several prose commentaries
collected under the title *The Fable of the Bees* (the best edition is by F. B. Kaye,
1924). Mandeville maintained that prosperity and employment were furthered by
spending, particularly on luxurious consumption, and that saving was detrimental

The Relevance of Ricardo

Should we have tariffs, quotas, and other devices that protect American industry and agriculture from foreign competition? Ricardo's analysis of these issues is still relevant today. He correctly perceived that measures intended to protect Americans from foreigners actually harm them in several ways. These measures increase the relative share of the pie distributed to some sectors of the economy at the expense of other sectors. Quotas, tariffs, and agreements that limit the importation of Japanese automobiles, for example, effectively redistribute real income away from purchasers of cars— including purchasers of American-made cars as well as Japanese cars—and toward labor, management, and stockholders in the automobile industry.

Ricardo's doctrine of comparative advantage demonstrates that the effect of impediments to free trade is to reduce the size of the world's economic pie. Subsidies to domestic agriculture throughout the world today are significantly reducing the well-being of most citizens of the earth.

The classical economists speculated about the long-run tendencies of capitalism. The economic future of humankind rests on the outcome of two broad forces: diminishing returns (emphasized by Ricardo), which *decrease* the incremental output of capital and labor applied in agriculture and industry; and technological development, which *increases* it. Which force will prevail? Economists have historically underestimated the rate of technological development, possibly because of an imperfect understanding of this process. Can we influence the rate of technological progress through public policy that encourages research and development expenditures? Even if we can do so, are expenditures to increase the rate of technological development also subject to diminishing returns, and is Ricardo's stationary state therefore inevitable? These are the questions raised by Ricardo's theory, and they remain to be answered.

---

to the economy because it led to lower levels of output and employment. He criticized his contemporaries because their views about saving and prosperity were inconsistent: "To wish for the Increase of Trade and Navigation, and the Decrease of Luxury at the same Time, is a Contradiction."[12]

Smith's Views of Aggregate Demand

Smith rejected the ideas of Mandeville and like-minded mercantilists. He praised frugality and saving; according to his analysis, it was capital accumulation that was the main determinant of prosperity and growth. He argued that the underconsumptionists, who believed that an insufficiency of consumption led to depression and low rates of growth, perceived the situation incorrectly because they failed to

[12] Bernard Mandeville, *A Letter to Dion,* ed. Bonamy Dobrée (Liverpool: University Press of Liverpool, 1954), p. 49.

understand the process of saving and investment and its impact on the economy. For Smith, saving does not reduce aggregate demand but merely rechannels demand from consumer goods to investment goods.

> Capitals are increased by parsimony and diminished by prodigality and misconduct. . . . As the capital of an individual can be increased only by what he saves from his annual revenue or his annual gains, so the capital of a society, which is the same with that of all individuals who compose it, can be increased only in the same manner. . . . What is annually saved is as regularly consumed as what is annually spent, and nearly in the same time too; but it is consumed by a different set of people.[13]

Malthusian Underconsumptionism

Those outside the field of economics usually associate Malthus only with his development of a theory of population. So did most economists until the writing of J. M. Keynes revived interest in Malthus's economic theories. In several pamphlets and particularly in his *Principles of Political Economy,* first published in 1820, Malthus set forth his economic theory, which differed from Ricardo's on a number of points. Our present interest is in Malthus's views on the economic consequences of saving, or capital accumulation. These views are set forth in his *Principles,* particularly in Book II, Chapter 1, "On the Progress of Wealth." (Book II, Chapter 1, refers to Malthus's second edition of *Principles,* which was published in 1836. This is the most readily available edition. The chapter is essentially the same as Chapter 7 of the first edition, published in 1820.)

Smith had concluded that economic progress depends on the size and efficiency of the labor force; the quantity and quality of natural resources; the institutional structure; and the amount of capital accumulation, which he considered the crucial determinant of economic development. Ricardo also regarded capital accumulation as the chief source of growth in the wealth of a nation. This analysis is based exclusively on the aggregate supply side: growth is limited only by the degree to which a nation can increase its supply of labor, capital, and natural resources. But what happens if aggregate demand for final output falls short of aggregate supply, producing less than full employment of resources, or depression?

The few mercantilists who had raised this possibility of *underconsumption* or overproduction were effectively silenced by Adam Smith's refutation of their positions. Nevertheless, the issue was again raised in the early 1800s. Lord Lauderdale (1759–1839) in *An Inquiry into the Nature and Origin of Public Wealth* (1804) and Jean Charles Sismondi (1773–1842) in *Nouveaux principes d'économie politique* (1819) questioned the ability of an economy to produce full utilization of its resources automatically. In 1820 Malthus also raised these questions, and a famous debate ensued between him and Ricardo. In Book II of the 1836 edition of his *Principles,* Malthus examined the alleged causes of economic growth

---

[13] Smith, *Wealth of Nations,* p. 321.

and criticized each as being inadequate, maintaining that it was necessary to consider the demand side, or what he called "effectual demand." Malthus never stated precisely what he meant by effectual demand, and his understanding of the issues raised by Say's Law is certainly confused. Yet he perceived that there were difficulties in maintaining full employment of resources, even though he had no clear grasp of the exact nature of these difficulties.

In Malthus's discussion of the process of capital accumulation, he presented both naive and more sophisticated analyses of the problem of maintaining full employment. His more naive argument is that labor does not receive the whole of the product, and labor demand by itself is not sufficient to purchase all final goods at satisfactory prices. Labor has the will to purchase goods, he said, but lacks the purchasing power, whereas the capitalists have the purchasing power but lack the will. This is certainly correct, but if the capitalists return their savings to the market in the form of demand for producer goods, there will be no deficiency of aggregate demand. Malthus accepted the notion that saving does not mean hoarding and that savings will flow back to the market as investment spending. He sometimes suggested other functions for money and questioned the Ricardian view that money is only a medium of exchange and that no one withholds purchasing power, but he never developed these insights into a monetary explanation of depressions.

His more sophisticated insight into certain problems of the economy suggests that the saving-investment process cannot go on indefinitely without leading to long-run stagnation. He contended that there is an appropriate rate of capital accumulation the economy can absorb and that too much saving and investment will cause difficulties. The process of saving leads to a reduction in the demand for consumer goods, and the process of investment leads to the production of more consumer goods in the future. Malthus recognized, moreover, that for full utilization of resources in a capitalist system to be maintained, the total level of output and consumption must keep expanding. As the Red Queen says in Lewis Carroll's *Through the Looking Glass,* "Now *here,* you see, it takes all the running you can do, to keep in the same place."

Malthus concluded that because there was insufficient effectual demand from the laborers and capitalists, the gap must be filled by those in the society who consume but do not produce. These unproductive consumers are those who provide services (teachers, servants, and public officials, among others) and the landlords. Thus, one of the social functions of the landlords is to consume without producing and therefore to help prevent depression and the eventual stagnation of the economy.

Say's Law

The orthodox classical economists rejected the criticisms of Lauderdale, Sismondi, and Malthus. Their position was most forcefully and explicitly developed by J. B. Say, James Mill, and Ricardo, who argued that in the process of producing goods, sufficient purchasing power was generated to take these goods off the market at satisfactory prices. They maintained that overproduction, or what they called *gluts,* might occur in particular markets but that it was impossible to have general overproduction for the entire economy. What declines did take place in the general level of economic activity would be of short duration, because the market would automatically return the system to a full utilization of its resources. Thus, the classicists insisted that in the long run there could be no excessive capital accumulation.

Admittedly, if an automobile is produced that sells for $9,000 and we deduct the payments made to the various factors of production, the residual will be zero. This is true by definition, because what is not wages, rent, or interest goes to the capitalists as profits. There is $9,000 worth of purchasing power now in the pockets of labor, landlords, and capitalists. The same holds true for the total economy; that is, the value of its yearly output is received as purchasing power by members of the economy. There can be no question, then, that sufficient purchasing power is always generated to take produced goods off the market. The classicals recognized, moreover, that demand and supply might not mesh in particular markets and that there could be overproduction of particular goods—an excess of supply in a given industry. This glut in a particular industry is a manifestation of market forces at work, on either the demand or the supply side. But an excess supply in one industry means that there must be an excess demand for the goods of another industry. Assuming a system of flexible prices and mobility of resources, factors of production will leave the industry with excess supply and flow into the industry with excess demand. Thus, full employment of all resources is assured in the long run.

Although sufficient purchasing power is generated to take all goods produced off the market, what assurance is there that this purchasing power will be exercised in the market? The answer contained in Say's Law is often simply stated as follows: supply creates its own demand. There can be no question that supply creates a potential demand, but what is crucial is whether that potential demand is exercised in the market as *effective* demand. Ricardo, James Mill, and Say dealt with this issue by simply asserting that all potential purchasing power was returned to the market as demand for either consumer or producer goods. Essentially, they returned to the Smithian position that a decision to save is a decision to invest. They denied the possibility of hoarding—no one locks gold in a box. Money was only a medium of exchange in their system; thus, they denied any possible monetary causes of depression or stagnation. Though the classical defense of Say's Law has some weak links, Malthus never clearly perceived these difficulties. He tried to disprove the theory while accepting all the assumptions necessary for its proof. He did suspect that the theory was incorrect, but he was never able to articulate this insight into a sound criticism or an alternative theory of the determinants of the level of income and rate of economic growth.

The Bullion Debates, Henry Thornton, and Ricardo's Monetary Theory

Ricardo's views on Say's Law were developed in debates that occurred in the early 1800s; these debates were called the *Bullion Debates.* At issue was what was the cause of the Napoleonic wartime inflation. The Bullionists argued that the cause of the inflation was the monetary expansion that occurred during the wars. The anti-bullionists maintained that the causes of the inflation were more complicated, but that they included real causes such as harvest failures. They favored the *Real Bills Doctrine:* the doctrine that if the issuance of money were related to short-term financial commercial operations (such as the financing of inventories), there could be no over-issuance of money. When monetary growth did not exceed the needs of real trade, the causes of inflation are not in the monetary sector. Robert Torrens (1780–1864) was a major supporter of this anti-bullionist position and his *Essay on Money and Paper Currency* (1812) is a good statement of the anti-bullionist position.

In this debate Ricardo soon became a major expositor of the Bullionist position, which is similar to a modern-day monetarist position—inflation is always a monetary phenomenon. For Ricardo, the "action" in the economy was in the real sector; his monetary theory reflected that view. Money was simply a veil hiding the real economy; his writings in the debate were designed to remove that veil.

Ricardo's authority led to his views' overshadowing those of Henry Thornton (1760–1815), a far more subtle and, when it came to monetary matters, more thoughtful, economist. In his most famous book, *The Paper Credit of Great Britain* (1802), Thornton set out a remarkably sophisticated analysis not only of the relationship between money and prices, but also of the path through which money affects prices. Thornton traced the effect of money through the interest rates and lending practices of banks, and in doing so he recognized the potential for monetary disequilibrium affecting the real economy, and hence for money to affect the real economy. Money was more than a veil to Thornton. In his discussion he even recognized the distinction between real and nominal interest rates. But as often happens in economics and other fields, these more sophisticated views fell by the wayside and the received classical monetary theory remained a simplistic theory centered around the version of the *quantity theory of money* favored by Ricardo in which monetary forces are simply a veil hiding real forces.

Technological Unemployment

In the third and last edition of *Principles,* published in 1821, Ricardo added a new chapter, "On Machinery," in which he analyzed the effect of the introduction of machinery on the economy. His previous view had been that the introduction of labor-saving machinery would not result in unemployment and would be beneficial to the entire society. There was a growing concern by labor that new machinery would create unemployment. Ricardo did not deal directly with this issue in the first two editions of *Principles,* but he concluded in his *Essay on Profits* that the introduction of machinery would raise the real wages of labor. In a speech in Parliament in 1819 and in a letter to his friend McCulloch, he maintained that the introduction of machinery did not reduce the demand for labor.[14] Ricardo evidently

[14] Ricardo, *Principles,* p. lviii.

changed his mind on this issue after reading and critically evaluating Malthus's *Principles*. In his new chapter "On Machinery," Ricardo stated: "That the opinion entertained by the labouring class, that the employment of machinery is frequently detrimental to their interests, is not founded on prejudice and error, but is conformable to the correct principles of political economy."[15]

Ricardo's discussion of the possibility of *technological unemployment* is not as inconsistent with his position on the impossibility of general gluts as the preceding quotation would imply. He believed that if newly introduced machinery is financed by the diversion of circulating capital into fixed capital, the wages fund will be reduced and unemployment will occur. He did not discuss how long this unemployment would persist or how changes in the market might bring about a new position of full employment. If the newly introduced machinery is financed out of savings rather than circulating capital, then no unemployment will occur. It seems clear, then, that Ricardo's views on the possibilities of unemployment caused by labor-saving machinery were changing and that he never fully reconciled these views with his defense of Say's Law.

Keynes on Malthus and Ricardo

Present-day interest in the controversy between Malthus and Ricardo over Say's Law and in Malthus's economic ideas, apart from his population thesis, is in large part a result of J. M. Keynes's macroeconomic theory and his praise of Malthus and criticism of Ricardo. Keynes presented his views on Malthus and Ricardo in a paper about Malthus that is most easily found in Keynes's *Essays and Sketches in Biography* and in *The General Theory*. Keynes's opinions raised three related issues: (1) the Malthus-Ricardo controversy over Say's Law; (2) the methodology appropriate to economics; and (3) the effect of Ricardo's triumph over Malthus with regard to both these issues on the subsequent development of economics as a discipline. In *The General Theory* Keynes states:

> The idea that we can safely neglect the aggregate demand function is fundamental to the Ricardian economics, which underlie what we have been taught for more than a century. Malthus, indeed, had vehemently opposed Ricardo's doctrine that it was impossible for effective demand to be deficient; but vainly. For, since Malthus was unable to explain clearly (apart from an appeal to the facts of common observation) how and why effective demand could be deficient or excessive, he failed to furnish an alternative construction; and Ricardo conquered England as completely as the Holy Inquisition conquered Spain. Not only was his theory accepted by the city, by statesmen and by the academic world. But controversy ceased; the other point of view completely disappeared; it ceased to be discussed. The great puzzle of Effective Demand with which Malthus had wrestled vanished from economic literature. You will not find it mentioned even once in

---

[15] *Ibid.*, p. 392.

the whole works of Marshall, Edgeworth and Professor Pigou, from whose hands the classical theory has received its most mature embodiment. It could only live on furtively, below the surface, in the underworlds of Karl Marx, Silvio Gesell or Major Douglas.

The completeness of the Ricardian victory is something of a curiosity and a mystery. It must have been due to a complex of suitabilities in the doctrine to the environment into which it was projected. That it reached conclusions quite different from what the ordinary uninstructed person would expect, added, I suppose, to its intellectual prestige. That its teaching, translated into practice, was austere and often unpalatable, lent it virtue. That it was adapted to carry a vast and consistent logical superstructure, gave it beauty. That it could explain much social injustice and apparent cruelty as an inevitable incident in the scheme of progress, and the attempt to change such things as likely on the whole to do more harm than good, commended it to authority. That it afforded a measure of justification to the free activities of the individual capitalist, attracted to it the support of the dominant social force behind authority.[16]

In his essay on Malthus, Keynes praises Malthus's understanding of an economy's difficulties in maintaining full employment, quoting letters from Malthus to Ricardo "to show Malthus's complete comprehension of the effects of excessive saving on output via its effects on profit."[17] Historians of economic thought agree that Keynes has read too much into Malthus's vague notions about the inability of an economy to reach full employment. Although Malthus's intuition may have been correct, his criticism of Ricardo was vague and deficient, and as Keynes correctly notes, he had no alternative theoretical construction to offer in place of Say's Law.

A closely related issue raised by Keynes concerns the different methodologies used by Malthus and Ricardo. We have previously noted that Ricardo represented a turning point in economic methodology, replacing Smith's combination of theory and historical description with highly abstract theoretical models. Though the first edition of Malthus's *Essay on Population* was strictly deductive, the second and subsequent editions were much more inductive. Keynes strongly approves of Malthus's methodology and criticizes Ricardo's abstract models. In the previous two paragraphs extracted from *The General Theory,* Keynes makes three references to methodology: one approving Malthus's "appeal to the facts of common observation" and two disparaging Ricardo's model, which "reached conclusions quite different from what the ordinary uninstructed person would expect" and had "a vast and consistent logical superstructure." Keynes heaps further praise on Malthus and others who, in "following their intuitions, have preferred to see the truth obscurely and imperfectly rather than to maintain error, reached indeed with clearness and consistency and by easy logic, but on hypothe-

[16] John Maynard Keynes, *The General Theory of Employment, Interest and Money* (New York: Harcourt Brace, 1936), pp. 32–33.
[17] Keynes, *Essays and Sketches in Biography* (New York: Meridian, 1956), p. 34.

ses inappropriate to the facts."[18] In his essay on Malthus, Keynes commends Malthus's methodology as "a method which to me is most sympathetic, and, as I think, much more likely to lead to right conclusions than the alternative approach of Ricardo."[19] Keynes's praise of Malthusian methodology is somewhat self-serving, being, as he defines it, similar to his own.

According to Keynes, "the complete domination of Ricardo's [approach] for a period of a hundred years has been a disaster to the progress of economics,"[20] and "if only Malthus, instead of Ricardo, had been the parent stem from which nineteenth-century economics had proceeded, what a much wiser and richer place the world would be today."[21] This view contains some truth and some error. Certainly, economics today would have a more developed understanding of the forces that determine the level of income and employment if the questions raised by Malthus had been more thoroughly discussed. An earlier development of macro theory might have avoided the great economic and social upheavals that took place between the two world wars; thus, conceivably, the economic and social forces that brought on World War II might never have developed. But the difficulty with Keynes's position is that it is rendered with hindsight. How are we to judge an economic proposition or theory at the time it is rendered? Should we accept the vague and intuitive feelings of a Malthus, whose position in part rationalizes the interests of the unproductive consumers, particularly the landlords, or the clear, consistent, and logical views of a Ricardo, whose position rationalizes the interests of the capitalists? It is possible that other agencies answer this question for us—that, as Keynes suggests, the accepted view must have "the support of the dominant social force behind authority."[22] We can hope that in the social sciences in general and in economics in particular, criteria for the acceptance of a theory will eventually be developed that are less politically biased.

SUMMARY

The first quarter of the nineteenth century brought many fresh contributions to economic theory. The only other short period of time of comparable significance occurred during the 1930s, when major depressions turned the attention of economists to new problems, just as rising agricultural prices, land rents, and the Corn Laws had caught the attention of Ricardo and others. David Ricardo was the right man at the right time; his clear, analytical mind was able to sort the important from the trivial and build a theoretical framework that dominated economic thinking for one hundred years. The scope of economics turned from an almost

---

[18] Keynes, *General Theory*, p. 371.

[19] Keynes, *Essays*, p. 23.

[20] *Ibid.*, p. 33.

[21] *Ibid.*, p. 36.

[22] Keynes, *General Theory*, p. 33.

exclusive concern with questions of economic growth to include the issue of changes in the functional distribution of income over time. Ricardo's concern with the distribution of income led him to give much greater attention than previous economists had to the micro issue of formulating a theory of value, or relative prices; thus, although Ricardo's major policy interest was in macroeconomic issues, he moved the focus of economics toward micro questions. His defense of Say's Law and the quantity theory of money also succeeded in precluding the examination of certain macro questions from subsequent orthodox economic literature.

Ricardo represents a distinct break from the Smithian method—a loose combination of theory and historical description—to a methodology of highly abstract theoretical models. With brilliant analysis, Ricardo was able to demonstrate the strengths and weaknesses of a labor cost theory of value and to illuminate the pressing policy issues of the time. He strengthened the Smithian case for laissez faire with his argument showing the gains in welfare from free and open international trade. He brought together the Malthusian population doctrine and the wages fund theory to demonstrate the impossibility of improving the lot of those in the lower-income groups. His defense of Say's Law silenced one set of critics who found flaws in the operation of a capitalist system, wherein decisions concerning saving and investment are made by private individuals. His economics undermined the position of the landlords, who were beginning to lose political power to the rising capitalist class. And his analysis of the impending stationary state cast a long shadow over the future of capitalism. By the middle of the nineteenth century, Marx had combined the Ricardian tools with other analysis to forge his theory that capitalism was just a phase in history and contained the seeds of its own destruction.

Key Terms

diminishing returns
dismal science
Malthus's population thesis
Poor Laws
functional distribution of income
labor cost theory of value
real wage
Corn Laws
neutral money
fixed coefficients of production
constant returns
economic actors
marginal product
intensive margin
extensive margin

marginal cost
single tax movement
opportunity cost
absolute value
residual theory of distribution
Say's Law
comparative advantage
absolute advantage
underconsumption theory
gluts
Bullion Debates
Real Bills Doctrine
quantity theory of money
technological unemployment

Questions for Review, Discussion, and Research

1. Explain and critically evaluate Malthus's population theory.
2. Contrast and compare Ricardo's and Smith's methodologies.
3. Indicate the difference between Smith's contextual and Ricardo's noncontextual policy analysis.
4. Explain Ricardo's theory of land rent and point out the relationship between viewing rent from the product side and the cost side.
5. Summarize Ricardo's labor theory of value.
6. Explain Ricardo's theory of distribution and his views about changes in the distribution of income over time.
7. State Ricardo's theory of comparative advantage and explain how people are made better off by free trade.
8. Critically evaluate the argument between Ricardo and Malthus concerning the stability of a market system.
9. Some historians hold that economic theory can be explained as an intellectual reaction to problems of the times. Use this thesis to explain Malthus's and Ricardo's contributions to economic thought.
10. Labor has always been concerned about being replaced by machines. Why do firms introduce labor-saving machinery? Do you think the introduction of labor-saving machinery is beneficial to society?
11. It seems that you can never escape that absent-minded professor. She has yet another job for you. She tells you that the following quotation appears somewhere in Ricardo's writing:

> The exportation of the coin is caused by its cheapness, and is not the effect, but the cause of an unfavorable balance: we should not export it, if we did not send it to a better market, or if we had any commodity which we could export more profitably.

She is quite—but alas, not absolutely—sure that it does not appear in Ricardo's *Principles,* but she cannot remember precisely where it does appear. Unfortunately for you, she wants to use it in her next article, which means that your assignment is to find the complete bibliographic citation for it.

Suggested Readings

Baumol, William J. "The Classical Dynamics." Chapter 2 in *Economic Dynamics.* New York: Macmillan, 1951.

Becker, Gary S., and William J. Baumol. "The Classical Monetary Theory: The Outcome of the Discussion." *Economica,* 19 (November 1952).

Blaug, Mark. *Ricardian Economics.* New Haven: Yale University Press, 1958.

Cannan, Edwin. *A History of the Theories of Production and Distribution in English Political Economy from 1776 to 1848.* London: Staples, 1917.

Cassels, John M. "A Re-Interpretation of Ricardo on Value." *Quarterly Journal of Economics,* 46 (May 1935).

Hollander, Samuel. "David Ricardo." *Oxford Economic Papers,* 33 (1981).

————. "The Development of Ricardo's Position on Machinery." *History of Political Economy,* 3 (Spring 1971).

————. *The Economics of David Ricardo.* Toronto: University of Toronto Press, 1979.

————. "On Malthus's Population Principle and Social Reform." *History of Political Economy,* 18 (Summer 1986).

Hutchison, T. W. "James Mill and the Political Education of Ricardo." *Cambridge Journal,* 7 (November 1953).

Keynes, John M. "Robert Malthus." In *Essays and Sketches in Biography.* New York: Meridian, 1956.

Malthus, Thomas R. *An Essay on Population.* 2 vols. London: J. M. Dent, 1914.

———— . *Principles of Political Economy.* New York: A. M. Kelley, 1951.

Ricardo, David. *On the Principles of Political Economy and Taxation.* In *The Works and Correspondence of David Ricardo.* Vol. I. Eds. P. Sraffa and M. Dobb. Cambridge: The University Press, 1953.

Robbins, Lionel. "Malthus as an Economist." *Economic Journal,* 77 (June 1967).

Spengler, Joseph J. "Malthus's Total Population Theory: A Restatement and Reappraisal." *Canadian Journal of Economics and Political Science,* 11 (February-May 1945).

Sraffa, Piero. "Introduction" to *On the Principles of Political Economy.* In *The Works and Correspondence of David Ricardo.* Vol. I. Eds. P. Sraffa and M. Dobb. Cambridge: The University Press, 1953.

Stigler, George J. "The Ricardian Theory of Value and Distribution," "Sraffa's 'Ricardo,'" and "Ricardo and the 93 Per Cent Labor Theory of Value." In *Essays in the History of Economics.* Chicago: University of Chicago Press, 1965.

Readings in Original Sources

All readings by David Ricardo are from *On the Principles of Political Economy and Taxation.*

Value: Chapters 1, 4, 20, 28, and 30.

Rent: Chapters 2, 3, 24, and 32.

Wages: Chapter 5.

Profits: Chapters 6 and 21.

6 J. S. Mill and the Decline of Classical Economics

"Through Mill we see the philosophical conflicts underlying classical economics."

—Todd G. Buchholz

J. S. Mill (1806–1873) was a most unusual and gifted thinker who contributed significantly not only to economics but also to political science and philosophy. His tremendous intellectual powers were complemented by an education of unique breadth and intensity. His father, James Mill, assumed the role of instructor to his young son, restraining him from the life of a normal child. At three years of age he was studying Greek, and by age eight he began Latin. After mastering mathematics, chemistry, physics, and logic, he started to study political economy at age thirteen. By his fifteenth year his formal education was finished, and he spent the next four years editing a five-volume work of Bentham. The psychological costs of this unusually intense education were finally manifested in a mental breakdown at the age of twenty, but following a period of depression Mill rallied and became one of the leading intellectuals of his and all time. His *Autobiography* contains an unusually honest and open examination of his early education and subsequent psychological difficulties.

Although J. S. Mill was an extremely capable economic theoretician, his intellectual background directed him toward much broader social issues than economists typically address. Mill was essentially a social philosopher intent upon improving the role of the individual in society; in place of the pessimism of his father and Ricardo, he advanced a guarded optimism that contemplated the development of a good society. Although he read widely, the major influences on his economic ideas were his early training in the classical economics of Smith, Ricardo, his own father, and Bentham; the socialist writings of Fourier and Saint-Simon; the writings of Comte, sometimes called the father of sociology, who led

Mill to view economics as only one aspect of human social activity; and, finally, his friend Harriet Taylor, who later became his wife and who taught Mill to be more receptive to the humanistic socialist ideas of his times. Mill was both a classical liberal and a social reformer.

J. S. Mill's position in the development of economic ideas is difficult to specify. He wrote at the end of the classical period, but his open-mindedness, one of his greatest assets, enabled him to modify classical doctrine in several ways. His economics is simultaneously the most mature statement of the classical position and the start of a new period in the development of economic thinking. His *Principles of Political Economy,* written in less than two years, was first published in 1848 and remained, in its subsequent seven editions, the standard in the field until the end of the century. The short period it took Mill to write the book reflected his view that the discipline was so well developed that few major problems remained to be solved. He believed that his major tasks were to write a lucid exposition of Ricardian doctrine and to incorporate into it the new ideas that had appeared during the second quarter of the nineteenth century. However, he was an original thinker who made important contributions, which he characteristically did not emphasize, in international trade theory as well as in supply-and-demand analysis.

In his *Principles of Political Economy* (1848), John Stuart Mill attempted to rescue the essential tenets of Ricardo's *Principles* from the avalanche of criticism that had begun shortly after its publication in 1817 and continued unabated throughout three decades. Mill's work, which dominated orthodox economic thought from its publication until the 1890s, represented the culmination as well as a significant revision of classical economic theory, because saving Ricardian theory was contingent upon repairing its major flaws. Before examining Mill's contributions, therefore, it is necessary to survey some of the many criticisms of Ricardian doctrine to which Mill was responding. These stemmed from three main sources. First, there was increasing evidence of a disparity between Ricardian doctrine and the empirical evidence gathered from the operation of the English economy. Contrary to the Malthusian population theory, which was an essential premise of Ricardo's system, there was growing evidence that real per capita income was increasing, not decreasing, as population increased; and with rapidly developing technology, agriculture was experiencing increasing, not diminishing, returns. Second, the discipline of economics was becoming increasingly professionalized and consequently more critical of received doctrine. Academicians began to work through Ricardo's theoretical structure, particularly his labor theory of value, and found his treatment of demand and of the role of profits in the determination of prices to be wanting. Third, a number of humanist and socialist writers, ignoring the technical content of economic thinking, delivered broadsides attacking the foundations of the emerging capitalistic economy that Ricardo's theoretical structure represented.

A number of subsequent developments in economic thought emerged from these criticisms of Ricardian thought. Say's Law, the theory advanced by Ricardo,

Say, and James Mill that states that the economy will automatically produce full employment, came to be rejected by certain heterodox economists, notably Marx. And a growing body of socialist literature by French, Swiss, German, and English writers questioned the classical notion that economic harmony was best achieved by means of the unimpeded workings of a capitalist economy. The culmination of this heterodox thought was Marx's *Kapital,* but J. M. Keynes in his *General Theory* likewise rejected the classical assertion that free markets constitute the most effective approach to economic harmony.

A more technical body of criticism was advanced by men who were studying economics more as a profession than as an avocation. These writers tried to spell out more explicitly the proper scope and method of economics and to identify the chief building blocks of the classical system. Their major thrust was to reject, in part, the Malthusian population doctrine, historically diminishing returns in agriculture, and the wages fund doctrine, and to replace the labor theory of value with a value theory in which profits were a determinant of price and in which the role of demand and utility in determining relative prices was enlarged. This line of analysis finally bore fruit in the marginal utility school, which began in the 1870s, as well as in the economics of Alfred Marshall.

Before examining J. S. Mill, we shall consider a number of developments that occurred primarily between 1800 and 1850, including revisions of attitudes toward the scope and method of economics and the rethinking of such pillars of classical economic thought as the Malthusian population doctrine, the concept of diminishing returns in agriculture, the wages fund doctrine, and the Ricardian concept of land rent. After this background we turn to John Stuart Mill, who dominated orthodox theory for much of the remainder of the nineteenth century.

POST-RICARDIAN DEVELOPMENTS

Early Critics of Classical Economics

Many early critics of classical economics have little in common other than their objection to the economics of Smith and Ricardo. Some are often called socialists, but that may be questioned. The unifying theme that binds this diverse group of so-called socialists is their view of the functioning of capitalism in nineteenth-century Western Europe as disharmonious. Most of these early pre-Marxian socialists advocated nonviolent means of eliminating the conflicts in society, although the remedies prescribed vary with each writer. The early socialists indirectly influenced the development of orthodox theory, directly influenced J. S. Mill, and had a major impact, particularly in England, on legislation and on the formation of the labor movement. One of the more careful scholars of the development of economic theory during this period believes that "in fact much of the theoretical development of the 1830s, particularly that related to the nature of profit as a source of income, was the result of a more or less conscious effort to counter the spread of socialist ideology."[1]

These early critics from the left who rejected the assumption of harmony had a diversity of ideas. Some used a labor theory of value to suggest that because labor is the source of value it should receive all or more of its output; some found the working of competitive markets to be undesirable; some recommended cooperatives; some wanted scientists and engineers through state planning to play larger roles in the economy; and some found the distribution of income to be inequitable and proposed various remedies—and even suggested returning to an economy and society, less dominated by the new and larger firms, in which artisans and small firms played larger roles. It is not, therefore, surprising that one of the most important post-Ricardian developments was a response to these attacks on the classical vision of a market society in which the capitalist was a key actor and benefactor. The reaction of the post-Ricardian classicals was to re-examine this vision, to make modifications, and to probe some of the technical parts of the theoretical structure, particularly the theory of interest and profits.

The Scope and Method of Economics

Ricardo, as we have seen, represented a change in the methodology of economics from Smith's loose combination of theory and historical description to abstract, deductive theoretical models. Ricardo seldom addressed himself directly to questions of methodology, but his followers later reached an almost complete agreement on the proper methodology for economics. Their new Ricardian methodology regarded economics as a discipline based upon certain simple assumptions. The task of the economist was therefore to correct the logic of the system to make certain that the conclusions followed from the given assumptions. Such a methodological position contributed significantly to the development of economic theory during the post-Ricardian period when conflicts appeared between economic theory and the available empirical data, for it caused economists to ignore the data. Our first task is to examine this methodological position and to demonstrate that although newly gathered statistical and historical material was contradicting the theory, the majority of economists held to the major Ricardian doctrines.

The two best and most explicit statements dealing with the proper scope and method of economics made during this period were by Nassau Senior (1790–1864) and J. S. Mill. We will use Senior's views as representative of the times. In *An Outline of the Science of Political Economy* (1836), Senior defined political economy as treating "the Nature, the Production, and the Distribution of Wealth."[2] The foundations of economics as a science rest on four self-evident principles, and

---

[1] Mark Blaug, *Ricardian Economics: A Historical Study* (New Haven: Yale University Press, 1958), p. 140.

[2] Nassau William Senior, *An Outline of the Science of Political Economy* (New York: Augustus M. Kelley, 1951), p. 1.

the task of the economist is to develop an accurate terminology and follow the rules of logic so that his or her conclusions follow from their premises. Senior believed that economists had wasted their time in trying to collect more empirical information and should orient their efforts toward improving the logical consistency of economic theory. The economist's

> premises consist of a very few general propositions, the result of observation, or consciousness, and scarcely requiring proof, or even formal statement, which almost every man, as soon as he hears them, admits as familiar to his thoughts, or at least as included in his previous knowledge; and his inferences are nearly as general, and, if he has reasoned correctly, as certain, as his premises.[3]

Senior's four elementary propositions on which the foundations of economics as a science rested were: (1) the principle of rationality, in that people are rational and calculating and will attempt to acquire wealth with a minimum of sacrifice; (2) the Malthusian population doctrine; (3) the principle of diminishing returns in agriculture; and (4) the principle of historically increasing returns for industry. This view of economics as a purely deductive discipline had important consequences for the development of economic theory; but before examining these consequences, we shall look at another interesting aspect of Senior's methodological position.

Senior was one of the first economists to maintain unequivocally that economics should be a positive science. Senior believed that the economist, as a scientist, should take care to distinguish between normative judgments and positive economic analysis. One example of this view in Senior's system is his distinction between (1) the universal laws governing the nature and production of wealth, and (2) the principles governing the distribution of income, which are relative to the particular customs and institutional structure of an economy. J. S. Mill later made this distinction between the laws of production and distribution a cornerstone of his system. Senior maintained that the economist, as a scientist, can point out the consequences of various economic actions or the possible means to achieve any given end, but that he should not leave the field of positive scientific analysis and make value judgments concerning the desirability of any given line of action. Simply stated, the economist should concern himself with what is, rather than what ought to be. The economist's "conclusions, whatever be their generality and their truth, do not authorize him in adding a single syllable of advice."[4]

The acceptance of the methodology that Ricardo practiced and Senior expounded had an unfortunate effect on post-Ricardian economics. The conflict between theory and reality, which became manifest in the 1830s and 1840s, was largely ignored; and although empirical evidence contradicted several basic premises of the Ricardian theoretical system, the economists doggedly adhered to the Ricardian model.

[3] *Ibid.*, pp. 2–3.
[4] *Ibid.*, p. 3.

One way to judge the adequacy of a theory is to test its ability to predict. Ricardian economics, although abstract in form, was formulated to provide solutions to significant political and economic questions of the times; therefore, it made certain predictions that could be empirically tested. By comparing these predictions with the empirical evidence, we can uncover the reasons for the decline of Ricardian economics. In order to do this we will turn to the post-Ricardian treatment of certain basic tenets of orthodox theory: Malthusian population theory, the wages fund doctrine, diminishing returns and rent, and the tendency of the rate of profits to decrease over time.

Malthusian Population Theory

In the period following the publication of Ricardo's *Principles,* economists, being deeply concerned with the population problem, had begun to suggest that the only way to avoid the dire consequences of overpopulation suggested by the Malthusian theory was for families to use some form of contraception. These conclusions were always subtly stated because of the strong reaction by the church and the general public against contraception. There is ample evidence that the private views of the leading economists of this period, with the exception of McCulloch, had been in favor of some form of contraception, but their public statements supporting contraception were made with caution.

Nassau Senior was typical of the economists of his time in his simultaneous acceptance and rejection of the Malthusian population theory. Although he characterized this theory in 1836 as one of the pillars upon which the science of economics was founded, as early as 1829 he had published correspondence between himself and Malthus, together with lectures he had given the year before, that seriously questioned Malthus's proposition that population tends to increase faster than the food supply. Senior had concluded that historical evidence indicated instead that the food supply increased faster than population.

In the Ricardian analytical scheme, Malthus's theory of population was an essential element. Ricardo held that the major purpose of economics should be to explain the forces that determine the distribution of income, and he was particularly interested in the forces causing changes in the distribution of income over time. Ricardo had solved this problem by means of a residual theory of income distribution. The rentless margin determines rent; the remainder of output is composed of wages and profits. It is at this point that Malthusian population theory plays a crucial role. The long-run wage rate is fixed at a subsistence level by the Malthusian theory, and therefore the residual can be easily divided into wages and profits. (See Figure 5.3 and the accompanying text for a full explanation of the Ricardian theory of income distribution.) Ricardo assumed (1) that the long-run level of real wages was fixed and known, and (2) that at this level of real wages, the long-run supply of labor was perfectly elastic. Suppose that the long-run level of population and the size of the labor force are *not* solely dependent on the real wage rate. Under these circumstances the distribution of income at a point in time, or changes in the distribution of income over time, cannot be determined in the

Ricardian system. In the example of the Ricardian theory of distribution shown in Figure 5.3, the level of subsistence wages (*EN*) was given by Malthusian population theory. If the subsistence level of wages cannot be determined, then the curve *EN* has an infinite number of possible positions and shapes, and the calculation of profits and wages at a point in time or changes in the distribution of income over time is indeterminate. Thus, Ricardian distribution theory was fundamentally dependent upon Malthusian population theory. But by the middle of the 1830s, enough historical evidence had been accumulated to completely discredit this theory—and along with it Ricardian economics, which could no longer fulfill its avowed purpose, to explain changes in the distribution of income over time.

Wages Fund Doctrine

Malthusian population theory was used to explain the level of real wages in the long run. Ricardian short-run explanations of wages were based on a supply-and-demand analysis known as the *wages fund doctrine*. It should be noted that "long run" in this context means a minimum of fifteen years. Under Malthusian population theory in its minimum subsistence form, an increase in real wages in the present year would not have repercussions on the future level of wages for some time, depending upon the age of entry into the labor force. If we assume that immediate increases in population take place when real wages rise, the supply of labor will not be affected for at least fourteen years.

The wages fund doctrine as a short-run theory of wages simply suggests that the wage rate depends on the supply and demand for labor. These are not actually supply-and-demand schedules as used in modern economics. The demand for labor is fixed by the size of the wages fund, that part of capital accumulated to pay labor. Given the size of the wages fund, the short-run wage rate is determined by dividing the number of persons in the labor market into the wages fund. In the short run, then, the wages fund is fixed in amount, the quantity of labor is fixed, and the wage rate is uniquely determined.

With the demise of Malthusian population theory the wages fund doctrine had to carry the weight of being both a short-run and a long-run theory of wages. This it was unable to do, because nothing in the wages fund doctrine said anything about the long-run supply of labor. The wages fund doctrine was used, however, by many popular writers as an argument against labor's attempts to raise wages, particularly through the formation of unions. In the writings by economists of this period, there appears to be no connection between views on the wages fund doctrine and attitudes toward labor unions: many economists holding to the wages fund doctrine explicitly approved of the formation of labor unions. Nevertheless, in the popular literature the wages fund doctrine became known as an anti-union economic argument; this, in part, accounts for J. S. Mill's famous rejection of the wages fund doctrine in 1869 and the importance placed by subsequent writers on Mill's disavowal .

Historically Diminishing Returns

In the Ricardian model the key element that is fundamental to Ricardo's economic analysis and to the policy conclusions flowing from it is the rate at which diminishing returns occur in agriculture as compared with the rate of increase in agricultural productivity resulting from technological progress. Ricardo maintained that with added doses of capital and labor and a fixed quantity of land, the marginal product of those doses would decrease as the margin was extended. Technological improvements in agriculture could just offset, fail to offset, or more than offset short-run diminishing returns; therefore, it is possible in the long run to have historically constant, decreasing, or increasing returns in agriculture. Ricardo, and most of the writers in the post-Ricardian period, believed that technological development would not offset short-run diminishing returns and therefore predicted *historically diminishing returns*. The issue is not theoretical, however, but empirical.

All the available data for the British economy indicated that the Ricardian predictions based on historically diminishing returns were wrong. During the first half of the nineteenth century, empirical evidence indicated that the growth of population in England greatly exceeded the growth of labor employed in agriculture. Most economists, particularly McCulloch and J. S. Mill, interpreted these data as indicating that returns had not, in fact, diminished during the period. Yet curiously, despite their cognizance of this evidence, the Ricardians continued to hold to their model and its prediction that returns would eventually diminish.

As Mark Blaug, who is arguably the most astute modern scholar of this period, has said, "The divorce between theory and facts was probably never more complete than in the heyday of Ricardian economics."[5] This divorce was embedded in Ricardian methodology. As practiced by Ricardo and articulated by Senior, the methodology exclusively emphasized the deductive process of reasoning from a given set of assumptions; thus, it allowed the Ricardians to ignore the contradictions between their model and fact and to busy themselves with refining the elegance of their theoretical structure. There is some question as to whether the lesson to be learned from a study of economic thinking during the Ricardian period has been absorbed by present-day economists. We will see later that one common element in most non-Marxian heterodox economic thinking is the assertion that orthodox economic theory manifests precisely those faults displayed by Ricardian economics: a conflict between orthodox models and facts and an obsession with refining the deductive process and the internal consistency of its theoretical structure.

Falling Rate of Profits

The Ricardian model also predicted that the rate of profits would tend to fall over an extended period of time. The theoretical basis of this prediction was, again,

---

[5] Blaug, *Ricardian Economics,* p. 187.

historically diminishing returns. When the costs of agricultural products increase, profits on the marginal land fall as rents rise on the intramarginal land. This tendency will persist, according to Ricardo, until the rate of profit approaches zero and the stationary state results from a redistribution of income toward the landlord and away from the capitalist. But the validity of this assertion, too, can be determined only by empirical evidence and not by theory. The statistical problems of measuring changes in the rate of profit for an economy over time are exceedingly difficult, and the statistical tools required for this measurement were certainly not available during the nineteenth century. Indeed, some question whether they are available today. In spite of their lack of empirical verification of historically diminishing returns in agriculture and of a falling rate of profits and the eventual coming of a stationary state, the Ricardians—particularly J. S. Mill— persisted in these predictions.

Theory of Profits (Interest)

Two other aspects of the Ricardian theory of profits need to be examined before we turn to J. S. Mill's statement of the classical position: (1) a theoretical failure of Ricardo's theory of value, and (2) its use by some to criticize the prevailing distribution of income. After wrestling for a long time with the role of profits in his value theory, Ricardo concluded that changes in the rate of profits played an insignificant role in explaining changes in relative prices over time. He decided that although relative prices depended theoretically upon the costs of both labor and capital, with the cost of capital being profits, the role played by profits in practice was so insignificant that they could be ignored. Thus, Ricardo's theory of value was in effect a cost of production theory with labor being the only cost. This aspect of Ricardo's theory of value attracted the attention of various economists who were compelled to improve the logical consistency of value theory by including capital costs as well as labor costs of production.

Such concern for the theory of profits was intensified by the attacks of the Ricardian socialists, who used Ricardo's value theory to show that labor was being exploited. They argued that labor produced the entire product but did not receive all its product as wages. Profits were a deduction from labor's rightful share; and the capitalists, like the landlords, were parasites in the system who received an income while performing no essential economic function. Their argument was simple, and for that reason it could be used effectively in popular criticism of the existing economic order. It was, then, both to correct the logical defects of Ricardo's value theory and to buttress the prevailing ideology against the attacks of the Ricardian socialists that economists turned their attention to profits.

The most significant contribution to profit and value theory in the early post-Ricardian period was by Nassau Senior, who first attempted to develop an *abstinence theory of interest*. In his value theory Senior gave greater emphasis to utility on the demand side than did Ricardo, and when he came to the supply side, he emphasized disutility as a real cost of production. Using the basic psychological assumptions of classical economics, he maintained that people were rational and calculating. Wages, he said, are the reward paid to labor for incurring the pain of working. If we are to produce capital goods, someone must abstain from consumption, and the capitalist will not abstain unless he is rewarded for this pain. Because both capital and labor are necessary to produce final goods, their price must be sufficient to pay both of these real costs of production. Thus, Senior developed a cost of production theory of value with wages being the return to labor and profits being the return to the providers of capital.

In classical economics no distinction was made between profits and interest. Senior attempted to develop a theory of interest, which was a predecessor to the Böhm-Bawerkian theory developed near the end of the nineteenth century. Senior actually developed only part of a theory of interest, for his discussion deals solely with the supply side, in keeping with classical tradition. He examined only the forces that determine the supply curve of savings, whereas a theory of interest would also have to account for the demand for investment. As an argument against the socialists, Senior's abstinence theory of interest has several defects. He suggested that the supply curve of savings is perfectly elastic (horizontal) and that the pain cost, or disutility, incurred in saving is the same for the wealthy as for the poor. Because he dealt with interest exclusively as a payment for the pain costs or disutility of forgoing consumption, no social or economic justification is given for the receipt of interest on capital that is acquired by inheritance or by gift. Thus, in the end, Senior's theory of interest probably raised more questions concerning the social justification for interest than it answered.

J. S. MILL: THE BACKGROUND OF HIS THOUGHT

Mill's Approach to Economics

Mill's views on the scope and method appropriate to economics are contained in an article published in 1836—the same year as Senior's *Outline of the Science of Political Economy,* with its heavy emphasis on methodology—and in his *Principles,* published in 1848. Mill's article on methodology is available in his *Essays on Some Unsettled Questions of Political Economy.*[6] He regarded economics as a hypothetical science using the *a priori method.* The economist makes certain assumptions and then deduces conclusions from these assumptions. Because the experimental method is not available to economists, they must rely on the deductive technique and cannot use the inductive techniques that have been so fruitful in the natural sciences. Mill is, however, careful to point out that the conclusions derived by economists from their deductive models should be verified by a comparison with the facts of life. A lack of agreement between the results predicted using the deductive model and the historical facts will, in Mill's view, reveal important "disturbing causes" that have been overlooked. These causes may

[6] John Stuart Mill, *Essays on Some Unsettled Questions of Political Economy,* 2nd ed. (New York: Augustus M. Kelley, 1968), pp. 120–164.

result in new fruitful hypotheses, which will yield new conclusions through deductive reasoning, or they may be the result of noneconomic factors the economist has failed to consider. Although Mill's statement on the proper methodology for economics is basically sound, he, like his contemporaries, did not practice what he preached. "Disturbing causes" became a rug under which orthodox economists swept any divergencies between the predictions of the Ricardian model and the empirical evidence.

Influenced by the ideas of Comte, Mill regarded economics as only a part of a much larger study of humankind. The economist assumed an abstract economic man who was motivated completely by the desire to possess wealth. Yet Mill recognized that although this abstraction yielded some useful conclusions, it ultimately had to be integrated into a more complex model of humans in their social activities. Mill's open-mindedness, breadth of knowledge, and social concerns led him to develop his own economic analysis on a much broader level than Ricardo had. The full title of his major economic work is *Principles of Political Economy with Some of Their Applications to Social Philosophy*. There are two outstanding editions of this classic. The one we will quote from was edited by W. J. Ashley.[7]

Whereas Senior distinguished between positive and normative economics in order to eliminate normative judgments from economic inquiry, Mill drew this division in order to reincorporate questions of social philosophy into the Ricardian model. Mill maintained that his single most important contribution to economic thinking was this differentiation between the laws of production and the laws of distribution. The laws of production, according to Mill, are laws of nature (like the law of gravity) that cannot be changed by human will or institutional arrangement. But the laws of distribution are not fixed; they result chiefly from particular social and institutional arrangements. Mill was reacting strongly to the way in which classical orthodox theory was being used. In particular, many efforts to improve the quality of life of the mass of society through social legislation, the trade union movement, and income redistribution policies had been countered by conservative arguments alleging that the laws of economics invalidated these attempts. Classical economics was used to show that the distribution of income was determined by fixed, immutable laws that could not be changed any more than the law of gravity could be changed—despite one's great sympathy for the downtrodden masses, one must not permit one's heart to rule one's head.

Mill wanted to show that most economists were wrong in believing that neither the laws of production nor the laws of distribution could be changed by the institutional structure of the society. The laws of production (e.g., the principle of diminishing returns in agriculture) are fixed, according to Mill, but the personal distribution of income is subject to change by social intervention.

[7] John Stuart Mill, *Principles of Political Economy with Some of Their Applications to Social Philosophy,* edited with an introduction by W. J. Ashley (London: Longmans, Green, 1929). Another excellent edition of Mill's *Principles* can be found in Volumes II and III of *Collected Works of John Stuart Mill* (Toronto: University of Toronto Press, 1965).

In his *Autobiography* Mill discussed the origins of his concepts of the *laws of production* and *laws of distribution,* citing the socialist writings of the Saint-Simonians as his chief inspiration and crediting Harriet Taylor for convincing him of the importance of distinguishing between the two. Thus, Ricardian theory's predictions of the stationary state at which wages would be at a subsistence level were countered by Mill's more optimistic conviction that over time, society would act in a wise and humane way, so that a more equal and equitable distribution of income would result. He therefore favored high rates of taxation on inheritances but opposed progressive taxation because he feared its disincentive effects. He also advocated the formation of producer cooperatives and believed that as workers received not only wages but also profits and interest from these cooperatives, they would have greater incentives to increase their productivity. Furthermore, he believed that the results of diminishing returns in agriculture could be mitigated by the increased enlightenment of the people and by the reduction of the rate of population growth by later marriage and by birth control.

Some of the purely economic implications of Mill's distinction between the laws of production and the laws of distribution require further discussion. Modern orthodox economic theory discloses a close relationship between the laws of production and the *functional* distribution of income. The forces determining the prices of final goods and services in retail markets are closely connected to the forces determining the prices of the various factors of production. The physical relationship between inputs and outputs, what economists call production functions, determines the marginal physical productivity of the various factors of production, and the price of a factor of production in the market is, in part, determined by this productivity. Modern orthodox theory has, however, very little to say concerning the forces that determine the *personal* distribution of income. The personal distribution of income depends upon a much broader set of non-economic variables such as the laws, customs, and institutional arrangements of a society and are, therefore, in the view of the orthodox economist, outside the discipline of economics. Furthermore, the orthodox theorist hesitates to examine issues connected with the personal distribution of income, because normative issues and value judgments are involved. If Mill's distinction between the laws of production and the laws of distribution is translated into the terms of modern theory (a translation that is arbitrary, because Mill made this distinction before the development of marginal productivity analysis), he would maintain that there is only a loose connection between the marginal productivity of the various factors and the personal distribution of income. Society cannot modify production functions, but it does have the ability to effect a distribution of personal income in keeping with its own value judgments.

Mill's Eclecticism

Mill's great strength, which was also the strength of the two most important post-Millian English economists, Marshall and Keynes, was his *eclecticism,* which was manifested in many ways: in his unwillingness to accept uncritically the economic theory of Ricardo and his followers; in his predominantly Smithian methodology; in his acceptance of Comte's view that economic activity must be studied in the broader context of all human social activity; in his acknowledged indebtedness to the French socialists and to Harriet Taylor; in his concern with social philosophy; and in his distinction between the laws of production and the laws of distribution.

Unaccountably, he sometimes tried to disavow this eclecticism by maintaining that in economic *theory* he was merely modifying Ricardian economics by incorporating into it the developments of the second quarter of the century. But in the area of economic *policy,* as he indicated in the preface to the first edition of his *Principles,* Mill admitted that he was breaking new ground. In his *Autobiography* and his *Principles* he expressly dissociated himself from the economists of the old school, declaring that "the design of the book is different from that of any treatise on Political Economy which has been produced in England since the work of Adam Smith."[8] Actually, although Mill wanted to incorporate new theoretical developments into Ricardian theory, his primary objective was to indicate clearly the applications of economic theory to policy.[9] Adam Smith had done this, but much of Smithian theory was now obsolete.

Jeremy Bentham's Influence

The most important influence on J. S. Mill's and his contemporaries' attempts to unite theory and policy was the work of the Englishman Jeremy Bentham (1748–1832). After Bentham's first important work was published in 1780, he became the intellectual leader of a group of reformers known as the *philosophical radicals,* or *utilitarians.* Historians of ideas disagree as to the degree of influence Bentham had on various writers, particularly on Ricardo and J. S. Mill. There is little question that James Mill was significantly influenced by Bentham and that Bentham and his followers had an important effect on economic, political, and social legislation and reform during this period. Even before Malthus wrote his essay on population, Bentham had proposed birth control; and Benthamites later advocated a long list of reforms encompassing adult suffrage (including women), prison reform, free speech and free press, civil service, and legalization of unions. Bentham started from the simple premise that people are motivated by two strong desires: to achieve pleasure and to avoid pain. If society could measure pleasure and pain, then laws could be created that would result in the greatest amount of happiness for the greatest number of individuals. The best way to measure pleasure and pain, according to Bentham, was by the measuring rod of money. Thus, Bentham and his followers hoped to make social reform an exact science by designing laws that would lead to the greatest good for the greatest number.

Although J. S. Mill, like the philosophical radicals, was strongly interested in political, economic, and social reform, he partially rejected some aspects of

---

[8] *Ibid.,* p. xxvii.

[9] Pedro Schwartz, *The New Political Economy of J. S. Mill* (Durham, N.C.: Duke University Press, 1972).

Benthamism that his father accepted. Before he was twenty years old J. S. Mill had edited a five-volume edition of Bentham's works and had been strongly indoctrinated into the Benthamite system by James Mill. How much of the severe psychological depression that overwhelmed him as he reached adulthood is attributable to his growing dissatisfaction with his father's and Bentham's views will never be known, but for the remainder of his life he continued to emulate Bentham's concern with social reform while eschewing certain aspects of his theoretical structure. Two parts of the Benthamite system disturbed him in particular. The first was a dogmatism in the views of the philosophical radicals, particularly evident in their insistence that the pleasure-pain calculus of *hedonism* could be used to analyze *all* human behavior. Influenced by Comte and others, Mill could not accept such a narrow view, which seemed to disregard many of the elements that distinguished humans from other animals. The second disturbing aspect of the philosophical radicals was that in some ways they were not radical enough. Though Mill's views, in historical perspective, may not seem particularly radical, he was nevertheless to the political left of his father and other strict adherents of the Bentham tradition. What most distinguished J. S. Mill from the utilitarians was his openness to new ideas, a trait that would have been foreign to a strict Benthamite.

Laissez Faire, Intervention, or Socialism?

Mill's eclecticism in economic theory carries over to his views on economic and social policy. His writing is such a strange admixture of opinions that he defies classification as an advocate of laissez faire, of intervention, or even of socialism. Possibly the best way by which to characterize such a subtle and complex thinker as Mill is to say that in terms of public policy he represents a midpoint between classical liberalism and socialism. His socialism was not Marxian, and Mill evidently had little contact with Marx. Yet he did distinguish between revolutionary socialists and philosophic socialists, his own views being more closely allied with the latter. The distinction usually made between left (revolutionary) and right (evolutionary) socialists is based on the strategy they consider appropriate to achieve the goals of socialism. However, Mill's preference for the right-wing evolutionary position of the philosophic socialists was based on their conception of the good society.

    What were Mill's views of the role of government in society and of the economic, political, and social framework of the good society? In his essay *On Liberty* (1859), Mill tried to state his view of the proper relationship between government and the people. A strong dose of classical liberalism is contained in his statement that the only rightful exercise of power by a government over an individual against his will is "to prevent harm to others. His own good, either physical or moral, is not a sufficient warrant."[10] In his discussion of practical social actions, however, Mill was forced to abandon this strong liberal position and found

---

[10] John Stuart Mill, *On Liberty,* People's ed. (London: Longmans, Green, 1913), p. 6.

exception upon exception to the general rule. At one place he makes a forceful liberal statement such as "Laissez-faire, in short, should be the general practice: every departure from it, unless required by some great good, is a certain evil."[11] At another, he backs away from a strict laissez faire position and asserts that "it is not admissible that the protection of persons and that of property are the sole purposes of government. The ends of government are as comprehensive as those of the social union. They consist of all the good, and all the immunity from evil, which the existence of government can be made either directly or indirectly to bestow."[12] In other words, Mill acknowledged that the absence of government intervention does not necessarily result in maximum freedom, for there are many other restraints on freedom that only legislation or government can remove.

Although Adam Smith considered the operation of the market to be fundamentally harmonious, he had acknowledged the existence of conflict in the fact that "landlords love to reap where they have never sowed." Mill, building on the foundation of Ricardian rent theory, similarly perceived a class conflict between landlords and the rest of society. His condemnation of the landlords was biting, and his policy recommendations would have taken all further increases in rent and land values away from landowners. Landlords "grow richer, as it were in their sleep, without working, risking, or economizing. What claim have they, on the general principle of social justice, to this accession of riches?"[13] He went on to advocate a tax on all increases in rent. Mill did not emphasize the existence of a class conflict between labor and the rest of society, particularly the capitalists; yet his entire social philosophy and the major programs he advocated, such as universal education, redistribution of income through inheritance taxes, the formation of unions, the shortening of the working day, and the limitation of the rate of growth of population, all implied that there were conflicts and disharmonies in the system besides those associated with land ownership.

Mill's treatment of private property in his system reflects his blend of classical liberalism with social reform. Property rights are not absolute, and society can abrogate or alter the right of property when it judges these rights to be in conflict with the public good. Indeed, in his chapter on property, in which he discussed communism as an alternative economic system, he said:

> If, therefore, the choice were to be made between Communism with all its chances, and the present (1852) state of society with all its sufferings and injustices; if the institution of private property necessarily carried with it as a consequence, that the produce of labour should be apportioned as we now see it, almost in inverse ratio to the labour—the largest portions to those who have never worked at all, the next largest to those whose work is almost nominal, and so on in a descending scale, the remuneration dwindling as the work grows harder and more disagreeable, until the most fatiguing and exhausting bodily

---

[11] Mill, *Principles,* p. 950.
[12] *Ibid.,* pp. 804–805.
[13] *Ibid.,* p. 818.

labour cannot count with certainty on being able to earn even the necessities of life; if this or Communism were the alternative, all the difficulties, great or small, of Communism would be but as dust in the balance.[14]

Mill then qualified this approval of communism by pointing out that it is not appropriate to compare communism at its best with the economic order of his time, and that if the laws of private property were changed to give a more equitable distribution of income and a closer conformity between contributions of individuals to the economy and their incomes, he would prefer a system of private property, at its best, to communism. If all these changes were made, "the principle of individual property would have been found to have no necessary connection with the physical and social evils which almost all Socialist writers assume to be inseparable from it."[15]

Just as he rejected the socialists' argument that private property was a major cause of the evils of society, Mill also failed to accept their argument that competition was a cause of social difficulties. In this regard Mill followed the tradition running from Adam Smith to modern orthodox theory that sees competition as beneficial and that predicts misallocation of resources in markets where monopoly power prevails. Competition is beneficial to society; "every restriction of it is an evil, and every extension of it, even if for the time injuriously affecting some classes of labourers, is always an ultimate good."[16] The inconsistency of these views favoring competition with Mill's support of trade unions and other attempts to improve labor's position through the exercise of monopoly power caused him some difficulty. In the course of rather tortuous reasoning, Mill concluded that trade unions, "far from being a hindrance to a free market for labour, are the necessary instrumentality of that free market; the indispensable means of enabling the sellers of labour to take due care of their own interests under a system of competition."[17]

A Different Stationary State

Mill's eclecticism and the humanism he brought to economics are nowhere better reflected than in his discussion of the long-run tendencies of the economy. Even though the empirical evidence was to the contrary, Mill stayed with the basic Ricardian model that predicted falling rates of profit and the stationary state. But *Mill's stationary state* was not the dismal one Ricardo envisioned; in contrast to nearly all orthodox economists up to the present, Mill was not certain if a nation with a growing economy, such as the England of his times, was a desirable place in which to live. Mill found reprehensible many aspects of a prosperous, growing economy, such as the "trampling, crushing, elbowing, and treading on each other's

[14] *Ibid.,* p. 208.
[15] *Ibid.,* p. 209.
[16] *Ibid.,* p. 793.
[17] *Ibid.,* p. 937.

heels."[18] In a famous chapter on the stationary state, Mill took a critical view of his own society and outlined his hopes for the future. Individual happiness, well-being, and improvement were Mill's criteria for a good society, and he clearly indicated that these things are not necessarily measured in material goods. Nor were growth of output and growth of population good in and of themselves. According to Mill, a stationary state might be a highly desirable society, as the pace of economic activity decreases and more attention is focused on the individual and his or her noneconomic and economic well-being. "It is only in the backward countries of the world that increased production is still an important object: in those most advanced, what is economically needed is a better distribution."[19]

Mill wanted to see a slowing of population growth in order to increase per capita income and to reduce population density. Growing population had made it difficult for people to find solitude or to enjoy the beauty of nature. In Mill's stationary state a gentler, less materialistic culture exists. A redistribution of income has occurred, and a reorientation of values ensures that "while no one is poor, no one desires to be richer, nor has any reason to fear being thrust back by the efforts of others to push themselves forward."[20] Finally, Mill hoped that the stationary state would result in an improvement in the art of living, which, he believed, had a stronger "likelihood of its being improved, when minds ceased to be engrossed by the art of getting on."[21] He looked at the society and economy of his time and asked whether technological development had really reduced human toil and drudgery. Although increased production had improved the lot of the middle classes and made large fortunes for some, Mill found the mass of society bypassed by the fruits of the Industrial Revolution and felt that his stationary state might bring about a good society.

Mill's Social Philosophy

The broad outline of Mill's social philosophy reflects the intellectual forces impinging upon his life. With his unique open-mindedness he was able to break away from the strict classical liberalism inculcated in his youth and to try to fuse theory and policy in an eclectic blend of liberalism and social reform. His view of the role of government in society is not dogmatic, and although his essay *On Liberty* takes a strong liberal position, when he turned to policy issues he acknowledged many exceptions to that position. Much more than Smith and Ricardo he recognized that the working of market forces did not necessarily bring about a harmonious economic and social order, and he was particularly aware of the conflict between the landlords and the society as well as the inequities of the existing order in income distribution.

[18] *Ibid.*, p. 748.
[19] *Ibid.*, p. 749.
[20] *Ibid.*
[21] *Ibid.*, p. 751.

Mill's Concern for Women's Rights

Of all Mill's writings on political or social causes, none was received with greater hostility than *The Subjection of Women,* published in 1869. This would not have entirely surprised Mill, as is clear from a letter he wrote in 1850 to the editor of the *Westminster,* which reflected his misgivings about speaking out on this issue: "My opinions on the whole subject are so totally opposed to the reigning notions that it would probably be inexpedient to express all of them."*

The first paragraph of *The Subjection of Women* succinctly states Mill's long-held views on equality of the sexes:

> The object of this essay is to explain as clearly as I am able, the grounds of an opinion which I have held from the very earliest period when I had formed any opinions at all on social or political matters and which, instead of being weakened or modified, has been constantly growing stronger by the progress of reflection and the experience of life: That the principle which regulates the existing social relations between the two sexes—the legal subordination of one sex to the other—is wrong in itself, and now one of the chief hindrances to human improvement; and that it ought to be replaced by a principle of perfect equality, admitting no power or privilege on the one side, nor disability on the other. (*Works,* XXI, 261)

Mill's biographer records one incredulous reader as having responded: "He leads us to suppose that the relation of men and women between themselves may work on a purely voluntary basis."**

Mill completed *The Subjection of Women* two years after the death of his wife, Harriet Taylor, but waited nine years before publishing it, no doubt because of its controversial nature. In a paper written jointly by Mill and Taylor between 1847 and 1850, however, they had already expressed their dismay at the anomalous situation of women in English society:

> In the first place it must be observed that the disabilities of woman are exactly of the class which modern times most pride themselves on getting rid of—disabilities by birth. It is the boast of England that if some persons are privileged by birth, at least none are disqualified by it—that anyone may rise to be a peer, or a member of parliament, or a minister—that the path of distinction is not closed to the humblest. But it *is* closed irrevocably to women. A woman is born disqualified, and cannot by any exertion get rid of her disabilities. This makes her case an entirely peculiar one in modern Europe. It is like that of the negro in America, and worse than that of the roturier formerly in Europe, for *he* might receive or perhaps buy a patent of nobility. Women's disqualifications are the only indelible ones. (*Works,* XXI, 380)

* Quoted in J. S. Mill, *Collected Works,* ed. John M. Robson (Toronto: University of Toronto Press, 1984), XXI, p. xxxi.
** Michael St. John Packe, *The Life of John Stuart Mill* (London: Secker and Warburg, 1954), p. 495.

Although he was influenced by the utopian socialists and by his wife, he could not accept uncritically two of their major arguments: that many of the faults of contemporary society were a result of the institutions of private property and of competition. Mill was concerned about the quality of life, and he found much in a materialistic, growth-oriented economy that turned people from self-fulfillment and improvement to baser pursuits. He accepted the Ricardian analysis of the long-run tendency of the economy to produce a stationary state, but with his optimistic humanism he foresaw a new, better society no longer oriented toward strictly materialistic pursuits, not the gloomy world of Ricardo. With this general overview of Mill's social philosophy, we now turn to examine his modifications of and contributions to the mainstream of orthodox theory.

MILLIAN ECONOMICS

The Role of Theory

Influenced by the literature of both orthodox and heterodox thinkers, Mill approached technical economic theory critically. Although he regarded himself as merely extending the basic Ricardian analysis, in a number of areas Mill made fundamental changes in Ricardo's theory of value. Richard Jones, in his *Essay on the Distribution of Wealth* (1831), had criticized Ricardo's theory of rent in particular and the classical position in general because their analysis ignored the historical and institutional circumstances of the economy. Jones has been called a forerunner of the historical school because he questioned the application of the Ricardian analysis to all times and places and advocated a more empirical approach in accounting for changes in institutional structure. "Of Competition and Custom," Book II, Chapter 4, of Mill's *Principles* implicitly recognizes this criticism of Jones and shows Mill's recognition that abstract economic theory must be tempered by an awareness of historically prevailing institutions. Mill maintained, therefore, that two forces, competition and custom, govern the distribution of income, and he criticized the orthodox line of English economists for emphasizing the role of competition while almost completely neglecting the role of custom. "They are apt to express themselves as if they thought that competition actually does, in all cases, whatever it can be shown to be the tendency of competition to do."[22]

Taking a relativistic historical position, Mill pointed out that the operation of competition in the market economy is a comparatively young historical phenomenon and that if we glance backward we find that custom has traditionally played a major role in solving the economic problems surrounding the distribution of income. Mill presented historical material describing a variety of institutional arrangements that existed in the past and that were present in the underdeveloped, less market-oriented economies of his own time. For example, he recognized that the Ricardian system assumes the existence in the economy of a set of actors, businessmen, who are motivated by a strong desire to make profits, and it is through their actions that resources are allocated and market equilibrium is reached. Yet there are economies without such actors, and even market economies

[22] *Ibid.*, p. 242.

in which "there are no enterprising competitors, those who have capital prefer to leave it where it is, to make less profit by it in a more quiet way."[23] Here, and elsewhere in his book, Mill was pondering the question of how much importance should be given to abstract theory and how much to institutional-historical material. This issue has been raised again and again by various heterodox economists and is still with us today.

In the face of social forces such as custom that modify or even negate predictions based on competitive processes, why do economists continue to use a competitive model? "This is partly intelligible," Mill said, "if we consider that only through the principle of competition has political economy any pretensions to the character of a science."[24] This curious conclusion makes sense only if we accept a certain definition of science—that to be scientific, economic theory or models had to be able to reach exact and certain conclusions. In other words, science requires that exact predictions be made and that the probability of their occurrence be equal to one. This view carried over then-prevalent notions of science to economics from the natural sciences. Today, however, we can accept as scientific areas of inquiry in which the probability of an expected occurrence is less than one. Thus, modern physics acknowledges that random phenomena can occur that prevent experiments from being repeated with perfect consistency. In his statement about competition and economic science, Mill seemed to accept a narrow conception of science. In much of his writing, however, he was much closer to the present-day view of science.

Mill on Contextual Analysis

Mill's views about the role of theory—of not accepting uncritically theoretical outcomes because in practice, in the context of a given society, other factors such as custom may modify theoretical predictions—distinguish him from Ricardo and return him to the Smithian view. In our examination of Adam Smith, we found that his economic policy pronouncements were not abstract theoretical tools applied to a mechanical society but were a contextual analysis that reflected his views of how pure theoretical propositions work out in a given social context.

The electicism of Mill that we found in his examination of the merits of capitalism and private property as compared with communism is also a reflection of this Smithian-type contextual analysis. Mill suggested he would choose pure theoretical communism as contrasted with existing capitalism, but he immediately exclaimed that this is not a proper basis for choice. Existing capitalism (and, indeed, socially reformed capitalism) compared with communism as it is likely to unfold throws the balance in favor of a system of private property capitalism.

Smith's and Mill's contextual analysis is fundamentally grounded in their broader approach to economics, to the view that economic activity is only a part

[23] *Ibid.*, p. 247.
[24] *Ibid.*, p. 242.

of all activities. This contrasts sharply with the more narrow focus of Ricardo and the legions of mainstream economists who followed his lead.

Value Theory

The theory of value, or relative prices, presented by Mill is a fundamental rejection of Ricardo's labor theory of value, although Mill characteristically stressed not his deviations from Ricardian dogma but the continuity between his theory and the past. He presented a cost of production theory of value in which money costs fundamentally represent the real costs or disutilities of labor and abstinence. In this regard Mill and Senior have comparable theories of value. However, Mill gave up the Ricardian search for absolute value based on some invariant measure of value, believing that the purpose of value theory is to explain relative prices. In his discussion of rent, he recognized that the opportunity cost of land is not always zero and that rent is a social cost of production in cases in which there are alternative uses of land. Although Mill did not distinguish between short run and long run in the manner of Marshall, he did seem to have a vague idea of this distinction and regarded his primary task as explaining how relative prices are determined in the long run. Though he did not explicitly formulate supply-and-demand schedules, his value theory clearly reflects a recognition that the quantities demanded and supplied are a function of price. For this reason we may present his theory of long-run prices in the familiar Marshallian form without doing an injustice to either Marshall or Mill.

For a good to have exchange value, or a price, it must be useful and difficult to obtain; but use value determines exchange value, or price, only in unusual circumstances. Mill discussed the price of a musical snuff-box using two hypothetical cases he borrowed from a contemporary writer: one set in London, where, he assumed, the boxes are produced under conditions of *constant costs;* the other on a boat on Lake Superior, where only one such box exists. Mill's purpose in this example was to demonstrate that prices will almost always depend on cost of production rather than on utility. Where supply is absolutely limited, the supply curve is perfectly inelastic (vertical) and price depends upon supply and demand (see "a" in Figure 6.1). This first class of commodities Mill regarded as relatively unimportant, because few commodities are perfectly inelastic in supply; it includes wines, works of art, rare books, coins, the site value of land, and potentially all land as population density increases. He also used this case to analyze monopoly situations in which the monopolist can artificially limit the supply. A second group of commodities, manufactured goods, has a perfectly elastic (horizontal) supply curve, and Mill concluded that the cost of production of these goods determines their price. Mill assumed that all manufacturing industries are constant-cost situations (see Figure 6.1b); that is, their marginal costs do not change as their output increases. For Mill's third group of commodities, those produced by agriculture, he assumed that marginal costs do increase as output expands *increasing costs;* the price of these commodities depends upon cost of production in the most unfavorable circumstances (see Figure 6.1c). Thus, he applied the principle

Figure 6.1   Mill on Value

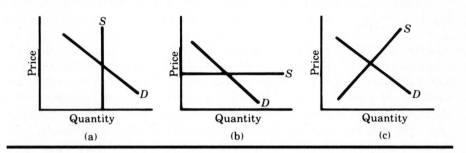

of diminishing marginal returns to agricultural production but not to manufactured goods. Although Mill was very careful to make clear that utility (demand) and difficulty of attainment (supply) must both exist before any commodity has a price, the terminology of his conclusions obscures the fundamental applicability of the laws of supply and demand to all three groups of goods.

He saw clearly how equilibrium prices are brought about in markets through the forces of demand and supply and that

> the proper mathematical analogy is that of an equation. Demand and supply, the quantity demanded and the quantity supplied, will be made equal. If unequal at any moment, competition equalizes them, and the manner in which this is done is by an adjustment of the value. If the demand increases, the value rises; if the demand diminishes, the value falls: again, if the supply falls off, the value rises; and falls if the supply is increased.[25]

Final equilibrium is reached when quantity demanded equals quantity supplied.

Even though Mill did not use mathematical equations, schedules, or supply-and-demand curves, his analysis of price determination is a notable advance over Ricardo's, particularly because Mill's conceptual apparatus was obviously set up in accord with supply-and-demand functions. The only group of commodities he failed to cover are those with decreasing costs and downward-sloping long-run supply curves.

He also made some original contributions to value theory in discussing non-competing groups (he recognized that in labor markets mobility was far from perfect), pricing where a firm produces two or more products in fixed proportions (wool and mutton), rent as price-determining when land has alternative uses, and economies of scale. His satisfaction with the development of value theory was manifested by his view that "Happily, there is nothing in the laws of value which

---

[25] *Ibid.*, p. 448.

remains (1848) for the present or any future writer to clear up; the theory of the subject is complete."[26]

A number of economists writing after Mill have been amused by this statement, and it was probably the reason why Marshall suggested that his own contributions to microeconomic theory would soon be obsolete. Yet it can be argued that our general understanding of the workings of supply and demand in allocating resources under competitive markets has not been fundamentally changed since Mill. Of course, many developments have occurred that permit more technical analysis and greater insights; but Mill, with cruder technical apparatus and a complete lack of mathematical notation, was able to carry out a significant analysis of markets with few analytical errors. The great gap in Mill's micro theory, a gap not filled until the 1930s, was his inability to analyze less than perfectly competitive markets. Some would say that this gap still remains to be filled.

International Trade Theory

Historians of economic analysis have praised Mill for his contributions to the theory of international trade. In particular, his analysis of the division of the gains from international trade among trading countries is probably his most important and lasting contribution to technical economic theory. By means of his comparative advantage argument, Ricardo had supported and extended Smith's analysis of the benefits of unregulated international trade. As we have seen, Ricardo argued that where comparative advantages exist, international trade will increase world output and benefit all trading economies, and that a range of international prices, or barter terms of trade, satisfactory to all the trading nations will be determined. In the simple model presented in Table 5.3, England would be willing to trade 1 yard of cloth as long as more than 2 gallons of wine was received in exchange, and Portugal would benefit by trading wine for cloth as long as less than 8 gallons of wine had to be given up to receive 1 yard of cloth. A range of prices, or barter terms of trade, between 7.9 gallons of wine for 1 yard of cloth and 2.1 gallons of wine for 1 yard of cloth would benefit both nations. Although Ricardo was able to show the gains from trade by using the comparative advantage argument, he did not indicate what the international price of wine and cloth would be, and consequently how the gains of trade would be distributed between the two countries. Obviously, England would prefer to gain as much wine as possible for a yard of cloth, and Portugal would prefer to give up as little wine as possible for a yard of cloth. Ricardo had simply suggested that the *terms of trade,* or international price, would be roughly halfway between the two domestic prices. From the data in Table 5.3, the price would be 5 gallons of wine for 1 yard of cloth.

Mill considered how the gains from trade would be divided and gave a surprisingly correct answer, in view of the fact that he used no mathematical techniques and that the concept of elasticity was yet to be developed. Marshall and

---

[26] *Ibid.,* p. 436.

Edgeworth, who were later to present Mill's argument more precisely with the aid of mathematical and diagrammatic techniques, both acknowledged and praised Mill's contribution. Mill concluded that the terms of trade would depend on the demands for the imported products by the two countries. If, in the example just cited, the strength of England's demand for imported wine was much greater than Portugal's demand for English cloth, the barter terms and gains from trade would favor Portugal: the international price would be closer to 2 gallons of wine for 1 yard of cloth. Portugal would not have to give up much wine to get cloth. The relative strength of the demands for imports will depend on the "inclinations and circumstances of the consumers on both sides," and the international price or terms of trade will be a value such that "the quantities required by each country, of the articles which it imports from its neighbor, shall be exactly sufficient to pay for one another."[27] Mill developed what he meant by "inclinations and circumstances of the consumers," indicating clearly that he was talking about the positions and elasticities of the demand curves. Although he never explicitly developed the concept of demand elasticity, he described the cases of elastic, inelastic, and unitarily elastic demand.

Mill's other contributions to trade theory were less important, but they do indicate his analytical abilities. He introduced the cost of transportation into the analysis of foreign trade and showed how transportation costs may produce situations in which trade will not occur even with differences in comparative costs. He also analyzed the influence of tariffs on the terms of trade, indicated how both price and income changes bring about trade equilibrium between countries, and showed the adjustments in trade brought about by unilateral transfer payments between countries. It was nearly one hundred years after Mill before major changes in the classical theory of international trade were made by Ohlin and Keynes.

Mill's Monetary Theory and Excess Supply: Say's Law Reconsidered

Concerned with the attacks made on Say's Law by Malthus, Chalmers, and Sismondi, Mill refuted these criticisms in an article titled "Of the Influence of Consumption on Production." It was written around 1830 but was not published until 1844 in *Essays on Some Unsettled Questions of Political Economy* and in Book III, Chapter 14, "Of Excess of Supply," of his *Principles*. Mill defended Say's Law to counter the argument of many underconsumptionists that the economy would be better off if the wealthy saved less and spent more on unproductive consumption. His defense was not equaled until the twentieth century. Mill acknowledged that there may be an excessive supply of individual commodities as the market reacts to changing conditions of supply and demand, but he argued that it was illogical to carry this analysis into macroeconomics and conclude that an excess of supply could exist permanently for all commodities. In his defense of Say's Law, Mill distinguished among three possible economies: a

[27] *Ibid.*, p. 587.

barter economy, an economy in which money is a commodity and no credit exists, and an economy in which credit money exists. By overtly introducing money into the discussion of possible general overproduction, Mill considerably improved the arguments in support of Say's Law previously given by Ricardo, James Mill, and Say himself.

Mill showed very clearly that there can never be an insufficiency of aggregate demand in a barter economy, for a decision to supply commodities presupposes a demand for commodities. In a simple barter economy, an individual or firm would produce and trade goods only out of desire for other goods. For example, a bootmaker will produce and trade his products because he needs clothes, food, and fuel, among other things. If money is introduced but its only function is as a medium of exchange, the conclusion is the same. If, however, money functions in part as a store of value, then a seller may not immediately return to the market to buy, and although sufficient aggregate purchasing power is generated to give full employment, it may not be exercised in the current period and thus can lead to general oversupply.

On these views Mill reintroduced Henry Thornton's sophisticated monetary analysis back into the classical view by developing a *psychological theory of business cycles*. Mill showed that when credit is introduced the possibility of general oversupply of commodities may exist. An overissue of credit during a period of expansion and prosperity may be followed by contraction of credit as a result of pessimism in the business community.

> At such times there is really an excess of all commodities above the money de-
> mand: in other words, there is an undersupply of money. From the sudden annihi-
> lation of a great mass of credit, every one dislikes to part with ready money, and
> many are anxious to procure it at any sacrifice. Almost everybody therefore is a
> seller, and there are scarcely any buyers.[28]

The introduction of credit money into an economy, according to Mill, permits the possibility of general oversupply, not because of overproduction in the Malthu-sian sense of general glut but because of the changing expectations of the business community. Mill said that any such oversupply will be of short duration and will be followed by full employment, as prices change in the economy. The net effect of Mill's discussion of the issues raised by Say's Law and the role of money in an economy is to defend this fundamental part of the classic system against Malthu-sianlike attacks and to develop a simple psychological theory of business fluctua-tions based on the interactions between credit money and business confidence.

The Currency and Banking Schools

Mill's views on monetary theory were developed in the context of the times and reflected his methodological approach in which reactions to practical problems directed theoretical inquiry, rather than letting theory develop separately from

---

[28] *Ibid.,* p. 561.

policy questions. The context of the times was an extension of the Bullion Debate and how to deal with the periodic recessions and financial disruptions that were occurring.

The extension of the Bullion debate is called the Currency School/Banking School debate. The *Currency School* carried through the Bullionist position, and argued that a mixed paper and gold standard should be subject to unbending rules and operate just as a strict gold standard. This policy, they argued, was the only way to prevent inflationary printing of money. The *Banking School* argued that a more flexible monetary policy was needed and that, as long as the Real Bills Doctrine was followed by banks, no control of the issuance of bank notes was needed. Interestingly, Robert Torrens, who was a major advocate of the Anti-Bullionist position, the forerunner of the Banking School position, switched sides and supported the Currency School.

Mill's monetary theory, which involved a modification of Ricardo's strict quantity theory, fit between the Banking and Currency Schools. Mill argued that the Banking School was correct during normal times when markets were quiet. But he disagreed that the Real Bills Doctrine would always be relevant; he argued that speculative financial booms could occur, and in such times the Currency School's policy of tying the issuance of notes to gold was the appropriate policy.

The Wages Fund: Mill's Recantation

The wages fund doctrine was used by some economists and a number of popular writers as an argument against the formation of labor unions. According to the wages fund theory, the wage rate was determined by the size of the labor force and the wages fund, and any attempt by labor to raise wages, by whatever means, would be fruitless. This is an example of how orthodox economic theory was used to prove that attempts to improve the welfare of the working class by a more equal distribution of income could not be successful. We have already seen that Mill believed that his unique contribution to economic thinking was a distinction between the fixed laws of production and the institutionally and culturally determined laws of distribution, and that his reason for drawing this separation was to allow his humanism to moderate the conservative conclusions of the Ricardians.

Even though Mill accepted the wages fund doctrine, he supported the formation of labor unions. In this he followed the reasoning of Adam Smith, who had pointed out that a single unorganized laborer was at a competitive disadvantage in bargaining over wage rates with an employer. Unions and strikes seemed to Mill to be appropriate tools for labor in its attempt to counterbalance the power of the employing firm. It is possible that Mill's adherence to the wages fund theory can be explained by his strong concern over the consequences of unregulated population growth. After the publication of the sixth edition of Mill's *Principles,* but before the publication of the seventh, Mill reviewed a book by William Thornton that was critical of the application of supply-and-demand analysis to labor markets and that rejected the wages fund doctrine. In his review Mill accepted nearly all of Thornton's arguments, concluding that the argument that unions cannot raise wages is invalid.

The wages fund doctrine asserted that the demand for labor was fixed absolutely by the size of the wages fund. Mill now retreated from this position to argue that whereas the *maximum* amount of funds that could be used to pay wages was fixed, a given labor force and wage rate might not exhaust this fixed amount. Under this reasoning the wage rate is not conclusively determined, and there is a range of possible wages. Labor unions can therefore raise wages through the bargaining process.

Although Mill rejected the wages fund doctrine in his 1869 review of Thornton's book, the seventh edition of his *Principles,* published in 1871, made no changes on this score, because Mill maintained that these new developments "are not yet ripe for incorporation in a general treatise on Political Economy."[29] This is quite puzzling, for in 1862 Mill had already concluded in the fifth edition of his *Principles* that wage rates depended on the bargaining power of the employer and employee and that one important way for labor to increase its power was through unionization.[30] This inconsistency is simply another example of Mill's attempts to stay within the general framework of classical economics, which he learned at a young age from his father, while giving vent to his humanistic feelings, which called for social reform centering around a more equal distribution of income.

SUMMARY

An examination of the development of orthodox economic theory in the fifty-odd years following the publication of Ricardo's *Principles* in 1817 reveals interesting contradictions and crosscurrents. The increased professionalization of economics, the growth of a socialist and humanistic literature, and the conflict between theory and fact all provoked criticism of the Ricardian analysis. Economists became more aware of their discipline and began to address themselves to the issues of the scope and method of economics and the distinction between positive and normative economic thinking. As the economy evolved and more data became available, a growing divergence between theory and fact became apparent, raising important questions about major Ricardian building blocks such as the Malthusian population theory, the principle of historically diminishing returns, and the prediction of a fall in the rate of profits over time.

Malthusian population theory was an important part of the Ricardian system, because it permitted the development of a residual theory of income distribution. With its gradual abandonment, the wages fund doctrine became both a short- and long-run theory of wages. Ricardian economics had deduced that returns would diminish over time because it assumed that technological development in agriculture could not offset short-run diminishing returns. The question of long-run

[29] *Ibid.,* p. xxxi.
[30] *Ibid.,* p. 937.

returns in agriculture is, however, an empirical, not a deductive, issue, and the available data appeared to contradict these predictions of the theoretical model. Ricardo had also deduced a falling rate of profit over time; but although neither statistical data nor techniques were available to measure the rate of profit, the increasing returns observed in agriculture cast doubt on the validity of this conclusion. One of the most interesting and amazing aspects of the post-Ricardian period is the tenacity with which economists clung to the predictions of the Ricardian model in the face of conflicting empirical evidence. This is largely accounted for by their enthusiastic acceptance of the very abstract and deductive Ricardian model. A growing awareness of the logical difficulties inherent in a strict labor theory of value and a reaction to the criticism levied by the Ricardian socialists led to the development of an abstinence theory of interest and a cost of production theory of value of which labor and capital costs were both a part.

This was the environment into which J. S. Mill emerged, trained at an early age in the Ricardian tradition but with strong and deep feelings about the injustices of the capitalist economy. He attempted to combine the hardheadedness of classical liberalism with the humanism of social reform to promote a society and economy less concerned with the business of business and more concerned with the art of individual improvement and self-fulfillment. He brought to economics an intellect so broad that he was able to contribute significantly to political science, philosophy, and belles-lettres as well as to economics. His original contributions to economic thought were somewhat obscured by his eclectic, open-minded incorporation of new developments into the Ricardian framework; and although he stressed the deductive character of economics as a discipline, he advocated a continuous re-examination of the relevance of theory to fact. Though his methodological position was sound, like that of most of his contemporaries, he failed to do what he advocated.

Mill's concern with social reform led him to stress insistently the distinction between the immutable laws of production and the changeable, institutionally determined laws governing the distribution of personal income. His efforts to establish a consistency between theory and policy application align him more with the tradition of Smith than of Ricardo. His eclecticism makes him difficult to classify ideologically; his writing contains strong strains of classical liberalism and laissez faire, yet he often advocates government intervention in the economy. For Mill, the clash between the interests of the landlords and those of the rest of society was a discordant element in the system. But he rejected the socialist condemnation of private property and competition, suggesting institutional adjustments that might retain their benefits and remove their glaring evils. His optimism led, moreover, to a new view of the stationary state freed of its dismal Ricardian overtones.

J. S. Mill made lasting and important contributions to economic theory. Although he did not admit it, he finally rejected the Ricardian labor theory of value and in its place developed a long-run cost of production theory of value that included both labor and capital costs. He extended the Ricardian theory of international trade to explain the terms of trade in a comparative advantage model and came close to explicitly developing the concept of price elasticity of demand.

His well-reasoned defense of Say's Law ultimately saved it from the onslaughts of heterodox criticism. His monetary theory allowed for the possibility of a psychological theory of business cycles. Toward the end of his career, he withdrew his support from the wages fund doctrine, removing an important economic argument from the arsenal of those who believed that the mass of society were unable to raise their wages through collective bargaining or political processes. Orthodox thinking was ruled by Millian economics until the end of the nineteenth century, largely ignoring the grumblings of the brilliant, bushy-bearded malcontent Karl Marx.

Key Terms

wages fund doctrine	Mill's stationary state
historically diminishing returns	constant costs
abstinence theory of interest	increasing costs
a priori method	terms of trade
laws of production	psychological theory of business
laws of distribution	cycles
Mill's eclecticism	Currency School
philosophical radicals (utilitarians)	Banking School
hedonism	

Questions for Review, Discussion, and Research

1. Write an essay about the divergent influences on J. S. Mill and how they produced his eclectic views on economic theory and policy.
2. Explain the problems encountered by Ricardian economics in the period from 1820 to 1850.
3. Critically evaluate Senior's views on the proper method for economics.
4. Write an essay on J. S. Mill's distinction between the laws of production and distribution and give your views on the validity of his distinction.
5. What were J. S. Mill's views about competition and private property as causes of social disorder? What are your views?
6. Mill turned the classical notion of a stationary state as a dismal outcome into a utopian vision. Explain.
7. Write an essay on Mill's views about women and equality. Do you think the problem of the subjection of women has been solved in the United States?
8. Explain how custom might negate or modify economic predictions based on competitive markets.
9. Explain Mill's theory of value and contrast it with Ricardo's.
10. Write an essay on how Mill was able to extend and improve Ricardo's theory of comparative advantage.
11. That absent-minded professor is back with another job for you. This time she's reviewing a recent book that argues that utility is interdependent, and that what matters is one's relative position, rather than one's absolute amount of income. She remembers that Mill had a discussion of that issue, and she believes the

quotation from Mill is: "Men do not desire to be rich, but to be richer than other men." She wants you to find the complete bibliographic citation for it.

Suggested Readings

Anschutz, R. P. *The Philosophy of J. S. Mill.* London: Oxford University Press, 1963.

Ashley, W. J. "Introduction" to J. S. Mill's *Principles of Political Economy.* London: Longmans, Green, 1909.

Bladen, V. W. "Introduction" to J. S. Mill's *Principles of Political Economy.* Vols. II and III. In *Collected Works of John Stuart Mill.* Toronto: University of Toronto Press, 1965.

————. "John Stuart Mill's *Principles:* A Centenary Estimate." *American Economic Review,* 39 (May 1949).

Fetter, Frank. "The Rise and Decline of Ricardian Economics." *History of Political Economy,* 1 (Spring 1969).

Gordon, Barry. "Criticism of Ricardian Views on Value and Distribution in the British Periodicals, 1820–1850." *History of Political Economy,* 1 (Fall 1969).

————. "Say's Law, Effective Demand and the Contemporary British Periodicals, 1820–1850." *Economica* (November 1965).

Grampp, William D. "Classical Economics and Its Moral Critics." *History of Political Economy,* 5 (Fall 1973).

de Marchi, Neil B. "The Success of Mill's Principles." *History of Political Economy,* 6 (Summer 1974).

Mill, John S. *Principles of Political Economy.* Ed. W. J. Ashley. London: Longmans, Green, 1909.

Packe, Michael St. John. *The Life of John Stuart Mill.* London: Martin Secker and Warburg, 1954.

Plamenatz, John. *The English Utilitarians.* Oxford: Basil Blackwell and Mott, 1958.

Schwartz, Pedro. *The New Political Economy of J. S. Mill.* Durham: Duke University Press, 1972.

Viner, Jacob. "Bentham and J. S. Mill: The Utilitarian Background." *American Economic Review,* 39 (March 1949).

Readings in Original Sources

All readings are from Mill's *Principles of Political Economy.*
Value: Book III, Chapters 1–4, 6, 15, and 16.
Rent: Book II, Chapter 16; Book III, Chapter 4, Section 6; Book III, Chapter 5.
Wages: Book II, Chapters 11–14.
Profits: Book II, Chapter 15.
Socialism: Book II, Chapter 1.
Custom and Competition: Book II, Chapter 4.

7 Karl Marx

"The fox knows many things, but the hedgehog knows one main thing."

—Isaiah Berlin

arl Marx (1818–1883) was more than just an economist—he was also a
philosopher, sociologist, prophet, and revolutionist. He is proof of the importance of economic thinking and ideas. His writing inspired generations of economic thinkers, and in his name entire societies were transformed. In the 1990s
many of the societies that had adopted Marxian ideology have abandoned it and
are experimenting with a transition to a "capitalist" society. Many of these
transitions are likely to be rocky and marked with much turmoil. Thus, in the 1990s
more than ever it is important to look at Marx's writings and ideas.

AN OVERVIEW OF MARX

Marx's Purpose

Marx was first and foremost a philosopher who felt that his job was not merely to
interpret and analyze society but also to promote the changes in society he
considered desirable. As a partisan advocate of change, he does not differ from
Smith, Ricardo, or J. S. Mill. In contrast to the classical economists, however,
Marx advocated a fundamental revolution, not small marginal changes in the
society and economy. Because Marx is popularly associated with the economic
systems of socialism and communism, people often assume that he wrote about
these systems. Nothing could be further from the truth. Marx studied what he
called capitalism—his major work is titled *Das Kapital,* or *Capital.* In all the vast
literature produced by Marx and his collaborator, Friedrich Engels (1820–1895),

What Is Communism According to *The Communist Manifesto?*

As communism undergoes change, it becomes difficult to determine what communism actually is. One way to decide is to look at its roots. In *The Communist Manifesto* (1848), Karl Marx and Friedrich Engels set forth the principles of modern communism. They said that communism means:

1. Abolition of property in land and application of all rents of land to public purposes.
2. A heavy progressive or graduated income tax.
3. Abolition of all rights of inheritance.
4. Confiscation of the property of all emigrants and rebels.
5. Centralization of credit in the hands of the state by means of a national bank with state capital and an exclusive monopoly.
6. Centralization of the means of communication and transport in the hands of the state.
7. Extension of factories and instruments of production owned by the state; the bringing into cultivation of waste lands; and the improvement of the soil generally in accordance with a common plan.
8. Equal obligation of all to work. Establishment of industrial armies, especially for agriculture.
9. Combination of agriculture with manufacturing industries; gradual abolition of the distinction between town and country by means of a more equitable distribution of the population over the country.
10. Free education in public schools for all children; abolition of child factory labor; combination of education with industrial production.

there is little reference to how a socialist or communist economy is to be organized, other than a short list of items characterizing the nature of communism that appeared in *The Communist Manifesto* (1848).

Marx's economic theory is an application of his theory of history to the capitalist economy. He wanted to lay bare the laws of the dynamics of capitalism. Whereas other classical economists focused on the static equilibrium of the economy, Marx focused on the dynamic process of change. Paul M. Sweezy, an important American Marxian economist, has suggested that Marxian economics is the economics of capitalism and that capitalist economics is the economics of socialism. In other words, Marxian economics helps one to understand the forces underlying the market, whereas the standard classical analysis is useful in organizing and operating a socialist economy. The late Oskar Lange, a Marxian who taught in the United States and later returned to his native Poland to become an economic planner, reiterated that view. He contended that Marxian and orthodox economic analysis should be looked upon as complementary rather than mutually exclusive. Whereas an understanding of the everyday operation of the market can be achieved by using neoclassical orthodox theory, an understanding of the evolutionary development of capitalism, Lange said, is possible only within the Marxian framework.

Intellectual Sources of Marx's Ideas

A study of Marx's life discloses the intellectual sources of his system. Born into a Jewish family that turned to Christianity, the young Marx began studying law but soon became interested in philosophy. Early in his studies he was attracted by the intellectual framework of Hegel, another German writer. That framework, as we shall see, became an important element in Marx's system. After receiving his doctorate in philosophy Marx was unable to find an academic appointment because of his radical views, so he turned to journalism. His political views, radical for the Germany of his time but still not socialistic, caused him to be expelled from Germany. In Paris and Brussels he began to study French socialist thought and classical political economy. Marx had tremendous intellectual powers coupled with a strong drive to read and study. After being expelled from Paris and Brussels, he moved to London and spent the last thirty-three years of his life reading and writing in one of the world's great libraries, the British Museum.

Marx's Theory of History

Marxist thought combines Hegelian philosophy, French utopian thought, and classical political economy—particularly Ricardian. Marx's analysis of capitalism is an application to his time of a theory of history derived from G. W. F. Hegel. Hegel maintained that history does not proceed cyclically through a series of recurring situations, as many people believe, but rather moves forward in a straight line, progressively, by the interaction of a triad of forces that he termed *thesis, antithesis,* and *synthesis.* Because these forces are ideological, it is in the study of ideas, not past events, that the laws of history can be found. At any given time, according to Hegel, an accepted idea, or thesis, exists but is soon contradicted by its opposite, or antithesis. Out of this conflict of ideas is formed a synthesis, representing a higher form of truth, which becomes a new thesis. The new thesis is likewise opposed by its antithesis and is transformed into a new synthesis, and so on and on. Thus, in a never-ending chain of ideas, each one approaching closer to truth, history evolves in an endless process in which all things become gradually more perfect by means of conflict-induced change. Hegel called this process, as well as the method for investigating it, dialectic.

Marx perceived a similar process in history—and in reality in general—and used a similar method to investigate it, which he also called dialectic. But the great difference between Hegel's and Marx's philosophies was that Hegel's was idealistic and Marx's materialistic. The reality in which change occurred for Hegel was ideas, but for Marx it was matter, which, he said, contained within itself the seeds of constant conflict. Marx's philosophy, therefore, is called *dialectical materialism.*

The grand questions that engaged Marx's attention are the following. Can one develop a theory to explain the different ways in which societies have been organized over time, and can this theory be used to predict the possible future organization of society? Are the societal structures we call feudalism and capitalism part of an evolutionary development capable of analysis, or are they merely a result of random historical occurrences?

Marx accused the capitalist bourgeois economists of writing as though there had been a past but would be no future—as though capitalism, a system evolved from previous systems, was somehow an ideal societal structure that would exist forever. Therefore, one important ingredient in the Marxian system is change: though we may not know exactly what the future will bring, Marx said, we do know it will be different from the past and the present.

In focusing on materialistic or economic forces as the primary (although not the sole) determinant of historical change, Marx revolutionized thinking in the social sciences. Marx's thesis has proved a fruitful hypothesis or first approximation for a good deal of important and useful work in the social sciences. Isaiah Berlin, a British critic and philosopher, applies the parable of the hedgehog and the fox to Marx's concentration on materialistic factors in explaining historical change. The fox knows many things, Berlin says, but the hedgehog knows one main thing. The scholarly Marx was clearly an intellectual fox, but in the elaboration of his historical theory he assumed the role of a hedgehog, ignoring many other relevant issues in order to focus on economic factors as the most important element in explaining the changing structure of society. The Marxian theory of history is most explicitly stated in *The Communist Manifesto* and in the Preface to the *Critique of Political Economy,* in which Marx explains:

> The general conclusion at which I arrived and which, once reached, continued to serve as the leading thread in my studies, may be briefly summed up as follows:
> In the social production which men carry on they enter into definite relations that are indispensable and independent of their will; these relations of production correspond to a definite stage of development of their material powers of production. The sum total of these relations of production constitutes the economic structure of society—the real foundation, on which rise legal and political superstructures and to which correspond definite forms of social consciousness. The mode of production in material life determines the general character of the social, political, and spiritual processes of life. It is not the consciousness of men that determines their existence, but, on the contrary, their social existence determines their consciousness. At a certain stage of their development, the material forces of production in society come in conflict with the existing relations of production, or—what is but a legal expression for the same thing—with the property relations within which they had been at work before. From forms of development of the forces of production these relations turn into their fetters. Then comes the period of social revolution. With the change of the economic foundation the entire immense superstructure is more or less rapidly transformed.[1]

Marx believed that all societies, except classless societies, can be divided analytically into two parts: the forces of production and the relations of production.

[1] Karl Marx, *A Contribution to the Critique of Political Economy,* trans. from the 2nd German ed. by N. I. Stone (Chicago: Charles H. Kerr, 1913), pp. 11–12.

The *forces of production* are the technology used by the society in producing material goods; manifested in labor skills, scientific knowledge, tools, and capital goods, they are inherently dynamic. The *relations of production* are the rules of the game. There are relations between one person and another, or social relations; and relations between people and things, or property relations. To carry on production, the problem of economic order must be solved; and the historically determined relations of production provide the institutional framework within which economic decisions are made. In contrast to the dynamic, changing forces of production, the relations of production are static and past-binding. The static nature of the relations of production is reinforced by what Marx called the social superstructure, whose function is to maintain the historically determined relations of production. The social superstructure consists of the art, literature, music, philosophy, jurisprudence, religion, and other cultural forms accepted by the society, and its purpose is to keep intact the relations of production—to maintain the status quo.

The static relations of production are the thesis in the Marxian dialectic, and the dynamic, changing forces of production are the antithesis. In the beginning of any historical period there is harmony between the forces and relations of production, but over time the changing forces of production bring about contradictions in the system as the existing relations of production (institutions) are no longer appropriate to the forces of production (technology). These contradictions will manifest themselves, Marx said, in a class struggle. Finally the contradictions become so intense that there is a period of social revolution, and a new set of relations of production is brought into being. The new relations of production are the synthesis that results from the conflict between the old thesis (relations of production) and the antithesis (forces of production), and these relations of production become the new thesis. At this point in history there is again harmony, but the dynamic, changing forces of production ensure that new contradictions will soon develop.

A Closer Look at the Dialectic

An examination of the Marxian concept of the social superstructure will help to clarify the Marxian theory of history and the Marxist attitude toward society. Marx was interested in individuals' fulfilling themselves. This interest comes out most clearly in his *Economic and Philosophical Manuscripts of 1844,* which were lost for eighty years and not published until 1932. In these early manuscripts Marx made clear his philosophical objection to capitalism and how he believed it alienates human beings from themselves. According to Marx, private property and the market devalue and demean all that they touch and thereby alienate individuals from their true selves. Thus, the very existence of markets—especially labor markets—undermines people's ability to achieve true happiness.

Because Marx's notions are themselves alien to much of current Western thinking, let us give some examples of similarities to Marx's ideas in current social mores. Current social mores generally hold that it is immoral to sell one's body for sex; doing so involves prostituting oneself and alienates one from one's body. The same applies with certain interactions among friends: you don't charge friends or relatives interest for loans, and you don't expect, or want, payment for acts of friendship.

Why does modern society have these social conventions? Because in these cases it sees the market as demeaning, as alienating the individual from one's true self. The market undermines love and friendship. Marx's analysis simply carried that morality further and extended the concept of *alienation* to all market transactions. To sell one's time to another is to alienate oneself from the realization of one's true self.

Marx argued that classical economics simply accepted markets and did not consider the nature of private property and the effect that the existence of markets had on people. He argued that it was necessary to study the connection between "private property, avarice and the separation of labor, capital, and landed property; between exchange and competition, value and the devaluation of men, monopoly and competition, etc.; the connection between this whole estrangement and the money system."[2] Thus, his central criticism of classical economics was that it did not consider how the forces of production would undermine the relations of production.

Marx argued that ultimately, once the market had created the forces of production that could meet people's material needs, the alienation inherent in property rights and markets would lead individuals to free themselves from the market and create a society that would eliminate private property and the alienation associated with it.

Given the moralistic grounding of Marx's thought, one would expect Marx to have had a positive view of religion. That was anything but the case. Marx said that religion validated the current alienation and was a part of the social superstructure; it was the opiate of the people. It prevented change rather than fostering change. He thought likewise about cultural aspects of society such as art, literature, music, and philosophy. Their function is to rationalize and support the existing institutional structure and to divert attention from the growing conflicts indicating that this institutional structure is no longer appropriate to the available technology. This accounts for the antireligious attitude of some Marxists as well as for their stance that the only acceptable literature, art, or music is that which recognizes and exposes the alienating aspect of private property and markets.

The Marxian theory of history traces the development of society from feudalism to capitalism and its further development, as predicted by Marx, into socialism and finally into communism. Marx argued that during the early feudal period the relations of production were appropriate to the existing forces of production, and these relations of production were supported and reinforced by the social super-

[2] Karl Marx, *Economic and Philosophical Manuscripts of 1844,* trans. Martin Milligen, ed. D. I. Struik (New York: International Publishers, 1964), p. 107.

structure. However, the changing forces of production soon destroyed this harmony, as the institutional structure of feudalism became incompatible with developing agricultural technology, increased trade, and the beginning of manufacturing. These conflicts between the forces and relations of production were manifested in a class struggle and finally produced a new set of relations of production, capitalism.

In *The Communist Manifesto* Marx described the harmony between the forces and relations of production that existed in early capitalism and the tremendous increase in output and economic activity that ensued. Capitalism, however, like feudalism, contains the seeds of its own destruction, as the inevitable conflicts develop with changes in the forces of production. With the fall of capitalism a new set of relations of production will emerge, which Marx called socialism; socialism, in turn, will finally give way to communism. Before we turn to Marx's detailed examination of capitalism, several other issues raised by the Marxian theory of history deserve attention.

Socialism and Communism

The terms *socialism* and *communism* have no exact meaning as they are used today, but in the Marxian system they refer to stages that will occur in the historical process. Socialism, a set of relations of production following capitalism, contains some vestiges of capitalism, according to Marx. One of the chief characteristics of capitalism, he said, is that the means of production, capital, are not owned or controlled by the proletariat. The major change that occurs in the transition from capitalism to socialism is that the expropriators are expropriated—the proletariat now owns the means of production. However, under socialism, the remaining vestige of capitalism is that economic activity is still basically organized through the use of incentive systems: rewards must still be given in order to induce people to labor.

Communism, as the concept was used by Marx, will emerge from the socialist economies. A communist economy would be quite different from a socialist economy. People are no longer motivated to work by monetary or material incentives, and the social classes that existed under capitalism, and to a lesser extent under socialism, have disappeared. Communism is a classless society in which the state has withered away. Under socialism each person contributes to the economic process according to his or her ability and receives an income according to his or her contribution; under communism each contributes according to his or her ability but consumes according to his or her needs.

As you can see, Marxian thought regards human beings as perfectible and human goodness as suppressed and distorted by existing society. This approach follows the intellectual lineage of the philosophical anarchists that began with William Godwin.

There are several levels at which one can analyze Marxian economics. The first is philosophical. Is it a correct reading of human nature to see the market as inherently alienating? Will a communistic society reveal that humans are basically good? A second level of analysis concerns practicality. Even if the market is alienating, is there a practical alternative to it? Some find the idea of a society of pure or ideal communism desirable, but they doubt its practicality. The fundamental issue dividing these views is which environmental or instinctive forces are more important in determining patterns of human behavior. In any event, one appealing facet of Marxism is the view that humans are basically good and that undesirable behavior is a result of the institutional environment.

Related to these issues is a criticism of Marx's dialectic in that the entire system is not truly an ongoing dialectic but is *teleological,* because all conflict between the forces and relations of production ceases with the emergence of communism. Marx's theory of history is directed toward an end, communism. But why would contradictions cease with the emergence of communism? Would it not be more reasonable to conclude that as long as the forces of production remain dynamic, contradictions will always exist within any society? To avoid this criticism, some modern Marxists, such as Richard Wolff and Stephen Resnick, have reinterpreted Marx's dialectic as overdeterminism. In an overdetermined theory, there can be many possible paths.

Such issues become especially important in terms of the recent developments in many changing countries. The Soviet Union no longer exists, and the emerging republics are attempting to institute market economies. Dramatic changes are also occurring in Eastern Europe. Throughout the socialist world, socialism and communism are being questioned and experimentation with new forms of social organization is taking place. Even in China, the one large country in which communists remain in control, a stock market now exists and the use of private property and markets is increasing.

These developments disprove the thesis that society is on a direct path to communism; for many, they argue strongly against Marxist economics. But others reject this view. They argue that socialism was not truly tried in these countries, that the communists simply became the oppressors and were, quite rightly, overthrown. Markets do alienate; this creates a contradiction in capitalist society that will ultimately lead to the overthrow of capitalism and the institution of a nonalienating economic system.

An interesting first presentation of the notion that the Soviet Union of Stalin's time was merely a transitional phase of the movement toward socialism and communism was made in 1957 by the Yugoslavian Milovan Djilas in *The New Class*.[3] Djilas's argument was that a new class had arisen that was, under the guise of being socialistic, exploiting the people of the Soviet Union and Yugoslavia and that a further revolutionary change would be necessary to remove the new oppressing class and continue the road to pure communism. Needless to say, Stalin

[3] Milovan Djilas, *The New Class: An Analysis of the Communist System* (New York: Praeger, 1957).

and Tito were not pleased with this Marxian analysis, so Djilas spent a good deal of time in prison in Yugoslavia. The West also had some trouble with this analysis, for although it was severely critical of so-called communism, it was framed in a Marxian theory of history.

Recent events in Eastern Europe, the former Soviet Union, and former Yugoslavia raise other interesting issues concerning ideal socialism and communism and human nature. Marxian theory, and almost all preceding socialist theory, has a strong idealistic belief in the perfectibility of humankind. One aspect of this belief concerns the ethnic and nationalistic feeling possessed throughout the world in countries with varying economic and political structures. Marxian theory maintains that people under socialism will set aside their ethnic and nationalistic allegiances and regard all persons as comrades: a common bond exists across ethnic and national boundaries that binds all together. Are ethnic and nationalistic feelings a product of capitalism that will disappear under socialism?

Marxists argued that World War I was a war by capitalists in imperialistic competition for raw materials and final goods markets. The proletariats of Germany, France, Britain, and all other countries should recognize their commonality and refuse to serve in their armies or to work in the factories; they should call for a general strike that would halt the conflict. Nationalistic feelings were evidently much stronger than these pleas, as evidenced by the fact that the death toll of World War I was about 10 million. Marxists respond that their pleas during World War I were ignored because the proletariat was caught in the ideology of capitalism. But was it?

Marxism has never been as important in American intellectual history as in European. The Marxists did assert that the shame of America, the discrimination against African-Americans, what the economist Gunnar Myrdal called the American dilemma, was an inherent part of capitalism; and they promised that after the revolution and movement to socialism discrimination would cease. It is interesting to juxtapose these claims of solidarity under socialism against recent history in the former Soviet Union and Yugoslavia. Seventy-plus years of socialism from 1917 until the breakup of the Union of Soviet Socialist Republics have evidently not cooled the intense ethnic and nationalistic sentiments that have existed for centuries. It may be true that people are basically good and that undesirable behavior results not from human nature but from the institutional structure. Recent experience indicates, however, that the culprit may not be capitalism but some other factor common to many economic systems.

MARX'S ECONOMIC THEORIES

Marx's system is a mixture of philosophical, sociological, and economic analysis; therefore, it is somewhat of an injustice to separate the purely economic theories from the rest. Convinced of the inevitable collapse of capitalism, Marx applied his theory of history to the society of his time as he searched for contradictions between the forces and relations of production. He maintained these contradictions would be made manifest in a class struggle, because, as he stated in *The Communist Manifesto,* the history of all societies is a history of class struggles. The fundamental determinant of the relations of production and thus of the institutional structure of a society will be the forces of production. With the hand mill the appropriate institutional structure is feudalism, Marx asserted, and with the steam mill it is capitalism. The logic of the technological process creates the conditions and forces that enable the steam mill to evolve out of the hand mill; and as the forces of production change, the old relations of production must give way to more appropriate institutional forms. Thus, Marx saw the present as part of the historical unfolding of the dialectic.

Marx's Methodology

Marx's approach to the study of the economy is unconventional. Orthodox economic theory, particularly microeconomic theory, attempts to understand the

---

The Forces of Production and the Demise of Communist Economies

History abounds with irony. One such irony concerns the recent breakup of communist economies. Marx wrote at a time when it seemed that technology was driving economies to larger and larger production units. Marx built this into his analysis and argued that smaller production units would be unable to compete with more efficient large production units. When communists took over countries, they built enormously large production units to take advantage of scale economies and to create a social production environment conducive to communism.

But a funny thing happened. As the information revolution became an important driving force of Western economies, the advantages of economies of scale decreased, and production units decreased in size in Western economies. The new information technology allowed a greater geographic dispersal of portions of the production process. Moreover, the service sector of industri-alized economies grew in relative importance and services generally do not require large production units.

What is ironic about this development is that it suggests that Marx was right to focus on the connection between technology and economic systems. As technological imperatives change, so too do the dynamic forces of change in society. Communist economies were built on a command-control system based on information processing at only the top levels of the system. That information processing system cannot be well integrated with the new technology, which requires free flow of information to all. Some claim that the information revolution was important in the fall of the communist economies. If they are right, then—ironically—the downfall of the communist economies is another example of the applicability of Marx's analysis of the dynamics of change in economies.

whole of the economy through an examination of its parts: households, firms, prices in markets, for instance. Marx, on the other hand, started at the level of the total society and economy and analyzed them by examining their influence on their components. Thus, in orthodox methodology the major causation runs from the parts to the whole, whereas in the Marxian scheme the whole determines the parts. This description of the different approaches of Marxian theory and orthodox economic theory is an oversimplification, because both allow for an interaction between the parts and the whole, but it does clarify a basic difference in orientation.

Commodities and Classes

Marx began by examining the exchange relationship between those who own the means of production, the capitalists, and those who sell only their labor in the market, the proletariat. He argued that one of the chief characteristics of capitalism was the separation of labor from the ownership of the means of production. Under capitalism labor no longer owns its workshops, tools, or the raw materials of the production process. Capitalism is therefore essentially a society of two classes, and one of the most important aspects of this society is the exchange, the wage bargain, that takes place between the capitalist and the proletariat. For this reason Marx developed a theory explaining commodity prices, or exchange values. Because he was particularly interested in explaining the source of property incomes, he examined the forces determining the prices of the commodities produced by labor and the price labor receives as payment for its productive efforts.

Ricardian economic theory, as well as the orthodox microeconomic theory that followed, also begins its analysis of the economy with the price of commodities. People often assumed, therefore, that Marx was interested in the same basic problem, namely, to explain the forces that determine commodity prices. Marx, however, was not primarily interested in developing a theory of relative prices. His interest was in wages, which he considered to be the most crucial element in the capitalist system, because they disclosed a contradiction that would help to explain the laws of motion of the capitalist system.

In precapitalist economies human goods were produced primarily for their use value; that is, commodities were produced for consumption by the producer. One of the chief characteristics of capitalism is that commodities are produced by the capitalist not for their use value but for their exchange value. An understanding of capitalism, therefore, requires an understanding of the exchange relationships that develop between owners of commodities, the most important being between the capitalist and the proletariat.

This can be expressed in another way. According to Marx, the prices of commodities in a capitalist system represent two different sets of relationships: (1) quantitative relationships between commodities (two beavers exchange for one deer), and (2) social, or qualitative, relationships between individuals in the economy. Wages, as prices in the economy, represent both a quantitative relation-ship and a social, or qualitative, relationship between the capitalist and the proletariat. Marx was interested in prices primarily insofar as they disclose these social relationships; he was only secondarily interested in prices as they reflect a quantitative relationship between commodities.

Marx's Labor Theory of Value

In developing a theory of relative prices, or the quantitative relationship between things or commodities, Marx essentially used Ricardo's theory of value. Because commodities manifest in their prices certain quantitative relationships, this means, according to Marx, that all commodities must contain one element in common that must exist in certain measurable quantities. Marx considered use value, or utility, as a common element but rejected this possibility. He then turned to labor as the common element and concluded that it is the amount of labor time necessary to produce commodities that governs their relative prices. As an advocate of a labor theory of value, Marx worked through the various problems inherent in the formulation of a labor theory of value, as Ricardo had before him, and essentially followed the Ricardian solutions. Marx was able to give a clearer presentation of the difficulties of a labor theory of value, but he was no more able to solve the problems than Ricardo.

To Marx the only social cost of producing commodities was labor. On the highest level of abstraction Marx disregarded the differing skills of labor and conceived of the total labor available to society for commodity production as a homogeneous quantity, which he called *abstract labor*. The production of any commodity requires the use of a part of the total supply of abstract labor. The relative prices of commodities reflect amounts of this abstract supply of labor, measured in clock hours, necessary to produce the goods. This raises what we have called the skilled labor problem, namely, that labor of varying skills will have varying outputs. Marx reduced the level of abstraction and met this issue by measuring the amount of labor required to produce a commodity by the socially necessary labor time, which is defined as the time taken by a worker possessing the average degree of skill possessed by labor at the time. Labor with skill greater than the average is reduced to the average by measuring its greater productivity and making an appropriate adjustment. If, for example, a given laborer, because of greater natural ability, produced 100 percent more than a laborer with average skills, each hour of the superior labor would count as two hours of average labor. In this manner all labor time is reduced to socially necessary labor time. We saw that Smith became involved in circular reasoning by measuring differences in labor skills by wages paid to labor. Marx sidestepped the entire issue by assuming that differences in labor skills are measured not by wages but by differences in physical productivity.

Another problem raised by a labor theory of value is how to account for the influence of capital goods on relative prices. Marx used Ricardo's solution to this problem, maintaining that capital is stored-up labor. The labor time required to produce a commodity is, then, the number of hours of labor immediately applied added to the number of hours required to produce the capital destroyed in the process. Marx's solution, like Ricardo's, is not completely satisfactory, because it fails to allow for the fact that where capital is used, interest may be paid on the funds used to pay the indirect labor stored in the capital from the time of the payment of the indirect labor until the sale of the product.

A labor theory of value must also address the issues raised by differing fertilities of land. Equal amounts of labor time will produce varying outputs when applied to land of different fertilities. The labor theory of value that Marx developed in the first two volumes of *Capital* completely neglects this problem, but in Volume III he met the question by adopting Ricardo's theory of differential rent: the greater productivity of labor on land of superior fertility is absorbed by the landlord as a differential rent. Competition will cause the rent on superior grades of land to rise until the rates of profit on all grades of land are equal. Rent, then, is price-determined, not price-determining.

A final difficulty inherent in a labor theory of value derives from the influence of profits on prices. In examining Smith's and Ricardo's versions of a labor theory of value, we found that when profits are a different percentage of the final price for commodities, relative prices cannot be measured correctly by labor alone. One of the crucial aspects of this problem involves labor-capital ratios in various industries. Industries that are highly capital-intensive will produce goods whose profits are a larger proportion of final price than industries of lesser capital intensity. Because of his close study of Ricardo, Marx was fully aware of this problem, but throughout the first two volumes of *Capital* he avoided the issue by assuming that all industries and firms have the same capital intensity. He dropped this assumption in Volume III, however, and attempted to work out an internally consistent labor theory of value. But he failed in this, as Ricardo had before him. Before examining this problem more closely, we need to become more familiar with some other Marxian concepts.

Marxian Algebra

Marx said that the value of a commodity can be broken down into three parts:

$$\text{value} = C + V + S$$

Constant capital (C) is defined as the expenditures of the capitalists for raw materials and depreciation charges on fixed capital. It is convenient to regard this as all nonlabor costs the capitalists incur in producing commodities. *Variable capital* (V) is defined as wage and salary expenditures. *Surplus value* (S) is a residual obtained by subtracting constant and variable capital outlays from the gross receipts of the capitalist. According to Marx, constant capital outlays result in receipts to the capitalist of an amount equal to these outlays; thus, the name constant capital. Variable capital outlays, where business is profitable, result in receipts greater than those outlays. By this means, Marx embedded in his system his fundamental assumption that only labor creates value.

It is important to understand clearly the nature and source of surplus value in the Marxian analysis of capitalism, because surplus value is in turn the source of property incomes. Because Marx assumed that all markets are perfectly competitive, his analysis focused almost exclusively on long-run, competitively determined equilibrium prices. One of the first uses to which he put his labor theory of value was to explain the nature and source of property incomes. How do property incomes, or surplus value, arise in competitive markets? According to Marx, the capitalist buys various inputs, paying their long-run competitive prices, and sells the final product at its equilibrium price. Surplus value or property incomes do not, then, arise from labor's being paid less than its competitive price or from final products' being sold at higher than competitive prices. It appears that no one is cheated, yet surplus value exists. Marx's solution was that the capitalist purchases one commodity, labor, which when used in the production process creates more value than it is paid. According to Marx, labor is the only commodity that has the ability to create surplus value.

The long-run competitive equilibrium price of labor is the equivalent of the socially necessary labor time required to produce the real wage of labor. If in four hours labor is able to produce enough commodities to purchase all the commodities necessary to maintain labor (food, clothing, and shelter), then the price of labor will be equivalent to four hours of labor time. A capitalist's variable capital outlays or daily wage bill for each laborer will, then, be the equivalent of four hours of labor time. If the working day were only four hours, then no surplus value or property income could arise, because the whole of final output would be used to meet the socially necessary wage bill. A longer working day—for example, eight hours—results in surplus value, for after labor has received its competitively determined wage equal to four hours of labor time, a surplus of commodities equal to four hours of labor time remains. Marx called the ratio of surplus value to variable capital outlays the rate of surplus value, or the rate of exploitation.

$$\text{rate of surplus value} = S' = \frac{S}{V}$$

In the preceding example, the rate of surplus value would be

$$\frac{4 \text{ hrs.}}{4 \text{ hrs.}} = 100 \text{ percent}$$

In this example, if one laborer produced one unit of output each day, the produced commodity would in fact sell in the market at a price equivalent to eight hours of labor time, which is its long-run equilibrium price in a competitive market. Labor, however, still has a price per day equal to only four hours of labor time. Thus, although ostensibly no one is cheated in the various market transactions, because they all take place at competitive prices, there is a rate of surplus value of 100 percent. Under capitalism, with its separation of labor from ownership of the means of production, labor has an option of working eight hours each day or not at all. Because of the capitalist's ownership and control of the means of production, he can require labor to work longer than is necessary to maintain itself and is thus able to realize a property income equal to the surplus value.

Surplus Value: A Digression

Marxian analysis, like other analyses, contains an objective part that puts certain aspects of the economy into perspective, but it also explicitly includes an element of ideology. Stripped of ideological overtones, Marx's message is simply that any economy will produce more goods and services than are needed to pay all the real social costs of production. It is useful to consider this phenomenon in a macroeconomic context. Subtracting from total yearly output in the United States all the real costs that must be paid to produce that output would yield a residual, which could be called surplus value. These real costs would include both labor and capital costs. Marx's surplus value is thus similar to the physiocrats' concept of net product. The Industrial Revolution has brought about large increases in the yearly surplus value created in the world. Marx raised a legitimate question: what is an equitable way to distribute this socially produced surplus among participants in the society?

But Marx was not content merely to raise this issue. Nor was he content to suggest that in his time the cutting of the social pie was inequitable, unjust, and unfair. Marx went beyond this and claimed with "scientific objectivity" that the surplus created by labor was taken from it because of its lack of ownership of the means of production. A revolution in which the means of production was taken from the capitalists would, therefore, return the surplus value to its creators, the laboring proletariat.

Back to the Marxian Algebra

The rate of surplus value can be increased by lengthening the working day, by increasing the productivity of labor, or by lowering the quantity of commodities that constitute the real wage of labor. The capitalist, Marx contended, is constantly trying to increase the rate of surplus value either by lengthening the working day or by increasing the productivity of labor. The individual capitalist can do little to lower the real wage of labor, because this wage rate is determined by competitive market forces. Technological improvements in producing goods consumed by wage earners can, however, result in an increase in the rate of surplus value.

The rate of profit is equal to the ratio of surplus value to total capital outlays:

$$\text{rate of profit} = P = \frac{S}{C + V}$$

The *organic composition of capital,* Marx's term for the capital intensity of a firm or industry, is equal to the ratio of constant capital outlays to total capital outlays:

$$\text{organic composition of capital} = Q = \frac{C}{C + V}$$

The rate of surplus value is equal to the ratio of surplus value to variable capital outlays:

$$\text{rate of surplus value} = S' = \frac{S}{V}$$

The greater this ratio, the more capital-intensive the firm or industry. Algebraic manipulation of the concepts of the rate of surplus value, the rate of profits, and the organic composition of capital shows that the rate of profit varies directly with the rate of surplus value and varies inversely with the organic composition of capital:[4]

$$\text{rate of profit} = P = S' (1 - Q)$$

Problems with Marx's Labor Theory of Value

In examining Smith's and Ricardo's labor theories of value, we found certain inherent difficulties. One problem a labor theory must solve is the role of profits in price determination. Smith was only vaguely aware of this issue as he wrestled with his labor cost and labor command theories of value in an advanced economy. Marx, like Ricardo, was fully aware of the theoretical issues but was unable to offer a satisfactory solution.

Marx assumed that competitive market forces will cause the rate of surplus value to be the same for all firms and industries. These same competitive forces will also result in a common rate of profit for all firms and industries. A higher rate of profit—for example, in one sector of an industry or of the economy—he says, will bring about a shift of resources that will result in a uniform rate of profit in the long run. If, however, both the rate of surplus value and the rate of profit are uniform throughout the economy, the organic composition of capital must also be uniform. This can easily be demonstrated. The rate of profit is given by the formula $P = S' (1 - Q)$. If the rate of surplus value (S') is everywhere the same because of competitive forces and if the rate of profit (P) is uniform throughout the economy for the same reasons, then the organic composition of capital (Q) must be the same in every firm and industry.

It is an observable fact, however, that capital-labor ratios and the organic composition of capital differ from one industry to another; an example will

---

[4] See Paul M. Sweezy, *The Theory of Capitalist Development: Principles of Marxian Political Economy* (New York: Monthly Review Press, 1956), p. 68, for a proof of this derivation.

illustrate the problems presented by a labor theory of value. Assume an economy with a rate of surplus value (S') equal to 100 percent; a capital-intensive industry, aluminum, wherein the organic composition of capital is 0.75 ($Q_A = 0.75$); and a labor-intensive industry, berries, wherein the organic composition of capital is 0.25 ($Q_B = 0.25$). Inserting these values into the Marxian formula, $P = S' (1 - Q)$, for determining the rate of profit gives:

$$\textit{Aluminum Industry}$$
$$P_A = S' (1 - Q_A)$$
$$= 1.00 (1 - 0.75)$$
$$= 0.25 \text{ or } 25 \text{ percent}$$

$$\textit{Berry Industry}$$
$$P_B = S' (1 - Q_B)$$
$$= 1.00 (1 - 0.25)$$
$$= 0.75, \text{ or } 75 \text{ percent}$$

This result contradicts the assumption that the rate of profit is equal in all forms of economic activity. It also shows, rather curiously, that if the rate of surplus value (S') is the same between industries, the rate of profit is higher in the labor-intensive berry industry than in the capital-intensive aluminum industry.

Back to Labor Cost and Labor Command

Now that we have come full circle, we can re-examine the difficulties encountered by Smith, Ricardo, and Marx in developing a labor theory of value. In analyzing Smith's value theory, we found that if labor-capital ratios varied between industries—in other words, if wage payments are not the same proportionate part of the final prices of all commodities—the set of relative prices given by a labor cost theory of value is different from that given by a labor command theory. Smith's perception of these difficulties led him (1) to abandon a labor theory of value for an advanced economy in which profits are paid, and (2) to opt for a cost of production theory of value.

When Ricardo attacked this problem, he found that a theory of value based on labor time alone would not satisfactorily explain relative prices where industries have different labor-capital compositions. Ricardo concluded that although differing labor-capital ratios theoretically prevent a pure labor theory of value from explaining all the variations in relative prices, this disturbing factor is quantitatively of minor importance. It is, therefore, hardly surprising to find that Marx could develop an internally consistent labor theory of value only on the restrictive assumption that all industries have the same organic composition of capital.

Marx's Solution and Some Implications

Marx followed Ricardo's procedure and thoroughly examined the nuances of this problem before finally removing it by assumption. The labor theory of value used throughout the first two volumes of *Capital* assumes that the organic composition of capital is the same for all industries. But in the third volume of *Capital,* Marx dropped this restrictive assumption and attempted to develop an internally consistent labor theory of value. This he failed to do. The internal inconsistency, which has been called the great contradiction in Marxian value theory, was immediately recognized by Eugen Böhm-Bawerk in a book translated as *Karl Marx and the Close of His System.* Considerably more work on the theoretical issues of this problem has been done by economists since the time of Marx. The difficulties with Marx's labor theory of value have become known as the *transformation problem,* because in Volume III of *Capital,* Marx attempted to transform his concept of the values of commodities into market prices, in order to include economies with industries of varying capital intensities. A number of later writers have also tried to solve this problem, beginning with L. Bortkiewicz in 1896. The discussion of the transformation problem was still in the journals as recently as the 1970s, when some of the best neoclassically oriented minds in the profession (such as Paul Samuelson and W. J. Baumol) added to the literature. It is an intriguing though esoteric theoretical problem, and debates about it are likely to continue.

What consequences does the failure of Marx's labor theory of value have for his analysis of capitalism? Value theory plays a central role in orthodox economic theory. Because one of the major tasks of orthodox theory is to explain the allocation of scarce resources among alternative uses, a failure of orthodox value theory involves a collapse of almost its entire theoretical structure. It is for this reason that most orthodox economists regard the inadequacies of Marx's theory of value as fatal to the whole of his system. It is certainly correct that the Marxian labor theory of value provides little help in understanding resource allocation and the formation of prices in a modern economy. Furthermore, planning a socialist economy by using only a labor theory of value to set relative prices would lead to undesirable results. But does the failure of the Marxian labor theory of value necessarily imply the failure of his complete system? Several answers have been given to this question.

Some orthodox economists accept the conclusion that Marx's entire system falls with the failure of his labor theory of value. Others argue that his primary purpose was to explain the laws of motion of capitalism and that he was interested to only a small degree in explaining relative prices. They therefore conclude that Marx's analysis of capitalism is only slightly damaged by the failure of his labor theory of value. Others argue that the labor theory of value in the Marxian system is designed purely to provide an ideological foundation for the revolutionary implications of the system. Admittedly, technical criticisms pointing to the internal inconsistencies of the labor theory of value do not impair the ideological use of the theory. There are also, of course, economists who reject Marx's analysis of capitalism on grounds other than the inadequacies of his value theory.

We agree that the labor theory of value fails to explain relative prices. But this failure does not vitiate Marx's complete system, for two major reasons. First, Marx was not primarily interested in questions concerning the allocation of resources and the formation of prices; he wanted to develop a theory to explain the dynamic changes taking place in the economy of his time. In this sense it is proper to regard Marx as a macroeconomist rather than a microeconomist. Second, the labor theory of value could be replaced in the Marxian system by other theories of value without changing either his essential analysis or his conclusions. Similarly, Ricardo's doctrine of comparative advantage is not dependent upon a particular value theory. Likewise, although the ideological force of Marx's system is certainly weakened by a refutation of the labor theory of value, he could raise the ethical questions that concerned him—namely, the serious inequities in the distribution of income under capitalism—without reference to this particular theory.

From the uses to which Marx put his labor theory of value, our view is that its primary role was ethical, or ideological. He wanted to show that the source of property income was exploitative, or unearned, incomes. He accomplished this by assuming that labor is the only commodity that creates surplus value. He maintained this position consistently throughout his analysis as he measured the rate of surplus value as a ratio of surplus value to variable capital outlays. One could, in principle, say that capital was the sole creator of surplus value and thus develop a capital theory of value, though it would come as no surprise to discover that a capital theory of value would contain some of the same inherent inconsistencies as a labor theory of value. As long as labor-capital ratios vary among industries, a capital theory of value cannot measure relative prices correctly. Although the ethical issues Marx raised concerning the proper distribution of income are important, he was mistaken in believing that he had demonstrated objectively and scientifically, by means of a labor theory of value, that the proletariat was being exploited by the capitalists. It may indeed have been exploited, but that conclusion involves an ethical judgment.

MARX'S ANALYSIS OF CAPITALISM

Marx applied his theory of history to the society and economy of his time in order to discover the laws of motion of capitalism and to identify contradictions in the system between the forces and relations of production. He was concerned with long-run trends in the economy; when he examined the present it was always in the context of the present as history. In his analysis of capitalism he formulated certain principles that have become known as Marxian laws and are treated with much the same reverence by some Marxists as the laws of supply and demand are by some orthodox economists. The Marxian laws of capitalism include the following: a reserve army of the unemployed, a falling rate of profit, business crises, increasing concentration of industry into fewer firms, and increasing misery within the proletariat.

In his analysis of the economics of capitalism, Marx used, with a few exceptions, the basic tools of classical economics, particularly Ricardian theory. Thus, he assumed (1) a labor cost theory explaining relative prices, (2) neutral money, (3) constant returns in manufacturing, (4) diminishing returns in agriculture, (5) perfect competition, (6) a rational, calculating economic man, and (7) a modified version of the wages fund doctrine. In most of his analysis he rejected Ricardian assumptions of fixed coefficients of production, full employment, and the Malthusian population doctrine.

It is important to realize that part of the difference between Marx and Ricardo in their analysis of the economics of capitalism does not proceed from any difference in their basic analytical framework; rather, it comes from a difference in their respective ideologies. Because Marx was critical of capitalism, he examined it with a view to finding faults or contradictions in the system; Ricardo basically accepted it and saw it as a harmonious working-out of the economic process. The chief actor in the Marxian model, as in the Ricardian model, is the capitalist. The capitalist's search for profits and reaction to changing rates of profits explain, in large part, the dynamics of the capitalist system. But whereas capitalists in the Marxian system rationally and calculatingly pursue their economic advantage and sow the seeds of their own destruction, in the Ricardian system these same rational and calculating capitalists, in following their own self-interest, promote the social good. Although the classical economists' long-run prediction of a stationary state is certainly pessimistic, it is not the fault of the capitalistic system but rather of the belief in Malthusian population doctrine and in historically diminishing returns in agriculture. For Marx, however, the capitalistic system produces undesirable social consequences; and as the contradictions in capitalism become more manifest over time, he said, capitalism as a phase of history will pass away.

The Reserve Army of the Unemployed

Marx rejected Malthusian population theory. In classical analysis this theory had been essential to explain the existence of profits. The classical economists maintained that capital accumulation leads to an increased demand for labor and a rise in the real wage of labor. If wages continued to rise with capital accumulation, the level of profits would fall. The Malthusian population doctrine, however, explained why wages do not rise to a level at which profits cease to exist: any increase in wages will lead to a larger population and labor force, and wages will then be pushed back to a subsistence level. The Malthusian population theory, therefore, not only accounts for the existence of profits in the classical system but also partly explains the forces determining wage rates.

Rejecting the Malthusian theory meant that Marx had to find some other vehicle to explain the existence of surplus value and profits. In the Marxian model, increased capital accumulation will increase the demand for labor. As wage rates rise, what keeps surplus value and profits from decreasing to zero? Marx's answer to this question lies in his concept of *the reserve army of the unemployed,* which plays the same theoretical role in his system as does the Malthusian population theory in the classical model. According to Marx, there is always an excess supply of labor in the market, which has the effect of depressing wages and keeping surplus value and profits positive. He saw the reserve army of the unemployed as recruited from several sources. Direct recruitment occurs when machines replace humans in production processes. The capitalists' search for profits leads them to introduce new machines, thereby increasing the organic composition of capital. The workers displaced by technology are not absorbed into other areas of the economy. Indirect recruitment results from the entry of new members into the labor force. Children finishing school and housewives who desire to enter the labor market as their family responsibilities change find that jobs are not available and enter the ranks of the unemployed. This reserve army of the unemployed keeps down wages in the competitive labor market.

The size of the reserve army and the level of profits and wages vary, in Marx's system, with the business cycle. During periods of expanding business activity and capital accumulation, wages increase and the size of the reserve army diminishes. This increase in wages ultimately leads to a reduction in profits, to which the capitalist reacts by substituting machinery for labor. The unemployment created by this substitution of capital for labor pushes down wages and restores profits.

The concept of the reserve army of the unemployed is counter to several aspects of orthodox analysis. Ricardo had suggested the possibility of short-run technological unemployment in a new chapter, "On Machinery," in the third edition of his *Principles.* Technological unemployment, or any unemployment other than frictional unemployment, is not possible in the long run in the classical system. Marx's assumption of long-run, persistent technological unemployment amounts to a rejection of Say's Law predicting full employment of resources. Most orthodox economic theorists have never been willing to accept Marx's reserve army of the unemployed for the following reasons. The notion of the reserve army implies the existence of an excess supply of labor, of a labor market that is not cleared. But if quantity supplied exceeds quantity demanded and competitive markets exist, economic forces will push down wages until quantity supplied equals quantity demanded and the market clears. Because Marx assumed perfectly competitive markets, an orthodox theorist would argue that the logic of Marx's own system invalidates his concept of persistent technological unemployment.

A Marxist would counter this argument by pointing out that the orthodox framework is one of comparative statics—that is, it assumes that as the forces of supply and demand work to lower wages and reduce unemployment, other things are equal and that, in particular, no replacement of people by machines takes place as the labor market clears. The Marxists would admit that the orthodox analysis is theoretically correct, given the static framework of orthodox theory, but they would argue that a more dynamic analysis of the labor market would allow for permanent disequilibrium. Modern orthodox macroeconomists who focus on dynamic search theory would agree that something that might look like long-run disequilibrium in a comparative static framework might exist, although they would argue that excess labor supply suggests that an average above–competitive equilibrium wage exists in an economy.

One possible means of exploring the validity of Marx's concept of a reserve army of the unemployed is to examine the level of unemployment over time. This procedure will not, however, give an unequivocal answer, as the definition of unemployment used for statistical measurement contains some anomalies. In most countries unemployed persons are considered to be the part of the labor force that is seeking jobs but cannot find them. Some members of the population are not seeking jobs precisely because they have been unable to find work in the past and have therefore dropped out of the labor force. For example, a worker who preferred to be employed might spend several months actively seeking work and then decide to drop out of the labor force. If employment opportunities should improve, that worker might re-enter the labor force. The ratio of those actively in the labor force to the total population, often called the participation ratio, varies directly with the level of business activity. A person who is working part-time but who would prefer full-time employment is usually considered to be employed. A Marxist would claim that both the dropout and the part-timer help to push down wage rates and should be included in the reserve army of the unemployed. A statistical rate of unemployment for the U.S. economy of say 6 percent is not, therefore, an adequate indication of the size of the reserve army of the unemployed, as it does not take into account the proportion of the labor force that is willing but unable to secure full-time employment.

Even if a satisfactory statistical measure of the size of the reserve army of the unemployed were available, it is not clear that it would validate or invalidate the Marxian notion that such a reserve army prevents wages from rising so that surplus value and profits are eliminated. How much unemployment is required to produce a positive rate of surplus value and profits? The issue is further clouded, perhaps hopelessly, by the fact that the Marxian model assumes competitive markets as contrasted with the oligopolistic firms and powerful labor unions of the modern economy. Thus, empirical work may never resolve the issue of whether or not there exists a reserve army of the unemployed.

Falling Rate of Profit

One of the important contradictions between the forces and relations of production that Marx said would lead ultimately to the destruction of capitalism is the falling *rate of profit*. Here he followed the classical tradition of Smith, Ricardo, and Mill, who had all predicted that the rate of profit would fall over the long run. In the Marxian model the rate of profit varies directly with the rate of surplus value and inversely with the organic composition of capital.

$$P = S' \, (1 - Q)$$

Assuming that the rate of surplus value remains unchanged over time, any increase in the organic composition of capital will result in a falling rate of profit. Marx maintained that competition in commodity and labor markets will increase the organic composition of capital and thus lead to a fall in profit rates. Competition in labor markets results in a fall in profits in the following way. There is a strong drive, according to Marx, for the capitalist to accumulate capital. Capital accumulation means that more variable capital will bid for labor, forcing up wages and reducing the size of the reserve army of the unemployed. The rate of surplus value will fall as wages rise; thus, the rate of profit will fall. Capitalists will react to these rising wages and falling profits by substituting machinery for labor; that is, by increasing the organic composition of capital. If the rate of surplus value remains unchanged, the increase in the organic composition of capital will push profit rates even lower. Marx was suggesting here that each individual capitalist, in reacting to rising wages and falling profits, will take actions that will effectively reduce still further the rate of profit in the economy.

Competition in commodity markets will also result in a continuous decrease in the rate of profit, because the capitalist will keep trying to reduce the costs of production in order to sell final output at lower prices. These competitive forces lead the capitalist to search for new, lower-cost methods of production that reduce the socially necessary labor time required to produce a given commodity. These new, more efficient production techniques almost always involve an increase in the organic composition of capital, which, given a constant rate of surplus value, will result in a falling rate of profit. Marx concluded, therefore, that competition in labor and commodity markets necessarily leads to an increase in the organic composition of capital, which in turn will result in falling rates of profit.

But it has been assumed in the foregoing analysis that the rate of surplus value does not change with increases in the organic composition of capital, that the rate of surplus value is determined by forces independent of those determining the organic composition of capital. Marx's analysis of the forces determining the rate of surplus value, however, indicates his own awareness that these two factors are, in fact, related. Increases in the organic composition of capital will result in a substitution of machinery for labor—and consequently a fall in wages, an increase in the rate of surplus value, and an increase in the rate of profit. Increases in the organic composition of capital, moreover, will increase the productivity of labor and, depending on how this increase in productivity is shared between capital and labor, are quite likely to lead to an increase in the rate of surplus value.

Whether the rate of profit will fall over time depends on the rate of change in the organic composition of capital as compared to the rate of change in the rate of surplus value. Because $P = S' (1 - Q)$, if Q increases at a greater rate than S', P will decrease; if Q and S' increase at comparable rates, P remains unchanged; and if Q increases at a slower rate than S', P will increase in the long run. The issue can be put in broader perspective in the following way. As capital accumulation occurs, diminishing returns on capital can be expected to lower profit rates. Capital accumulation is, however, associated with technological development, which reduces costs and thereby raises the rate of profit. Whether the rate of profit will decrease over time depends on the rate of capital accumulation as compared to the rate of technological development. The outcome of these opposing forces cannot be determined theoretically; it is an empirical question.

Although Marx's analysis of the falling rate of profit assumed a constant rate of surplus value, he was aware that there were many forces operating to increase the rate of surplus value over time. For example, one reaction of the capitalist to a falling rate of profit is to increase the length of the working day or to increase output per worker-hour by means of better management. Also, increases in the organic composition of capital will enlarge the size of the reserve army of the unemployed, with a consequent fall in wages and increase in the rate of surplus value. Women and children can be hired at lower wages than other workers, which will increase the rate of surplus value. If goods such as food, which are an important part of the real income of labor, can be purchased from foreign countries more cheaply than they are produced in the home country, the effect is again to reduce variable capital outlays in the form of money wages and to increase the rate of surplus value. Finally, Marx recognized that technological improvements may permit replacement of manufacturing equipment by equipment with a lower money cost. A plant that produces 10,000 pairs of shoes and costs $1 million today may be replaced in the future by a plant producing the same quantity of output with only a $750,000 capital outlay. In short, increasing the output from capital equipment does not necessarily mean increasing the monetary value of that equipment. This is important, because the rate of profit and the organic composition of capital are monetary computations.

It must be concluded, therefore, even keeping within the structure of the Marxian model, that over time there are forces that will increase the rate of surplus value and the organic composition of capital. What course the rate of profits takes over time will depend upon the relative rates of increase in these two variables. Marx nevertheless posited a constantly declining rate of profit, although his model affords no theoretical grounds for doing so. Marx, Smith, Ricardo, and J. S. Mill all reached this conclusion for essentially the same reason.

The crucial unknown element here, one that is difficult to predict, is the rate of technological development. Other things being equal, increased investment spending or capital accumulation will result in a falling rate of profit because of the principle of diminishing returns. Other things being equal, technological development can be expected to result in higher rates of profit. Will technological development take place in the future at a rate sufficient to offset diminishing

Figure 7.1   The Falling Rate of Profit

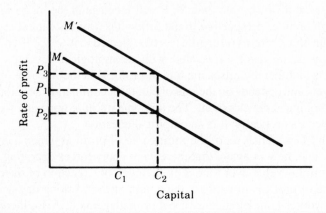

returns from capital accumulation? This question is difficult to answer, largely because economists have no theory that satisfactorily explains the rate of techno-logical development. In the absence of such a theory, economists have been inclined to underestimate the expected future rate of technological development. That is why Smith, Ricardo, and J. S. Mill all concluded that the rate of profit will decrease over the long run. It is why Malthus concluded that population tends to increase at a faster rate than the supply of food. The issue can be put into sharper focus by the aid of the simple diagram in Figure 7.1.

Diminishing returns to increased capital accumulation, or investment spending as it is known today, are represented by the downward-sloping curve M. Other things being equal, increased capital accumulation of $\Delta C = (C_2 - C_1)$ results in a fall in the rate of profit from P_1 to P_2 because of diminishing returns. Other things being equal, technological development implies that the rate of profit increases and thus can be graphically represented by an upward shift of the M curve to M'. Thus, increased capital accumulation is represented by movements along the horizontal axis, and technological development is represented by upward shifts in the M curve. In the example represented in Figure 7.1, technological development has more than offset the diminishing returns associated with increased capital accumulation so that the rate of profit has increased from P_1 to P_3. It is easy to see that two other possibilities exist: M' may shift out just far enough that the rate of profit remains unchanged, or the rate of profit may fall over time. Again, what will happen to the rate of profit over time can be determined only by reference to empirical information, not by pure theory. Unfortunately, the statistical problems of measuring changes in the rate of profit over time for an economy are very difficult.

In any event, Marx maintained that the rate of profit would decrease over time and that this was one manifestation of a contradiction in the system between the forces and relations of production. The falling rate of profit, he claimed, is brought about by the activities of the capitalists, who are therefore part of the mechanism that will bring about the ultimate collapse of the system. Thus, although a falling long-run rate of profit leads to a stationary state in the classical model, it is an ingredient in the collapse of capitalism in the Marxian model. Moreover, Marx's belief in the falling rate of profit forms a part of his theories of business crises, the increasing concentration of industry, and the Marx-Lenin concept of imperialism.

The first generation of modern twentieth-century Marxian economists (e.g., Paul Sweezy and Joan Robinson) argued that Marx was incorrect in his conclusion of a falling rate of profit under capitalism. This conclusion is not accepted by some of today's Marxists, who find a falling rate of profit under capitalism to be part of the basis for the instability of the system.

The Origin of Business Crises

One anomaly of Marx's analysis of capitalism is that although he repeatedly referred to business crises under capitalism (what today we call depressions), he had no clearly formulated theory of a *business cycle*. His entire analysis of the causes of fluctuations in the general level of economic activity is combined with his more general description of the contradictions inherent in the capitalist system. It is therefore incorrect to refer to Marx's own theory of a business cycle, as opposed to the theories of his followers. He suggested a number of causes of economic fluctuations, but these suggestions were never clearly delineated in his writing. There can be no question, however, that Marx contended that one of the major contradictions between the forces and relations of production under capitalism is the periodic depressions that are inherent in a capitalist economy. Although Marx himself did not clearly distinguish among his various insights into the source and nature of economic fluctuations, for the sake of clarity we will do so here.

Marx's view that periodic fluctuations are an integral part of the capitalist process is a definite departure from his usual adherence to the classical model and its assumptions. As one of its major premises classical economics accepted Say's Law: that apart from minor fluctuations in total output, a capitalist economy tends to operate at a level of full employment. Marx attacked this classical position, alleging that it presents a distorted and unhistorical view of capitalism. Marx maintained that in a simple barter economy, people produce goods either for the use value they achieve by directly consuming these commodities or for the use value they obtain by bartering the produced goods. Under these circumstances production and consumption are perfectly synchronized. A household produces shoes for its own use or to trade for food it will consume. The entire motive behind economic activity or production is, then, to obtain use values. Introducing money into such an economy does not necessarily change the orientation of production from use value. In a money economy, people produce commodities that they exchange for money; money is in turn exchanged for commodities that render use value to the consumer. Money in such an economy is merely a medium of exchange that facilitates the division of labor and trade. These two economies can be schematically represented as follows:

$$\text{simple economy} \quad C \longrightarrow C \qquad\qquad C = \text{commodities}$$

$$\text{money economy} \quad C \longrightarrow M \longrightarrow C \quad M = \text{money}$$

But according to Marx, capitalism is not just a simple, or barter, economy to which money as a medium of exchange has been added. Capitalism represents a change in the orientation of economic activity from the production of use values to the production of exchange values. The capitalist, who directs the production process, wants to make profits. He enters the market with money, purchases the various factors of production, and directs their activities toward the production of commodities. He then exchanges these commodities for money in the market. His success is measured by the surplus value he makes, the difference between the amount of money he begins with and the amount he ends with. A capitalist economy is represented as

$$M \longrightarrow C \longrightarrow M'$$

The difference, ΔM, between M' and M is the surplus value realized by the capitalist. Marx repeatedly stressed the orientation of economic activity under capitalism toward exchange value and profits. He criticized Ricardo's acceptance of Say's Law on the grounds that Say's Law implies that there is no basic difference between a barter economy and a capitalist economy and that money is merely a medium of exchange that facilitates the division of labor and trade.

In a barter economy or an economy in which money is only a medium of exchange and in which economic activity is oriented toward producing use values, there can be no problem of overproduction. People will produce goods only when they want to consume these goods or trade them and consume other commodities. Under capitalism, which is oriented toward exchange values and profit, overproduction becomes a possibility. Marx's basic approach to a study of economic fluctuations is to examine the capitalist's reactions to changes in the rate of profits; that is, to changes in the ratio of $\Delta M/M$ or P. Marx concluded that changes in the rate of profit will result in changes in investment spending, and he cited this volatility of investment spending as the major cause of fluctuations in the total level of economic activity. Marx's interest in investment spending is shared by many modern macroeconomic theorists.

Cyclically Recurring Fluctuations

One model of economic fluctuation suggested by Marx is a recurring cycle. Impressed by the dramatic growth of the textile industry in England, he hypothesized that a burst of technological change could generate a business cycle. A technological burst will produce increased capital accumulation and an increased demand for labor. The size of the reserve army will fall, wages will rise, surplus value will fall, the rate of surplus value will fall, and the rate of profit will decrease. The falling rate of profit will result in decreased capital accumulation as the economy spirals downward into depression. But depression, according to Marx, contains elements that will sooner or later generate a new expansion in economic activity. As total output falls, the size of the reserve army of the unemployed is enlarged. The competitive pressure of this unemployed labor will bring down wages and thus provide greater profit opportunities. These larger profits will stimulate more capital accumulation, and economic activity will increase as the upward stage of the cycle begins. Marx suggested that another self-corrective aspect of depressions was their destruction of capital values. Because profit is a money calculation, businesses that were not profitable because of the inflated value of their capital assets carried over from the prosperity phase of the cycle become profitable as asset values are lowered during the depression. A cycle started by a technological burst may generate further cycles in the future as capital equipment wears out. If all plants and equipment were replaced evenly over time, there would be a constant level of investment to replace worn-out capital goods. A replacement cycle can be generated, however, when the capital goods put into place during the technological burst suddenly require immediate replacement.

Disproportionality Crises

Once an economy moves from the barter stage to a high degree of labor specialization and the use of money and markets, there may be difficulty in coordinating the levels of output of its various sectors. Under capitalism the market mechanism performs this function, but Marx questioned the ability of the market to reallocate resources smoothly. Suppose there is an increase in the demand for the products of industry A and a decrease in demand for the commodities produced in industry B. In a smoothly functioning capitalist economy, prices and profits in industry A would increase and prices and profits in industry B would decline. In reaction to these changing profits, capitalists would move resources from the contracting to the expanding industry. The excess supply or overproduction of industry B would thus be of short duration and would have no perceptible influence on the general level of economic activity. Overproduction in one industry, what Ricardo called a partial glut, would not spread to the rest of the economy and cause a general decline in economic activity, or a depression.

Marx contended that supply and demand will not always mesh this perfectly in an economy's various submarkets and that the entire process of resource reallocation therefore will not work as smoothly as in the classical model. His theory is that the unemployment created in industry B as demand decreased could spread to the rest of the economy and result in a general decline in economic activity, a view that directly opposes the orientation of the orthodox classical theorists. Classical theory looks to the market to solve problems of resource allocation. It stresses equilibrium, maintaining that positions of disequilibrium are of short duration and that a smooth transition occurs between equilibria. Marx assumed disharmony in the system and looked for basic contradictions in the workings of market forces. Orthodox theory has not paid much attention to Marx's *disproportionality crises* theory, arguing that an individual industry is so small relative to the entire economy that the spread of overproduction from one industry to produce a general decline is unlikely. They also argue that the mobility of resources is much greater than Marx admitted. Overproduction in a major industry such as automobiles, however, might conceivably spread to the rest of the economy.

The Falling Rate of Profit and Business Crises

The two Marxian theories of business crises we have examined so far, cyclically recurring fluctuations and disproportionality crises, explicitly reject Say's Law. Marx integrated his law of the falling rate of profit into these two theories. Thus, his theories that depressions result when technology fails to develop smoothly, that disproportionality crises will occur because overproduction in one industry can adversely affect the rest of the economy, and that the rate of profit will steadily decline are all facets of a single integrated view that capitalism will fail to provide stable levels of economic activity at a full utilization of resources.

Marx had another explanation for depressions—or crises, as he called them—that is unusual in that it accepts Say's Law. He said that even if we make all the necessary assumptions so that Say's Law holds, capitalism will still fail because of inherent contradictions that will bring about business crises. In the Marxian model a capitalist economy clearly depends on the behavior of the capitalist, whose reactions to changing rates of profits and changing expectations of profits form a central part in the explanation of business crises. Marx used his law of the long-run, continual fall in the rate of profits to explain short-run fluctuations in economic activity, asserting that in their search for greater profits, the capitalists increase the organic composition of capital and thereby cause the rate of profit to fall. The capitalists will periodically react to this fall in profit rates by reducing investment spending, causing fluctuations in economic activity, which will engender crises. Thus, Marx deduced crises even in a model that accepts Say's Law.

Business Crises: A Summary

Marx's explanation of the source and nature of the business cycle is intertwined with his broader analysis of capitalism and is incompletely developed. He did not take any one theory and develop its full meaning and implications. This has resulted in a good deal of controversy among Marxians themselves and among historians of economic thought as to the nature and significance of Marx's contributions to business-cycle theory. Although the relative importance of Marx's various theories of crises is disputed by historians of economic thought, there is general agreement that he did offer three distinct explanations of fluctuations in business activity: the falling rate of profit, the uneven introduction of new technology, and disproportionalities that develop in one sector of the economy and spread to cause a decrease in the general level of economic activity. Marx's writing also contains some even vaguer hints of an underconsumptionist explanation of economic fluctuations, but these are never pursued.

Although Marx did not fully develop his theories of business crises, he clearly argued that periodic fluctuations in economic activity were a fundamental part of a capitalist economy and one more manifestation of the basic contradictions in capitalism that would lead to its ultimate destruction. It is also important to recognize that he saw these periodic fluctuations as inherent in the system, because they are based on the activities of the capitalists as they search for profits and react to changes in the rate of profits. Whatever Marx's theories of business crises may lack in internal consistency, there can be no doubt that his view of capitalism as basically unstable and subject to periodic fluctuations in economic activity because of internal contradictions represents an important insight into capitalism as an economic system. Nevertheless, the Marxian vision of capitalism as inherently unstable was largely ignored by orthodox economic theory until the 1930s.

The Concentration and Centralization of Capital

Although the basic Marxian model assumes perfectly competitive markets with a large number of small firms in each industry, Marx was aware of the growing size of the firm, the consequent weakening of competition, and the growth of monopoly power. He concluded that this phenomenon derives from the increasing concentration and centralization of capital. Increasing concentration of capital occurs as individual capitalists accumulate more and more capital, thereby increasing the absolute amount of capital under their control. The size of the firm or economic unit of production is increased correspondingly, and the degree of competition in the market tends to be diminished.

A more important reason for the reduction of competition is the centralization of capital. Centralization occurs through a redistribution of already existing capital in a manner that places its ownership and control in fewer and fewer hands. Marx maintained that larger firms would be able to achieve economies of scale and produce at lower average costs than would smaller firms. Competition between the larger, lower-cost firms and the smaller firms will result in the elimination of the smaller firms and the growth of monopoly.

The battle of competition is fought by cheapening of commodities. The cheapness of commodities depends, ceteris paribus, on the productiveness of labor, and this again on the scale of production. Therefore, the larger capitals beat the smaller.[5]

The increasing centralization of capital is furthered by the development of a credit system and of the corporate form of business organization. Although the corporation was just beginning to assume importance during Marx's time, he demonstrated a remarkable insight into some of the long-run consequences of the growth of the corporate economy. *Corporate capitalism* is characterized by the fact that its

enterprises assume the form of social enterprises as distinguished from individual enterprises. It is the abolition of capital as private property within the boundaries of capitalist production itself. Transformation of the actually functioning capitalist into a mere manager, an administrator of other people's capital, and of the owners of capital into mere owners, mere money capitalists.[6]

Marx's view is that capital accumulation, economies of scale, the growth of credit markets, and the dominance of the corporation in business organization would lead to the concentration and centralization of capital into fewer and fewer hands. Competition ends by destroying itself, and the large corporation assumes monopoly power. With the large corporation comes a separation of ownership and control, along with a number of undesirable social consequences:

a new aristocracy of finance, a new sort of parasites in the shape of promoters, speculators, and merely nominal directors; a whole system of swindling and cheating by means of corporation juggling, stock jobbing, and stock speculation. It is private production without the control of private property.[7]

Possibly no other vision of the future of capitalism advanced by Marx has been more prophetic than his law of the concentration and centralization of capital. Yet this prediction was not backed up by any substantial reasoning, for Marx did not fully develop an explanation of the forces that would bring about the growth of the corporation and monopoly power. According to Marx, the growth of the large firm with its monopoly power is merely another example of the contradictions within capitalism between the forces and relations of production that will lead to the ultimate destruction of capitalism.

---

[5] Karl Marx, *Capital: A Critique of Political Economy,* ed. Friedrich Engels, trans. from the 3rd German ed. by Samuel Moore and Edward Aveling, revised and amplified from the 4th German ed. by Ernest Untermann, 3 vols. (Chicago: Charles H. Kerr, 1926), I, p. 686.
[6] *Ibid.,* III, p. 516.
[7] *Ibid.,* p. 519.

Increasing Misery of the Proletariat

Marx called another contradiction of capitalism that will lead to its collapse the *increasing misery of the proletariat*. Three separate, though not necessarily contradictory, interpretations of this much-debated doctrine have been offered. (1) Absolute increasing misery of the proletariat implies that the real income of the mass of society decreases with the development of capitalism. If this is what Marx meant, history has clearly proved him wrong. (2) Relative increasing misery of the proletariat means that the proletariat's share of the national income declines over time. Real income could increase for each member of the proletariat, yet relative income could decrease. But historical evidence in developed countries indicates that wages have constituted a remarkably constant proportion of national income over time; so if this is what Marx meant, he was wrong. (3) A final interpretation of the increasing-misery doctrine is that it concerns noneconomic aspects of life. With the advance of capitalism the quality of life itself declines as people become chained to the industrial process. It makes no difference, according to Marx, whether the income of the proletariat rises or falls, because "in proportion as capital accumulates, the lot of the laborer, be his payment high or low, must grow worse."[8] With the growth of capital accumulation goes the "accumulation of misery, agony of toil, slavery, ignorance, brutality, mental degradation."[9] Because there is, at present, no accepted measure of the quality of life, this prediction cannot be tested. It is interesting to note that a number of economists from Adam Smith to J. K. Galbraith have questioned whether rising per capita income must be associated with the development of a good society.

Marx actually subscribed to each of these three doctrines of increasing misery at one time or another. The doctrine of absolute increasing misery was advanced in his early writings. But sometime between the publication of *The Communist Manifesto* in 1848 and the first volume of *Capital* in 1867 he abandoned this position. It has been suggested that Marx's long period of study in the British Museum made him aware of the rising standard of living of the industrial worker and led to this recantation. He did, however, continue to maintain that the relative income position of the proletariat would fall over time even though its real income would rise. Marx used the term *subsistence wage* to identify the lower limit to which wages may be pushed. This refers to a cultural subsistence, not a biological subsistence; he recognized that over time the cultural subsistence level of wages would rise. Finally, and most important, Marx consistently maintained that one of the most undesirable consequences of capitalism is a deterioration of the intangible factor known as the quality of life. Laboring in a capitalistic society no longer gives people the pleasure that work can give. Specialization and division of labor and all the factors resulting in increased labor productivity also beget a laborer who is "crippled by life-long repetition of one and the same trivial operation, and

[8] *Ibid.*, pp. 708–709.
[9] *Ibid.*, p. 709.

thus reduced to the mere fragment of a man."[10] Whatever material benefits capitalism may bring to society, Marx concluded, it brings them with great intangible costs to the individuals who constitute the masses.

SUMMARY

Marx's analysis transcends pure economics. He combined economic analysis with philosophical and sociological elements in a unique way that makes it difficult to consider his economic contribution separately.

Marxian analysis represents a combination of Hegelian philosophy, French socialist thought, and classical political economy. Marx's avowed purpose was to explain the laws of motion of capitalism, and to this end he applied his theory of history, dialectical materialism. Being critical of capitalism, he looked for contradictions in the system, between the dynamic forces of production and the static relations of production, that would lead to the collapse of capitalism and the emergence of a new economic order, socialism. While he departed from orthodox purpose and method, he borrowed many aspects of Ricardian theory, and his different ideological position led him to conclusions quite different from those of classical analysis.

He used the labor theory of value to show that under capitalism the proletariat was being exploited, as well as to explain the forces determining relative prices. He failed in the latter task just as Ricardo had; but this failure does not impair Marx's analysis of the laws of motion of capitalism, for his analysis does not depend on a labor theory of value. His critique of capitalism—clearly the most significant element of his work—must be evaluated separately from his value theory. Marx's description of the laws of motion of capitalism—the reserve army of the unemployed, the falling rate of profit, the inevitable occurrence of business crises, and the concentration and centralization of capital—lacks technical theoretical analysis and tends toward vague generalizations that have given rise to many contradictory interpretations. Yet behind all the generalization there remains a vision, unsurpassed by his predecessors, of capitalism as a dynamic and changing economic order. Laissez faire capitalism does manifest difficulties in maintaining prosperity and preventing unemployment and depressions, and out of the competitive struggle have emerged large corporations with separation of ownership and control.

An aspect of Marx's macroeconomic writing that is one of the most relevant to modern-day economists is his analysis of business crises. Of his microeconomics the concentration and centralization of capital are still of interest today. Neither issue has been adequately dealt with by modern-day economic theorists.

[10] *Ibid.*, p. 534.

With the transformation of many of the formally socialist countries, some economists have argued that Marx is no longer relevant. We believe that view is wrong. Marx's predictions did not hold true; but mainstream economists' predictions have often been wrong, and that does not necessarily undermine their insights.

The same can be said about Marx's idea of a good society. The fact that Plato's ideal of a good society is directly at odds with our current Western idea of a good society does not mean that Plato's ideas are irrelevant. So, too, with Marx. With the demise of the former Soviet Union, and, we hope, a lessening of world ideological warfare, it is possible that Western economists will be able to deal more objectively with the concept of alienation and the philosophical and ideological underpinnings of market economies and capitalism.

Key Terms

thesis	constant capital
antithesis	variable capital
synthesis	surplus value
dialectical materialism	organic composition of capital
forces of production	transformation problem
relations of production	reserve army of the unemployed
alienation	rate of profit
socialism	business cycle
communism	disproportionality crises
teleological	corporate capitalism
abstract labor	increasing misery of the proletariat

Questions for Review, Discussion, and Research

1. Explain Paul Sweezy's statement that "Marxian economics is the economics of capitalism and capitalist economics is the economics of socialism."
2. Contrast and compare Marx's and Hegel's theories of history.
3. Using Isaiah Berlin's analogy of hedgehogs and foxes, would you classify Marx as a fox, or a hedgehog? Why?
4. Explain Marx's distinctions among capitalism, socialism, and communism.
5. Write an essay on problems inherent in a labor theory of value, and Marx's solutions to these problems.
6. What is the so-called transformation problem in Marxian theory? Trace the origin of this problem in Adam Smith's theory of value and explain Ricardo's and Marx's handling of this problem.
7. Marx's theory of a falling rate of profit under capitalism has similarities to both Smith's and Ricardo's. Explain.
8. Write an essay on whether Marx should be considered a classical economist.

9. Modern New Classical and New Keynesian theories of macroeconomics are beginning to endogenize technological change as an explanation of real business cycles. They argue that these technological business cycles are equilibrium business cycles reflecting a combination of people's desires and technological realities. How does Marx's explanation of business cycles caused by technological change differ from these new theories?

10. It can be argued that modern microeconomic search theory explanations of unemployment are more consistent with Marx's concept of a reserve army of the unemployed than are neoclassical theories of unemployment. In what sense is this true, and in what sense is it not?

11. That absent-minded professor is back with another job for you. This time, she remembers a discussion of Marx's writings about what distinguishes "the worst architects from the best of bees." She's doing a paper comparing Marx's thought with Mandeville's thought and thinks this discussion might be relevant. Your assignment is (1) to find the complete bibliographic citation, and (2) to explain why it is or is not relevant.

Suggested Readings

Berlin, Isaiah. *Karl Marx: His Life and Environment.* New York: Oxford University Press, 1959.

Bober, M. M. *Karl Marx's Interpretation of History.* Cambridge, Mass.: Harvard University Press, 1948.

Bose, Arun. "Marx on Value, Capital, and Exploitation." *History of Political Economy,* 3 (Fall 1971).

Bronfenbrenner, M. "The Vicissitudes of Marxian Economics." *History of Political Economy,* 2 (Fall 1970).

Burns, Emile. *A Handbook of Marxism.* New York: International Publishers, 1935. This is a good collection of original sources on Marx.

Elliot, J. E. "Marx and Schumpeter on Capitalism's Creative Destruction: A Comparative Restatement." *Quarterly Journal of Economics* (August 1980).

King, J. E. "Marx as an Historian of Economic Thought." *History of Political Economy,* 11 (Fall 1979).

Marx, Karl. *Capital.* 3 vols. Chicago: Charles H. Kerr, 1926.

————. *Economic and Philosophical Manuscripts of 1844.* Trans. Martin Milligen, ed. D. J. Struik. New York: International Publishers, 1964.

Marx, Karl, and F. Engels. *The Communist Manifesto.* Chicago: Appleton Century-Crofts, 1955.

Meek, Ronald L. *Studies in the Labour Theory of Value.* London: Lawrence and Wishart, 1956.

Robinson, Joan. *An Essay on Marxian Economics.* New York: St. Martin's Press, 1967.

Roll, Eric. "Marx." In *A History of Economic Thought.* Englewood, N.J.: Prentice-Hall, 1956.

Schumpeter, Joseph A. "The Marxian Doctrine." In *Capitalism, Socialism, and Democracy.* New York: Harper, 1950.

Sherman, Howard J. "Marxist Models of Cyclical Growth." *History of Political Economy,* 3 (Spring 1971).

Sweezy, Paul M. *Four Lectures on Marxism.* New York: Monthly Review Press, 1982.

————. *The Theory of Capitalist Development.* New York: Monthly Review Press, 1956.

Wolff, Richard, and Stephen Resnick. *Economics: Marxian versus Neoclassical.* Baltimore, Md.: Johns Hopkins University Press, 1987.

Wolfson, Murray. "Three Stages in Marx's Thought." *History of Political Economy,* 11 (Spring 1979).

Neoclassical
Economic Thought

Clockwise from top left: William Stanley Jevons, Carl Menger, Léon Walras, Alfred Marshall

In the early 1870s three writers from three different countries and with three different backgrounds independently suggested that the value, or price, of a commodity depends upon the marginal utility of the commodity to the consumer. In 1871 W. S. Jevons published his *Theory of Political Economy* in English and Carl Menger published his *Principles of Economics* in German. Three years later a French economist who taught in Switzerland, Léon Walras, published his *Elements of Pure Economics* in French. The important contribution of these writers—as well as of Alfred Marshall, who had these ideas in the late 1860s but did not publish them until 1890—was the use of marginal analysis in economic theory. Their work was the beginning of what would come to be known as neoclassical economic thought.

By the 1890s a number of economists, realizing that this tool could be applied to the forces that determined the distribution of income, developed the concept of the marginal productivity of factors. The growth of marginal analysis during this period resulted in an almost exclusive focus on problems of microeconomic theory. Thus, orthodox or neoclassical economic theory from 1870 to 1930 largely ignored macro-economic questions, namely, the forces that determine the level and the rate of growth of income. Within the area of microeconomic theory, the new analysis was principally applied to the way in which competitive markets allocated scarce resources among alternative uses. Marginal analysis was fundamentally deductive in its approach, using highly abstract models of households and firms, which were assumed to be trying to maximize utility and profits. The development of these abstract models led to controversies over methodology, which we will examine.

Although Jevons, Menger, and Walras were all significant in the emergence of marginal analysis, Jevons and Menger focused on the use of marginal analysis, Jevons at the level of the household, and Menger at the level of both the household and the firm. For Walras the use of marginal analysis was but a steppingstone in formulating a general equilibrium model. Jevons and Menger looked for simple lines of causation; Walras saw the interrelatedness of all economic variables. Marshall used marginal analysis as a building block in his partial equilibrium system and also saw the interrelatedness of all prices and economic activity. It was the greater theoretical sophistication of

Walras and Marshall that accounts for their profound influence on subsequent economic thought.

Walras's work differed from Marshall's in that the analysis was structured so that all markets were simultaneously analyzed, providing a general equilibrium rather than a partial equilibrium approach. The differences in approaches represented diverse methodological views about the purpose of economics. Marshall regarded economics as an engine of analysis to consider real-world issues. He recognized general equilibrium issues but believed that they were to be kept at the back of one's mind, to be pulled out when needed. Walras was more concerned about the formal logic of the theoretical structure and less about applying it to real-world policy issues.

Alfred Marshall and Léon Walras each have claim to being the father of modern neoclassical economics, which sees price as determined by both supply and demand and recognizes the complex interrelatedness of all economic activity. The dual determination of prices and awareness of the interdependency of all variables marked the death of the classical labor theory of value,

the classical cost of production theory of value, and the classical residual theory of income distribution.

Because the formation of neoclassical analysis was actually part of a series of several somewhat unrelated developments, we shall divide our discussion of the period from 1870 to 1900 into several chapters. Chapter 8 examines some of the forerunners of marginal analysis and the economists Jevons, Menger, and Walras, who applied it largely to the theory of demand in the early 1870s. The application of marginal analysis to the theory of production, and the resulting notion of marginal productivity, as well as the contributions to capital and interest theory that followed, are studied in Chapter 9. The next two chapters present the contributions of the two individuals who forged complete theories of markets. Chapter 10 examines the general equilibrium model first presented by Léon Walras in 1874. Chapter 11 explores the economics of Alfred Marshall, who developed the basic framework of present partial equilibrium or supply-and-demand analysis and attempted to resolve many of the theoretical and methodological questions raised during this period.

8 Jevons, Menger, and Austrian Foundations of Marginal Analysis

"In commerce, bygones are for ever bygones; and we are always starting clear at each moment, judging the values of things with a view to future utility."

—William Stanley Jevons

IMPORTANT WRITERS

ANTOINE AUGUSTIN COURNOT	*Researches into the Mathematical Principles of the Theory of Wealth* 1838
H. H. GOSSEN	*Development of the Laws of Human Relationships* 1854
J. H. VON THÜNEN	*The Isolated State* 1826–1863
W. S. JEVONS	*Theory of Political Economy* 1871
CARL MENGER	*Principles of Economics* 1871
LÉON WALRAS	*Elements of Pure Economics* 1874
FRIEDRICH VON WIESER	*Natural Value* 1889
EUGEN VON BÖHM-BAWERK	*Positive Theory of Capital* 1889

The final three decades of the nineteenth century witnessed the birth of modern microeconomic theory. During this period the forging of a new set of analytical tools helped transform classical economics into neoclassical economics. The most important of these tools was marginal analysis. Aside from its obvious usefulness, its development was significant because it initiated an appreciable increase in the use of mathematics in economic analysis. The acceptance of marginal analysis and full realization of its importance and implications did not occur overnight, however; they developed slowly throughout the period from 1870 to 1900. Its first notable application was to the theory of demand. In the early 1870s, three academicians independently applied marginal analysis to demand theory and developed the concept of marginal utility. Two of these, Léon Walras and Carl Menger, also applied marginal analysis to the theory of the firm. Walras even went beyond the application of marginal analysis and formulated general equilibrium analysis, which will be treated in Chapter 10.

The marginalists were in agreement that economics was largely concerned with resource allocation, or microeconomics, but they had different views about the appropriate methods to be used: Jevons advocated greater empirical work; Menger, abstract deductive logic; and Walras, mathematics.

We will close this chapter with an evaluation of the influence of these three great marginalists on the subsequent development of economic thought.

HISTORICAL LINKS

Marginal analysis is now thoroughly ingrained in economics. The historical significance and status of economic thinking in the late nineteenth century become clear when compared with the prominent ideas of classical economics in the preceding century.

The early classicals, exemplified by Adam Smith, provide a striking contrast. They were interested mainly in analyzing the process of economic development and discovering and implementing policies that would achieve high rates of economic growth. Smith was a contextual policy-oriented, developmental macroeconomist with little interest in abstract economic theory. Smith's method, which reflected his broad training in the humanities and social sciences, loosely intermingled theory with history and description, unlike the more mathematical methodology to come.

Early in the nineteenth century, Ricardo transformed both the scope and the method of economics. First, he switched from contextual analysis to more abstract deductive analysis, emphasizing the importance of internal logical consistency in abstract models. In doing so he provided the methodological rudiments for neoclassical economics. Second, Ricardo believed that economics should not focus on developmental issues but should instead focus primarily on the forces that determine the functional distribution of income over time. This led him to examine what was then known as value theory or price theory, which is now known simply as microeconomic theory. In analyzing the forces determining the distribution of income over time, Ricardo began to use marginal analysis in his theory of land rent, which would later become a key element of microeconomic theory.

In the period immediately following Ricardo, economic theory and the capitalist system itself were subjected to a number of criticisms by humanists and socialists. Although these criticisms had little effect on the technical content of economic theory, they did call into question the classical assumption that laissez faire was an ideal government policy, and they initiated changes that further prepared the profession for developments between 1870 and 1900. As economics became more professionalized, economists began to scrutinize the technical content of classical theory, particularly the labor theory of value. Classical economics in the hands of J. S. Mill and Nassau Senior adopted a cost of production theory of value, with capital costs as well as labor costs included.

Another contribution to the evolution of this era was the growing contradiction between Ricardian theory and the actual operation of the British economy. In particular, increases in population were occurring simultaneously with a rising real income for the masses. Empirical evidence refuted the Malthusian population doctrine, but economists of the time clung to it as a basic postulate of the classical system. When J. S. Mill finally withdrew his allegiance from the wages fund doctrine in 1869, the decline of the classical system was nearly complete. By that time, three of the basic tools and assumptions of the Ricardian system—the labor theory of value, the Malthusian population doctrine, and the wages fund doctrine—had, in effect, been abandoned. In 1874, in *Some Leading Principles of Political Economy Newly Expounded,* J. E. Cairnes (1823–1875) tried to salvage the classical system, but to no avail. Nevertheless, the century of orthodox economics in Britain from 1770 to 1870, the period of classical political economy, can be seen as a time of significant change in the scope, method, and tools of economics; it laid the foundation for the reformation in economics that came in the last three decades of the nineteenth century.

Forerunners of Marginal Analysis

Classical economics did not become neoclassical economics overnight; the recasting of perspectives and theoretical structure occurred gradually. For example, the idea of utility had existed in economic literature for a long time. Aristotle had used the concept of use value some two thousand years earlier, and Jeremy Bentham had used the concept of utility in utilitarian philosophy in the latter part of the eighteenth century.

In the nineteenth century a host of minor writers had a clear conception of the principle that as an increasing quantity of a good is consumed, the good will yield diminishing marginal utility to the consumer. None of these writers, however, had been able to elaborate in full the concept of diminishing marginal utility or to apply it to the solution of economic problems. In retrospect, and with nearly perfect hindsight, one can see marginal analysis emerging as early as 1834, when Samuel Mountifort Longfield (*Lectures on Political Economy*), being critical of the labor theory of value, developed a marginal productivity theory. W. F. Lloyd in his *Lecture on the Notion of Value* (1837), Jules Dupuit in an article titled "On the Measurement of the Utility of Public Works" (1844), Hermann Heinrich Gossen in *Development of the Laws of Human Relationships* (1854), and Richard Jennings in *Natural Elements of Political Economy* (1855) all displayed some understanding of the usefulness of the marginal utility approach to a theory of demand. Although Antoine Augustin Cournot, in his *Researches into the Mathematical*

Principles of the Theory of Wealth (1838), did not present utility theory, he was an original and seminal thinker who used marginal tools to develop a fairly thorough analysis of the economics of the firm. He was able to define demand and to determine that at lower prices quantity demanded would increase.

Another important economist was J. H. von Thünen. J. A. Schumpeter has characterized von Thünen as an economist who wrote before his time. In several books published collectively as *The Isolated State* (1826–1863) von Thünen applied marginal analysis through calculus, realizing important insights into a marginal productivity theory of wages, diminishing returns, and rent. He and Cournot were the first of the mathematical economists. Some of these writers would be discovered later as "neglected economists," but others, especially Cournot and von Thünen, whose influence Alfred Marshall acknowledged, contributed notably to subsequent economic theory.

George Stigler, writing about the development of utility theory, has observed that

> the principle that equal increments of utility-producing means (such as income or bread) yield diminishing increments of utility is a commonplace. The first statement in print of a commonplace is adventitious; it is of no importance in the development of economics, and it confers no intellectual stature on its author. The statement acquires interest only when it is logically developed or explicitly applied to economic problems, and it acquires importance only when a considerable number of economists are persuaded to incorporate it into their analysis. Interest and importance are of course matters of degree.[1]

Following Stigler, our criterion for determining the writers we will examine intensively is their influence on subsequent economic thinking and policy.

JEVONS, MENGER, AND WALRAS

Between 1871 and 1874, Jevons, Menger, and Walras all published books that influenced the development of orthodox economic theory. Their influence was not immediate, but it developed over the last quarter of the century as the followers of these three men, the second generation of marginal utility theorists, fought for and slowly gained acceptance for some of the "new" ideas. The positions of Jevons, Menger, and Walras on the forces determining the value, or price, of final products are similar enough that we may examine them by subject rather than treating them individually.

There were, among these developers of marginal analysis, some very important differences, which we will investigate later in this chapter. In particular they had different views on the proper methodology for economics. Menger deserves

---

[1] George Stigler, *Essays in the History of Economics* (Chicago: University of Chicago Press, 1965), p. 78.

special attention because modern Austrians claim him as their intellectual spring. However, Walras's general equilibrium analysis, as well as his integration of marginal concepts into general equilibrium theory, were unique because of their subsequent importance in modern micro theory; and they are important enough to warrant a separate chapter.

A Revolution in Theory?

All three of these economists, working independently of one another, were convinced that they had developed a unique, revolutionary analysis of the forces explaining the determination of relative prices. Jevons stated this most succinctly:

> Repeated reflection and inquiry have led me to the somewhat novel opinion,
> that value depends entirely upon utility. Prevailing opinions make labour rather
> than utility the origin of value; and there are even those who distinctly assert that
> labour is the cause of value.[2]

Menger's statement was more personally modest, although nationalistic:

> It was a special pleasure to me that the field here treated, comprising the most
> general principles of our science, is in no small degree so truly the product of
> recent development in German political economy, and that the reform of the
> most important principles of our science here attempted is therefore built upon a
> foundation laid by previous work that was produced almost entirely by the indus-
> try of German scholars.[3]

Walras, noted for his general equilibrium analysis, also believed in the originality and uniqueness of his contribution:

> I am now able to start publishing a treatise on the elements of political and social
> economy, conceived on a new plan, elaborated according to an original method,
> and reaching conclusions which, I venture to say, differ in several respects from
> those of current economic science.[4]

Are Jevons, Menger, and Walras justified in claiming that their work was both original and revolutionary? On this issue we must clearly separate the contributions of each. Jevons's contribution to economic theory was largely in the application of marginal analysis to the side of demand. Menger's contribution was in the application of marginal analysis to both the demand and the supply side. Walras's was in the application of marginal analysis to both demand and

---

[2] W. S. Jevons, *The Theory of Political Economy* (New York: Kelley and Millman, 1957), p. 1.

[3] Carl Menger, *Principles of Economics,* trans. and eds. James Dingwall and Bert F. Hoselitz, with an introduction by Frank H. Knight (Glencoe, Ill.: Free Press, 1950), p. 49.

[4] Léon Walras, *Elements of Pure Economics or the Theory of Social Wealth,* trans. William Jaffé (Homewood, Ill.: Richard D. Irwin, 1954), p. 35.

supply *and* in the formulation of a general equilibrium model of an economy. Yes, they were original, insofar as their ideas influenced the subsequent development of economic theory in a way that the ideas of previous writers using marginal analysis did not (e.g., Gossen and Cournot). But to what extent their work is revolutionary can be determined only by comparing their views with previous classical theory and against the subsequent development of neoclassical micro-economic theory.

Inadequacies of the Classical Theory of Value

All three writers found the classical theory of value inadequate to explain the forces determining prices. Their principal criticism was that the cost of production theory of value lacked generality, because there were a number of goods whose prices could not be analyzed within the classical framework. They criticized Ricardo's labor theory of value and Senior's and Mill's cost of production theories because those theories required a separate explanation for the prices of goods of which there was a fixed supply. The value, or price, of goods with a perfectly inelastic (vertical) supply curve—for example, land, rare coins, paintings, or wines—did not depend on their costs of production. Cost of production theory of value was also problematical in that it suggested that the price, or value, of a good comes from cost incurred in the past. Jevons, Menger, and Walras all maintained that large costs incurred in producing goods will not necessarily result in high prices. According to the marginal utility theory, value depends instead upon utility, or consumption, and comes not from the past but from the future. No matter what costs are incurred in producing a good, when it arrives on the market its price will depend upon the utility the buyer expects to receive. Producers who incorrectly forecast the demand for their products are painfully aware of this. The term *dead stock* was used to refer to goods for which the demand had so declined that their prices were less than their costs of production. Jevons put this tartly: "The fact is, that labour once spent has no influence on the future value of any article: it is gone and lost forever. In commerce bygones are for ever bygones."[5]

The problem these three writers were addressing was, therefore, whether value was produced in final goods by the *factors of production* (as the classical value theory held) or whether final goods determined the values of the factors of production. The marginal utility school asserted that factors of production were valuable but that the extent of their value was determined by the marginal utility received from consuming the final products produced by these factors. However, factors of production, or intermediate goods, do not confer value on final goods. Richard Whately, an early critic of the Ricardian labor theory of value, had put it very neatly in the 1830s when he said that pearls are not valuable because men have dived for them, but men dive for them because they are valuable.

Another fundamental flaw in preclassical and classical economic theory, according to the marginal utility writers, was its failure to recognize that the significant element in price determination is not total or average utility, but

[5] Jevons, *Theory,* p. 164.

Table 8.1   Menger's Table (marginal utility in Arabic numerals)

	Classes of Commodities									
	I	II	III	IV	V	VI	VII	VIII	IX	X
Marginal Utility	10	9	8	7	6	5	4	3	2	1
	9	8	7	6	5	4	3	2	1	0
	8	7	6	5	4	3	2	1	0	
	7	6	5	4	3	2	1	0		
	6	5	4	3	2	1	0			
	5	4	3	2	1	0				
	4	3	2	1	0					
	3	2	1	0						
	2	1	0							
	1	0								
	0									

marginal utility. Adam Smith had exhumed from earlier literature the old *diamond-water paradox*: that diamonds have high prices but little utility, whereas water has a low price but high utility. The classical theorists were unable to elucidate the paradox because they thought in terms of the total utility diamonds and water give to consumers and did not understand the importance of their marginal utility. The paradox is easily illustrated in Table 8.1, which is patterned after the one used by Menger.

The Roman numerals represent classes of commodities of varying importance. The higher the number, the less essential the commodity. Thus, water might be in class I and transportation in class V. The declining Arabic numerals represent the diminishing marginal utility of the commodities as more of them are consumed. The marginal utility of a class I good is 10 for the first unit, but it declines as successive units are consumed. Suppose that the class I good is water and the class VIII good is diamonds. If a consumer had already consumed 8 units of water and none of diamonds, the marginal utility of another unit of water would be only 2, but it would be 3 for the first unit of diamonds. The total utility of water, which is the sum of marginal utilities, is clearly greater than that of diamonds, yet the value of another unit of diamonds is greater than that of another unit of water. According to the marginal utility writers, the failure of the classical writers to recognize the importance of this principle in explaining prices was one of the major reasons why they were unable to develop a correct theory of prices. The value of diamonds is greater than the value of water because it is marginal utility that determines consumer choice, and hence value.

What Is Utility?

The marginal utility writers followed orthodox classical economic theory in assuming that individuals are rational and calculating. In making buying decisions, consumers or households consider the marginal utility they expect to enjoy from the consumption of goods. This raises two questions: what is utility, and how is it measured? Jevons, Menger, and Walras were almost identical in their approaches to these issues: they did not directly engage them at all. None used the term *marginal utility;* Menger did not even use the word *utility,* preferring to speak of the "importance of satisfactions." All three simply assumed that utility existed and that individual introspection would disclose the varying utilities of different final goods. For them, utility is evidently a psychological phenomenon with unspecified units of measurement. Is it measured in linear space (as an inch), in volume (as a quart), or in weight (as an ounce)? They considered utility to be a characteristic of final or consumer goods, but what about factors of production and goods consumed only indirectly? Menger gave this last problem more attention than did Jevons or Walras. How are we to measure the utility of goods that are acquired not for consumption but to be exchanged for other commodities? These goods acquire their utility from the consumption goods for which they are finally exchanged. Jevons called the utility of such goods "acquired utility."

Thus, without clearly explaining the nature of the utility concept, Jevons, Menger, and Walras assumed what is now known as the principle of *diminishing marginal utility,* which states that as the consumption of a good increases, its marginal utility decreases. This is based on the assumption that whatever marginal utility is, it can be measured. Menger and Walras did not discuss measurability. Jevons stated that although we are presently unable to measure utility, further developments may permit such measurement in the future. From the examples given in their writings, however, it is clear that all three assumed the cardinal measurability of utility.

Jevons and Walras, using mathematical presentations of utility functions, assumed as a first approximation that both the quantity of goods consumed and the quantity of utility were continuously divisible. Both recognized the unreality of this assumption and made allowance in their presentations for nondivisibility, which would give rise to discontinuous functions. Because Menger's approach made no use of mathematics other than arithmetic tables, all his functions were discontinuous. Continuous functions when plotted have smooth curves, but discontinuous functions have steplike curves. This has some minor theoretical importance. For example, Gossen's Second Law asserts that consumers will maximize their total utility by purchasing so that the last unit of money spent for any one good gives the same marginal utility as the last unit spent for any other. An algebraic statement of this *utility maximization* proposition is:

$$\frac{MU_A}{P_A} = \frac{MU_B}{P_B} = \frac{MU_C}{P_C}$$

If the utility functions are continuous (with smooth curves), small variations in quantity and utility can occur and the equality will still be satisfied. However, if the utility functions are discontinuous, then the consumer may be at a maximum without the equality's being satisfied.

Comparisons of Utility

Assuming that utility can be measured, another series of questions arises. All three writers assumed, without examining the issue, that an individual was capable of making comparisons between the utilities of different commodities. Thus, the marginal utility of another glass of beer can be compared to the marginal utility of another pair of shoes. A more important issue is involved in the making of *interpersonal comparisons of utility.* Is it possible to compare the utility one person receives from consuming another glass of beer with the utility another person would receive from consuming another pair of shoes or another beer? Menger and Walras never addressed this question, but their analysis does not depend on the assumption that interpersonal comparisons are possible. Jevons argued that such comparisons were impossible, but (in a manner typical of his writing) he made them anyway.

We shall return later to interpersonal comparisons of utility, because they have importance for certain questions of public policy and welfare economics. In the meantime, a brief look at one of Jevons's examples will be helpful. Jevons believed that an additional amount of income given to a person with a high income will yield less marginal utility than the same amount given to someone with a low income. This assumes that interpersonal comparisons of utility are possible. Jevons did no more than to suggest that interpersonal comparisons of utility could be made, but let us nevertheless spell out certain implications of such comparisons. If we assume that interpersonal comparisons of utility are possible and that all individuals have the same functions relating utility to income (e.g., that the marginal utility of a 999th dollar of income is the same for everyone), some interesting conclusions follow. Given these two assumptions, an ideal distribution of income (i.e., one that would maximize the total utility for a society) would be an equal distribution of income. This conclusion can be seen from Figure 8.1.

Our two assumptions permit us to represent the marginal utility functions with respect to income of both rich and poor in one curve (II'). (An implicit third assumption is that the principle of diminishing marginal utility applies to income.) Suppose that Rich's income is OR and that Poor's income is OP. A dollar in taxes taken from Rich reduces Rich's total utility by RA, and this dollar if given to Poor increases Poor's total utility by PB. The transfer of income from Rich to Poor increases the total utility of the society, because $PB > RA$. Furthermore, if this process were to be repeated, total utility for the society would be increased until the incomes of both Rich and Poor were equal.

Suppose we change one of our assumptions and assume that individuals have different functions relating utility to income and that the marginal utility of income functions of upper-income receivers lie above those of lower-income receivers. This model is represented in Figure 8.2. The curve rr' represents the diminishing marginal utility of income for Rich and the line pp' the marginal utility of income for Poor. The relative positions of the curves show that Rich is able to receive more marginal utility from a given amount of income than is Poor.

Figure 8.1   Robin Hood Effect

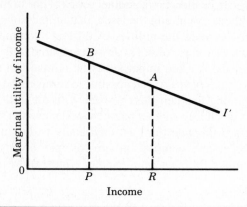

If the initial distribution of income is represented by Poor's having *OP* income and Rich's having *OR* income, then an ideal distribution of income, which would maximize total utility for the society, would be achieved by taking income from Poor and giving it to Rich, because *RA* > *PB*. This could be called the reverse Robin Hood effect. It should be apparent that a different initial distribution of income or different positions of the curves *pp'* and *rr'* could lead to a different conclusion.

Neither Jevons, Menger, nor Walras investigated the implications of their theories for the distribution of income because they maintained—Jevons explicitly, Menger and Walras implicitly—that interpersonal comparisons of utility were

Figure 8.2   Reverse Robin Hood Effect

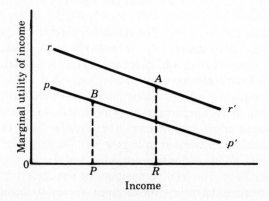

not possible. We will return to some of the issues raised by interpersonal comparisons of utility and the normative issues raised by questions on the distribution of income when we examine the twentieth-century development of microeconomic theory in Chapter 15.

Utility Functions

Although Jevons, Menger, and Walras did not explicitly examine the exact form and nature of utility functions, Jevons and Walras did write out equations relating total utility to the quantities of goods consumed, and Menger's verbal and arithmetical examples indicate that his conception of the total utility function was the same as that of Jevons and Walras. The utility an individual receives from consuming a good depends, according to these writers, exclusively on the quantity of that good consumed. It does not depend on the quantities of other goods consumed. For example, the marginal utility received from consuming another glass of beer depends only on the quantity of beer consumed and does not depend on the quantity of wine consumed (a substitute good) or on the quantity of pretzels consumed (a complementary good). The total utility function, the utility received from consuming all goods, is therefore an *additive function,* which Jevons and Walras represented in the following form:

$$\text{total utility} = f^1\,(Q_a) + f^2\,(Q_b) + f^3\,(Q_c) + \ldots$$

This indicates that total utility is a function of, or depends upon, the quantity of good A consumed plus the quantity of good B consumed, and so on, which denies the existence of any complementary and substitute relationships between goods. In modern micro theory these complementary and substitute relationships are not denied and the total utility function is written in a more general form, such as:

$$\text{total utility} = f\,(q_A, q_B, q_C, \ldots)$$

Utility, Demand, and Exchange

What set Jevons, Menger, and Walras apart from their predecessors, with the exception of Gossen, is that they not only postulated the principle of diminishing marginal utility but also attempted to determine the conditions that would hold when a consumer is maximizing utility, and to develop a theory of exchange. Jevons and Walras went so far as to investigate the relationship between utility and demand. Because of Walras's greater mathematical ability, he was the most successful of the three in these endeavors. Although he was less concerned about the concept of diminishing marginal utility, he had a much more sophisticated understanding of the interrelatedness of the various sectors of an economy.

Gossen's Second Law states that a consumer maximizes utility by spending a limited income so that the last unit of money spent for any particular good yields the same marginal utility as the last unit spent for any other good.

$$\frac{MU_A}{P_A} = \frac{MU_B}{P_B} = \frac{MU_C}{P_C}$$

Although both Menger and Jevons established the essence of this proposition (Menger with verbal explanations and crude arithmetic examples, Jevons with more sophisticated mathematical notation), it remained for Walras, in his justly famous Lesson 8, to derive mathematically the equations that hold when a consumer is maximizing utility.

If individual consumer utility is the underlying force explaining individual and market demand, it is necessary to show the relationship between utility functions and demand curves. Menger did not attempt this process and did not deal directly with demand curves either verbally, graphically, or arithmetically. Jevons used demand functions in his analysis but failed to establish a relationship between utility and demand. Walras was able to establish the relationship between utility and demand and to show that the fundamental force lying behind demand is marginal utility.

All three pioneers attempted to show the relationships between marginal utility, maximization of consumer satisfaction, and the exchange of goods in a market. Menger was the least successful. Jevons was able to show these relationships in a simple market of two goods and two individuals. If individual A owns corn and individual B owns beef, and they barter, the final position of equilibrium can be concisely stated: "The ratio of exchange of any two commodities will be the reciprocal of the ratio of the final degrees of utility of the quantities of commodity available for consumption after the exchange is completed."[6] Jevons's statement can be translated into the following equation:

$$\frac{MU \text{ of corn to A}}{MU \text{ of beef to A}} = \frac{MU \text{ of corn to B}}{MU \text{ of beef to B}} = \frac{\text{quantity of beef traded}}{\text{quantity of corn traded}} = \frac{\text{price of corn}}{\text{price of beef}}$$

Walras was able to demonstrate the relationship between marginal utility, maximization of consumer satisfaction, and exchange in a much more thorough and generalized manner than either Jevons or Menger.

The Value of Factors of Production

The early writers who emphasized the role of utility criticized the classical theory of value, which held that relative prices depend upon cost of production. This implied, they said, that value comes from the past; they argued instead that value comes from the future, from the expected utilities to be enjoyed when consuming final goods. How did these marginal utility writers explain the prices of the factors of production? On this issue there are important differences between Jevons and Menger, on the one hand, and Walras, on the other.

Jevons and Menger both discussed this question, and although Menger's treatment was much more complete than Jevons's, both came to essentially the

---

[6] *Ibid.*, p. 95. The complete sentence is italicized in the original.

same conclusion. Arguing that value causation runs not from cost of production to final prices but in the opposite direction, they maintained that factors of production are not *price-determining* but *price-determined*. The price of a final good depends upon its marginal utility, and the price of factors of production (otherwise known as intermediate goods, or goods of higher order) depends upon the utility of the produced final good. Thus, Jevons and Menger treated the causal relationship between a final good and its factors of production in a partial equilibrium framework. Because Walras formulated his consideration of value in his general equilibrium analysis, he understood the issue much more fully than did Jevons or Menger and saw the causal relationships as more complex.

Evaluation of Jevons and Menger

That Jevons's and Menger's criticisms of the classical theory of value are incorrect and inadequate in a number of ways can be seen by comparing their value theories with J. S. Mill's. As we saw in Chapter 6 and in Figure 6.1, Mill envisioned three possible cases of value: a perfectly inelastic (vertical) supply curve; a perfectly elastic (horizontal) supply curve representing manufacturing, which Mill assumed was composed of constant-cost industries; and an upward-sloping supply curve representing agriculture, which Mill assumed was an increasing-cost industry. Mill concluded that in constant-cost industries, cost of production alone determines price. Jevons and Menger were unable to refute this.

For commodities whose supply is fixed, and which therefore have a perfectly inelastic (vertical) supply curve, Mill maintained that supply and demand determine price. Jevons and Menger could not refute this proposition either. Instead they said that given supply, demand determines price. They could just as reasonably have said that given demand, supply determines price. Mill's case of upward-sloping supply curves of increasing-cost industries was not analyzed by Jevons and Menger because they always assumed that supply was given. This does not imply that there were no weaknesses in Millian value theory, but it does show that Jevons and Menger were not able to support all their claims.

Menger stated his criticism of classical value theory succinctly: "Among the most egregious of the fundamental errors that have had the most far-reaching consequences in the previous development of our science is the argument that goods attain value for us because goods were employed in their production that had value to us."[7] Menger asserted that it is utility, not cost of production, that determines value: "The value of goods arises from their relationship to our needs, and is not inherent in the goods themselves."[8] Because Jevons's statement is even stronger, he is somewhat more vulnerable: "Repeated reflection and inquiry have led me to the somewhat novel opinion that value depends entirely upon utility."[9]

[7] Menger, *Principles,* p. 149.

[8] *Ibid.,* p. 120.

[9] Jevons, *Theory,* p. 1.

The examples used by Jevons and Menger indicate that value, or price, does not depend entirely upon utility or demand, but upon both supply and demand. Although these writers and their disciples claimed that value depends solely on utility, their own analysis refutes this assumption. Jevons is the best example of this. The second paragraph of his *Political Economy* opens with the sentence we have just quoted. After making this strong statement, Jevons proceeded in the next four sentences to refute himself.

> Prevailing opinions make labour rather than utility the origin of value, and there are even those who distinctly assert that labour is the cause of value. I show, on the contrary, that we have only to trace out carefully the natural laws of the variation of utility, as depending upon the quantity of commodity in our possession, in order to arrive at a satisfactory theory of exchange, of which the ordinary laws of supply and demand are a necessary consequence. This theory is in harmony with the facts; and, whenever there is any apparent reason for the belief that labour is the cause of value, we obtain an explanation of the reason. Labour is found often to determine value, but only in an indirect manner, by varying the degree of utility of the commodity through an increase or limitation of the supply.[10]

Jevons further destroyed (1) his argument that value depends entirely upon utility, and (2) his claim to have refuted the classical theory of value, in Chapter 4 of *Political Economy,* which develops his theory of exchange. Here he showed correctly that assuming a fixed supply of two goods held by two individuals, the prices of these goods and the quantities exchanged will depend upon the marginal utilities of the two goods to the two individuals. Although this proposition is formally correct, it does not cover the usual economic situation in which supply is not fixed but variable. When Jevons dropped the assumption that supply is fixed and analyzed the relationship between cost, supply, marginal utility, and price, he arrived at the following causal relationships:

> Cost of production determines supply;
> Supply determines final degree of utility;
> Final degree of utility determines value.[11]

The proposition can be criticized on several grounds. First, Jevons offered no theory of cost or supply. Furthermore, the proposition suggests that a chain of causation runs from cost of production to value, or price. If such a chain of causation did exist, it would be possible to omit the middle part of the chain and conclude that cost of production determines value. Jevons and Menger erred in trying to find a simple one-way, cause-and-effect relationship between marginal utility and price. They did not perceive that cost, supply, demand, and price are interdependent and mutually determine each other.

---

[10] *Ibid.,* p. 165.

[11] *Ibid.* The complete sentence is italicized in the original.

Classical versus the Emerging Neoclassical Theory of Value

Let us return to Mill's three cases of value and determine the strengths and weaknesses of the classical position as compared with the alternative theory offered by Jevons and Menger. Where supply is perfectly inelastic (vertical), as in Mill's first case, the classical cost of production theory of value does not adequately explain the determination of price. Under these circumstances, price depends upon supply and demand, and cost of production may have no influence on supply. But the Jevons-Menger position that price depends only upon demand is also unsatisfactory, for it assumes that the supply is fixed. A few examples of situations that come under Mill's first case may make this clear. Suppose that only one curious misprinting of a postage stamp is known to exist. The supply is fixed at one stamp and, given this fixed supply, the price will be fixed by the level of demand. That the price depends upon both supply and demand can be demonstrated by assuming that ten more of these stamps are discovered, in which case the supply curve would shift to the right and price would fall. For a second example, assume that a grocer holds perishable fruits that must be marketed on a given day. As the day passes the grocer will lower the price to capture whatever demand exists, because acquiring some revenue is better than failing to sell a perishable commodity before it spoils. A third example of Mill's first case would be a manufactured product that is fixed in supply but held at a certain price by the producer-seller. Such a price is often called a "reservation price" and might well be determined by the producer according to the cost of production. In this example the supply curve would look like a backward capital L, with the horizontal portion being the level of costs and the vertical portion representing the total existing stock of the good.

In Mill's second case, in which supply is perfectly elastic (horizontal) and constant costs exist, price depends entirely on cost of production. Here classical value theory, as represented by Mill, is perfectly correct and the Jevons-Menger position completely fails.

As in the first case, both the Jevons-Menger and the classical theories fail to explain the determinants of price in Mill's third case, in which the supply curve is upward-sloping (characterized by increasing costs). Under these circumstances Mill concluded that price depends upon cost of production in the most unfavorable circumstances. In modern terminology, he was saying that price depends upon the marginal cost of the last good produced. Given demand, cost of production, or supply, determines price. Jevons and Menger concluded that price depends upon marginal utility: given supply, demand determines price. Because price in this case depends upon both supply and demand, both positions are erroneous. Jevons and Menger and the classicals, moreover, all made the same error of trying to find a simple causal chain to explain prices: the classical cause and effect runs from cost of production to price, whereas the Jevons-Menger cause and effect runs from utility to price. They all failed to see that these variables are interdependent and mutually determine each other's values. As we will see in Chapters

10 and 11, it took the brilliance of Walras and Marshall to comprehend this interdependence.

Jevons and Menger had some problems and gaps in their exposition of marginal analysis; these were recognized and improved upon by later writers. Jevons, for example, solved only half of the puzzle of maximization, confining his attention to consumers. Menger saw and solved both sides of the puzzle; the household and the firm. None of the three founders of marginalism followed through from final goods markets to factor markets and developed the notion and implications of marginal productivity analysis. These advancements are significant enough to warrant special attention in Chapter 9.

Jevons and Walras had no immediate followers who tried to "clean up" their first approximations. Menger was fortunate enough to have two students who immediately took up the cause of utility and marginalism, and we will now inspect their contributions to the flow of economic thought.

SECOND-GENERATION AUSTRIANS

Friedrich von Wieser

Wieser (1851–1926) was twenty years old when Menger published his *Principles* in 1871. He was a student of Menger, along with Eugen von Böhm-Bawerk (1851–1914), and later took Menger's Chair at the University of Vienna in 1903. Böhm-Bawerk also taught at the University. Not only did they continue to expand on and improve some of Menger's original ideas, they had as students Ludwig von Mises (1881–1973) and Joseph Schumpeter (1883–1950). Mises spawned still another generation of economists. The influence of Menger and the University of Vienna has led historians of thought to refer to an *Austrian school,* which we will examine in this and some of the following chapters.

Wieser, like Menger, did not use any mathematics and developed his arguments by using abstract Robinson Crusoe verbal models. He was the first to use the term marginal utility, which became the accepted expression of economists. Wieser's seminal work concerned costs and factors of production; he demonstrated how inputs or factors of production receive their value from final goods through a process of *imputation.* Value causation ran in a single line from the marginal utility of the marginal or final consumer good back through to the various inputs that had produced the consumer good. The classicals had maintained that factors of production were price-determining. Wieser concluded that they were price-determined. His failure to use any but the most simple mathematics as examples prevented him from pursuing his important insights into the cost side and from developing marginal productivity analysis.

The issue of whether factors of production are price-determined or price-determining can be clarified with the use of Figure 8.3. Assume that we have three final goods—apples, bananas, and carrots—and that a single factor of production, labor,

Figure 8.3 Value Causation

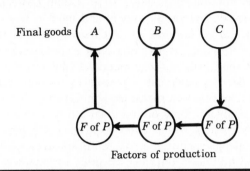

can be used to produce these goods. Also assume that quantities of the final goods consumed and their marginal utilities are such that the marginal utility of another unit of A is greater than that of B, and the marginal utility of another unit of B is greater than that of C. Carrots (C) are the marginal good produced, and apples (A) and bananas (B) are referred to as *intramarginal final goods*. Using Figure 8.3, the Austrians would assert that the marginal utility of good of the marginal good C determines the value of the marginal factor of production, and, therefore, the value of a factor of production is price-determined. The value of the intramarginal final goods A and B depends on the value of the factor of production used in their creation, and, therefore, the factors of production are price-determining for intramarginal final goods.

Marginal utility writers found the classical economists wrong in asserting that prices depend upon cost of production. Figure 8.3 discloses the exact nature of this alleged misconception. If one looks only at intramarginal goods or superficially at price formation, it seems that causation runs from factors of production to price, that factors are price-determining. A closer look at the process, according to this view, reveals that the price of a factor of production is measured by the marginal utility it yields in the marginal, or last, final good produced, carrots (C) in our example.

Eugen von Böhm-Bawerk

Böhm-Bawerk and Wieser were the same age; both were students of Menger and were friends and brothers-in-law. Wieser's influence was largely in Austria and Germany, whereas Böhm-Bawerk became much better known in England and the United States. Following the publication of his first book, Böhm-Bawerk acquired a disciple in England, William Smart, who translated his *Capital and Interest* in 1890 and *The Positive Theory of Capital* in 1891. One reason for the smaller influence of Menger in English-speaking countries is that his *Principles* was not translated until 1950. Böhm-Bawerk was a profound scholar whose work in the area of capital and interest was published in three volumes. The first, *Capital and Interest: A Critical History of Economic Theory,* covers more than 150 writers from as far back as the Greeks. It took him some twenty years to finish the trilogy, during much of which time he was an important figure in the Austrian government. His contributions to economics included his book on Marx, which was mentioned in Chapter 7; his lucid exposition and extension of Menger's ideas on marginal utility; and his development of a theory of capital and interest, which will be explored in Chapter 9. Like his teacher, Menger, and his colleague and friend, Wieser, Böhm-Bawerk used no mathematics. He expounded his views on value or price formation with a monocausal line of reasoning and saw none of the mutual determination pointed out by Walras and Marshall, which has become an important building block in modern economic thought.

Which Way to Go? The Changing Scope and Method of Economics

Jevons, Menger, and Walras made important contributions to the technical apparatus of modern economics. They also had a profound influence on the scope and method of ensuing economic thinking.

All three writers were significantly concerned with resource allocation, or what has come to be called microeconomic theory. We must qualify this broad statement with respect to Menger, who in Part V of *Principles* examined the role and influence of knowledge in the progress of human welfare. Here Menger wanted to supplement and improve upon Adam Smith's emphasis on the division of labor as the primary cause in the improvement of national well-being. Unfortunately, Menger's insights into the role of knowledge as a factor in economic growth and development were not pursued by the following generation of economists, who became almost exclusively interested in resource allocation. During the period from 1870 to 1900 economics turned from the issues that concerned Smith, Ricardo, and Mill toward an investigation of how a price system functions to allocate scarce resources.

Although there was near unanimity from Jevons, Menger, and Walras on the proper scope of economics, there was diversity in their views concerning proper methodology. Jevons followed in the line from William Petty and advocated a greater use of statistical procedures to establish causal relationships between economic variables. Menger pointed to the greater use of abstract reasoning and the building of intellectual models through the use of deductive logic. In this his lineage is Ricardian. Menger's work is devoid of mathematics, statistics, and discussion of historical processes or institutional arrangements. Walras's methodology is also in the same rarified air of abstraction from time or place, but he was convinced that through the use of mathematics the interrelatedness and mutual causation of market societies could be understood.

The mainstream of economics went largely along two paths: greater use of abstract reasoning in mathematical form, the path suggested by Walras; and greater importance on the necessity of testing theoretical propositions through the use of statistical procedures, the path suggested by Jevons. We will return to some of these issues in Part V, Understanding the Present Through the Past.

The Influence of Jevons, Menger, and Walras on Subsequent Writers

One influence of these writers was on the scope and method of economics. What was their more direct influence on subsequent economic theorists? Jevons never developed a following, so there is no Jevonian school of economic thought. What ideas he did contribute were smothered by Marshall's domination of British economic thinking. Jevons's lack of a following can also be explained by his early death at the age of 46 in a swimming accident. Walras's contributions to marginal analysis were totally overshadowed by his general equilibrium formulation. Menger's influence on writers and the subsequent development of economics is still being worked out. A meaningful number of economists influenced by Menger have taught and researched in Germany, England, and the United States: the older group includes Mises and Schumpeter, and a younger group includes Friedrich von Hayek (1899–1992), Gottfried Haberler (1900–   ), and Oskar Morgenstern (1902–1977). Some of these economists have gone their own way and have not followed an Austrian tradition in any important manner; but others do fit a pattern and consitute the early Austrian school of economics. The methodology advocated by Menger was not accepted by mainstream economic thinkers who embraced the greater use of mathematics and statistics. However, the Austrian tradition is of enough interest that we will peruse its modern champions in Chapter 14, which covers some of modern nonmainstream economic thought.

Many, but not all, of those influenced by Menger are defenders of market-driven economies and are critical of alternatives offered by socialists. Mises and Hayek played important roles in the arguments that began in the 1920s concerning (1) the ability of socialistic economies to allocate resources effectively, and (2) the relationships among capitalism, socialism, and economic and political freedom. We will turn to these issues in Chapter 13, where we examine Austrian and other writers who addressed capitalism and socialism.

SUMMARY

In their contributions to marginal analysis Jevons, Menger, and Walras began neoclassical economics. Jevons and Menger believed they were revolutionizing economic theory by replacing a supply-oriented cost of production theory of value with a demand-oriented marginal utility theory of value. Their hopes were not realized, however, because their exclusive emphasis on the demand side was as deficient as the classical stress on the supply side. Jevons and Menger's conception of the value problem was, in fact, fundamentally unsound, as they looked for a simple cause-and-effect relationship between marginal utility and price. Whereas the classical economists had in essence assumed that demand was given and concluded that supply determined price, Jevons and Menger assumed that supply was given and concluded that demand determined price. Walras had a much clearer understanding of the value problem in that he recognized the mutual interdependence of the parts of an economy.

The three writers made five lasting contributions to economic theory. (1) Their emphasis on marginal utility and the role of demand caused subsequent economists to pay greater attention to this part of value theory. (2) Their use of marginal analysis led to a recognition of the more general applicability of this technique, a recognition that was to have important consequences for the development of economic theory. By 1890 marginal analysis had been extended to cover not only the household demand side and the supply side of the firm but also the demand side of the firm for factors of production. (3) Jevons and Walras's use of mathematics in economic theorizing made economists more aware of the power of this analysis and ultimately led to the present dominance of mathematical models in economic thinking. (4) Walras's general equilibrium model was seminal in providing insight into the interrelatedness of the sectors of a market economy and furnishing a basis for subsequent theoretical work. (5) Jevons's use and endorsement of statistics was another important step toward the emergence of the testing of theory with econometric techniques.

The spread of marginal analysis was not rapid, however, and many controversies arose concerning the new technique. We will study the growth of marginalism and neoclassical microeconomics in the last three chapters of Part III.

Key Terms

dead stock	additive function
factors of production	price-determining
marginal utility	price-determined
diamond-water paradox	Austrian school
diminishing marginal utility	imputation
utility maximization	intramarginal final goods
interpersonal comparisons of utility	

Questions for Review, Discussion, and Research

1. Menger and Jevons made an error that might be described as the mirror of the error of the classical economists. Describe.
2. Explain how Jevons used the phrase *bygones are for ever bygones* to criticize the labor theory of value.
3. How does marginal utility explain the diamond-water paradox?

4. What difference does it make if one can make interpersonal comparisons of utility?

5. Are factors of production price-determined or price-determining? What difference does it make?

6. Contrast the scope and method of economics according to Jevons, Menger, and Walras.

7. Using Gossen as an example, discuss the criteria one should use in selecting people to study in a course on the history of ideas (the first to express an idea versus the developer of an idea that influenced subsequent thought).

8. Write an essay on this statement: classical value theory explains what determines prices in the long run, whereas marginal utility theory explains prices in the short run.

9. Marginal utility theory is an example of a broader principle of going to the margin in order to understand economic activity. Explain this statement and give other examples of marginal analysis used by economists.

10. Write an essay in which you evaluate the claim that a revolution in economic theory took place during the 1870s.

11. That absent-minded professor is back with another job for you. This time, she's writing a Principles textbook and wants to include a variety of definitions of economics. She remembers that Jevons had the following definition:

> To satisfy our wants to the utmost with the least effort, to procure the greatest amount of what is desirable at the least expense of the least that is undesirable, in order words, to maximize pleasure, is the problem of Economics.

Your assignment is to find the full bibliographic citation and to explain how this definition differs from that found in recent texts.

Suggested Readings

Caldwell, Bruce J., ed. *Carl Menger and His Legacy in Economics*. Durham, N.C.: Duke University Press, 1990.

History of Political Economy, 4 (Fall 1972). This entire issue is devoted to papers on the marginal revolution in economics.

Howey, R. S. *The Rise of the Marginal Utility School, 1870–1899*. Lawrence, Kan.: University of Kansas Press, 1960.

Hutchison, T. W. *A Review of Economic Doctrines, 1870–1929*. Oxford: Clarendon Press, 1953.

Jaffé, William. "The Birth of Léon Walras' Elements." *History of Political Economy,* 1 (Spring 1969).

————. "Léon Walras' Role in the Marginal Revolution of the 1870s." *History of Political Economy,* 4 (Fall 1972).

Jevons, W. S. *The Theory of Political Economy*. New York: Kelley and Millman, [1871] 1957.

Keynes, J. M. "William Stanley Jevons." In *Essays and Sketches in Biography.* New York: Meridian, 1956.

Menger, Carl. *Investigations into the Method of the Social Sciences with Particular Reference to Economics.* Trans. Francis J. Nock, ed. Lawrence White. New York: New York University Press, [1883] 1985.

————. *Principles of Economics.* Glencoe, Ill.: Free Press, [1871] 1950.

Schabas, Margaret. "Some Reactions to Jevons' Mathematical Program: The Case of Cairnes and Mill." *History of Political Economy,* 17 (Fall 1985).

Schumpeter, Joseph A. "Carl Menger." In *Ten Great Economists.* New York: Oxford University Press, 1951.

Stigler, George J. "The Development of Utility Theory." In *Essays in the History of Economics.* Chicago: University of Chicago Press, 1965.

Viner, Jacob. "The Utility Concept in Value Theory and Its Critics." In *The Long View and the Short.* New York: Free Press, 1958.

9 The Transition to Neoclassical Economics: Marginal Analysis Extended

"The value of the orchard depends upon the value of its crops: and in this dependence lurks implicitly the rate of interest itself."

—Irving Fisher

IMPORTANT WRITERS

FRANCIS Y. EDGEWORTH	*Mathematical Psychics* 1881
FRIEDRICH VON WIESER	*On the Origin and the Principal Laws of Economic Value* 1884
EUGEN VON BÖHM-BAWERK	*Capital and Interest* 1884
PHILIP HENRY WICKSTEED	*An Essay on the Co-Ordination of the Laws of Distribution* 1894
KNUT WICKSELL	*Interest and Prices* 1898
JOHN BATES CLARK	*The Distribution of Wealth* 1899
IRVING FISHER	*The Rate of Interest* 1907
JOSEPH A. SCHUMPETER	*Theory of Economic Development* 1912
FRANK H. KNIGHT	*Risk, Uncertainty, and Profit* 1921

The first generation of marginal theorists, Jevons, Menger, and Walras, transformed economic methodology by introducing marginal analysis. Like most developments in intellectual history, the new economics of the early 1870s evinced both continuity and change, harking back to fundamental ideas and methods of the past but, more notably, breaking with the classical economics of J. S. Mill. These writers had discovered a tool, marginal analysis, whose usefulness they could only partially imagine. The full weight of their discovery eluded them: they all stressed the difference between the *content* of their theories and those of the classical school rather than their departure from classical *methods*.

235

Ricardo was a master builder of highly abstract models based on a few rigid assumptions. J. S. Mill represented a return to a methodology much closer to Adam Smith's in his attempt to weave description and history into a theoretical analysis of the English economy. Because the early marginalists so strongly emphasized their differences with the conclusions of Ricardo's labor theory of value, they failed to recognize their affinity with his abstract model building. Ricardo had also used marginal analysis in his explanation of the forces determining the rent of land. Thus, marginal analysis and abstract model building were not new to the early 1870s. What was new was the slowly developing recognition of the importance of marginal analysis and the detailed application of marginalism to all parts of microeconomic theory as the period progressed. These developments were advanced tremendously by the use of mathematical tools, particularly differential calculus. Jevons and Walras both had training in mathematics, although Menger did not. The second generation of marginal theorists, with the exception of the Austrian disciples of Menger, all used calculus to push forward the frontiers of economic theory.

The trends set into motion by the first generation of marginal theorists have persisted to the present. Highly abstract models, developed with an impressive array of mathematical techniques, are now the order of the day. These developments have been resisted by some, notably Alfred Marshall, the German and English historical schools, the American institutionalists, neo-Austrian economists, radical economists, and a number of economists who would otherwise be classified as mainstream.

MARGINAL ANALYSIS EXTENDED: THE SECOND GENERATION

It is helpful to examine the weaknesses in micro theory as it was presented by Jevons, Menger, and Walras before studying the specific contributions of the second generation of marginal theorists to the theory of production, costs, prices of factors of production, and the distribution of income. After studying the second generation of marginal theorists we will examine Léon Walras's general equilibrium model. Finally, we will explore Alfred Marshall's attempts to solve the many theoretical and methodological issues raised during this period.

Although Jevons, Menger, and Walras contributed significantly to the development of microeconomic theory by their expansion of the use of marginal analysis, the content of their theories was deficient in a number of ways. They had applied marginal analysis almost exclusively to the theory of demand and almost completely ignored the theory of supply. Jevons and Menger paid little attention to supply because they were obsessed with the notion that value depended almost exclusively on marginal utility. Walras did not explicitly pursue the supply side because his general equilibrium model concentrated on the interrelatedness of economic variables.

For the most part, their models assumed that supply was given and that the resource allocation problem was merely one of allocating a fixed supply among alternative uses. More specifically, they had no explanation of the forces that determined the prices of the factors of production when the supply of these factors was not fixed; no explanation of the forces determining the distribution of income; no significant analysis of the economics of the firm; and no insight into the unique problems that must be solved in developing theories to explain wages, rents, profits, and interest.

In fact, marginal analysis had already been applied to factor pricing and the distribution of income by two earlier writers, although their efforts, like Gossen's, were ignored for the most part by contemporary economists. In *Lectures on Political Economy* (1834), Mountifort Longfield (1802–1884) criticized the labor theory of value and presented a marginal productivity theory of distribution. Unknown to Jevons, Menger, Walras, and Marshall, his work was brought to the attention of the profession by E. R. A. Seligman in 1903. And though Johann H. von Thünen (1783–1850) had even greater insight into the issues of microeconomics, Alfred Marshall appears to be the only one of the early discoverers of marginal productivity to have been influenced by him.

Von Thünen appears, in fact, to have been the first to apply calculus to economic theory. His mathematical abilities gave him insight into the interdependence of markets, which he represented in a series of simultaneous equations. He was able not only to develop the idea of the marginal products of the various factors but also to present a reasonably correct theory of distribution based upon these principles. After wrestling for nearly twenty years with the problem of embodying in a simple statement all the economic forces determining the prices of factors, von Thünen was so pleased with his final result that he requested that his formula for the wage of labor be inscribed on his tombstone. But his achievement unfortunately had almost no direct impact on subsequent economic thinking, although Marshall generously acknowledged his debt to von Thünen.

The second generation of marginalists came to economic theory with a new tool that had broad applicability to the theories of both demand and supply. It had been used almost exclusively to analyze the demand side, however, particularly the theory of the household, and rarely to analyze the theory of supply or the firm. In the following presentation we will record the contributions of this second generation of marginalists without stressing either the originators of new concepts or the slight differences among writers.

Writers from Austria, England, Sweden, and the United States all contributed notably to this body of theory, which demonstrates not only that these developments represented the combined efforts of many scholars but also that economics as an academic endeavor was becoming increasingly professionalized. Although our discussion of some topics will extend well into the twentieth century, we will reserve the bulk of our critical evaluation of this theory until we have presented the economics of Alfred Marshall, who polished his own ideas for more than twenty years before publishing his *Principles* in 1890.

MARGINAL PRODUCTIVITY THEORY

Introduction

The *principle of diminishing returns* plays a fundamental role in modern economic theory. In micro theory it explains the shapes of the short-run supply curves of firms and the shapes of firms' demand curves for factors of production.

This concept was recognized early by economic theorists and applied by Ricardo to his analysis of land rent. Ricardo studied what today would be called *production functions* for agriculture; that is, the relationship between physical input and physical output for land. He assumed that the ratio of capital to labor in a production process was fixed by the available technology and that doses of capital and labor in these technologically fixed proportions were added to a fixed quantity of land. On the basis of these assumptions, he concluded that the resulting output would display the characteristic of diminishing marginal product for the successive doses of capital and labor.

Ricardo and his followers did not grasp all the implications of this analysis, such as the difference between diminishing average product and marginal product, nor did they recognize the broader applicability of the concept of diminishing returns. One of the anomalies of the history of economic analysis is that nearly seventy-five years elapsed between Ricardo's application of marginal productivity analysis to the determination of land rent and its general application to all factors of production. A parallel anomaly is that the marginal analysis Ricardo developed for use on the supply side saw its first significant extension in the 1870s, when it came to be used to analyze not marginal productivity but marginal utility. A second generation of marginalists finally worked out the elements of what has become known as the marginal productivity theory of distribution. The most important of these writers were the Austrians Friedrich von Wieser (1851–1926) and Eugen von Böhm-Bawerk (1851–1914); an American, J. B. Clark (1847–1938); a Swede, Knut Wicksell (1851–1926); and the English writers P. H. Wicksteed (1844–1927) and F. Y. Edgeworth (1845–1926). These writers, along with Jevons, Menger, Walras, and Marshall, were the intellectual giants of this period of orthodox economic theory. Their first major works appeared between 1871 and 1893.

Principle of Diminishing Returns

If we hold one factor of production constant and add a variable factor to it, the resulting output will often first increase at an increasing rate, then increase at a decreasing rate, and finally decrease. An example of this relationship between physical input and physical output is shown in Table 9.1.

The data shown in this production function would presumably be arrived at empirically in the following way. If we held the quantity of land constant at 100 acres, for example, and applied 1 man-year, we would find that total product was 10 tons of corn. We would then repeat the experiment, using 2 man-years, and record an output of 21 tons of corn, and so on. Note that the Total Product of Labor

Table 9.1   A Production Function

Labor	Total Product of Labor (tons of corn)	Average Product of Labor (tons of corn)	Marginal Product of Labor (tons of corn)
0	0	0	
		>	10
1	10	10.0	
		>	11
2	21	10.5	
		>	12
3	33	11.0	
		>	13
4	46	11.5	
		>	12
5	58	11.6	
		>	10
6	68	11.3	
		>	7
7	75	10.7	
		>	5
8	80	10.0	
		>	3
9	83	9.2	
		>	0
10	83	8.3	
		>	−3
11	80	7.3	

column data in Table 9.1 are assumed to be the maximum product that can be produced given the quantities of the fixed inputs and variable inputs. In short, it is assumed that maximum technological efficiency is achieved. Furthermore, the level of technology is assumed to continue unchanged as we record these input-output relationships.

The average and the marginal products of the variable input, labor, are shown numerically in Table 9.1 and are presented graphically in Figure 9.1. The *average product* of labor, computed by dividing total product by the quantity of labor, is plotted in relationship to the total product curve in the two panels of Figure 9.1. The *marginal product* of labor, often more precisely called the marginal physical product of labor, is defined as

$$MPP_L = \frac{\Delta TP}{\Delta L}$$

Geometrically it is the slope of the total product curve, or the first derivative of total product with respect to labor. It is also plotted in Figure 9.1. When the quantity of labor is q_1, the marginal product of labor is at a maximum; at q_2 the average product of labor is at a maximum, and marginal and average product are equal; and at q_3 the total product is at a maximum and the marginal product of labor is zero. Quantities of labor beyond q_3 result in decreasing total product and negative marginal product of labor.

The exact properties of production functions and the implications of these properties were slowly worked out during the close of the nineteenth century. It is possible to represent and compute the marginal product of any factor of

Figure 9.1   Total Product, Average Product, and Marginal Product

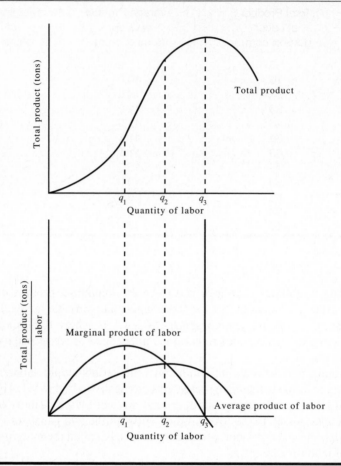

production. We might, for example, hold the quantity of labor fixed and thereby derive the marginal product curve for land.

The New and the Old

With this greater understanding of production relationships came the realization that the demand curve for factors of production could be derived from marginal product curves. Assume that a firm in a perfectly competitive industry uses only one variable factor of production, labor. The firm sells its final product in perfectly competitive markets, so the price of the final product does not change as the firm's sales vary. In other words, the firm faces a perfectly elastic demand curve for its final product. The firm buys the variable input in perfectly competitive markets, so the price of that input to the firm does not vary with the quantities purchased. In other words, the firm faces a perfectly elastic supply curve for the variable input. Optimally, the firm will hire the variable input up to the point at which the last unit of input purchased adds as much to the total revenue of the firm as to its total cost. This condition can be stated as follows:

price of labor = (marginal physical product of labor)(price of output)

The left side of the equation measures the addition to total cost of hiring another unit of labor. The right side measures the addition to total revenue derived from the sale of the added product of labor. It is commonly referred to as the *value of the marginal product*.

Given the data presented in Table 9.1, assume that the price of labor is $10,000 per man-year and the price of the final product is $1,000 per ton. If the firm in our example employs 5 units of labor, the equation for the optimum hiring of labor would give the following values:

$$P_L = MPP_L \cdot P_O$$
$$\$10,000 < 12 \cdot \$1,000$$
$$\$10,000 < \$12,000$$

The last unit of labor hired added $10,000 to total cost and $12,000 to total revenue; thus, profits were increased by $2,000. The firm interested in maximizing profits would then increase its use of the variable input, labor. As it did, the marginal physical product of labor would decrease. The sixth unit of labor hired adds $10,000 to total costs and $10,000 to total revenue. The seventh unit of labor adds $10,000 to total cost but only $7,000 to total revenue. The optimum quantity of labor is 6 units, because the price of labor is then equal to the value of the marginal product of labor.

However, because most production processes involve several inputs, a more general rule for the optimum hiring of inputs is needed. Assume we have several inputs, $A, B, C, \ldots, N$. We represent their marginal physical products as MPP_A, MPP_B, $MPP_C, \ldots, MPP_N$, and their prices as $P_A, P_B, P_C, \ldots, P_N$. These inputs are being used in an optimum way when the following condition holds:

$$\frac{MPP_A}{P_A} = \frac{MPP_B}{P_B} = \frac{MPP_C}{P_C} = \ldots = \frac{MPP_N}{P_N}$$

The equation states that inputs are optimally utilized when the last dollar spent in the purchase of each input yields the same marginal physical product. If this condition does not hold, it would be possible to alter the purchase of inputs and produce more final product with the same total costs, or, what is the same thing, to produce a given final output at lower total costs.

The demand for an input can now be easily derived. Demand for an input is defined as the quantities the firm would hire at various prices. Suppose we start with a firm that is hiring inputs optimally; that is, the ratios of marginal physical products to the prices of inputs are equal. If we were to lower the price of an input, the firm would use more of that input until the last dollar spent on the input would give the same marginal physical product as the last dollar spent for all other inputs. Marginal productivity theory also indicates that when firms in competitive markets are optimally hiring inputs, all inputs will receive a price equal to the value of their marginal products.

These new notions concerning marginal productivity are closely related to Ricardo's theory of land rent, as some of their originators recognized. In analyzing land rent, Ricardo reduced a three-input model to a two-input model by assuming that capital and labor are applied as if they were a single variable input to the fixed input, land, in proportions fixed by technology. To illustrate the affinity between the newly developed marginal productivity theory and Ricardo's theory of land rent, let us consider a model with only two inputs, labor and land. In such a model Ricardo would measure the rent of land in the way indicated in Figure 9.2.

In panel (a) of Figure 9.2 the quantity of land is assumed to be the fixed input, and the quantity of labor the variable input. The curve ABM represents the marginal physical product of labor. If a quantity of labor equal to OC is used, total product is the area $OABC,$ the sum of the marginal products. Ricardo, however, did not focus on marginal products, although he assumed a diminishing marginal product; he focused on the determination of rent. He concluded that rent would be the area DAB. Each laborer receives a wage $OD = BC,$ and the total wage bill is the area $ODBC$. Subtracting total wages from total product gives the residual $DAB,$ which goes as rent to the fixed factor of production, land.

But suppose, now, that we hold the quantity of labor fixed and vary the quantity of land. This is done in panel (b) of Figure 9.2, with the curve FGN measuring the marginal physical product of land. The total product would be equal to the area $OFGH,$ the same as the total product $OABC$ produced in panel (a). Each unit of

Figure 9.2   Wages as Rent and Rent as Wages

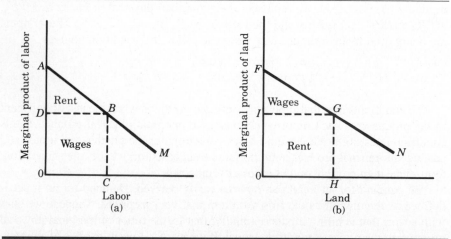

land would receive a rent $OI = HG$, and total rent would be $OIGH$. Wages are now measured as a residual accruing to the fixed factor, labor, and are equal to IFG.

One of the consequences of this new theory of marginal productivity was, thus, to reorient and generalize Ricardo's theory of rent. Ricardo had stressed not the marginal product of the variable input but the residual accruing to the fixed factor. The new theory, however, concentrated on the marginal product of the variable input. Whereas Ricardo applied marginal productivity analysis only to the determination of land rent, the new theorists recognized that any of the inputs could be varied and their marginal products computed. They saw, too, that the firm would hire inputs until their prices were equal to the value of the variable input's marginal product. These new ideas raised a number of issues that were extensively debated during this period.

Product Exhaustion

Ricardo's theory of distribution is a residual theory in the sense that rent is what remains after wages and profits have been deducted from total product, and profit is what remains after wages, determined by the Malthusian population doctrine, are deducted from wages and profits. (See Figure 4.3 of Chapter 4 and the accompanying explanation of Ricardo's procedure.) With a residual theory of distribution, there is no question of whether the payments to the various factors of production are equal to the total product, since the method of determining the payments to the factors ensures that the total product is distributed.

Let us assume a simple economy with two inputs, labor and land. If we explain the distribution of income using Ricardian residual theory, our reasoning would be as follows: panel (a) of Figure 9.2 shows that the total product in the economy is equal to $OABC$, labor's share is equal to $ODBC$, and rent is the residual, or the difference between total product and total wage payments. Since rent is computed as a residual, wages plus rent must equal the total product. A marginal productivity theory of distribution, however, does not reach this conclusion so obviously. If in competitive markets each factor receives the value of its marginal product, is there any reason to suppose that the sum of all these marginal products will be exactly equal to the total product?

The newly developed marginal productivity theory held that each factor would receive its marginal product. By referring to panel (a) of Figure 9.2, we concluded that the marginal physical product of labor is BC and that the total wage bill is quantity of labor used, OC, times the marginal product of labor, which yields the area $ODBC$. In panel (b) of Figure 9.2 the marginal physical product of land is GH and the total rent is the marginal product of land, GH, times the quantity of land OH, or the area $OIGH$. Will the sum of wages plus rent, if both are computed by the marginal product method, equal the total product? Will the area $ODBC$ (wages) plus the area $OIGH$ (rent) equal the area $OABC$ (total product)? In other words, will wages computed by the marginal product ($ODBC$) equal wages computed by the residual method (IFG)? The same can be asked about rent: will $OIGH$ equal

DAB? The proposition that payments to the factors of production will equal the total product can be stated in equation form:

$$Q = MPP_L \cdot L + MPP_T \cdot T$$

Here Q is the physical amount of output (total product), MPP_L and MPP_T are the marginal physical products of labor and land, and L and T are the quantities of labor and land.

J. B. Clark stated that paying each factor of production its marginal product would just exhaust the total product, but he offered no proof of this proposition. A controversy over the issue developed in the 1890s and continued into the twentieth century. The most important economists involved were Wicksteed, Wicksell, Barone, Edgeworth, Pareto, and Walras.[1] We will confine our comments to Wicksteed and Wicksell, whose contributions significantly influenced the development of marginal productivity theory.

In 1894 P. H. Wicksteed published a small pamphlet titled *An Essay on the Co-Ordination of the Laws of Distribution* in which he argued that classical theory was deficient in requiring separate explanations of the payments to land, labor, and capital but that the marginal productivity theory was a better theory in that one unifying principle explains the return to any factor of production. Wicksteed concluded that in competitive markets each factor would have a price equal to the value of its marginal product—which, he recognized, raised the question of whether the total product will be exhausted if all factors receive their marginal products. He attempted to prove that this result, referred to as *product exhaustion,* will occur. Although Wicksteed failed in this attempt, he did point out that for product exhaustion to take place, competition must exist and the production functions of firms must manifest certain properties. In a review of Wicksteed's *Co-Ordination* A. W. Flux also contributed to these developments.[2] He demonstrated that product exhaustion would result only from production functions with certain mathematical properties that had been previously examined by a Swiss mathematician, Leonhard Euler, whose name has consequently become associated with issues concerning product exhaustion.

When total product is exactly exhausted by payments to each factor for its marginal product, the production function must exhibit the property that a given proportionate increase in all inputs will increase output or total product by the same proportion. In our example, if the quantity of labor and land is doubled, then total output doubles; if both inputs are trebled, then output triples, and so forth. The mathematical phrase applied to these functions is that they are *homogeneous to the degree one.* These functions are also described as "linearly homogeneous," although such a description may mislead the nonmathematician because they are not necessarily linear. A production function homogeneous to a degree less than

---

[1] The acknowledged best summary of this issue is contained in George Stigler's *Production and Distribution Theories* (New York: Macmillan, 1941), Chapter 12, "Euler's Theorem and the Marginal Productivity Theory."

[2] A. W. Flux, *Economic Journal,* 4 (1894), pp. 305–308.

one produces a situation in which a proportionate increase in all inputs leads to a *less* than proportionate increase in output. If the production function is homogeneous to a degree greater than one, a proportionate increase in all inputs leads to a more than proportionate increase in output.

Economists use the phrase *returns to scale* to describe the way output or costs behave in response to proportionate increases in all inputs. If all inputs are increased proportionately and total output increases by the same proportion, average costs do not change: this result is called *constant returns to scale*. Constant returns to scale are given by production functions homogeneous to the degree one. If all inputs are increased proportionately and total output increases by a smaller proportion, there are *decreasing returns to scale* and increasing average costs. Decreasing returns to scale are given by production functions homogeneous to a degree less than one.

A firm selling its output and buying its inputs in perfectly competitive markets with a production function yielding constant returns to scale will find that if all inputs are paid the value of their marginal product, the total revenues of the firm will be completely exhausted by these payments. Competition in the factor market will cause each input to receive the value of its marginal product, and competition in the final goods market will result in zero profits' being earned by the firm. If zero profits are earned, then total revenue for the firm must equal total cost; and because total cost is the payment to the various inputs, product exhaustion has occurred.

A simple algebraic representation may clarify the problem. The issue as stated by Wicksteed and discussed during this period was whether paying each input its marginal product would exhaust the total output of a firm. We previously stated this in equation form for a simple labor and production function:

$$Q = MPP_L \cdot L + MPP_T \cdot T$$

Multiplying by the price of the final good

$$PQ = P \cdot MPP_L \cdot L + P \cdot MPP_T \cdot T$$

Now $P \cdot MPP_L$ = value of the marginal product of labor (VMP_L), and $P \cdot MPP_T$ = value of the marginal product of land (VMP_T). Therefore,

$$PQ = VMP_L \cdot L + VMP_T \cdot T$$

The right side of the equation shows the total payments to labor and the total payments to land. It therefore represents the total costs to the firm. The left side represents the total revenues of the firm. Under perfect competition all inputs receive the value of their marginal product and profits are zero, which means that total revenue of the firm will equal total cost. The payments to the factors of production, then, exhaust the total revenues of the firm.

A production function homogeneous to a degree greater than one gives *increasing returns to scale* and decreasing average costs. This means that marginal costs must be less than average costs and that the marginal physical product of an input will be greater than the average product of that input. If inputs are purchased in competitive markets, the firm must pay each input the value of its marginal product. But if all inputs receive the value of their marginal products, the total revenues of the firm will be less than the payments to all of the inputs. This result can be demonstrated by approaching the issue from either a cost or an output point of view. If a firm experiencing decreasing average costs behaved competitively and sold its output at a price equal to marginal cost, it would operate at a loss; that is, total costs would exceed total revenues. Similarly, if the marginal physical products of inputs are greater than their average products, and if inputs receive payments equal to their marginal products, the payments to inputs will exceed total output and the firm will operate at a loss.

A production function homogeneous to a degree less than one gives decreasing returns to scale, or increasing average costs. Here marginal costs are greater than average costs, and the marginal physical product of an input will be less than the average product of that input. A firm behaving competitively will equate marginal cost to price and at that output will earn profits. This implies that when all factors receive the value of their marginal product, the payments to inputs will be less than total output. Under these circumstances total revenues exceed total costs and the firm earns profits.

Wicksell on Product Exhaustion

Knut Wicksell, a Swedish economist who made a number of important contributions to both macro- and microeconomic theory, was an early independent discoverer of the marginal productivity theory. He became interested in questions relating to Euler's theorem and product exhaustion and contributed more to solving them than any other economist of his time. In his earlier writing on the subject he had thought, like most other economists, of a given firm or industry as displaying either increasing, constant, or decreasing returns to scale. These categories seemed to be mutually exclusive. In 1902 Wicksell reached a quite different conclusion, namely, that a given firm could pass through all three phases of returns to scale. A firm expanding output would first experience increasing returns to scale but would sooner or later encounter decreasing returns to scale. At the level of output at which returns change from increasing to decreasing, constant returns to scale must occur. Wicksell was explicitly developing the concept of the long-run, U-shaped average cost curve for a firm, showing average costs decreasing, then reaching a minimum point, and finally increasing. Wicksell argued that it was not necessary that a firm's production function be homogeneous to the degree one for product exhaustion to occur. If firms are producing at the level of output that occurs at the minimum point of the long-run average cost curve and profits are zero, product exhaustion takes place. Wicksell reasoned that perfectly competitive markets will produce these results, because competition will result in each firm's producing at minimum cost and making zero profits. Thus, even though the production function of a firm would yield increasing, constant, and diminishing returns, competition will guarantee that in long-run equilibrium the firm is operating at the point on its production function at which constant returns exist, at which the function is homogeneous to the degree one, and at which average costs are a minimum.

Wicksell's solution to the problem of product exhaustion raised new and interesting theoretical issues, which economists pursued well into the twentieth century. Wicksell suggested some explanations for the shape of the long-run average cost curve, but these issues were not fully understood until the 1930s.

Ethical Implications of Marginal Productivity Theory

John Bates Clark (1847–1938) independently discovered and developed the ideas of both marginal utility and marginal productivity. His development of marginal utility theory was not as penetrating as that of Jevons, Walras, or Menger, but his contributions to the marginal productivity theory of distribution equaled those of the second generation of British and European economists. Clark acknowledged that his development of marginal productivity theory was in response to issues raised by the American social critic Henry George.[3] We saw in Chapter 5 that Henry George had concluded that the return to land was an unearned income and thus had questioned the social legitimacy of rent. George's assertions led Clark to attempt to identify the product resulting from individual factors of production and thus to marginal productivity theory. J. B. Clark's son, J. M. Clark, also became an important economist. In an article summarizing his father's contributions to economic theory and the intellectual and social forces that influenced the content of his father's ideas, the younger Clark maintained that J. B. Clark's ethical statements on marginal productivity "are oriented at Marx, and are best construed as an earnest, and not meticulously qualified, rebuttal of Marxian exploitation theory."[4] J. B. Clark's development of marginal productivity theory, therefore, might be explained as a reaction to the economic ideas of Henry George and Karl Marx.

An interest in ethical issues is clearly manifest in Clark's early writings, which were not as theoretically oriented as his contributions to marginal productivity theory. Yet his *Distribution of Wealth,* which contains the essence of his marginal productivity theory of distribution, also contains an extensive development of the desirable ethical results that flow from competitive markets. It is not necessary to develop Clark's contributions to marginal productivity theory in detail. The relevant point here is his conclusion that under perfectly competitive markets, each factor of production would receive a return equal to the value of its marginal product. This return measures the contribution of a factor both to the particular product being produced and to society. The return to capital is justified by the fact that capital is productive: the return is not robbery but honest, fair, and just. The return to land is, likewise, not an unearned income but a return to the productivity

[3] J. B. Clark, *The Distribution of Wealth* [1899] (New York: Kelley and Millman, 1956), pp. viii, 84–85.

[4] J. M. Clark, "J. M. Clark on J. B. Clark," in *The Development of Economic Thought,* ed. H. W. Spiegel (New York: Wiley, 1952), p. 610.

of land. The same applies to the return to labor. Clark's conclusion is that the distribution of income that results from perfectly competitive markets is an ethically correct distribution in that it rewards the factors of production according to their economic contributions to the social product. Theories of exploitation and unearned incomes are naive, he contended, because they fail to understand the working of market forces in an economy.

J. B. Clark's contributions to marginal analysis, particularly to marginal productivity theory, gained him worldwide recognition. It is fair to say that he was the first American economist to make important contributions to economic theory. Yet the ethical conclusions he drew from marginal productivity theory have attracted more critical attention than his contributions to positive theory. There may be some justice in this, in that Clark regarded his ethical conclusions as his most important contributions.

How much merit is there in his argument that competitive markets result in an ethically desirable distribution of income? The most important problem is its violation of Hume's Dictum: it draws an ethical implication from a nonethical analysis. What a person "should" earn may have little relation to what he or she does earn. Numerous other problems have been identified. For example, even given the assumption of perfectly competitive markets, there are no grounds for concluding that because each *factor* receives the value of its marginal product, each *individual* receives a return that measures his or her contribution to the economy and society. An individual's income will depend on the price of the factors he or she sells in the market and the quantity of factors sold. Individuals owning capital and land will receive incomes from these sources, but these payments represent the contribution of the factors, not the individuals.

Another difficulty with Clark's ethical conclusions is their reliance on perfectly competitive markets. Clark was aware of monopoly power in both firms and labor unions and tried to address its influence on the distribution of income and on his ethical conclusions. His particularly optimistic viewpoint led him to regard these deviations from competitive markets as quantitatively unimportant. It is interesting that one of his most brilliant undergraduate students, Thorstein Veblen, was to view the same economy and society as J. B. Clark and come to quite a different conclusion about their ethical outcome.

Marginal Productivity as a Theory of Employment

Although marginal productivity analysis was originally developed to explain the forces determining the prices of factors of production and the distribution of income, it was soon believed that the theory could also be applied to the forces determining the level of employment. In a partial equilibrium analytical framework, if the price of labor is increased, a firm will hire less labor until the value of the marginal product of labor is equal to the higher price of labor. Hiring less labor will result in an increase in the marginal physical product of labor and thus in the value of the marginal product of labor. At the industry level the price of labor will depend upon the demand for labor, which is derived from the value of the marginal product of labor and the supply of labor. If the price of labor in an industry is above an equilibrium level, the quantity of labor supplied will exceed the quantity of labor demanded—there will be a surplus of labor, or unemployment.

When marginal productivity analysts extended this theory to the entire economy, they concluded that unemployment exceeding frictional unemployment of 3 percent was caused by prevailing wages' being higher than at equilibrium. An excess supply of labor, like that of any other commodity, is explained by supply-and-demand analysis. Given the analysis and flexible wage rates, a market system will automatically correct the unemployment as wages fall. Unemployment is a manifestation of disequilibrium in labor markets; when labor markets return to equilibrium, the unemployment will be eliminated. On the basis of this application of marginal productivity theory to the economy, a number of policy conclusions have been drawn at various times: that wages should be kept flexible and that any impediments to flexible wages, such as union contracts or minimum-wage legislation, are undesirable; that unions and minimum-wage legislation could cause unemployment; that if a depression produced unemployment, institutional factors that render wages inflexible could prevent the market from automatically removing the unemployment by lowering wages.

The macro policy conclusion drawn from marginal productivity theory was that depressions and unemployment could be eliminated by permitting wages to fall. Although some economists were reluctant on social grounds to advocate lowering wages to remove unemployment and depressions, there is little doubt that orthodox theory came to these conclusions. In discussing this issue Alvin Hansen cites A. C. Pigou's writings of the 1920s, which described such a relationship between employment and wages. Hansen says that he cites "Pigou as the most eminent (and withal one of the most socially minded) representative of thinking generally current among economists in the twenties; innumerable references from a host of economists (including paragraphs from my own earlier writings) could easily be added by anyone who will take the trouble to do so."[5] These views, which flowed from marginal productivity theory, continued to be held by orthodox theorists until they were seriously criticized by J. M. Keynes in the mid-1930s. The Nobel Prize–winning economist J. R. Hicks devoted two chapters of his *Theory of Wages* (1932) to a discussion of wage regulation and unemployment. Hicks concluded that wages artificially set above competitive equilibrium wages either by union pressure or by legislation would result in unemployment and that "the unemployment must go on until the artificial wages are relaxed, or until competitive wages have risen to the artificial level."[6]

We can illustrate this reasoning by simple supply-and-demand analysis in Figure 9.3. The demand curve for labor, DD', is the value of the marginal product of labor. At a wage of W_1, the quantity of labor hired will be OQ_1. Firms will hire

[5] Alvin H. Hansen, *Business Cycles and National Income* (New York: Norton, 1951), p. 518, fn. 6.

[6] J. R. Hicks, *The Theory of Wages* (London: Macmillan, 1932), p. 181.

Figure 9.3   The Labor Market in Disequilibrium

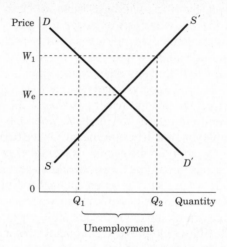

labor up to the point at which the wage paid is equal to the value of the marginal product of labor. At a wage of W_1 the quantity of labor supplied will be OQ_2. The excess supply of labor at a wage of W_1 is equal to Q_1Q_2 and is called unemployment. If markets are free to operate, wages will fall to an equilibrium wage, W_e, and the unemployment will be eliminated. Unemployment, therefore, is a result of (1) a temporary disequilibrium in labor markets, or (2) certain impediments that prevent wages from falling.

Marginal productivity theory coupled with the strong laissez faire market orientation of American economists led them to suggest that the best policy to alleviate the depression in the early 1930s was to keep the government out of the economy and let the market work to lower wages. Let us briefly examine Keynes's major criticism of marginal productivity theory as a theory of employment. The theory states that wages will equal the value of the marginal product of labor in competitive markets. The value of the marginal product of labor is the marginal physical product of labor multiplied by the price of the final good. Keynes pointed out that even though wages are a cost from the viewpoint of the firm, they are income from the viewpoint of the worker. Thus, whereas a cut in wage rates would lower costs for firms, it would also lower the income of labor. When labor incomes begin to fall, the demand for and the price of final goods would fall as well. This decrease in the price of final goods would result in a fall in the value of the marginal product of labor. The difficulty with the marginal productivity theory as a theory of employment is that it assumes that lowering wages will not lower the demand for final goods; in other words, that aggregate supply and aggregate demand are not interconnected. The theory concentrates on the cost side of wage reductions and ignores what Keynes called aggregate demand.

Marginal Productivity Theory Criticized

Almost from the time of its first formulation, marginal productivity theory was criticized; and some of this criticism has continued to the present. The early criticism included broad attacks on the general theory of marginal productivity, whether it was applied to labor, capital, or land, and specific discussion of the special problems arising when the theory was applied to the determination of profits and interest. We will discuss these special problems in the next section and look now at the most significant early criticism of marginal productivity theory, namely, that it is impossible to measure the marginal product of a factor of production.

The final output of a firm, industry, or the economy is the result of a joint effort of labor, land, and capital, and it is impossible, said the critics, to separate out the marginal products of the contributing factors. F. W. Taussig (1859–1940), a commanding figure in the early development of Harvard's economics department, asserts in his influential *Principles of Economics* that in a process using capital and labor "there is no separate product of the tool on the one hand and of the labor using the tool on the other. . . . We can disengage no concretely separable product of labor and capital."[7] A more popular version of this criticism is contained in George Bernard Shaw's delightful *Intelligent Woman's Guide to Socialism and Capitalism*. Shaw maintained that whereas it might be desirable to reward labor by giving to each what he or she produces, this is impossible: "When a farmer and his laborers sow and reap a field of wheat nobody on earth can say how much of the wheat each of them has grown."[8] Suppose, for another example, that a house is being constructed by carpenters (labor) using hammers (capital). If another carpenter is added, what is his marginal physical product? In any production process the addition of labor usually requires the simultaneous addition of capital, thereby creating a difficulty in separating the marginal product of the added labor from that of the added capital. Marshall's solution to this problem would be to measure the net product of labor by deducting the cost of the capital from the value of the marginal product of the additional labor and capital. J. B. Clark offered another solution, suggesting that the amount of capital be held constant but that its form be allowed to vary. However, because the form of capital could only vary over time, Clark's solution suggests a longer-run view of the problem of computing marginal products.

PROFITS AND INTEREST

Some of the early developers of marginal productivity theory, particularly Eugen Böhm-Bawerk, perceived that although marginal productivity analysis was a

---

[7] F. W. Taussig, *Principles of Economics,* 3rd ed. (New York: Macmillan, 1924), II, pp. 213–214.
[8] G. B. Shaw, *The Intelligent Woman's Guide to Socialism and Capitalism* (New York: Brentano's, 1928), p. 21.

satisfactory explanation of the return to labor and land, it failed to explain the returns known as profits and interest. In retrospect, we can see that the problems associated with explaining the nature and amount of profits and interest had not even manifested themselves prior to the development of marginal productivity analysis.

Classical economic theory had, for the most part, divided the factors of production into labor, land, and capital. The return to labor is wages; to land, rents; and to capital, profits. The term profits, as used by classical economists, includes what is today called profits and interest. Even those classical writers who developed theories of interest called their theories "profit theories." The failure to distinguish between profits and interest as returns is understandable, because the typical firm of the times combined the roles of the capitalist and the entrepreneur. The supplier of capital funds and the manager were one and the same, so no distinction was made between profits and interest. One of the accomplishments of the period we are studying was a recognition of the need to distinguish between the two.

Can we use marginal productivity theory to explain not only the wages of labor, the rent of land, and the interest on capital, but also the profits that flow to entrepreneurs? The writers of the time concluded that whereas marginal productivity theory could satisfactorily explain wages and rents, the problems peculiar to profits and interest required more sophisticated theories.

Profit Theory

Although the classical economists had applied the term *profits* indiscriminately to all the income of the capitalist-entrepreneur, they did recognize that this income was a payment containing at least three distinct elements: a payment for the use of capital, a payment to the entrepreneur for management services rendered, and a payment that compensated for the risks of business activity. Payments to the firm for the use of capital (assuming this payment involves no risk) fall under the modern classification of *interest,* which we will discuss in the next section. Can we identify entrepreneurship as a fourth factor of production, defining the marginal product of the entrepreneur as the measure of his or her contribution to the firm for management services and assumption of risk?

J. B. Clark was the most important early developer of marginal productivity theory to recognize that this solution is not satisfactory. The return to the entrepreneur as a manager is not profit, but a wage. Profit—or, to be more exact, *pure profit*—must be defined as a residual remaining after all the inputs used by a firm are paid a price equal to their opportunity cost. Perfectly competitive markets in long-run equilibrium result in all factors' receiving the value of their marginal product, which is also equal to their opportunity cost. Assuming a homogeneous production function, these payments are costs of the firm and when subtracted from total revenues yield a zero rate of profit. The existence of profit must then be explained as a consequence either of competitive markets' not being in long-run equilibrium or of actual markets' not being perfectly competitive.

Long-run competitive equilibrium is, of course, a theoretical construct to which no market ever conforms. Let us keep the competitive assumption, however, while analyzing the emergence of profit in a market or an economy not in long-run equilibrium. When businesses buy inputs to produce an output, they assume risks. The final price of the output must be estimated, and the price of and payments to the inputs become contractual obligations. If the total revenues of the firm exceed the payments to the inputs, profits accrue; if revenues are less than payments, losses occur. Profits in perfectly competitive markets might, then, be explained as the result of disequilibrium occurring while the economy moves to a new position of long-run equilibrium.

An explanation of profits as temporary income resulting from dynamic changes in the economy was suggested by J. B. Clark, Alfred Marshall, and J. A. Schumpeter. Assume that an economy is in long-run equilibrium with all factors receiving a return equal to their opportunity cost and that the revenues of a typical firm are equal to its costs. A change in preferences of consumers or a change in technology will lead to profits in some industries. These profits will be eliminated, however, by competitive forces as capital moves to those markets having above-normal rates of return. Thus, profit is not a return to a factor of production but a windfall associated with dynamic elements in an economy.

F. H. Knight (1885–1972) significantly integrated and extended prior theories of profit by combining in one theory the factors of risk, managerial ability, and economic change. In *Risk, Uncertainty, and Profit* Knight distinguished between risks businesses take that can be insured against and risks for which no insurance is available.[9] A firm, for example, may lose its plant through fire, but actuarial knowledge permits this risk to be covered by insurance. The insurance premium becomes a part of the firm's costs. This kind of risk is therefore not a source of profit. Profits exist because there are uncertainties in the market that are not insurable, arising from dynamic changes in the market. However, if we drop the assumption of perfect competition, profits may arise for a number of reasons, the most important being monopoly or monopsony power.

Capital and Interest Theory

With the development of marginal productivity theory, economists began to distinguish more carefully between profits and interest. This has permitted the development of a generally accepted theory of profit; however, capital and interest theory has remained controversial to the present day. Robert M. Solow wrote that "when a theoretical question remains debatable after 80 years there is a presumption that the question is badly posed—or very deep indeed."[10] C. E. Ferguson has suggested several reasons for the unsettled nature of capital theory:

[9] F. H. Knight, *Risk, Uncertainty, and Profit* (Boston: Houghton Mifflin, 1921).
[10] Robert M. Solow, *Capital Theory and the Rate of Return* (Amsterdam: North-Holland, 1963), p. 10.

Everyone knows, or has strongly suspected, that capital theory is difficult. There is a superficial reason for this in that so much of the literature of capital theory has been mired in polemics and semantics. There is a more fundamental reason, however. Capital theory necessarily involves time; and time involves expectations and uncertainty, although we generally abstract from them by assuming a stationary state or a golden-age growth path.[11]

We shall first survey the development of the theory of capital and interest since 1890. One set of writers, including Schumpeter, Fisher, and Knight, made a broad philosophical inquiry into the nature of capital and the reasons for the *existence* of interest. Another set of writers, touching only superficially on the reasons for the existence of interest, concentrated on explaining the economic forces determining the *rate* of interest. Theories of the forces determining the rate of interest can be classified as nonmonetary, monetary, and neo-Keynesian, the last being a synthesis of the other two approaches in a model first suggested by J. R. Hicks. The nonmonetary theories of interest concentrate on long-run real forces that fix the rate of interest; they are therefore in the classical tradition. Nonmonetary theories persisted from the end of the mercantilist period until the 1930s. Monetary theories of the rate of interest include the loanable funds theory and the liquidity preference theory. The three most important writers on interest theory from 1890 to the 1930s were Böhm-Bawerk, Knight, and Fisher, whose theories we examine in this chapter.

The mercantilists emphasized the role of money in the economy and consequently developed monetary theories of interest. They maintained that increases in the quantity of money not only would raise the general level of prices and lower the value of money but also would lower the general level of interest rates. Some writers on interest theory during the latter part of the mercantilist era developed more penetrating analyses. Although Richard Cantillon presented a nonmonetary theory of interest, he also pointed out that increases in the quantity of money could lead to either an increase or decrease in interest rates. If the increase in the money supply went first to savers, the interest rate would fall. But if it went to spenders, the interest rate would rise, because the increased spending would cause increased investments by businessmen and a consequent increase in the demand for loanable funds.

Classical theory, with its focus on the long-run real forces that determine the wealth of nations, developed nonmonetary, or real, theories of interest. The classical economists maintained that the rate of interest depends on the rate of return on investment spending. Monetary forces may in the short run alter the rate of interest, but in the long run it is the productivity of capital, a real force, that fixes interest rates. Ricardo put it most succinctly when he said that the interest rate depends

[11] C. E. Ferguson, "The Current State of Capital Theory: A Tale of Two Paradigms," *Southern Economic Journal*, 39 (October 1972), p. 173.

on the rate of profits which can be made by the employment of capital, and which is totally independent of the quantity, or of the value of money. Whether a Bank lent one million, ten million, or a hundred million, they would not permanently alter the market rate of interest, they would alter only the value of the money they had thus issued.[12]

We could quote other passages from Ricardo indicating that he did recognize that the rate of interest is not "totally independent" of the quantity of money. The point is that the classical economists' focus on long-run forces in the economy led them to de-emphasize monetary forces because these had only short-run influences on the rate of interest and could not change the productivity of capital, which was the real force fixing interest rates in the long run. In broad perspective there were some 250 years, from 1500 to 1750, when monetary theories of interest were in vogue; then 180 years, from 1750 to 1930, when nonmonetary theories were advanced by the orthodox theorists. Two new monetary theories of interest emerged during the 1930s, the liquidity preference and loanable funds theories, and with them came a realization that a theory of interest developed in a general equilibrium framework must include both monetary and real forces.

The Problem of Interest

The development of economic theory shows that a new theory that answers an old question often raises new questions. We have already seen that the development of marginal productivity analysis shattered the old classical theory of distribution. The classical theory had divided the population into workers, capitalists, and landlords; and it had explained the payments to these factors as wages, profits, and rents. Because the classical theory of distribution was a residual theory, the problem of product exhaustion—determining whether the payments to the factors equaled the amount of the total product—was not a theoretical issue. It was the marginal productivity theory that first raised the new issue. The marginalists concluded that given perfectly competitive markets, the sum of the value of the marginal products would equal the total product in long-run equilibrium. They didn't worry that this conclusion required linear homogeneous production functions. If that assumption was needed, they would simply assume it. The concept of product exhaustion raised new and complex issues concerning interest and capital. We turn now to an explanation of these issues, which we will call collectively the problem of interest, before examining the answers offered by subsequent theorists.

Under long-run equilibrium in perfectly competitive markets, all the revenues from the sale of final products will be received by the factors of production. This

---

[12] David Ricardo, *On the Principle of Political Economy and Taxation*, in *The Works and Correspondence of David Ricardo*, eds. Piero Sraffa and M. H. Dobb, I (Cambridge: Cambridge University Press, 1953), pp. 363–364.

conclusion of marginal productivity theory raised the following question: how are we to explain the return to capital called interest? Capital is a produced good made with labor and land previously applied, whereas labor and land are original factors of production. The marginal productivity theory holds that the return to capital must exactly equal the value of the labor and land used to create the capital. If this is true, why does capital receive a further return in the form of interest? In other words, why is the payment to capital more than is necessary to pay for the labor and land used to produce capital? Capital appears to be unique among the factors of production in creating a surplus value that flows to its owner in perpetuity.

An obvious answer would be that capital is productive, and that this accounts for the existence of interest. This answer, however, is not satisfactory. Capital is productive in that labor and land used with capital produce a greater output. But the marginal productivity theory holds that the productivity of capital results in a higher return to the labor and land used to produce the capital, which means that there could be no net return to capital. The return to capital in long-run equilibrium must be exactly equal to the cost of producing the capital, yet in the real world we observe that interest income is constantly flowing to the owner of capital. The issue is complicated still further by the fact that present capital is the product of past labor, land, and capital. The marginal productivity theory holds that the market will impute the value of the productivity of present capital to the factors of production used to produce it. If we go back through the production process, using this procedure, we will be left with only the original factors of production, labor and land. To clarify the problem of interest, let us examine another factor of production, labor. Labor is productive, but the flow of income to labor, or wages, measures and is equal to its productivity. There is no net return to labor as there appears to be to capital. The problem of interest was recognized by Böhm-Bawerk but was given its most lucid exposition by Schumpeter in Chapter 5 of his *Theory of Economic Development,* which was first published in German in 1912.

How can we explain the source, the basis, and the persistence of *interest*? In the course of examining some of the issues concerning profits, we found that in long-run equilibrium, profits disappear and become zero. Interest, however, is observed to persist even in long-run equilibrium. Schumpeter not only succinctly posed the problem of interest but also suggested a framework within which to examine possible answers. Three possible solutions to the problem of interest exist. One is that there are not two but three original factors of production and that interest is a return to the third factor. A second is that marginal productivity theory is incorrect in holding that in long-run competitive equilibrium, revenues from the sale of final goods will exactly equal the flow of payments to the factors of production. A third solution is that marginal productivity theory is a theory of competitive, static markets; because the real economy is neither competitive nor static, noncompetitive or dynamic elements in the economy can produce a positive rate of interest. So much for the problem of interest. Let us now examine some of the solutions offered during the period from 1890 to 1930.

Böhm-Bawerk's Theory of Interest

Early in his career, Eugen Böhm-Bawerk, a follower of Menger, was drawn to the problem of capital and interest theory. There were two reasons for this. First, he recognized the existence of the problem of interest and understood the theoretical issues involved. Second, like Menger and Austrian economists in general, Böhm-Bawerk was disturbed by the Marxist-socialist attacks that condemned profits and interest as forms of capitalistic exploitation. Menger manifested these same concerns in his *Principles:* "One of the strangest questions ever made the subject of scientific debate is whether rent and interest are justified from an ethical point of view or whether they are 'immoral.' . . . But it seems to me that the question of the legal or moral character of these facts is beyond the sphere of our science."[13]

Böhm-Bawerk's *Capital and Interest, a Critical History of Economical Theory,* published in German in 1884, critically evaluated previous theories of interest. He was unmerciful in his criticism of these earlier theories and voiced particularly strong views about the exploitation theory of the socialists, which, he said, "is not only incorrect, but in theoretical value, even takes one of the lowest places among the representatives of some of the other theories, I scarcely think that anywhere else are to be found together so great a number of the worst fallacies—wanton, unproved assumption, self-contradiction, and blindness to facts."[14]

In 1888 Böhm-Bawerk offered his own ideas on capital and interest theory in *The Positive Theory of Capital:* "Present goods are, as a rule, worth more than future goods of a like kind and number. This proposition is the kernel and center of the interest theory which I have to present."[15] Given the existence of a positive rate of interest, the statement is clearly correct. Under these circumstances an individual would prefer $1 today as against $1 a year from now, because the $1 received today could be lent and thus be worth more in the future. However, Böhm-Bawerk's statement does not immediately explain the reason for the existence of interest, although it suggests that the fundamental reason for the existence of interest is that present goods are worth more than an equal amount of future goods.

Böhm-Bawerk's examination of previous theories of interest in *Capital and Interest* led him to the conclusion that no one had yet explained the causes of interest. He maintained that the causes of interest are to be found not in the institutional structure of the society but in technological and economic considerations that are independent of social forms. In particular, he wanted to establish that the exploitation theories of interest advanced by Marx and other socialists were incorrect and that the phenomenon of interest would exist even in a socialist

---

[13] Carl Menger, *Principles of Economics* (Glencoe, Ill.: Free Press), p. 173.

[14] Eugen Böhm-Bawerk, *Capital and Interest,* trans. William Smart (New York: Brentano's, 1922), pp. 390–391.

[15] Eugen Böhm-Bawerk, *The Positive Theory of Capital* [1888], trans. William Smart (London: Macmillan, 1891), p. 237.

society, because even in such a society present goods would be worth more than an equal amount of future goods.

Böhm-Bawerk offered three reasons for the higher value of present goods. "The first great cause of difference in value between present and future goods consists in the different circumstances of want and provision in the present and future."[16] In support of this first reason, he gave the following argument. Because the value of goods depends upon marginal utility, and because marginal utility decreases as the quantity of goods increases, present goods are worth more than future goods for individuals who expect a larger flow of income and goods in the future. Such individuals might include those who are urgently in need of present goods because of illness, a loss from bad harvests or fire, and so forth. But the problem with these examples, which Böhm-Bawerk recognized and attempted to solve, is that many individuals might equally well prefer future to present goods because of "different circumstances of want and provision in the present and future." Many wage earners expect their income flow to be less in the future than at present and would therefore find the marginal utility of present income to be less than that of future income. Böhm-Bawerk attempted to meet this difficulty by suggesting that these individuals who expect declining income will hold money, because it is durable and nearly costless to store. If they hold money and do not spend their higher present income on goods, the marginal utility of present goods is not less than that of future goods.

The examples Böhm-Bawerk used to illustrate his first reason for the existence of interest led him into some implications and contradictions of which he was not aware. If individuals want to use money as a store of value in order to transfer purchases of goods from the present to the future, then a demand for money exists that is separate from its use as a medium of exchange. This proposition contradicts the orthodox view persisting from Smith to Keynes that money was only a medium of exchange. We might conclude from Böhm-Bawerk's discussion of these issues that an economy composed largely of wage earners who expect declining future incomes and therefore prefer future to present goods would have a positive rate of interest because of the demand for money and the scarcity of its supply.

The second reason for placing a higher value on present goods is that "we systematically underestimate future wants, and the goods which are to satisfy them."[17] Böhm-Bawerk supported this statement by noting a general lack of imagination and willpower in individuals, as well as an uncertainty regarding the length of life. This second reason threatens the entire theoretical structure of orthodox economic theory. Either humans are rational and calculating or they are not. It is hard to justify assuming the existence of an economic man for some purposes and disclaim it for others. Böhm-Bawerk recognized this difficulty by choosing the activities of savages and children to illustrate the underestimation of future wants: "How many an Indian tribe, with careless greed, has sold the land of its fathers, the source of its maintenance, to the palefaces for a couple of casks

[16] *Ibid.*, p. 249.
[17] *Ibid.*, p. 253.

of 'firewater'!"[18] This is certainly a curious view of American history and does not support the existence of interest. Uncertainty about the length of life is also not a strong argument for the preference of present over future goods, as few individuals would plan to consume all of their savings before death. Individuals may well want to leave an inheritance for their children, making future goods more desirable than present goods. And even if they did not, financial instruments such as death-related annuities (which allow people to spend all their wealth and still have an assured income until they die) can essentially eliminate the uncertainty factor.

Böhm-Bawerk was arguing that for psychological reasons individuals will prefer present to future goods. Present goods command a premium, or agio, over future goods that can be measured by the interest rate individuals are willing to pay for funds that permit them to buy present goods. Observe that these first two arguments apply only to the market for consumer loans.

Böhm-Bawerk's third explanation for the existence of interest, however, addresses the market for producer loans. It states that interest exists because of the technical superiority of present goods over future goods. Böhm-Bawerk's explanation is not completely clear, and J. B. Clark and Irving Fisher were quick to point out its difficulties.

In his criticisms of previous theories of interest, Böhm-Bawerk had rejected the idea that interest is a payment for the productivity of capital. He acknowledged that capital is productive but perceived that the marginal productivity theory of distribution, which holds that the higher productivity of capital would result in a higher payment to the factors of production used to produce capital, precludes the possibility of a net return to capital because of its productivity. The assertion that present goods are technically superior to future goods is an attempt to explain why capital goods earn interest. To understand what Böhm-Bawerk meant by the technical superiority of present goods, we must examine his notion of the roundabout method of production.

According to Böhm-Bawerk, two methods can be used to produce final goods: a direct method and a roundabout, or capitalistic, method. The direct method involves no capital goods; an example would be catching fish by hand. The roundabout method is capitalistic in that it uses capital goods and requires time. Our fisherman could spend time to make a net and then fish. The time for the production process could be further lengthened if the fisherman built a boat and made a net. The direct method takes less time, but it is less productive than a roundabout method. The roundabout method is more productive, but it requires more time. Böhm-Bawerk then asserted that the law of diminishing returns applies to roundabout production processes. On the whole, it may be said that not only are the first steps more productive, but every lengthening of the roundabout process is accompanied by a further increase in the technical result; however, as the process is lengthened the amount of the product, as a rule, increases in a smaller proportion.

[18] *Ibid.*

This proposition is based on experience, and only on experience.[19] Böhm-Bawerk illustrated the correspondence of diminishing returns to the length of the production process with the data given in Table 9.2.[20] A unit of labor in a production process requiring one year will yield 100 units of final product. If the production process is lengthened (in our example, by making a net), the yield of final product that emerges at the end of two years is 200 units; but as the production process is lengthened and the roundaboutness increases, the flow of final product increases at a decreasing rate. The technical superiority of present over future goods is disclosed by examining the columns for This Year and Next Year in the table. A unit of labor applied today will yield 280 units of final product three years from the present, but if that unit of labor is not applied until next year, the yield of final product three years from the present is only 200 units.

Böhm-Bawerk's concept of the technical superiority of present over future goods raised a number of issues that were extensively discussed in the literature of the time, particularly in his controversies with J. B. Clark and Irving Fisher. These issues were re-examined as late as the 1930s in a controversy involving F. H. Knight and Nicholas Kaldor. A number of the minor issues related to this topic are discussed in the suggested readings for this chapter.

Böhm-Bawerk maintained that the third reason for the existence of interest was independent from his first two reasons. But Irving Fisher argued correctly that the greater productivity of roundabout methods would not result in a positive rate of interest in the absence of Böhm-Bawerk's first two reasons. The first two reasons stated in essence that for psychological reasons individuals prefer present over future goods. Let us suppose that individuals do not prefer present over future goods and examine the third reason by itself. Given the assumption that capital is productive and that lengthening the productive process will increase the flow of final goods, in the absence of a time preference, a society would want to maximize the quantity of final goods emerging from the productive process regardless of the date of their emergence. If society were indifferent to the time at which it consumed final goods, the technical superiority of present goods would not result in indi-

Table 9.2 Roundaboutness and Diminishing Returns

Years from Present to Final Product	Units of Product for Labor Applied	
	This Year	Next Year
1	100	—
2	200	100
3	280	200
4	350	280
5	400	350

[19] *Ibid.*, p. 84.
[20] *Ibid.*, p. 262.

viduals' being willing to pay interest to consume goods today rather than in the future. Böhm-Bawerk formulated all the necessary elements for a consistent theory of interest but incorrectly concluded that the productivity of capital separate and apart from time preference would result in a positive rate of interest. Irving Fisher took Böhm-Bawerk's seminal but confused notions, discarded some of the nonessential elements, and articulated the essential points of the currently accepted theory of interest.

Fisher on Interest

Although Irving Fisher adopted many of the basic concepts of Böhm-Bawerk's theory of interest, his approach represents a distinct break with Böhm-Bawerk. Classical theory had proceeded on the basis that reasonably sharp distinctions could be made between the factors of production and that the returns to these factors could be distinguished as wages, rent, interest, and profits. Böhm-Bawerk continued in this tradition; his discussion of interest theory is therefore predicated on the belief that the return to capital is interest and that a special theory is needed to explain interest as opposed to wages and rent. Fisher first presented his views in his work *The Rate of Interest* (1907), and later in a considerably revised and polished version titled *The Theory of Interest* (1930).

Fisher objected to the prevailing manner of classifying incomes as wages, rent, profits, and interest. He saw interest not as a share of income received by capital but as a manner of examining income flows of every kind. All productive agents yield flows of income over time. If these flows of income are discounted at the current rate of interest, their capitalized value is obtained. An owner of a productive agent computes the interest return on that agent by comparing its capitalized value with the flow of income. Some examples will clarify Fisher's viewpoint. Land is said to receive a return called rent; yet if we compare the flow of income called rent with the capitalized value of the land, the return is interest. As Fisher said, "Rent and interest are merely two ways of measuring the same income."[21] Frank Knight agreed with this perspective on interest theory and expounded on it throughout his writings on the subject. Knight claimed that "only historical accident or 'psychology' can explain the fact that 'interest' and 'rent' have been viewed as coming from different sources, specifically natural agents and capital goods."[22] The return to labor that has historically been called wages can also be looked upon as interest. An investment in vocational training will increase a worker's future income flow. Thus, the productive agent that is usually called labor can be viewed as capital, with interest being the rate at which the income stream must be discounted to equate it to the cost of training. From this perspective Fisher

---

[21] Irving Fisher, *The Theory of Interest* [1930] (New York: Kelley and Millman, 1954), p. 331.
[22] Frank Knight, "Capital and Interest," in *Readings in the Theory of Income Distribution* (Philadelphia: Blakiston, 1949), pp. 391–392.

concluded that "interest is not a part, but the whole, of income."[23] Fisher discarded Böhm-Bawerk's classification of factors and his entire concept of the period of production, contending that interest is produced by individuals adjusting their income flows in the marketplace. The rate of interest measures the price individuals will pay to receive income now rather than in the future. The owner of any productive agent always has the option to alter the flow of income. Present consumption expenditures may be reduced in order to buy or build machinery that will increase future income flows or to invest in the training required for a future high-paying job.

Two kinds of forces will determine interest rates in a market economy: subjective forces, which reflect the preferences of individuals for present over future goods or income; and objective forces, which depend upon the available investment opportunities and the productivity of the factors used to produce final goods. Individuals can change their income flows by borrowing, lending, investing, or disinvesting. Their actions will depend upon their time preferences, the rates of return available on different investments, and the rate of interest in the market. Böhm-Bawerk believed that the productivity of capital alone, what he called the technical superiority of present goods, could account for the existence of interest. Fisher claimed that both the productivity of capital and individual time preferences are necessary to explain the existence of interest. In other words, the productivity of capital will result in a demand for income to be deferred from current consumption to future consumption; but unless individuals prefer present to future goods, no positive rate of interest will prevail.

Although Fisher's exposition of his interest theory introduces indifference curve analysis when it is applied to simple cases, and mathematics when it is applied to a number of individuals and a number of time periods, we can understand the essence of his approach by using the more conventional supply-and-demand analysis. Individuals can alter their income flows by saving (investing) or by dissaving (borrowing). The supply of savings is a function of the interest rate: at higher rates of interest, the quantity of savings will increase. An individual will have a preference between present and future income and will save or disinvest until his or her marginal rate of time preference between future and present income is equal to the rate of interest. The demand curve for investment is also a function of the interest rate; and at lower rates of interest, the quantity demanded will increase. The expected rate of profit on investment Fisher called the marginal rate of return over cost; this is analogous to Keynes's concept of the marginal efficiency of capital. By saving and dissaving, individuals can alter their income flows; the equilibrium, or optimum, position for an individual would require that the marginal rate of return over cost be equal to the rate of interest. Market equilibrium is achieved when the quantity of funds borrowers want to borrow equals the quantity of funds lenders want to lend. Interest rates will change until this occurs. For example, if at the existing rate of interest, desires to lend exceed desires to borrow, the rate will fall. In long-run equilibrium the action of individuals in altering their

[23] Fisher, *Theory,* p. 332.

income flows will result in the rate of interest equaling the marginal rate of time preference and the marginal rate of return over cost. Fisher's position, which is actually more sophisticated than we have shown in our summary, represented an important advance over previously existing notions concerning the nature of interest and the forces determining the rate of interest.

The Problem of Interest: A Summary

Around the turn of the century, orthodox economists began to apply marginal analysis to the pricing of the factors of production and to a theory of distribution. The marginal productivity theory raised the issue of product exhaustion in concluding that under perfectly competitive markets, the sum of the marginal products of the factors would exhaust the total product. This raised serious theoretical questions with respect to the return on capital. Capital appeared to receive a return in the form of interest in perpetuity; but if the value of the final product was completely absorbed by the factors of production, there would be nothing left to provide an interest return on capital. The value of the product of a capital good would flow backward into higher values paid to the factors of production used to produce the capital good.

Böhm-Bawerk's and Fisher's theories of interest resolve this apparent contradiction, accounting for the existence of interest in long-run competitive equilibrium by the fact that individuals prefer present goods to an equal amount of future goods. Because of this time preference, the payment made today to a factor of production will be less than the value of the final goods produced tomorrow. Factors of production will receive the discounted values of their marginal products; the difference between these discounted values and the value of the marginal product when the final goods are produced will be interest.

SUMMARY

The 1890s witnessed important new developments in microeconomic theory. Although the early marginalists had emphasized the differences in content between their views and those of classical orthodoxy, economists gradually realized that the important difference was in their method; that is, in their use of marginalism and abstract model building. The first generation of marginal writers had applied their technique almost exclusively to the demand side and the household and had developed few theoretical constructs to explain supply, the prices of factors of production, the distribution of income, and the special problems associated with interest and profits. But the new technique of examining the economic forces at work at the margin was employed to derive demand curves for factors of production and to indicate the optimum way for firms to hire several factors. The marginal productivity theory of distribution was developed, raising new and interesting theoretical issues. Because the classical economists had used a residual theory of distribution, the sum of the payments to the factors had necessarily been equal to the total product. The new theory held that each factor received its marginal product, thereby raising the issue of product exhaustion. The mathematical properties that production functions must have to cause product exhaustion were discovered, and it was argued that perfectly competitive markets in long-run equilibrium satisfied these prerequisites. But this solution led to other problems, such as the economic forces determining the long-run average cost curves of firms and the compatibility of constant returns to scale with competition.

J. B. Clark tried to draw ethical conclusions from the marginal productivity theory. Others used it to explain depressions. It was criticized on a number of grounds, the most important being that it was impossible to determine the marginal product of cooperating factors. Economists soon recognized that profits and interest were returns that required special study. A number of theories of profits were offered, all of which essentially concluded that profits arise either because of monopoly power or because of temporary disequilibria in perfectly competitive markets. The classical tradition of explaining interest as a nonmonetary phenomenon continued, but individual time preferences were acknowledged as a subjective cause of interest in addition to the classical objective cause, the productivity of capital. As a result, interest theory could be fitted into the basic supply-and-demand framework that was emerging during the period. After we have examined Marshallian economics in Chapter 11, we shall be able to summarize and evaluate the relative merits of the marginal utility school's emphasis on demand, the classical emphasis on supply, and Marshall's attempt to deal with these issues.

Key Terms

principle of diminishing returns	returns to scale
production functions	constant returns to scale
average product	decreasing returns to scale
marginal product	increasing returns to scale
value of the marginal product	profits
product exhaustion	interest
homogeneous to the degree one	pure profit

Questions for Review, Discussion, and Research

1. The classical theory of distribution is not concerned with the issue of product exhaustion, as is the marginal productivity theory of distribution. Explain.
2. Write an essay in which you explain the distribution of income in the United States, using marginal productivity theory. What are some of the weaknesses of using marginal productivity theory to explain the distribution of income in the United States?
3. Why did J. B. Clark maintain that perfectly competitive markets would give a just and fair distribution of income?
4. What were the errors in J. B. Clark's argument that an ethically ideal distribution of income would result from competitive markets?

5. Discuss the problems of any argument's trying to ethically justify a given distribution of income.
6. Explain the role of marginal productivity concepts in arguments that minimum wage legislation causes unemployment.
7. Explain why marginal productivity theory cannot be used to explain profits.
8. Write an essay in which you examine the role of risk and dynamic economic change in explaining profits.
9. The rate of interest depends upon supply and demand. Explain the forces that are behind supply and demand.
10. How could you determine the rate of return (interest) on your college education?
11. That absent-minded professor is back with another job for you. This time, she's doing an article on John Bates Clark's theory of distribution. As is her way, she has jotted down the following quotation:

> . . . moreover, we need a knowledge of three laws, of which the first is one that we may term the law of the varying efficiency of consumers' wealth, which is the basis of natural value; the second is the law of the varying efficiency of producers' wealth, which is the basis of natural interest; and the third is the law of varying efficiency of labor, which is at the bottom of natural wages. These are among the universal truths of economic science.

As usual, she does not remember where she found the quotation. Your assignment is to find the full bibliographic citation.

Suggested Readings

Allen, William R. "Irving Fisher, F.D.R., and the Great Depression." *History of Political Economy,* 9 (Winter 1977).

Böhm-Bawerk, Eugen. *The Positive Theory of Capital,* trans. William Smart. London: Macmillan, 1891.

Clark, John Bates. *The Distribution of Wealth.* New York: Kelley and Millman, 1956.

Conrad, J. W. *An Introduction to the Theory of Interest.* Berkeley: University of California Press, 1959.

Hutchison, T. W. *A Review of Economic Doctrine, 1870–1929.* Oxford: Clarendon Press, 1953.

Knight, Frank H. *Risk, Uncertainty, and Profit.* Boston: Houghton Mifflin, 1921.

Robertson, Dennis H. "Wage-Grumbles." In *Readings in the Theory of Income Distribution.* Philadelphia: Blakiston, 1949.

Schumpeter, Joseph A. *The Theory of Economic Development.* Cambridge, Mass.: Harvard University Press, 1955.

Stigler, George J. *Production and Distribution Theories.* New York: Macmillan, 1941.

Weston, J. Fred. "The Profit Concept and Theory: A Restatement." *Journal of Political Economy,* 62 (April 1954).

10 | Walras and General Equilibrium Theory

"If one wants to harvest quickly, one must plant carrots and salads; if one has the ambition to plant oaks, one must have the sense to tell oneself: my grandchildren will owe me this shade."

—Léon Walras

WALRAS'S GENERAL EQUILIBRIUM SYSTEM

In Chapter 8 we introduced Jevons, Menger, and Walras, who led the marginalist fight against the classical economists. In Chapter 9 we saw how the marginalist analysis was extended to factor markets. In this chapter we consider one of the two ways in which the supply side and demand side were integrated. In doing so we look more closely at the contribution of one of the originators of marginal analysis, Léon Walras.

Walras's use of marginal analysis was only a part of his contribution to modern economics. His work on marginalism was in many ways more sophisticated than that of Jevons and Menger, but because it was in French it did not have the same impact on their fellow economists. We devote an entire chapter to Walras because of his general equilibrium theory. That work has had an enormous impact on the economics profession, and it places him with Marshall as a candidate for father of one of the two branches of modern neoclassical economics.

What Is General Equilibrium Theory?

General equilibrium theory is an analysis of the economy in which all sectors are considered simultaneously. Thus, one considers both the direct and the indirect effects of any shock to the system, and one considers the cross market effects simultaneously with the direct effects. This interrelationship of the sectors of the economy is relatively simple to conceptualize, but it is an enormously complicated

266

idea to put down formally. Walras's contribution was to model the general equilibrium system in a formal manner.

Early Precursors of General Equilibrium Theory

Because general equilibrium is relatively easy to conceptualize, it shouldn't be surprising that it was not a new idea in 1874 when Walras published *Elements of Pure Economics*. Earlier writers had a clear vision of an economy consisting of many interconnected parts. For example, Quesnay had given this vision form in his economic table, which traced the flow of annual production among the various sectors of the economy. Similarly, in vivid descriptions of market processes Adam Smith showed deep insight into the relationships among the various parts of the economy. But although they explained the interconnection, they did not formally model it.

In 1838, A. Cournot (1801–1877) made an enormous advance in formalizing the interrelatedness of the economy while analyzing certain microeconomic problems. He was able to express some of the problems of the theory of the firm in mathematical form and used calculus to prove that profits are maximized when marginal cost is equal to marginal revenue. In doing so he did for the theory of the firm what Jevons and Menger did for choice theory: he formulated it in marginal terms. In addition, Cournot went beyond Jevons and Menger, whose heuristic and arithmetical expositions had limited their insights. Cournot's abstract mathematical orientation assisted him considerably in comprehending relationships within the economy and helped him to anticipate Walras. Cournot correctly concluded that "for a complete and rigorous solution of the problems relative to some parts of the economic system, it [is] indispensable to take the entire system into consideration."[1]

Cournot felt, however, that mathematical analysis was not sufficiently developed to permit the formulation of a general equilibrium model. J. H. von Thünen (1783–1850) also applied calculus to the solution of problems in economic theory; and as in the case of Cournot, this mathematical orientation led him to see the possibility of presenting a general equilibrium model as a system of simultaneous equations. Perhaps due to the fact that they were better mathematicians than Walras (Walras had not been accepted into the prestigious École Polytechnique in France because he failed the mathematics section of the entrance exam, whereas Cournot was considered a brilliant mathematician), Cournot and von Thünen did not attempt to address the complicated interrelationships of general equilibrium theory because of the many assumptions that were required to make the problem tractable and the inability to measure the concepts.

For whatever reason, Walras forged ahead where others feared to tread; so it was Léon Walras who was first able to give the general equilibrium vision clarity and precision by formulating a model of an economy through the use of mathematical

---

[1] Antoine Augustin Cournot, *Researches into the Mathematical Principles of the Theory of Wealth,* trans. Nathaniel T. Bacon (New York: Macmillan, 1897), p. 127.

notation. For this accomplishment he is justly praised as an important predecessor of modern economic theory, with its heavy emphasis on abstract model building and the use of mathematics.

We will describe a Walrasian model in words and discuss some of the theoretical issues it raises, and then we will present a mathematical model to give the mathematically untrained reader some idea of the highly abstract nature of Walrasian models. Before we do that, however, it is helpful to consider the difference between a general and a partial equilibrium model.

Partial and General Equilibrium Analysis

By their very essence, models and theories assume that certain elements are held constant so that they will not influence the behavior of the variables in the model. In the physical sciences, where the laboratory method has proved so fruitful, the researcher conducts repeated experiments in which all variables except two are held constant. One variable—for example, the heat applied to a mass of water—is permitted to vary, and the effect on the other variable is observed. If the water is observed to boil at 212 degrees Fahrenheit in repeated experiments, we conclude that with certain factors held constant—in this case constant pressure would be crucial—water boils at that temperature. The Latin phrase *ceteris paribus* is a shorthand expression used by economists to express the fact that all other factors are assumed to be held constant when statements are made about the action of an independent variable upon a dependent variable. *Ceteris paribus* means "other things being equal."

Economists distinguish between partial and general equilibrium models in terms of the degree of abstraction in the model. More factors are assumed to be held constant in partial analysis than in general equilibrium analysis. *Partial equilibrium analysis* allows only a small number of variables to vary; all else is assumed constant. General equilibrium analysis allows many more variables to change. It does not allow all variables to vary, and thus to influence the model, however, but only those regarded as within the scope of economics. General equilibrium models, for example, assume as given the tastes or preferences of individuals, the technology available for producing goods, and the institutional structure of the economy and society. Because the scope of economics as a social science has historically been limited by orthodox theory to variables that appear to be quantifiable, a mathematical general equilibrium model appears feasible.

Most partial equilibrium models, following the tradition of Alfred Marshall, limit themselves to the analysis of a particular household, firm, or industry. Suppose we want to analyze the influence on beef prices of a reduction in costs in the beef industry. Using the partial equilibrium approach, we would start with the industry in assumed equilibrium, disturb the equilibrium by making the cost reduction, and then deduce the new position of equilibrium. During this analysis, all other forces in the economy are assumed to be fixed and to have no influence on the beef industry. The reduction in costs in the beef industry would result in the supply of beef increasing and the price of beef falling to a new equilibrium level.

Suppose we make our model less restrictive and include in the analysis both the pork and the beef industries. The immediate effect of lower costs in the beef industry is to lower beef prices as the supply of beef increases. The fall in the price of beef will, however, also influence the demand for pork. As beef prices fall relative to pork prices, the demand for pork will decrease as the quantity of beef demanded increases: consumers will substitute beef for pork. The decrease in demand for pork will result in a fall in the price of pork, which will result in a decrease in the demand for beef and a further fall in its price. This fall in the price of beef will further decrease the demand for pork and, again, lower its price. The interaction between prices and demands for the two goods will continue, with the resulting changes in prices and outputs becoming smaller and smaller, until new equilibrium conditions are established in both industries.

In our partial equilibrium model, the beef industry is assumed to be isolated from the rest of the economy. We can plot a simple graph showing the consequence of a reduction in costs in the beef industry by means of supply-and-demand curves. The supply curve of beef moves out and to the right, and a new equilibrium emerges. But if we show the interactions between the beef and the pork industries, the resulting graphs become more complex. Figure 10.1 indicates the shift in the supply curve of beef from S to S_1, as a result of the decrease in costs in the beef industry. This falling price of beef results in an immediate decrease in the demand for pork from d to d_1, which lowers the price of pork. The falling price of pork brings a decrease in the demand for beef from D to D_1. The successive interactions between prices and demand for these two products is indicated by the downward shift of demand curves until a final equilibrium is reached.

Partial equilibrium analysis is an attempt to reduce a complex problem to a more manageable form by isolating one sector of the economy, for example one industry, and ignoring the interaction between that sector and the rest of the economy. It is useful for contextual argumentation. The gains in clarity and

Figure 10.1   The Interdependence of Industries

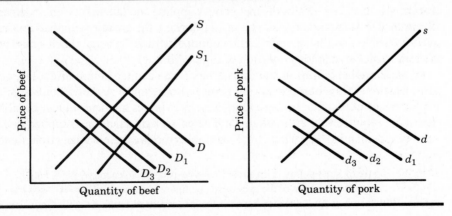

analytical neatness, however, are achieved at the expense of theoretical rigor and completeness.

If we were to move toward a more general equilibrium model by adding a third and fourth industry to our example, the analysis would become so complex that diagrammatic representation would produce more confusion than clarity. Walras's great contribution was his recognition that the complex interdependence of industries could best be understood and communicated mathematically. His general equilibrium analysis is useful for noncontextual argumentation.

Walras in Words

Before proceeding to our study of Walras's general equilibrium model, let us think through a partial equilibrium problem in mathematical form. Suppose we are interested in price and output in the beef industry. The demand and supply for beef can be expressed as equations relating price to quantity supplied and quantity demanded. Although there are three variables in the model—price, quantity supplied, and quantity demanded—at equilibrium there are only two unknowns, because quantity demanded equals quantity supplied. The problem of finding the equilibrium price in the beef industry, then, consists of an equation for supply, an equation for demand, and two unknowns.

Let us now move from this partial equilibrium model to a more complex general equilibrium model. Even in a general equilibrium model it is necessary to disregard certain aspects of a complex economy, so we will assume an economy made up of only two sectors, firms and households, and ignore the government and foreign sectors. We will assume, moreover, that firms do not buy intermediate goods from each other, that household preferences do not change, that the level of technology is fixed, that full employment exists, and that all industries are perfectly competitive. A schematic representation of such an economy is presented in Figure 10.2.[2]

Households enter the markets for final goods with given preferences and limited incomes and express a dollar demand for these goods. Firms enter the final markets willing to supply goods; thus, a supply of final goods flows from firms to households. It is in these markets, represented by the upper part of Figure 10.2, that the prices and quantities of final goods supplied and quantities demanded are determined. For these markets to be in equilibrium, the quantity supplied and the quantity demanded for each particular commodity must be equal. Factor markets are represented by the lower portion of Figure 10.2.

In these markets, firms demand land, labor, and capital from households, and there is a dollar flow of income from firms to households. As households supply the factors of production in these markets, factor prices are determined. Equilibrium here requires that all markets be cleared so that quantities supplied equal quantities demanded for each factor. Households receive their incomes from factor

---

[2] The use of a figure such as this to illustrate various aspects of an economy has a long history. For an interesting account of the uses of such a figure in the present context, see Don Patinkin, "In Search of the 'Wheel of Wealth': On the Origins of Frank Knight's Circular-Flow Diagram," *American Economic Review* (December 1973).

Figure 10.2   The Interdependence of Sectors of the Economy

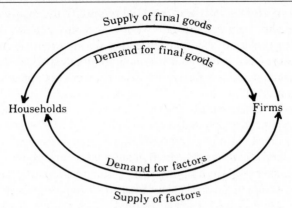

markets and spend them in markets for final goods. For households to maximize the satisfaction they receive from consuming final goods, given their limited income, they distribute their expenditures so that the last dollar spent on any particular good yields the same marginal utility as the last dollar spent on any other good (Gossen's Second Law). The flow of income between firms and households represents the national income of the economy; for this to be in equilibrium, households must spend all the income they receive. The distribution of income is determined in factor markets and depends upon the prices of the various factors and the quantities of factors sold by each household.

When firms in a market economy look one way, they face the prices for final goods; when they look the other way, they face prices for the various factors of production. Given these prices and the technology available, they combine inputs to produce outputs in a manner that will maximize their profits. This requires that they combine inputs so as to produce a given output at the lowest possible cost and that they produce at a level of output that maximizes profits. Competitive forces will result in a situation at long-run equilibrium in which the price of final goods is just equal to their average cost of production. For the level of national income to be in equilibrium, firms must spend all their receipts from final markets in factor markets.

The first and most obvious lesson from this somewhat abstract example of an economy is that the various parts of the economy are interrelated. It is misleading to think of one variable in the system as determining another variable. If equilibrium exists, all the variables are simultaneously determined. Suppose that we disturb the equilibrium by changing the price of a single final good. This will have repercussions throughout the entire system as consumers change their spending patterns and as firms change their outputs. These changes will make themselves felt in the factor markets as firms change their demands for inputs, thereby bringing about a new constellation of input prices and a different distribution of income.

Smith, Quesnay, and others had recognized the interdependence of the various parts of a market economy. But to go beyond the simple statement that everything depends on everything else, it was essential to specify the relationships between the various sectors in greater detail. Walras's genius enabled him to lay the groundwork for this more exact specification through the use of mathematics. When the economy is considered in an explicitly mathematical Walrasian model with mathematical notations, questions arise that were not apparent in our verbal analysis of his model.

The demands of households for final goods can be expressed as equations relating price to quantity demanded for each household. The market demand for a given final good can also be expressed as an equation obtained by summing the household demand equations. The market supply for final goods can be obtained in a similar manner by summing the firm's equations relating price to quantity supplied. Equilibrium in the markets for final goods requires that quantity supplied equal quantity demanded for each final good. Market demand and supply equations can be derived analogously for factor markets, with the equilibrium condition being that all markets clear. For households an equation can be derived with one side indicating income (the sum of the prices of each factor sold times the quantity sold for each factor) and the other side indicating expenditures (the sum of the price of each final good bought times the quantity purchased for all goods purchased). For the household to be in equilibrium, income must equal expenditures and expenditures must be made so as to maximize utility. The equilibrium conditions for the firm to maximize profits, and for its average costs to equal price through the force of competition, can likewise be expressed in equations.

Thus, we arrive at a system of simultaneous equations that indicates the interrelatedness of the sectors of the economy. The Walrasian formulation of the working of a market economy raises some new questions. For example, is a general equilibrium solution possible? Will the equilibrium conditions produced by the market in the various sectors of the economy be consistent with a general equilibrium for the entire economy? How does production fit into the model? The unknowns determined by the market and given by a general equilibrium solution are (1) the prices of final goods, (2) the prices of factors, (3) the quantities of final goods supplied and quantities demanded, and (4) the quantities of factors supplied and quantities demanded. Is there only one set of prices and quantities that will result in equilibrium for the entire economy, or are there many possible equilibria? If a solution to this problem does exist, is it a solution that is economically meaningful, or will it yield negative prices and quantities? Will the solution be a *stable equilibrium* or an *unstable equilibrium*? Is the system determinate? Several possibilities exist. The very process of the market working may result in shifting mathematical functions that will not result in final equilibrium. Another possibility is that a final equilibrium will be reached but that its position will depend upon the path followed by the variables in the system. This suggests that different final equilibrium values are possible. Finally, how will the equilibrium be achieved? Who sets the price? What happens if there is disequilibrium trading? Walras was aware of some of these problems, though others were not identified or solved for nearly sixty years after 1874.

Walras did not answer any of these questions satisfactorily. Thus, the historical judgment must be that if he is the father of modern neoclassical economics, he did not make it to the promised land. Instead, he promised much and delivered only an abstract framework containing many holes. Despite this negative judgment, even the harshest critic must agree that he did present a model that afforded great insight into the workings of a market and that could serve as a foundation for further theoretical developments. When one considers the development of economics over the ninety years since his death, one can say that he has had an enormous impact on economics.

Walras in Equations

Walras's general equilibrium model, presented in Lesson 20 of his *Elements*, assumes a market economy made up of households and firms with no government or foreign sector. Walras used the following symbols for his analysis of this economy. There are *n* factors of production.

$T, T', T'', \ldots$ are different kinds of land

$P, P', P'', \ldots$ are different kinds of labor

$K, K', K'', \ldots$ are different kinds of capital goods

There are *m* final goods represented by $A, B, C, \ldots$

The marginal utility function for an individual is written as $r = \phi_q$

Prices for final goods are written as $p_b, p_c, p_d, \ldots$

Prices for factors of production are written as $p_t, p_p, p_k, \ldots$

Households start with given quantities of factors of production, which are written as $q_t, q_p, q_k, \ldots$

The quantities of factors of production offered by households are written as o_t, $o_p, o_k, \ldots$ These values are positive when households offer factors and negative when households demand factors.

The demands of households for final goods are represented by $d_a, d_b, d_c, \ldots$

The first aspect of market equilibrium that Walras analyzed concerns the household or individual. Because his system does not contain money as a unit of account, what Walras called a *numeraire* is needed. Consumer good *A* fills this need; its price is equal to one ($p_a = 1$). The prices of all final goods and factors of production are measured in terms of this unit. In equilibrium the flow of income to the household will be equal to the expenditures of the household. The flow of income from the sale of land is measured by the amount of land offered (o_t) times the price of land (p_t). The income from the sale of other factors is given by a similar product. The expenditure of a household for a given final product is the product of its price times the quantity consumed, or demanded, in equilibrium. Setting income equal to expenditure gives the first equilibrium condition for a household.

$$o_t p_t + o_p p_p + o_k p_k + \ldots = d_a + d_b p_b + d_c p_c + \ldots \tag{10.1}$$

The household or individual is faced with the prices of final goods and factors of production in the market. The first task Walras undertook was to determine the quantities of the n factors offered by households $(o_t, o_p, o_k, \ldots)$, of which there are n factors and therefore n unknowns, and the quantities of the m final goods demanded by households $(d_a, d_b, d_c, \ldots)$. Because there are m final goods and n factors, the number of unknowns is $m + n$.

For households to maximize their utility, the marginal utilities of final goods purchased must be proportional to their prices, and the marginal utilities of factors of production not offered on the market but retained by households for their own use must be proportional to their prices. Because there are n factors of production, this gives n equations.

$$\phi_t (q_t - o_t) = p_{t\phi a} (d_a)$$
$$\phi_p (q_p - o_p) = p_{p\phi a} (d_a) \qquad (10.2)$$
$$\phi_k (q_k - o_k) = p_{k\phi a} (d_a)$$

There are m final goods, but because final good A is the numeraire, only $m - 1$ equations of the following type represent household equilibrium in the market for final goods.

$$\phi_b (d_b) = p_{b\phi a} (d_a)$$
$$\phi_c (d_c) = p_{c\phi a} (d_a) \qquad (10.3)$$
$$\phi_d (d_d) = p_{k\phi a} (d_a)$$

We are trying to find the household's supply functions for n factors of production and its demand functions for m final goods. The number of unknowns is $n + m$. The conditions for household maximization of utility give us n equations of the type (10.2) and $m - 1$ equations of the type (10.3). Equation (10.1) can be used to determine the demand for final good A, so we have $n + m$ equations to solve for $n + m$ unknowns.

The demand functions of a household for final goods indicate that demand is a function of utility; of the household's incomes that are reflected in the prices of factors of production; of the price of the final good; and of the prices of all other final goods. There are $m - 1$ of these equations. The demand for good A is given by equation (10.1).

$$d_b = f_b (p_t, p_p, p_k, \ldots, p_b, p_c, p_d, \ldots)$$
$$d_c = f_c (p_t, p_p, p_k, \ldots, p_b, p_c, p_d, \ldots) \qquad (10.4)$$

The household's supply functions of factors of production indicate that supply is a function of the utility of retained factors of production, the price of the factor, the prices of all other factors, and the prices of final goods. There are n of these equations.

$$o_t = f_t (p_t, p_p, p_k, \ldots, p_b, p_c, p_d, \ldots)$$
$$o_p = f_p (p_t, p_p, p_k, \ldots, p_b, p_c, p_d, \ldots) \qquad (10.5)$$

In considering the equilibrium of the household, we may take as given the prices of the final goods and the prices of the factors of production. It is then possible to derive the household's supply functions of factors of production (equation 10.5) and the household's demand functions for final goods (equation 10.4). In analyzing general market equilibrium, it is not permissible to assume that either final or factor prices are given; they become unknowns. In discussing general market equilibrium, Walras introduced several other concepts expressed in symbols.

The technical coefficients of production express the quantities of land, labor, and capital that must be used to produce one unit of a given final product. Thus, a_t, a_p, a_k represent the quantities of land, labor, and capital necessary to produce one unit of the final good A. Walras assumed these coefficients to be fixed in the first three editions of his *Elements*; but in the fourth edition, published in 1900, he dropped the restrictive assumption.

Market demand and supply are represented by capital letters. For example, the market demand for final good A is written as D and is obtained by summing the demands of all the households for good A ($D_a = \Sigma d_a$). The market supply of factors is written and derived in a similar manner, $O_t = \Sigma o_t$.

In general market equilibrium there are $2m + 2n - 1$ unknowns. This can be ascertained by examining Table 10.1. Four systems of equations will provide these $2m + 2n - 1$ unknowns.

The quantities of factors supplied in the market are functions of the prices of the factors and final goods. There are n equations of this type.

$$O_t = F_t (p_t, p_p, p_k, \ldots, p_b, p_c, p_d, \ldots)$$
$$O_p = F_p (p_t, p_p, p_k, \ldots, p_b, p_c, p_d, \ldots) \qquad (10.6)$$

The quantities of final goods demanded in the market are also functions of the prices of factors and final goods. There are $m - 1$ of these equations, and one equation expressing the demand for good A, the numeraire, for a total of m equations.

$$D_b = F_b (p_t, p_p, p_k, \ldots, p_b, p_c, p_d, \ldots)$$
$$D_c = F_c (p_t, p_p, p_k, \ldots, p_b, p_c, p_d, \ldots) \qquad (10.7)$$

Table 10.1 General Market Equilibrium Unknowns

Unknowns	Number of Unknowns
Prices of final goods (p_b, p_c, p_d, ...)	$m - 1$
Prices of factors (p_c, p_p, p_k, ...)	n
Quantities of final goods demanded	
(D_a, D_b, D_c, ...)	m
Quantities of factors offered	
(O_t, O_p, O_k, ...)	n
Total	$2m + 2n - 1$

and

$$D_a = O_t p_t + O_p p_p + \ldots - (D_b p_b + D_c p_c + \ldots)$$

The quantities of factors used by firms must, in equilibrium, equal the quantity offered. There are n equations of this type.

$$O_t = a_t D_a + b_t D_b + c_t D_c + \ldots$$
$$O_p = a_p D_a + b_p D_b + c_p D_c + \ldots \tag{10.8}$$
$$\cdots \cdots \cdots \cdots$$

Final costs of production must, in equilibrium, equal prices. There are m equations of this type.

$$1 = a_t p_t + a_p p_p + a_k p_k + \ldots$$
$$p_b = b_t p_t + b_p p_p + b_k p_k + \ldots \tag{10.9}$$
$$\cdots \cdots \cdots \cdots$$

These four systems of equations, (10.6), (10.7), (10.8), and (10.9), and equation (10.1) provide a total of $2m + 2n$ equations. One of these equations is not an independent equation, because it does not supply new information. Eliminating this equation, we are left with $2m + 2n - 1$ equations to find an equal number of unknowns.

General Equilibrium, Complexity, and the Limits of the Human Mind

In teaching economics to undergraduates, economics professors generally use examples of two goods that fit nicely into geometric presentations, such as analyzing individual choice through indifference curve analysis. In such examples, strong rationality assumptions make intuitive sense. Then we economics teachers wave our hands and extend the analysis to "n" goods without pointing out that, with each additional good, the computational requirements necessary for a decision-maker to make this jump increase exponentially. In some ways it is the equivalent to showing how a person can jump, and then assuming the individual can fly.

The reality is that in order to reach a general equilibrium with large numbers of goods, individuals would need brains with far more computing power than they currently have, and even then individuals would need to spend all their time processing information so they could remain rational. The point is that when there is a cost to thinking, too much "rationality" does not make sense. So when people are irrational, they are probably being rational.

Recent work in the analysis of complex systems suggests that when such decision complexity exists, the nature of the aggregate system changes and that to understand complex systems one must approach the problem in a fundamentally different way. If that is correct, in the future Walras's general equilibrium theoretical foundation for economic analysis may well be displaced by some other foundation for economic thinking.

Walras in Retrospect

Walras's high place in the history of economic theory rests partly on his independent discovery of marginal utility theory, but more on his conceptualization of the interdependence of the sectors of a market economy. Although others before him had perceived the interrelatedness of households, firms, prices of final goods, prices of factors of production, and quantities supplied and quantities demanded of all final and intermediate goods, no one had been able to express this perception as precisely as Walras did by stating it as a system of simultaneous equations. Now it was possible to see that equilibrium of the household and equilibrium in the markets for final goods were consistent with equilibrium for the firm and equilibrium in factor markets. The attempts by Jevons and Menger to find a simple causal relationship between marginal utility, the prices of final goods, and the prices of factors of production seem unsophisticated compared with Walras's general equilibrium model. Walras clearly demonstrated the power of mathematics as a tool of economic analysis, although full acceptance of his message did not come until well into the twentieth century. The extent and manner of the use of mathematics is still being debated by some today.

Walras's marginal analysis was more sophisticated than either Jevons's or Menger's. He did not see a simple direction of causation from subjective utility to value; instead, he saw a complexly interrelated system. Because Walras was focusing on the interdependence of sectors, and in a sense only working backward to demand, he did not fall into some of the traps that Jevons and Menger did. Whereas Jevons and Menger were content to search for a one-way cause and effect relationship among utility, prices of final goods, and prices of factors of production, Walras's general equilibrium model showed that they were all interconnected. In the Walrasian system, all prices are mutually determined and it is not possible to assign value causation in either direction. The prices of final goods influence and are influenced by the prices of factors of production. In a general equilibrium model, everything depends upon everything else. It is not at all clear that this sophisticated exposition was the result of understanding, and not a byproduct of Walras's focus on general equilibrium rather than on utility. Utility was not the focus of Walras's analysis. For Walras, utility was merely something he needed to assume to get to the demand curves he wanted. Thus, rather than providing a full utility underpinning of demand analysis, Walras only hinted at the underpinning.

Walras, Marginal Productivity, and the Interdependence of the Economy

Walras's general equilibrium theory was dependent not only upon demand and, therefore, utility but also upon supply and, therefore, diminishing marginal productivity. Here, too, there is much ambiguity in Walras's exposition. In Lesson 20 of the first three editions his model used constant coefficients of production, which is to say that there is no marginal product because one factor cannot be varied independently of another. Thus, his early exposition of general equilibrium theory did not have the second underpinning of a full general equilibrium model. Despite this, he stated that the analysis can be extended to include variable coefficients of production. The reader is left to accept that possibility on faith.

Walras recognized the problem and in the late 1800s asked a colleague how he could extend his analysis to include variable factors of production. Thus, in 1900 in the fourth edition, he incorporated variable factors of production and, thereby, the marginal productivity underpinnings of supply. Yet Walras's incorporation of marginal productivity came six years after Philip Wicksteed had formally developed the marginal productivity concept and had publicized its importance. Because of this, Walras's contribution to marginal analysis on the supply front is in question. As was the case with marginal utility, his interest was in the supply function that he needed for his general equilibrium theory, not in the production function that underlay it.

Walras was aware of some of the deficiencies of his model. Other problems were not identified or solved for nearly sixty years after 1874, and some are still not solved. To see some of these problems, consider the following questions.

Is a general equilibrium solution possible?

Some individuals thought that simply by counting equations and unknowns the existence of a general equilibrium could be deduced. Abraham Wald in 1933 showed that that was not the case and that proving the existence of a solution was far more complicated; it was only in 1954 that Gerard Debreu and Kenneth Arrow were able to prove the existence of a general equilibrium solution.

If a solution does exist, is it a solution that is economically meaningful, or will it yield negative prices and quantities?

Just because one can mathematically prove the existence of general equilibrium does not mean that it has any relevance to the real world. Because the connection between general equilibrium and the real world is so tangential, it is not at all clear that the mathematics is relevant. It has been called the celestial mechanics of a nonexistent world.

How does production fit into the Walrasian system?

Although the Walrasian system seems to include production, careful consideration reveals that it is primarily a model of exchange and that production has been inappropriately related to it. As long as there are constant returns to scale, this presents no problem; but if there are increasing returns to scale, the model has serious problems.

Will the equilibrium conditions produced by the market in the various sectors of the economy be consistent with a general equilibrium for the entire economy?

Walras thought he had answered this complicated question, but he hadn't. There are strict conditions under which such consistency will be achieved.

The unknowns determined by the market and given by a general equilibrium solution are: (1) the prices of final goods, (2) the prices of factors, (3) the quantities of final goods supplied and quantities demanded, and (4) the quantities of factors supplied and quantities demanded. Is there only one set of prices and quantities that will result in equilibrium for the entire economy, or are there many possible equilibria?

Walras recognized the possibility of multiple general equilibria, and general equilibrium analysis still must contend with it. General equilibrium theorists can show the conditions under which there will be a unique equilibrium, but they cannot show that those are the conditions we would expect in the economy. The matter becomes even more complicated when one tries to include expectations in the model as one does in what are called *sunspot models*. Multiple equilibria abound in these models. The possibility of *multiple equilibria* is one of the greatest limitations of applying the general equilibrium model to the real world. How do multiple equilibria make a difference? Even though the market solution may be an equilibrium, it need not be the best equilibrium; a preferable equilibrium might exist. Moreover, if a preferable equilibrium exists, a disequilibrium to that preferable equilibrium might actually be preferable to the equilibrium the market achieves.

Is the equilibrium stable or unstable?

An equilibrium is not necessarily stable; if the model is thrown out of equilibrium, will it return to equilibrium? This issue was answered relatively quickly and the conditions necessary for stability were shown. What was not shown was whether those conditions fit reality. Several events might actually undermine stability. The very process of the market at work may cause shifting mathematical functions that will not result in final equilibrium. In another scenario, a final equilibrium may be reached but its position may depend upon the path followed by the variables in the system. Thus, different final equilibrium values may be possible.

How will the equilibrium be achieved? Who sets the price, and what happens if there is disequilibrium trading?

Walras struggled with this question, which is now playing a significant role in modern macroeconomic debates. He proposed numerous schemes involving written and oral pledges and a *tatonnement process* in which an auctioneer (who has since acquired the name the *Walrasian Auctioneer*) processes all the bids and offers, determines which prices will clear all markets, and only then allows trading. Donald Walker, who has examined these schemes in depth, has concluded that the model is fatally flawed because Walras did not endow it with enough viable features. Walker's conclusion is extremely damaging to the new classical branch of macroeconomics, which bases its analysis on the reasonableness of the assumed auctioneer.

These problems are substantial but do not undermine Walras's achievement. He set the framework within which many of the best minds in modern economics have posed questions. Issues of existence and stability of general equilibrium occupied economists well into the 1950s. Other questions are still occupying them. Even though Walras's formulation was less than perfect mathematically, it has been the framework for advanced research since the 1950s.

The source of Walras's success, his use of mathematics, was also the cause of some of the failures of general equilibrium theory. The highly abstract model offered insight into the interrelatedness of the economy, but Walras made no attempt to measure the concepts in his model empirically. They were not designed to be measured; it was theory without empirical application. The difficulty of measuring the concepts has remained a criticism of general equilibrium theory through modern times. Thus, although it demonstrates the relationships existing within an economy in equilibrium, it does not explain what happens in that economy when the factors that Walras took as fixed actually change.

The conclusion of most scholars is that although the general equilibrium model has tremendous potential for use in answering questions concerning the consequences of alternative economic policies, such potential has yet to be realized. Frank Hahn, a general equilibrium theorist, writes:

> It was Adam Smith who first realized the need to explain why this kind of social arrangement does not lead to chaos. Millions of greedy, self-seeking individuals, in pursuit of their own ends and mainly uncontrolled in these pursuits by the State, seem to "common sense" a sure recipe for anarchy. Smith not only posed an obviously important question, but also started us off on the road to answering it. General Equilibrium Theory as classically stated by Arrow and Debreu [1954 and 1959] is near the end of that road. Now that we have got there we find it less enlightening than we had expected.[3]

Walras and Marshall on Method

It is instructive to briefly compare Walras with the Marshallian approach. Walras was interested in technique and form. He was looking for the most general mathematical exposition of a model of the economy. Marshall regarded economic theory as an engine of analysis; it must relate to the real world, or should be forgotten, or perhaps simply kept at the back of one's mind, to bring into the analysis when relevant.

There could not have been two more different approaches. As we will see in the chapter on modern microeconomics, Marshallian economics rules in many undergraduate courses but Walrasian economics has become the mainstream graduate microeconomics. Despite its victory, the problems of the Walrasian

---

[3] Frank Hahn, "General Equilibrium Theory," *Public Interest,* Special Issue (1980), p. 123. Parenthetical dates are ours.

approach are significant and leave modern microeconomics vulnerable to much criticism.

Walras on Policy

Walras regarded his pure economics as a tool to be used in formulating economic policy. He regarded himself as a socialist but strenuously objected to the views of Marx and the utopian socialists such as Saint-Simon. He argued that economic theory had failed to demonstrate rigorously that an optimum allocation of resources takes place under perfect competition. In Lessons 8, 22, 26, and 27 of his *Elements,* he examined these issues and concluded that "production in a market ruled by free competition . . . will give the greatest possible satisfaction of wants" and that "freedom procures, within certain limits, the maximum of utility."[4]

He therefore advocated that the state attempt through legislation to create systems of perfectly competitive markets. At the same time, Walras was not a thoroughgoing proponent of laissez faire: he found many areas in which government intervention was desirable. He might reasonably be characterized as an advocate of market socialism. He followed Mill in maintaining that land rents represented unearned income and should therefore accrue to the government. With perfectly competitive markets and the abolition of rents as a source of private income, Walras reasoned, the resulting distribution of income would not contain major inequities. In general he tried to take a policy line between the socialists of the left and the hard-line proponents of laissez faire. His attempt to prove that general equilibrium in competitive markets results in a maximum of utility for society has been largely ignored or forgotten by economists. Knut Wicksell (1851–1926) was later to prove that Walras's conclusion would hold only if all individuals had the same utility functions and equal incomes.[5]

Walras's socialist views of the implications of his model were extended by theorists in the 1930s and beyond in what has become known as the socialism-capitalism debate, which we will review in Chapter 13.

VILFREDO PARETO

Vilfredo Pareto (1848–1923) was a disciple of Walras and an early supporter of general equilibrium theory. He carried through the reasoning Walras used in general equilibrium theory and extended the analysis to consider welfare implications of various policies. Pareto tried to extend Walrasian economics into policy. Pareto lays claim to being one of the fathers of modern *welfare economics,* the

[4] Léon Walras, *Elements of Pure Economics* (Homewood, Ill.: Richard D. Irwin, 1954), pp. 255–256. All quoted words are italicized in the original.
[5] Knut Wicksell, *Lectures on Political Economy,* trans. E. Classen, ed. with an introduction by Lionel Robbins (New York: Macmillan, 1934), pp. 72–83.

other being A. C. Pigou, who extended the welfare implications of Marshallian economics.

Pareto addressed the issue of how to evaluate the efficiency of resource allocation for an economy or for a particular market structure within an economy. Adam Smith had concluded that perfectly competitive markets resulted in desirable consequences, particularly higher long-term rates of growth for an economy. Increased interest in microeconomics, which began in the 1870s, led to questions concerning the efficiency of resource allocation and to the development of criteria for evaluating the merits of different economic policies that impact upon an economy.

Adam Smith's advocacy of laissez faire was not based on a theoretically rigorous model; it focused more on the macro consequences of markets coupled with a minimum of government intervention. Pareto began evaluating microeconomic performance with the new marginal tools in the 1890s and became the father of the branch of welfare economics that works largely in a general equilibrium framework. Pareto also represents a continental (particularly French and Italian) approach as opposed to the British framework based on the partial equilibrium structure laid down by Alfred Marshall. This line of welfare economics began with Henry Sidgwick (1838–1900), a political philosopher who contributed to economics. Sidgwick published his *Principles of Political Economy* in 1883. It was Marshall's successor at Cambridge, Arthur C. Pigou (1877–1959), who became the father of the partial equilibrium branch of welfare economics by extending and refining Sidgwick's and Marshall's insights into market failures and externalities.

Pareto's answer to the question of evaluating the efficiency of resource allocation was straightforward: a change in resource allocation will improve welfare if one person can be made better off with no other person's being made worse off. An ideal or optimum distribution of scarce resources, a *Pareto optimum,* is defined as one in which it is impossible to make someone better off without making someone else worse off. Pareto recognized that his concept of optimality was not of particular relevance for real-world problems, and in his book *Mind and Society* (1916) he explained the necessity of making interpersonal comparisons in real-world welfare analysis. However, he regarded his Pareto optimal criteria as a useful analytic extension of Walras's general equilibrium theory.

Pareto optimal policies acquired a special significance when it was determined that competitive markets will lead to a Pareto optimal position—a position from which no one can be made better off without making someone else worse off. This is one of the important conclusions that flowed from general equilibrium analysis, and it has deepened our understanding of markets. This judgment underlay the theoretical support of the market that was used in the formal aspect of the socialist-capitalist debate, which we consider in Chapter 13. But it missed important other aspects of the broader debate of the use of markets, and it made the market process seem mechanistic.

In so doing it directed welfare economics away from real-world issues and the use of economics as an engine of analysis, as Marshall wanted to use it, and toward a set of formalist deductive proofs that have little direct relationship to reality. The reality is that any policy helps some people and hurts others; thus, if economists are only to make judgments on policies that fit the Pareto optimal criteria, they must separate their analysis from the real world.

SUMMARY

Walrasian general equilibrium analysis is impressive; but there were many problems in Walras's formulation, only some of which have been resolved today. The same can be said for its competitor, Marshallian partial equilibrium analysis, which we will consider in the next chapter. Despite their flaws, the accomplishments of both Walras and Marshall were considerable. They provided vehicles to integrate the work of the marginalists on both the supply and the demand side, and as such providers they deserve to be called the fathers of neoclassical economics.

Key Terms

general equilibrium theory
ceteris paribus
partial equilibrium analysis
stable equilibrium
unstable equilibrium
numeraire

sunspot models
multiple equilibria
tatonnement process
Walrasian Auctioneer
welfare economics
Pareto optimum

Questions for Review, Discussion, and Research

1. Which is preferable: general or partial equilibrium analysis? Why?
2. Are Quesnay and the physiocrats more related to Walras or to Marshall? Why?
3. "For Walras, utility was only something he needed to assume to obtain the demand results he wanted." Discuss this statement.
4. Why is an equal number of equations and unknowns insufficient to prove the existence of general equilibrium?
5. What difference would the existence of multiple equilibria make for general equilibrium analysis?
6. If there is no Walrasian Auctioneer, how is the Walrasian model changed?
7. What relevance does the absence of a Walrasian Auctioneer have to the new classical model?
8. If a policy affects relative prices, is it likely to meet the Pareto optimal criteria? Why or why not?
9. A policy transfers income from individual A, who gets zero marginal utility from his marginal income, to individual B, who gets a high marginal utility from income. Will this policy be a Pareto optimal policy? Why or why not?

10. Walras accomplished in equations what Adam Smith accomplished in words. Explain.
11. That absent-minded professor is becoming a pain, but a job is a job. This time, she's doing an article titled "Walras and the Art of Economics." She knows that somewhere in his writings, Walras discussed Coquelin's distinction between the art of economics and the science of economics, but she doesn't remember where. Since you've been so good at finding other citations, she sends you off to find Walras's. After you find it she wants you to compare it with J. M. Keynes's distinction discussed in this text.

Suggested Readings

Hutchison, T. W. *A Review of Economic Doctrines, 1870–1929.* Oxford: Clarendon Press, 1953.

Jaffé, William. "The Birth of Léon Walras' Elements." *History of Political Economy,* 1 (Spring 1969).

————. "Léon Walras' Role in the Marginal Revolution of the 1870s." *History of Political Economy,* 4 (Fall 1972).

Schumpeter, Joseph A. "Marie Esprit Léon Walras." In *Ten Great Economists.* New York: Oxford University Press, 1951.

Stigler, George J. "The Development of Utility Theory." In *Essays in the History of Economics.* Chicago: University of Chicago Press, 1965.

Walker, Donald A. "Léon Walras in the Light of His Correspondence and Related Papers." *Journal of Political Economy,* 78 (July/August 1970).

————. "The Markets for Circulating Capital and Money in Walras's Last Monetary Model." *Économie Appliquée,* 3 (1991).

————. "The Written Pledges Markets in Walras's Last Monetary Model." *Économie Appliquée,* 3 (1991).

Walras, Léon. *Elements of Pure Economics.* Homewood, Ill.: Richard D. Irwin, 1954.

11 Alfred Marshall and Neoclassical Economics

"Economic doctrine is not a body of concrete truth, but an engine for the discovery of concrete truth."

—Alfred Marshall

A lfred Marshall (1842–1924) is considered one of two contenders for the title of father of modern orthodox microeconomic theory (the other being Léon Walras). Building on the work of Smith, Ricardo, and J. S. Mill, Marshall developed an analytical framework that still serves today as the structural basis of current undergraduate economic theory and most economic policy. A truly thorough examination of his ideas would include nearly all of present-day partial equilibrium microeconomic theory; what follows in this chapter should be viewed as the barest introduction to the works of this great thinker.

MARSHALL'S CLAIM TO BEING THE FATHER OF NEOCLASSICISM

Marshall came to economics with an undergraduate training in mathematics and with strong humanitarian feelings about improving the quality of life of the poor. His early education and home environment oriented him toward ordination in the Anglican church, but his undergraduate study at Cambridge revealed a strong preference and aptitude for mathematics. He therefore remained at Cambridge after graduation to teach mathematics. Soon, however, he was caught up in reading metaphysics, ethics, and economics. By the late 1860s he had developed such a consuming interest in economics that he decided to become a scholar-teacher rather than a clergyman. He began teaching economics at Cambridge; and under the influence of the writings of two early mathematical economists, Cournot and von Thünen, he began to translate Ricardo's and J. S. Mill's economics into mathematics.

Marshall began his study of economics at a historically propitious time. We have already noted the crumbling of the foundations of classical theory. Malthusian population doctrine maintained that real wages would fall as population increased, but English economic history continued to demonstrate the contrary. J. S. Mill had become so dissatisfied with the wages fund theory that by 1869 he expressly rejected it. Karl Marx had constructed a novel analysis on a foundation of classical theory and invoked revolution. The German historical school and certain English writers, such as Leslie and Bagehot, had taken exception to several fundamental tenets of classical economic theory. In 1871 Jevons and Menger had attacked its almost exclusive emphasis on supply. The policies arising from classical theory were also under siege. Laissez faire, for example, seemed hardly appropriate in light of the poor living and working conditions of the growing population of English factory workers. Thus, the time was ripe for the appearance of Alfred Marshall, a man of immense scholarship and wisdom who from 1867 to 1890 carefully forged the principles of supply-and-demand analysis.

Jevons rushed into print claiming to have destroyed the classical theory of value and to have revolutionized economic theory, but Marshall tried his ideas on his students and colleagues for more than twenty years before cautiously presenting them in 1890 in his *Principles of Economics*. As Keynes has aptly said, "Jevons saw the kettle boil and cried out with the delighted voice of a child; Marshall too had seen the kettle boil and sat down silently to build an engine."[1] The engine of analysis that Marshall built reflects both his personality and the environment in which he was reared. His early religious beliefs, later expressed as a mellow humanitarianism, evoked in him a deep concern for the poor as well as an optimistic conviction that the study of the economy might provide the means of improving the well-being of the entire society. His scholarship had familiarized him with the attacks of the historically oriented economists, who objected to the notion that economic theory was a body of absolute truths applicable to all times and places. In an inaugural lecture given on his election to professorship at Cambridge in 1885, he addressed himself to this criticism: "For that part of economic doctrine, which can alone claim universality, has no dogmas. It is not a body of concrete truth, but an engine for the discovery of concrete truth."[2]

Marshall was trying to combine his early mathematical training with his background in history to construct an engine of inquiry adaptable to the changing times. Yet, being aware of J. S. Mill's hasty conclusion in 1848 that the theory of value was complete, Marshall expected his own contributions to economics to become obsolete as new theories arose to meet the needs of a continually changing society. He was aware, too, of Jevons's claim to originality and belief that he had replaced the classical cost of production theory of value with a theory that value depends entirely upon demand. Marshall hoped, of course, that his own ideas might be both original and enduring, but most of all he wanted to be understood—

[1] J. M. Keynes, *Essays and Sketches in Biography* (New York: Meridian, 1956), p. 58.
[2] A. C. Pigou, ed., *Memorials of Alfred Marshall* (New York: Kelley and Millman, 1956), p. 159.

not only by his fellow economists but by the community at large, particularly the businessmen. Thus, even though he had begun to work out the fundamental mathematical structure of his theory by 1870 and later developed the basic technique by which to illustrate supply-and-demand analysis with graphs, he did not actually publish his findings until 1890—and then only with the mathematics and graphs in footnotes and appendixes. Marshall, a strange admixture of theoretician, humanitarian, mathematician, and historian, tried to point the way out of the methodological controversy of his time while simultaneously tempering the best of classical analysis with the new tools of the marginalists to explain the forces that determine prices and the allocation of resources.

Although Marshall is a towering figure in the development of economic theory, his refusal to take rigid positions on theoretical and methodological issues has caused succeeding generations of economists a good deal of pain. In attempting to achieve balanced judgments, he was sometimes vague and indecisive. He often seemed to be saying that it all depends: Ricardo was right but also wrong; abstract theory is good and bad; the historical method can be helpful but theory is needed, too; payments to the factors of production are price-determining from one point of view but price-determined from another. Some readers see this flexibility with regard to issues of theory and method as a sign of true wisdom, but others, particularly the more abstract mathematical economists, chafe at what they regard as indecisiveness in Marshall's economics. Nevertheless his style has given rise to a vast body of literature that tries to uncover what Marshall "really meant."

Scope of Economics

Book I, Chapter 1, of Marshall's *Principles of Economics* begins with a broad, flexible definition of economics: "Political Economy or Economics is a study of mankind in the ordinary business of life; it examines that part of individual and social action which is most closely connected with the attainment and with the use of the material requisites of well being."[3]

An interesting and somewhat ironic aspect of this definition is that the concept is referred to by two different terms, *political economy* and *economics*. Given his broad definition of economies, one would have expected Marshall to use the broader political economy terminology. Marshall's use of both terms reflects some of the methodological issues of his time. The term political economy, which was more common than economics at the time, implies that economics and politics are related and that economics, as a discipline in the social sciences, is intimately connected with normative judgments. But John Neville Keynes, a colleague and friend of Marshall who was particularly interested in methodological issues, published a work in 1891 titled *The Scope and Method of Political Economy* in which he clearly distinguished three branches of economics: *positive economics,* encompassing the scientific branch of economics; *normative economics,* which considered what the goals of society should be; and an *art of economics,* which

[3] Alfred Marshall, *Principles of Economics,* 8th ed. [1920] (London: Macmillan, 1948), p. 1.

related the insights of the positive science branch to the goals determined in the normative branch. Keynes asserted that in discussions of the positive branch, the terms economics or economic science were preferable to political economy, because these names stressed the nature of economics as a science. Unlike Ricardo and J. S. Mill, Marshall chose to call his book *Principles of Economics* rather than *Principles of Political Economy,* and eventually he dropped the term political economy in favor of the term economics. What is ironic about his choice of the term economics is that he, more than almost any of his contemporaries, practiced the art, not the science, of economics. He focused on applied theory and was uninterested in the pure science of economics. There are two likely reasons for the shift. The first may have been Marshall's desire to differentiate his approach from Marx's approach, which was often referred to as political economy. The second is that Marshall was attempting to gain acceptance of a separate field of study in economics at Cambridge where he taught, and the term political economy, which suggested an overlap among fields, was not helpful in that attempt.

Another interesting aspect of the definition is its breadth and flexibility—some might say its flabbiness. According to the definition, how can economics be distinguished from political science, sociology, psychology, anthropology, and history? Marshall's loose definition springs not from careless, unfocused thinking but from a conscious reluctance to sharply divide economics from the other social sciences. Nature draws no such sharp lines, he pointed out, and the economist accomplishes nothing by defining the scope of the discipline too narrowly. In Appendix C, titled "The Scope and Method of Economics," Marshall considered (in his characteristically compromising fashion) the relative merits and feasibility of developing a unified social science as opposed to allowing each discipline to develop separately. The idea of unifying the social sciences appealed to him, but he recalled that both the great Comte and Herbert Spencer failed in their attempts to accomplish it. On the other hand, he observed, the physical sciences had made great strides by means of specialization. He decided ultimately that the issue could not be resolved in the absence of some concrete question:

> Economics has made greater advances than any other branch of the social sciences, because it is more definite and exact than any other. But every widening of its scope involves some loss of this scientific precision; and the question of whether the loss is greater than the gain resulting from its greater breadth of outlook, is not to be decided by any hard and fast rule.[4]

Marshall suggested that each economist define the scope of economics to suit his own inclination, that some economists are more likely to do their best work within a rather narrow definition of the scope of economics while others work within a broader framework. Those who choose a broad definition of economics and extend their analysis toward other areas of the social sciences must exercise extreme caution, he warned, but if they work carefully they perform a great service to economics and the other social sciences.

[4] *Ibid.,* p. 780.

Marshall introduced one other interesting issue in his discussion of the scope of economics, namely, the complexity of the relationship between the wants of society and its economic activity. Could economics be described as a study of the ways in which economic activity satisfies the wants of society? Marshall rejected this definition because it suggests that wants are an independent given, to which economic activities are secondary. In his discussion of the relationship between wants and activities in Book III, Chapter 2, Marshall tried to correct what he considered the incorrect conclusion reached by Jevons and Menger and their predecessors, who seemed to regard "the theory of consumption as the scientific basis of economics." He assessed the relative importance of demand (wants) and supply (activities) in the broadest possible context. His position is that our wants are not something that arise within us independent of our activities; on the contrary, many of our wants are direct outgrowths of our activities. To apply this thinking to the 1990s, it would be wrong to view a "yuppie" family's desire for a minivan as the starting point of economic analysis, because this want probably arises from the family's perception of its role in the society. Marshall suggested that economists begin with a preliminary study of demand, proceed to activities and supply, and then return to demand. This, he contended, will enable them to appreciate the complex interconnections between wants and activities. Forced to choose between the supremacy of either wants or activities in economic analysis, Marshall would opt for activities; this reflects his affinity for classical economics, which emphasized supply, and contrasts him with Jevons and Menger, who emphasized demand:

> For much that is of chief interest in the science of wants is borrowed from the science of efforts and activities. These two supplement one another; either is incomplete without the other. But if either, more than the other, may claim to be the interpreter of the history of man, whether on the economic side or any other, it is the science of activities and not that of wants.[5]

Marshall's religiously based humanitarian concerns led him to regard the elimination of poverty as the chief task of economics. He maintained that the key to solving these problems lay in the facts and theories of the economists, and his fondest hope was that the engine of inquiry he was constructing might uncover the causes of poverty and eventually discern how to remedy it. In Appendix B of his review of the history of economic theory he castigated the classical theorists, particularly Ricardo, for not recognizing that poverty breeds poverty, because the poor do not have sufficient income to attain the health and training that would enable them to earn more. In contrast to the classicals, Marshall wholeheartedly believed in the possibility of significantly increasing the well-being of the working classes.

His discussion of the scope of economics reveals his desires to respond to the criticisms of the historically oriented economists who wanted a broader definition of economics; to discuss the question of whether economics should develop as a

[5] *Ibid.,* p. 90.

narrow, abstract discipline or develop into a unified social science; to answer the marginal utility writers, who insisted that the theory of consumption should take precedence over the theory of cost and supply; and to take issue with the part of classical economics that had troubled J. S. Mill because it held out so little hope for the elimination of poverty. As usual, Marshall tried to present a balanced judgment on these issues and seldom took a clear-cut position.

Marshall on Method

Marshall's training and background are also reflected in his views on methodology. His mathematical ability made him fully aware of the power of mathematics as a tool in the hands of the economist, and his close study of Ricardo revealed the insights to be gained by building abstract models. His wide reading of history and of the historical economists convinced him of the value of their approach and of the validity of their attacks on classical theory. He realized that the chief fault of classical economics, especially Ricardian economics, was its failure to recognize that society changes. But he saw that a combination of abstract theory and historical analysis could correct this defect, and in Appendix B he praised Adam Smith as a model of method. In Appendix C, "The Scope and Method of Economics," and Appendix D, "The Uses of Abstract Reasoning in Economics," he bestowed lavish praise on the historical method and the German historical school. Marshall's own methodology attempts to blend the theoretical, mathematical, and historical approaches. He acknowledged that some economists prefer to rely heavily on a single methodology, and he did not object to this. For Marshall, the use of a different methodology did not imply conflict or opposition, because all economists are engaged in a common task. Each methodology will throw its particular light on the working of the economy and thus increase our understanding of it.

Marshall's attempt to reconcile the methodological controversies of his time made him vulnerable from all sides. The historically oriented economists of Germany and England found his economic methodology too abstract and rigid. In the twentieth century a strong attack against his method was led by an American, Thorstein Veblen, and the so-called institutionalists who followed him. The advocates of an abstract mathematical methodology were irritated by his praise of the historical method and his pointed remarks concerning the limitations of theory and mathematics. In a letter written in 1906 to A. L. Bowley, a friend who was very involved with the use of mathematics and statistics in economic research, Marshall made a comment that hit at the heart of the abstract mathematical approach:

> I have not been able to lay my hands on any notes as to Mathematico-economics that would be of any use to you: and I have very indistinct memories of what I used to think on the subject. I never read mathematics now: in fact I have forgotten how to integrate a good many things.
>
> But I know I had a growing feeling in the later years of my work at the subject that a good mathematical theorem dealing with economic hypotheses was very

unlikely to be good economics: and I went more and more on the rules—(1) Use mathematics as a shorthand language, rather than as an engine of inquiry. (2) Keep to them until you have done. (3) Translate into English. (4) Then illustrate by examples that are important in real life. (5) Burn the mathematics. (6) If you can't succeed in (4), burn (3). This last I did often.[6]

Marshall's *Principles* includes steps (3) and (4) and is written in a style intended not for his fellow economists but for any educated reader. His mathematics are placed either in footnotes or in a mathematical appendix. Even though Marshall went to great lengths to avoid the jargon of economics and illustrated each principle with examples from either current or historical economic experience, underneath it all is a strong, tight, highly abstract theoretical structure.

Just as Marshall refused to provide a neat and tidy definition of economics, so he generally avoided precise definitions of a number of economic concepts. Classical economics had given the concepts of land, labor, and capital, the so-called factors of production, a much more precise meaning than was appropriate. In the economy land, labor, and capital are often so intermingled that only a gross abstraction can disentangle them. Marshall therefore suggested that "we . . . arrange the things that are required for making a commodity into whatever groups are convenient, and call them its *factors of production*."[7] No hard and fast definition is laid down: the problem at hand dictates how the factors will be defined. Similarly, in analyzing supply Marshall had to address the issue of costs. If supply depends upon the normal costs of a firm, which firm is to be selected as normal? Here again Marshall demonstrated his flexibility, stating that "for this purpose we shall have to study the *expenses of a representative producer* for that aggregate volume."[8] His concept of the average, or representative, firm is not a statistical one, such as an arithmetic mean, mode, or median. Rather, he suggested that an industry be surveyed to locate firms managed by people of normal or average ability, firms that are neither newcomers to the industry nor old and established, firms whose costs disclose that they have normal access to the available technology.

It is important to recognize that Marshall's seeming vagueness, changeability, and occasional lack of theoretical rigor do not result from a disorderly mind; his is a carefully considered methodological position. Marshall's understanding of micro theory and his mathematical ability would have enabled him to present his *Principles,* which is some seven hundred pages long, in a much more concise form. He did this, in fact, in his mathematical appendix. But the economy is actually far more complex than can be shown by mathematical economics. Marshall worked out the pure theory of a market economy early in his career; it was reasonably complete by about 1870. Mathematical Note XXI is a one-page version of a general equilibrium model showing the relationships among the demand for final products, the supply of final products, the demand for factors of production, and

---

[6] Pigou, *Memorials,* p. 427.
[7] Marshall, *Principles,* p. 339.
[8] *Ibid.,* p. 317.

Marshall, Walras, and Complexity

Partial equilibrium analysis is often seen as an approach that is complementary to a Walrasian general equilibrium approach; they simply start at opposite ends. Marshall looked initially at small issues; Walras looked initially at big issues; but eventually the two would be combined.

Modern work in the analysis of complex systems suggests that such a view may be wrong. According to this new work, general equilibrium may require information processing that significantly exceeds the computing capabilities of the human mind. If that is the case, the two approaches are not compatible, since one cannot build down from an equilibrium that is beyond the informational capabilities of the individuals in the system. In that case, the system ac-

quires a life of its own not directly related to the decisions of individuals.

To arrive at an analysis of the aggregate economy one must approach it through partial equilibrium and then modify that partial equilibrium to be "less partial" and "even less partial." Ultimately one might be able to extend Marshallian analysis to a consideration of the aggregate economy. But one will not get there by an analysis of the general equilibrium.

Robert Clower and Axel Leijonhufvud's interpretation of Keynesian macroeconomics follows this line of reasoning and suggests that Keynesian economics was the beginning of a Marshallian approach to an analysis of the aggregate economy.

the supply of factors of production. In 1908 Marshall wrote to J. B. Clark: "My whole life has been and will be given to presenting in realistic form as much as I can of my Note XXI."[9] In his *Principles* Marshall explicitly defended his lack of exactness. After spelling out briefly the conditions that would exist in an economy in long-run equilibrium, Marshall went on to point out that

> nothing of this is true in the world in which we live. Here every economic force is constantly changing its action, under the influence of other forces which are acting around it. Here changes in the volume of production, in its method, and its cost are ever mutually modifying one another; they are always affecting and being affected by the character and the extent of demand. Further all these mutual influences take time to work themselves out, and, as a rule, no two influences move at an equal pace. In this world therefore every plain and simple doctrine as to the relations between costs of production, demand and value is necessarily false: and the greater the appearance of lucidity which is given to it by skillful exposition, the more mischievous it is. A man is likely to be a better economist if he trusts to his common sense, and practical instincts, than if he professes to study the theory of value and is resolved to find it easy.[10]

[9] Pigou, *Memorials,* p. 417.
[10] Marshall, *Principles,* p. 368.

Understanding the Complex: The Marshallian Method in Action

Marshall had two reasons for regarding the study of an economy as complex and difficult. On the one hand, everything seems to depend upon everything else: there is a complex and often subtle relationship among all the parts of the system. On the other hand, "time is a chief cause of those difficulties in economic investigations which make it necessary for man with his limited powers to go step by step."[11] Causes do not instantaneously bring final effects; they work themselves out over time. But as one cause, such as an increase in demand, is making its influence felt, other variables in the economy may independently change (e.g., supply may increase), so it is often difficult to isolate a single cause and be certain of its effects. If only the laboratory technique of the physical sciences (whereby it is possible to hold constant all influences except one and then observe the results of repeated experiments) were available to the economist, this problem would not exist. But because the methodology of the laboratory is not available to economists, an alternative must be used. Marshall provided this alternative when he carefully developed his basic thought system.

According to this system, because economists cannot hold constant all the variables that might influence the outcome of a given cause, they must do so on the theoretical level by assumption. In order to make some headway in analyzing the complex interrelationships in an economy, we hypothesize that changes in certain elements occur *ceteris paribus,* "with other things being equal." At the start of any analysis, many elements are held constant; but as the analysis proceeds, more elements can be allowed to vary, so that greater realism is achieved. The *ceteris paribus* technique permits the handling of complex problems at the cost of a certain loss of realism.

Marshall's first and most important use of the *ceteris paribus* technique was to develop a form of *partial equilibrium* analysis. To break down a complex problem we isolate a part of the economy for analysis, ignoring but not denying the interdependence of all parts of an economy. For example, we analyze the actions of a single household or firm isolated from all other influences. We analyze the supply-and-demand conditions that produce particular prices in a given industry, ignoring for the moment the complex substitute and complementary relationships among the products of the industry under analysis and of other industries. One important use of the partial equilibrium approach is to make a first approximation of the likely effects of a given cause. It is therefore particularly useful for dealing with policy issues—for example, predicting the effect of a tariff on imported watches. Simple supply-and-demand analysis can be used within a partial equilibrium approach to predict the immediate implications of such a policy. Marshall's procedure is first to limit a problem very narrowly in a partial equilibrium framework, keeping most variables constant, and then to broaden the scope of the analysis slowly and carefully by permitting other things to vary. His method has been called, appropriately, the *one-thing-at-a-time method.*

---

[11] *Ibid.,* p. 366.

The Problem with Time

One of the chief difficulties in economic analysis is that causes take time to work out their effects. Any analysis or conclusion that correctly explains the short-run effects of a given cause may be incorrect in its conclusions with regard to long-run effects. Marshall's use of the *ceteris paribus* technique corresponds to his method of dealing with time. In the market period, sometimes called the immediate period or very short run, many factors are held constant. More and more constants are permitted to vary as the time period is extended to the short run, the long run, and the secular period, which is also referred to as the very long run. The passage of time influences demand somewhat, but it can be far more disruptive to the analysis of supply.

To address the problems caused by time, Marshall defined four time periods. He acknowledged that his distinctions were purely artificial, for "nature has drawn no such lines in the economic conditions of actual life."[12] Marshall's concept of time is not chronological time measured in clock hours; rather, it is an analytical construct. The various time periods are defined in terms of the economics of the firm and of supply. The *market period* is so short that supply is fixed, or perfectly inelastic. Under these circumstances there is no reflex action of price on quantity supplied, as the period is too short for firms to be able to respond to price changes. The *short run* is a period in which the firm can change production and supply but cannot change plant size. Here there is a reflex action, as higher prices cause larger quantities to be supplied and the supply curve slopes upward. In the short run, the total costs of the firm can be divided into two components: costs that vary with output, which Marshall termed special, direct, or *prime costs;* and costs that do not vary with output, which Marshall termed *supplementary costs* and modern texts often call fixed costs. The distinction between variable and fixed costs in the short run was evidently drawn from Marshall's observation of the business world. It became an important analytical tool in analyzing the actions of the firm. In the *long run,* plant size can vary and all costs become variable. The supply curve becomes more elastic in the long run than in the short run, as firms are able to make full adjustment to changing prices by altering plant size. The long-run supply curve for an industry can take three general forms: it can slope up and to the right (costs may increase); it can be perfectly elastic (costs may be constant); or, in unusual situations, it can slope down and to the right (costs may decrease). The *secular period,* or very long run, permits technology and population to vary, so Marshall used this construct when he analyzed the movement of prices from one generation to another.

Clearly, Marshall's time periods are not measured in days but refer instead to conditions of supply for the firm and industry. For example, the short run in a very capital-intensive industry in which plant size can be changed only very slowly, such as the steel industry, may be as long in chronological time as the long run in an industry in which plant size may be altered rather quickly. Although Marshall

---

[12] *Ibid.,* p. 378.

contributed to nearly every part of microeconomic theory, the major focus of his attention and the source of his greatest contributions was his analysis of the influence of time on supply. He found the chief difficulties in the analysis of price to be in determining the influence of time, and he asserted later in life that much more work needed to be done in this area. In a letter to J. B. Clark written in 1908, he listed five topics that still needed an immense quantity of work, and at the top of his list was "elaborating the influence of time."[13]

The Marshallian Cross

During the last quarter of the nineteenth century, a controversy arose among economists concerning the relative importance of demand and supply in price, or value, theory. Classical economics as set forth in the *Principles* of J. S. Mill had emphasized supply; however, Jevons, Menger, and Walras had stressed demand; and Jevons and others went so far as to assert that value depends entirely upon demand. It is difficult to assess the impact of this controversy on the content and form of Marshall's theory of relative prices. He asserted that the essential elements of his own views on value and distribution were worked out before 1870 but that it would be "foolish if he troubled himself to weigh and measure any claims to originality that he had."[14] Marshall was vexed by criticisms of his supply-and-demand analysis that suggested he had tried to reconcile the positions of the classical and marginal utility schools. He was looking for truth, not just peace, he asserted; moreover, his supply-and-demand analysis had been formulated before Jevons, Menger, and Walras began to write on the subject.

Marshall believed that a correct understanding of the influence of time and an awareness of the interdependence of economic variables would resolve the controversy over whether cost of production or utility determines price. The demand curve for final goods slopes downward to the right, as individuals will buy larger quantities at lower prices. The shape of the supply curve depends upon the time period under analysis. The shorter the period, the more important the role of demand in determining price; the longer the period, the more important the role of supply. In the long run, if constant costs exist and supply is therefore perfectly elastic, price will depend solely on cost of production. In general, however, it is fruitless to argue whether demand or supply determines price. Marshall used the following analogy to show that causation is not a simple matter and that any attempt to find one single cause is doomed to failure:

> We might as reasonably dispute whether it is the upper or under blade of a pair of
> scissors that cuts a piece of paper, as whether value is governed by utility or costs
> of production. It is true that when one blade is held still, and the cutting is ef-
> fected by moving the other, we may say with careless brevity that the cutting is
> done by the second; but the statement is not strictly accurate, and is to be excused

[13] Pigou, *Memorials,* p. 417.
[14] *Ibid.,* p. 418.

only so long as it claims to be merely a popular and not a strictly scientific account of what happens.[15]

Possibly even more important is Marshall's insistence that marginal analysis had been misused by many economists. They wrote, he said, as though it is the marginal value (whether cost, utility, or productivity) that somehow determines the value of the whole. For example, in analyzing the prices of final goods it is not correct, according to Marshall, to say that marginal utility or marginal cost determines price. Marginal analysis simply suggests that "we must go to *the margin to study the action of those forces which govern* the value of the whole."[16] Marginal utility or marginal cost does not determine price, for their values along with price are mutually determined by factors acting on the margin. Here again Marshall provided a very apt analogy to illustrate his point. Jevons had isolated the essential elements in price determination: utility, cost, and price. But he was mistaken in trying to find a single cause and in viewing the process as a chain of causation, with cost of production determining supply, supply determining marginal utility, and marginal utility determining price. Marshall maintained that this is mistaken because it ignores the interrelationships and mutual causation among these elements. If we place three balls in a bowl, one being marginal utility, one being cost of production, and the third being price, it is clearly incorrect to say that the position of any one ball determines the position of the others. But it is true that the balls *mutually* determine one another's positions. Thus, demand, supply, and price interact with one another at the margin and mutually determine their respective values.

In Appendix I and the last paragraph of Book V, Marshall attempted to place his theory of price in the context of both Ricardo's theory of value and the controversy over whether it is utility or cost of production that determines price. Marshall believed that his own theory of price was fundamentally in the Ricardian line. Although the marginal utility writers would hardly have agreed, he suggested that Ricardo recognized the role of demand but gave it limited attention because its influence was so easy to understand, devoting his energies instead to the much more difficult analysis of cost. Marshall found Ricardo's cost of production theory of value to include both labor and capital costs. Most historians of economic theory consider this an overly generous interpretation of Ricardo. The main defects in Ricardo's value theory, according to Marshall, were his inability to handle the influence of time and to express his ideas clearly. Marshall rejected the claim of Jevons and other marginal utility writers that they had effectively demolished Ricardo's theory of value and replaced it with a correct version by emphasizing demand almost exclusively. Viewing his own contribution as merely an extension and development of Ricardo's ideas, Marshall felt that his treatment of Ricardo left the basic foundation of the Ricardian theory of value intact. We will postpone our evaluation of Marshall's value theory until we have surveyed his other ideas.

---

[15] Marshall, *Principles,* p. 348.
[16] *Ibid.,* p. 410.

Marshall on Demand

Marshall's suggestion that the influence of demand on price determination is relatively easy to analyze may well be correct. Yet there were problems with the theory of demand that Marshall was not able to solve satisfactorily. He seemed to recognize these difficulties and avoided them by assumption. His most important contribution to demand theory was his clear formulation of the concept of *price elasticity* of demand. Price and quantity demanded are inversely related to each other; demand curves slope down and to the right. The degree of relationship between change in price and change in quantity demanded is disclosed by the coefficient of price elasticity. The coefficient of price elasticity is

$$e_D = -\frac{\text{percent change in quantity demanded}}{\text{percent change in prices}} = -\frac{\dfrac{\Delta q}{q}}{\dfrac{\Delta p}{p}}$$

Because price and quantity demanded are inversely related, the computed price elasticity of demand coefficient would be negative. By convention, to express the coefficient as a positive number, a negative sign is added to the right side of the equation. The price of a product times the quantity demanded will equal the total expenditure of the buyers or, alternatively, the total revenues of the seller ($p \times q$ = TE = TR). If price decreases by 1 percent and quantity demanded increases by 1 percent, total expenditure, or revenue, will remain unchanged and the coefficient will have a value of 1. If price decreases and total expenditure or revenue increases, the coefficient will have a value greater than 1 and the commodity is said to be *price elastic*. If the price decreases by a given percentage and quantity demanded increases by a smaller percentage, total expenditure or revenue will decrease, the coefficient will have a value less than 1, and the commodity is said to be *price inelastic*. Marshall also applied the elasticity concept to the supply side, and in so doing gave economics another extremely useful tool. Although the notion of price elasticity had been suggested in earlier literature, it was Marshall, with his mathematical ability, who was able to express it precisely; he is therefore considered its discoverer.

According to Marshall, individuals desire commodities because of the utility received through their consumption. The form of the utility function used by Marshall was additive; that is, he derived total utility by adding the utilities received from consuming each good. The utility received from consuming good A depends solely on the quantity of A consumed, not on the quantities of other goods consumed. Thus, substitution and complementary relationships are ignored. An additive utility function is given as

$$U = f_1 q_A + f_2 q_B + f_3 q_C + \ldots + f_n q_n$$

The utility function used in contemporary practice explicitly recognizes complementary and substitute relationships and is expressed as

$$U = f(q_A, q_B, q_C, \ldots, q_N)$$

F. Y. Edgeworth and Irving Fisher were two of Marshall's contemporaries who suggested the more generalized utility function now used. The most important implication of Marshall's use of the additive utility function, which we will discuss shortly, concerns income effects.

Marshall assumed that utility was measurable through the price system. If an individual pays $2 for another unit of good A and $1 for another unit of good B, then A must give twice the utility of B. He also argued that intergroup comparisons of utility were possible because in group comparisons personal peculiarities are washed out.

In Marshall's framework the most important task of the theory of demand is to explain the shape of the demand curve. If, as more of a commodity is consumed, its marginal utility decreases, does it follow that individuals will pay lower prices for larger quantities? Are demand curves, then, negatively sloped? Marshall accepted diminishing marginal utility (Gossen's First Law) and formulated the equilibrium condition that would give maximum utility for an individual consuming many commodities (Gossen's Second Law):

$$\frac{MU_A}{P_A} = \frac{MU_B}{P_B} = \ldots \frac{MU_N}{P_N} = MU_M \tag{11.1}$$

In equilibrium the consumer will spend so that the last dollar spent for any final good will have the same marginal utility as that spent for any other good. The ratios of these marginal utilities to prices will be equal to, and thus disclose, the marginal utility of money. The marginal utility of money is the marginal utility received by the last dollar of expenditure. If saving is considered as a good, then the marginal utility of money is the utility received from the last dollar of income. The marginal utility of a single good is equal to its price times the marginal utility of money:

$$MU_A = P_A \cdot MU_M \tag{11.2}$$

Let us work through the derivation of a demand curve in order to see some of the problems encountered and Marshall's solution to these problems. If we begin with an individual who is maximizing utility and then lower the price of one good, we can derive the relationship between price and quantity demanded. Using equations (11.1) and (11.2), we see that lowering the price, P_A, of good A will lead to an increase in quantity demanded only under certain conditions. Lowering the price of good A will have two effects. The *substitution effect* reflects the fact that good A is now relatively cheaper than its substitutes, so that the individual's consumption of good A will therefore increase. The substitution effect will always lead to greater consumption at lower prices and less consumption at higher prices. The *income effect* produced by price changes is more complex. Lowering the price of good A increases an individual's real income. At the lower price the individual can buy the same quantity of good A as before and have income left over that can be spent on good A or on other goods. For example, if the price of good A was $1 and 10 units were previously purchased, lowering the price of good A to $0.90 increases real income by $1.00. A *normal good* is one whose consumption increases with increases in income. If good A is a normal good, its demand curve will slope down and to the right. Lowering its price will increase the quantity demanded under both the substitution and the income effect.

If good A is an *inferior good,* other complications occur. An inferior good is one whose consumption decreases with increases in income. Hamburger might well be an inferior good in a consumer's budget. As income increases, the quantity of hamburger consumed will decrease as better cuts of beef replace hamburger. If good A is an inferior good, then a fall in its price will lead to an increase in its consumption, because of the substitution effect, but a decrease in its consumption because of the income effect. If the substitution effect is stronger than the income effect, the demand curve will be negatively sloped; but if the income effect is stronger than the substitution effect, the demand curve will be positively sloped. The possibility of upward-sloping demand curves is extremely disturbing to the theory of demand. The theoretical possibility exists, but no empirical information has yet been produced to indicate the actual occurrence of upward-sloping demand curves.

Marshall first stated the general law of demand: "The amount demanded increases with a fall in price, and diminishes with a rise in price."[17] He then noted that information gathered by Robert Giffen suggests that the demand curve of poorer individuals for bread may slope up and to the right. In other words, for these individuals a rise in the price of bread results in a reduction in the consumption of meat and of more expensive foods, and a rise in the consumption of bread. For this reason, inferior goods with a more powerful income effect than substitution effect are referred to as *Giffen goods* in the theoretical literature. Again, although a considerable body of theoretical literature exists about the so-called Giffen paradox, no acceptable statistical information showing actual upward-sloping demand curves has been produced.

Let us return to the theoretical problems of deriving demand curves and how Marshall handled them. Because he worked with an additive utility function, he ignored substitution and complementary relationships in his formal mathematical treatment of deriving demand curves—although, characteristically, he did discuss these issues. Marshall simply assumed that the income effect of small price changes is negligible; that is, that the marginal utility of money remains constant for small changes in the price of any single commodity. Thus, if we lower the price of good A in equation (11.1), quantity demanded increases and the marginal utility of good A decreases until the ratio MU_A/P_A is brought into equality with the ratios for other commodities, and all are again equal to the constant marginal utility of money. Marshall's procedure can be studied from another perspective. Using equation (11.2), a fall in the price of good A (assuming that the marginal utility of

---

[17] Marshall, *Principles,* p. 99.

money is constant) must lead to an increase in its consumption because of the principle of diminishing marginal utility.

Marshall had two reasons for dismissing these theoretical difficulties by assuming that the marginal utility of money was constant: first, he did not have the theoretical tools to distinguish clearly between the substitution and income effects; second, he claimed that the income effect of minor changes in the price of a good was so small that no harm was done by ignoring it.

Consumers' Surplus

Marshall's belief that the marginal utility of money was constant for small changes in prices permitted him (or so he thought) to draw certain conclusions in the area now known as welfare economics. In this case, too, Marshall's first ventures into the new areas of economic theory have been followed by a large volume of literature interpreting and extending his analysis. The concept of *consumers' surplus,* first suggested by Marshall, is still being discussed in the literature of welfare economics.

Using equation (11.2), $MU_A = P_A \cdot MU_M$, and assuming that the marginal utility of money is constant, the price of good A and the marginal utility of good A are directly related. Marshall concluded that the price of good A is a measure of the marginal utility of good A to a consumer. Demand curves slope down and to the right because of diminishing marginal utility. Their downward slope indicates that consumers will be willing to pay more for earlier consumed units of a commodity than for later consumed units. In the market, however, consumers are able to buy all the units consumed at one price; because this price measures the marginal utility of the last unit consumed, consumers obtain the earlier units, the intramarginal units, at a price less than they would be willing to pay. The difference between the total expenditures consumers would be willing to pay and what they actually pay constitutes consumers' surplus.

Marshall wished to use the concept of consumers' surplus to draw welfare conclusions; therefore, he was concerned with the surplus of consumers as a group rather than with the individual consumer's surplus. He worked with market-demand curves, not individual-demand curves. Given a market-demand curve as shown in Figure 11.1, we can analyze consumers' surplus. If the market price is *OC,* the quantity demanded will be *OH*. Because *DD'* is a market-demand curve, there are buyers who would have been willing to pay a higher price than OC. The OMth buyer would have been willing to pay a price of *MP* but paid only a price of *MR*. *RP* then represents that consumer's surplus. All the other intramarginal buyers also account for a consumers' surplus; the total consumers' surplus is equal to *CAD,* which is the difference between what consumers spent to buy the commodity, or *OHAC,* and what they would have been willing to spend, or *OHAD*.

CAD is, then, a measure of the monetary gain obtained by consumers in purchasing a commodity. To express this result a little differently, a monopolist practicing perfect price discrimination will work the consumers down their de-

Figure 11.1   Consumers' Surplus

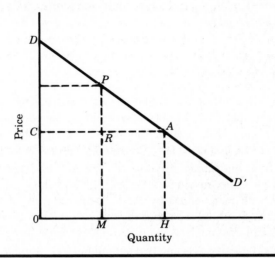

mand curve and in the process collect total revenues of *OHAD;* but in a competitive market in which all consumers buy at the single price of *OC*, the total expenditures of consumers are *OHAC. CAD* is therefore the amount the consumers save, or their monetary gain. Marshall, however, wanted to measure the gain in utility, and the monetary gain can be expressed as a gain in utility only if there is an invariable measure to transform price into utility. If the marginal utility of money remains constant as we move down the demand curve from price *OD* to *MP* to *HA,* then Marshall's consumers' surplus is an acceptable means of representing the gain in utility from consuming the good.

Marshall's use of prices to measure utility depends upon two assumptions: (1) that there is an additive utility function that ignores substitution and complementary relationships; and (2) that the income effect from small price changes is negligible; that is, that the marginal utility of money is constant. Using a more generalized nonadditive utility function, Edgeworth had suggested and Irving Fisher had shown that although utility could be measured by using additive utility functions, this would not be possible if substitution and complementary effects were permitted. Furthermore, there was general criticism of the hedonistic element in the theory of demand presented by Marshall and others. Marshall responded to these criticisms by making some minor terminological changes, such as satisfaction for utility, but he basically held to the position that price could be used as a measure of utility. Marshall's awareness of the problems associated with measuring consumers' surplus led him to use the measure only for small changes in price in his applications to welfare economics. For small changes in price (e.g., around the price *HA* of Figure 11.1), the assumption of constant marginal utility of money does not appear to be unrealistic, particularly if expenditures on the commodity in question represent only a small part of total consumer expenditures. The income effect of small price changes for most commodities is likely to be so small that it can be ignored.

Taxes and Welfare

Marshall used his concept of consumers' surplus to analyze the welfare consequences of taxes. The essence of the analysis can be appreciated by examining the simplest case, a constant-cost industry represented by the perfectly elastic supply curve shown in Figure 11.2. Assume the industry in equilibrium, with demand being *DD'*, supply SS', and price HA. Consumers' surplus is SAD. Now a tax of *Ss* is levied, shifting the supply curve to *ss'*. The loss of consumers' surplus is SAas, and the gain in tax revenues is SKas. The loss in consumers' surplus is greater than the gain in revenues by *KAa*. Taxes on constant-cost industries, therefore, appear undesirable. The analysis can be similarly used to show that a subsidy to a constant-cost industry is undesirable, because its net costs would be greater than its net benefits. Assume that demand is *DD'*, supply is ss', and price is ha. A subsidy in the amount of Ss will shift downward the supply curve to *SS'*. The gain in consumers' surplus is SAas, which is ALa less than the total expenditure for the subsidy *SALs*.

Marshall then extended the analysis to cover industries with diminishing returns (upward-sloping supply curves) and those with increasing returns (downward-

---

Figure 11.2 Taxes, Subsidies, and Consumers' Surplus

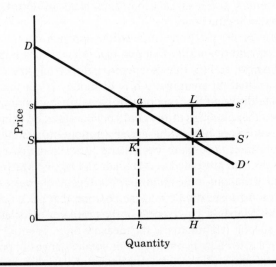

sloping supply curves).[18] Assuming that decreasing returns exist, a tax will result in increased welfare if the supply curve is sloped steeply enough that the gain in the tax is greater than the loss in consumers' surplus. In the same way, a subsidy to a decreasing-cost industry will increase welfare, because the gain in consumers' surplus will be greater than the cost of the subsidy. Marshall thus concluded that there might be advantages to the society from taxing certain decreasing-returns industries and using the collected revenues to subsidize increasing-returns industries. Since the entire analysis rests on the dubious notion that utility can be measured by consumers' surplus, its practical value for use in making policy is questionable. Marshall's purpose in presenting the analysis was not so much to give a set of precise rules for taxes and subsidies as to show that unregulated markets do not always result in an optimum allocation of resources. A. C. Pigou took these seminal suggestions to form an extended theory of welfare economics.

Marshall on Supply

Marshall laid the foundation for the currently accepted analysis of cost and supply that is taught in undergraduate courses. His most important contribution to the theory of supply was his concept of the time period, particularly the short run and the long run. He correctly perceived the shapes of industry supply curves in the market period, short run, and long run, even though his explanation of the economic reasons for these shapes was often deficient and confused and sometimes incorrect.

The market period causes no difficulties; here supply is perfectly inelastic. In the short run, modern micro theory explains the shape of supply curves for the firm and for the industry as depending upon the principle of diminishing returns. Marshall pointed out that for analytical purposes it is useful to divide the firm's costs in the short run into fixed costs and variable costs. Marshall did not, however, establish a precise relationship between his distinction between fixed costs and variable costs and the derivation of the short-run cost curves of the firm based on the principle of diminishing returns. His main application of the principle of diminishing returns was to land, usually in the context of long-run analysis.

He did use his distinction between fixed and variable costs in the short run to show that a firm would continue to operate in the short run even if it was incurring a loss, as long as it was covering its total variable costs. Under these circumstances the firm actually minimizes losses by operating: shutting down would result in a loss equal to total fixed costs, but the losses incurred by operating are less than total fixed costs as long as total revenue exceeds total variable costs. The supply curve of the firm in the short run in a perfectly competitive industry is, therefore, equivalent to that portion of its marginal cost curve above its average variable cost

[18] Marshall, *Principles,* pp. 468–476.

curve. With characteristic realism, Marshall went on to conclude that the real supply curve for the firm in the short run is not likely to be its marginal cost curve when prices have fallen below average costs and losses are incurred. He said that firms would be hesitant to sell at a price that does not cover all their costs, both fixed and variable, because they are concerned about "spoiling the market." Spoiling the market means selling at low prices today and preventing the rise of market prices tomorrow, or selling at prices that incur the resentment of other firms in the industry. Thus, the true short-run supply curve, when losses are incurred, is not the portion of the marginal cost curve between the average variable and average cost curves, but a supply curve to the left of the marginal cost curve. In this discussion Marshall dropped the assumption of perfectly competitive markets, because under a strict definition of perfect competition, no firm would be concerned about glutting the market or about the consequences of its actions on other firms in the industry. The inspiration for Joan Robinson's *Imperfect Competition* and E. H. Chamberlin's *Theory of Monopolistic Competition* can be found in part in Marshall's discussion of the operation of markets when the assumption of perfect competition is discarded.

Although Marshall's discussion of long-run firm cost curves and supply curves and industry supply curves is clearly deficient by modern standards, his early attempts in these areas provoked an interesting series of articles in the 1920s and 1930s, the most important being by Clapham, Knight, Sraffa, and Viner. Marshall indicated the long-run forces that determine the shape and position of the firm's cost and supply curves. First are the forces internal to the firm. As the size of the firm is increased, *internal economies* of scale lead to decreasing costs and internal diseconomies result in increasing costs. Marshall's discussion of the economic reasons for internal economies of scale is reasonably satisfactory; his discussion of internal diseconomies is minimal, and he did not really confront the issue of the relationship between economies and diseconomies and its influence on the optimum size of the firm.

Marshall's discussion of *external economies* and diseconomies nevertheless precipitated a plethora of literature on the theoretical issues implicit in his analysis. Marshall wanted to reconcile the upward-sloping short-run supply curves of firms and industries with historical evidence suggesting that in some industries, costs and prices have decreased over time. He based this reconciliation on his notion of external economies. External economies—Marshall never made it clear whether these are external to the firm or to the industry—result in the downward shift of firm and industry cost curves and supply curves as an industry develops. Under these circumstances the industry's long-run supply curve will slope downward: larger quantities will be supplied at lower prices. The major causes of external economies are the reductions in costs that take place for all firms in an industry when all the firms locate together and share their ideas. Localization also brings cost-saving subsidiary industries and skilled labor to the area.

Marshall's examination of costs and supply raised a number of important theoretical issues that were examined between 1900 and 1940. What are the economic reasons for the shape of cost and supply curves? Why do supply curves rise in the short run while costs and prices fall in the long run for some industries? Are internal and external economies compatible with competitive markets?

Marshall on Distribution

Marshall's explanation of the forces determining the prices of the factors of production and the distribution of income was consistent with the rest of his analysis. Here, as elsewhere, he often generously acknowledged the merits of criticism of his theories, for example, those attacking his marginal productivity theory of distribution. The same basic supply-and-demand analysis and the distinction between short run and long run used to explain the prices of final goods are also used to explain rents, wages, profits, and interest. The demand for a factor of production is a derived demand that depends upon the value of the marginal product of the factor. Marginal products are, however, difficult to disentangle, because technology usually requires that an increase in one factor will require more of other factors. Marshall solved the problem of measuring marginal products by computing what he termed the net product at the margin. If an additional laborer requires a hammer, then the net product of the labor is the laborer's addition to total revenue minus the added cost of the hammer. Marshall then pointed out that it is incorrect to call the theory of factor pricing a marginal productivity theory of distribution, because marginal productivity measures only the demand for a factor, and factor prices are determined by interaction of demand, supply, and price at the margin. After explaining his concept of marginal productivity and its measurement with respect to labor and wages, Marshall advocated a cautious interpretation of the marginal productivity theory:

> This doctrine has sometimes been put forward as a theory of wages. But there is no valid ground for any such pretension. The doctrine that the earnings of a worker tend to be equal to the net product of his work, has by itself no real meaning; since in order to estimate net product, we have to take for granted all the expenses of production of the commodity on which he works, other than his own wages.
>
> But though this objection is valid against a claim that it contains a theory of wages, it is not valid against a claim that the doctrine throws into clear light the action of one of the causes that govern wages.[19]

The proportions in which factors are combined, he said, will depend upon their marginal products and their prices. An entrepreneur interested in maximizing profits will want to produce a given level of output at the lowest possible cost, which will lead the firm to use factors of production in such a way that the ratios of their marginal physical products to their prices will be equal. Otherwise it will be possible to substitute at the margin and achieve lower costs. Marshall did not dwell on the issue of product exhaustion and Euler's theorem; he accepted the

[19] *Ibid.*, p. 518.

Wicksteed-Flux conclusion that in long-run competitive equilibrium, the total product is exhausted when each factor receives the value of its marginal product. Marshall's analysis of the returns to the separate factors of production—wages, rents, profits, and interest—is not particularly interesting. However, his development of the concept of quasi-rent in connection with his theory of factor prices and distribution deserves attention.

Quasi-Rent

With his concept of *quasi-rent,* Marshall not only provided insight into the workings of a market system but also threw new light on an aspect of the controversy between classical and marginal utility economists. Classical economics had contended that payments to the factors of production, with the exception of land, were price-determining. Prices of final goods depended upon costs of production at the margin. Because there is no rent at the margin, the classical doctrine (in the hands of J. S. Mill) held that wages, profits, and interest were price-determining. Prices were thus determined on the side of supply. The marginal utility writers joined the early critics of the classical cost doctrine in asserting that payments to the factors of production are price-determined. Marshall's analysis indicates that whether a factor payment is price-determining or price-determined depends upon the time period under consideration (which significantly influences the elasticity of the supply curve of the factors) and the particular perspective from which the analysis is made. Let us examine the payments called rent, wages, profits, and interest.

The return to land has historically been termed rent. In analyzing land rent, Ricardo had assumed that the supply of land was perfectly inelastic and that there were no alternative uses of land. The payment to the landlord for the use of land was price-determined rather than price-determining. The high price of corn was the cause of high rents. Although there were some criticisms of this theory from minor economists, the basic Ricardian analysis of rent remained unchanged through the time of J. S. Mill to the time of Marshall. Marshall recognized that the issues were much more complex. Whereas the rent of land, when viewed from the perspective of the entire economy, was price-determined and therefore not a cost of production, from the perspective of the individual farmer or firm, rent was a cost of production and therefore price-determining. The farmer who wants to rent land to grow oats must pay a price sufficient to keep the land from alternative uses. Unless the rent the oat farmer is willing to pay is higher than that of the barley farmer or the real estate developer, the oat farmer will not be able to rent the land in a competitive market. From the perspective of the individual farmer or firm, therefore, land rent is a cost of production that must be paid just as labor and capital costs must be paid.

Marshall also argued that under certain circumstances land rent was price-determining even from the point of view of the entire economy. For an economy with unsettled land that costs nothing, like the United States in the nineteenth century, rent may be considered as price-determining. Marshall reasoned that the original pioneers considered as part of their return for land settlement not only the immediate return from farming but also the appreciation in land prices that would take place as population moved toward the frontier areas. This expected land price appreciation is, therefore, part of the necessary supply price that must be paid in order to induce individuals to endure the hardships and dangers of frontier life. The rising land prices, equal to the capitalized value of the rising rents, can therefore be considered as a social cost. Rent under these circumstances is price-determining from the perspective of the economy. From the perspective of the economy, the supply curve of land is perfectly inelastic in a country in which all the land is settled, and rent is therefore price-determined. For a country with unsettled land, the supply curve of land slopes up and to the right; with higher rents, larger quantities of land will be settled and rent is price-determining. In a letter to Edgeworth, Marshall commented that

> it is *wisest* not to say that "Rent does not enter into cost of production": for that will confuse many people. But it is *wicked* to say that "Rent *does* enter into cost of production," because that is *sure* to be applied in such a way as to lead to the denial of subtle truths.[20]

Marshall went on to show how the returns called wages, profits, and interest in the short run have some of the characteristics of rent. The wage paid to a particular type of labor (e.g., an accountant) in long-run equilibrium will be just sufficient to bid those persons in that occupation away from other occupations and hold them in their present use. This long-run wage is the supply price that must be paid by society in order to elicit the quantity supplied. Wages are therefore price-determining. Suppose there is an increase in the demand for the services of accountants and thus an increase in the wage of accountants. In the short run the supply of accountants is less elastic than in the long run. Increases in wages will not greatly influence quantity supplied, so the short-run wage will rise above the long-run wage. The higher short-run wage has no connection with the price necessary to keep individuals in the occupation and is therefore price-determined, not price-determining. The key to understanding these issues is in the elasticity of the supply curve. In the very short run, the supply curve of a particular kind of labor can be thought of as perfectly inelastic. An increase in demand will result in higher wages, with the quantity of labor supplied remaining constant. During the short run the wage will fall slightly as individuals with acceptable training who were working in other occupations enter the occupation. In the long run the supply curve will become even more elastic, as wages fall to the long-run equilibrium value, the necessary supply price. In the short run and market period, therefore, wages are price-determined and are like rent. Marshall called these payments quasi-rents. "And thus even the rent of land is seen, not as a thing by itself, but as the leading species of a large genus."[21] With his concept of quasi-rent Marshall

---

[20] Pigou, *Memorials,* p. 436.
[21] Marshall, *Principles,* p. 412.

illuminated the controversy over whether the payments to the factors of production are price-determining or price-determined. It all depends on the time period: in the long run wages are price-determining, but in the short run wages are price-determined and therefore like rent.

Marshall also applied his concept of quasi-rent to the analysis of profits in the short run. In perfectly competitive markets in long-run equilibrium, each firm will earn only a normal rate of profits. Normal profits are a cost of production and must be paid by the firm to hold capital in the firm, just as normal wages must be paid to attract and hold labor. If a firm does not earn normal profits in the long run, capital will leave the firm for other firms and industries in which a normal rate is earned. Thus, in the long run, normal profits are a necessary cost of production and therefore are price-determining. But in the short run the return called profits can be considered a quasi-rent, and they are price-determined. In the short run the costs of the firm can be divided into variable and fixed costs. The revenues of the firm must be sufficient in the short run to pay the opportunity costs of all the variable factors, or they will leave the firm. What is left over is the return to the fixed factors, which in the short run are perfectly inelastic in supply. Profits in the short run are a quasi-rent to the fixed factors and are price-determined. If total revenues exceed total costs, above-normal profits are made; but where competition prevails these will be eliminated in the long run. If total revenues exceed total variable costs but are less than total costs, losses are incurred; but these losses will disappear in long-run equilibrium. Profits, like wages, can be either price-determining or price-determined, depending upon the time period under examination.

The concept of quasi-rent was applied to the analysis of interest in the short run. In the long run there will be a normal rate of interest, which is a necessary cost of production and therefore price-determining, although an old capital investment may earn above or below a normal rate of interest, depending upon supply and demand in the market. But because the capital is fixed, or sunk, in the short run, its return is a quasi-rent.

The analysis of quasi-rent in the broadest perspective can be used to point out some of the essential differences between classical economics, which emphasized the supply side, and the marginal utility writers, who emphasized demand. If the supply of factors of production is fixed, any factor's return is a quasi-rent and factor prices are price-determined. The return to the factors is considerably influenced by the level of demand. In the long run the supply of factors is not fixed, and long-run equilibrium prices of final goods must therefore be sufficient to pay for all the socially necessary costs incurred in production. Under these circumstances the payments to the factors of production are price-determining, and the analysis of final prices must give greater attention to the role of supply. Analytically the returns called wages, profits, rents, and interest have much in common over the various time periods. Although, admittedly, nature provides no sharp divisions between time periods, Marshall's theory of generalized time periods and its accompanying doctrine of quasi-rent penetrated deep into the complex issues raised by the forces determining relative prices.

Stable and Unstable Equilibrium

Marshall regarded demand schedules as indicating the maximum price individuals would be willing to pay for a given quantity of a commodity. Quantity is thus the independent variable, and demand price is the dependent variable. Supply schedules, on the other hand, indicate the minimum price at which sellers would be willing to supply a given quantity of a commodity. Again, quantity is the independent variable and price the dependent variable. In Book V, Section III, paragraph 6, of his *Principles of Economics,* Marshall explained the process of reaching equilibrium in markets. Because he regarded quantity as the independent variable, the adjustments that bring about equilibrium are discussed largely in terms of quantity adjustments. If, at a given quantity, demand price exceeds supply price, "then sellers receive more than is sufficient to make it worth their while to bring goods to market to that amount; and there is at work an active force tending to increase the amount brought forward for sale."[22]

Figure 11.3 reproduces Marshall's graphic representation of the process by which equilibrium is reached. At quantity R_1 demand price R_1d_1 exceeds supply price R_1s_1; thus, a larger quantity will be brought to the market by sellers. At quantity R_2 supply price R_2s_2 exceeds demand price R_2d_2 and sellers reduce the quantity brought to the market. Equilibrium is brought about by changes in quantity as sellers respond to the relative level of demand and supply prices. The equilibrium achieved is a *stable equilibrium,* because any displacement from equilibrium will produce forces returning the market to equilibrium.

Figure 11.3   Reaching Equilibrium

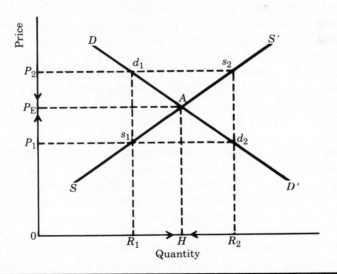

[22] Marshall, *Principles,* p. 345.

Walras and current economic theory follow a different set of behavioral postulates in analyzing market forces, regarding price as the independent variable. For them, demand schedules show the quantities individuals are willing to buy at various prices, and supply schedules indicate the quantities sellers are willing to offer at various prices.

Which is correct: to regard price as the independent variable, as Walras did, or quantity as the independent variable, as Marshall did? Because this question involves assumptions about the way in which buyers and sellers behave in a market, it can be decided only through empirical research. However, the analytical consequences of these two ways of describing market behavior can be theoretically deduced. Marshall concluded that it made no theoretical difference, but he was wrong.

The issue is further confused by a historical anomaly: although modern theory followed Walras in regarding price as the independent variable, it followed Marshall in placing price on the vertical axis in supply-and-demand graphs. Mathematical convention places the dependent variable on the vertical axis. An equation of a linear demand curve written $p = a - bq$ implies that price is the dependent variable, yet the behavioral postulates of modern theory regard price as the independent variable.

It is true that Walras and Marshall reached the same conclusions if the demand curve is downward-sloping and the supply curve is upward-sloping. Referring again to Figure 11.3, we see that under Marshall's analysis changes in quantity would bring about an equilibrium quantity of OH. Walras and modern theory, however, using price as the independent variable, would analyze the forces bringing about equilibrium as follows. At a price of P_2 quantity demanded is P_2d_1, which is less than quantity supplied, P_2s_2, so there is an excess supply. Competition among sellers will force price down until a price is reached at which the market clears; that is, at which quantity supplied equals quantity demanded. At price OP_1, which is less than the equilibrium price, there is an excess demand; quantity supplied, P_1s_1, is less than quantity demanded, P_1d_2. Competition among buyers will, therefore, force price up until the market clears.

A market represented by the supply-and-demand curves of Figure 11.3 will reach a stable equilibrium. Using the analysis of Walras and modern theory, any price other than OP_E will set in motion forces that will return price to OP_E. OP_E is an equilibrium price, because if price is at OP_E it will remain there. The equilibrium is stable; if something should cause the price to move from OP_E, it will return to OP_E. But the equilibrium is also stable equilibrium under Marshall's analysis. Quantity OH is a stable equilibrium quantity, because for any quantity other than OH, demand price would be either greater or less than supply price and market forces would return the quantity to OH.

Unstable equilibrium is possible when the supply curve is downward-sloping. In unstable equilibrium, if price or quantity attain their equilibrium values, they will remain there; but if the system is disturbed, it will not return to these equilibrium values. An egg laid on its side is in stable equilibrium; if disturbed it will return to its original position of rest. But an egg laid on its end is in unstable equilibrium; if left alone it will remain on its end, but if disturbed it will not return to its original state of equilibrium. Panel (a) of Figure 11.4 represents stable equilibrium using Marshall's analysis with quantity as the independent variable.

At a quantity greater than OH, supply price exceeds demand price; that is, the minimum supply price sellers will accept exceeds the maximum price buyers are willing to pay, and sellers will consequently reduce quantity offered to OH. If quantity were less than OH, sellers would expand quantity, because demand price would exceed supply price. However, if price is the independent variable, panel (a) of Figure 11.4 represents an unstable equilibrium. At a price less than OP_E, quantity supplied exceeds quantity demanded and competition among sellers will force the price further down. If price were higher than OP_E, the excess demand would force price further up.

Panel (b) of Figure 11.4 shows that a stable equilibrium when quantity is the independent variable can be an unstable equilibrium when price is the independent variable. A comparison of panels (a) and (b) indicates that when a supply curve slopes down and to the right, the stability of equilibrium will depend upon the relative slopes of the supply-and-demand curves and upon the behavioral assumptions used. Marshall and Walras did have an element in common, which led them both to conclude that with upward-sloping supply curves stable equilibrium is achieved. Both their analyses were in a static framework. For Walras, quantity supplied and quantity demanded in the present period depend upon price in the present period; for Marshall, supply price and demand price in the present period depend upon quantity in the present period. Thus, both Marshall and Walras assumed static behavior.

Figure 11.4   Stable and Unstable Equilibria

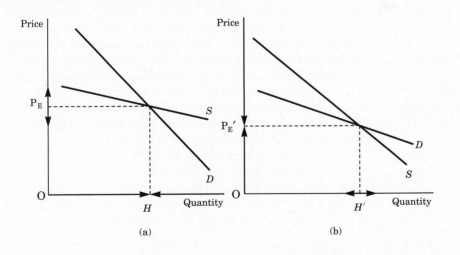

Economic Fluctuations, Money, and Prices

Although Marshall's overriding concern was with microeconomic theory, he contributed significantly to macroeconomics by studying the influence of monetary forces on the general level of prices. Although some of Marshall's earliest writings (1871) concerned the quantity theory of money, he did not publish any systematic work on money until 1923, in a book titled *Money, Credit, and Commerce*. His ideas on macroeconomic topics, though not yet published, were well developed in his lectures and in evidence presented before governmental commissions. The first five editions of his *Principles* carried the subtitle "Volume 1," but in the sixth edition (1910) he changed this to "An Introductory Volume." In 1895, with the publication of the third edition of the *Principles,* Marshall announced three prospective volumes: *Modern Conditions of Industry and Trade*; *Credit and Employment*; and *The Economic Functions of Government*. He published *Industry and Trade* in 1919 but never was able to write the other two volumes. What Marshall did write on macroeconomics primarily concerns economic stability or instability and the forces determining the general level of prices.

Marshall essentially accepted J. S. Mill's views on the stability of the economy: there can never be an insufficiency of aggregate demand, because a decision to save involves a decision to invest. It is impossible to have general overproduction. This line of reasoning was initiated by Adam Smith; elaborated by James Mill, Ricardo, and J. B. Say; and is now known in the literature as Say's Law. There were, of course, fluctuations in economic activity during Marshall's time; and some writers, particularly J. A. Hobson in England, were advocating underconsumptionist theories. Marshall believed that an understanding of the causes of economic fluctuations was "not to be got by a study of consumption, as has been alleged by some hasty writers."[23] Marshall's explanation of the causes of economic fluctuations follows J. S. Mill, who stressed the influence of business confidence. During an upswing, business confidence is high and credit expands rapidly; during a downswing, businesses become pessimistic and credit rapidly contracts. Mill's acceptance of Say's Law led him to assert that depressions could not be attributed to any fundamental problem within the system. Marshall suggested two public policies to address depression and unemployment. The first is to control markets so that credit is not overexpanded in periods of rising business confidence, because overexpansion may lead to recession. If depression does occur, governments can help restore business confidence by guaranteeing firms against risks. Marshall was not totally satisfied with this solution, because it would be difficult to implement without some adverse results. Guaranteeing businesses against risk, for example, would insure both competent and incompetent businessmen and thus interfere with market processes that reward the capable and punish the incapable.

Although Marshall's contribution to the understanding of the causes of business fluctuations was meager, his explanations of the forces that determine the general level of prices are significant. He recognized that his microeconomics analysis

---

[23] Marshall, *Principles,* p. 712, fn.

was based on the assumption that full employment existed and that there were no important changes in the general level of prices. His analysis of the determinants of the general level of prices is a quantity theory of money constructed within the framework of his supply-and-demand analysis.

SUMMARY

Although over a century has passed since Marshall began his study of economics, his contributions to microeconomics still provide the basis of orthodox undergraduate theory. Like most writers of economics, he built upon the work of great theorists of the past; unlike many other great thinkers and innovators, however, Marshall did not stress his differences with past writers but acknowledged that he had borrowed from their ideas. He regarded his work as a continuation of the work of Smith, Ricardo, and J. S. Mill and was always generous in his interpretation of theirs. His writing is characterized by modesty, a quality rare in the writings of seminal thinkers.

Marshall came to economics with a strong background in mathematics and a deep humanitarian desire to help those in lower-income groups. Yet he contended it was possible to separate the normative and positive elements of economics and busied himself in developing what he regarded as a positive, value-free science based on the theory that if we understand what is, society can make better choices about what ought to be. He addressed many methodological and theoretical issues, some of which had been discussed in the literature of economics since the 1830s.

Classical orthodox theory had not agreed upon a uniform methodology. Adam Smith had amalgamated theory, history, and description in the *Wealth of Nations;* his weakest link was theory. Although Ricardo was not specifically concerned with methodology, he had presented, without using mathematics, a methodology almost completely in the abstract, deductive, theoretical mold. Ricardo's weak points were history and description. J. S. Mill followed Smith in attempting to forge a structure in which theory, history, and description reinforced and complemented one another. Yet these men had many elements in common. They presumed that economic theory was universally true, equally applicable to different periods in history and to societies with markedly different structures. They also commonly assumed that an understanding of the entire economy was best achieved by starting at the level of the household and the firm. Human nature and behavior were antecedent to the culture. Another common element was an overriding belief that economic conflicts were harmoniously worked out in free markets. Whatever the inadequacies of free markets, they were preferable to government intervention in the economy. The only obvious flaw in this harmonious natural order was the conflict between the landlords and the industrialists. Aside from that, scarce resources would be efficiently allocated by the market without government direction, and the free play of markets would guarantee a full utilization of resources. In the classical analysis of the forces determining relative prices, prices were commonly assumed to depend upon the cost side or the supply side in the long run.

These classical ideas were not accepted by everyone. A literature developed in the post-Ricardian period criticized the classical theory of value and further suggested that utility and demand were the crucial factors in determining relative prices, rather than cost and supply. Other writers used the Ricardian labor theory of value to show that labor was being exploited, thereby calling into question the harmonious operation of the economic process in the classical system. This line of thinking reached its fruition in Marx, who used the classical tools to reach quite different conclusions. The systems presented by Auguste Comte, Karl Marx, and Herbert Spencer called into question the methodological foundations of classical theory, which defined the scope of economics narrowly and viewed human behavior as antecedent to culture and society. Some writers in Germany and England attacked the abstract nature of classical theory and tried to formulate a broader, historically oriented approach to understanding the economy. Finally, the basic theoretical structure was assailed by Jevons, Walras, and Menger, who wanted to replace the cost of production theory of value with an almost exclusive emphasis on the role of demand and marginal utility.

Marshallian economics is the product of these methodological and theoretical controversies. Marshall consistently refused to take a partisan approach to these issues, and his conclusions therefore failed to satisfy the dogmatic thinkers on both sides. He maintained there was merit in a narrow definition of the scope of economics, but he also held out the hope that a unified approach in the social sciences would prove fruitful. Because each methodological approach has its benefits as well as its costs, he considered it pointless to waste time arguing over a unique methodology for economics. Economists should use the approach that fits their training and temperament, and different methodologies should be regarded as complementary rather than mutually exclusive. Equally pointless are controversies over whether prices are determined by supply alone or by demand alone. Prices, Marshall pointed out, are the result of a vast set of complex, interacting forces. It is incorrect to view the process of price determination as a simple chain of causal relationships in which utility determines demand, which then determines price, or cost determines supply, which then determines price. Nor do marginal values, whether on the side of utility or of cost, determine prices. We go to the margin to examine the forces at work and to improve our understanding of them, but when we go to the margin we find that utility, cost, and price mutually determine one another's values and that simple causal chains do not exist. The margin, partial equilibrium, *ceteris paribus,* time periods, the representative firm, and factors of production are all abstract theoretical constructs that help us to break up complex problems for analysis. This analytical progress is achieved, however, at a cost of realism, and the economist must therefore supplement pure theory with descriptive and historical material.

Although Marshall attempted to take noncommittal positions on many of the methodological and theoretical issues of his time, he usually leaned in the direction of certain elements in the classical theory. He defined the scope of economics more broadly than Jevons, Menger, and Walras and preferred the methodology of Smith and J. S. Mill. He claimed that although prices depend upon a complex set of forces in the long run, the classical economists were basically correct in emphasizing the importance of cost and supply. The concept of opportunity cost gives some insights into the allocation of resources in the short run when supply is relatively fixed, but in the long run a more fundamental insight into the pricing process can be achieved by considering the real costs of production, the efforts of labor, and the waiting or abstinence of the capitalists. Marshall was never able to dispense completely with Bentham's hedonistic psychology, although he was well aware of the criticism it incurred.

The fundamental framework of present-day partial equilibrium microeconomic theory derives from Marshall's *Principles*. Although there have been many important contributions to micro theory since then, most have been additions to technique, not to substantive analysis. A primary exception is the contribution to the theory of market structures initiated by Joan Robinson and Edward Chamberlin in the 1930s; and many of their ideas are suggested by Marshall. One great weakness in Marshall's system was his failure to examine the forces determining the levels of income and employment. But when that treatment was undertaken in the 1930s by J. M. Keynes, it was formulated within the Marshallian framework of supply-and-demand analysis applied to aggregate variables.

Key Terms

political economy	price elasticity
economics	price elastic
positive economics	price inelastic
normative economics	substitution effect
art of economics	income effect
ceteris paribus	normal good
partial equilibrium	inferior good
one-thing-at-a-time method	Giffen goods
market period	consumers' surplus
short run	internal economies
prime costs	external economies
supplementary costs	quasi-rent
long run	stable equilibrium
secular period	unstable equilibrium

Questions for Review, Discussion, and Research

1. Explain Keynes's comment, "Jevon saw the kettle boil and cried out with the delighted voice of a child; Marshall too had seen the kettle boil and sat down silently to build an engine."

2. Distinguish between Walras's general equilibrium approach and Marshall's partial equilibrium approach.
3. Marshall is essentially irrelevant because all he ever says is, "It depends." Do you agree or do you disagree?
4. In what way was it ironic that Marshall started using the term *economics* rather than *political economy*?
5. Most modern economists regard tastes as outside the purview of economics; how would Marshall be likely to view this development?
6. Marshall stated that his entire life had been and would be given to presenting in realistic form as much as he could of a certain mathematical note. What was that note, and was Marshall accurate?
7. In what way is Marshall's analysis different in its treatment of time?
8. What are two limitations of Marshall's analysis of consumers' surplus?
9. Marshall said, "It is *wisest* not to say that 'Rent does not enter into cost of production': for that will confuse many people. But it is *wicked* to say that 'Rent *does* enter into cost of production,' because that is *sure* to be applied in such a way as to lead to the denial of subtle truths." Discuss.
10. Draw supply and demand curves that will be Marshallian stable and Walrasian unstable. Explain why.
11. That absent-minded professor is back with another job for you. This time, she's doing an article on methodology and remembers the following quotation from Marshall's *Principles:*

> We have seen that the economist must be greedy of facts; but that facts by themselves teach nothing. History tells of sequences and coincidences; but reason alone can interpret and draw lessons from them. The work to be done is so various that much of it must be left to be dealt with by trained common sense, which is the ultimate arbiter in every practical problem.

Alas, she does not remember where she found this quotation. Your assignment is to find the full bibliographic citation, and to explain and compare this view of methodology to the one found in your microeconomics text.

Suggested Readings

Biggs, R. J. *Cambridge and Monetary Theory of Production. The Collapse of Marshallian Macroeconomies.* London: Macmillan, 1990.
Coats, A. W. "Sociological Aspects of British Thought." *Journal of Political Economy,* 75 (October 1967).
Eastern Economic Journal, 8, No. 1 (January/March 1982). The entire issue is on Alfred Marshall.
Frisch, Ragnar. "Alfred Marshall's Theory of Value." *Quarterly Journal of Economics,* 64 (November 1950).
Guillebaud, Claude W. "Some Personal Reminiscences of Alfred Marshall." *History of Political Economy,* 3 (Spring 1971).

Homan, Paul T. "Alfred Marshall." In *Contemporary Economic Thought*. New York: Harper, 1928.

Keynes, J. M. "Alfred Marshall." In *Essays and Sketches in Biography*. New York: Meridian, 1956.

Marshall, Alfred. *Principles of Economics*. 9th ed. London: Macmillan, 1961.

Marshall Studies Bulletin (various issues).

Petridis, Anastasios. "Alfred Marshall's Attitudes to the Economic Analysis of Trade Unions: A Case of Anomalies in a Competitive System." *History of Political Economy,* 5 (Spring 1973).

Pigou, A. C., ed. *Memorials of Alfred Marshall*. New York: Kelley and Millman, 1956.

Review of Social Economy. 17, No. 4 (1990). The entire issue is on Alfred Marshall.

Robertson, H. M. "Alfred Marshall's Aims and Methods Illustrated from His Treatment of Distribution." *History of Political Economy,* 2 (Spring 1970).

Shove, G. F. "The Place of Marshall's 'Principles' in the Development of Economic Thought." *Economic Journal,* 52 (December 1942).

Viner, Jacob. "Marshall's Economics, in Relation to the Man and to His Times." *American Economic Review,* 31 (June 1941).

Whitaker, John K. "Alfred Marshall: The Years 1877 to 1885." *History of Political Economy,* 4 (Spring 1972).

―――――. *The Early Economic Writings of Alfred Marshall, 1867–1900*. New York: Free Press, 1975.

―――――. "Some Neglected Aspects of Marshall's Economic and Social Thought." *History of Political Economy,* 9 (Summer 1977).

Heterodox Economic
Thought

Clockwise from top left: Thorstein Bunde Veblen, John R. Commons, Joseph Alois Schumpeter, Ludwig von Mises

In Parts I, II, and III, we traced the unfolding of economic thought from the preclassical scholastics, mercantilists, and physiocrats; through the classicals, especially Adam Smith, David Ricardo, and J. S. Mill; and into the neoclassical period, which began in the 1870s and extends into the present. These parts concentrated on mainstream, *orthodox* economic thinking, but even with that focus we have seen that not all economists were in agreement over the proper scope, method, and content of economics. We saw that Malthus, for example, questioned some of the macro conclusions of classical theory and that Karl Marx used parts of the classical apparatus to question the very foundations of mainstream economic thought. There were also instances in which economists, in the excitement of discovering new insights, thought they were breaking new ground that would revolutionize accepted theory. Some of these "revolutions," however, came to be incorporated into the prevailing theory, and the "revolutionaries" eventually were accepted as seminal mainstream thinkers.

There have been individual writers and groups of writers, on the other hand, whose objections exerted little direct impact on current orthodox theory; pre-1930s Marxist theory and the German historical school would be prime examples of this. Other writers who contributed ideas to the mainstream had other views rejected by orthodox theorists—Thomas Robert Malthus and William Stanley Jevons are examples. In fact, every theorist is unique in this regard, no one being orthodox or heterodox on every issue.

In assessing *heterodox* ideas it is important to remember that the heterodox of today might become the mainstream of tomorrow—although some heterodox ideas are rejected by prevailing opinion and remain forever outside theory. Other theories, however, may be rejected at first but finally, sometimes long after their introduction, accepted because they are introduced in a new context or by an economist who has impeccable orthodox credentials. For example, the view that capitalism internally generates fluctuations in the level of economic activity took at least one hundred years to find its way into orthodoxy via Keynesian theory.

It is difficult to appreciate fully the development of economic thought without an examination of both orthodox and heterodox economic ideas. Thus, we have found it important to look at Malthus's underconsumptionist views, to discover how even orthodox economists such as J. S. Mill strayed from the fold, and to devote a complete chapter to the economic thought of Karl Marx.

In Part IV we bring together a number of older heterodox economists who have influenced modern economic thought, and some contemporary or modern heterodox writers who are striving to gain broader acceptance of their views. Sometimes these critics have enough in common to be classified as a school of their own—a "nonmainstream" or "heterodox" school. A school (at least the group of economists who have been included in a school) interacts with the mainstream profession to a greater or lesser extent, depending upon the personalities of the individuals and the nature of their deviation from the mainstream model. This interaction sometimes leads to conflict and change in the mainstream model; sometimes to a slow but certain modification of mainstream thinking that accommodates the heterodox insight; sometimes to entrenchment and fortification of the mainstream. Whatever the outcome, to understand mainstream economics it is absolutely necessary to understand heterodox thinking.

THE ROLE OF HETERODOX ECONOMISTS

Lakatos's "competing research program" approach to methodology envisions various groups competing for students to further their research programs. The group that is most successful in competing becomes the mainstream, and groups that are less successful but do attract some researchers become nonmainstream. Some economists who use the Lakatosian approach tend to regard mainstream theory as the "best" theory—whatever "best" might mean—but there is, in fact, no guarantee that mainstream theory constitutes the best theory or the truth. Because there are many areas of economics in which empirical testing is difficult, if not impossible, it is hard to devise tests that will cause the dominant view to be discarded. Theories are chosen for many reasons. Modern rhetorical and sociological approaches to methodology suggest that criteria irrelevant to the appropriateness of a theory play an important role in determining whether a theory is or is not studied, which makes an understanding of heterodox thought all the more important.

Defining Heterodoxy

Before we can discuss heterodox economics, we must establish a criterion for heterodoxy. Because empirical testing is difficult, the mainstream of economics itself includes divergent approaches. For example, in modern mainstream microeconomics two types of economic thought are generally included, one being characteristic of the

University of Chicago and the other, of the Massachusetts Institute of Technology. These are classified as mainstream because most mainstream economists regard both approaches as legitimate; in fact, graduate schools often try to have some representation from both groups to maintain a "balanced" program. Conversely, one defining characteristic of a heterodox school is "revealed illegitimacy." If the mainstream sees little or no value in a group's views, we define that group as heterodox. This does not mean that a heterodox economist cannot teach at a mainstream school; but most who do so have done some mainstream work and have later been converted to heterodoxy, or have a foot in both camps. The revealed illegitimacy criterion is not unambiguous. For example, mainstream graduate schools tend to take a narrower view of allowable mainstream thought than do undergraduate liberal arts schools, which are more likely to value diversity of thought. Nonetheless, the criterion of revealed illegitimacy provides some guidance in identifying heterodoxy.

How Dissenting Economists Influence Economic Thought and the Profession

One way to appreciate the role of the dissenting economists is to consider a segment of the history of economic thought. A history of economic thought is a history of change, and what is heterodox in one time period can find a place in the mainstream in another. For example, the heterodox views of Malthus, Tugan-Baranowsky, and Marx were partially reflected in the Keynesian revolution. These shifts occurred because some economists were willing to take a heterodox stance and then to convince others of its correctness. As they did so, sometimes their views became integrated into the mainstream.

Nonmainstream schools play important roles in the evolution of a discipline: they pollinate the mainstream view and keep it honest by pointing out its shortcomings or inconsistencies. An example of the interaction between heterodox thinking and mainstream developments can be seen in the development of the economics of Alfred Marshall, who was able to found neoclassical economics by wrestling with the competing claims of historically oriented economists and abstract theorists. But Marshallian economics was too formal and abstract for most American economists in the late nineteenth century; and when the American Economic Association was formed in 1885, it was largely in the control of economists sympathetic to the German historical school. There was open hostility between those who advocated historical-institutional methodological approaches and those who insisted that the future of economics lay in abstract-mathematical modes of analysis; their conflict has played an important role in shaping modern economics. The importance of the historical-institutional approach in American universities decreased during the first half of the twentieth century, and neoclassical economics (first Marshallian and finally Walrasian) emerged as the American mainstream.

Problems of Heterodox Economists

It is not easy being a heterodox economist. The profession does little to encourage heterodoxy and questions the legitimacy of its views. Because of this, heterodox economists generally tend to focus on methodology, because through methodology they can question the legitimacy of the assumptions, scope, and methods that mainstream economists take as given. A problem faced by almost all heterodox groups is that of moving beyond methodology to establish their own analysis and provide a viable competing research program. There is truth in the saying that a theory can be replaced only by another theory.

Another problem faced by heterodox groups is that people attracted to heterodox theory are often individualistic; they are as little prone to compromise with their heterodox colleagues as they are with mainstream economists. Consequently, the body of heterodoxy is almost inevitably riddled with dis-

sension. Heterodox thinkers, in fact, often save their most vituperative invective for their fellow heterodox economists.

Some heterodox economists tend to have "a chip on the shoulder"; contending that the mainstream has been unfair to them, they lose their ability or desire to communicate with the rest of the profession. That chip may well be warranted, because mainstream economists often do unfairly reject heterodox arguments; but without communication there can be no hope that mainstream economics will ever seriously consider heterodox thought.

STRUCTURE OF PART IV

In Part IV we review the major groups of heterodox thinkers over the past one hundred years. In Chapter 12 we consider some early critics of neoclassical economics, the German historical school and American institutionalists. In Chapter 13 we review a number of writers who have examined the theoretical foundations of socialistic economies, and we discuss the work of J. A. Schumpeter, who speculated about the future of capitalism. Finally, in Chapter 14 we examine several modern heterodox groups who are still playing a role in the evolution of economic thought.

12 Early Critics of Neoclassical Economics

"Man is not simply a bundle of desires but rather a coherent structure of propensities and habits which seeks realisation and expression in an unfolding society."

—Thorstein Veblen

IMPORTANT WRITERS

FRIEDRICH LIST	*The National System of Political Economy* 1841
WILHELM ROSCHER	*Outline of Lectures on Political Economy Based on the Historical Method* 1843
KARL KNIES	*Political Economy from the Standpoint of the Historical Method* 1853
T. E. CLIFFE LESLIE	*Essays in Political Economy* 1879
ARNOLD TOYNBEE	*Lectures on the Industrial Revolution of the Eighteenth Century in England* 1884
JOHN A. HOBSON	*The Physiology of Industry* 1889
GUSTAV VON SCHMOLLER	*The Mercantile System and Its Historical Significance* 1897
WERNER SOMBART	*Der Moderne Kapitalismus* 1902, 1927
THORSTEIN VEBLEN	*The Theory of Business Enterprise* 1904
WESLEY CLAIR MITCHELL	*Business Cycles* 1913
JOHN R. COMMONS	*Institutional Economics* 1934

Neoclassical economics did not come into being without controversy. As it was emerging, the German historical school challenged its methodological foundations; and throughout the late 1880s there was a vigorous debate between the Austrians, particularly Menger, and some members of the German historical school over the proper method for economics. Neoclassical economics swept through England and France but not Germany. When it tried to move to the United States, it was met with resistance. Around the turn of the century it was still commonplace for American graduate students in economics to study for their Ph.D.s in Germany. Many of these scholars returned home with a full knowledge and sympathetic view of the position of the German historical school. Added to this "imported" criticism of neoclassical theory were some distinctly American elements that had roots in the populist and progressive movements of the Middle West.

This chapter first summarizes the controversy over method that took place largely between German-speaking economists. It then considers the contributions of certain non-Marxian American heterodox economists of the current century, focusing on a group of U.S. writers who often are referred to as institutionalists.

Even with this limited focus it was not easy to decide which writers to include. We emphasize Gustav Schmoller in the historical school because of his importance in the debate. Veblen was chosen from the Americans writing earlier in the twentieth century because of his acknowledged influence on subsequent heterodox thought, Mitchell because of his pioneering work in collecting and analyzing data relevant to economic fluctuations, and Commons because of his impact on present social theory and legislation. Finally, we chose Hobson, an Englishman, as a representative of non-American heterodox economists because of his influence on contemporary English attitudes toward social policy.

Early dissent from orthodoxy had two major aspects: first, a dissent from orthodox theory's scope and method and from other elements in its theoretical core; second, a dissent from the overriding view of orthodox theory that a market system generally results in a harmonious resolution of economic forces and that laissez faire is therefore the best policy for a government to follow.

METHODOLOGICAL CONTROVERSY

Even before Menger, Jevons, Walras, and Marshall had begun to apply marginal analysis to the theory of value and distribution, orthodox classical theory was being criticized by certain nonsocialist German writers. Although there were some notable differences among the views of these writers, they had enough in common to be referred to collectively as the German historical school. The influence of this school began in Germany during the 1840s and extended into the present century. Many historians divide it into an older and a younger historical school, noting differences of opinion—largely resulting from changing problems in Germany and reactions to orthodox theory—between the earlier and the later writers.

Criticism of orthodox classical theory and advocacy of the so-called historical method also appeared in England in the 1870s independently of the German historical school. These English advocates of the historical method, however, formed no cohesive group, so it would be improper to speak of an English historical school. These German and English writers deserve our attention because of the influence they had on certain neoclassical economists, particularly Alfred Marshall. The Germans also influenced economic theory and policy in the United States because of the number of American economists who received graduate education in Germany.

The Older Historical School

The important writers of the *older historical school* are Friedrich List (1789–1846), Wilhelm Roscher (1817–1894), Bruno Hildebrand (1812–1878), and Karl Knies (1821–1898). They contended that classical economic theory did not apply to all times and cultures and that the conclusions of Smith, Ricardo, and J. S. Mill, though valid for an industrializing economy such as England's, did not apply to agricultural Germany. There was a great deal of nationalistic feeling in the economic analysis of these writers. Furthermore, they asserted that economics and the social sciences must use a historically based methodology and that classical theory was mistaken in attempting to ape the methodology of the physical sciences, particularly in the hands of Ricardo and his followers. Some of the more moderate members of the school acknowledged that theoretical-deductive methods and historical-inductive methods were compatible; but others, particularly Knies, objected to any use of abstract theory.

List expressed particularly strong nationalist views and refused to admit that the laissez faire conclusions of classical theory were applicable to countries less developed than England. Where classical theory held that national well-being would result from the pursuit of individual self-interest in an environment of laissez faire, List argued that state guidance was necessary, particularly for Germany and the United States. He contended that whereas free trade would be beneficial to England, given the advanced state of its industry, tariffs and protection were necessary for Germany and the United States. He spent five years in the United States, from 1825 to 1830, and some ten years later published *The National System of Political Economy* (1841), which drew on his experience here. His protectionist views were so warmly received in the United States that he is often called the father of American protectionism.

What was the historical method advocated by these writers? Their works reflect a belief that the chief task of economics is to discover the laws governing the stages of economic growth and development. For example, List stated that economies in the temperate zone will go through five stages: nomadic life; pastoral life; agriculture; agriculture and manufacturing; and manufacturing, agriculture, and commerce. Hildebrand asserted that the key to understanding the stages of economic growth was to be found in the conditions of exchange; thus, he posited three economic stages based on barter, money, and credit. These descriptions of growth by stages obviously contain a certain amount of theory, and they are highly abstract. However, the writers did collect large quantities of historical and statistical information to support their analyses of economic development. In more recent times, W. W. Rostow (1916–   ) has advanced a theory of economic development by stages, which is in the tradition of the older historical school.[1] As might be expected, his book has been much better accepted by those in other social sciences than by economists themselves.

The Younger Historical School

The second generation of the German historical school was represented by one outstanding leader, Gustav von Schmoller (1838–1917). Like the members of the older historical school, these writers attacked classical economic theory, particularly the view that it was applicable to all times and places. Generally much less ambitious than the older school in their application of the historical method, they were content to write monographs on various aspects of the economy and society rather than to formulate grand theories of the stages of economic development. In this endeavor they preferred to use inductive methods and seemed to think that after enough empirical evidence had been gathered, theories might emerge. They also were very interested in social reform through state action. Because of this they were called "socialists of the chair," an epithet they happily accepted, contending that their critics who would not accept proposals such as income taxation were reactionaries.

The application of marginal analysis and the construction of abstract deductive models by Menger, Jevons, and Walras in the early 1870s had little or no influence in Germany. Although Menger, an Austrian, wrote his *Principles* in German, it was not studied in the German universities because they subscribed exclusively to the historical method. Though Schmoller, in his earlier writings, did not recommend the construction of abstract theoretical models, he was willing to admit that both methodologies had a place in economic investigation. In 1883 Menger published a book on methodology, *Inquiries into the Method of the Social Sciences and Particularly Political Economy,* which began a long, dreary, and ultimately fruitless controversy that extended into the twentieth century. This *Methodenstreit* (controversy over method) was one of the most intense methodological controversies ever to occur in the development of economic theory; it was equaled only by the later controversy in the United States between the institutionalists and the orthodox theorists. Menger's book included a general survey of the methodological issues in economics and the social sciences, but he also launched a polemic against the errors of the historical approach. Schmoller responded to the bait, and the battle commenced. Menger published a refutation of Schmoller's response, and others joined in the fun. Both sides put their backs to the wall and argued for the virtually exclusive use of their own methodological approach. As Schumpeter has pointed out, both used honorific terms to describe their own methodology—empirical, realistic, modern, and exact—while referring to the competing methodology as speculative, futile, and subordinate.

---

[1] W. W. Rostow, *The Stages of Economic Growth* (Cambridge: Cambridge University Press, 1960).

From one point of view, the controversy could be regarded as a mere wasteland of economic literature and a detriment to the development of economics as a discipline, because capable minds occupied their time in pointless argument. On the other hand, it may be that the controversy helped economists to recognize that theory and history, deduction and induction, abstract model building and statistical data gathering are not mutually exclusive within their discipline.

Although individual economists may be inclined to devote the majority of their efforts exclusively to one of these methods, a healthy, developing discipline requires a variety of methodological approaches. Because neither methodology can be accepted to the complete exclusion of the other, the real issue is the priority to be given to each one. In our view the internal development of the discipline will determine this issue, so it is pointless to debate it.

There is another lesson to be learned from the controversy. If practitioners of a particular methodological approach become so convinced of its correctness that they will not permit other points of view to be represented at the universities where research and the training of graduate students occur, the development of economics will suffer. This happened in Germany, where the self-righteous and rigid intellectual leadership of Schmoller was so influential that abstract theoreticians who pursued the lines laid down by Menger, Jevons, Walras, and Marshall were unable to find academic employment. As a result, the mainstream of economic thinking passed by German economists, and economics as an intellectual discipline suffered in Germany for several decades.

The Historical Method in England

During the last quarter of the nineteenth century, a number of English writers criticized orthodox classical theory and advocated the historical approach to the study of economics. These writers did not form a cohesive group as in Germany, nor were they influenced directly by the German writers. The English tradition in economic thought was no stranger to the historical inductive approach. Adam Smith's *Wealth of Nations* was a blend of historical and descriptive material tied together with a loose theoretical structure. Ricardo represented a major shift in the methodology of economics toward the building of abstract deductive models almost completely devoid of any historical or institutional content. Senior supported and extended Ricardo's use of deductive reasoning. J. S. Mill and Alfred Marshall, however, moved back in the direction of Smith's methodology, using his great scholarship and knowledge of historical and institutional material to give substance to his theoretical structure.

The leading English advocate of the historical method was T. E. Cliffe Leslie (1827–1882), who directed his criticism of the methodology of classical economics largely toward Ricardo and his followers. Leslie maintained that Smith's economic theory was not applicable to the contemporary English situation but that on balance Smith's methodology was reasonably sound, because Smith made extensive use of historical material in arriving at his conclusions. Although Arnold Toynbee (1852–1883) died at a young age and his great promise as an economic historian was never fully realized, his *Lectures on the Industrial Revolution of the Eighteenth Century in England* (1884) are a magnificent example of the use of the historical approach to understanding the fundamental changes that took place in England and the resulting problems of an industrial economy. It was Toynbee who coined the term *Industrial Revolution*. The works of William Ashley (1860–1927) and William Cunningham (1849–1919) on English economic history are still highly respected. Other writers used the historical method to analyze specific topics: Walter Bagehot (1826–1877) wrote *Lombard Street* (1873), a classic study of English banking; and John K. Ingram (1823–1907) published *History of Political Economy* (1888), the first systematic book on the history of economic theory written in English.

Although the historical school has not had a major impact on recent developments in theory, its lessons remain valid and have influenced many of the critics of economic theory whom we will consider in the next part of this chapter and in Chapter 14.

THORSTEIN VEBLEN

Thorstein Bunde Veblen (1857–1929) is the intellectual father of the branch of American heterodoxy often called *institutionalism*. His scientific and ethical dissent from orthodox theory greatly influenced the development of heterodox thinking in the United States. Veblen's views are in part explained by his background. The son of Norwegian immigrants, he was reared in rural Wisconsin and Minnesota. When he entered Carleton College, his command of English was as deficient as his knowledge of American society, and he never became fully integrated into the American mainstream. He was like a man from Mars observing the absurdities of the economic and social order with satirical wit. At Carleton his brilliance was recognized by J. B. Clark, who was then making seminal contributions to marginal analysis; with Clark's encouragement, Veblen went east to graduate school. He received his Ph.D. in philosophy from Yale but was unable to obtain a job in teaching, apparently because of his atheistic views. So Veblen returned to the farm, married his college sweetheart, and spent seven years reading and thinking.

At the age of thirty-five he secured a postdoctoral fellowship at Cornell. Still unable to find an academic appointment, he received a fellowship to the University of Chicago, where he was finally appointed instructor of economics and given the editorship of the *Journal of Political Economy*. He was never popular with university administrators, never reached the rank of full professor, and spent the rest of his life moving from college to college. It is not clear whether his failure to receive the professional recognition his scholarship warranted was a result of his penetrating criticism of American capitalism, his almost complete disregard for all but the best of his students, or his personal life, which was complicated by affairs and marital difficulties. In the mid-1920s, however, after several years of political infighting, the American Economic Association offered Veblen its presidency on the condition that he join the association and deliver an address. He refused the offer, asserting that it had not come at the time when he needed it.

Veblen's isolated agrarian upbringing, his training in philosophy, his wide reading in the social sciences, and his deep appreciation of the significance of the Darwinian revolution are reflected in his analysis of American capitalism. His style and choice of words give his works a quality that some writers have found highly entertaining and others have deplored. He was a phrasemaker who loved to make his readers uncomfortable by using terms like *conspicuous consumption* to describe the purchasing patterns of the emerging affluent society. We are either members of the *kept classes* or the *underlying population.* University presidents are *captains of erudition* and the chief service of businessmen is to *practice sabotage.* Industry is *inordinately productive* and profit making requires *a conscientious withdrawal of efficiency.* Veblen described the church as "an accredited vent for the erudition of effete matter from the cultural organism." W. C. Mitchell has suggested that one needs a sense of humor to appreciate Veblen; perhaps this is why he is so little appreciated by economists.

Veblen's Criticism of Orthodox Theory

Veblen's criticisms of orthodox theory are contained throughout his works, although a collection of his essays, *The Place of Science in Modern Civilization,* contains most of his explicitly methodological writings. His training in philosophy partly explains the nature of his attack on the accepted economics of his time. Veblen was not interested in making small changes in the theoretical structure, for example, in correcting minor logical flaws in the system. He struck at the heart of neoclassical theory, asserting that the basic assumptions of received doctrine were unscientific. Such an assault on the fundamental tenets of a theoretical structure leaves those trained in that structure with two choices: they may accept the criticism and build a new theory on altered premises, or they may reject the criticism. Criticism of a theoretical structure that accepts its basic premises but offers new, more logical, or more empirically correct conclusions can also be accepted or rejected; but in such a case acceptance is much less painful for those already trained in the discipline, because it demands no drastic reordering of their training and orientation. Veblen was clearly no Ricardo, Marshall, or Keynes trying to improve the theoretical structure of classical economics while accepting its premises as laid down by Smith; he wanted to tear down the entire structure and rebuild a unified social science from economics, anthropology, sociology, psychology, and history. It is interesting to note that Veblen criticized prior heterodox thinking on the same grounds as those on which he criticized orthodoxy, contending that both the historical school and Marxian economics were deficient because their basic assumptions and preconceptions were unscientific.

It was Veblen's view that although the terminology of orthodox economic theory had changed from the time of Smith, its basic assumptions and preconceptions remained the same. Before Smith much analysis of the economy and society had been based on the preconception that society was ordered by supernatural forces so as to obtain desirable results. Later the appeal to supernatural forces or God was replaced with the idea that natural laws existed in the economy and society, just as in the physical sciences, and that appropriate investigation and study would reveal the workings of these natural laws.

Veblen said that all of orthodox economic theory from Smith through Marshall was based on the same assumption: that there is harmony in the system, or what Veblen called a "meliorative trend." This appears in Smith's concept of natural price and in the workings of the invisible hand that turns private vices into public benefits. Marshallian theory reflects this belief in its notions of normal price and equilibrium and in its expectation of beneficial results from perfectly competitive markets in long-run equilibrium. J. B. Clark's conclusion that long-run competitive equilibrium produces an equitable distribution of income is a particularly striking example of the presumption of harmony in the economy. To Veblen the concept of equilibrium as used by orthodox theorists was normative: they imply, without proof, that equilibrium is good and that the results produced by markets in equilibrium are socially beneficial.

Let us examine this point from a different perspective and integrate it with another of Veblen's criticisms of orthodox theory. Borrowing concepts from philosophy and biology, Veblen concluded that orthodox theory was *teleological* and, therefore, pre-Darwinian. It was teleological because it depicted the economy as moving toward an end—namely, long-run equilibrium—that was not attained empirically, but given before the analysis began. It was therefore pre-Darwinian because, as Veblen interpreted Darwin, evolution was a purely mechanical process by which living things developed over time in response to environmental circumstances. There was no purpose or design in evolution.

Classical thought was also pre-Darwinian in refusing to admit that the economy was constantly changing and evolving and in focusing instead on its static aspects. The static, pre-Darwinian economic theory, Veblen contended, should be replaced by a dynamic Darwinian analysis of the evolution of the economy and society. Veblen made this same point in biological terminology, accusing orthodox theory of being *taxonomic* and therefore, again, unscientifically pre-Darwinian. It is taxonomic in that it classifies the economy and its parts but has no explanation or conception of them as a set of evolving, changing institutions. In its focus on price theory, orthodox economics assumes many things as given or fixed (e.g., tastes or consumer preferences, technology, the organizational arrangements of the society and economy, and so forth). Veblen suggested that economists not only study the formation of prices and the allocation of resources but investigate the very factors they held constant. He had some kind words for Marshall in his attempt to break from static analysis but concluded that Marshall was unsuccessful in this endeavor.

One reason Veblen gave for the unscientific nature of economics was that it had never been purged of Adam Smith's concept of the invisible hand. It was founded, therefore, on an assumption that was never examined: that making money could be equated with making goods. According to orthodox theory, the businessman in pursuit of profit will produce at the lowest possible cost those goods that consumers want. Competitive markets make the self-interest of the businessman correspond to that of the society. Each individual businessman following his own self-interest promotes the social good. Veblen maintained that it was obvious to all but economists that producing goods and making profits were two different things, that the business community's striving for profits often has deleterious effects on the economy and society, and that each individual businessman following his own self-interest will promote only his own self-interest. It has been suggested that this conception of the economy and society came to Veblen at a young age when he moved from a Lutheran family on a frontier farm in Minnesota to Carleton College, which was attended mainly by the children of moneymakers from New England with a Congregational background.[2] The growth of the size and power of the large corporation and the formation of the trusts in the last quarter of the nineteenth century also influenced Veblen. In addition, the agrarian populist hostility toward business—the grain elevator, the railroad, the farm equipment manufacturers, and the banks—must have run deep in his family.

Veblen contended that in Adam Smith's time there was a reasonably close connection between making profits and producing goods serviceable to the society. But this changed as the economy developed. He drew a sharp distinction between those who are involved in producing goods—production managers, foremen, and workers—and those who are involved in the management of firms. The aim of business is pecuniary gain, and Veblen delighted in pointing to examples in which the general interest is damaged by the pursuit of profit. His view is that increased profits result from a reduction of output, which is obviously detrimental to society. The purpose of the larger corporations that were being formed during Veblen's time was not to increase efficiency but to acquire monopoly power and restrict production. He pointed to the advertising activities of firms, questioning their serviceability to the community at large. Competition between firms for international markets led to conflicts and ultimately to wars. The pecuniary activities of the captains of industry will inevitably lead to depressions and mass unemployment. In essence, Veblen rejected the orthodox assumption of perfectly competitive markets and the idea that markets under the control of businessmen would produce socially desirable results. Where orthodox theory found harmony under capitalism with an efficient allocation of resources and full employment, Veblen found discord, with the businessman sabotaging the system in order to make profits and, ultimately, bringing about depression.

The pre-Darwinian, teleological preconceptions of orthodox theory reflected the failure of economics to keep abreast of developments in the physical and biological sciences. Orthodox economic theory was also culpable in ignoring developments in psychology, sociology, and anthropology, and in building a model based upon unscientific notions of human nature and behavior. Orthodox theory, according to Veblen, was based upon the assumption that humans are driven by the desire to maximize pleasure and minimize pain, on hedonistic psychology.

[2] W. C. Mitchell, *Types of Economic Theory* (New York: Augustus M. Kelley, 1967), p. 619.

Given this assumption, economists correctly deduced its logical consequences. The logic was impeccable, but the assumption was wrong. Veblen maintained that orthodox economics was the study of man, with man abstracted out of the analysis. In some of his most biting prose, he ridiculed the accepted theory of consumer behavior:

> The psychological and anthropological preconceptions of the economists have been those which were accepted by the psychological and social sciences some generations ago. The hedonistic conception of man is that of a lightning calculator of pleasure and pains, who oscillates like a homogeneous globule of desire of happiness under the impulse of stimuli that shift him about the area, but leave him intact. He has neither antecedent nor consequent. He is an isolated, definitive human datum in stable equilibrium except for the buffets of the impinging forces that displace him in one direction or another. Self-imposed in elemental space, he spins symmetrically about his own spiritual axis until the parallelogram of forces bears down upon him, whereupon he follows the line of the resultant. When the force of the impact is spent, he comes to rest, a self-contained globule of desire as before.[3]

A final criticism of orthodox theory by Veblen, one less explicitly stated than the others, was its failure to reconcile the theory of the economy with the facts of the economy. Thus, Veblen's writing includes an implicit plea for more empirical work and a greater emphasis on inductive research.

Veblen's Analysis of Capitalism

Veblen insisted that the subject matter of economics should be something quite different from that of the prevailing economic theory. Orthodox theory in Veblen's time was largely interested in how society allocates its scarce resources among alternative uses. Veblen contended that economics should be a study of the evolving institutional structure, defining institutions as habits of thought that are accepted at any particular time. In this definition of the subject matter of economics, Veblen accorded to some extent with Marx; both were attempting to explain the forces that shape society and the economy. What orthodox economic theory assumed as given, the particular institutions of a culture, Veblen tried to explain. An explanation of the prevailing culture required an evolutionary approach, he held, for any culture can be understood only by its antecedents:

> The growth of culture is a cumulative sequence of habituation, and the way and means of it are the habitual response of human nature to exigencies that vary incontinently, cumulatively, but with something of a consistent sequence in the cumulative variations that so go forward—incontinently, because each new move creates a new situation which induces a further new variation in the habitual man-

---

[3] Thorstein Veblen, "Why Is Economics Not an Evolutonary Science?" in *The Place of Science in Modern Civilization* (New York: B. W. Huebsch, 1919), pp. 73–74.

ner of response; cumulatively, because each new situation is a variation of what has gone before it and embodies as causal factors all that has been expected by what went before; consistently, because the underlying traits of human nature (propensities, aptitudes, and what not) by force of which the response takes place . . . remain substantially unchanged.[4]

To understand the development and present functioning of the industrial society, we must understand the complex set of interrelationships that exist between traits of human nature and the culture:

> Not only is the individual's conduct hedged about and directed by his habitual relations to his fellows in the group, but these relations, being of an institutional character, vary as the institutional scheme varies. The wants and desires, the end and aim, the ways and means, the amplitude and drift of the individual's conduct are functions of an institutional variable that is of a highly complex and wholly unstable character.[5]

As individuals emerge within the culture, they find themselves acting in accordance with established patterns of behavior that are a legacy of past interaction between individuals and culture, and that have taken on an institutional character and force. These relatively fixed underlying traits of human behavior Veblen called *instincts*. He was much influenced by the contemporary development in psychology that emphasized the role of instincts in guiding human behavior. Veblen regarded the most important instincts that shape human economic activities as the parental instinct, workmanship, idle curiosity, and acquisitiveness. The parental instinct is originally a concern for family, tribe, class, nation, and humankind. The instinct of workmanship makes us desire to produce goods of high quality, to be proud of and to admire workmanship, and to be concerned with efficiency and economy in our work. Idle curiosity leads us to ask questions and seek explanations for the world around us. It is an important element in accounting for the development of scientific knowledge. The acquisitive instinct is the opposite of the parental in that it leads the individual to regard his or her own welfare rather than that of others.

The Dichotomy

The instinctive drives of human beings create certain tensions. The instincts of parenthood, workmanship, and idle curiosity would lead humans to produce high-quality products with great efficiency that would be of benefit to their fellow humans. The acquisitive instinct, however, because it is self-regarding, leads to behavior that benefits the individual, even though it might have deleterious consequences for the rest of society. An analysis of the economy, Veblen said,

---

[4] Thorstein Veblen, "The Limitations of Marginal Utility," in *The Place of Science in Modern Civilization*, pp. 241–242.
[5] *Ibid.*, pp. 242–243.

discloses this fundamental tension and antagonism, which is basic in human nature. Every culture can be analyzed by observing two aspects of human behavior: one that promotes the economic life process, and another that inhibits the full development of the productive powers of the society and has negative effects on the welfare of humankind.

Veblen called the activities that flow largely from the instincts of parenthood, workmanship, and idle curiosity *industrial* (or *technological*) *employments*. They involve matter-of-fact, cause and effect relationships. He engaged in conjectural history—although he had severely criticized orthodox theory for this practice—and explained that in the distant past humans attempted to explain the unknown by appealing to supernatural forces to bring about effects by casting spells, to grow corn by dancing around the stalk. This noninstrumental, nontechnological, prescientific manner of approaching the unknown and seeking explanations or effects Veblen called *ceremonial behavior*. Ceremonial behavior is static and past-binding. It manifests itself in totem and taboo, in an appeal to authority or emotion, and it has undesirable consequences for the welfare of humankind. Industrial or technological employments are, however, dynamic, and the more we approach problem-solving with a scientific, matter-of-fact point of view, the more our tools, technology, and problem-solving capacities increase. Technology does not look back, but ceremonial behavior is rooted in the past.

Veblen's analysis of the culture and economy of his time is founded upon this dichotomy. Nearly all his papers and books set forth this theme again and again. He contended that this framework and its application involved no normative judgments but constituted a matter-of-fact, positive analysis of the development and current structure of the culture and society. The purely economic applications of the dichotomy are most clearly seen in his essay "Industrial and Pecuniary Employments" and in possibly his best single book of economic analysis, *The Theory of Business Enterprise* (1904). Ceremonial behavior in the modern culture manifests itself in what Veblen called *pecuniary* (or *business*) *employments*. In the handicraft period, which preceded the emergence of the industrial economy, the craftsman owned his tools and materials, used his own labor, and produced commodities that gave expression to his instincts for workmanship and parenthood. The income derived from these activities was a fair measure of the effort exerted. As the economy developed, much changed. The worker no longer owned the tools of production or the materials, and the owner of the firm now became more interested in making money than in making goods; acquisitive instinct overrode instincts of workmanship and parenthood. Moneylending developed, absentee ownership became more common, and individuals now had "prescriptive rights to get something for nothing." The captains of industry emerged and a period of intense competition followed. The captains of industry soon recognized that competition was undesirable; and holding companies, trusts, and interlocking directorates were formed through the instrumentality of the investment bankers. The One Big Union of the vested interests and absentee owners was formed. All the developments resulted in different habits of thought, both for the workers and engineers and for the captains of industry and absentee owners. The workers and engineers are involved on a daily basis in industrial employments—

the making of goods. This leads them to think in terms of cause and effect and gives expression to their instincts of workmanship and parenthood. But the captains of industry and the absentee owners are concerned with profits, and it is Veblen's view that quite often, making profits conflicts with making goods.

The major thrust of Veblen's analysis of the industrial society of his time is that orthodox theory is incorrect in holding that an economy directed by businessmen will promote the social good. He pointed relentlessly to the "illfare" caused by the businessman. Firms with monopoly power practice "advised idleness" in order to make larger profits. This reduction in output, which enhances profits, leads to a "capitalization of inefficiency." "Industry is carried on for the sake of business, and not conversely."[6] A good deal of activity is misdirected into producing goods of no service to humankind and into marketing and advertising. The businessman is not the benefactor of society, but its saboteur.

The Leisure Class

The ceremonial-industrial dichotomy was also applied to what Veblen called the *leisure class*. In 1899 Veblen published what proved to be his most widely read book, *The Theory of the Leisure Class;* it became the favorite of many intellectuals of his time. Here he used his basic dichotomy to discuss conspicuous consumption, conspicuous leisure, conspicuous waste, pecuniary emulation, and dress as an expression of the pecuniary culture. Veblen reasoned that in less developed cultures the predatory powers of a man or tribe were held in high esteem, giving honorific status to their holders. In the modern industrial economy these predatory powers manifest themselves in employments that result in high incomes for a few members of the society. However, the large incomes are of little value if they cannot be recognized, so our culture supplies a number of mechanisms to permit this display. Because emulation is a powerful motive, these wealth-displaying activities quickly spread throughout the society.

Conspicuous consumption in the articles we buy is a most efficient means of displaying our predatory abilities. Our automobiles, housing, and especially our clothes give a clear indication of our place in the predatory order. If the male of the household is too busily involved in his predatory activities, his wife is expected to carry the burden of displaying the family wealth. She does this in dress and the display of other articles as well as by carefully avoiding any sort of work—the number of servants employed is a good index of economic capacity. Moreover, because the leisure class is the high-income class, what work is done should be in strictly pecuniary employments; absentee ownership is preferred, but if some actual work must be done, high management, finance, or banking are ceremonially acceptable. Law is a good profession because "the lawyer is exclusively occupied with the details of predatory fraud."[7] Our leisure activities, too, reflect this desire

[6] Thorstein Veblen, *The Theory of Business Enterprise* (New York: Charles Scribner's Sons, 1904), p. 26.
[7] Thorstein Veblen, *The Theory of the Leisure Class* (Boston: Houghton Mifflin Company, 1973), p. 156.

Veblen on Higher Education

In 1918 Veblen applied his analysis to the university in a work titled *The Higher Learning in America*. The subtitle of the book, "A Memorandum on the Conduct of Universities by Business Men," reflects the ceremonial-industrial dichotomy, the theme of the treatise. Veblen reasoned that knowledge is acquired and advanced through the institution of the university when free play is given to idle curiosity and the instinct of workmanship. But universities have become contaminated by the values of the culture, which give a high place to ceremonial behavior and the pursuit of pecuniary employments. University policy is in the control of governing boards of trustees who are businessmen, or politicians and clergy controlled by business-men. Veblen found it quaint that individuals who have demonstrated their predatory powers by the pursuit of profit should later be expected to know anything about the pursuit of knowledge:

> Indeed except for a stubborn prejudice to the contrary, the fact should be readily seen that the boards are of no material use in any connection; their sole effectual function being to interfere with the academic management in matters that are not of the nature of business, and that lie outside their competence and outside the range of their habitual interest.*

*Thorstein Veblen, *The Higher Learning in America* (Stanford: Academic Reprints, 1954), p. 66.

---

for honorific status in the culture, said Veblen. Higher education, which makes a person unfit for honest work, is of great value. The leisure class has also cultivated a great interest in sporting activities and rationalizes this on the grounds of promoting physical well-being and manly qualities. Veblen remarked that "It has been said, not inaptly, that the relation of football to physical culture is much the same as that of the bull-fight to agriculture."[8]

Whereas individuals associated with technological employments, such as inventors and engineers, are bold and resourceful, Veblen contended, American businessmen exhibit a spirit of quietism, "compromise, caution, collusion, and chicane."[9] But the businessmen reap the benefits of the technological society in unearned income. He remarked that "There is a homely but well-accepted American colloquialism which says that 'The silent hog eats the swill.'"[10] It was Veblen's view that scholarly and scientific training makes an individual unsuited for business and that business experience is incompatible with the pursuit of knowledge.

Moving from the governing boards to academic administration, he called university presidents "captains of erudition." Though they are often former scholars, he said, they become caught up in the pecuniary values of our culture

[8] *Ibid.*, pp. 173–174.
[9] Thorstein Veblen, *The Higher Learning in America,* p. 70.
[10] *Ibid.*, p. 71.

and misdirect the efforts of the university; like their counterparts in business, they become confused between means and ends. Universities compete with each other in a waste of resources comparable to that of their counterparts in business; the president and board become more interested in buildings, grounds, and real estate than in educational programs and policies; resources are wasted on athletics, law and business schools, ceremonies, and pageants that are neither of value to the university nor of service to the society. Veblen did not spare "the professoriate," who think "their salaries are not of the nature of wages," have no collective bargaining rights, and aspire to be "country gentlemen." To control the faculty, the presidents appoint deans and others who have "a ready versatility of convictions and a staunch loyalty to their bread."[11] The major program of action that Veblen recommended to return the university to the pursuit of knowledge is an elimination of the president and the board of governors. It is difficult to tell how serious Veblen was about this satirical proposal, but at least he recognized that it would be highly unlikely to take place.

The Stability and Long-Run Tendencies of Capitalism

Veblen applied his distinction between pecuniary and industrial employments to the development of a business cycle theory as well as to speculation on the tendencies of capitalism in the very long run. During the prosperity phase of the cycle, the pecuniary activities of the businessmen lead to an expansion of credit, and higher values are placed on the intangible ability of corporations to earn profits. The increased value of capital serves as collateral for additional credit. This process is self-reinforcing for a while, as the quantity of credit and collateral value of capital goods keep expanding with the increase in the prices of capital goods. But it soon becomes apparent that a wide gap exists between the earning power of capital goods and their values as manifested in security prices, and a period of liquidation and retrenchment begins.

Falling prices, output, employment, and reduced credit lead to a recapitalization of firms on a more realistic basis. During the depression phase of the cycle, weaker firms are forced out or acquired by larger, stronger firms and the concentration of the ownership and control of American industry into fewer hands proceeds. The depression phase of the cycle contains self-correcting forces, because real wages fall and profit margins increase. Finally, the excess credit is wrung out of the economy and the pecuniary value of business as reflected in balance sheets reflects a more reasonable evaluation of industrial output.

Although all of Veblen's writings speculate about the long-run tendencies of the system, he dealt with these issues most explicitly in *The Theory of the Leisure Class, The Theory of Business Enterprise,* and an essay, "Some Neglected Points in the Theory of Socialism." Veblen was as critical of the Marxian analysis of

[11] *Ibid.,* p. 94.

capitalism as he was of orthodox theory. In one sentence he disposed of the Marxian law of the increasing misery of the proletariat:

> The claim that the system of competition has proved itself an engine for making the rich richer and the poor poorer has the fascination of epigram; but if its mean-ing is that the lot of the average, of the masses of humanity in civilized life, is worse to-day, as measured in the means of livelihood, than it was twenty, or fifty, or a hundred years ago, then it is farcical.[12]

Veblen's speculations about the future are in terms of the conflicts and tensions created by the clash of pecuniary and industrial employments. His analysis in *The Theory of the Leisure Class* suggests that emulation, adulation, and the making of invidious comparisons in the consumption of goods will lead to an economy devoted to conspicuous consumption, conspicuous waste, and increased advertis-ing and marketing costs. As long as industry is controlled by businessmen in search of profits, we can expect an increased flow of goods that impede the progress of mankind. If, however, the working population and engineers, through their daily association with the matter-of-fact, cause and effect relationships engendered by industrial employments, should gain control of the system, the industrial economy might fulfill its promise.

Although Marx was wrong, according to Veblen, in his prediction that capital-ism might fall through revolutions brought about because the poor had grown poorer, capitalism may end because the working classes will have a feeling of being *relatively* poorer as the system grows. Veblen believed that the emulation in consumption patterns generated under capitalism is such a strong force that it may create tensions in the system and discontent on the part of the working classes and lead to the end of private property. No amount of increase in the absolute real income of individuals can relieve these tensions, for individuals want more than others, not just more:

> Human nature being what it is, the struggle of each to possess more than his neighbor is inseparable from the institution of private property. . . . The inference seems to be that . . . there can be no peace from this—it must be admitted—igno-ble form of emulation, or from the discontent that goes with it, this side of the abolition of private property.[13]

The suggestion that capitalism may end because of individuals' concern about their own relative well-being is another example of the paradoxical quality of Veblen's analysis. Here Veblen is suggesting, in contrast to Marx, that capitalism will cease not because of its failure but because of its success.

Veblen refused, however, to commit himself completely and suggested that not all of this may not actually come about. The future of capitalism and pri-vate property is uncertain. One possibility is that the growing scientific and

---

[12] Thorstein Veblen, "The Theory of Socialism," in *The Place of Science in Modern Civiliza-tion,* p. 391.
[13] *Ibid.,* pp. 397–398.

technological attitudes generated among the working classes and engineers will lead to a replacement of the businessman, and control of the economy will pass into the hands of technocrats. If these developments occur, said Veblen, it will mean an end to absentee ownership, financial manipulation, and the search for profits, and industry will be so directed as to produce goods serviceable to humankind.

It is also possible that a genuine socialist revolution may take place, thus ending class discrepancies, dynastic politics, and international animosities. Another possibility is an economic and political movement to the right as the working class and engineers lend themselves to nationalist ambitions and warlike aims and democracy subsides into a police state. Being deeply rooted in the Darwinian theory of evolution, Veblen would not make the error of Marx and predict the future with certainty. The only inevitability in Veblen's view of the future is change. Whether imbecile institutions will triumph over matter-of-fact technology remains to be seen:

> Which of the two antagonistic factors may prove the stronger in the long run is something of a blind guess; but the calculable future seems to belong to one or the other. It seems possible to say this much, that the full dominion of business enterprise is necessarily a transitory dominion.[14]

Veblen's Contribution

Heterodox economic theory in general, and Veblen in particular, are often omitted from books on the history of economic theory, probably because they had very little direct effect on modern orthodox economic theory. Veblen was highly critical of the orthodox economic theory that had received its most mature statement in the economics of Alfred Marshall. He wanted to scrap the system because he considered its approach wrongheaded. Veblen asserted that orthodox theory was atomistic in approach, attempting to understand the economy as a whole by proceeding from an initial analysis of its parts, the household and the firm. But the whole is different from the sum of the parts; Veblen argued that a proper approach should start at the level of the culture, society, and economy.

Some people say that Veblen was not an economist at all, but a sociologist, which to some economists simply means a fuzzy-thinking social scientist. But this view of Veblen as something other than an economist is at least consistent with both his approach and his contribution. One of Veblen's theories was precisely that we cannot understand what we call the economy by isolating the economic behavior of the human race from its other activities. Veblen was, therefore, actually suggesting an amalgamation of the social sciences.

Veblen was not interested in the same set of problems as orthodox theorists. He wanted to understand the development of the institutional structure formed by the habits of thought that guide our economic activity. From this perspective Veblen's

---

[14] Thornstein Veblen, *Theory of Business Enterprise*, p. 400.

contribution could be regarded as complementary to orthodox theory. However, Veblen would argue that once the changing institutional structure was understood, a solution of the more limited and narrow problems addressed by orthodox theory would require a different set of assumptions and tools from those currently used by the economist. He insisted that economics must use an evolutionary approach and drop its teleological notions of natural, normal, and equilibrium; must integrate with the other social sciences; must drop its unrealistic assumptions of competitive markets and hedonistic households; must recognize that its implicit assumption of harmony in the system invalidates much of its analysis; and must supplement its sterile, deductive approach with more fact-finding and statistical work.

Veblen found many flaws in economics, but the alternatives he offered have not yet been very fruitful. He built no grand model with easily identifiable assumptions and a logical superstructure leading inexorably to unambiguous conclusions. The instinct psychology that he substituted for the hedonism of orthodox theory has subsequently been rejected by psychology.

Orthodox theorists have responded to Veblen's criticism of their use of hedonistic concepts by substituting a less objectionable terminology, but their basic model still assumes rational, calculating households and firms. The perfectly competitive market assumption that Veblen attacked has not been notably modified by the theories of monopolistically competitive and oligopoly markets, although Chamberlin, one of the developers of such theories, acknowledged some debt to Veblen. Theories of these markets are at present still unsatisfactory. As a result of developments in welfare economics and of the Keynesian conclusion that equilibrium may coincide with mass unemployment, equilibrium per se is no longer considered desirable. Veblen's attack on the concept of consumer sovereignty and his analysis of the role of emulation and advertising in the economy have been carried further in the theories of imperfect markets and in the works of J. K. Galbraith. His view of evolutionary change received some attention as concern shifted in the post–World War II period to problems of growth and development in the underdeveloped nations of the world.

Another of Veblen's contributions, though, resulted from what he sometimes preached but never practiced—namely, the scientific method, with its collection of factual material to test hypotheses. He criticized orthodox theory on the grounds that it was a wholly deductive system that failed to empirically test either its assumptions or its conclusions. Yet Veblen's own theories are not presented in a form suitable for testing, nor did he document his assertions with statistical material. Veblen's criticism of orthodox theory did, to some extent, compel economists to be more concerned with facts; the fantastic growth of empirical work in economics during the past sixty years may be partly explained as an intellectual response to Veblen's legacy. We shall shortly examine some of the contributions of W. C. Mitchell, a student of Veblen who became a pioneer in the collection of data for analyzing the business cycle.

Finally, we must acknowledge Veblen's normative contribution to economics. Running throughout his writings is not only a scientific dissent from orthodoxy but an ethical dissent. Whereas orthodox theorists, such as Veblen's teacher J. B. Clark, were amazed at the material welfare produced by the modern industrial economy, Veblen used his satire and posture of objectivity to describe an economy shot through with illfare. Veblen became a rallying point for many who felt that government action might remedy some of the most glaring faults of a pecuniary culture.

WESLEY CLAIR MITCHELL

In 1896 Wesley Clair Mitchell (1874–1948) entered the University of Chicago to study classics. After taking courses from John Dewey and Thorstein Veblen, he became more interested in philosophy and economics and finally decided to pursue economics. Mitchell went on to become a leading American economist of the twentieth century: an authority on business cycles, a pioneer in establishing a research agency for studying the economy, and an astute observer of the development of economic theory. Although Mitchell did not fully accept many of Veblen's ideas, his economics was not orthodox, so he is usually identified with the so-called institutionalist school. He accepted and amplified some of Veblen's criticisms of orthodox economic theory, but he made no attempt to build a complete theoretical structure to explain the evolution of the industrial economy. Mitchell attempted to follow what Veblen recommended in his essays on methodology, researching carefully and grounding all his theoretical work in empirical information. His example as a scholar and researcher and his work in setting up the National Bureau of Economic Research to collect and analyze macroeconomic data have been more important than his contributions to pure theory.

Mitchell's views about orthodox economic theory are expressed in a number of his essays and in his *Lecture Notes on Types of Economic Theory*.[15] In an unusually candid letter to J. M. Clark, he revealed the turn of mind that deflected him from the mainstream of economic theory.[16] Mitchell said that at a young age he began to prefer concrete problems and methods to abstract ones. He recalled a great aunt who "was the best of Baptists, and knew exactly how the Lord had

[15] These notes were taken by a student, John Meyers, in the academic year 1926–1927 and reproduced in mimeographed form. Additions were made by Meyers in subsequent years until 1935, when that version was some 30 percent larger than the 1926–1927 version. Mitchell died in 1948, and a 1949 mimeographed version was published by Augustus M. Kelley. The best source is in book form edited by Joseph Dorfman, who also wrote an introduction. See W. C. Mitchell, *Types of Economic Theory*, ed. Joseph Dorfman (New York: Augustus M. Kelley, 1967).

[16] This delightful letter can be found in a number of places, including Lucy Sprague Mitchell's "A Personal Sketch" in *Wesley Clair Mitchell: The Economic Scientist,* ed. Arthur F. Burns (New York: National Bureau of Economic Research, 1952), pp. 93–99; and J. M. Clark, *Preface to Social Economics* (New York: Farrar and Rinehart, 1936), pp. 410–416. We cite Clark.

planned the world."[17] Mitchell remembered how he developed "an impish delight in dressing up logical difficulties which my great aunt could not dispose of. She always slipped back into the logical scheme, and blinked the facts in which I came to take proprietary interest."[18]

Mitchell accounted for his particular approach to economics by the fact that when he went to Chicago he studied both philosophy and economics. He found economics easier than philosophy and thought the economic theories from Quesnay to Marshall "were rather crude affairs compared to the subtleties of the metaphysicians. . . . The technical part of the theory was easy. Give me premises and I would spin speculations by the yard. Also I knew that my 'deductions' were futile."[19] Mitchell was impressed with Veblen and felt "that few could match him in spinning out theories." Yet Mitchell recognized that Veblen's system had the same methodological weakness as did orthodox theory; both failed to test either their assumptions or their conclusions satisfactorily. "But if anything were to convince me that the standard procedure of orthodox economics could meet no scientific tests, it was that Veblen got nothing more certain by his dazzling performances with another set of premises."[20]

This particular attitude is manifested in two of Mitchell's lifelong efforts. In his study of the history of economic ideas, he was not interested in what particular theorists said, but in why they attacked certain problems and not others; why they accepted certain premises without question; and why their contemporaries accepted their conclusions and thought them significant. Mitchell's work in the history of economic theory possibly represents the best of the relativist position. He concluded that economic theory can be largely explained as an intellectual reaction to problems of the times. This attitude is also manifested in his work on business cycles. He left behind no theory of cycles founded upon abstract premises from which conclusions could be deduced. His approach was a careful construction and explanation of time series as a preliminary step to checking the tentative theories he offered. At times his work on business cycles appears almost atheoretical, yet there is a theoretical structure underlying the entire analysis.

Mitchell criticized the abstract models of orthodox theory. "Economic theory of the speculative kind is as cheap and easy to produce as higher mathematics or poetry—provided one has the gift. And it has the same problematical relation to reality as do those products of imagination."[21] He also objected to the hedonistic psychological assumptions of orthodox theory but did not accept Veblen's instinct theories. He claimed that the social sciences could develop a better explanation of the activities of humans by basing it upon empirically grounded behaviorist psychology, and he advocated a more generalized approach to studying human

[17] *Ibid.*, p. 410.
[18] *Ibid.*
[19] *Ibid.*, p. 411.
[20] *Ibid.*, p. 412.
[21] W. C. Mitchell, "Institutes for Research in the Social Sciences," *Journal of the Proceedings of the Association of American Universities* (1929), p. 63.

behavior than could be achieved by letting the various branches go their own ways. Orthodox theory had incorrectly focused on normality and equilibrium in the system instead of examining its dynamic interrelationships.

Mitchell particularly emphasized the evolutionary cumulative causation approach in his study of the business cycle. Implicit in Mitchell's writings is an ethical dissent as well as a scientific dissent from orthodox theory. Mitchell, who hoped to use economic knowledge to improve welfare, maintained that a study of the economy revealed a need for national planning to achieve better integration of the activities of firms and better control of fluctuations in economic activity.

Mitchell took Veblen's distinction between pecuniary and industrial employments as a broad guide in his approach to the study of business cycles. Fluctuations in economic activity can be accounted for largely by the reactions of businesses to changing rates of profit. Because business decisions are made in a setting of expectations and uncertainty, the businessman's investment decisions always reflect either optimistic or pessimistic outlooks for the future. Fluctuations in economic activity are to be expected in economies with developed monetary systems; therefore, orthodox theory with its conceptual framework of normal, static, and equilibrium is not appropriate. Mitchell did not attempt to build another abstract model of the business cycle. He tried instead to explain what happens during the business cycle, giving what he called a descriptive analysis of the cycle. Because each cycle is unique, the possibility of developing a general theory is restricted; yet all cycles have certain similarities, because all reveal the interactions of economic forces during the various phases of depression, revival, prosperity, and crises.

Although others before Mitchell had seen the cycle as a self-generating process, he was the first to give this conception explicit form and to support it with extensive empirical data. His explanation of the cycle is based on business reactions to changing levels of profits. A depression carries the seeds of the subsequent revival as interest rates fall, inefficient firms are eliminated, both fixed and variable costs decline, inventories decrease, and so on. Prosperity also carries the seeds of crisis and subsequent depression as costs rise with a consequent squeeze on profits.

Mitchell's descriptive analysis, reflecting as it does a scholar's judicious blend of theory, description, and history devoid of mathematical encumbrances, is somewhat like Marshall's. Yet the hard theoretical core that underlay Marshall's micro analysis was missing, to such an extent that some call Mitchell's work measurement without theory. Others, with post-Keynesian hindsight, find in it the multiplier process, the accelerator principle, and a counterpart to Keynes's marginal efficiency of capital and liquidity preference. Mitchell believed that business cycles cannot be considered apart from the rest of the economy; they are part and parcel of the system and are, in fact, generated by the system. As each phase of the cycle evolves into the next phase, the institutional structure of society changes so that "economists of each generation will see reason to recast the theory of business cycles which they learned in their youth."[22]

---

[22] W. C. Mitchell, *Business Cycles* (New York: Burt Franklin, 1913), p. 583.

In 1920, at the age of forty-five, Mitchell founded the National Bureau of Economic Research. This private, nonprofit organization has been tremendously important in financing economic research in the United States. Although its most important efforts have been concerned with the measurement of national income and business-cycle research, it has sponsored research in nearly all areas of the economy. If we were studying the development of economic research in the United States, Mitchell's role would require at least one long chapter. In Chapter 17 we will see some direct influences of Mitchell in the work of some of his students—Simon Kuznets, for example—and some indirect influences in the work of economists who were more interested in measuring economic activity than in producing abstract deductive models.

JOHN R. COMMONS

John R. Commons (1862–1945), five years younger than Veblen but twelve years older than Mitchell, was another heterodox economist from the midwestern United States. Born in Ohio and reared in Indiana, he attended Oberlin College and received the standard classical education of the time, which included a heavy dose of theology dispensed by professors who were quite often members of the clergy. He did graduate work in economics at Johns Hopkins, where he was strongly influenced by Richard T. Ely.

Because Ely had studied in Germany and had been influenced by the German historical school, political economy at Johns Hopkins included economics, political science, sociology, and history. Ely's interest in labor economics—he published *Labor Movement in America* in 1886, two years before Commons went to Johns Hopkins—was transmitted to his student, and Commons contributed to this area of economics throughout his career. Commons left Johns Hopkins after two years and taught at several places before finally following Ely to Wisconsin in 1904.

At the University of Wisconsin an approach to economics was developed (largely under the influence of Commons, sometimes called the *Wisconsin school*) that was important in sustaining economic heterodoxy in the United States and in initiating reforms that have changed the structure and functioning of the economy. Before going to Wisconsin, Commons was unable to remain long at any university, possibly because of his political and economic views and possibly because he was not well received as a teacher of undergraduates. At Wisconsin, however, he found fertile soil for his visionary dissent and even received encouragement from progressive politicians who were eager to find academic experts willing to support social reform.

During his twenty-eight years at Wisconsin, until his retirement in 1932, Commons made significant contributions to economics in three broad areas: social reform, graduate education, and labor economics. Perhaps his most significant contribution was the social legislation he was instrumental in formulating. This legislation has changed the structure of the economy. Commons's first book, *Distribution of Wealth* (1893), was not well received. Critics found it an unsatisfactory attempt to establish a scientific basis for his socialist ideas. Yet Commons was not a revolutionary attempting to change the structure of a private-property, free-enterprise society. He believed that the essentials of capitalism could and should remain intact, but that changes in the working rules of the economic order were needed to remove the obvious faults of a laissez faire economy. In Wisconsin he found support for his position from Governor La Follette.

During Commons's years at Wisconsin (1904–1932) a relationship developed between academics and politicians that was repeated on a national scale in the *New Deal* of Franklin Roosevelt, a relationship that has become commonplace today. The state government of Wisconsin made extensive use of the faculty at Madison as a brain trust for new ideas, as drafters of legislation, and as members of appointed commissions. A history of Commons's career at Wisconsin reveals that he spent a great deal of time helping to draft, pass, and implement social legislation.

In these efforts a discernible pattern developed. Commons would thoroughly study a problem, often with the help of his graduate students. He would then discuss the issues with those in the economy who would be influenced by any new legislation and get the support of the more progressive businesses or labor leaders. After the legislation was passed, he would travel and use other means to promote the spread of the new legislation to other states. There is little doubt that a number of ideas that took shape in social legislation of the New Deal came from Wisconsin. And there is no question that many economists and others trained at Madison moved to Washington, D.C., in 1932.

Commons has been described as "the intellectual origin of the movement toward the welfare state."[23] The year after his arrival in Madison in 1904, he drafted a civil service law for Governor La Follette; in subsequent years he influenced social legislation in the following areas: regulation of public utilities, industrial safety laws, workmen's compensation, child labor laws, minimum wage laws for women, and unemployment compensation laws. The unemployment compensation legislation was possibly Commons's greatest achievement in social legislation. His reaction to the depression of 1920 and his study of European unemployment compensation programs led him to draft a bill for the Wisconsin legislature. Versions of this bill were introduced again and again until finally in 1932 a former student of Commons, Harold Groves, then both a senator and a professor of economics specializing in public finance at the university, introduced the bill that finally passed. In 1934, when Roosevelt urged Congress to pass an unemployment compensation law, he formed a Committee on Economic Security to propose legislation; its director was a student of Commons, E. E. Witte, then a professor of economics at Wisconsin.

The efforts of Commons in these areas of social legislation proceeded from his conviction that the modern industrial economy required government intervention

[23] Kenneth Boulding, "A New Look at Institutionalism," *American Economic Review,* 48 (May 1957), p. 7.

if it were to function properly and if social justice were to be achieved. Much of the legislation originating in Wisconsin would not strike modern readers as particularly radical, visionary, or even socialistic. Yet in Commons's time these ideas for social reform were not generally accepted in the United States. Commons represents, on this score, an unusual type of heterodox economist. He did more than merely object to the orthodox theory that for the most part the market was best left alone to allocate resources; he was interested in changing the situation through social legislation and participated actively in the endeavor to do so. Not all his efforts were successful; for example, he did not succeed in achieving a national health insurance program.

A second contribution of Commons is related to his endeavors in the area of social reform. The economics department of the University of Wisconsin became known as a major graduate training center for economists throughout the world. At one time more Ph.D. degrees in economics were being granted by Wisconsin than by any other university. More important, Commons's particular approach to economics became embedded in the fabric of the department; thus, until the 1980s, a "Wisconsin school" approach was maintained. This legacy is in sharp contrast to that of Veblen or Mitchell, who had no lasting impact on any graduate program.

The economics departments of the University of Texas at Austin under the leadership of C. E. Ayres and of the University of Maryland under Allan Gruchy also sustained particular heterodox approaches for short periods of time, but the number of Ph.D. degrees granted by those institutions and their influence was small compared to Wisconsin's. More historical perspective will be needed to understand the demise of the Wisconsin school approach and, more generally, the end of the concentration of graduate education in heterodox economics in particular departments. With the exception of a few members of their faculties, Wisconsin, Texas, and Maryland seem safely back in the orthodox fold.

In any event, it appears that Commons's approach was not sustained or carried to other universities by its graduates because the economists trained at Wisconsin were, for the most part, oriented toward applied fields of economics rather than economic theory. Legions of them went out to serve in government, in research agencies, and in universities. But being interested in issues such as labor, public finance, and public utilities, they took little interest in orthodox theory, which was then almost exclusively microeconomic. Commons, as we will see, criticized orthodox theory but spent most of his time in applied fields and in social reform.

The Wisconsin school approach, which was heavily indebted to Commons, is dead in the sense that the Ph.D. program at Madison is now in the same tradition as programs at other universities in the United States. During the Commons period, however, and even for a time after World War II, it was possible to earn a Ph.D. at Wisconsin with less training in orthodox economic theory than the average undergraduate economics major receives today in the standard intermediate theory course. (This is no longer true.) Nevertheless, the influence of Commons resulted in Wisconsin's turning out a large number of economists over a period of nearly fifty years who carried their predilection for applied economics and social reform into research agencies, government, and other universities.

A third major contribution of Commons was to the field of labor economics. When his teacher, Richard T. Ely, a labor economist, moved from Johns Hopkins to Wisconsin, he brought Commons with him. Because Ely was interested in the history of the labor movement, he began to collect documents in labor history. He wanted Commons to produce from these materials a definitive history of labor in the United States, a work that was to occupy a good part of Commons's academic time at Wisconsin. Aided extensively by his graduate students, in 1910 Commons published *A Documentary History of American Industrial Society,* a ten-volume collection of major documents pertaining to labor history. This was followed by two volumes in 1918 and two in 1935 of the four-volume *History of Labor in the United States*. Commons became a recognized authority on labor in the United States, and Wisconsin became the leading university for producing labor economists. Its most notable graduate may be Selig Perlman, whose *Theory of the Labor Movement* (1928) is still a classic.

Commons's Economic Ideas

Although Commons arrived independently at his criticism of orthodox economic theory, it parallels that of Veblen and Mitchell. His entire approach to social problems rejected the narrow, static, deductive approach of neoclassical theory. Commons tried to bring all the social sciences, with the addition of history and law, into the analysis. He viewed society and the economy as evolving and changing and sharply objected to the almost exclusively deductive orthodox approach with its assumptions of hedonistic agents and competitive markets. Finally, Commons found that the implicit assumption of harmony in the economy, on which the laissez faire policy was based, was contrary to his empirical observations.

The starting point for Commons's analysis of American capitalism was the same as that of orthodox price theory, but the analyses themselves were quite different. He asserted that the orthodox theory of price formulation and exchange was unrealistic. It assumed rational individuals acting almost mechanically in competitive markets. Commons said that it is not atomistic, hedonistic individuals acting in competitive markets that form the exchange relationships connecting the separate parts of the economy. Orthodox price theory might satisfactorily explain exchange and price in a few very special situations, such as highly organized commodity or security markets, for in these markets there are exchanges but no *exchange relationships*. In these markets, where there is complete anonymity between buyer and seller, habit, custom, and all the cultural, sociological, and psychological forces that impinge on usual market transactions are absent. Transactions became a key element in Commons's theoretical structure:

> In fact, transactions have become the meeting place of economics, physics, psychology, ethics, jurisprudence and politics. A single transaction is a unit of observation which involves explicitly all of them, for it is several human wills, choosing alternatives, overcoming resistance, proportioning natural and human

resources, led on by promises or warnings of utility, sympathy, duty or their opposites, enlarged, restrained or exposed by officials of government or of business concerns or labor unions, who interpret and enforce the citizens' rights, duties, and liberties, such that individual behavior is fitted or misfitted to the collective behavior of nations, politics, business, labor, the family and other collective movements, in a world of limited resources and mechanical forces.[24]

Commons found three types of transactions in the economy. "Bargaining transactions *transfer ownership* of wealth by voluntary agreement between legal equals."[25] Legal equality does not imply equal economic power. *Bargaining transactions* that determine prices in final and factor markets are the subject matter of orthodox price theory, but this theory is really applicable only to the unusual situation of competitive markets in which bargaining power, coercion, persuasion, habit, custom, and law are ignored by assumption. A second type of transaction is the *managerial transaction,* which involves commands by legal and economic superiors to inferiors. "It is the relation of foreman and worker, sheriff and citizen, manager and managed, master and servant, owner and slave."[26] Managerial transactions involve the creation of wealth. The third type of transaction Commons identified is *rationing transactions*. They involve "the negotiations of reaching an agreement among several participants who have authority to apportion the benefits and burdens to members of a joint enterprise."[27] Commons then moved on to define what he called institutions:

> These three types of transactions are brought together in a larger unit of economic investigation, which, in British and American practice, is named a Going Concern. It is these going concerns, with the working rules that keep them going, all the way from the family, the corporation, the trade union, the trade association, up to the state itself, that we name Institutions. The passive concept is a "group"; the active is a "going concern."[28]

Institution is defined as collective action in control, liberation, and expansion of individual action. Economic transactions involve conflict—the more I receive, the less you receive. These conflicts are not manifest in most transactions, because over time, precedents are established by custom, habit, law, and so forth, which bring order out of conflict. Commons called these precedents working rules of the going concerns.

With this bare outline of Commons's approach, it is possible to outline his analysis of American capitalism. Neoclassical theory held that the conflicts arising from problems of scarce resources could be solved in impersonal competitive markets, which by assumption removed all cultural, sociological, psychologi-

---

[24] John R. Commons, *Legal Foundations of Capitalism* (New York: Macmillan, 1924), p. 5.
[25] John R. Commons, *Institutional Economics* (New York: Macmillan, 1934), p. 68.
[26] *Ibid.,* p. 64.
[27] *Ibid.,* pp. 67–68.
[28] *Ibid.,* p. 69.

cal, and legal elements from the analysis. It maintained that for the most part the working out of these conflicts in competitive markets led to results that were superior to any results that might be achieved through government intervention.

The basic thrust of Commons's approach was to include the social sciences, history, and law in his analysis and to recognize that government intervention was often necessary to bring about desirable social consequences. Most of our economic activity is not individual activity; we act as members of groups that are guided and molded by the working rules of the going concerns. Although the function of the working rule is to bring order out of conflict, at times conflict develops as changes are brought about by history. These conflicts or disputes are then settled, and the old working rules are modified in an endless, ongoing process. The proper subject matter of economics, Commons maintained, is the institutions that shape our lives and society by means of collective action. This collective action not only controls individual action but also liberates it by freeing the individual "from coercion, duress, discrimination, or unfair competition, by means of restraints placed on other individuals. And collective action is more than restraint and liberation of individual action—it is an *expansion* of the will of the individual far beyond what he can do by his own puny acts."[29]

Because an unregulated economy produces undesirable social consequences, capitalism needs to be modified by governmental intervention. Monetary policy to prevent depression, legislation to recognize the right of labor to organize, workmen's compensation to assist the unemployed, health and accident insurance to care for the unfortunate, regulation of public utilities to prevent monopoly practices, and other social reforms were advocated by Commons. Thus, although he made almost no impact on orthodox theory, the reforms he advocated and helped to implement have significantly influenced the institutional structure of American capitalism.

JOHN A. HOBSON

Although England has been the citadel of orthodox economic theory from Smith through Marshall, with its main tenet's being that unregulated markets will produce a maximum of social welfare, there have been legions of heretics. Possibly the most influential of these was John A. Hobson (1858–1940), whose heterodox ideas became the intellectual fountain of the present English welfare state. Hobson's academic career was ended shortly after the publication of his first book on economics. He lost his job because of "the intervention of an Economics Professor who read my book and considered it as an equivalent in rationality to an attempt to prove the flatness of the earth."[30] An independent income allowed him to

---

[29] *Ibid.,* p. 73.

[30] John A. Hobson, *Confessions of an Economic Heretic* (New York: Macmillan, 1938), p. 30.

continue his attack on orthodox theory, however, and he published nearly forty books as well as a large number of articles. His works were never well received in academic circles until Keynes praised him in the *General Theory;* and although Hobson's impact has been almost negligible in pure theory, he has been important in shaping English economic policy. Hobson is like many heterodox economists who had a vision of the inadequacies of orthodox theory and were able to describe them but who were never able to formulate a theoretical structure capable of overthrowing accepted doctrine.

In broad perspective Hobson's heterodoxy was an attack on the accepted doctrine that laissez faire is the best policy, because markets will produce a maximum of social welfare. Orthodox theory held that competitive markets will, for the most part, produce the goods that sovereign consumers desire at the lowest possible social costs. The distribution of income that flows from these markets rewards the participants according to their productivity. Furthermore, the operation of these economic forces will produce a full utilization of society's resources. Because prices are, in general, good measures of the costs incurred and the utilities produced in the economy, they are indexes of the welfare achieved by a society.

Although Hobson accepted some of the major assumptions of orthodox theory, he came to quite different conclusions about the adequacy of a laissez faire market economy. He found three major faults with the workings of the English economy of his time. First, it failed to provide full employment because there existed chronic underconsumption or oversaving. Second, the distribution of income unjustly rewarded those in upper-income groups, largely because of their superior bargaining power. Third, the market is not a good measure of social costs and social utilities produced, for the entire price system is oriented toward monetary profit. Whereas orthodox thinkers found harmony in the economy and then built a theory to demonstrate that harmony, Hobson assumed the negative influence of the laissez faire economy and then attempted to build a theoretical structure to remedy the faults of the existing industrial society. Hobson contended that if the goals of a society were clearly defined, a knowledge of economic theory would permit the society to achieve "the good life."

He objected to John Neville Keynes's position that we can distinguish between what is and what ought to be, and to the orthodox tendency to confine activities to an analysis of what is. For Hobson, economic theory was useful precisely insofar as it would assist society to achieve "oughts." The normative-positive dichotomy attempted by orthodox theory was impossible, because the same facts are both ethical and economic. Hobson's attack on orthodox theory began in his co-authored first book, with a rejection of Say's Law:

> We are thus brought to the conclusion that the basis on which all economic teaching since Adam Smith has stood, viz. that the quantity annually produced is determined by the aggregates of Natural Agents, Capital, and Labour available, is erroneous, and that, on the contrary, the produced, while it can never exceed the limits imposed by these aggregates, may be, and actually is, reduced far below

this maximum by the check that undue saving and the consequent accumulation of over-supply exerts on production.[31]

The argument in support of the contention that oversaving leads to depression is deficient largely because Hobson and his coauthor, A. F. Mummery, accepted the orthodox position that all saving is returned to the income stream as investment spending.

In subsequent writings Hobson never wavered from his conclusion that capitalism tends to produce depression because of oversaving at full employment. In 1902 he published *Imperialism,* which asserted that the colonial expansion of the capitalist countries served largely as an outlet for the oversaving and excess supply of goods generated at full employment. Lenin borrowed heavily from Hobson's imperialism thesis. Hobson concluded that full employment could be achieved by imperialistic practices, by expenditures for war, by governmental expenditures designed to improve the conditions of the working classes, by a domestic increase in the consumption of luxury goods, and by a more equal distribution of income. The ethically correct alternatives were clear: a redistribution of income by taxation combined with governmental expenditure to improve the condition of the poor.

Hobson wrote extensively about the distribution of income. He rejected the marginal productivity theory of distribution on the grounds that it is impossible to impute marginal products to the separate factors. In a modern complex economy, production is a social or cooperative enterprise; we beg the ethical questions surrounding the distribution of income if we attempt to identify the marginal contributions of the various factors of production by means of differential calculus. Furthermore, orthodox theory implicitly assumes in its analysis of factor price determination that equal bargaining power exists among the various factors of production. Observation of the economy, however, reveals that labor's bargaining position is relatively weak, which results in low wages. Payments to the various factors of production can be analytically separated into three parts: (1) a payment that will just permit the factor to maintain itself; (2) a payment that will allow the factor to increase in quantity and productivity; and (3) a payment in excess of what is necessary for maintenance and improvement, which Hobson called "unproductive surplus." The modern industrial economy produces an output more than sufficient to pay for the maintenance of the various factors, and it is the bargaining process of factor market pricing that determines which factors receive an unproductive surplus. Hobson claimed that land receives an unproductive surplus because of its natural scarcity and that capital receives an unproductive surplus because of its superior bargaining power and the artificial scarcity that flows from monopoly power. A more equal distribution of income, one that grants higher wages for labor, would not only be more just but would also increase the productivity of labor. Furthermore, greater equality will increase consumption and

---

[31] A. F. Mummery and J. A. Hobson, *The Physiology of Industry* (New York: Kelley and Millman, 1956), p. vi.

reduce saving, thereby enabling the economy to avoid depression. Hobson was not content to rest his case against orthodox theory at this point.

He went on to make a fundamental and sweeping attack on the orthodox analysis of the meaning of the price system. Orthodox theory, according to Hobson, erroneously holds that prices are a reflection of the social costs of producing goods and the social benefits received from consuming goods. Hobson found prices to be inadequate measures of welfare on both the cost and the benefit side. "A science which still takes money as its standard of value, and regards man as a means of making money, is, in the nature of the case, incapable of facing the deep and complex human problems which compose the Social Question."[32]

Hobson's solution was that we should calculate *human* costs, which are different from costs expressed in prices, and *human* utility, which is not the same as market prices. In this analysis Hobson addressed what modern welfare theory refers to as externalities, on both the supply-cost side and the demand-benefit side. His analysis of the demand side reflects the influence of Veblen; he pointed to the waste created by conspicuous consumption and to the fine art of salesmanship as practiced in the modern economy. Hobson's solution was to remove the laissez faire approach of government and the profit-oriented nature of the modern economy. "The substitution of direct social control for the private profitseeking motive in the normal processes of our industries is essential to any sound scheme of social reconstruction."[33]

This brief look at Hobson does little more than give the flavor of his broadside attack on orthodox theory. He rejected Say's Law, objected to the orthodox theory of distribution, found the price system an inadequate measure of social welfare, rejected the normative-positive dichotomy of orthodox theory, explicitly called for the injection of ethical considerations into economic analysis, found the profit motive to have negative effects on society, and above all, called for the end of laissez faire. He suffered the fate of many seminal heterodox thinkers: he was unable to obtain employment in an academic community controlled by orthodoxy. His ideas were usually rejected without close examination. In 1913 J. M. Keynes remarked that "One comes to a new book by Mr. Hobson with mixed feelings, in hope of stimulating ideas and of some fruitful criticisms of orthodoxy from an independent and individual standpoint, but expectant also of much sophistry, misunderstanding and perverse thought."[34]

Later, as Keynes rejected Say's Law and moved from the orthodox position, his evaluation of Hobson changed accordingly. In 1936 he praised Hobson's *Physiology of Industry* as "the first and most significant of many volumes in which for nearly fifty years Mr. Hobson has flung himself with unflagging, but almost unavailing, ardour and courage against the ranks of orthodoxy. Though it is so

---

[32] John A. Hobson, *The Social Problem* (London: J. Nisbet, 1901), p. 38.

[33] John A. Hobson, *Work and Wealth* (New York: Macmillan, 1914), p. 293.

[34] J. M. Keynes, *Economic Journal,* 23 (September 1913), p. 393.

completely forgotten today, the publication of this book marks, in a sense, an epoch in economic thought."[35] Keynes went on to contend that Hobson belongs to an important group of underconsumptionist heterodox economists "who, following their intuitions, have preferred to see the truth obscurely and imperfectly rather than to maintain error, reached indeed with clearness and consistency and by easy logic, but on hypotheses inappropriate to the facts."[36]

As with most heterodox writers, Hobson's intuitive insights did not lead him to a consistent, well-ordered theoretical structure. Thus, there are no identifiably Hobsonian elements in present orthodox theory. He exposed issues that the orthodox economist was content to sweep under the rug. When these issues finally had to be addressed, the solutions were proposed by economists other than Hobson. Nevertheless, Hobson had an important effect on British economic policy, where his ideas became the dominant intellectual influence in the Labour Party. With its social control of industry and full-employment policies, the British Labour program in the post–World War II period was rooted in the economics of John A. Hobson.

SUMMARY

The early critics of neoclassical economics had little in common other than an objection to orthodoxy. This objection was manifested in various ways by various writers; but in general it is a dissent from the scope, method, and content of orthodox theory, as well as a rejection of the orthodox economists' view that harmony prevails in a market economy and that laissez faire is therefore the proper governmental policy. Thus, the heterodox dissent is a scientific as well as an ethical dissent. Many heterodox writers explicitly charged orthodox theory with containing normative or ethical judgments that it attempted to hide by pretending to develop a positive science.

The German historical school objected to the abstract theorizing of the Austrians, particularly Menger, and a famous debate took place between German-speaking economists over the proper method for economics. The historical school also objected to the classical view that their economic theory and policy was applicable to the less developed countries such as Germany as well as to industrialized countries such as England. They wanted to protect their "infant industries" and advocated a much larger role for government than did the laissez faire classicals.

Veblen, who preached the scientific method but practiced impressionistic writing, taught Mitchell, who practiced science but was reluctant to reach any theoretical conclusions from the data he collected. Neither writer offered a theoretical structure to replace the model he was criticizing. Commons did offer an alternative structure, but it was not seriously considered by subsequent

---

[35] J. M. Keynes, *The General Theory of Employment, Interest, and Money* (London: Macmillan, 1936), pp. 364–365.
[36] *Ibid.*, p. 371.

economists—either orthodox or heterodox. Hobson, like Commons, influenced economic policy significantly, but his theoretical contributions were largely ignored for nearly a third of a century until others looked back and recognized the value of his insights.

All these writers, to varying degrees, reached conclusions that call for much more governmental intervention in the market than do most orthodox economists'. Some commentators have concluded that because particular versions of heterodox theory have failed to replace orthodox theory, heterodox theory has been a failure. Our view is different. An examination of heterodox thinking reveals that although it has not replaced the accepted stream of economic thought, it often forces orthodox theory into new channels and sometimes offers seminal ideas that become part of the accepted theoretical structure. These contributions to the direction and content of the flow of ideas cannot be ignored.

Institutionalist and other heterodox criticisms of neoclassical economics did not end with the early critics but have continued (and in certain instances have even grown stronger) in their assaults on orthodox theory, but not necessarily in their assaults on policy. This is because many of the policy changes nonorthodox economists were suggesting were actually implemented during the twentieth century. Hobson and other British reformers influenced British social policy, and many of the ideas of the U.S. institutionalists were implemented in the New Deal. Thus, nonorthodox economists had an enormous effect on the institutional structure of capitalism, and many of their criticisms were blunted because of reaction to those criticisms.

In theory, however, they had less impact. As the institutional structure of Western economies changed, neoclassical theory, based on an institutional structure most relevant for a pure market economy, did not change; instead, it simply retreated deeper into pure abstract theory with little or no direct policy relevance. As we will see in Chapter 14 when we examine recent heterodox economic thought, challenges to mainstream thinking that are institutionalist in that they are the intellectual heirs of Veblen, Commons, and Mitchell focus more and more on the separation of orthodox theory from reality.

Key Terms

orthodox	ceremonial behavior
heterodox	pecuniary employments
older historical school	leisure class
younger historical school	Wisconsin school
Methodenstreit	New Deal
institutionalism	exchange relationship
conspicuous consumption	bargaining transactions
teleological	managerial transactions
taxonomic	rationing transactions
instincts	institution
industrial employments	

Questions for Review, Discussion, and Research

1. The philosopher Henri Bergson has described time as a device that prevents all things from happening at once. What is the implication of this statement for orthodox economic theory, and how does it relate to the historical school?
2. Which would the historical school more strongly object to, Marshall's or Walras's version of orthodox economic theory? Why?
3. How would current economic theory be different if the historical school had won the *Methodenstreit*?
4. Who are "captains of erudition," and how might Veblen's use of such terms have influenced his career?
5. Mitchell often used Veblen as the best example of why one should eschew theory. Why? Was Mitchell correct?
6. Summarize the recurring themes in the institutionalist thought of Veblen, Mitchell, and Commons.
7. Distinguish the institutionalist thought of Veblen, Mitchell, and Commons.
8. How would Veblen respond to the argument that the market directs self-interest toward societal interest?
9. Why was Mitchell's antitheoretical position more successful than Veblen's alternative theoretical position?
10. What part, if any, of neoclassical theory would Hobson be willing to accept?
11. That absent-minded professor is back with another job for you. This time, she's doing an article on demography, and she remembers that Veblen had something witty to say about conspicuous consumption by children. She even jotted it down. It was:

> The conspicuous consumption, and the consequent increased expense, required in the reputable maintenance of a child is very considerable and acts as a powerful deterrent. It is probably the most effectual of the Malthusian prudential checks.

Alas, she does not remember where she found this quotation. Your assignment is to find the full bibliographic citation.

Suggested Readings

Commons, John R. *Institutional Economics*. New York: Macmillan, 1934.
————. *Myself*. New York: Macmillan, 1934.
Dorfman, Joseph. *Thorstein Veblen and His America*. New York: Viking, 1934.
Dowd, Douglas F., ed. *Thorstein Veblen: A Critical Reappraisal*. Ithaca: Cornell University Press, 1958.
Gruchy, Allan G. *Contemporary Economic Thought*. Clifton, New Jersey: Augustus M. Kelley, 1972.
————. *Modern Economic Thought*. New York: Prentice-Hall, 1947.
Harter, Lafayette G., Jr. *John R. Commons*. Corvallis: Oregon State University Press, 1962.

Hirsch, Abraham. "Mitchell's Work on Civil War Inflation in His Development as an Economist." *History of Political Economy,* 2 (Spring 1970).

Homan, Paul T. "John A. Hobson." In *Contemporary Economic Thought.* New York: Harper, 1928.

Hutchison, T. W. "J. A. Hobson." In *A Review of Economic Doctrines.* Oxford: Clarendon Press, 1953.

Leathers, Charles G., and John S. Evans. "Thorstein Veblen and the New Industrial State." *History of Political Economy,* 5 (Fall 1973).

Mitchell, Lucy Sprague. *Two Lives.* New York: Simon and Schuster, 1953.

Mitchell, Wesley Clair. *The Backward Art of Spending Money.* New York: Augustus M. Kelley, 1950.

————. *Business Cycles and Their Causes.* Berkeley: University of California Press, 1941.

————. *Types of Economic Theory.* New York: Augustus M. Kelley, 1967.

Veblen, Thorstein. *The Place of Science in Modern Civilization.* New York: B. W. Huebsh, 1919.

————. *The Theory of Business Enterprise.* New York: Charles Scribner's Sons, 1904.

13 Austrians, Neoclassicals, and Socialists on Socialism and Capitalism

"With all these economic doctrines, decaying and reviving, jostling each other, half understood, in the public mind, what basic ideas are acceptable, and what rules of policy are derived from them?"

—Joan Robinson

IMPORTANT WRITERS

J. C. L. SISMONDI	*New Principles of Political Economy* 1819
HENRI DE SAINT-SIMON	*Du système industriel* 1821
ROBERT OWEN	*What Is Socialism?* 1841
ALBERT SCHAFFLE	*The Quintessence of Socialism* 1874
VILFREDO PARETO	*The Socialist Systems* 1902
ENRICO BARONE	"The Ministry of Production" 1908
LUDWIG VON MISES	"Economic Calculation" 1920
F. A. VON HAYEK	*Collectivist Economic Planning* 1935
	The Road to Serfdom 1944
OSCAR LANGE	"On the Economic Theory of Socialism" 1936
JOSEPH SCHUMPETER	*Capitalism, Socialism, and Democracy* 1942
MILTON FRIEDMAN	*Capitalism and Freedom* 1962

Contributors to both orthodox and heterodox economic ideas have at times written about capitalism and socialism. Sometimes these writings have been highly technical, addressing the theoretical requirements for optimum resource allocation under any economic system; sometimes they have been broad-brushed, speculating about the long-run possibilities of socialism or capitalism. Surveying these views gives a better perspective on the historic changes that are occurring in formerly socialist countries. Examining these views highlights some of the strengths and weaknesses of various theories and approaches.

The issue of the economic and institutional structure of a socialist society has been examined at two levels. At a highly theoretical level, economists have examined the conditions necessary to achieve efficiency in a society in which many nonlabor resources are publicly owned. The workability of socialism has also been discussed in very broad terms that integrate analysis and ideology. One of the key questions in the broader examination of socialism concerns the compatibility of socialism and freedom.

We make no claim of providing a fully acceptable treatment of these issues, but we consider them too important to ignore. After briefly reviewing pre-Marxian socialist thought we will consider the important ongoing debate that started in the 1920s on the ability of a socialist economy to allocate resources efficiently and the compatibility of a socialist society with freedom. We will then review the contributions of Soviet economists to an understanding of some of the problems of their planning system and to solutions to these problems.

Recent events in the former Soviet Union have also led to speculation about the future course of socialist societies and of capitalist systems as well. After briefly addressing the possible convergence of different economic systems, we close the chapter with a very provocative set of conjectures about the future of capitalism put forth by Joseph Schumpeter.

DEFINING CAPITALISM AND SOCIALISM

The words *capitalism* and *socialism* have general but not precise meaning. They combine characteristics of an economy with ideology; to some they mean good and bad, and to others bad and good. One could theoretically define these words with some precision; but if one did so, any given society (e.g., England) might not fit enough of the criteria to be said to be described by one term or the other. On the one hand, we have a theoretical idea of what capitalism and socialism are; on the other hand, we have existing systems that contain elements of both theoretical capitalism and socialism. This last point becomes relevant when advocates of each system structure their arguments for the system of their choice in theoretical terms but structure evidence against their opponent's in terms of an existing society. We will frame our discussion in this chapter largely in theoretical terms.

In capitalism, economic decision making is done by individuals largely in their roles as consumers, owners of factors of production, and managers of firms; most economic resources are privately owned. In socialism, economic decision making is done by individuals largely in their roles as voters, politicians, and managers of firms; economic resources may be privately or publicly owned but the control over resource allocation is by government, not by the owners of the resources.

These definitions center on economic criteria, but they inevitably interrelate with political and social issues. Freedom (economic and political) and democracy can be highly developed or retarded under either system. Advocates of capitalism often assert that freedom is possible only under capitalism (read "theoretical capitalism") and does not exist in a significant way under socialism (read "actual socialism"). Defenders of socialism often maintain that true freedom is not possible under capitalism (read "existing capitalism") and is truly attainable only under socialism (read "theoretical socialism"). We will return to this issue of capitalism, socialism, and freedom, because recently it has been extensively discussed.

The two social systems are quite different in terms of their origins. Capitalism is a system that developed historically and then, as economists tried to explain the workings of that system, became an intellectual or theoretical structure. Socialism, in contrast, developed first intellectually as an alternative theoretical structure to existing systems and then was tried as an existing system.

Both systems have been continually evolving in their theoretical and, especially, in their actual forms. Part of the evolution has occurred because our theoretical understanding of the two systems as ideal types has advanced. Another part has occurred because existing systems change over time. Because of change, capitalism and socialism today are quite different from what they were fifty years ago; these changes complicate analysis.

In the 1930s through the 1960s it was capitalism that was changing—theoretically and in practice. The definition of capitalism became more and more compatible with positions of government control of capitalism and separation of ownership and control, because of either managerial control of firms or governmental regulation. In the 1980s and 1990s, it has been socialism that has been changing; markets and private ownership in theory and in practice are now seen as consistent with socialism. Thus, there has been a movement in both theoretical and actual socialism toward greater use of the institutions of capitalism, and a shift in both theoretical and actual capitalism toward greater use of the institutions of socialism. These observations have led some to speculate that the two systems are converging, each shedding the faults of its pure form and moving toward a common denominator.

THE EMERGENCE OF CAPITALISTIC THOUGHT

Capitalism was like Topsy—it just grew. Without foresight or plan, in Western Europe and England a social organization emerged and developed into what Marx called capitalism. Previous societies were substantially past-bound: tradition and authority in the form of religion and political forces prevented change. One essential ingredient in the emergence of capitalism was the freeing of individuals from the church, the guilds, and the state. New categories of economic goods emerged with capitalism—labor, land, and capital, which people were free to buy and sell.

The land was owned by landowners who received rent; labor was controlled by workers who received wages; and capital was controlled by capitalists who received profits. These groups constituted distinct social as well as economic groups and served as the basis of classical analysis. What were the forces that determined the distribution of income among these groups? What were the dynamics of growth of the system? The capitalist owners of production were seen as providing the dynamics of growth—hence the name, *capitalism.*

Under feudalism the uses of labor, land, and capital were determined not by market activities but by tradition and authority. With the rise of the new form of social and economic organization appeared a new actor, the entrepreneur, who became the agent of change under capitalism. What was crucial is that capitalism, as contrasted with feudalism, had embedded in its system the machinery for further change. This is one of the most important insights one achieves in studying those great students of capitalism: Adam Smith, Karl Marx, and Joseph Schumpeter.

Although the entrepreneur was the causal factor in the dynamic change in capitalism, there was another element that permitted, if it did not initiate, evolutionary reformation. Under feudalism and mercantilism one of the functions of the state had been to constrain the forces that produced change. Under mercantilism the state had been extensively used by special interest groups to protect vested interests, particularly of business groups. With the growth of markets there also occurred a significant restructuring of political life, and more democratic political arrangements coupled with the changing economy produced democratic capitalism. Democracy was important because it permitted change but preserved the underlying political and institutional structure. The revolutionary changes that have recently occurred in socialist societies are partly explained by this lack of institutional structure that would tolerate small changes while protecting the basic integrity of the system.

The new society that replaced feudalism had two interesting elements: one, the entrepreneur, which gave the system dynamism; and another, democracy, which facilitated new arrangements without tearing the basic fabric of the society.

Markets coordinate, given a property rights structure. Markets allow people to trade and thereby increase the value of their initial endowment of rights. But markets do not solve the problem of initially unacceptable or unjust property rights, or of allocation when property rights have not yet developed. Democracy is a system of government that allows voting by people to determine governmental policy and modify existing property rights to keep the system sufficiently just that people will accept it. Under capitalism we have seen enormous modification of property rights through taxation, regulation, and empowerments while the basic market framework was being maintained.

The precursors of classical political economy, the classicals, and the neoclassicals examined this emerging and changing system and gave us a theoretical understanding of capitalism from a particular ideological perspective. As the market system began to emerge, prices played a larger role as coordinators of individual economic activities. This vision of the function of markets was faintly seen by the preclassicals, seen with great clarity by Adam Smith and the classicals, and expressed by the neoclassicals not simply as a vision but in formal models detailing the conditions that would result in an efficient allocation of resources. Neoclassical economic theory became a system to explain how markets operated, given the institution of private property. In this sense the resulting neoclassical economic theory is capitalist economic thought.

THE DEVELOPMENT OF SOCIALIST ECONOMIC THOUGHT

While mainstream economic thinkers were writing an ode to capitalism, others were coming to different conclusions. Even before the birth of Christ, some viewed with serious misgivings the greater attention being given to the economic aspect of life. Before capitalism was fully formed during the Industrial Revolution, some writers had seen enough of nascent capitalism to judge its impact on individuals and society objectionable.

These early philosophers and moralists were predecessors of early and middle socialist thought, what Marx termed *utopian socialists*. The pre-Marxian socialists oriented their writings toward a criticism of capitalistic society and devoted little attention to an exposition of what the essentials of the society they were advocating (socialism) would be like. They paid particularly little attention to the economic organization of socialism.

Early Writing about Socialism

Some early critics of capitalism have so little in common that it may be questionable to refer to them as socialists. One common thread that does bind this diverse group is their view of the functioning of capitalism in nineteenth-century Western Europe as disharmonious. Nearly all the early pre-Marxian critics of capitalism advocated nonviolent means of eliminating the conflicts in society, although the remedies prescribed vary with each writer.

One of the earliest uses of the term socialism is in the writing of Louis Blanc (1811–1882). He argued that an economic system should provide everyone with a job, and he defined socialism as a system in which all individuals have jobs paying fair wages. The term quickly changed to include government as the provider of those jobs through its control of the means of production. Blanc coined the phrase, "from each according to his ability, to each according to his needs."

Robert Owen (1771–1858), an important early English socialist, was a successful industrialist who turned his attention to the evils of capitalism. He followed the Godwin tradition, which asserted that people are perfectible and that the evils in society result from environmental factors. He therefore advocated educational reform and the substitution of cooperatives for the competitive market process. It is interesting that he rejected any notion of a class conflict in the society of his time.

Another group of English writers came to conclusions similar to Owen's; but because their critical analysis of the faults of society started with a labor theory of value, they have become known as *Ricardian socialists*. In Ricardo's system the landlord is a parasite who receives part of the social dividend while performing no essential economic function; these writers used Ricardo's labor theory of value to conclude that because labor is the source of all value, the capitalist exploits labor by depriving it of a portion of its fruits. The most important of these writers were John Bray (1809–1897), John Gray (1799–1883), Charles Hall (c. 1740–c. 1820), Thomas Hodgskin (1787–1869), and William Thompson (1775–1833).

The most prominent of the early French socialists were Henri de Saint-Simon (1760–1825), Charles Fourier (1772–1837), and Pierre-Joseph Proudhon (1809–1865). Saint-Simon was impressed with the possibilities of expanding economic output by state planning in which the scientist and engineer played key roles; Fourier's conception of the good society envisioned cooperatives in which a minimum income was guaranteed to all; and Proudhon, distrusting state action, recommended an anarchy in which credit would be granted to all without any interest's being charged to a borrower.

Although the early German socialists had little direct or indirect influence on the development of economic theory, a Swiss writer, J. C. L. Sismonde, now known as Sismondi (1773–1842), who is classed more properly as a social reformer than as a socialist, deserves closer attention. Sismondi was a prolific writer of history who produced a sixteen-volume history of Italy and a history of France comprising thirty-one volumes. His major contributions to economic thought are contained in his *Nouveaux principes d'économie politique* (1819). In his early writing, Sismondi had followed Adam Smith in perceiving the economy as fundamentally harmonious and believing that a governmental policy of laissez faire would most benefit society. But in his *Nouveaux principes* he concluded that Smith, Ricardo, and Say had overestimated the benefits of laissez faire. He attacked Say's Law, contending that a laissez faire policy would result in unemployment and misery for a large mass of the population. Though he was convinced that the distribution of income achieved by laissez faire markets was not fair, just, and equitable, he agreed with Ricardo that the distribution of income was the most important question in economics. Sismondi was concerned about the slow but certain disappearance of the small-farm owner and small-shop owner; he envisioned a society of class conflicts, rather than harmony, as society became more and more polarized between the proletariat and the capitalists. He believed that the large increases in total output resulting from increased industrialization were not being passed on to the average citizen as increased welfare. Thus, the major thrust of Sismondi's criticism of orthodox doctrine was to reject the harmony of classical liberalism and find instead a discord manifested in the system's failure to provide full employment and, consequently, in growing class conflict. Sismondi is an obvious predecessor of Marx.

Sismondi's appreciation of the failures of capitalism was more intuitive than analytical; the remedial policies he advocated were vague and, in part, internally inconsistent. To Sismondi the primary causes of periodic fluctuation in the level of economic activity were the uncertainty of competitive markets and the elimination of the small farmer and artisan. His remedies were to slow down the increases in production caused by capitalism and to return to an economy in which the separation of labor and capital was minimal and production would more closely mesh with the ability of the economy to consume.

His advocacy of the small-scale, independent industrial and agricultural economic unit led him to defend private property, a view opposed to the general tenor of socialist writing during this period. Solving the problem of overproduction by limiting, if not contracting, total output was not likely to attract much support during the nineteenth century from either the capitalist or the laboring classes of France or England. Whether Sismondi should even be called a socialist is subject to question. In any event, his rejection of Say's Law and his replacement of the harmony of the classical system with disharmony proceeding from a class conflict between capitalists and laborers place his ideas in sharp contrast to the Smithian tradition that Sismondi at one time had accepted.

Speculating About Socialism

Some interesting discussions of the economics of socialism occurred in Germany, Sweden, and Italy. Although they had almost no direct influence on the subsequent literature, they laid down the essential framework for the great debate that began in the 1920s on the economics of socialism.

In 1874 Albert Schaffle (1831–1904), a German, published a book that was translated some twenty years later as *The Quintessence of Socialism*. Schaffle was a nonsocialist with an affinity for the German historical school who became interested in the issues raised by socialism. He advanced two questions, which have proved to be the chief issues in the succeeding literature on the economic theory of socialism. First, what mechanism will be used to allocate scarce resources? Schaffle contended that if a socialist economy based its prices on a theory of value that did not consider use value and focused exclusively on the cost side, presumably labor cost, it could not effectively allocate resources. The second issue raised by Schaffle addressed the possibility of conflict between socialism and freedom. His position was that the advantages of socialism might be offset by loss of individual freedom. Two of Schaffle's contemporaries, Lujo Brentano (1844–1931) and Erwin Nasse (1829–1890), extended Schaffle's ideas about socialism and freedom, maintaining that socialism and planning were incompatible with freedom.

The Swedish economist Gustav Cassel (1866–1945) became interested at the turn of the century in the marginal utility idea of the Austrians. Among the concerns examined in his *Outline of an Elementary Theory of Price* (1899) was whether an economy not based on private property could efficiently allocate resources. He concluded that a fundamental defect of socialism is that it cannot correctly price the factors of production and, therefore, cannot correctly direct production.

Vilfredo Pareto had turned his attention to the economics of socialism in *Les systèmes socialistes,* published in two volumes in 1902–1903. Applying his Pareto optimal welfare theory to a socialist economy, he found no reason why maximum welfare could not be achieved under socialism. A follower of Pareto, the Italian Enrico Barone (1859–1924), further explored these questions. In 1908 Barone became the first economist to systematically examine the conditions necessary to achieve an optimum allocation of resources under a socialist regime.[1] Barone first showed the conditions that lead to maximum welfare under capitalism with perfectly competitive markets and then built a model in which all resources other than labor are collectively owned and a ministry of production controls the economy. He concluded that if the ministry will set prices so that they are equal to costs of production and if costs of production are at a minimum, an optimum allocation of resources exists and maximum welfare is achieved. Writing in 1947, Paul Samuelson said that "it is a tribute to his work that a third of a century after it was written there is no better statement of the problem in the English language to which the attention of students may be turned."[2]

Marx, Marxists, and Socialist Theory

Marx wrote about capitalism; there is no explanation about the mechanism one would use to allocate resources under socialism. Curiously enough, socialist writers following Marx did not seriously examine this question until the 1930s. As with most developments in economic theory, the graveyard of economic ideas contains writers who examined this issue prior to the 1920s. Schaffle, Brentano, Nasse, Cassel, Pareto, and Barone all wrote about socialism; but there was no living theory of socialism, possibly because there had been no successful revolutions and the attention of socialists had been directed exclusively toward the overthrow of capitalism.

As we saw in Chapter 7, Marx developed a theoretical structure to explain changes in institutional structures. Therefore, he did deal with one aspect of socialism that we need to explore: the emergence of socialism. In Marx's dialectic the contradictions between forces and relations would become so large that a historically sudden period of change would bring from the failure of capitalism a new system called socialism. What is not clear in Marx's writings is whether the new system will emerge by historical inevitability or whether the change will require nurture and support by interested parties. Marx had several sides to his personality—one being the disinterested scholar-philosopher writing about scientific socialism, the other being the political activist-revolutionist. Marx the creator of the dialectic is not clear on this point; Marx the revolutionist is.

[1] This article has been translated as "The Ministry of Production in a Collectivist State" and can be found in *Collectivist Economic Planning,* ed. F. A. Hayek (London: George Routledge, 1935).

[2] P. A. Samuelson, *Foundations of Economics* (Cambridge, Mass.: Harvard University Press, 1955), p. 217.

Post-Marxian socialist theory engaged this question, which became known in the literature as the *transition from capitalism* to socialism. Two important opposing views developed. One set of writers contended that socialism would emerge from capitalism in an orderly, nonrevolutionary, nonviolent way, with major roles being played by the labor movement, political parties, and changed legislation; these thinkers have become known as evolutionary or right-wing socialists. Probably the best known of these evolutionary socialists are represented by the Fabian socialists in England, the best known of whom are Sidney and Beatrice Webb and George Bernard Shaw. The evolutionary socialists in England were the intellectual founders of the British Labour Party, the aim of which is to remake British society and economy through peaceful political forces. The other view held that capitalism would not fall merely because of its failures and would be brought down only by bloody violent revolution. Marx's writings give some support to what have become known as left-wing socialists or communists.

Although Marx and post-Marxian socialists until the 1930s did not intensively examine how socialism would allocate resources, they did speculate on the transition from capitalism to socialism. This background is interesting in the context of the changes currently taking place in the remaining and former socialist countries. Whatever one chooses to call these systems in the 1980s and 1990s, it is clear that they are moving toward a new set of social arrangements.

The Great Debate over Theoretical Socialism

The debate about socialism has actually been two debates—one a broad-brush debate, the other a technical debate. The broad-brush debate has filtered down to the general public; it is a debate that touches all aspects of the economic and political system. The technical debate, although much narrower in focus, has sharpened our understanding of microeconomic theory and the limitations of that theory.

The essential question of the technical debate asks how resources will be allocated under socialism. Marx said nothing; no one paid attention to the literature on this question, from Schaffle to Barone, or to the economics of socialism in general, until the 1920s. Ludwig von Mises (1881–1973), an Austrian, had a good deal of influence on subsequent developments on this issue, possibly because of the force of his attack on socialism or because he concentrated on these issues for a good part of his life. He was later joined in this issue by his student Friedrich von Hayek (1889–1992).

In 1920 Mises published an article in which he contended that a rational allocation of resources was not possible under socialism.[3] Mises observed the operation of markets under capitalism and pointed particularly to the key role played by factor markets. In these markets owners of land, labor, and capital supply

---

[3] This article, originally published in German, has been translated as "Economic Calculation in a Socialist Commonwealth" and can be found in *Collectivist Economic Planning,* ed. F. A. Hayek.

the factors of production to firms demanding them. Prices emerge, and on the basis of these prices and the available technology, firms make decisions on the most economical way to combine factors to produce final products. Under socialism the factors of production are, for the most part, not individually owned; they are owned by the community. Mises contended that because there are no independent owners of the factors of production, there would be no factor markets and no set of prices emerging from these markets. Rational decision making for resource allocation is not possible without factor prices: "As soon as one gives up the conception of a freely established monetary price for goods of a higher order [factors of production], rational production becomes completely impossible. Every step that takes us away from private ownership of the means of production also takes us away from rational economics."[4]

Although the earlier work of Pareto and Barone had already allegedly demonstrated that Mises' argument was erroneous, his position was challenged by F. M. Taylor in his presidential address to the American Economic Association in 1928.[5] Taylor claimed that the problem of allocating resources could be rationally solved under socialism. He suggested that income be distributed by the state in accordance with whatever objectives were accepted and that the household be permitted to spend its income in free markets. State-owned firms would plan production to meet consumer demand so that price equaled cost of production. The prices of factors of production would be determined by a process of imputation. Trial and error would disclose to the planners equilibrium prices for the factors. Thus, no fundamental resource-allocation problem existed under socialism.

The debate grew as F. A. Hayek, later a Nobel Prize winner, and Lionel Robbins (1898–1984) started a new argument. They contended that although the solution to the allocation problem under socialism was theoretically possible, it was practically impossible. To appreciate their argument, think of the economy as a giant computer. For each commodity demanded by a household, there is an equation; for each commodity supplied by a firm, there is an equation; and so forth. Hayek and Robbins insisted that it would be impossible for socialist planners to collect the mass of data necessary for rational allocation, let alone solve the equations simultaneously.

This phase of the debate was effectively closed by Oskar Lange (1904–1965) in two essays published in 1936–1937, which were revised and published under the title *On the Economic Theory of Socialism.*[6] Lange, like many other writers on these issues, also made important contributions to welfare economics. He was a socialist who taught in the United States at the University of Chicago and then returned to Poland following World War II. In responding to the argument of Mises, Hayek, and Robbins, Lange claimed that once it is recognized that factor prices can be used for rational allocation whether the factor prices emerge from

[4] *Ibid.,* p. 104.
[5] This paper is reprinted in *On the Economic Theory of Socialism,* ed. B. Lippincott (Minneapolis: University of Minnesota Press, 1938).
[6] In the Lippincott anthology, *supra.*

competitive markets or are set by state planners, their arguments fail. Market prices are really just indexes of the alternatives offered to buyers and sellers. In competitive markets under capitalism, the households selling factors and the firms buying factors have no real knowledge of the forces determining these prices. But that lack of knowledge does not influence their actions. They take the prices as parameters and act accordingly. By trial and error the planners will find the prices that will make quantity supplied equal to quantity demanded and thus clear the markets.

Lange went on to point out that under competitive capitalism, neoclassical theory has found that three conditions obtain in equilibrium. (1) Both consumers and producers are in maximizing positions; (a) consumers are spending their limited income so as to maximize satisfaction, and (b) producers are maximizing profits. (2) Every price is such that quantity supplied equals quantity demanded, such that all markets are cleared. (3) Incomes from consumers will be equal to their receipts from the factors sold plus profits. Under planned socialism equilibrium (1a) is unchanged. Thus, Lange argued that consumers would be able to spend their income to maximize satisfaction. Condition (1b) no longer holds under socialism, because state-owned firms are not interested in profit maximization. Lange would replace condition (1b) by requiring producers to follow two rules: first, that they produce every output at the lowest possible cost; second, that they choose the scale of output so that price equals marginal cost. Condition (2) is brought about in capitalism by free-market forces. Lange contended that the clearing of markets under socialism would be brought about by state planners adjusting prices on a trial-and-error basis. A price that is too high would bring about surpluses and indicate to the planners the necessity of lowering prices. Too low a price would result in shortages. Condition (3) would hold under socialism except that there would be no profits.

Lange recognized that his essay was just an extension and elucidation of Taylor's argument. There is no more need to have a huge computer solving supply-and-demand equations under socialism than under capitalism. The Pareto-Barone-Taylor-Lange-Lerner[7] argument essentially states that a socialist economy would allocate resources most efficiently if, by planning and direction, it brought about the same results as would exist under perfectly competitive markets. Thus, the state firm would meet consumer demands by operating at the minimum point of its long-run average cost curve, where marginal cost would equal price.

By 1940 there was agreement in the profession that Mises and Hayek had been wrong and that socialism could rationally allocate resources. This acceptance is manifested by an article written in 1948 by Abram Bergson (1914–   ) in a two-volume collection of survey articles under the sponsorship of the American Economic Association, which was designed to be used by economists to bring them up to date with accepted thought in various fields.

---

[7] A. P. Lerner (1903–1982) was also an important contributor to this literature on the economics of socialism. See in particular his *Economics of Control* (New York: Macmillan, 1946).

In his survey of socialist economic theory, Bergson notes that "by now it seems generally agreed that the argument on those questions advanced by Mises . . . is without much force."[8] He goes on to suggest that some of Hayek's contributions to the debate concerning the monitoring of state firms and the knowledge necessary for planners to acquire to give efficiency "exaggerate the difficulties of the problems."[9]

One of the reasons why Mises, Hayek, and others were unable to effectively communicate their criticisms of theoretical and practical socialism as worked out by Lange and others was the state of the economic model in the 1930s and 1940s. It was essentially an equilibrium model. There was little discussion of how disequilibrium adjustments would come about and individual entrepreneurial action was not part of the formal model. Because that disequilibrium adjustment was not part of the formal model, criticism of an argument based on the need for such actions was not acceptable.

To have accepted the Austrian argument would have damaged the theoretical case for socialism; it also would have undermined the formal theoretical case for capitalism, because that too was based on the static general equilibrium model and did not have any explicit role for individual entrepreneurial actions.

It was only in the 1970s that these issues were raised again. From the 1930s to the 1970s the central argument that socialism was theoretically and practically able to rationally allocate resources was accepted by the economics profession, nonsocialists and socialists, with few exceptions.

Socialism and Freedom

We have already seen that by the 1890s Schaffle, Brentano, and Nasse had openly questioned the compatibility of socialism and freedom. In the twentieth century this issue was forcibly brought to the attention of social scientists by developments in Germany, Italy, and the Soviet Union between the two World Wars. Among English-speaking economists the issue was again raised by F. A. Hayek in his *The Road to Serfdom* (1944).

In this book and in other writings, Hayek maintained that socialism is incompatible with freedom. An economic plan cannot simply exist; it requires a specific course of action. Because planners cannot know the preferences of everyone in the society, they must necessarily "impose their scale of preferences on the community for which they plan."[10] The socialist blueprint suggesting that market socialism will permit freedom of consumer and occupational choice within a planned economy is, therefore, false, because planning and freedom of choice are incompatible, Hayek contended.

---

[8] Abram Bergson, "Socialist Economics," in *A Survey of Contemporary Economics,* Vol. I, ed. Howard S. Ellis (Homewood, Ill.: Richard D. Irwin, 1948), p. 412.

[9] *Ibid.,* p. 435.

[10] F. A. Hayek, *The Road to Serfdom* (Chicago: University of Chicago Press, 1944), p. 65.

Probably reflecting the attitude of the majority of mainstream economists in 1948, Bergson responded to this new tack in a manner that is interesting from the hindsight of today:

> Unfortunately, it does not seem possible to refer also to recent contributions to the discussion of the other basic issue in the larger controversy over socialism, that concerning planning and freedom. In view of the special circumstances in which the Russian Revolution has unfolded, the experience of that country perhaps is not so conclusive on the question of planning and freedom as is sometimes supposed. It must be conceded too that the emphasis that critics of socialism have lately placed on this issue sometimes has the appearance of a tactical maneuver, to bolster a cause which Mises' theories have been found inadequate to sustain. But certainly arguments revolving around the question of planning and freedom must be given the most serious consideration; without reference to them, one obviously is in no position to strike a balance for socialism.[11]

The question of the relationships between economic and political freedom, socialism, and capitalism falls outside the normal scope of mainstream economics, but it has been pursued by a number of writers. The line of argument that finds planning incompatible with freedom, and capitalism compatible with freedom, has been espoused by a number of economists. The most notable are Frank

The Fatal Conceit

When Western economists went to formerly socialist countries in the early 1990s, one of the economists that formerly socialist economists most wanted to examine was F. A. Hayek, particularly the ideas in his *The Road to Serfdom* (1944) and *The Fatal Conceit* (1988), subtitled "The Errors of Socialism." These books, they felt, captured the problems these countries had undergone. In these books Hayek draws a correlation between markets and political freedom.

Recent changes in the former Soviet Union appear to acknowledge that achieving a tolerable degree of economic efficiency requires greater political freedom than was permitted before.

It is clear that recognizing the issue of the relationship of various economic systems to freedom is important in assessing the performance and acceptability of competing institutional arrangements. There are broad philosophical issues of interest and importance as well as more technical questions of interest largely to economists. One specific issue concerns freedom not merely as an end in itself but as a means to an end—in particular, how much freedom is necessary to achieve the economic goals of efficiency and reasonable growth. Hayek's early recognition of this connection is a tribute to his understanding of economic systems.

[11] Bergson, "Socialist Economics," pp. 412–413.

Knight, Henry C. Simons, and most recently Milton Friedman and Henry Wallich.[12]

Even writers sympathetic to socialist ideas have expressed concern about the failure of Marxist socialist governments to permit political freedom. Robert Heilbroner is of the opinion that

> Democratic liberties have not yet appeared, except fleetingly, in any nation that has declared itself to be fundamentally anticapitalist, which is to say within the self-styled "Marxist" socialist ambit. The tendency in all these nations has been toward restrictive, usually repressive governments that have systematically compressed or extinguished political and civil liberties.[13]

THE FORMER SOVIET UNION AND RESOURCE ALLOCATION

After the revolution in Russia the communists were faced with the problem of organizing economic activity; Marx's writings were no help. An approach was taken whereby five-year plans were developed; much attention was paid to physical output and meeting quotas, and little concern was given to prices or issues of efficiency. Some problems were encountered: for example, farmers were not given prices high enough to encourage them to be productive and surrender their output to the government to supply food and materials for the urban sector. Rather than use incentive pricing, it was decided to collectivize the farms and thereby ensure the supply of agricultural products. Collectivization "solved" the problem of supply but exacerbated the problem of lack of efficiency.

Some Soviet writers recognized the inefficiencies in the Soviet system of material balances planning; they are the intellectual founders of the movement toward perestroika and glasnost that developed during the 1980s. To understand their contributions to modern economic thought, it is necessary to see why Marxian theory had inhibited economic planning.

Marxian Theory and Planning

Marx used a labor theory of value to identify the conflict under capitalism between labor and capital. A labor theory of value, however, places certain ideological constraints on rational resource allocation. One of the thrusts of modern Soviet economic theory that began in the 1930s is an awareness that Marx's labor theory is a positive hindrance to sound economic planning. The assault on this Marxian

---

[12] For Friedman's views, see Milton Friedman, *Capitalism and Freedom* (Chicago: University of Chicago Press, 1962) and Milton Friedman and Rose Friedman, *Free to Choose* (New York: Harcourt Brace Jovanovich, 1979). For Wallich's, see Henry Wallich, *The Cost of Freedom* (New York: Harper, 1960).

[13] Robert Heilbroner, *The Nature and Logic of Capitalism* (New York: Norton, 1985), p. 126.

pillar came about not as a broadly conceived thrust but as a byproduct of attempts to solve everyday problems in planning. The strength of ideology and the authoritarian nature of the Soviet system are evidenced by the time lag between the publication of papers in 1939 by L. V. Kantorovich, who later was awarded a Nobel Prize, and V. V. Novozhilov, and the fuller discussion of these issues that began with Khrushchev's sanction in the early 1960s.[14] These men were the first to implicitly question the labor theory of value.

Shadow Prices

Kantorovich, a mathematician by training, was asked to help solve a scheduling problem in the plywood industry. Soviet mathematicians long before had developed certain techniques that could be applied in industry. Because the particular problem presented to Kantorovich was not adaptable to existing techniques, however, he developed a new method for its solution. Kantorovich thus became the originator of *linear programming,* a technique independently discovered in the United States in 1947.

In the solution of a linear programming problem, certain so-called multipliers are derived. Although Kantorovich did not immediately perceive their importance and implications, his further investigations into the application and economic significance of linear programming made apparent their usefulness in economic planning. These multipliers are what economists refer to as *shadow prices,* and they reflect the scarcity value of commodities.

It soon became clear to many Soviet economists that planners employing shadow prices as indicators of value would achieve a much more efficient allocation of resources than planners using prices set by a planning board and derived from some mixture of ideology and expediency. Others were equally quick to see that the shadow prices generated by linear programming implied that relative prices are not just a function of labor time but that they also depend upon the scarcity value of capital and land. Use of shadow prices was therefore an obvious and fundamental attack on the labor theory of value.

Opportunity Costs

The other pincer in the movement against Marxian orthodoxy also started as an attempt to solve limited practical problems of planning. Suppose that a planning board must choose among several investment alternatives. Should it allocate funds (capital) to build a hydroelectric plant, a steel mill, or a machine tool plant? A labor theory of value that excludes interest from consideration does not help to solve this everyday problem even in an economy organized like that of the former Soviet

[14] Kantorovich's essay has been translated as "Mathematical Methods of Organizing and Planning Production," *Management Science* (July 1960); Novozhilov's essay has been translated as "On Choosing Between Investment Projects," *International Economic Papers,* No. 6, 1956.

Union. This is one example of a series of problems that can be solved only by admitting the productivity and scarcity value of capital.

Problems such as these engaged the attention of the economist Novozhilov in the late 1930s and led him to write a series of papers. His solution to the problems of rational calculation is complicated in its details but clear in its outline and main thrust. He proposed to measure value or price by what economists term *opportunity costs* and thereby allow not only for labor costs but also for capital and land costs. By expressing his concept of opportunity costs in units of labor, he gave the impression of remaining within the tent of Marxian orthodoxy.

In the post-Stalinist period there was a relatively free and open discussion of Kantorovich's and Novozhilov's proposals, and the pot started to boil.[15] These early discussions of resource allocation were studied by others and led in the 1960s to a critical re-examination of economic planning in the Soviet Union. An economist, Evsei Gregorevich Liberman (1897–1983), suggested giving the state firm greater latitude in making decisions and reducing the number of production targets assigned to the firm by the state planners; this was a strong suggestion for greater decentralization. Liberman also advocated the discontinuation of paying bonuses to firms based on output because more production of unwanted or inferior goods was wasteful. Instead, he recommended that bonuses be based on the profitability of firms.

Slowly the tide began to turn: witness the post-Stalinist period, the era of Khrushchev, and the collapse of the Soviet Union under Gorbachev. With these events came profound changes in many countries of Eastern Europe.

Planning and Economic Theory: An Assessment

With the fall of many of the socialist economies in the 1990s, and their attempts to introduce markets into their economies, it is helpful to go back and consider the debate on socialist economic planning from this historical perspective. It seems that, in practice, mainstream economists were wrong, and Mises and Hayek were right. Planning in socialist countries did not lead to anything like efficient allocation of resources; it led to distributional equality. It did not lead to what most people would call increases in personal freedom; most people in the socialist countries felt that the Communist party was simply an oppressor.

What is not clear is whether that failure is endemic to socialism or occurred for other reasons. Making a judgment based on history is difficult. We will, however, offer the opinion that the disequilibrium adjustment process, which involves knowledge acquisition, freedom, and entrepreneurs, is an important part of the understanding of an economy, and that the events in the formerly socialist countries should reinforce the need for the mainstream to consider that disequilibrium process more carefully. One such economist, who specifically considered

[15] For a discussion of their contributions to economic thinking in the Soviet Union during this period, see Robert W. Campbell, "Marx, Kantorovich, and Novozhilov: *Stoimost* versus Reality," *Slavic Review* (October 1961).

Convergence of Economic Systems

The movement toward greater use of market mechanisms in the former Soviet Union and the greater use of government to control both the macro and micro parts of Western economies has led to speculation concerning likely outcomes of these processes. It is suggested that all societies are pragmatic and that they will discard the parts of their systems that are undesirable. Thus, the former Soviets will become more like us as they use markets and incentives to achieve greater efficiency, and we will use more planning in order to remove the major fault of our economy—its inability to produce full utilization of resources.

A number of writers who represent a wide spectrum of political ideology and professional training have concluded that a convergence of capitalism and socialism is going to take place—Erich Fromm, Arnold J. Toynbee, Robert Heilbroner, and Jan Tinbergen, to name just a few.

In some ways, they are certainly right. Until the 1970s most Western economies were introducing more planning in their economies. In the 1970s however, things changed and Western economies seemed intent on limiting government involvement. In the 1980s and 1990s, with the downfall of many of the formerly socialist economies and their attempts to introduce market economies, the convergence seemed to be occurring more on the market side. So recently, there has been an asymmetric convergence. Whether that trend will continue or whether some new form of economic organization will develop is still an open question.

the process of disequilibrium, is Joseph Schumpeter. His analysis of growth and economic systems may provide a foundation for future work.

SCHUMPETER: A RENAISSANCE MAN IN THE TWENTIETH CENTURY

Joseph A. Schumpeter is one of the towering intellectuals of the twentieth century. He produced many books and articles that brought great admiration from fellow economists but few imitators. There were a number of ironies to Schumpeter's career as a social scientist. Before he was thirty years old he laid the foundation for his theory of economic growth in *The Theory of Economic Development,* first published in 1912 and translated into English in 1934. A brilliant conception, it has lain almost dormant because it is so broad-based that it does not lend itself to the economic model building that has been the vogue of mainstream economics for some fifty years. In the foreword to Eduard Marz's recent study of Schumpeter, Nobel Prize winner and model builder James Tobin comments that Schumpeter's "theories of development and business cycles were difficult to incorporate into the style and method that came to dominate economics, especially American economics, over the past fifty years."[16] Ironically, Schumpeter was a strong proponent of the greater use of mathematics in economics and econometric testing of hypotheses, the areas in which he was at a comparative disadvantage. Schumpeter's two-volume study, *Business Cycles,* was almost completely eclipsed by the interest of the economics profession in Keynesian economics. He turned his earlier *Economic Doctrine and Method* (1914) into an awe-inspiring example of scholarship, *History of Economic Analysis,* which was published after his death. His most popular book was written as much for the layperson as for his colleagues; in *Capitalism, Socialism, and Democracy* (1942) he presented many themes that are of interest to us. Journals in the history of economic thought are still filled with articles that refer to Schumpeter's view of a particular writer, period, or concept as compared with the authors'.

Schumpeter was born in Austria and studied under Menger's students Wieser and Böhm-Bawerk. By his own admission there were stronger influences on him than the Austrians, and these were manifested in his earliest writings during his twenties. From his first years in economics, Schumpeter had a natural inclination toward its larger issues; he showed little interest in making minor additions to accepted theory. It is therefore hardly surprising to find that he was significantly influenced by the work of Walras. He also admitted the strong influence of Marx. He admired Marx's scholarship and attempted to understand the development of capitalism. In his own work Schumpeter forcefully rejected what he regarded as the ideological elements in Marxian analysis. Politically Schumpeter was a conservative; so where Marx regarded evolving capitalism with disdain, Schumpeter praised it and mourned its eventual demise, which he foresaw. He came to America in 1932 and taught at Harvard until his death in 1950.

Schumpeter's explanation of the process of economic growth does not fit into the orthodox mold because he stressed the noneconomic causes of growth. Though he examined some strictly economic factors, he insisted that the principal elements in the past growth of the system and the elements that will reduce growth in the future are noneconomic.

First let us look at his novel analysis of economic factors. He essentially accepted Say's Law, although he recognized and analyzed the fluctuations in economic activity under capitalism. To him depressions were self-correcting, and there could be no equilibrium at less than full employment. Where Marx had seen depressions as a manifestation of the contradictions in the system that lead to its ultimate collapse, Schumpeter considered depressions beneficial to the system; they were an integral part of the entire process of economic growth. Growth was tied to the prosperity stage of the cycle, because this phase represented the ultimate outcome of the introduction of new products and technology into the economy. But excesses develop as credit is overexpanded and businesses overextend themselves. The resulting depression is beneficial in that it shakes out the economy,

---

[16] James Tobin, foreword to Eduard März, *Joseph Schumpeter: Scholar, Teacher, and Politician* (New Haven: Yale University Press, 1991), p. x.

removing the less efficient firms, and thereby prepares the way for a growing economy of healthy, well-managed, efficient firms.

But the principal agents of economic growth are noneconomic, according to Schumpeter, and are to be found in the institutional structure of the society. Schumpeter attributed to the activities of what he called *entrepreneurs* the tremendous growth that took place in the industrialized world. An entrepreneur to Schumpeter is not just a businessperson or manager; this person is a unique individual who is by nature a taker of risks and who introduces innovative products and new technology into the economy.

Schumpeter clearly distinguished between the process of *invention* and that of *innovation*. Only a few far-sighted innovative businesspersons are able to grasp the potential of a new invention and exploit it for personal gain. But their gain is the economy's gain. After the introduction of a successful innovation by the entrepreneur, other businesspersons will follow suit and the new product or technology will spread throughout the economy. The real source of growth in the economy, therefore, is found in the activities of the innovative entrepreneur, not in the activities of the mass of the business community, who are risk-averting followers.

Therefore, economic growth is fostered by an institutional environment that rewards and encourages the activities of entrepreneurs; early capitalism, with its private property and laissez faire government, was ideally suited to economic growth. Insofar as it stresses the importance of incentive and laissez faire government, this part of Schumpeter's analysis is in theoretical and ideological accord with the classical theory of growth; but where classical theory stressed the economic factor of the size of capital accumulation, Schumpeter emphasized a noneconomic, cultural, sociological factor in his analysis of the role of the entrepreneur. The contrast between this view of growth and that of mainstream neoclassical economics was stated succinctly by Schumpeter:

> What we are about to consider is that kind of change arising from within the system *which so displaces its equilibrium point that the new one cannot be reached from the old one by infinitesimal steps.* Add successively as many mail coaches as you please, you will never get a railway thereby.[17]

Still more novel are Schumpeter's observations about the future growth and development of capitalism. Where Marx had predicted that the demise of capitalism would proceed from its contradictions, Schumpeter speculated that its end would be the product of its success. He was an ideologically conservative economist who had a somewhat romantic vision of the growth of the economy as proceeding from the daring deeds of swashbuckling entrepreneurs. He wished to see the continuation of this process, yet he expected capitalism to be brought to a halt because of its success. The main elements in this scenario were the demise of the entrepreneur and, to a lesser extent, the greater role of the intellectual as the

---

[17] J. A. Schumpeter, *The Theory of Economic Development,* trans. Redvers Opie (Cambridge, Mass.: Harvard University Press, 1934), p. 64. Italicized in the original.

society became more affluent. The successful entrepreneur will promote the growth of a large firm that will eliminate by competition the less efficient, risk-averting firms in an industry. But the large firm will soon become risk-averting and cautious and will be run by bureaucratic committees, not by innovating entrepreneurs. The bureaucratized giant firm will then eliminate the entrepreneurs and replace them with "prudent" managers. As the hired managers replace the entrepreneurs, ownership of the large corporation will become an absentee ownership. "The true pace makers of socialism," Schumpeter said, "were not the intellectuals or agitators who preached it but the Vanderbilts, Carnegies, and Rockefellers."[18]

Once the giant firm has eliminated many of the small, owner-operated firms, a large part of the political support for capitalism will have been removed. The success of capitalism will destroy, moreover, the old conception of private property and the willingness to fight for it, Schumpeter contended. Once the entrepreneur is gone, the paid manager and the stockholders will no longer defend the concept of private property. Their attitude will also prevail among the working class and public at large. "Eventually there will *nobody* left who really cares to stand for it—nobody within and nobody without the precincts of the big concerns."[19] Again, the success of capitalism will speed this process, for the increases in income and wealth produced by capitalism will permit the growth of an intellectual group in the society who "wield the power of the spoken word" and who have "no direct responsibility for practical affairs."[20] The success of capitalism will permit these intellectuals to live off the fruits of the system but, at the same time, to criticize it. They will radicalize the labor movement; although they will not usually run for public office, they will work for and advise the politician. Occasionally they will become part of the government bureaucracy; but most important, with the ever-increasing growth of mass communication they will be able to disseminate throughout the society a discontent with and resentment of the institutions of capitalism.

Schumpeter envisioned the end of the system he loved approaching slowly but surely. He feared that with the demise of the entrepreneur and the end of laissez faire, government will intervene more and more in the economy. Some, like Keynes, welcomed this intervention as a way of saving capitalism, but to Schumpeter it was a sign of the imminent end of capitalism. With what Schumpeter called "Evaporation of the Substance of Property" and the end of the entrepreneur, the dynamic element in the economy accounting for its past growth will disappear. Socialism, having bureaucrats not unlike the risk-averting corporate managers of mature capitalism, will not be capable of achieving the dynamic burgeoning of earlier capitalism; Schumpeter rejected the arguments that socialism could not rationally allocate resources.

[18] J. A. Schumpeter, *Capitalism, Socialism, and Democracy,* 3rd ed. (New York: Harper, 1950), p. 134.
[19] *Ibid.,* p. 142.
[20] *Ibid.,* p. 147.

SUMMARY

Socialism and capitalism are difficult to define except in the context of a particular time. The theoretical definitions of socialism and capitalism have changed over time, as have the existing systems. One difficulty in evaluating the merits of these alternative ways of organizing societies is the divergence between purely theoretical systems and existing systems. Advocates of a particular system are prone to comparing the faultless, purely theoretical system they prefer with the wart-marked actual system they reject.

As it developed with democracy, capitalism contained two elements that gave it a dynamic as well as a stability: the entrepreneur gave it change and growth; democracy facilitated changes in the institutional structure of capitalism without destroying the basic institutions of the market. Neoclassical economic thought explains how markets operate in a private property system and is, therefore, capitalist economic thought.

Socialist economic thought was in part a reaction to the "failures" of a capitalistic society. Most socialists—utopian, Marxian, and post-Marxian—concentrated on an analysis of the faults of capitalism and wrote little about how they expected a socialist society to be economically organized. Some writers around the turn of the nineteenth century raised two questions about socialism that are still important today. Can socialism rationally allocate resources? Are socialism and freedom compatible?

These questions lay dormant until the beginning of the 1920s, when Ludwig von Mises asserted that socialism could not efficiently allocate resources. His charge initiated a debate that continues today. His student, Friedrich von Hayek, supported Mises' claim about resource allocation and also charged that socialism was incompatible with economic and political freedom. The continuing debate has given us a better understanding of the strengths and weaknesses of theoretical systems and has also shown some of the strengths and weaknesses of the neoclassical microeconomic model. The debate about socialism was conducted at a theoretical level largely within the framework of neoclassical theory and at a broad-based level with arguments from throughout the social sciences and history.

At the theoretical-technical level it was found that by giving instructions to plant managers and by setting factor prices by trial and error, socialism could produce results comparable to purely competitive markets and, therefore, could rationally allocate resources. In the technical-mechanistic model, the reason for this conclusion was that the working of the economy was reduced to an abstract set of equations. In this humanless model all knowledge about how to produce efficiently was known by assumption. The plant manager was a bureaucrat who was assumed to behave like an entrepreneur. All this was possible because the neoclassical model of capitalism made no provision for the entrepreneur's discovering through experimentation how to produce efficiently. Although the debate apparently disclosed the ability of socialism to efficiently allocate resources in the neoclassical model, it also showed the limitations of that model.

The broad-based debate was far less conclusive and continues today. Some argue that freedom is possible only under socialism, and others find a historical and theoretical relationship between capitalism and freedom.

All these discussions led some writers to speculate on the possibility of a convergence between socialism and capitalism. Joseph Schumpeter provided an alternative, broader interpretation of capitalism. Although his prediction of the demise of capitalism has not come true, it is an enormously insightful and provocative analysis.

Key Terms

capitalism   shadow prices
socialism   opportunity costs
utopian socialists   entrepreneurs
Ricardian socialists   invention
transition from capitalism   innovation
linear programming

Questions for Review, Discussion, and Research

1. Write an essay in which you describe some of the difficulties of defining capitalism and socialism.
2. One can construct a convincing argument for an economic system by comparing a theoretical system to an existing system. Explain.
3. When capitalism emerged from socialism, it brought with it seeds for change within the system in the role of the entrepreneur. Explain.
4. The recent dramatic changes in some formerly socialist countries have given us greater insight into the stabilizing role that democracy plays in any system. Explain.
5. What were the key issues in the debate about socialism that began in the 1920s?
6. How could rational prices be determined for factors of production in a socialist society in which there are no markets for nonlabor factors of production?
7. If the conditions that hold under perfectly competitive capitalism could be duplicated under socialism, socialism could rationally allocate resources. Explain.
8. What do you think is the relationship between economic systems and freedom?
9. Write an essay on the progress made by economists in the former Soviet Union in understanding the difficulties of allocating resources in a system in which prices do not reflect social costs.
10. Explain Schumpeter's view of the long-run tendencies of capitalism.
11. That absent-minded professor is back with another job for you. This time, she is doing an article on fascism and economics, and she remembers that Hayek

had some interesting things to say on the subject in *The Road to Serfdom*. She has jotted down the following quotation:

> Although few people, if anybody, in England would probably be ready to swallow totalitarianism whole, there are few single features which have not been advised by somebody or other. Indeed, there is scarcely a leaf out of Hitler's book which somebody or other in England or America has not recommended us to take and use for our own purposes.

Alas, she does not remember where she found this quotation and fears it is not correct. Your assignment is to find the full bibliographic citation and confirm its correctness.

Suggested Readings

Bergson, Abram. "Socialist Economics." In *A Survey of Contemporary Economics,* Vol. I. Ed. H. S. Ellis. Homewood, Ill.: Richard D. Irwin, 1948.

Friedman, Milton. *Capitalism and Freedom.* Chicago: University of Chicago Press, 1962.

Hayek, Friedrich A., ed. *Collectivist Economic Planning.* London: Routledge and Kegan Paul, 1935.

———. "The Fatal Conceit: The Errors of Socialism." In *The Collected Works of F. A. Hayek,* Vol. I. Ed. W. W. Bartley III. Chicago: University of Chicago Press, 1989.

———. *Individualism and Economic Order.* Chicago: University of Chicago Press, 1948.

Kirzner, Israel M. "The Economic Calculation Debate: Lessons for Austrians." *Review of Austrian Economics,* 2 (1988), 1–18.

Lavoie, Don. *Rivalry and Central Planning: The Socialist Calculation Debate Reconsidered.* Cambridge: Cambridge University Press, 1985.

Lerner, Abba P. *The Economics of Control.* New York: Macmillan, 1946.

März, Eduard. *Joseph Schumpeter: Scholar, Teacher, and Politician.* New Haven: Yale University Press, 1991.

Vaughn, Karen I. "Economic Calculation under Socialism: The Austrian Contribution." *Economic Inquiry,* 18 (1980), 535–554.

14 The Development of Modern Heterodox Economic Thought

"There is much of the past that is in the present, so also there is much of the present that will be in the future."

—John Kenneth Galbraith

IMPORTANT WRITERS

JOSEPH SCHUMPETER	*The Theory of Economic Development* 1912
GUNNAR MYRDAL	*The Political Element in the Development of Economic Theory* 1930
MICHAL KALECKI	"Essays on Business Cycle Theory" 1933
F. A. HAYEK	"Economics and Knowledge" 1937
MAURICE DOBB	*Political Economy and Capitalism* 1937
LUDWIG VON MISES	*Human Action* 1940
JOAN ROBINSON	*An Essay on Marxian Economics* 1942
PAUL SWEEZY	*The Theory of Capitalist Development* 1942
CLARENCE AYRES	*The Theory of Economic Progress* 1944
JOHN KENNETH GALBRAITH	*American Capitalism* 1952
PIERO SRAFFA	*Production of Commodities by Means of Commodities* 1960
VERNON SMITH	"An Experimental Study of Competitive Market Behavior" 1962
JAMES BUCHANAN AND GORDON TULLOCK	*The Calculus of Consent* 1962
PAUL BARAN AND PAUL SWEEZY	*Monopoly Capital* 1966
PAUL DAVIDSON	*Money and the Real World* 1972
I. M. KIRZNER	*Competition and Entrepreneurship* 1973
SAMUEL BOWLES AND HERBERT GINTIS	*Schooling in Capitalist America* 1976

380

Previous chapters have recounted the ideas of some of the most important past critics of mainstream economics who helped shaped the profession from outside orthodox theory. These critics were not simply voices crying in the wilderness, and kindred spirits have maintained the voice of dissension to the present. As in the past, there are important heterodox figures within the profession who are helping to shape and determine the economics of the future. This chapter will examine modern heterodoxy to determine its characteristics, its chief figures, and how it has evolved.

Heterodox thinkers are even more difficult to organize into schools than mainstream thinkers, because dissenters are often free-thinking, iconoclastic individuals who tend to disagree with other dissenters as much as with the mainstream. Organizing such writers into schools of thought thus does them some injustice. But to fail to present their views because of this difficulty would be an even greater injustice. Hence, this chapter should be seen as a somewhat oversimplified guide to further reading rather than as a definitive interpretation.

Modern heterodox thinkers fall roughly into six dissident groups: radicals, modern institutionalists, post-Keynesians, public choice advocates, neo-Austrians, and experimental economists. The first five schools represent "traditional heterodoxy," differing as they do with the mainstream on policy issues, assumptions, and (often) methodology. Members of the sixth group, the experimental economists, do not differ from orthodox economists on policy issues but are heterodox in a possibly more fundamental methodological way.

Five of these groups are organized in Table 14.1 according to political points of view, ranging in varying degrees from liberal to conservative. We do not list experimental economists in this group because their heterodoxy is of a different, nonpolitical sort. In looking at the table, remember that our discussion of heterodox economists is intended to give evidence of the diversity of modern American heterodox thought and to provide a brief introduction to some interesting reading; it is in no way intended to be exhaustive. As a summary, Table 14.1 blurs important differences within a given school.

RADICALS

Bongo: Human beings should not eat each other.
Wowsy: Good Gooey Gow! You can't dictate to people what they're going to eat and what they're not going to eat. Men have always eaten each other and always will. It's natural. You can't change human nature.
Bongo: I love my fellow men.
Wowsy: So do I—with gravy on them.

The conservative economists, like Wowsy, argue that people are born with certain ideas—such as eating people, or holding slaves, or being a competitive capitalist—and that there is no way to change those ideas. . . .

Table 14.1   Heterodox Economists

	Radicals	Institutionalists
Views on individual rationality	Individuals follow class beliefs; self-expression is extremely difficult in a capitalistic society.	Individualist psychology is incorrect; people learn tastes through culture.
Policy view	Government reflects ruling class; major changes in form of government are necessary for serious reform.	Favor more government intervention.
Theory of production	Some hold labor theory of value; some reject labor theory of value; capitalists extract surplus from workers.	Firms use rule of thumb to determine prices; focus on institutional constraints on pricing.
Theory of distribution	Class theory of distribution based on power of ruling groups.	Distribution determined by institutions and legal structure; market is less important.
Some leading living advocates	David Gordon, Anwar Shaikh, Samuel Bowles, Herbert Gintis.	Mark Tool, John Adams, Wallace Peterson, Warren Samuels.
Primary journal	*Review of Radical Political Economics.*	*Journal of Economic Issues.*
Main graduate schools emphasizing their view	University of Massachusetts, New School for Social Research, University of Utah.	Colorado State University, University of Nebraska, Michigan State University.
Macroeconomic views	Economy tends toward crisis and unemployment without massive state intervention.	Oppose neoclassical models; relevant models must have more institutional structure; generally support Keynesian policies.

Post-Keynesians	Public Choice Advocates	Neo-Austrians
Uncertainty makes individual rationality difficult.	Individuals are rational in all aspects of life, including politics; rent-seeking is important.	Radical individualism; close association with libertarian philosophy.
Tend to favor government intervention.	Government is a reflection of individuals' political interest. The less government involvement, the better. Strongly oppose government intervention as a form of rent-seeking.	Strongly oppose government intervention on moral grounds; it violates individuals' rights.
Firms use cost-plus pricing; margin determined by need for reinvestment.	Profit maximization on individual level. Generally accept mainstream views, although rent-seeking can lead to monopolization.	Profit-maximizing firms.
Macroeconomic distribution theory determined by profit-wage mix.	Marginal productivity theory of distribution modified by rent-seeking.	Marginal productivity theory; focus on property rights.
Paul Davidson, Jan Kregel.	Gordon Tullock, James Buchanan, Robert Tollison.	Murray Rothbard, Don Lavoie, Ludwig Lachmann, Israel Kirzner.
Journal of Post-Keynesian Economics.	*Public Choice.*	*Cato Papers.*
University of Tennessee.	George Mason University.	New York University, George Mason University.
Oppose IS-LM. Uncertainty makes modeling difficult. Believe in multiple equilibria.	Take an essentially microeconomic view; a separate macro-economics does not exist.	The market process is important; mainstream models lose the required focus on markets.

By contrast with conservatives, radical economists believe that all ideas and preferences—such as our desire for Cadillacs—are shaped by the society in which we live. . . . Since our ideology is determined by our social environment, radical economists contend that a change in our socioeconomic structure will eventually change the dominant ideology. . . . There is thus hope of a completely new and better society with new and better views by most people.[1]

The preceding paragraphs are quoted from the beginning of Hunt and Sherman's radical introductory economics textbook. The quotation demonstrates an important aspect of the way in which radicals view the economy. They believe orthodoxy accepts too much of the status quo; radicals want to change it, not accept it.

Twentieth-Century Parents of Modern Radicals

The radical school has its origins in Marx's analysis but it has both extended Marxian economic analysis and moved beyond it. At the turn of the century, as neoclassical economics was being established, Marx had few followers among Western economists, in part because of his inherent anticapitalist views. Societies and their institutions will not support analysis that advocates their own destruction. Marx's analysis did attract followers among noneconomists, however, and a few Marxian economists have achieved some status in the economics profession. A number of important works in *Marxian economics* were published between the 1930s and the 1970s, including Maurice Dobb's *Political Economy and Capitalism* (1937), Joan Robinson's *An Essay on Marxian Economics* (1942), Paul Sweezy's *The Theory of Capitalist Development* (1942), and Paul Baran and Paul Sweezy's *Monopoly Capital* (1966). Active discussion of Marxian issues has been kept alive in the *Monthly Review,* and the Monthly Review Press has been an outlet for book-length Marxian analysis.

Maurice Dobb (1900–1976) was the foremost British academic Marxist from the 1930s through the 1960s. He published his first book on entrepreneurship at twenty-five and continued an active scholarly life with contributions on Russian economic development, Marxian theory, economic history, underdeveloped countries, welfare economics, and the history of economic thought. With Piero Sraffa (1898–1983), he edited the *Works and Correspondence of David Ricardo.*

Joan Robinson (1903–1983), without doubt the most prominent woman economist, burst on the scene as a mainstream economist with her impressive *Economics of Imperfect Competition,* published in the same year (1933) as E. H. Chamberlin's *Theory of Monopolistic Competition.* In that work she exhibited great skill as a microeconomic theorist in using marginal analysis to clarify and extend Marshall's hints concerning markets situated somewhere between pure competition and pure monopoly. For several years before the publication of Keynes's *General Theory,* there was considerable interest in a Chamberlin-Robinson analysis of imperfectly competitive markets. As an important member of the small group of economists

---

[1] E. K. Hunt and Howard Sherman, *Economics,* 4th ed. (New York: Harper and Row, 1981), p. xxiv.

from Cambridge and Oxford who helped J. M. Keynes develop the ideas that became the *General Theory,* she gained further prestige. In 1937 she published *Introduction to the Theory of Employment,* an outstanding introduction to Keynes's ideas. Robinson's intellectual and political life manifested a gradual movement away from orthodoxy. Her *An Essay on Marxian Economics* (1942) remains an excellent short analysis of Marx. In the 1950s she offered a new analysis of capital theory that rejected much of mainstream neoclassical capital and marginal productivity theory. Moving further from orthodoxy, she authored an introductory economics text intended to convey her ideas to a broader audience, but it was not commercially successful.

As Joan Robinson grew older, there was considerable speculation each year that she might win a Nobel Prize in economics. Many in the profession, from the most orthodox to the very heterodox, were puzzled when each year went by without this honor's being given to so outstanding an economist. We too have pondered this question. We speculate that the reasons were not that others were more deserving, not that she was a woman, but that her movement out of neoclassical and Keynesian theory had brought her into the muddy waters of heterodoxy. Nevertheless, Joan Robinson was an important precursor of the post-Keynesians and may have had the most significant non-Marxian influence on modern radical economics.

Paul M. Sweezy (1910–   ) published a seminal article in 1939 developing the kinked demand curve as a tool in the analysis of oligopoly. Sweezy was at Harvard when Keynes's ideas were brought to the United States, but he preferred to stay within the Marxian tradition. He left the academic world when he was still a young man and has spent the rest of his life trying to adapt Marx to the twentieth century. He and Leo Huberman edited the *Monthly Review,* a major journal for the dissemination of heterodox Marxist ideas. His *Theory of Capitalist Development* (1942) is probably the best published presentation of Marx's economic thought. In 1966 he and Paul Baran published *Monopoly Capital,* an adaptation of Marx's analysis of capitalism to the Keynesian world of the 1960s. This book became a starting point for many of the radical economists generated by the period of the Vietnam War. It also refocused attention on the problem of marginal productivity theory and imperialism raised by John A. Hobson at the turn of the century.

Paul Baran (1910–1964), born in Russia and educated in Europe, came to the United States during the 1930s, like many other scholars. After a variety of experiences, he became a professor at Stanford. Baran's economics professorship at a major American graduate school was considered unique, because he was an acknowledged Marxist. The fact that Marxists have not been given professorships at major centers of graduate education in the United States is not without interest to students of the history of economic thought. We cannot pursue this issue here but refer interested readers to the provocative note written by Martin Bronfenbrenner to the *American Economic Review* on the occasion of Baran's death.[2]

---

[2] Martin Bronfenbrenner, "Communications: Notes on Marxian Economics in the United States," *American Economic Review,* 54 (December 1964), 1019–1026.

Possibly the most provocative work in stimulating radical theorists has been Baran and Sweezy's *Monopoly Capital* (1966). Essentially Marxist, the book (1) introduces into radical economics some of Michal Kalecki's ideas and some elements from the theory of monopolistic competition and oligopoly, while (2) implicitly dropping Marx's labor theory of value. Baran and Sweezy pointed to Marx's astuteness in predicting the growth of oligopoly but saw his analysis as faulty in claiming that competition would generate falling rates of profit over time. They maintained that profits would rise over time with the increasing concentration of capital—monopoly capital. Crises in the capitalist period of history would be brought about, they said, not by falling profits but by underconsumption. They predicted that the capitalist reaction to underconsumption would be to create even larger firms, more wasteful consumption, and more expenditures by government in order to stabilize the failing system. As a result of *Monopoly Capital* and the literature it generated, one could be a radical without accepting all the older Marxian positions—in particular, the labor theory of value, a class analysis, and the inevitable fall in the rate of profits under capitalism.

Contemporary Radical Economics

Radical economics, based in part on Marx, evolved into a school of thought in its own right in the late 1960s and 1970s, partly in response to the social strains of the Vietnam War. In 1968 a group of young economists formed the Union of Radical Political Economy. This organization publishes the *Review of Radical Political Economics,* a central journal of radical economic thought. It is supplemented by the *Monthly Review, Science and Society,* and *Cambridge Journal of Economics.* Although radical views are diverse, certain ideas about what is wrong with neoclassical economics and market-oriented economics bind them together. The radical position encompasses the following three points:[3]

1. Radical economists think that "major socioeconomic problems can be solved only through a radical restructuring of our society." They argue that poverty, racism, sex discrimination, destruction of the environment, alienation of workers, and imperialism "are not pathological abnormalities of the system, but rather are derived directly from the normal functioning of capitalism."
2. Radicals argue that there are major inconsistencies between neoclassical theory and real-world experience. Where mainstream economists see social harmony, radicals see conflict.
3. Following their Marxist heritage, radicals view society as an "integrated social system existing in concrete historical circumstance." They believe that mainstream economics simply accepts existing institutions, such as the market, as given and does not consider a wide variety of proposals to change those institutions. They see the incremental changes advocated by mainstream eco-

---

[3] This section relies heavily on Eileen Applebaum, "Radical Economics," in *Modern Economic Thought,* ed. Sidney Weintraub (Oxford: Basil Blackwell, 1977), p. 560.

nomics as hardly worth considering. As Eileen Applebaum states, radicals "are interested in ending—not salvaging or stabilizing—monopoly capitalism" and replacing it with "a socialist society based on participatory planning, public ownership of the means of production, the elimination of private appropriation of profit, and a genuinely egalitarian redistribution of income and wealth."

Given these views, radical analysis of the economy is significantly different from mainstream analysis. The radical premise, as Applebaum says, is that the problems of Western society "are inevitable consequences of the capitalist institutional structure." Radicals emphasize in their analysis that technology embodies the social relations between individuals and that any analysis must study why capitalism exists rather than take it as given. Many radicals explain the existence of capitalism by means of class analysis, contending that any useful economics must incorporate class analysis. Most radicals also believe that capitalism embodies internal contradictions that inevitably will bring the system down, although this process is slowed by the repressive state, which exists to serve the interests of the capitalist class, and by institutions such as schools, which are arms of the state.

Since the mid-1970s, radicals have played a smaller role in mainstream economic debate. The reasons for this are varied. Some radicals have turned inward to debate doctrinal Marxian issues, such as the tendency for the rate of profit to fall and the transformation problem (how one can move from a labor theory of value to a set of values or prices of goods in a multi-industry model). But other radical work of the 1970s has influenced mainstream analysis. An example is Steven Marglin's "What Do Bosses Do?" Marglin argued that technology is not given but is chosen by a particular group of individuals within the society.[4] In capitalism this group is the managers, or "bosses," who choose the technology that provides them with the strongest role. In stating his argument, Marglin reconsiders Adam Smith's example of the pin factory, which Smith used to demonstrate the advantages of the division of labor. Marglin argues that by bringing all the workers under one roof, the bosses (organizers) gained control over the workers, securing their own role in the production process and allowing them to extract a larger surplus from the workers. Although this analysis is not found in introductory textbooks, it is known to most economic organizational specialists.

A second radical argument that has gained recognition within mainstream economics concerns the economics of education. The mainstream analysis of schooling holds that individuals invest in schooling and receive a return in the form of increased future earnings. The investment makes them and society better off. Significant empirical research has gone into showing what that return is, and neoclassical economics has concluded on the basis of this research that we have underinvested in schooling. Samuel Bowles and Herbert Gintis disagree, arguing that schooling does not necessarily enhance the well-being of society. Their

---

[4] Stephen Marglin, "What Do Bosses Do?" *Review of Radical Political Economics,* 7 (Summer 1974), pp. 60–112.

hypothesis is that the higher earnings of educated persons are sometimes simply a return for being allowed into a monopoly. Schooling, they contend, does not necessarily increase the true value of workers; it may merely provide a union card that allows individuals into a set of professions they could not enter without it. Bowles and Gintis assert that because econometric work cannot separate these two hypotheses, the question of education's contribution to society remains open.

Another inroad of radical thought into mainstream economics came from a "more acceptable" radical (so acceptable that he might not even be considered radical). That inroad is Michael Piore's *dual labor market* analysis. Piore argues that it is wrong to view the labor market as a single market, because major structural and social constraints limit the mobility of labor. For example, a worker hired as a shipping clerk will find it almost impossible to be promoted to a managerial position, no matter how capable he or she is. It follows that the relative desirability of various jobs cannot necessarily be ranked by pay, because a position with possibilities of upward mobility may initially pay less than a position without such possibilities. Because each job is done by a separate class within labor, Piore says, neoclassical analysis of the labor market as competitive does not fit the reality. One should instead analyze the labor market as a structurally constrained market, which he calls a dual labor market. Although this analysis conforms to Marxian analysis in that it incorporates a type of class distinction, the dual labor market has become part of mainstream Keynesian analysis.

With the demise of many of the world's socialist economies, radical economists have been pressed to explain how they can maintain their position when the type of economy they proposed has failed. Their response is that the so-called socialist economies of Eastern Europe, for example, did not really try true socialism but that their economies were subverted by capitalist influences and individuals who had lost sight of socialist ideals. Moreover, the failure of socialist economies has little or nothing to do with the problem of inequalities that radical economists see as existing (or inherent) in capitalist economies.

MODERN INSTITUTIONALISTS, QUASI-INSTITUTIONALISTS, AND NEOINSTITUTIONALISTS

Institutionalists from the turn of the century to the 1930s played a more significant role in economics than do contemporary institutionalists because the former were involved in implementing significant policy changes in the U.S. economy. Except for Marxists, the institutionalists have the longest history as a nonmainstream heterodox American school of economic thinking. In Chapter 12 we introduced the three central figures that represent the institutionalists of the early twentieth century: Thorstein Veblen, Wesley C. Mitchell, and John R. Commons. They spawned a school of thought, persisting until the present day, that has influenced a wide variety of heterodox economists. Consequently, the label "institutionalist" often extends far beyond describing the followers of these three. For this reason we have divided our description of *institutionalists* into three sections: (1) traditional institutionalist economics in the tradition of Veblen, Mitchell, and Commons; (2) what we call the *quasi-institutionalists*—writers whose ideas resemble those of the institutionalists but who are too iconoclastic to fit the traditional institutionalist mold; and (3) *neoinstitutionalists*—economists who write in a neoclassical choice-theoretic tradition but who believe that institutions must be far better integrated into current practice than is currently done, both in theory and in practical applications of theory.

Traditional Institutionalist Followers of Veblen, Mitchell, and Commons

American institutionalism reached its peak in the late 1920s and early 1930s, but by the late 1930s it began to wane. In his *Theory of Economic Progress* (1944), Clarence Ayres described the victory of the neoclassical over the institutionalist approach as complete. Since that time institutionalists have been outside the discipline: they are simply given credit for having called attention to important matters that economists should not overlook but that lie outside the scope of economic analysis.

It is important to recognize that being outside the scope of modern economic analysis does not necessarily make the institutionalists wrong. As we discussed in the introductory chapter, mainstream is not to be equated with right. Institutionalists forcefully argue that interactions between economic, cultural, and sociological issues are too great to warrant the isolated focus on economic forces that constitutes the thrust of much modern economic thought. In assessing mainstream economics they would agree with Kenneth Boulding, who called neoclassical economics the celestial mechanics of a nonexistent world, and they would argue that much of the work in modern economics is elaborate game-playing.

The University of Wisconsin, once the haven of thoroughgoing institutionalism, now offers an otherwise mainstream curriculum whose only vestige of institutionalism is its strong focus on empirical research. Most modern institutionalists continue to draw chiefly on Veblen, Mitchell, and Commons and express their ideas in the *Journal of Economic Issues*. Although they persist in opposing mainstream economics, for the most part they have been little heeded by the mainstream. Of the leaders of institutionalist thought in post–World War II America (e.g., Allan Gruchy, Wallace Peterson, and Clarence Ayres), none has achieved the preeminence of these earlier figures, no doubt partially because their views are chiefly elaborations of those of the earlier institutionalists. We will briefly examine those of Clarence E. Ayres (1891–1972) as an example of post–Veblen-Commons-Mitchell institutionalists.

Ayres has been the most visible of the institutionalists in post–World War II America. He spent most of his academic life at the University of Texas at Austin, which became the main source of institutionally trained economists after the University of Wisconsin moved into the mainstream. In his most important book, *The Theory of Economic Progress* (1944), Ayres accepted and elaborated the basic dichotomy between technological employments and ceremonial activities that permeates much of Veblen's work. Providing examples from cultural anthropology to illustrate that much of business activity was comparable to the totem and taboo behavior of technologically ignorant societies, he was able to distinguish between those matter-of-fact technological activities that furthered what he termed the "life process" and those that hindered achievement of "full production." Ayres also strongly stressed the Veblenian view that economics, with its fixation on equilibrium, was a nonevolutionary science and that the static neoclassical framework needed to be replaced by an evolutionary dynamic one. Borrowing from various fields in the social sciences, he valiantly struggled to incorporate the concept of "instrumental value," expounded by the American philosopher John Dewey, into economics. Marc Tool (1921–   ), a modern institutionalist, has continued to follow this avenue of Ayresian theory.

Heterodox schools, as we have noted, are often at odds with one another. For example, Ayres criticized the Austrian theory of capital as put forth by Böhm-Bawerk. On the other hand, Keynesian ideas were accepted by Ayres largely because an element of underconsumption notions runs throughout his own macro theory. A number of other institutionalists continue in the lineage of Veblen-Ayres.

QUASI-INSTITUTIONALISTS

Modern institutionalists remain a relatively tightly knit group intent on sustaining an ongoing dialogue among themselves, dispensing the insights of Veblen, Commons, Mitchell, and their followers. There exists another group of writers who accept many of the insights of the institutionalists and who were strongly influenced by them, but who are too individualistic and iconoclastic to fit the institutionalist mold. These include Joseph Schumpeter, Gunnar Myrdal, and John Kenneth Galbraith, all of whom deserve comment.

Joseph Schumpeter

Because Schumpeter's provocative views on capitalism were treated in the previous chapter, we need only briefly examine his contributions in the context of their relationship to heterodox economic ideas. Schumpeter came to the United States in the early 1930s and taught at Harvard, hardly a hotbed of heterodoxy. Yet he befriended the young Paul Sweezy; and although Schumpeter was clearly a conservative and not a Marxian, he acknowledged the power of Marx's vision of historical change. One element in Schumpeter's heterodoxy was a lack of interest in the equilibrium focus of neoclassical theory. He concerned himself instead with the dynamic aspects of theory, as manifested in *The Theory of Economic Development* (1912) and *Business Cycles* (1939), and especially in the delineation of the entrepreneur, a key figure in all of his analysis. Schumpeter, who like many heterodox economists painted with a broad brush, found the very abstract model of orthodox theorists too limiting. He continuously demonstrated the heterodox proclivity of drifting outside the intellectual boundaries of neoclassical theory as he poached on the preserves of sociology, history, and political science.

Although he unflinchingly declared his interest in and support of the orthodox paradigm, in his work he ignored the practices he advocated. For example, he avidly supported greater use of mathematics and econometrics in economics, but his own work was almost completely devoid of these orthodox tools. Another example of this curious tendency to say one thing and do another can be seen in his encyclopedic *History of Economic Analysis* (1954). In the introduction, Schumpeter promises to present a history of economic analysis and to hold to the absolutist's interpretation of the development of economic theory—namely, that modern theory contains an analytical positive core free of value judgments and that past contributions to theory are interpreted through the use of modern standards and are valued because of their role in providing a better understanding of the modern economy. His plan was to show how there has been a steady progression from error to greater and greater truth. However, the book is not a history of economic *analysis* but a history of economic *thought*. Nevertheless, Schumpeter is complex, multifaceted, and in his own way mainstream: this is reflected in the fact that he reserved his highest honors for those economists who created modern, abstract general equilibrium theory.

Schumpeter formed no school to carry on his economics, but his dynamic approach to economic institutions and development is reflected in the work of Richard Nelson and Sidney Winter, and also in the work of Nathan Rosenberg and L. E. Birdzell, Jr. His focus on entrepreneurial activity also lives on in the works of I. M. Kirzner, Harvey Leibenstein, and Mark Casson.

Gunnar Myrdal

Our second quasi-institutionalist is Gunnar Myrdal (1898–1987), one of many Swedes who have made important contributions to economics. In this tradition Knut Wicksell is the most eminent, but after Wicksell there are many of nearly equal stature in the development of economic theory. We have chosen Nobel Prize–winning economist Gunnar Myrdal not because he is typical of the Swedish economists but because he represents distinctly heterodox views. Myrdal came to be an international figure whose interests led him to study economic policy issues around the world, though early in his career he was more interested in technical questions of pure theory. His classic study of the relationship between ideology and theory, *The Political Element in the Development of Economic Theory* (1930), manifests interests ranging throughout the social sciences and humanities. In the early 1940s he ventured into sociology with a book on the population problem and a major study of blacks in America. In the Southern states, Myrdal's reputation was established with the publication of *An American Dilemma: The Negro Problem and Modern Democracy* (1944), which figured significantly in the legal battles for greater civil rights for blacks in the post–World War II period. When he came, later in his career, to focus his attention on planning in developed and underdeveloped countries, he brought to this task a rich experience as professor of economics, member of parliament, cabinet minister, sociologist, and international civil servant.

Myrdal is critical of orthodox economic theory, yet his criticism is not as strident as that of Veblen, Commons, or Hobson. Temperamentally more like Wesley Mitchell, he objects quietly and then busies himself with the tasks at hand. His major criticisms of orthodox economic theory center on the role of value judgments in theory, the scope and methodology of theory, and the implicit laissez faire bias of theory.

Myrdal maintains that attempts by orthodox theorists to develop a positive science free of normative judgments have failed. In his view, it is impossible to completely separate the normative from the positive, to achieve an analysis devoid of *oughts*. The orthodox attempt, he asserts, merely produced a body of propositions in which normative judgments were implied but never made explicit. Yet economists are and should be interested in questions of policy, Myrdal points out; thus, their choice of subjects to study and methods to use will necessarily reflect value judgments.

In the original Swedish edition of *The Political Element in the Development of Economic Theory,* he had concluded, however, that although ideology and positive theory were often intimately associated in the early stages of the formation of new theories, over time the normative or ideological elements would be purged and a pure, positive, scientific theory would remain. Economists could then use this positive, value-free body of knowledge in conjunction with the normative values implicit in any given set of goals to make policy. An English translation of this book was published some fifteen years later. Its preface reveals that Myrdal completely reversed his position on this important question:

> This implicit belief in the existence of a body of scientific knowledge acquired independently of all valuation is, as I now see it, naive empiricism. Facts do not organize themselves into concepts and theories just by being looked at; indeed, except within the framework of concepts and theories, there are no scientific facts but only chaos. There is an inescapable *a priori* element in a scientific work. Questions must be asked before answers can be given. The questions are an expression of our interest in the world, they are at bottom valuations. Valuations are thus necessarily involved already at the stage when we observe facts and carry on theoretical analysis, and not only at the stage when we draw political inferences from facts and valuations.
>
> I have therefore arrived at the belief in the necessity of working always, from the beginning to the end, with explicit value premises. The value premises cannot be established arbitrarily; they must be relevant and significant for the society in which we live.[5]

---

[5] Gunnar Myrdal, *The Political Element in the Development of Economic Theory* (Cambridge, Mass.: Harvard University Press, 1955), pp. vii–viii.

A second criticism leveled by Myrdal against orthodox theory concerns its scope and method. In common with many other heterodox economists, he maintains that economics is too narrowly defined by orthodox theory. Myrdal wants to bring into his analysis material from all the social sciences, particularly psychology and sociology. He also criticizes the focus of economics on short-run issues, whether they involve the allocation of resources or fluctuations in economic activity. Myrdal is more interested in the longer-run questions concerning economic growth and development and believes that much of the analytical framework and concepts of orthodox theory are inappropriate for this task. Myrdal finds the orthodox fixation on equilibrium particularly inappropriate in trying to explain the economic, social, and political changes taking place throughout the world. He abandons the static equilibrium analysis of conventional theory and develops instead a notion of cumulative causation. His idea of cumulative causation is, in essence, a general, dynamic equilibrium framework in which the term *general* implies that other than purely economic factors enter the analysis. This idea will be demonstrated later with an example from Myrdal's analysis of the economics of underdevelopment.

Finally, Myrdal is critical of what he regards as the bias of orthodox theory, which assumes that there is harmony in the system and that laissez faire is therefore the best policy for all nations to follow regardless of their stage of economic development. Myrdal views the long-run development of the Western industrialized nations as passing from a period of mercantilist governmental controls, to a period of liberalism and laissez faire, to a period of welfare politics in which governments intervene on a more or less pragmatic basis to ease pressing social problems, to a final period of planned economy, which has not yet been reached by some industrial countries, particularly the United States. The end of laissez faire is marked by increasing government involvement and intervention on a piecemeal basis with no overall coordination. Present experience, according to Myrdal, reveals the necessity of planning the macro goals of the economy and letting the market and, for the most part, private enterprise allocate resources within this plan. Without the overall planning to take us beyond the welfare state, he says, we will have an economy characterized by inflation, unemployment, and balance of payments difficulties. Myrdal's model of planning is not that of Soviet economics, nor is it as complete as indicative planning. It supposes national planning of the macro variables with a minimum of bureaucracy and maximum decentralization of economic decision making. Looking into the future, Myrdal sees the need to extend planning to the international level so that the fruits of the Industrial Revolution can be extended to everyone as we achieve a global welfare society.

Myrdal took an interest in underdeveloped countries and the world economy as well as in the special problems of affluent economies. Many of his books have been read in the United States by people other than economists; these books include *An International Economy* (1956), *Rich Lands and Poor* (1957), *Beyond the Welfare State* (1960), *Challenge to Affluence* (1962), *Asian Drama* (1968), and *The Challenge of World Poverty* (1970). In his study of the underdeveloped nations, Myrdal found that orthodox economic theory was not very helpful. There are two major areas in which it fails. On the one hand, orthodox international trade theory gives incorrect answers when applied to the foreign trade problems of developing nations. On the other hand, orthodox theory seems incapable of formulating internal policies that will lead to economic growth and development.

Let us examine one element of Myrdal's criticism of orthodox theory to obtain an idea of his approach. Myrdal maintains that there is a widening gap in real income between the rich and poor nations. Orthodox economic theory has no satisfactory explanation for this widening gap, nor does it offer any suitable policies to reverse these trends. The definitions economists use are too narrow, and the models for economic development are in the basic tradition of static equilibrium models; they fail to grasp the complex interrelationships among economic, sociological, political, and psychological factors that mold economic development. Myrdal argues that in order for anyone to understand economic development, "history and politics, theories and ideologies, economic structures and levels, social stratification, agriculture and industry, population developments, health and education, and so on, must be studied not in isolation but in their mutual relationship."[6]

The orthodox theorist believes that increased capital formation will lead to economic growth and therefore concludes that an unequal distribution of income is desirable, because it will result in less aggregate consumption and more saving and investment. Yet this is too narrow a view of the concept of investment. Myrdal contends that labor efficiency is very low in underdeveloped countries partly because of all the evils associated with poverty. Increased consumption for the laboring classes, he contends, will therefore lead to better health, greater productivity, and better attitudes toward work. Thus, what an orthodox economist would call consumption expenditure is in this case an investment in human capital. The failure to define expenditures in terms of their impact on productivity "is one reason for doubting the usefulness for South Asia of Western-type economic models which stress the relationships among output, employment, savings, and investment."[7]

Some thirty years of studying economic and social problems convinced Myrdal of the necessity for an end to laissez faire and for a thoroughgoing program of planning on both the national and the international levels. Coordinated national planning consistent with freedom has been implemented in Western European countries, although some difficulties with planning remain to be solved. The United States, Myrdal believes, has failed to recognize the necessity of planning its economy, in spite of the obvious social and economic costs of not planning. And the underdeveloped countries cannot afford the luxury of evolving planning systems in the manner of the Western European countries—the stages of laissez faire, piecemeal intervention, and then national planning. The poor countries must begin, Myrdal reasons, with comprehensive national planning if they hope to

---

[6] Gunnar Myrdal, *Asian Drama,* 3 vols. (New York: Pantheon, 1968), I, p. x.
[7] *Ibid.,* p. 530.

stimulate their static, past-bound, stagnant economies; to solve their population problems; and to significantly increase their per capita incomes so as to promote the long-cherished Western ideal of social justice.

John Kenneth Galbraith

John Kenneth Galbraith (1908–   ) represents the first American economist since Veblen to be widely read by intellectuals among the general public. Born in Canada, he took graduate work at Berkeley and majored in agricultural economics. His experiences have been varied: he has been a government official during World War II, an editor of *Fortune* magazine, an adviser to Democratic politicians on the state and national levels, ambassador to India, professor of economics at Harvard, and president of the American Economic Association. An unusually gifted writer, he has published a number of books on subjects outside the scope of economics as well as many in that field. His writings in economics have been addressed to a large audience; several, in fact, have been bestsellers on the nonfiction lists. Annoyed by his criticism of orthodox economic theory and by his popularity, some of his academic colleagues have tended to regard him as a fuzzy-thinking social critic rather than as an economist. But with his usual wit and charm, he has replied to these charges by admitting his guilt in writing in clear English so that he can be understood rather than following the lead of fellow economists and being incomprehensible.

Like many other heterodox writers, Galbraith has offered a criticism of accepted economic theory without providing a well-defined and logically consistent alternative. He long ago gave up trying to change the profession; he does not seem to mind whether or not any new theoretical structure emerges to conform to his vague, tentative formulations. Similarly, his analysis of the American economy is more concerned with explaining its present operation than speculating about its future course: "On the whole, I am less interested in telling where the industrial system is going than in providing materials for consideration of where it has arrived."[8]

To give an idea of Galbraith's approach, let us briefly consider three of Galbraith's major economics books, *American Capitalism* (1952), *The Affluent Society* (1958), and *The New Industrial State* (1967), and then attempt to discover unifying themes within them.

Countervailing power.   *American Capitalism* begins with a long criticism of orthodox economic theory. The major deficiencies of conventional theory, Galbraith contends, are that (1) it is too narrow in its conception of the scope of economics—it does not address issues of economic and political power, and (2) it draws incorrect conclusions concerning the working of the American economy. One of the major conclusions of theory is that any deviation from competition in

[8] J. K. Galbraith, *The New Industrial State* (Boston: Houghton Mifflin, 1967), p. 324.

markets will result in a less than optimal allocation of resources. Yet an examination of the American economy reveals that monopoly and oligopoly are not mere aberrations from some normal or usual market structure; rather, they are the essence of the economy. Applying orthodox theory to the prevailing economy, we would have to conclude that resources are not efficiently allocated. But Galbraith asserts that the economy has performed rather well and that resources are not being inefficiently allocated. Thus, he points to a paradoxical situation: "In principle the economy pleases no one; in practice in the last ten years it has satisfied most."[9]

Galbraith then offers a new analysis of American capitalism to explain why the economy continued to work when (according to orthodox theory) it was seriously out of kilter. He contends that when competition began to decline and the economic power came to be concentrated more and more in the hands of large corporations, new forces arose to restrain or "countervail" against the power of the corporations:

> In fact, new restraints on private power did appear to replace competition. They were returned by the same process of concentration which impaired or destroyed competition. But they appeared not on the same side of the market but on the opposite side, not with competitors but with customers or suppliers. It will be convenient to have a name for this counterpart of competition and I shall call it countervailing power.[10]

Competition as the regulatory mechanism of the economy, then, has been superseded by *countervailing power,* says Galbraith. Like competition, countervailing power is a self-generating regulatory force: power arising at one point in the economy begets a countervailing power. Galbraith then proceeds to give examples of this hypothesis: the growth of large corporations led to the growth of powerful unions in the same industry; the power of the large manufacturer was countervailed by the power of the large retailer; and the continuing government policy has facilitated the growth of countervailing power. Although he identifies areas of the economy in which countervailing forces do not effectively subdue the exercise of economic power, Galbraith contends that it is a singularly important factor in most of the economy. *American Capitalism* leaves anyone who accepts Galbraith's argument feeling generally optimistic about the workings of the economy.

The orthodox theory that equates monopoly power with illfare, Galbraith says, is wrong. The self-generating character of countervailing power results in an economy shot through with monopoly power, but one that nevertheless produces welfare for its society. Galbraith's invisible hand has replaced Adam Smith's invisible hand. He does note one significant case in which countervailing power does not operate: "It does not function at all as a restraint on market power when there is inflation or inflationary pressure on markets."[11] During these periods the

---

[9] J. K. Galbraith, *American Capitalism* (Boston: Houghton Mifflin, 1952), p. 90.

[10] *Ibid.,* p. 118.

[11] *Ibid.,* p. 133.

powerful unions and corporations find "it is to their mutual advantage to effect a coalition and pass the costs of their agreement along in higher prices."[12] We will return to the concept of countervailing power after reviewing two other works by Galbraith.

The Affluent Society.   Whereas the tone of *American Capitalism* is optimistic, the tone of *The Affluent Society* is mixed. In this book Galbraith extends some of the material only briefly outlined in the earlier work and concludes that a fundamental misallocation of resources is occurring in the economy. Whereas *American Capitalism* focuses on the efficiency of resource allocation in the private sector, *The Affluent Society* is concerned with the division of total output between the public and private sectors. Galbraith begins with another attack on orthodox theory and, phrasemaker that he is, coins a term to apply to theories he rejects: the *conventional wisdom*. Because the conventional wisdom of orthodox price theory was formulated at a time when societies were concerned about providing basic necessities, the theory focuses on scarcity. Observation of the American economy reveals, however, that for the most part we have solved the problem of scarcity and are now providing, in the private sector of the market, goods of a low order of urgency. Galbraith finds it interesting that as our production of goods has increased, our concern for producing even more goods has increased as well. Part of the reason for our fixation on production, for our GDP cult, is that the problems of unequal distribution of income, individual insecurity, and depression are relieved or solved by an ever-growing output. But the primary reason is that consumer wants are manipulated by the producers so that consumers feel a deep need for the products of an affluent society. Orthodox price theory assumes that individual consumer wants are given; they come from within the individual. It is the sovereign consumer that directs the allocation of resources to meet his or her needs. Galbraith maintains that this theory is not applicable to the modern affluent society, in which producers create the desire for their products. The process by which "wants are increasingly created by the process by which they are satisfied"[13] Galbraith terms the *dependence effect*.

The proposition that consumer wants are for the most part created by producers through the dependence effect does serious damage to orthodox price theory; it demands, in fact, that the entire theory of consumer behavior be rewritten and that the notion of consumer sovereignty be completely exploded. Concern for production and economic growth is seen to be misguided. "One cannot defend production as satisfying wants if that production creates wants."[14] Welfare economics becomes a shambles. But the main purpose of the concept of the dependence effect in the Galbraithian system is to cast light on problems concerning the proper size of the public and private sectors of the economy. Even though consumers are

---

[12] *Ibid.,* p. 138.

[13] J. K. Galbraith, *The Affluent Society* (Boston: Houghton Mifflin, 1958), p. 158.

[14] *Ibid.,* p. 153.

constantly being reminded of their immediate needs for a new automobile, an electric toothbrush, or a deodorant that will improve all aspects of their lives, there is no comparable dependence effect for public goods. This leads to a social imbalance, in that we produce and consume large volumes of high quality consumer goods and low amounts of inferior public goods. Galbraith graces this point with some of his best satirical writing:

> The contrast was and remains evident not alone to those who read. The family which takes its mauve and cerise, air-conditioned, power-steered, and power-braked automobile out for a tour passes through cities that are badly paved, made hideous by litter, blighted buildings, billboards, and posts for wires that should long since have been put underground. They pass on into a countryside that has been rendered largely invisible by commercial art. (The goods which the latter advertise have an absolute priority in our value system. Such aesthetic considerations as a view of the countryside accordingly come second. On such matters we are consistent.) They picnic on exquisitely packaged food from a portable ice box by a polluted stream and go on to spend the night at a park which is a menace to public health and morals. Just before dozing off on an air mattress, beneath a nylon tent, amid the stench of decaying refuse, they may reflect vaguely on the curious unevenness of their blessings. Is this indeed, the American genius?[15]

Orthodox theorists, quick to recognize the damage that the concept of the dependence effect does to price theory, have not accepted this Galbraithian thesis. But he anticipates rejection of his ideas by the keepers of the conventional wisdom and envisions them saying, "It is a far, far better thing to have a firm anchor in nonsense than to put out on the troubled sea of thought."[16]

The New Industrial State.   Nine years after the publication of *The Affluent Society,* Galbraith again set sail on the troubled sea of thought in *The New Industrial State.* Characteristically, he provokes orthodox theorists with biting comments. "The problem of economics . . . is not one of original error but of obsolescence."[17] As an example of the conventional wisdom, Galbraith selects Nobel Prize–winning Paul Samuelson's elementary textbook, which dominated the market in elementary textbooks in economics from 1947 until the 1970s. Those purveying the conventional wisdom say, "Better orderly error than complex truth."[18] In *The New Industrial State* Galbraith raises new questions and comes to new conclusions about American capitalism. In his previous work he suggested in his discussion of the dependence effect that the orthodox theory of demand was incorrect. In *The New Industrial State* he completes his criticism of orthodox price theory by criticizing the theory of firm behavior and supply. He then ties it all

---

[15] J. K. Galbraith, *The Affluent Society* (Boston: Houghton Mifflin, 1958), p. 253.
[16] *Ibid.,* p. 160.
[17] J. K. Galbraith, *New Industrial State,* p. 62.
[18] *Ibid.*

together to reveal that the orthodox description of the market process is largely wrong.

The utilization of modern technology requires large-scale firms. With the growth of these firms has come a separation of ownership and control; those who control firms are paid managers who form part of the technostructure of the society. In order to avoid risk and eliminate uncertainty, the firms encourage the government to stabilize the economy; they cooperate with unions; they invest out of retained earnings as much as possible; but above all they manage the preferences of consumers. Although this involves planning, firms do not plan in order to maximize profits, as is assumed by orthodox price theory; their primary goal is continuity of operation or survival of the firm. Once the firm achieves this security, it begins to think about growth in sales. Thus, Galbraith extends and amplifies his concept of the dependence effect—that wants are created by the process by which they are satisfied—to show (1) that the growth of technology and large-scale firms has created a necessity for order in the economy with a minimum of risk and uncertainty; and (2) that planning, which includes the management of consumer preferences, is now an essential part of the economy. Orthodox theory states that the market works through sovereign consumers, who give instructions to profit-maximizing firms by means of market prices. Galbraith calls this myth "the accepted sequence." He suggests that in markets in which the corporation is large and powerful, "the producing firm reaches forward to control its markets and on beyond to manage the market behavior and shape the social attitudes of those, ostensibly, that it serves."[19] He calls this more accurate description "the revised sequence."

Let us now state the thrust of Galbraith's criticism of orthodox price theory. He maintains that its theories of consumer and firm behaviors are incorrect and that their view of the firm's responding to the direction of the household is wholly inaccurate when the firm is large and powerful. If he is correct, then it follows that the policy recommendations of orthodox theory are without foundation, especially the view that with laissez faire there will be an optimum allocation of resources:

> Once it is agreed that the individual is subject to management in any case—once the revised sequence is allowed—the case for having him free from (say) government interference evaporates. It is not the individual's right to buy that is being protected. Rather, it is the seller's right to manage the individual.[20]

One of the undesirable consequences flowing from the new industrial state, Galbraith further contends, is that our social attitudes are shaped by the technostructure. The technostructure produces goods and identifies social welfare with output, thereby rationalizing its role in society and providing a national purpose for itself. The state supports the technostructure in promoting social attitudes that extol the quantity of goods produced by the economy as opposed to the quality of life in the society. Our educational system has already to some extent joined in

[19] *Ibid.*, p. 212.
[20] *Ibid.*, p. 217.

Modern Quasi-Institutionalists and Socioeconomics

Most people reading Schumpeter, Myrdal, and Galbraith, even if disagreeing with the authors' policy recommendations, will find much good sense in what they say, just as earlier readers found good sense in traditional institutionalism. But good sense does not necessarily lead to influence and change, and it is fair to say that their thinking has had little influence on the economics profession. Still, it is hard to hold down good sense; and there are, today, a number of quasi-institutionalists about whom future historians of thought well may ask, why did they have so little influence?

One of these groups has organized itself loosely under the banner of "socioeconomics." Organized by Amitai Etzioni, it has its own journal, the *Journal of Socio-Economics*. Like institutionalists, socioeconomists believe that social forces must be more strongly integrated into economic models than they currently are in neoclassical models. They propose a far more complicated psychological foundation for the utility function, one in which people are seen as more than simply self-interested profit maximizers.

Socioeconomists argue for a communitarian approach to value. Their theory holds that individuals are guided by their concern for community as well as by self interest, and that policy needs to be aimed at building communities.

---

this cult of GDP, although there is still a possibility that the uneasiness educators and others feel with regard to the country's obsession with production will manifest itself in a critical reappraisal of the direction of our economy and society. "The danger to liberty lies in the subordination of belief to the needs of the industrial system."[21]

An overview of Galbraith's evolving thought reveals some contradictions. *American Capitalism* projects a basically optimistic outlook about the future of capitalism, because countervailing power can be expected to lead to reasonable efficiency in the economy. The power of the large corporation is not necessarily undesirable if it is countervailed. Although we cannot see the future with certainty, the picture sketched by Galbraith in *The Affluent Society* and *The New Industrial State* is dark and gloomy. He is suggesting in these works that even though technological development has made it possible to solve our problems of production and scarcity, we now stand in great danger of becoming servants of the industrial system rather than its masters. Some hope exists if the intellectuals will reflect on these questions and become a force to redirect our society away from its concern for more production and toward a better quality of life. But what will happen remains to be seen:

> If the educational system serves generally the beliefs of the industrial system, the influence and monolithic character of the latter will be enhanced. By the same to-

---

[21] J. K. Galbraith, *New Industrial State*, p. 398.

ken, should it be superior to and independent of the industrial system, it can be the necessary force for skepticism, emancipation, and pluralism.[22]

NEOINSTITUTIONALISTS

Neoclassical economics leaves out institutions or, to be more precise, posits the institutions it needs to make the available mathematical techniques work. Initially this led to the use of static analysis, then comparative static analysis, then differentiable calculus, and later, set theory, measure theory, and optimal control theory. An interesting aspect of neoclassical economics is that, in part, technique has driven the questions it has addressed and the answers it finds.

The science of economics is far less likely to explicitly include institutions, for the simple reason that the analysis of institutions is messy and the search in science is for elegant underlying relationships that fit into existing techniques. Avoiding the explicit analysis of institutions, however, does not free the science of economics from them: neoclassical economics includes a variety of *implicit* assumptions about institutions in its underlying structural model. For example, consider "the firm"—the production unit of modern neoclassical economics. It is composed of many individuals and is enormously complicated, but neoclassical theory reduces its goals to a single goal—profit maximization—without explaining how that goal can be consistent with utility maximization of individuals within the firm. For example, will managers and other employees engage in activities that benefit them at the expense of profits? The same applies to markets: neoclassical economics assumes the existence of particular types of markets with specific mathematical characteristics; it does not explain how such markets have come about, how they might change, whether their existence might influence individuals' behaviors and preferences, or whether those markets are close approximations of what we see in the real world. Thus, it has a very narrow focus.

Such narrowing of focus and theoretical simplifications rule out many of the questions posed by critics of economics; thus, heterodox economists who have been consistent critics of society have also focused more heavily on explicit analyses of institutions than have neoclassical economists.

Some neoclassical economists believe that the messiness of institutions must be addressed, and they propose to do it within a neoclassical framework. These "neoinstitutionalists" include more institutional detail in their theoretical models than is usual for neoclassical economists, but they retain the conventional individual maximization procedures of the neoclassical model. Transaction costs play a central role in their analysis. Ronald Coase's article on the theory of the firm (1937) is a seminal article for these neoinstitutionalists. It argues that firms develop because the transaction costs of the market are too high for interfirm transactions.

---

[22] *Ibid.*, p. 370.

Neoinstitutionalism is sometimes also called rent-seeking analysis or neoclassical political economy. Its proponents contend that rational individuals try to improve their well-being not only within a given institutional structure but also by changing that structure. Economic analysis, they contend, must include a consideration of the forces determining that institutional structure. An *equilibrium institutional structure* is one in which it is not worthwhile for individuals to expend further effort in changing the institutions. Only on the basis of an equilibrium institutional framework, they say, can one produce relevant analysis. These neoinstitutionalists argue that a competitive institutional structure is unstable because some individuals have a strong incentive to change the institutional structure to benefit themselves, and this incentive is not offset by incentives to support a competitive structure. Perfect competition loses out in the competition of institutional structures. Accordingly, neoclassical economics is irrelevant, not because of its maximizing assumption but because its assumed institutional structure is not an equilibrium institutional structure. The maximization assumption has not been carried far enough. These ideas, unlike those of the few remaining followers of the original institutionalists, have provoked mild interest within the profession. Oliver Williamson's studies of the firm are in what we call the neoinstitutionalist mold.

POST-KEYNESIANS

In our consideration of macroeconomics, we saw that mainstream macroeconomics has followed only one of the many threads found in Keynes's writings. This situation arose partly from the general inability of economists to reach a consensus on what exactly Keynes was saying about the working of the macro-economy. In the 1970s, therefore, a group led initially by Sidney Weintraub and Paul Davidson on this side of the Atlantic and by Joan Robinson and John Eatwell in England joined forces in articulating a criticism of the mainstream neo-Keynesian model specific enough to allow its authors to view themselves and be viewed as an economic school. Calling themselves *post-Keynesians,* they held an organizational meeting in 1974 at which they founded their publication, the *Journal of Post-Keynesian Economics (JPKE).* In the inaugural issue of that journal, the various founders and supporters attempted to state what post-Keynesian economics meant to them.[23] Joan Robinson called it a "method of analysis which takes account of the difference between the future and the past"; J. K. Galbraith said it considers that "an industrial society is in a process of continuous and organic change, that public policy must accommodate to such change, and that by such public action performance can, in fact, be improved." Other writers focused on different issues, but all agreed that neoclassical and neo-Keynesian economics are inappropriate. They came to view themselves, therefore, as the true

[23] *Journal of Post-Keynesian Economics,* 1 (Fall 1978).

keepers of the Keynesian faith, calling mainstream macroeconomics "bastard Keynesianism."

British Post-Keynesians

The general statements that embody the concepts underlying most post-Keynesian analysis have not proved particularly problematical, but the specifics drawn from them have. The British post-Keynesians (sometimes called *neo-Ricardians*) believe the correct approach is to go back to the Ricardian theory of production and supplement it with a Kalecki class theory of business cycles. Following the work of Piero Sraffa in *Production of Commodities by Means of Commodities: Prelude to a Critique of Economic Theory* (1960), they argue that the distribution of income between wages and profits is indeterminate and independent of total output. Hence, the distribution of income is determined not by marginal productivity but by other forces, which are macroeconomic in nature. In this view they follow a model similar to one presented by Michal Kalecki in 1933, which he summed up in the statement that workers spend what they get and capitalists get what they spend.[24]

Kalecki makes three central assumptions in his model. First, he assumes that firms use a cost-plus method of pricing. Capitalists determine the profit rate and the wage rate but not the total profit or the total level of wages, because they are determined by the total level of output. Second, no saving is translated into spending, so the total level of output is determined by the level of total demand in a type of Keynesian multiplier fashion. Third, workers spend 100 percent of their income, so their marginal propensity to consume is 100 percent.

Capitalists' spending on investment tends to be arbitrary and unrelated to their level of profits (which constitute savings). If they spend all their profits, demand is sufficient to buy all the production; total output and profits will be high. If capitalists become pessimistic and do not spend but save their profits, aggregate demand and total output will be low, profits will be low (though the profit rate will remain the same), and unemployment will follow. Thus, the distribution of income between wages and profits is determined by macroeconomic forces, not marginal productivity. Most of the assumptions in this simple model can be modified, making the results somewhat more ambiguous, without invalidating the general insight that the macroeconomic level of activity is a determinant of the distribution of income.

American Post-Keynesians

The American branch of post-Keynesian theory is more diffuse than the British, but all its elements are variations on the theme that the economy is "in time." Alfred Eichner has extended the microeconomic analysis of the firm, which he calls the

[24] Michal Kalecki, "An Essay on the Theory of the Business Cycle" [1933], translated in his *Studies in the Theory of Business Cycles: 1933–1939* (London: Basil Blackwell, 1966).

megacorp, arguing that it determines investment internally from retained profits. Hence, to understand investment—and thereby total output—one must understand the modern corporation.

In *Money and the Real World,* Paul Davidson (1930–   ) contends that understanding money's role is central to understanding how the macroeconomy works and that neoclassical economics has not adequately addressed its role. In developing the post-Keynesian role of money, he emphasizes the existence of *irreversible time* and *true uncertainty,* which cannot be reduced to a probability distribution and hence cannot be changed to risk and then to certainty equivalents. These two interrelated characteristics of the economy have "led man to develop certain institutions and rules of the game, such as (i) money, (ii) money-contracts and a legal system of enforcement, (iii) sticky money-wage rates, and (iv) spot and forward markets."[25] Thus, institutions change the way in which the macroeconomy operates. Davidson's view resembles somewhat that of Hyman Minsky (1919–   ), another well-known post-Keynesian, who argues that the financial system is like a house of cards in imminent danger of collapse.

Post-Keynesian growth theory emphasizes methodological issues and, therefore, is a matter of perspective. It emphasizes growth as an important aspect of the economic process, whereas until recently mainstream economists emphasized static issues. For example, Roy Harrod and Evsey Domar's analysis of growth, which in the 1950s was a fundamental part of mainstream macroeconomics, now rarely appears in mainstream intermediate macroeconomics textbooks. Instead new books discuss stable, endogenous growth. This partially accounts for the post-Keynesian focus on instability, because the Harrod-Domar model suggested that equilibrium in the economy is always on a knife-edge bordering boom and bust.

In post-Keynesian work as a whole, one sees a consistency of conceptualization, if not of models. An enduring concept is that the economy is not stable: the invisible hand of the market does not work as well as neoclassical theory suggests. It follows that post-Keynesians see a much stronger role for government action in correcting the problems of capitalism than does orthodox theory. Post-Keynesians are best known for their support of tax-based incomes policies (TIP).

The Mainstream Response to the Post-Keynesians

The mainstream's response to American post-Keynesians has been to completely disregard them or to assume the attitude "What else is new?" Robert Solow sums it up as follows:

> I am very unsympathetic to the school that calls itself post-Keynesian. First of all,
> I have never been able to understand it as a school of thought. I don't see an intel-

[25] Paul Davidson, *Money and the Real World* (Cambridge: Cambridge University Press, 1976), p. 360.

lectual connection between a Hyman Minsky, on the one hand, who happens to be one of the oldest friends I have, and someone like Alfred Eichner, on the other, except that they are all against the same thing, namely the mainstream, whatever that is.

The other reason why I am not sympathetic is that I have never been able to piece together (I must confess that I have never tried very hard) a positive doctrine. It seems to be mostly a community which knows what it is against but doesn't offer anything very systematic that could be described as a positive theory. I have read many of Paul Davidson's articles and they often do not make sense to me. Some of post-Keynesian price theory comes forth from the belief that universal competition is a bad assumption. I have all my life known that. So I have found it an unrewarding approach and have not paid much attention to it.[26]

Mainstream economists also argue that "there is no correct neo-Ricardian proposition which is not contained in the set of propositions which can be generated by orthodoxy."[27]

PUBLIC CHOICE ADVOCATES

Economists assume that individuals are rational in economic affairs; why not assume that they are rational in other affairs as well? This is the question James Buchanan and Gordon Tullock asked in the early 1950s and so began the *public choice school*. Tullock and Buchanan left the University of Virginia in the 1960s, partly because of their unorthodox policy positions, and founded the Public Choice Center at the Virginia Polytechnic Institute, moving it in 1983 to George Mason University.

The central idea of the public choice school is that individuals are as rational in their interactions with government as they are in their economic affairs. Government is not an agency for good or for bad; it is simply an agency by which individuals achieve their economic goals through politics. The public choice theorists have devised an economic theory of politics; using the same framework that classical and neoclassical theory uses in modeling household and firm behavior, they analyze political, or public, choice.

The important insights of public choice theorists have sometimes been obscured by the anti-statist views of a number of public choice adherents, just as the insights of economists such as Galbraith have been obscured by their pro-statist views. This is unfortunate on both sides. Public choice theorists have made important contributions to our understanding of both policy issues and economic theory.

[26] Arjo Klamer, *Conversations with Economics* (Totowa, N.J.: Rowman and Allanheld, 1984), pp. 137–138.

[27] Frank Hahn, "The Neo-Ricardians," *Cambridge Journal of Economics,* 6 (1982), 363.

Economists of all political persuasions agree that *government failures*—governmental policies that do not achieve the social good—exist and must be included, along with *market failures,* in our analysis of policy. Of all the critical schools of thought we mention, the public choice school has been the most successful and their analysis of rent-seeking activities has spread into the mainstream. A number of introductory textbooks with a public choice flavor have been widely adopted. James Buchanan's selection for a Nobel Prize in 1986 also reflects some acceptance from the mainstream. For the most part, however, mainstream economists hesitate to fully accept public choice theory.

AUSTRIAN ECONOMICS

In Chapter 8 we examined the role Karl Menger played in the early development of marginal utility theory. Later we looked at some of Menger's students, such as Böhm-Bawerk and Wieser. In turn, their students and their students' students set up a coherent and well-organized approach to economics that has come to be known as the "neo-Austrian," or simply the Austrian, school. Austrian economists parted company from the mainstream for much the same reason that post-Keynesians did—the formalization of economics, which, they argue, has lost or abandoned many insights of earlier writers. Until 1960 *Austrian economics* was considered part of the mainstream; but as neoclassical economics became more formalized, the Austrians re-emerged as dissenters.

This is not to say that they did not have differences; they had substantial differences with the mainstream even then. For example, the Austrian analysis of production sees capital as an intermediate good that can be understood only in stages of production analysis. Similarly, Austrians maintained a steadfast adherence to viewing individuals as purposeful actors, not as a type of utilitarian machine that reacted to pleasure or pain. This, in part, led to a strong Austrian emphasis on entrepreneurship. They also maintained a different approach to costs, which they saw as individually subjective, rather than as objectively determined as in the classical school and in some interpretations of neoclassical cost analysis.

These differences, while substantial, did not place Austrians out of the mainstream until the 1960s. But in the 1960s, with (1) the increasing formalization of economics; (2) the almost total dominance by general equilibrium theory of the mainstream; and (3) the increasing tendency for mainstream economics to see itself as a science in which truth is determined solely by econometric testing, Austrian economics departed from the mainstream. Recent generations of what are now called neo-Austrian economists—especially Ludwig von Mises, Friedrich Hayek, and their students Murray Rothbard, Israel Kirzner, and Ludwig Lachman—contend that many of Menger's chief insights have been lost.

A central Austrian economic theme is that economic analysis is a process, not a static interaction of individuals, and that time is an essential consideration. It sees competition as a dynamic process through which high profits are eliminated over time. But those high profits play a very important role in driving the system. In Austrian economics, individuals are assumed to operate in a changing environment in which information is limited and the future unknown. The most interesting analysis, in their view, derives from studying not equilibrium itself but the process through which individuals grope toward equilibrium, a process that emphasizes the entrepreneur and what neoclassical economics calls disequilibrium.

Until recently there were strong political overtones in Austrian economics. It remains difficult to find an Austrian who is not a conservative; most simply assume the market is desirable and necessary for achievement of individual freedom. Many Austrians themselves, however, would characterize their political views not as "conservative" but as "radical libertarian" or "anti-statist." They argue that such views follows naturally from a study of history.

Austrian economists object, from time to time, to econometric work and attempts to prove economic theorems empirically. Following von Mises' "praxeology," they perceived their task as one of deriving conclusions deductively from the logic of human action. Conclusions and theories thus derived need not be tested, in their view, because truth had already been logically established. Recently, however, they have taken a somewhat more conciliatory position, arguing that it is the *type* of empirical work mainstream economics does—which does not include historical and heuristic elements—that is inappropriate.

Key seminal works in Austrian literature are Hayek's 1937 *Economica* article, "Economics and Knowledge," and a 1945 *American Economics Review* article, "The Uses of Knowledge in Society." Hayek raises the legitimate question of how the knowledge presumed to be held by market participants in equilibrium is acquired by the participants. Neoclassical theory assumes the knowledge is given. Hayek finds that an important role of markets and the process of competition is the discovery of knowledge not previously available. Hayek argues that equilibrium is a situation in which all agents' plans are synchronized; knowledge, expectations, and beliefs are therefore central elements of any economic analysis.

Scientism vs. Science

Austrian economists pride themselves on being *nonscientistic*. They do not think the proper methodology of economics should be application of the principles of natural science to the study of human action. They are more interested in a basic understanding than in an impressive appearance, which is what they mean by scientistic (as opposed to scientific). Hayek, the strongest advocate of this terminology, who won the Nobel Prize in 1974, evolved in his writing from economics to a study of the underlying legal and constitutional structure of society. In doing so he considered many of the same issues as did the institutionalists, and brought to that study a sense of history as well as of economics.

Because of uncertainty, coordination of individuals' plans is difficult and beyond a single individual's comprehension. Only through the *spontaneous order* that develops through the market does our system work. Hayek's policy position follows from his attitude toward knowledge and uncertainty, namely, that we do not know the ultimate effects of our actions. Thus, we should accept institutions that have developed spontaneously, particularly the market, which solves our economic problems much more efficiently and effectively than do political processes.

Although many mainstream economists seem willing to grant the Austrians their acceptance of existing institutions and belief in the importance of uncertainty, which makes formal modeling and empirical work difficult, they argue that the Austrians (1) overemphasize the difficulties, (2) have not developed an acceptable alternative, and (3) have allowed value judgments to creep into their heuristic analysis.

EXPERIMENTAL ECONOMISTS

The claim that economics is a science has long been treated skeptically, partly because of its inability to perform controlled experiments to test its theories. Recently, though, one group of economists has begun to undertake what might indeed be called controlled experiments. Using animals or people to act as buyers and sellers of an unnamed commodity, and knowing the underlying supply and demand conditions, they determine whether the theory correctly predicts the results that occur in an experiment. Sometimes called "rat economists" (because they sometimes use rats to test propositions) but more commonly *experimental economists,* they claim to have proved various economic propositions through their experiments.

Let us consider a test they did using a procedure called a "double oral auction market," in which buyers and sellers publicly announce bid and offering prices. Vernon Smith, a leader and developer of much of this work, conducted a laboratory experiment in 1956 to test whether equilibrium would be achieved in a double oral auction market. Students took roles as suppliers and demanders and called out their prices: within fifteen minutes, with a market of fourteen students on each side, the price came very close to the equilibrium price; once it arrived there, it tended to stay there. When demand shifted (when students were given sheets of paper telling them different demand conditions), the price adjusted relatively quickly to the new equilibrium price. This experiment has been replicated by a number of other economists.

Such an approach has several possible uses. By using the experimental method, economists can see how markets react under different institutional conditions. In a recent experiment, researchers tested a posted-price market and compared it to a double oral auction market. In a posted-price market, firms and buyers post a price for a period of time and stick to it. Researchers found that prices tended to be higher in posted-price markets than in double oral auction markets, a finding that led the U.S. Department of Transportation to ask the help of experimental economists in solving a problem concerning the pricing of railroads and barges. The railroads had asked the Department of Transportation to switch from privately negotiated freight rates to publicly posted rates, arguing that public posting would protect both themselves and small barge owners from unannounced price-cutting by large barge owners. When experimenters simulated the two types of markets, however, they found the opposite to be the case: price posting tended to yield higher prices than private negotiation and hurt small barge operators. The railroads dropped their request.

Another test done by experimental economists was of the *Coase theorem,* which states that parties who are capable of harming one another but who can negotiate will bargain to an efficient outcome, regardless of which side has the legal right to inflict damage. The experimental results confirmed this prediction. However, the experiment found that when individuals were endowed with the legal right by means of a coin flip, they almost inevitably did not extract the full individual rational share of the bargaining surplus that is predicted by game theory. Instead, the bargainers almost inevitably shared the surplus equally; this suggests that a fairness ethic, not pure rational individual maximization, governs distribution. This in turn suggests that individuals do not perceive asymmetric property rights as legitimate if they are awarded randomly. However, when property rights were awarded to the individual who won a game of skill before the experiment, the experimenters noted that two thirds of the individuals with the property right obtained most of the joint surplus, whereas under the random assignment treatment none did.

Given the problems of mainstream economists in empirically testing their theories, it is not surprising that they generally welcome this new work, though somewhat skeptically. But most have not considered its wide-ranging implications. To adopt such procedures would require significant changes not only in the training of economists but also in their role in society and their entire approach to economic problems. In view of the upheaval in the profession that such changes would entail, we suspect that experimental economics will gain adherents only in the face of considerable mainstream resistance.

SUMMARY

Heterodox economists have little in common besides an objection to orthodoxy. While manifesting their objections in differing ways, they constitute a dissent from the scope, method, and content of orthodox theory. Radicals, institutionalists, and post-Keynesians reject the orthodox view that harmony prevails in a market economy and that laissez faire is therefore a proper governmental policy. Public choice advocates and neo-Austrians, who tend to be to the political right of mainstream economics, are uneasy with the degree of governmental intervention in markets, which orthodox theory finds acceptable. The dissent of nonmainstream economists, whether to the left or to the right of the mainstream, is often ethical as well as scientific.

Interesting contrasts and comparisons exist among the heterodox groups. First, even though they often disagree among themselves about the shortcomings of mainstream economics, they nearly always concur on the necessity of extending the scope of mainstream analysis. For example, even though public choice theorists and radicals fall on opposite sides of the political spectrum, they agree that politics and economics cannot be separated. Second, even though heterodox economists are often ignored by the mainstream, they nonetheless influence it. As they do, and as their ideas are sometimes incorporated into the mainstream, their role as heterodox economists is reduced. Thus, longevity is not necessarily a positive attribute of heterodox thought. Third, heterodox economists have a tendency to turn inward and separate themselves from the profession—in which case their analysis becomes a separate field of study that either totally replaces mainstream economics or continues its existence independently of the mainstream. Fourth, nearly all heterodox schools are partisan; and for a group to have a significant impact on theory it must appear nonpartisan, associated with neither the left nor the right.

In the 1990s public choice seems close to being absorbed by the mainstream. With the development by more liberal economists of rent-seeking analysis and its use of neoclassical tools, it offers the highest potential for having its views integrated into the profession. Neo-Austrians are less likely to be absorbed. However, they will probably be able to continue their struggle, partly because significant funding is available to them to provide publishing outlets and other means by which they can influence economic thought. Radicals find themselves in a more difficult position; they receive less outside funding and thus have fewer publishing outlets, and some of their best ideas have been incorporated into "widely construed" mainstream theory. Without an outside political force radical- izing the population, they are unlikely to significantly affect mainstream econom- ics. Institutionalists have followed the inner-directed route. They have little contact with the profession and desire little, although some of their insights are working their way into mainstream economics via neoinstitutionalist analysis. The same is true to a great extent of the post-Keynesians, although they are a much more diverse group, some of whom do play a more active role in the mainstream profession.

Experimental economics still constitutes a very small part of economic research, but its potential for changing the direction of mainstream economics is considerable. It offers enormous numbers of workable dissertation topics; and at a time when faith in the empirical content of present economics is at a low point, it provides a method of empirically testing economic propositions. Because of economists' perceived need for a more empirical method, the growth of the new behavioral economics may be an important heterodox phenomenon in the future.

Some commentators have concluded that because particular versions of heterodox theory have failed to replace orthodox theory, heterodox theory has failed. For this reason heterodox theory is often omitted from histories of economic theory. Our view is different. An examination of heterodox thinking reveals that although it has not replaced the accepted stream of economic thought, it often forces orthodox theory into new channels and sometimes offers seminal ideas that are destined to become part of the accepted theoretical structure. These contributions to the direction and content of the flow of ideas cannot be ignored. They may well be the ideas historians of the twenty-first century look back on as forerunners of mainstream thought.

Key Terms

Marxian economics

radical economics

dual labor market

institutionalists

quasi-institutionalists

neoinstitutionalists

countervailing power

conventional wisdom

dependence effect

equilibrium institutional structure

post-Keynesians

neo-Ricardians

irreversible time

true uncertainty

public choice school

Austrian economics

government failures

market failures

spontaneous order

experimental economics

Coase theorem

Questions for Review, Discussion, and Research

1. Given the economic failure of socialism, all radical economists should become neoclassical economists. Discuss this statement.
2. Do you accept Bowles and Gintis's argument that school is primarily a means of providing individuals with a union card to higher-paying jobs? How would you test this theory?
3. Explain and critically evaluate Gunnar Myrdal's argument concerning the impossibility of developing economic theory that is free of value judgments.
4. What is Galbraith's theory of countervailing power, and how does it modify mainstream conclusions?
5. "It is a far better thing to have a firm anchor in nonsense than to put out on a troubled sea of thought." Discuss this statement in relationship to nonmainstream methodology.
6. How would a traditional institutionalist be likely to respond to a neoinstitutionalist?

7. Post-Keynesians differentiate between risk and uncertainty. What is the distinction, and what relevance does it have for economic theory?
8. How does government work, according to the public choice theorists? What are the implications of this for making and executing economic policy?
9. Explain the Austrian criticism of mainstream economics concerning the assumption of perfect knowledge and evaluate the significance of this critique.
10. How far can experimental economics go in testing economic theories?
11. That absent-minded professor is back with another job for you. This time, she's doing an article on economic planning, and she remembers that somewhere Galbraith had an entire chapter devoted to the future of economic planning. Your assignment is to find it.

Suggested Readings

Ayres, Clarence E. *The Theory of Economic Progress*. Chapel Hill: University of North Carolina Press, 1944.

Baran, Paul A., and Paul M. Sweezy. *Monopoly Capital*. New York: Monthly Review Press, 1966.

Blaug, Mark. "A Methodological Appraisal of Radical Economics." In *Methodological Controversies in Economics: Historical Essays in Honor of T. W. Hutchison*. Ed. A. W. Coats. Greenwich, Conn.: JAI Press, 1983.

Bowles, Samuel, and Herbert Gintis. *Schooling in Capitalist America: Educational Reform and Contradictions of Economic Life*. New York: Basic Books, 1976.

Buchanan, James M., and Gordon Tullock. *The Calculus of Consent*. Ann Arbor: University of Michigan Press, 1962.

Coase, Ronald. "The Nature of the Firm." *Economica,* New Series 4 [1937], pp. 386–405.

Dobb, Maurice H. *Political Economy and Capitalism*. London: Routledge & Kegan Paul, 1937.

Eichner, Alfred S. *Toward a New Economics: Essays in Post-Keynesian and Institutionalist Theory*. Armonk, N.Y.: M. E. Sharpe, 1985.

Galbraith, John Kenneth. *American Capitalism*. Boston: Houghton Mifflin, 1952.

————. *The New Industrial State*. Boston: Houghton Mifflin, 1967.

Hayek, Friedrich A. *Individualism and Economic Order*. Chicago: University of Chicago Press, 1948.

Kalecki, Michal. *Studies in the Theory of Business Cycles: 1933–1939*. London: Basil Blackwell, 1966.

Klamer, Arjo. *Conversations with Economists*. Totowa, N.J.: Rowman and Allanheld, 1984.

Lindbeck, Assar. *The Political Economy of the New Left*. Foreword by Paul Samuelson. New York: Harper and Row, 1971.

Mises, Ludwig E. von. *Human Action*. 3rd ed. New York: Henry Regnery, 1966.

Myrdal, Gunnar. *Against the Stream*. New York: Pantheon, 1973.

————. *The Political Element in the Development of Economic Theory.* Cambridge: Harvard University Press, 1955.

Robinson, Joan. *Economic Philosophy.* London: C. A. Watts, 1962.

————. *An Essay on Marxian Economics.* 2nd ed. London: Macmillan, 1966.

Schumpeter, J. A. *Capitalism, Socialism, and Democracy.* 3rd ed. New York: Harper, 1950.

Sraffa, Piero. *Production of Commodities by Means of Commodities.* Cambridge: Cambridge University Press, 1960.

Sweezy, Paul M. *The Theory of Capitalist Development.* New York: Oxford University Press, 1942.

Weintraub, Sidney, ed. *Modern Economic Thought.* Oxford: Basil Blackwell, 1977.

Wolff, Richard, and Stephen Resnick. *Economics: Marxian versus Neoclassical.* Baltimore, Md.: Johns Hopkins University Press, 1987.

Recent Economic Thought: Understanding the Present Through the Past

Clockwise from top left: Irving Fisher, John Maynard Keynes, Paul Samuelson, Milton Friedman

Courses in the history of economic thought often end their coverage of the subject with the 1930s, partly because their authors think that not enough time has elapsed to allow for the development of an adequate historical perspective on later economic literature. We sympathize with the view that we are still too immersed in current thought to stand back and view it. If other economics courses provided students with a broad perspective on recent developments in the field, this book too would end with the previous chapter. But more often than not, other courses do not address the historical context of recent developments: modern theory typically is presented in a historical vacuum. Thus, we believe it necessary to provide at least a minimal account of recent developments in economic thought in the context of forces that have shaped them and their relationship to earlier theory.

In doing so, we have tried to avoid duplicating what will be taught in other courses; instead, we have attempted to complement them by providing the needed historical perspective. We recognize, too, that many courses (especially in schools on the quarter system) won't make it through all the material, so we present it at a level that allows students to follow it independently. Students who do so, we believe, will find the chapters intellectually stimulating as well as relevant enrichments of other courses. We emphasize, however, that these chapters reflect a point of view more critical of much research in modern economics than is typical of economists at large. As we stated in the first chapter, we believe that incorporating personal points of view enlivens the presentation and stimulates critical thinking.

THE AUTHORS' POINT OF VIEW

Our underlying point of view is expressed as "Let a thousand flowers bloom." But we realize that there are roses and dandelions, and we prefer roses. We contend that the modern economics profession, especially in the United States, has become mired in technique for the sake of technique and has lost sight of one of the purposes of economics, which is to relate economic theory to the normative goals of society—what J. N. Keynes characterized as "the art of economics." By using the same methodology for both the development of abstract theory and the application of that theory, the profession has constrained both. The story we will tell of modern economics is one of primarily abstract theoretical developments—of economists developing more and more nebulous abstract models and generalizing and mathematicizing (or formalizing) the insights of earlier economists until they have come to constitute an enigma to all but the most skilled mathematicians. They are dandelions gone to seed and blowing in the wind.

Still, it is beginning to look as if generalizations have served a useful purpose: they have demonstrated the enormously strong assumptions needed for a model of the economy to arrive at unique aggregate equilibrium. Interdependent expectations can cause expectational bubbles and sunspot equilibria: a small change can lead to a major shift from one relative price equilibrium to another, and there is no good reason, therefore, to assume uniqueness of aggregate equilibrium.

Dealing with these complicated analytic problems has led to chaos (and chaos theory) in modern macro theory. In the 1990s there is no one accepted paradigm; macroeconomists differ radically in both theory and policy prescriptions.

Microeconomics, which appears to be in a much more settled state of affairs, has maintained an ostensible order chiefly by declining to address some complex issues that are central to its logical coherence. For example, no resolution to the product exhaustion or summing up problem has been advanced. Few economists have attempted to address the implications of the complexities of multiple aggregate equilibria for individual markets. If individual choices can cause shifts from one aggregate equilibrium to another, individuals may well take such effects into account; hence they must be included in the model. Similarly, any realistic theory of macroeconomics must incorporate the concept of money and allow for the fact that money can impose institutional constraints on individual decisions. The relevant microeconomics of a monetary economy can be quite different from the relevant microeconomics of a nonmonetary economy.

Problems also plague modern econometric practices. Empirical testing is often done perfunctorily, and what is done is often inappropriate. For example, as Edward Leamer points out, no economist believes the strong purchasing power parity proposition, but almost inevitably that is what is empirically tested.

Clearly, *some* economists *are* dealing with these issues. We are happy to say that more and more are. But what we do believe is that it has taken too long for these issues to be raised and addressed, and one of the reasons for that is a lack of knowledge of the history of economic thought. When difficult questions have been addressed, they have been dealt with not as problems needing to be solved but as technical puzzles, their broad, genuine, economic implications being ignored.

Technical puzzles lead to technical solutions, even though the assumptions embodied in these technical solutions might not fit the reality. A quiet conspiracy developed in the profession not to raise these issues; and any subject that raised them, like the history of economic thought, had to be purged from the curriculum as subversive. Don't ask big questions; ask only little ones. The purging occurred initially in graduate schools but soon filtered down into undergraduate programs—as might be expected, because people usually teach what they have been taught. This is but one aspect of the increasing spread of the technique orientation from the graduate school to undergraduate education. This tendency of the profession to deal with the trees rather than the forest is rooted in the incentive structure of the academic profession. "Publish or perish" may be good for journal publishers, but it takes its toll on relevance.

RECENT ECONOMIC THOUGHT

Chapters 15 through 17 survey recent developments in microeconomics, macroeconomics, and econometrics and relate them to earlier work. Rather than repeating accounts of techniques covered in other courses, these chapters concentrate on adding perspective, on helping the student see the forest rather than the trees. Chapter 15 recounts recent developments in microeconomics and focuses on the increased formalization of microeconomics as modern economists have moved farther and farther away from Marshallian partial equilibrium theoretical analysis and contextual policy application toward a Walrasian general equilibrium theoretical mode and a noncontextual policy framework.

Chapter 16 traces the development of modern macroeconomics starting with the Keynesian "revolution" of the 1930s. Just as much of the profession from Ricardo to Keynes ignored macroeconomics, microeconomics played a secondary role during the 1940s and 1950s. But beginning in the 1960s, puzzling theoretical issues in macroeconomics led to a growing interest in how to relate microeconomics and macroeconomics. Modern macroeconomics is shown to be characterized chiefly by conflicts, because Keynesians, classicals, neoclassicals, neo-Keynesians, new classicals, and new Keynesians all present different models.

Although William Petty initiated political arithmetic in the late 1600s, sophisticated use of statistical analysis in economics is a twentieth-century phenomenon. In Chapter 17 we survey the movement in economics from com-

Nobel Prize Winners in Economics

1969	Ragnar Frisch and Jan Tinbergen	1980	Lawrence Klein
1970	Paul Samuelson	1981	James Tobin
1971	Simon Kuznets	1982	George Stigler
1972	John R. Hicks and Kenneth Arrow	1983	Gerard Debreu
1973	Wassily Leontief	1984	J. Richard Stone
1974	Gunnar Myrdal and F. A. Hayek	1985	Franco Modigliani
1975	Leonid Kantorovich and Tjalling Koopmans	1986	James Buchanan
1976	Milton Friedman	1987	Robert Solow
1977	Bertil Ohlin and James Meade	1988	Maurice Allais
1978	Herbert A. Simon	1989	Trygve Haavelmo
1980	Theodore W. Schultz and W. Arthur Lewis	1990	H. M. Markowitz, Marcus Hay Miller, and W. F. Sharpe
		1991	Ronald H. Coase
		1992	Gary Becker

monsense empiricism, to statistical analysis, to modern econometrics. This is an interesting history that is only now beginning to receive the attention it deserves. Many statistical techniques have been borrowed by economists from fields of study in which controlled experiments are the usual method of establishing knowledge. Unfortunately, because controlled experiments are very difficult to perform in economics, major problems have arisen in econometrics. These problems are put into perspective in the final chapter.

15 The Development of Modern Microeconomic Theory

"To a person of analytic ability, perceptive enough to realize that mathematical equipment was a powerful sword in economics, the world of economics was his or her oyster in 1935."

—Paul Samuelson

IMPORTANT WRITERS

F. Y. EDGEWORTH	*Mathematical Psychics* 1881
SIMON NEWCOMB	*Principles of Political Economy* 1886
ALFRED MARSHALL	*Principles of Economics* 1890
IRVING FISHER	*Mathematical Investigations in the Theory of Value and Prices* 1892
GUSTAV CASSEL	*Theory of Social Economy* 1918
FRANK KNIGHT	*Risk, Uncertainty, and Profit* 1921
PIERO SRAFFA	"Laws of Return under Competitive Conditions" 1926
JACOB VINER	"Cost Curves and Supply Curves" 1931
E. H. CHAMBERLIN	*Theory of Monopolistic Competition* 1933
JOAN ROBINSON	*Economics of Imperfect Competition* 1933
JOHN R. HICKS	*Value and Capital* 1939
JOHN VON NEUMANN AND OSKAR MORGENSTERN	*Theory of Games and Economic Behavior* 1944
PAUL A. SAMUELSON	*Foundations of Economic Analysis* 1947
KENNETH ARROW	*Social Choice and Individual Values* 1951
MILTON FRIEDMAN	*Essays in Positive Economics* 1953
HERBERT SIMON	*Models of Man* 1957
GERARD DEBREU	*Theory of Value, an Axiomatic Analysis of Economic Equilibrium* 1959

RONALD COASE   "The Problem of Social Cost" 1960
GEORGE STIGLER   "Information in the Labor Market" 1962
GARY BECKER   *Human Capital* 1964

When British and American students, graduate and undergraduate, studied economics in the early 1900s, they studied a form of Marshallian economics that blended equilibrium analysis, historical and institutional facts, and common sense. Although much of the historical and institutional material, as well as some of the common sense, has disappeared, the undergraduate microeconomics taught today (at least that which is found in the most popular introductory and intermediate texts) is still strongly rooted in Marshallian economics.[1] Graduate microeconomics, however, is now almost totally devoid of Marshallian analysis. Depending heavily on mathematical modeling and Walrasian general equilibrium economics, it focuses on topics such as dynamic optimization, game theory, set theoretic choice theory, and principal-agent problems. The story of how and why we moved from an emphasis on Marshallian economics at both the graduate and undergraduate levels to this bifurcated state is an important part of the story of the development of modern microeconomics. The first episode of this story recounts the development of micro theory from the Marshallian economics at the turn of the century to the 1950s, when the core of modern graduate school theory began to emerge.

THE MOVEMENT AWAY FROM MARSHALLIAN ECONOMICS

Marshall's engine of analysis, combining supply and demand curves with common sense, could answer certain questions, but others exceeded its scope. Supply-and-demand analysis was partial equilibrium analysis applied to problems of relative prices. But many of the questions economists were trying to answer, such as what determines the distribution of income or what effect certain laws and taxes would have, either introduced problems beyond the applicability of partial equilibrium analysis or violated its assumptions. Nonetheless, economists continued to apply partial equilibrium arguments to such issues, assuming that the aggregate market must constitute some as-yet unknown combination of all the partial equilibrium markets.

Most economists were content with this state of affairs for quite a while. After all, Marshallian economics did provide a workable, if not formally tight, theory that was able to answer many real-world questions. It was the middle ground. Marshallian economists were engineers rather than scientists, and engineers are interested not in pondering underlying forces but in building something that works.

---

[1] In some higher-level intermediate books, Marshallian economics is disappearing and is being relaced by Walrasian general equilibrium economics.

Marshallian economists were interested in the art of economics, not positive or normative economics. As Joan Robinson put it, Marshall had the ability to recognize hard problems and hide them in plain sight.

Marshallian economics attempted to walk a fine line between a formalist approach and a historically institutional approach. It is not surprising that in doing so it created critics on both sides. In the United States, a group called the institutionalists wanted simply to eliminate the theory, arguing that history and institutions should be emphasized and the inadequate theory dropped. Other critics, whom we will call formalists, went in the opposite direction: they believed economics should be a science, not an engineering field. These formalists agreed with the institutionalists that Marshallian economic theory was inadequate, but their answer was not to eliminate the theory; they wanted to provide a better, more rigorous general equilibrium foundation that could adequately answer more complicated questions.

THE FORMALIST REVOLUTION IN MICROECONOMICS

The Marshallians remained the predominant group in the United States until the 1930s, but in the mid-1930s the formalists began a program of theoretical research that would eventually reformulate microeconomics into its present highly mathematical structure. This program, which we will call the *formalist revolution,* remained within the general sphere of neoclassical economics but significantly altered its methods. Consequently, modern economics is essentially neoclassical economics altered by mathematical economists in four ways.

1. The formalists provided greater range and precision to the existing theory. As economists moved away from Marshall and toward a more formal analysis, they also adopted a more formal language of exposition—mathematics. Marshall's immediate followers used geometry to extend and formalize his analysis. During the late 1930s and the 1940s Marshallian geometry was gradually replaced by multivariate calculus, which could be used to model multidimensional problems instead of the two or three dimensions graphical techniques allowed. Later, new techniques were added, such as optimal control theory (the calculus of functions rather than of variables), game theory, and set theory.
2. The new methods expanded the existing theory to include a wider range of phenomena. For example, modern graduate microeconomics analyzes choice under uncertainty, whereas in Marshall's day economics had no such formal analysis.
3. Economics moved from contextual to noncontextual argumentation, rendering it less representative of the real world and more abstract.
4. Although the new methodology was generally more abstract, some very practical mathematical techniques developed, such as linear programming, which are now commonly used by businesses to study the efficient use of resources.

Historical Roots of Modern Microeconomics

The formalist revolution that engendered modern graduate microeconomics is rooted in the thought of several nineteenth- and early twentieth-century figures discussed in our earlier chapters on neoclassical economics. The first of these great pioneers in stating hypotheses in mathematical form was A. Cournot, who published his *Researches into Mathematical Principles* in 1838. Cournot expected that his attempts to bring mathematics into economics would be rejected by most economists, but he adhered to his method nonetheless because he found the literary expression of theory that could be expressed with greater precision by mathematics to be wasteful and irritating.

Léon Walras and Vilfredo Pareto, who succeeded Walras as professor of economics at Lausanne, were other early devotees of mathematical economics. Whereas Marshall had focused on partial equilibrium, Walras, using algebraic techniques, focused on general equilibrium. His general equilibrium theory has substantially displaced Marshallian partial equilibrium theory as the basic framework for economic research. Jevons, in his influential *Theory of Political Economy* (1871), also advocated a more extensive use of mathematics in economics.

Jevons was followed by another pioneer in formalist economics, F. Y. Edgeworth (1845–1926), who pointed out in 1881 that the basic structure of micro theory was simply the repeated application of the principle of maximization. This finding raised the question, Why re-examine the same principles over and over again? By abstracting from the specific institutional context and reducing a problem to its mathematical core, one could quickly capture the essence of the problem and apply that essence to all such microeconomic questions. Following this reasoning, Edgeworth declared that both an understanding of the economy and a basis for the formulation of proper policies were to be found in the consistent use of mathematics. He accused the Marshallian economists of being seduced by the "zigzag windings of the flowery path of literature."[2]

As this extension was occurring, there was a simultaneous attempted extension of mathematics not only into positive economics but also into questions of economic policy. Vilfredo Pareto, whose name is familiar to many students of economics from its use in the phrase *Pareto optimal criteria,* extended Walras's general equilibrium analysis in the early 1900s to questions of economic policy. Thus, in the push for formalization little distinction was made between positive economics and the art of economics, John Neville Keynes's distinction between the two was lost, and the same formal methodology was used for both.

Irving Fisher (1867–1947), writing in the last decade of the nineteenth century, was an early American pioneer of formalism who supported and extended Simon Newcomb's (1835–1909) advocacy of increased use of mathematics in econom-

---

[2] F. Y. Edgeworth, *Paper Relating to Political Economy* (New York: Burt Franklin, 1925), II, p. 282. See Bruce Larson, "Edgeworth, Samuelson and Operationally Meaningful Theorems," *History of Political Economy,* 19, No. 3 (1987), pp. 351–357, who argues that Edgeworth is a precursor of Samuelson.

ics. The formalist position was not well received in the United States, however, until nearly the middle of the twentieth century. All these pioneers were, therefore, unheeded prophets of the future. Inattention to their efforts can be attributed partly to the strength of Marshall's analysis, a judicious blend of theory, history, and institutional knowledge. Unable to compete with the Marshallian approach, early mathematical work in economics was practically ignored by mainstream economists until the 1930s.

In the early 1930s this situation began to change. Expositions of the many geometric tools that now provide the basis for undergraduate microeconomics began to fill the journals. The marginal revenues curve, the short-run marginal cost curve, and models of imperfect competition and income-substitution effects were "discovered" and explored during this period. Though rooted in Marshall, these new tools *formalized* his analysis, and as they did so they moved farther and farther from the actual institutions they represented. The Marshallian approach to interrelating theory and institutions had been like a teeter-totter: it had worked as long as the two sides balanced. But once the theory side gained a bit, the balance was broken and economics fell hard to the theoretical side, leaving history and institutions suspended in air.

History and institutions were abandoned because the new formalized tools required stating precisely what was being assumed and what was changing, and stating it in such a way that the techniques could handle the entire analysis. History and particular institutions no longer fit in. One could no longer argue, as in the earlier Marshallian economics, that "a reasonable businessman" would act in a certain way, appealing to the reader's sensibility to know what "reasonable" meant. Instead, "reasonableness" was transformed into a precise concept—"rational"— that was defined as making choices in conformance with certain established axioms. Similarly, the competitive economy was defined as one in which all individuals are "price takers." Formalism required noncontextual argumentation, abstracted from any actual setting, in which assumptions are spelled out.

Though the use of geometry as a tool in Marshallian analysis was a relatively small step, it was the beginning of the end for Marshallian economics. When geometry disclosed numerous logical problems with Marshallian economics, the new Marshallians responded with further formalization. Thus, by 1935 economics was ripe for change. Paul Samuelson summed up the situation: "To a person of analytic ability, perceptive enough to realize that mathematical equipment was a powerful sword in economics, the world of economics was his or her oyster in 1935. The terrain was strewn with beautiful theorems waiting to be picked up and arranged in unified order."[3]

Because many economists had by this time acquired the requisite analytic equipment, the late 1930s and early 1940s witnessed a revolution in microeconomic theory, which formalism won. Cournot, Walras, Pareto, and Edgeworth

[3] Paul A. Samuelson, "The General Theory: 1946," in *Keynes' General Theory: Reports of Three Decades,* ed. Robert Lekachman (New York: St. Martin's Press, 1964), p. 315.

unseated Marshall to become the forefathers of modern graduate microeconomics, relegating Marshallian economics to a role in undergraduate education.

The first step in the formalization of micro theory was to extend the marginal analysis of the household, firm, and markets and to make it more internally consistent. As economists shifted to higher-level mathematical techniques, they were able to go beyond partial equilibrium to general equilibrium, because the mathematics provided a method by which to keep track more precisely of items they had formerly kept somewhat loosely in the back of their heads. The second step was to reformulate the questions in a manner consistent with the tools and techniques available for dealing with them. The third step was to add new techniques to clarify unanswered questions. This process is continuing today.

These steps did not follow a single path. One path had strong European roots; it included generalizing and formalizing general equilibrium theory. An early pioneer on this path was Gustav Cassel (1866–1945), who simplified the presentation of Walras's general equilibrium theory in his *Theory of Social Economy* (1918; English versions 1924, 1932), making it more accessible.

In the 1930s two mathematicians, Abraham Wald (1902–1950) and John von Neumann (1903–1957), turned their attention to the study of equilibrium conditions in both static and dynamic models. They quickly raised the technical sophistication of economic analysis, exposing the inadequacy of much of previous economists' policy and theoretical analysis. Their work was noted by economists such as Kenneth Arrow (1921–   ) and Gerard Debreu (1921–   ), who extended it and applied it to Walras's theory to produce a more precise formulation of his general equilibrium theory. Following Wald's lead, Arrow and Debreu then rediscovered the earlier writings of Edgeworth. So impressed were they by these writers that they declared Edgeworth, not Marshall, to be the rightful forefathers of modern microeconomics. The work of these theorists, in turn, has continued a highly formalistic tradition of general equilibrium theorists.

Some of the questions that general equilibrium analysis has addressed are Adam Smith's questions. Will the unfettered use of markets lead to the common good, and if so, in what sense? Will the invisible hand of the market promote the social good? What types of markets are necessary for that to be the case? Because they involve the entire system, these are essentially general equilibrium questions, not questions of partial equilibrium. They could not, therefore, be answered within the Marshallian framework, although they could be discussed in relatively loose terms, as indeed they were before formal general equilibrium analysis developed.

General equilibrium theorists have found the answer to the question "Does the invisible hand work?" to be yes, as long as certain conditions hold true. Their proof, for which Arrow and Debreu received Nobel prizes, was a milestone in economics because it answered the conjecture Adam Smith had made to begin the classical tradition in economics. Much subsequent work has been done in general equilibrium theory to articulate the invisible-hand theorem more elegantly and to modify its assumptions, but by first proving it Arrow and Debreu earned a place in the history of economic thought.

Paul Samuelson

Another path was somewhat less formal, but was still highly formal relative to Marshallian economics. This work had a major influence on the economics presented in economic texts.

Of the many economists involved in this formalization, Paul Samuelson is probably the best known. Born in 1915, Samuelson began graduate economics studies at Harvard in 1935 after acquiring a strong undergraduate background in mathematics. There he proceeded to publish significant articles applying mathematics to both micro- and macroeconomic theory. He received his Ph.D. in 1941 at the age of twenty-six, and by the time he was thirty-two had become a full professor at the Massachusetts Institute of Technology and the first recipient of the American Economic Association's John Bates Clark Award, which is given to economists under forty years of age who have made significant professional contributions. Samuelson later became the first American to receive the Nobel Prize in economics.

The sources of Samuelson's intellectual inspiration were Cournot, Jevons, Walras, Pareto, Edgeworth, and Fisher, all of whom contributed piecemeal applications of mathematics to economic theory. Using his mathematical background, Samuelson extended their work and laid down the mathematical foundations of orthodox economic theory. Like Edgeworth, he had harsh words for Alfred Marshall, whose ambiguities, he said, "paralyzed the best brains in the Anglo-Saxon branch of our profession for three decades."[4] He went on to say:

> I have come to feel that Marshall's dictum that "it seems doubtful whether any one spends his time well in reading lengthy translations of economic doctrines into mathematics, that have not been done by himself" should be exactly reversed. The laborious literary working over of essentially simple mathematical concepts such as is characteristic of much of modern economic theory is not only unrewarding from the standpoint of advancing science, but involves as well mental gymnastics of a peculiarly depraved type.[5]

Samuelson's works provide an interesting perspective on the methodological changes in economics since the time of Marshall.

The direction Samuelson's contribution to economic theory would take is evident in his Ph.D. dissertation, completed in 1941 and published in 1947 as *Foundations of Economic Analysis*. A subtitle, "The Operational Significance of Economic Theory," was eliminated in the published edition, and the statement "Mathematics Is a Language" was added to its title page. The book undertakes to analyze mathematically the foundations of modern micro and macro theory. In the introductory chapter, Samuelson explains that his purpose is to work out the

---

[4] Paul A. Samuelson, "The Monopolistic Competition Revolution," in *Competition Theory,* ed. R. E. Kuenne (New York: John Wiley, 1967), p. 109.
[5] Paul A. Samuelson, *Foundations of Economic Analysis* (Cambridge, Mass.: Harvard University Press, 1955), p. 6.

implications for economic theory of the following statement: "The existence of analogies between central features of various theories implies the existence of a general theory which underlies the particular theories and unifies them with respect to those essential features."[6]

Equilibrium and Stability

According to Samuelson, the theoretical structure that underlies and unifies the individual elements of micro and macro theory rests on two very general hypotheses concerning the conditions, first, of equilibrium and second, of its stability. For problems of comparative statics, the conditions of equilibrium can be placed in the familiar maximization framework in which much of the previous work in micro theory had been done. Samuelson illustrates the unity of this approach by working through the firm's minimization of costs and maximization of profits, the consumer's maximization of satisfaction, and welfare theory. Whereas previous economists had paid less attention to dynamic analysis, Samuelson demonstrates that once the dynamic properties of a system are specified, its stability can be assessed. Equilibrium and stability conditions thus emerge as the two-part structure underlying economic theory.[7]

Although Samuelson's *Foundations* and his subsequent work have dealt almost exclusively with mathematical economic theory, he is sensitive to the relationship between mathematical economics and the process of economic research. He consistently attempts to formulate operationally meaningful, not merely elegant, theorems—in other words, to provide testable hypotheses useful in economic research. "By a *meaningful theorem*," he says, "I mean simply a hypothesis about empirical data which could conceivably be refuted, if only under ideal conditions."[8]

Formalists, Mathematics, and Pedagogy

Mathematical economics has made it possible to state economic theory concisely and precisely and, by mathematical manipulations, to deduce the theoretical implications of a given set of assumptions. The formalists mathematically exposed inconsistencies and corrected logical errors in the literary reasoning that had been used to extend partial equilibrium analysis. Moreover, they showed that various aspects of the Marshallian model, such as demand theory and production theory, were simply specific applications of a generalized constrained maximization model. As they did, their mathematical techniques undermined the reason for using partial equilibrium analysis. Recognizing this, Samuelson went back to

---

[6] *Ibid.,* p. 3. (Complete sentence is italicized in the original.)

[7] In his Nobel lecture, Samuelson demonstrated more skepticism about relating dynamics and stability.

[8] Samuelson, *Foundations,* p. 4.

Walras to observe how he approached interconnected markets. Starting from Walras's analysis and applying algebra and calculus, Samuelson was able to determine the stability conditions necessary for equilibrium. This provided economic reasoning with a much more solid theoretical ground and an analytical core of multimarket equilibrium that would serve as the foundation of modern microeconomics.

But the introduction of formalism presented a pedagogical problem: the Walrasian general equilibrium approach is very difficult. In order to master it, one must learn a new language (mathematics) and be able to grasp highly abstract, noncontextual argumentation. But most economics undergraduates have no intention of becoming economists and hence have little incentive to acquire the considerable mathematical skill necessary to comprehend the complexities of general equilibrium interactions. This pedagogical problem has occasioned the current bifurcation of microeconomics, because the preferred graduate economics theory is too difficult for the typical undergraduate. Paul Samuelson responded to the special needs of undergraduate education by writing an elementary economics textbook, which has sold several million copies and gone through many editions. Samuelson's text dominated the field for some thirty years from its first edition in 1947, and most other introductory texts have copied his format. This elementary text shaped modern undergraduate economics, just as his *Foundations* did graduate economics.

In his undergraduate text Samuelson graphically presented microeconomics as a logical extension of the interactions of rational individuals within a competitive market structure. Retaining the Marshallian tools but eliminating most of the platitudes and homey analogies of earlier economics texts, Samuelson constructed a largely noncontextual theory that is more consistent with general equilibrium analysis. Thus arose the current divided worlds of graduate and undergraduate economics. Undergraduate introductory texts kept the Marshallian approach, emphasizing two-dimensional graphical techniques rather than multivariate calculus, and graduate microeconomics moved on to the formalist approach that is far more consistent with Walras and Cournot than with Marshall. With the ever-increasing sophistication of the techniques used in graduate micro theory, the split has widened.

Some carryover from graduate education has occurred, because once graduate students become teachers, they naturally tend to teach what they have been taught. Upper-level textbooks in subjects such as public finance and intermediate microeconomics are beginning to reflect the change and are becoming less Marshallian. But because introductory texts have not changed, the dichotomy between undergraduate and graduate microeconomics continues to be significant in the most widely used undergraduate texts.[9]

---

[9] In 1993 Joseph Stiglitz published an introductory text that followed a format more closely related to work done in graduate schools. It remains to be seen whether this book will gain wide acceptance.

THE MONOPOLISTIC COMPETITION REVOLUTION

In the 1930s, few would have predicted the future formalist direction of micro-economics. Instead, most thought that Marshallian economics would be fused with the real world in variations of one of two models—Joan Robinson's imperfect competition or Edward Chamberlin's monopolistic competition. Let's begin our discussion of this topic with some background as to why the monopolistic and imperfect competition models were important developments.

Marshall's Vague Use of the Term *Competition*

For classical economists up to and including Marshall, *competition* was a vague term. Marshall assumed perfect competition in his formal models, but in accompanying discussions he often relaxed his model to deal informally with markets in between monopoly and competition. Classical economists no doubt felt they knew what they meant by competition and did not need to define it. Their vague use of the term allowed competition to serve as the answer to all economic problems. In laissez faire economic philosophy, the consensus was that competition would solve any problem that arose. Once the formalists began to scrutinize laissez faire thought, however, they demanded a precise definition of this pivotal concept and reproached Marshall for continuing to use the term without providing one.

Some economists argued, too, that Marshall's analysis did not correspond with empirical observation. In *Risk, Uncertainty, and Profit* (1921), for example, Frank Knight (1885–1972) argued convincingly that the theoretical model of competitive markets failed to correspond to the markets actually found in the economy. The major empirical problem was that for Marshallian competition to work, there had to be many small firms; but during this period large firms were becoming increasingly powerful, which lessened the impact of competition on the market. John Clapham similarly pointed out in 1922 that many of the concepts concerned with cost conditions in industries, such as increasing, constant, and decreasing costs, were empty economic boxes.

In 1926 Piero Sraffa (1898–1983) challenged Marshall, contending that there was an internal inconsistency in the Marshallian analysis of decreasing-cost situations: decreasing costs "are clearly incompatible with the conditions of particular equilibrium of a commodity."[10] If decreasing costs are incompatible with perfectly competitive markets, Sraffa declared, then downward-sloping cost curves implied that the deterrent to selling larger quantities of output

---

[10] Piero Sraffa, "The Laws of Returns under Competitive Conditions," *Economic Journal* (1926). The quotation is taken from a reprint in American Economic Association, *Readings in Price Theory* (Chicago: R. D. Irwin, 1952), p. 185.

was not on the side of supply and cost but of demand.[11] If costs were continually declining, competition could not continue to exist, at least as Marshall had described it; monopoly, not competition, would be the dominant market structure. Marshall and some subsequent theorists had devoted some attention to monopoly, but their analysis generally continued to assume perfectly competitive markets. Because of the persistent divergence between empirical observation and theory, greater interest was aroused in the structure of markets at intermediate stages between monopoly and perfect competition.

These criticisms occasioned a number of works that had significant implications for modern theory, including Jacob Viner's (1892–1970) integration of firms' long-run and short-run cost curves, Joan Robinson's (1903–1983) theory of imperfect competition, and E. H. Chamberlin's (1899–1967) theory of *monopolistic competition*. Viner reconciled observation with theory by formally separating the long run from the short run. In his model, which has since become the mainstream model, capital is assumed to be fixed in the short run and diminishing marginal returns cause the short-run marginal cost curve to be upward-sloping regardless of whether there are increasing, decreasing, or constant returns to scale. Mathematically this solved the problem of reconciling theory with empirical observation—as long as one analyzed only the short run and did not try to integrate it with the long run. That is what economists did with general equilibrium theory; and the basic long run–short run distinction that underlies the definition of capital stems from Viner's work.

One of Joan Robinson's major contributions (which she later disavowed) was the rediscovery of the marginal revenue curve. Cournot had used this tool in 1838, but because Marshall had passed it by, it was rediscovered by Robinson and others. Her model of "imperfect competition," in which a firm equates marginal revenues and marginal cost, is now standard economics. Chamberlin's work, though similar to Robinson's, was more far-reaching. It attempted a thorough reconstruction of the theory of value. Chamberlin writes, "Monopolistic competition . . . is a challenge to the traditional viewpoint of economics that competition and monopoly are alternatives and that individual prices are to be explained in terms of either the one or the other."[12] The subtitle of his book, "A Re-orientation of the Theory of Value," reflects Chamberlin's belief that this new theory "contains, not a technique, but a way of looking at the economic system; and changing one's

---

[11] Joan Robinson wrote at the beginning of her book, "Mr. Sraffa's article must be regarded as the fount from which my work flows, for the chief aim of this book is to attempt to carry out his pregnant suggestion that the whole theory of value should be created in terms of monopoly analysis." Joan Robinson, *The Economics of Imperfect Competition* (London: Macmillan, 1933), p. v.

[12] E. H. Chamberlain, *The Theory of Monopolistic Competition,* 6th ed. (Cambridge, Mass.: Harvard University Press, 1950), p. 204. The ideas were first presented in 1927 in a doctoral thesis, and the first edition of *Monopolistic Competition* was published in 1933.

economic *Weltanschauung* is sometimes very different from looking into the economics of the individual firm or adding new tools to one's kit."[13]

Chamberlin conceived of markets as a spectrum with monopoly and perfect competition at the extremes, but with most real markets lying somewhere in between. Where the Marshallian analysis concluded that in the absence of unusual situations that might create monopoly, the outcome of free-enterprise laissez faire would be competitive markets, Chamberlin held that the outcome would be monopolistically competitive markets. A close examination of any "new" or "revolutionary" idea often reveals that it has fairly deep roots in the past. We saw in Chapter 11 that Marshall, with his great desire to make his economics realistic, had discussed in footnotes and asides some of the market characteristics that Chamberlin labeled monopolistic competition. There was also a long list of literature on markets with two sellers, or duopoly. But Marshall's writings on monopolistically competitive markets and the literature on duopoly both were subsidiary to other theories, and no one had ever developed a formal theoretical way to handle these markets. Not only did Chamberlin develop a formal theoretical structure for these markets, but he made them the basis of his main theory, with monopoly and competition being the side issues.

The Revolution That Wasn't

Chamberlin drew broad implications from his ideas. He noted that for a long time economic theory had loosely identified free enterprise with competition, but when he examined the actual outcome typical of a free enterprise system, he found not pure competition but monopolistic competition. An essential characteristic of free enterprise seemed to be "the attempt by every businessman to build up his own monopoly, extending it wherever possible and defending it against the attempts of others to extend theirs."[14] If Chamberlin is correct, we can no longer follow the Smithian-Marshallian tradition of equating perfectly competitive markets with the ideal for purposes of welfare economics. Chamberlin maintained that in many cases it would be impossible to establish perfectly competitive markets; he even questioned the desirability of such markets. The overstandardization of products that might result from them, for example, would not necessarily be desirable: "Differences in taste, desires, incomes, and locations of buyers, and in the uses buyers wish to make of commodities all indicate the need for variety." Such problems, he felt, dictate "substituting for the concept of a 'competitive ideal' an ideal including both monopoly and competition. How much and what kinds of monopoly, and with what measure of social control, became the questions."[15]

There was so much common sense and insight in the monopolistic competition model that many economists in the late 1930s and early 1940s expected it to revolutionize mainstream economics. That didn't occur. By the mid-1950s the

[13] *Ibid.*, pp. 204–206.
[14] *Ibid.*, pp. 213–214.
[15] *Ibid.*, pp. 214–215.

monopolistic competition revolution was being relegated to undergraduate and history of thought textbooks.

Why Did the Monopolistic Competition Revolution Fail?

A central reason why the monopolistic competition revolution failed was that it was difficult to formalize and draw implications from it. It was difficult, if not impossible, to separate out selling costs from product differentiation costs and hence to determine what to include as a cost and what to include as a variable that changed the demand curve. (If you buy a case of Pepsi or Classic Coke because these products are consumed regularly by sexy-looking people on television, it is not easy to separate out the product from the advertising.) Also, because most U.S. industries are, in effect, oligopolies, there is interdependence among the decisions of various firms; in making any decision, each firm takes into account the expected reaction of other firms in the industry. Chamberlin tried to solve these problems analytically, but he lacked the technical ability to do so adequately.

A second reason for the failure of Chamberlin's theory concerns oligopoly. Chamberlin believed that the various models of duopoly and Marshall's entire analysis of markets were all based upon a fundamental error: they ignored the interdependence of firms. This point needs to be examined closely, not only because it is the key to understanding Chamberlin's contribution but also because it provides an insight into what may well be a major theoretical issue in present-day micro theory. Marshall's analysis of competitive markets assumes an "industry" made up of a "large" number of firms. The concept of an industry is vague; for his theory to be logically consistent, however, it must be defined as a number of firms selling identical or homogeneous goods in identical markets. Similarly, a "large" number of firms must mean a number sufficient to ensure that no single firm has any control over price. But the crucial aspect of Marshall's analysis is that firms are independent of each other. If, for example, one firm places a large supply on the market, this action must have neither a direct effect on the market nor an indirect effect resulting from the reaction of another firm in the industry. Even though the firms are mutually interdependent, the theory requires that they do not recognize their independence. If they do and if, as in the case of farmers, they resort to the government or some form of cooperative to regulate the industry, the market is no longer one of pure competition.

Before Chamberlin various writers had tackled the interdependence problem largely by making assumptions that removed the problem. In Cournot's model, for example, a firm chooses an optimum output assuming competitors hold their given output. Nearly fifty years later J. Bertrand built a model in which each rival assumes that the other's price is fixed. F. Y. Edgeworth used a different set of assumptions about the behavior of rival sellers and reached different conclusions. On Cournot's assumptions, price would be somewhere between the price in a monopoly market and a perfectly competitive market; on Betrand's assumptions, price would be a competitive price; and on Edgeworth's assumptions, the price

New Directions in Monopolistic Competition Theory

Recent research has been directed toward an examination of monopolistic competition. Work by Darius Gaskins, Steven Salop, and Joseph Stiglitz has examined strategic pricing and has shown that when interfirm responses are considered, competition will not lead to efficient pricing. Joseph Stiglitz, George Akerlof, and Janet Yellen, among others, have explored the monopolistically competitive underpinnings of a macro model and found that these underpinnings lead to Keynesian conclusions. This work, unlike Chamberlin's and Robinson's, is more formal and uses complex mathematical techniques. Thus, whereas the work of these earlier writers was not compatible with modern micro theory, the new work is, and the lost revolution may yet occur.

The re-emergence of the monopolistic competition revolution is also occurring from another direction, namely, from economists who contend that the domain of modern microeconomics is too narrow and needs to be expanded to include political and anticompetitive actions. An early statement of this view was Gordon Tullock's analysis of the welfare loss due to monopoly. Tullock argued that the loss in efficiency from monopoly that traditional welfare economics focuses on is only a small part of the actual welfare loss; the time and money spent on achieving monopoly is far more significant.

Similar arguments were proposed by Jagdish Bhagwati (1934–   ) and Mancur Olson (1932–   ), whose combined work has been called *neoclassical political economy.** This theory assumes that people maximize not only *within* an assumed institutional structure but also *to achieve* an institutional structure most beneficial to them, and that these two maximizing procedures must be analyzed simultaneously. This approach has led to the reintroduction of a type of monopolistic competition, because it accords with Chamberlin's thesis that individuals are continually trying to create monopolies for themselves. But the emphasis is reversed: the new analysis yields not monopolistic competition but competitive monopolies, in which the desire to achieve monopoly is the central driving force, held in check only by the attempts of others to get a part of that monopoly for themselves. Thus, the creation of monopoly provides competition for existing monopolies, and that competition occurs only in the presence of monopoly.

*David Colander, ed., *Neoclasssical Political Economy* (Boston: Ballinger, 1984).

would be unstable and would oscillate between a perfectly competitive price and a monopoly price.

Chamberlin's work led to so many new theories of markets in which firms recognize their interdependence that it was suggested that there were as many theories of oligopoly as microeconomists. Chamberlin's work did not spawn a theory of oligopoly but theories of oligopoly, and thus it failed as a theory.

The formalists were not able to solve the problem of rival interdependence, although they tried in what has become known as game theory. One can, for example, program a computer to play games like chess or checkers because any given move of a rival has certain probabilities of success computed on predictions of the rival's reaction to a given action. Thus, one can formulate a mathematical theory of oligopoly that explicitly recognizes rival interaction. Firm interaction in markets is not, however, like chess, checkers, or games in which all the needed information to make rational, probabilistic decisions is known. Markets are more like poker games in which information about rivals is not known (cards are in the deck or hidden in rivals' hands). Markets are also more like poker games in that rivals may engage in practices designed to supply misinformation—bluffing, for example.

A third reason for the failure of the monopolistic competition revolution was that Chamberlin's analysis was essentially partial equilibrium with acknowledged Marshallian roots. In 1940 Robert Triffin raised questions concerning the integration of monopolistic competition with general equilibrium analysis, and at present general equilibrium theory is still largely formulated in terms of the competitive model.[16] The departure of graduate economics into Walrasian general equilibrium left behind the monopolistic competition revolution, which in the 1930s had seemed a contribution equal to Keynes's. But the fact that the monopolistic revolution died in no way negated the problems it had attempted to address. Even though most industries continue to be positioned somewhere between monopoly and competition, much of modern economic theory does not address this reality.

A final reason for the failure of the monopolistic competition revolution is that many economists have concluded that it was unnecessary. It is argued that although theories of market structures between pure monopoly and pure competition are more descriptive of actual markets, these theories are not superior to the polar models as predictors of economic behavior. This view asserts that the criterion of theory acceptance is not congruence with reality in its descriptive features but an ability to predict correctly.

MILTON FRIEDMAN AND THE CHICAGO APPROACH TO MICROECONOMICS

One of the reasons why the imperfect or monopolistic competitive revolution did not take place was that an important group of Marshallians (generally centered around Chicago, and sometimes called the Chicago school of economics) opposed it. They saw it as a useless appendage that added nothing to the analysis of competition and monopoly. This split within the Marshallians opened the way for the Walrasian formalists' domination of higher level economic theory.

The Chicago school is characterized by a belief that markets work better than the alternatives as a means of organizing society. Milton Friedman (1912–   )

---

[16] Robert Triffin, *Monopolistic Competition and General Equilibrium Theory* (Cambridge, Mass.: Harvard University Press, 1940).

has been a counterweight to Paul Samuelson throughout the modern period of economics. Friedman summarized his Chicago approach as follows:

> In discussions of economic policy, "Chicago" stands for belief in the efficiency of the free market as a means of organizing resources, for skepticism about government affairs, and for emphasis on the quantity of money as a key factor in producing inflation.
>
> In discussions of economic science, "Chicago" stands for an approach that takes seriously the use of economic theory as a tool for analyzing a startlingly wide range of concrete problems, rather than as an abstract mathematical structure of great beauty but little power; for an approach that insists on the empirical testing of theoretical generalizations and that rejects alike facts without theory and theory without facts.[17]

Friedman's approach to economics is Marshallian rather than Walrasian. He sees economics as an engine of analysis for addressing real problems and as something that should not be allowed to become an abstract mathematical consideration devoid of institutional context and direct relation to real world problems.

In his consideration of policy issues he combines a strong belief in individual rights and liberty and in the effectiveness of the market in protecting those rights (see *Capitalism and Freedom,* 1962). His political orientation is basically pro-market anti-government. He has advocated many policy proposals that at first were seen as radical but later became more acceptable: financing education with vouchers, eliminating licensing in professions, and legalizing drugs.

Around 1950 Friedman produced a number of provocative papers on methodology and also a paper on the Marshallian demand curve and the marginal utility of money. In the late 1950s he made contributions to macroeconomics in his *Studies in the Quantity Theory of Money* (1956). His column in *Newsweek* has been read by many, and a TV series titled "Free to Choose" has given him greater notoriety than most theorists. His standing in the profession is manifested by the fact that he won the John Bates Clark Medal of the American Economic Association in 1951 and the Nobel Prize in economics in 1976.

Even as Friedman was becoming well known, his Marshallian approach was dying. In part this was because it was seen by many as ideologically or normatively tainted, causing researchers to revert to formalism to avoid ideological bias.

An example of what some economists considered to be the normative bias in the Chicago approach to economics can be seen in the Coase theorem, named for Ronald Coase (1910–   ), another influential Chicago economist whose work led to the recent field of law and economics. The Coase theorem was a response to the Pigouvian approach, which saw the existence of externalities as a reason for government intervention.

In "The Problem of Social Cost" Coase argued that in theory, externalities were not a reason for government intervention because any party helped or hurt by an

---

[17] Milton Friedman, as quoted in Warren Samuels, "The Chicago School of Political Economy: A Constructive Critique," in *The Chicago School of Political Economy,* ed. Warren Samuels (New Brunswick, N.J.: Transactions Publications, 1992).

action was free to negotiate with others to eliminate the externality. Thus, if there were too much smoke from a factory, the neighbors hurt by the smoke could pay the factory to reduce it.

The Coase theorem has been much discussed in the literature. The general conclusion is that in and of itself the theorem is no more ideological than is the theory of externalities that predisposes one toward government intervention. Issues involving government intervention are complicated, and there is no answer that follows from theory; in modern economics a theory of government failure exists side by side with a theory of market failure. Which is more appropriate depends upon the relative costs and benefits, issues upon which individuals may disagree.

Nonetheless, the Chicago approach has stimulated many new ideas and it, rather than the more formalist approach, may sow the seeds for major developments in microeconomics in the twenty-first century. Among those new ideas that have been stimulated has been Armen Alchian's (1914–   ) and Harold Demsetz's (1930–   ) work on property rights as underlying markets. The Chicago view is that it is best to assume that markets work efficiently, so much of the discussion of inefficiency in markets (such as might be produced by monopolistic competition) is misplaced. But markets depend upon property rights; thus, the study of property rights is of paramount importance to economics. What are the underlying property rights? How do they develop? How do they change?

TOPICS IN MODERN MICROECONOMICS

Although we cannot provide more than an overview of the changes currently under way in microeconomic theory, we can illustrate some of their implications by discussing areas that have seen substantial change. These include two general areas—the domain of microeconomics and the techniques of microeconomics— and two specific areas—demand theory and welfare theory. We conclude this section with a general discussion of problems in modern microeconomics.

The Expanding Domain of Microeconomics

Economists have applied the micro model that explains household consumer behavior and firm behavior using the tools of rationality and maximization to areas that were formerly the exclusive province of sociology and political science. In this sense, economists have become imperialistic in the post–World War II period. The formalization of theory as a methodological program, which now dominates economics, has also infiltrated other disciplines, notably political science, history, sociology, and geography. Techniques developed largely by econometricians are widely used in the social sciences and history. One example of this expanded use of economic models to explain what was previously regarded as noneconomic behavior is the work of Gary Becker (1930–   ), who won the Nobel Prize in economics in 1992.[18] He has used microeconomic models to study decisions about crime, courtship, marriage, and childbearing.

The simple-maximization micro model based on the assumption of rational individuals has potentially infinite applications, and recent years have seen it used in widely diverse areas. These incursions of economic theory into other disciplines have sometimes been treated facetiously by those who claim that the economic approach is too simple. In one sense they are right. The ideas and policy conclusions of the "economics of everything" are often simple. But mere simplicity does not make them wrong. Market incentives make a difference in people's behavior, and noneconomic specialists have often not included a sufficient consideration of these incentives in their analyses. But analyses can go astray when only economic incentives are considered and insufficient attention is paid to institutional and social incentives. Unfortunately, given modern economists' training in noncontextual modeling, this is often what occurs.

Evolving Techniques

The evolution of microeconomics has entailed a progression from one mathematical language to another, each of which has been able to resolve some of the ambiguities that marred its predecessor. Initially, economists such as Paul Samuelson and John Hicks (1904–1989) translated the geometry of the 1930s into the multivariate calculus of the 1960s. The partial differentials of calculus represented the interrelationships among sectors; the sign of the second partial derivative illustrated stability conditions; and the sign of the first derivatives captured the interactive effects. Cross-partial elasticities of demand, linear homogeneous production functions, homothetic demands, and constant elasticity of substitution (CES) production functions all appeared in microeconomic terminology. The results of the mathematical reformulation of microeconomics are impressive. As economists worked through the problems, they began to perceive the relationship between prices and *Lagrangian multipliers* (the values of the constraints). The question of whether prices were inherent in economic systems had been debated previously, but now mathematical economists could show that prices occurred naturally in a maximization process and that even in the absence of markets, constrained maximization will still have a "price" (called a *shadow price*). If prices do not exist, another rationing device must replace price.

They also showed how one can easily reformulate a maximization problem subject to a constraint into a constrained minimization problem: by switching constraints and objective functions, the problem "Maximize output subject to technical production constraints" is equal to the problem "Minimize cost subject to producing a certain output." Such a reformulation, which is known as "analyzing the dual," affords insight into the nature of the maximization problem by showing how slight changes in the output or constraints change the situation.

---

[18] See Richard B. McKenzie and Gordon Tullock, *The New World of Economics* (Homewood, Ill.: R. D. Irvin, 1975), for other examples.

These developments had both practical and theoretical significance. On the practical side, the understanding of shadow prices and duals led to significant developments in modern management techniques. On the theoretical side, the analysis of the dual added to economists' analysis of scarcity a symmetry that deepened their understanding of the problem. What previously took volumes to present (often incorrectly) could be covered in one or two pages (for those who knew the language). Given the earlier misuse of informal models and confusion about their implications, most economists saw these developments as a significant gain. The 1987 winner of the Nobel Prize in economics, Robert Solow, commented:

> I detect a tendency . . . to idealize the old, nonformalist days in economics. I lived
> through those days and I was educated when that was the way economics was
> done, and let me tell you—they were not so great at all. They were pretty awful,
> in fact. My nonformalist education was full of vagueness and logical inconsis-
> tency and wishful thinking and mere prejudice and *post hoc propter hoc,* and pon-
> tification was everywhere in the classes I took and the lectures I went to.[19]

But the reformulation of microeconomic theory in terms of multivariate calculus also had problems. Multivariate calculus requires an assumption of continuity and poses the maximization problem in a highly rarefied way. In response to these shortcomings of calculus, economists modified the maximization problem in a number of ways—some of which made microeconomics more practical and useful in business, while others provided deeper understanding of the economy.

By the 1970s the possibilities of comparative static calculus had begun to be exhausted, and the cutting edge of theoretical work was being done in *dynamic calculus,* in which time is explicitly taken into account. To see why dynamic calculus is relevant, consider the production problem. The intermediate micro approach is to say that the firm faces a production problem: given a set of inputs and relative prices, it chooses an optimal quantity of output. But where is time in the model? It is suppressed, so how the model actually works is unclear. Adopting a *comparative static interpretation* provides a somewhat temporal dimension. The problem is considered twice: before and after a single change. Thus, it becomes an analysis of two points in time. No consideration is given, however, to how one gets from one point to the other or to how long that time period is.

For a better analysis of the process of getting from one point to the other, the mathematical formulation of the problem must explicitly include the time path along which one goes from the initial state to the end state. The calculus that accomplishes this is *optimal control theory.* Students typically learn optimal control theory in the calculus course following differential equations, which follows multivariate calculus. The solution sets are similar, but instead of being expressed in Lagrangian multipliers, they are expressed in Hamiltonians and bordered Hessians.

---

[19] Unpublished transcript of a comment by Robert Solow on a paper presented by David Colander at the 1986 American Economic Association meetings.

After increasing the complexity of the calculus it used, micro analysis expanded away from it, for both practical and theoretical reasons. Practically, it moved toward linear models because linear algorithms existed by which one could more easily compute numerical solutions. Thus, a simple linear formulation was more relevant to real-world problems, and linear, network, and dynamic programming were added to the economist's tool kit. In theoretical work, the formulation of the general equilibrium problem soon went beyond calculus to *set theory* and *game theory*. Economists preferred these approaches because they were more precise and did not require assumptions of continuity, as calculus did. As the techniques changed, so did the terminology; terms such as *upper-semi continuous* and *a Cournot-Nash equilibrium* became commonplace in graduate micro courses.

Another significant change in microeconomics is evident in its handling of uncertainty. Economic decisions must be made in the face of an uncertain future. Marshall did not attempt to tackle the uncertainty problem directly. Modern microeconomics, however, formally confronts uncertainty, though often with stochastic rather than static processes. To analyze such models, microeconomics uses *applied statistical decision theory,* a blend of statistics, probability theory, and logic.

As is often the case, one can look at developments in a field in both a positive and a negative light. Take game theory, for example, which we have presented briefly as simply an alternative, more elegant and precise, way of performing general equilibrium analysis. It is that, but it is also much more. It is the most general analysis of human interaction that exists, and it offers ways in which economists can analyze interdependent actions that they otherwise have to assume away. Thus, it offers practical models for understanding oligopoly behavior, which comprises large portions of most Western economies. Similarly, it offers enormous insight into social problems, as it does in Thomas Schellings's (1921–   ) work, such as *The Strategy of Conflict* (1960). Alternatively, it offers a method of synthesizing all the social sciences, as it does in Martin Shubik's (1926–   ) *Game Theory in the Social Sciences* (1982).

Thus, the logic of game theory is as compelling today as it was when John von Neumann and Oskar Morgenstern first published *The Theory of Games and Economic Behavior* in 1944, and it may well become the basis for the microeconomics of the twenty-first century.

The Progression of Demand Theory

In the neoclassical model, the theory of demand—that as price falls the quantity demanded will increase—was based upon assumptions about utility maximization. Marshall assumed that the utility received from consuming a good depends exclusively upon the quantity of that good consumed. In mathematical terms he assumed that individuals' utility functions were additive. Marshall's theory of demand also assumed that utility was cardinally measurable and that the principle of diminishing marginal utility held true.

A key debate in the early 1900s concerned the validity of the law of demand. Some economists questioned the assumptions, arguing either that utility was not cardinally measurable or that the theory of diminishing marginal utility did not hold true. Others, using data collected by Robert Giffen, argued that empirical evidence contradicted the law of demand. Still others contended that demand theory was based on an inadequate, hedonistic psychology. Modern demand theory evolved, in part, in response to economists' attempts to answer these questions.

Although a number of economists contributed to the revision of demand theory, the work of J. R. Hicks has had the greatest impact. In 1934 Hicks and R. G. D. Allen restructured demand theory by demonstrating that basing demand on indifference curves eliminates the assumptions of cardinal measurement of utility and diminishing marginal utility. They also showed that a generalized utility function allows for substitute and complementary relationships. Although indifference-curve techniques had been developed by Edgeworth, Pareto, and Fisher, they had not been used in the literature to any extent since their initial development. With their reintroduction in the 1930s, however, indifference curves became an accepted and frequently used tool of microeconomic theory.

Giffen's statistics were alleged by some to give an example of an upward-sloping demand curve; thus, they provoked further interest in a study of demand. With his new technique of indifference curves, Hicks was able to theoretically separate the income and substitution effect. If the price of good A is decreased, the substitution effect will produce an unambiguous result: the quantity demanded will increase. In cases involving what are now called *Giffen goods,* in which the good is strongly inferior, the income effect can offset the substitution effect and cause the demand curve to slope upward. Although these developments demonstrated the theoretical possibility of upward-sloping demand curves, no one could empirically demonstrate such a demand curve.[20]

The problem of inadequate psychological foundations. Developments of demand and utility theory expanded the applicability and clarified the meaning of the theory of consumer behavior, but they did not answer criticism of its underlying hedonistic psychological assumptions. The intellectual origins of utility theory can be found in the work of Jeremy Bentham. By the 1930s psychologists had rejected Bentham's explanation of behavior, asserting that economics was built upon false psychological premises. Psychologist William McDougall stated this criticism succinctly early in the 1920s:

> Political economy suffered hardly less from the crude nature of the psychological assumptions from which it professed to deduce the explanations of its facts and its prescriptions for economic legislation. It would be a libel, not altogether de-

[20] Hicks and Allen referred to a 1915 work by E. Slutsky that distinguished between normal and inferior goods. But not until Hicks and Allen discovered this earlier work was it generally introduced into the literature, which demonstrates that a first statement of a theoretical proposition is not as significant as a meaningful application of a proposition.

void of truth, to say that classical political economy was a tissue of false conclusions drawn from false psychological assumptions.[21]

Attacked on this issue by those outside the profession as well as by heterodox
economists, especially Thorstein Veblen, mainstream economists became uneasy.
Marshall attempted to ameliorate the situation by changing some of his terminology in subsequent editions of his *Principles*. But because he had no alternative
explanation, he never succeeded in purging hedonistic psychology from his theory
of consumer behavior. Some economists argued that indifference-curve techniques solved these problems by explaining consumer behavior without assuming
cardinal measurement of utility or diminishing marginal utility. But most economists disagreed, because indifference curves contain most of the inherent assumptions of cardinal measurement and diminishing utility.[22]

Though most modern economists use indifference-curve techniques, many
recognize their limitations, one of which is that the concept of a consumer's being
"indifferent" to various bundles of goods is nonoperational. The concept of the
indifference curve is completely theoretical: there is no way of empirically
measuring "indifference" or constructing indifference curves. Furthermore, the
theory still rests on two major psychological assumptions that consumers are
introspective and that they are trying to maximize. Because the indifference curve
is merely a construct without empirical content, the theory of consumer behavior
becomes tautological. First we assume that consumers are free to purchase any
goods consistent with their incomes and preferences. Because we have no way of
determining preferences except as revealed by actual purchases, it follows that
what is actually purchased must be preferred. Because the consumer is assumed
to be maximizing, purchase equals maximizing. Such a tautological theory tells
us nothing about consumer behavior.

Versions of this critique have been expressed by eminent orthodox theorists.
George Katona has suggested that "statements about 'maximizing' are too general
to contribute to a real understanding of consumer motivation."[23] The tautological
nature of the theory is suggested by the fact that it tells us only that "a person does
what he deems best."[24] James Duesenberry comments on existing theory as
follows:

> The preference system analysis of consumer behavior is a somewhat remarkable
> tour de force. It seems to say something about consumer behavior without saying
> anything about the motivation of the consumers in question. In its present form it

---

[21] William McDougall, *An Introduction to Social Psychology* (Boston: John W. Luce, 1923),
pp. 10–11.

[22] F. H. Knight, "Realism and Relevance in the Theory of Demand," *Journal of Political
Economy* 36 (December 1944); Dennis Robertson, "Utility and All What?" *Economics Journal* 64 (December 1954).

[23] George Katona, *Psychological Analysis of Economic Behavior* (New York: McGraw-Hill,
1951), p. 70.

[24] *Ibid.*

is a more or less deliberate attempt to sidestep the task of making any psychological assumptions.[25]

Paul Samuelson's view in 1947 of the theory of demand based upon indifference techniques was also critical:

> Thus, the consumer's market behavior is explained in terms of preferences, which are in turn defined only by behavior. The result can very easily be circular, and in many formulations undoubtedly is. Often nothing more is stated than the conclusion that people behave as they behave, a theorem which has no empirical implications, since it contains no hypothesis and is consistent with all conceivable behavior, while refutable by none.[26]

The revealed preference approach.   Out of this dissatisfaction with the indifference-curve approach emerged a new theory of demand, but it retreated even further from any assumptions about psychological motivation and the concept of utility. Known as the *revealed preference approach,* its major developer was Paul Samuelson. The primary assumption required for this theory to deduce a downward-sloping demand curve is that the consumer's preferences are consistent, or "transitive." Whether the consumer is maximizing or merely following Freudian urges is of no consequence to the theory: it is completely behavioristic, requiring the economist merely to record the consumer's choices as manifested in the market. Unfortunately, the revealed preference approach was not proven operationally significant. Although it freed micro analysis from its tautological theory of utility maximization, revealed preference is a theory of demand without a theory of consumer behavior; it is thus without much operational content.

Recent developments in utility theory.   Along with the increasing formalization of demand theory and the utility theory underlying it, there have been other changes, two of which deserve attention. One is an extension of utility analysis to include risk; the second is a modified conceptualization of the utility approach. The inclusion of risk allows utility analysis to focus on choices made under uncertainty. It is based on the *theory of expected utility* developed by John von Neumann and Oskar Morgenstern in 1944 and extended by J. L. Savage in 1953. They listed a series of reasonable axioms about human behavior and deduced a method of changing uncertainty states into certainty equivalents consistent with those axioms. For example, suppose one must decide whether to go fishing or to study. Going fishing would yield ten "utiles." Studying would result in a 50 percent chance of getting an A, which would yield fifteen utiles, and a 50 percent chance of not getting an A, or a yield of zero utiles. Given this information, along with

[25] James Duesenberry, *Income, Saving, and the Theory of Consumer Behavior* (Cambridge, Mass.: Harvard University Press, 1952), p. 17.

[26] Samuelson, *Foundations,* pp. 91–92.

Herbert Simon and Bounded Rationality

One economist who has taken the psychological foundations of economics seriously is Herbert Simon (1916–   ), who in 1978 won the Nobel Prize in economics for his work. Simon has always been interested in understanding how real people—not infinitely wise, infinitely rational and intelligent people—make decisions. That interest led him into an analysis of cognitive psychology, human information processing, and information processing more generally, which is the precursor to work in artificial intelligence.

Although his work is often highly mathematical and abstract, he continually attempted to relate it to the real world. He proposed that a better approach to rationality would be to assume what is called "bounded

rationality," which took into account the limitations of the brain in processing information. On the basis of bounded rationality, it is irrational to be fully rational as assumed by neoclassical theory. This led to a "satisficing model" of the firm in which profit maximization was not the primary goal. Instead, firms established profit margin and sales goals.

Simon's work has had limited impact on the profession. When he won the Nobel Prize in 1978, many economists had not heard of him. Recently his work has begun to receive more serious attention by mainstream economists. It remains to be seen whether he is a prophet ahead of his time or a minor player in the game of economics.

one's risk preference, we can calculate expected utiles for each alternative by multiplying the probability of occurrence by the utility one derives from the occurrence of that event. Assuming one is risk-neutral, in this case one would choose fishing, because it yields 10 expected utiles compared to 7.5 expected utiles for studying.

Another method of extending utility theory to address uncertainty is Kenneth Arrow's *state preference theory*, which is used to extend general equilibrium theory to include risky situations. Commodities in state preference must always be considered contingent on things outside themselves; thus, "a suit" would not be a sufficient description of a commodity whose preference order can be determined. Instead, one must rank all contingent commodities (e.g., a blue suit if Ellen calls; a brown suit if Bill calls; jeans if Joe calls). Individuals are assumed to have clear preferences among *contingent* commodities, not simply among commodities.

The second change in utility theory that deserves mention involves modified conceptualizations of the theory. Probably the best known and most widely used of these new conceptualizations of utility theory is the *human capital approach*, which explicitly treats time as a commodity and develops a household production function. Important contributors to this development include Theodore W. Schultz (1902–   ) and Gary Becker. They played an important role in extending economic analysis to issues previously considered outside of economics, making economic analysis important to other social sciences such as sociology. The importance of time was generally recognized before their work, but except for analysis of labor supply, it was not formally built into the analysis and the myriad logical results of its inclusion had not been drawn.

Kelvin J. Lancaster's (1924–   ) *characteristic analysis* provides an alternative method of expanding utility theory to capture a broader range of issues. Rather than specifying commodities, such as a car, as arguments in the utility function, it specifies characteristics. A commodity is a bundle of characteristics—in this case, a red, fourteen-foot-long, five-foot-high, gas-powered mode of transportation. Lancaster argues that individuals' preferences are for characteristics, not for commodities. Using Lancaster's approach, marginal decisions are impossible and the decision process is modeled as a linear-programming (nonmarginal) maximizing problem.

Modern demand theory in perspective.   The primary function of a theory of demand or household consumer behavior is to explain the shape of demand curves. Demand theory has come almost full circle, starting with J. S. Mill and ending with revealed preference theory. Mill was one of the first to recognize a functional relationship between price and quantity demanded, although he did not graph demand curves or explicitly state them in mathematical form. After the time of J. S. Mill, economists tried to tie demand theory to notions of measurable utility based upon hedonistic psychological assumptions. As psychologists backed away from pleasure-pain theories, so did economists, but with considerable reluctance. Marshall tried to purge hedonism from his demand theory by changing the terminology but retaining the essence of his analysis.

Modern demand theory is a theory of demand without a theory of consumer behavior; this seems to indicate that economists would be better off without the assistance of psychologists. The attention given the theory of demand today seems disproportionate to the benefits to be gained from it; its contribution amounts to little more than a statement that demand curves are negatively sloped because that is what we find in the marketplace. In considering recent developments in utility theory, moreover, one is left with the feeling that although its theoretical underpinnings have been intensively explored, these explorations have had little effect on the way in which economics is practiced.

The Progression of Welfare Economics

A second area of economics that demonstrates the development of modern microeconomic theory is its focus on policy and how theory and policy fit together. In modern economics this relationship has become known as *welfare economics*. Welfare economics constituted an integral part of classical economics, most of whose theoretical arguments were specifically designed to support policy positions. But as classical economics evolved into neoclassical economics in the last quarter of the nineteenth century, economists began to distinguish between economic theory and policy. Increased attention to demand theory helped to change economists' thinking about welfare. To Smith, Ricardo, and J. S. Mill, increasing welfare had meant, for the most part, increasing output; but with developing notions of marginal utility in the 1870s, the concept of welfare came to be framed in terms of psychology rather than physical output.

As this change occurred, the classical "invisible hand" theory (that laissez faire would produce maximum welfare) came under attack and some economists began to investigate aspects of the economy in which unregulated markets did not necessarily achieve this goal. As the debate proceeded, the loose, contextual classical argument in favor of laissez faire as a policy prescription became a formal, noncontextual argument centered on whether the market will optimally allocate a fixed quantity of resources among alternative uses within the framework of a subjective theory of prices. Discussions of growth, political and economic interaction, and evolving institutions disappeared and were replaced by an abstract, noncontextual theoretical model.

Henry Sidgwick (1838–1900), a moral philosopher who addressed economics in his *Principles of Political Economy* (1883), devoted a good deal of attention to exceptions to the general rule that laissez faire will produce maximum welfare. A sensitive liberal humanitarian, he noted with approval the movement toward greater government intervention in the economy; yet he also firmly believed in the beneficial effects of an economic structure that rewarded individual incentives and would change it only where it proved to be deleterious.

As economic theory became more formal, so too did the determination of when welfare actually increased. Building on Sidgwick's work, A. C. Pigou, who succeeded Marshall at Cambridge, tried to develop a formal welfare theory that could be applied to economic policy. Although Pigou distinguished between normative and positive analysis, he, unrecognized by himself, made some obvious value judgments: that working at home is better than working in a factory, that browsing in a museum is preferable to drinking in a pub. Such judgments, because they were agreed upon by most learned individuals, seemed acceptable in Marshallian contextual analysis, but in subsequent formalist noncontextual arguments they were not.

In the attempt to develop a value-free welfare economics, economists went back to the Italian economist Vilfredo Pareto, who initially proposed ordinal measurement of utility. Pareto argued that individuals in a market will voluntarily exchange as long as there is some benefit to them, and that production and exchange will cease at maximum welfare. At a *Pareto optimum* it is not possible to make someone better off without making someone else worse off. Economists in the 1930s thought they could use Pareto optimality to evaluate the performance of an economy without making value judgments. Accordingly, they tried to precisely formulate the conditions under which the general economy would reach a Pareto optimum. This writing was extremely fertile, leading to a much better understanding of the welfare implications of the economy and the allocation of resources in social economic systems. Three Nobel Prize winners in economics, Arrow, Samuelson, and Hicks, contributed significantly to this literature. As economists adopted Pareto optimality as their central welfare criterion, income distribution lost its role as a key economic issue, because Pareto optimality considers welfare implications *given* the distribution of income.

Despite its widespread use by economists, however, as elegantly pointed out in the work of A. K. Sen (1933–   ), Pareto optimality does not provide a value-free welfare economics.[27] It assumes that if a move makes everyone better off, society is better off. This may be an unobjectionable value judgment for many, but it is a value judgment nonetheless. Using Pareto optimality as a criterion to determine welfare violates Hume's dictum that you cannot derive a "should" from a fact. Even if one accepts Pareto optimality as being acceptably free of normative elements, it does not provide much help in policy-making. Most real-world political actions will hurt some people in helping others, even if only in a small way. For example, any action will affect the entire price vector of all goods, inevitably helping some and harming others. Pareto optimality provides no guide to dealing with such effects.

The limitations of Pareto optimality occasioned much literature on the subject. Some economists suggested, for example, the *compensating variation approach,* in which the gainers could compensate the losers. This led to a number of paradoxes. Tibor Scitovsky (1910–   ) demonstrated that there are a number of cases in which gainers can compensate losers, but in which losers can also compensate gainers. A second, more widely used approach was introduced by Abram Bergson (1914–   ) in 1938. He included welfare criteria in initial assumptions by using a *social welfare function* in an ordinal form to specify the preferences of society. Because this is the approach used by most economists today, there has been widespread discussion of what form this social welfare function should take. Proponents from several camps have advanced a variety of functions, including the additive, multiplicative, and the Maximin (maximizing the welfare of the least-well-off individual), which was proposed by the philosopher John Rawls.[28] These unspecified, abstract social welfare functions are so formalized that most models are never applied to policy. Although they theoretically resolve the problem of introducing normative arguments into economics, they serve little practical role.

The concept of the social welfare function did, however, raise a number of theoretical issues. Some economists asked, for example, whether it was possible to move from individuals' welfare functions to a social welfare function, and by what means. Voting was suggested as a means, which led to Kenneth Arrow's famous work on the voting paradox, *Social Choice and Individual Values* (1951), in which he demonstrated that given some reasonable assumptions, it is impossible to arrive at a unique social welfare function. Arrow's work opened up a new branch of highly abstract welfare economics called social choice theory.

---

[27] A. K. Sen, *Social Choice and Welfare* (Oxford: Basil Blackwell, 1982).
[28] John Rawls, *A Theory of Justice* (Cambridge, Mass.: Harvard University Press, 1971).

Externalities.   Even though Pareto optimality has proven to be an insufficient base for developing a solid welfare theory, it has left its mark on the profession. Specifically, it is central to the question of whether perfectly competitive markets lead to an optimum allocation of resources; hence it is basic to the structure of modern micro theory. A. C. Pigou was one of the first economists to specifically introduce such considerations into economic analysis. Pigou showed that firms' marginal cost functions may not accurately reflect the social costs of production and that the demand curves of individuals may not accurately reflect the social benefits of consumption. He examined the divergencies between private benefit and social benefit, and between private costs and social costs. These divergencies, known variously as *externalities,* third-party effects, and spillover effects, are considered to justify government action. The costs a firm considers in its profit-maximizing decisions are private costs borne by the firm. But social costs, such as pollution, are not borne by the firm; thus, there is a divergence between private and social cost at the margin. A free market will therefore result in the production of an excessive quantity of goods whose marginal social cost exceeds their marginal private cost.

Let us express this in the broadest possible terms. One problem of economics is to analyze the relative scarcity arising because the desires of individuals for goods and services exceed the ability of the economy to provide them. A conflict then exists between the benefits derived from consumption and the costs incurred in production. According to marginal analysis, the optimum solution to this conflict is to produce and consume goods up to the point at which marginal benefits equal marginal costs. Ignoring issues of the distribution and level of income, a free competitive market would provide a maximum of economic welfare and optimally resolve this conflict, as long as market demand and supply curves correctly reflect all costs and benefits in the society. Pigou's contribution to welfare economics was an analytic framework to deal with externalities by which market demand and supply curves do not adequately reflect social benefits and costs.

Whereas the externality structure is generally accepted, the policy implications are not. Externalities are difficult, if not impossible, to measure, and some economists joke that a Chicago economist is an economist who has yet to see one. Moreover, even if externalities exist, it is not clear that anything should be done about them. Given the influence of politics on economic policy, the actual policy undertaken by government may not in any way reflect the "theoretically correct" policy. Consideration of these issues has led to a burgeoning "public choice" literature focusing on the interrelationship of economics and politics.

Welfare economics in perspective.   Even if all the issues raised by recent work in theoretical welfare economics could be successfully handled, some fundamental questions remain to be answered. Suppose we had a theory that gave unambiguous answers about the economic welfare consequences of various actions or policies. Presumably, welfare theorists would regard this as a significant contribution to the larger task of answering questions about social welfare. But policies have other

The Evolving Art of Economic Policy

Modern microeconomics combines positive economics, the art of economics, and normative economics and has used the same formalistic methodology to consider all three branches. Thus, whereas J. N. Keynes saw each as having a separate methodology—positive economics a highly formal methodology, and the art of economics a loose, non-formal methodology*—modern economics used the same formalistic methodology in each and, in fact, combined the three in what came to be known as welfare economics. This combining of the three branches of economics changed the way in which economic theory was conceptualized and used. Classical economists were primarily interested in policy, or what Keynes called the art of economics. In practicing this art, some (especially Ricardo) saw a need to develop the positive theory of economics to guide one's thinking; but when discussing policy, even Ricardo reintegrated sociological and political insights into the analysis. This led many early writers, such as those in the German historical school, to separate out a distinct art of economics—or, alternatively, to argue that only an art of economics existed.

The neoclassical economic revolution was marked by fights between those who focused on economics as art (the historical and institutional approaches) and those who focused on economics as science (the Walrasian school and English economists such as Edgeworth and Jevons). Marshall tried to merge the two, and the result was Marshallian economics. It was a revolt against this merging that led to the modern mathematical revolution and the strong emphasis on economics as science.

A few mainstream economists, most notably Milton Friedman, maintained their Marshallian roots, but these individuals became increasingly rare in the twentieth century. As Marshallians became rarer, and abstract mathematical economists more prevalent, there were strong tendencies toward reintroducing the art of economics into mainstream economics. This would occur through a welfare economics that would once again become real-world applied economics, which would take into account the historical and institutional context of problems and would use a less formal method of analysis appropriate for such real-world considerations.

*J. N. Keynes did not discuss what he considered the appropriate methodology for normative economics.

than purely economic effects. So while the economic part of the jigsaw puzzle would be solved, a complete solution would await developments in the other social sciences and possibly in the humanities.

A number of writers from the nineteenth century through the present have questioned this fragmented approach to questions of social welfare. Although the criticism has taken various forms, its basic thrust is that one part of social welfare, economic welfare, cannot be isolated for analysis. Social welfare, according to these critics, is not many separate problems but one big problem. Economists have been reluctant to tackle the question of social welfare for a number of reasons, the most important being the desire to keep economics a positive science.

Problems in Modern Microeconomics

This discussion of the successes of modern microeconomics should be seen as both a tribute to the field's accomplishments and a prelude to our consideration of the problems it still faces. Most economists would agree that the formalization of economics has made some significant gains, but it has also had its costs. Each advance we have discussed has deepened our understanding of a particular area, but one cannot avoid concluding that the overall improvement to microeconomic theory is not equal to the sum of its parts; in some ways, an improved part may even be a step backward for the whole. A primary example is the significant shift in the method of argumentation from contextual analysis to noncontextual analysis that has accompanied the expression of formalist economics. Contextual analysis assumes that the reader will understand the nature of the decision maker and the institutional structure.

For example, say you are talking about a businessperson. Contextual analysis assumes an institutional structure that limits choice. The businessperson might not maximize profit but might instead set certain sales goals and minimum profits or use cost plus pricing procedures. On the basis of contextual analysis, if economists knew this was how decisions were made, they would not need to relate these procedures to first principles. Because such knowledge is taken as given, only the particular context that the writer is introducing need be considered. Most classical analysis was contextual; most modern analysis is noncontextual.

Contextual analysis is efficient in the sense that it avoids deducing all actions from first principles, but it is also subject to misinterpretation if the assumptions of the writer do not correspond with those of the reader. Incompletely explored assumptions can lead to significant misunderstanding. This is why economics evolved to noncontextual analysis, which avoids the problems of contextual analysis by spelling out each assumption and relating all actions back to first principles. But because of the need to fully specify the assumptions and to take nothing for granted, noncontextual analysis creates a danger of its own: the analysis becomes lost in itself. This is what some critics argue has happened to economics.

To see more clearly the problem that can develop from noncontextual argumentation, let us consider the underlying theory of modeling. A model is a simplified representation of reality. It makes an enormous number of simplifying assumptions, but if it is a good model the incorrect assumptions on both sides will cancel each other out. Ideally, as a model is expanded—if it is to remain a good representation of reality—there must be an equal marginal relaxation of assumptions so that the balance remains. But the decision as to what an equal marginal relaxation of assumptions actually is can be made only contextually, with knowledge of institutions and reality, because reality is ultimately what the model is designed to describe. This skill is exactly what is no longer taught. The models that have been developed do not allow equal marginal relaxations of the assumptions; thus, their results do not accord with reality. More complicated models do not necessarily add more insight; because the assumptions of the model are often interrelated, relaxing one assumption without relaxing the opposing interrelated assumption often yields a poorer, not a better, model.

With formalization has also come a loss of applicability. In Marshallian economics, the focus was on applicability; economics was seen as an engine of analysis. Modern formalist economics often gets so lost in specifics—relating the analysis back to first principles—that the applications are lost or become irrelevant because the analysis violates the law of significant digits. It is like carrying out multiplication to ten digits when in the application one is going to round off to the nearest whole number.

Many critics believe that modern economics has lost sight of which questions are important and which are not, and that economists spend inordinate amounts of time discussing (in a highly abstract, formal manner) the modern-day equivalent of how many angels can dance on the head of a pin. Kenneth Boulding (1910–) expressed the problem somewhat differently when he called modern economics "the celestial mechanics of a nonexistent world."

This loss of applicability was inevitable; as the tools of microeconomics have become more and more complicated, so have the areas of inquiry. The training of economists focuses so much on mathematics and techniques that sensitivity and workable rules of thumb for applying the analysis to reality must be discarded. Economists today are forced to concentrate on one subarea and one set of tools. Thus, the formalist approach has led to a breakdown of communication among economists. A search theorist will often have little to say to a social choice theorist, who in turn will have little to say to a general equilibrium theorist. The tools they use and the questions they ask are different.

Critics argue that in the absence of a set of general directions of inquiry, sociological factors direct the profession: economists ask the questions that meet their own immediate needs, questions that can be most easily developed into articles and thereby lead to tenure and promotion, not the questions whose solutions are most relevant to society as a whole. Modern microeconomics has resolved problems, but not in the way that best fits reality. Rather, it has done so in a way that best fits the mathematics.

All this is not to say that the formalist revolution should never have taken place. There were serious problems with Marshallian economics. But there were also advantages to the Marshallian approach, and these were lost. The current goal is not to abandon the advances but to find a way to integrate the best of both approaches.

SUMMARY

Our treatment of developments in modern micro theory has not included all the additions to present-day theory. For example, we haven't discussed the many improvements made in the theory of supply and costs that remove some of the internal inconsistencies in the Marshallian formulation. Nor have we presented the theoretical developments in various applied fields such as international trade, labor, and public finance, which fall into the domain of micro theory. Our treatment has been selective, principally addressing (1) the increased formalization of economic theory, and (2) topics in the theory of monopolistic competition, demand theory, and welfare theory. Nonetheless, the chapter conveys a sense of the direction micro theory has taken.

During the period from 1890 to the 1930s, microeconomists worked to both improve the logical structure of micro theory laid down by Marshall and apply the Marshallian apparatus to questions of economic welfare. Some economists during this period, unconvinced by Marshall's arguments against the use of mathematics in economics, advanced an even more rigorous theoretical structure for micro theory. The most important advocates of this new mathematical economics were Vilfredo Pareto in Europe, F. Y. Edgeworth in England, and Irving Fisher in the United States.

The most fundamental contribution in the period from 1930 to the present was more methodological than theoretical; we have called this the formalization revolution in microeconomics. Economists soon found that the increased mathematical precision they sought could not be achieved within the Marshallian framework; so modern microeconomic theory rejected Marshall's attempt to blend theory and institutions in a partial equilibrium framework. Instead, they adopted a general equilibrium framework that was almost devoid of contextual argument and analysis. Although a number of theorists from Europe and the United States have spearheaded these modern developments, the most important has been Paul Samuelson. E. H. Chamberlin's theory of monopolistic competition, on the other hand, runs counter to the increased formalization of economic theory. Though rich in contextual argument, it could not be used in a mathematical or general equilibrium framework.

Although some within the profession are alarmed by the increased formalization of economic reasoning over the past fifty years, the mainstream microeconomics taught and researched at most graduate schools in the United States is now highly mathematical. The study of economic history, the history of economic theory, and institutions in the applied fields has almost ceased.

Key Terms

formalist revolution	Giffen good
Pareto optimal criteria	revealed preference approach
monopolistic competition	state preference theory
neoclassical political economy	characteristic analysis
Lagrangian multipliers	welfare economics
shadow price	compensating variation approach
comparative static interpretation	social welfare function
optimal control theory	externalities

Questions for Review, Discussion, and Research

1. Explain some of the reasons why many in the profession left Marshallian economics and focused on Walrasian economics.
2. Is it possible that Marshallian economics may make a comeback? Why or why not?
3. In what four ways has modern economics modified neoclassical economics?
4. Edward Leamer, an economist at UCLA, has suggested that the profession should distinguish between a mathematical economist and an economic theorist. What do you think he means?
5. What does Paul Samuelson mean by a meaningful theorem? Are there other interpretations?
6. The domain of economic reasoning is expanding to the other social sciences. Is this a gain, or a loss?
7. What is the revealed preference approach, and what implications does it have for utility theory?
8. What are some of the limitations of modern welfare economics?
9. Which is preferable: contextual or noncontextual analysis?
10. Why did the monopolistic revolution die out, and why is it re-emerging?
11. That absent-minded professor is back with another job for you. This time, she's doing an article on reconstructing general equilibrium theory and remembers that Paul Samuelson had an interesting statement:

    > The concept of an equilibrium system outlined above is applicable as well to the case of a simple variable as to so-called general equilibrium involving thousands of variables. Logically the determination of output of a given form under pure competition is precisely the same as the simultaneous determination of thousand of prices and quantities.

    Alas, she does not remember where she found this quotation. Your assignment is to find the full bibliographic citation.

Suggested Readings

Backhouse, Roger. *A History of Modern Economic Analysis.* New York: Basil Blackwell, 1985.

Becker, Gary. *A Treatise on the Family.* Cambridge, Mass.: Harvard University Press, 1981.

Chamberlin, Edward H. *The Theory of Monopolistic Competition.* Cambridge, Mass: Harvard University Press, 1962.

Clapham, J. H. "Of Empty Economic Boxes." *Economic Journal,* 32 (1922), 305–314.

Cournot, Antoine Augustin. *Researches into the Mathematical Principles of the Theory of Wealth.* 1838. Trans. Irving Fisher. New York and London: Macmillan, 1927.

Friedman, Milton. "The Marshallian Demand Theory." *Journal of Political Economy,* 57 (December 1953), 463–495.

———. "The Methodology of Positive Economics." In *Essays in Positive Economics.* Chicago: University of Chicago Press, 1953.

Hicks, John R. *Value and Capital.* Oxford: Clarendon Press, 1946.

Hirsch, Abraham, and Neil de Marchi. *Milton Friedman: Economics in Theory and Practice.* Ann Arbor: University of Michigan Press, 1990.

Lancaster, Kevin J. "A New Approach to Consumer Theory." *Journal of Political Economy,* 74 (April 1966), 132–157.

Little, I. M. D. *A Critique of Welfare Economics.* London: Oxford University Press, 1957.

Musgrave, Richard A. *The Theory of Public Finance.* London: McGraw-Hill, 1959.

Reder, Melvin W. "Chicago Economics: Permanence and Change." *Journal of Economic Literature,* 1 (March 1982), 1–38.

Robinson, Joan. *The Economics of Imperfect Competition.* London: Macmillan, 1933.

Samuels, Warren. "The Chicago School of Political Economy: A Constructive Critique." In *The Chicago School of Political Economy.* Ed. Warren Samuels. New Brunswick, N.J.: Transactions Publications, 1992.

Samuelson, Paul A. *Foundations of Economic Analysis.* Cambridge, Mass.: Harvard University Press, 1955.

Sraffa, Piero. "The Laws of Returns under Competitive Conditions." *Economic Journal,* 36 (December 1926), 536–550.

16 The Development of Modern Macroeconomic Thought

"Keynes said some things that were new and some things that were true; unfortunately the things that were new weren't true, and the things that were true weren't new."

—Frank Knight

IMPORTANT WRITERS

Interest in macroeconomic issues has fluctuated throughout the years, reaching its nadir around the turn of the century. The attitude of the economics profession toward macroeconomic thought at that time could be characterized as one of benign neglect. The macroeconomic thinking that did exist, moreover, was somewhat confused. Alfred Marshall, who had codified and organized microeconomics in his *Principles of Economics,* always intended to do the same for macroeconomics, but he never did. He limited his discussion of macroeconomics to a determination of the general level of prices, as did F. W. Taussig in his introductory textbook that was popular during the first part of the twentieth century, and F. B. Garver and Alvin H. Hansen in their leading book of the 1930s. This is in striking contrast to the typical modern text, half of which may concern macroeconomic issues.

HISTORICAL FORERUNNERS OF MODERN MACROECONOMICS

Mercantilists specifically wanted to understand the forces that determine the capacity of an economy to produce goods and services and to ascertain whether the actual level of output reached the potential level. Many mercantilists perceived a fundamental conflict between private and public interest and therefore believed that the economy would fail to achieve its output potential unless the government intervened. Their argument was twofold: first, following Jean Bodin, they believed that private interest led to monopoly and that monopoly restricted output; second, they believed that when individuals either saved or bought foreign goods, a shortage of demand for domestic goods ensued, which weakened the economy. The mercantilist position was that the government should regulate domestic and foreign trade so that the economy would show a balance-of-payments surplus and increase the country's gold, which served as its money supply.

As mercantilism evolved into classical economics, attitudes toward government intervention changed dramatically. Unlike the early mercantilists, Adam Smith believed that competitive market forces were sufficiently strong that private interests, as though led by an "invisible hand," would be directed to work for the public interest. The economy would reach its output potential only if the government followed a laissez faire policy. Smith's analysis in favor of laissez faire was a contextual argument made in view of feasible alternatives. He agreed with the mercantilists that monopolies reduced output, but he asserted that the methods intended to control them—government control of trade and allocation of monopolies—made matters worse, not better. Thus, he argued that the preferable policy was to rely on laissez faire and competition to bring about utilization of resources as fully as possible.

The mercantilist *underconsumption arguments* came under much heavier attack by Smith and other classical economists. They argued that savings would automatically be translated into investment spending, because a decision to save is a decision to invest. The proposition that a laissez faire economy would automatically produce full utilization of resources was called Say's Law, and it became a central element of pre-Keynesian economic thinking. Classical economists also attacked the mercantilist argument for increasing the stock of gold by running a trade surplus, contending that the wealth of a nation is measured not in precious metals but by real output, and that a country would be better off allowing free trade, thereby gaining the advantage of foreign competition.

Classical economists, particularly Smith and J. S. Mill, agreed that market forces did not work perfectly but maintained that the market worked better than the alternatives. With the exception of Thomas Malthus, it was left from 1800 through 1930 to such heterodox, nonmainstream economists as Karl Marx, Mikhail Tugan-Baranowsky, and J. A. Hobson to assert that the economy might have an aggregate, or macroeconomic, problem. The classical conviction that markets could be relied upon to control the economy shifted the focus of economic inquiry from monetary and financial forces to real forces, and the classical analysis of macroeconomic issues generally accepted a dichotomy between real and nominal forces.

Quantity Theory of Money

Orthodox theory maintained an interest in at least one macro question: what determines the general level of prices? A few orthodox theorists also paid some attention to the question of stability, in their study of business cycles. First let us examine the attempts to explain the forces determining the general level of prices; that is, the forces determining the value of money. Then we will examine pre-Keynesian business cycle theory.

One way in which orthodox theory addressed the question of the value of money, or the general level of prices, was by utilizing the supply-and-demand approach developed in micro theory. The supply of money was assumed to be determined by the monetary authorities, so some orthodox economists contended that the basic issues to be analyzed were on the side of demand. The household and firm are assumed to be rational and to have a demand for money to be used for various purposes. Walras, Menger, and others developed a supply-and-demand analysis to explain the value of money, but the most famous of these theories is probably the one developed by Marshall, which has become known as the Cambridge cash-balance version of the quantity theory of money.

The first clear statement of the *quantity theory of money* was made by David Hume in 1752. This theory, as it came down through the literature, held that the general level of prices depended upon the quantity of money in circulation. Marshall's version of the quantity theory was an attempt to give microeconomic underpinnings to the macro theory that prices and the quantity of money varied directly. He did this by elaborating a theory of household and firm behavior to explain the demand for money. Marshall reasoned that households and firms would desire to hold in cash balances a fraction of their money income. If M is money (currency plus demand deposits), PY is money income, and k is the proportion of their income that households and firms desire to hold in the form of money, then the fundamental cash-balance equation is

$$M = kPY$$

Because Marshall accepted Say's Law, full employment is assumed. An increase in the quantity of money, assuming k remains constant, will lead to an increase in money income, PY. Because full employment is assumed, an increase in the quantity of money will result in higher prices and a consequent increase in money income; real income, however, will not change. Decreases in the quantity of money will result in a fall in money income as prices fall; real income again will remain constant. We shall not examine the many different aspects of Marshall's formulation; the important point is that Marshall's version of the quantity theory made an attempt to integrate the microeconomic behavior of maximizing firms and households with the macro question of the general level of prices.

A group of economists, the most prominent being the American Irving Fisher (1869–1947), developed another form of the quantity theory known as the transactions version. However, they showed little interest in finding a micro foundation for the macro analysis of the general level of prices. In this version,

$$MV = PT$$

where M is the quantity of money, V is the velocity of money, P is a measure of the price level, and T is the volume of transactions.

Although these two approaches have important differences, they have one element in common: they were both designed to explain the forces that determine the general price level. They were not used to explain the level of real income, which was assumed to be at full employment and fixed by nonmonetary forces in the economy. Knut Wicksell (1851–1926) was not satisfied with the quantity theory of money because it failed to explain "why the monetary or pecuniary demand for goods exceeds or falls short of the supply of goods in given conditions."[1] Wicksell tried to develop a so-called income approach to explain the general level of prices; that is, to develop a theory of money that explains fluctuations in income as well as fluctuations in price levels. Although he was not successful in developing a complete theory of income determination, he did manage to state a reasonably complete theory of the forces determining the level of investment expenditures. J. M. Keynes (1883–1946), a student of Alfred Marshall, used the basic Cambridge cash-balance version of the quantity theory of money in his *Tract on Monetary Reform* (1923), which was seen as the most up-to-date statement of the quantity theory in the 1920s. By 1930, however, he had moved to an income approach to the theory of money:

> Formerly I was attracted by this line of approach. But it now seems to me that the merging together of all different sorts of transactions—income, business and

[1] Knut Wicksell, *Lectures on Political Economy* (London: Routledge and Kegan Paul, 1935), II, 160 (originally published in Swedish in 1901 and 1906).

financial—which may be taking place only causes confusion, and that we cannot get any real insight into the price-making process without bringing in the rate of interest and the distinctions between incomes and profits and between savings and investment.

The "Real-balances" Equation discussed above is descended from a method of approach long familiar to those who have heard Professors Marshall and Pigou in the lecture-rooms of Cambridge. Since this method has not been employed elsewhere in recent times I call it the "Cambridge" Quantity Equation; but it has a much longer descent, being derived from Petty, Locke, Cantillon and Adam Smith.[2]

Thus, in 1930 Keynes broke with the classical-neoclassical "traditional method of setting out from the total quantity of money irrespective of the purposes on which it is employed"[3] and developed an analysis based on income flows. Several other writers employed the income approach, but none of them (including Keynes in his *Treatise* and Wicksell) attempted to formulate a theory explaining the determination of the level of income, nor did they reject the proposition of Say's Law that the automatic forces of the market would produce full employment.

Business Cycle Theory

Although fluctuations in business activity and in the level of income and employment had been occurring since the beginning of merchant capitalism and were acknowledged by orthodox theorists, economists made no systematic attempts to analyze either depression or the business cycle until the 1890s. Heterodox theorists, the most important of whom was Marx, had pursued these issues with greater vigor. But Marx's works were largely ignored by orthodox theory. Thus, until the last decade of the nineteenth century, orthodox economic theory consisted of a fairly well developed theoretical micro structure explaining the allocation and distribution of scarce resources, a macro theory explaining the forces determining the general level of prices, and a loose set of notions concerning economic growth. Prior to 1890, orthodox "work on depressions and cycles had been peripheral and tangential."[4]

One major exception to this generalization is the work of Clement Juglar (1819–1905), who in 1862 published *Des crises commerciales et de leur rétour périodique en France, en Angleterre et aux États-Unis*. The second edition of this work, published in 1889, was considerably enlarged with historical and statistical material. Juglar is a spiritual predecessor of W. C. Mitchell in that he did not build a deductive theory of the business cycle, but rather collected historical and statistical material that he approached inductively. His main contribution was his

[2] J. M. Keynes, *A Treatise on Money* (New York: Harcourt Brace, 1930), I, 229.

[3] *Ibid.,* I, 134.

[4] Alvin Hansen, *Business Cycles and National Income* (New York: W. W. Norton, 1951), p. 225.

statement that the cycle was a result not of forces outside the economic system but of forces within it. He saw the cycle as containing three phases that repeated themselves in continuous order:

> The periods of prosperity, crisis, liquidation, although affected by the fortunate or
> unfortunate accidents in the life of peoples, are not the result of chance events,
> but arise out of the behavior, the activities, and above all out of the saving habits
> of the population, and the way they employ the capital and credit available.[5]

Although Juglar's work initiated the study of the business cycle, the modern orthodox macro analysis of economic fluctuations is grounded in the writings of a Russian, Mikhail Tugan-Baranowsky (1865–1919). His book *Industrial Crises in England* was first published in Russian in 1894; German and French editions followed. After reviewing past attempts to explain the business cycle, he pronounced them all unsatisfactory. The chief intellectual influences on Tugan-Baranowsky were Juglar and Marx, particularly Marx. Tugan-Baranowsky's main contribution to our understanding of the business cycle was his statement of two principles: (1) that the economic fluctuations are inherent in the capitalist system because they are a result of forces within the system, and (2) that the major causes of the business cycle are to be found in the forces determining investment spending. The modern Keynesian analysis of income determination, with its emphasis on the inherent instability of capitalism and the role of investment, runs from Marx through Tugan-Baranowsky, Juglar, Spiethoff, Schumpeter, Cassel, Robertson, Wicksell, and Fisher on the orthodox side; and from Marx, Veblen, Hobson, Mitchell, and others on the heterodox side.

The history of the part of macroeconomics that addresses forces determining the level of income is one of a number of individual considerations of cyclical fluctuation that were overwhelmed by the logic of Say's Law. Some of the mercantilists, the physiocrats, and a host of heterodox economists who followed had suggested earlier that there were forces inherent in capitalism that would bring about depressions, but their theories were almost universally repudiated by Say's Law. Even mainstream economists' consideration of cycles, such as Jevons's sunspot cycle, were generally disregarded. After 1900 more serious work was done on business cycles by orthodox theorists, but curiously enough this work existed alongside a continuing fundamental belief that the long-run equilibrium position of the economy would provide full employment. Thus, we see economists such as Friedrich Hayek (1889–1992) exploring problems of aggregate fluctuation as a coordination failure while maintaining a solid belief in the self-equilibrating properties of the market economy. No one, neither heterodox nor orthodox, had been able to challenge this belief, because no one had built a theory of income determination to show that equilibrium was possible at less than full employment. When J. M. Keynes in 1936 developed a theory arguing that equilibrium at less

---

[5] Clement Juglar, *Des crises commerciales,* 2nd ed. (Paris: Guillaumin, 1889), p. xix, quoted in T. W. Hutchison, *A Review of Economic Doctrines 1870–1929* (Oxford: Clarendon Press, 1953), p. 372.

than full employment could exist, a new phase of orthodox macro theory commenced. The developments that followed and Keynes's contributions to them are discussed in the remainder of this chapter.

Neoclassical Macroeconomics

Why did Marshall, and others using his framework, have a problem with macro-economics? The reason is inherent in the partial equilibrium nature of supply-and-demand analysis. It analyzes a specific market, holding everything else constant. To use supply and demand curves correctly, one must assume that everything in the market being analyzed remains constant except price and quantity. But because all other things cannot be assumed to remain constant in an entire economy, Marshall's framework is inappropriate. The only way to extend the arguments from partial to general equilibrium is to use complicated mathematics or simply to have faith; early twentieth-century neoclassical economists used little of the former and much of the latter, especially when the aggregate economy seemed to be working.

A few economists anticipated the problems to come. In the early 1900s two Swedish economists, Gunnar Myrdal (1898–1987) and Erik Lindahl (1891–1960), working from the writings of Knut Wicksell, examined the possibility of an inequality between savings and investment. They argued that a difference between ex-ante and ex-post savings and investment could significantly affect the aggregate economy. Although their work had been done in the 1920s and early 1930s, it was not translated into English until the late 1930s, after the Depression had necessitated a reconsideration of the problem of unemployment and other macroeconomic issues by the British neoclassicals.

The work done by British economists influenced by these events is now called the disequilibrium monetarist approach, or neoclassical monetary theory. Its most notable representative, Dennis Robertson (1890–1963), maintained that there could be temporary monetary disturbances in which the flow of savings would not equal the flow of investment. Although he accepted Say's Law for the long run, Robertson contended that disequilibrium could occur because individuals had to make plans before knowing the plans of others, so their actions in the market would not be coordinated. These temporary disturbances would cause fluctuations in real income. Ultimately the economy would right itself, but there could be a sequence of time periods within which the interconnected flows would be in disequilibrium.

In their research, these disequilibrium monetary theorists sought to determine exactly how individuals' adjustments affected the aggregate economy. Robertson considered a "sequence equilibrium" in which individuals *progressively* adjusted their plans; then he analyzed a series of these sequence disequilibria in order to discover how the long-run forces pushing toward equilibrium interacted with the short-run disequilibrium forces. His model allowed for temporary unemployment but held that unemployment caused by too little investment spending would be eliminated in time. It followed that something other than lack of investment would be the cause of extended unemployment. Robertson's painstaking theoretical work became so enormously complicated that few economists of his time read it. Modern researchers have rediscovered him, however, and his analysis has provided the basis of some recent work in macroeconomic theory.

Another economist working with Robertson to extend neoclassical monetary theory was J. M. Keynes. His work focused on potential short-run problems with the quantity theory. In his two-volume *Treatise on Money,* Keynes argued that the velocity of money could fluctuate in the short run and that there would be temporary unemployment as it did. Such temporary unemployment was not inconsistent with Say's Law, which stated only that these problems would adjust in the long run.

Most neoclassical economists of this period were not disequilibrium monetary theorists; rather, they subscribed to a different view of the cause of unemployment. Using a supply-and-demand approach set largely in a partial equilibrium framework, they focused on disequilibrium in labor markets as the cause of any extended unemployment, believing that the real wage must be above a market-clearing wage in order for unemployment to occur. Something had to be preventing the real wage from falling, and many neoclassical economists considered unions the culprit. Their approach to eliminating unemployment was to reduce union power and let markets lower real wages and increase employment.

The Depression of the 1930s changed the context within which society and economists viewed the market. Prior to that time, the neoclassical arguments in favor of laissez faire had been based not only on economic theory but also on a set of philosophical and political judgments about government. The general political orientation of almost all individuals except radicals in the early 1900s was against major government involvement in the economy. Within that context the concepts of many government programs we now take for granted, such as Social Security and unemployment insurance, would have seemed extreme. But with the onset of the Depression, attitudes began to change. Many people felt that if the free market could lead to such economic distress as existed during the Depression, it was time to start considering alternatives. As economists began to analyze the aggregate economy in greater detail, many became less confident of their policy prescriptions and much more aware of the shortcomings of neoclassical theory. Consequently, economists began to advocate a variety of policy proposals to address unemployment that were inconsistent with their mainstream neoclassical views. In the early 1930s, for example, A. C. Pigou in England and several University of Chicago economists in the United States advocated public works programs and deficits as a means of fighting unemployment.

KEYNESIAN MACROECONOMICS

Modern macroeconomics developed within the context of economic upheaval, concern over unemployment, and a questioning of the underlying neoclassical theory. A history of modern macroeconomics must begin with a consideration of Keynes, the economist most responsible for changing the focus of economics.

Keynes the Man

John Maynard Keynes's father, J. N. Keynes, was an important economist in his own right, but his son's accomplishments quickly eclipsed his own. In this and in several other ways J. M. Keynes's life is like that of J. S. Mill. Both had fathers who were contemporaries and friends of brilliant economists: James Mill was a friend of David Ricardo, and J. N. Keynes was a friend of Alfred Marshall. Both the younger Keynes and the younger Mill received the high-quality education typically provided to children of intellectuals, an education that equipped their innately brilliant minds to break new ground and to persuade others through the force of their writing. Both Mill and Keynes rejected the policy implications of their fathers' economics and proceeded in new directions. But here the similarities end, for J. S. Mill was unable to break completely with the theoretical structure of his father and Ricardo; ultimately, he constructed a halfway house between classical and neoclassical theory. Keynes's break with the past—that is, with the laissez faire tradition running from Smith through Ricardo, J. S. Mill, and Marshall—was more complete. Although he was familiar with the basic Marshallian partial equilibrium analysis, he constructed a new theoretical structure to address the aggregate economy that had significant effects on both economic theory and policy.

Keynes does not fit the stereotype of the intellectually narrow twentieth-century economist. He was criticized, in fact, for devoting too little of his time to economic theory and spreading his interests too broadly. Even as a student at Eton and Cambridge he displayed this proclivity to pursue a wide range of interests; hence he came to be known as a dilettante. His education completed, he entered the British government's India Office as a civil servant, where he remained for two years before returning to Cambridge. He was never exclusively an academic. His continuing interest in economic policy led him to take a number of government posts throughout his life. He was active in business affairs both for himself and as bursar of King's College, and his ability in business is manifested by the fact that his net worth rose from near bankruptcy in 1920 to more than $2 million by the time of his death in 1946. Keynes was interested in theater, literature, and the ballet; he married a ballerina and associated with a group of London intellectuals known as the Bloomsbury group, which included such notables as Clive Bell, E. M. Forster, Lytton Strachey, and Virginia Woolf. His unique mixture of talents enabled him to be an accomplished mathematician as an undergraduate, to write a book on probability theory, and to be a powerful and effective prose stylist, which is evident in the sheer literary mastery of both his *Economic Consequences of the Peace* and his essays, collected into two books as *Essays in Persuasion* and *Essays in Biography*.

The single most important aspect of Keynes the economist is his orientation toward policy. He attended the Versailles peace conference as a representative of the British Treasury Department but resigned abruptly in 1919; he was disgusted by the terms of the Versailles treaty, which imposed on Germany large reparations that he thought could never be paid. He received international acclaim for his criticism of the terms of the treaty, published in 1919 in his *Economic Conse-*

quences of the Peace. In 1940 he wrote *How to Pay for the War,* and in 1943 he advanced a proposal called the Keynes Plan for an international monetary authority to be put into effect after World War II. As head of the British delegation to Bretton Woods, he was instrumental in the formation of the International Monetary Fund and the International Bank. But his most important contributions to policy and theory are contained in his book *The General Theory* (1936), which created modern macroeconomics and still forms the basis of much of what is taught in undergraduate macroeconomics. Paul Samuelson captured its importance when, reflecting on the Keynesian era, he wrote, "*The General Theory* caught most economists under the age of thirty-five with the unexpected virulence of a disease first attacking and decimating an isolated tribe of South Sea Islanders."[6]

The Contextual Nature of *The General Theory*

Possibly no book in economic theory has a more presumptuous first chapter than Keynes's *General Theory.* To be sure, other economists had proclaimed their own originality and brilliance, but Keynes did it with such force that it seemed convincing. This lack of modesty apparently went back to Keynes's youth. When he took the civil service exam upon graduation from college and did not receive the top score in economics, his response was, "I evidently knew more about economics than my examiners."[7] While Keynes was working on *The General Theory,* he wrote to George Bernard Shaw that he was writing a new book that would revolutionize the way in which the world thinks about economic problems. The first chapter of *The General Theory* is one paragraph long. Here Keynes simply states that his new theory is a general theory in the sense that previous theory is a special case to be placed within his more general framework. By "previous theory" Keynes meant both classical and neoclassical economics, which he defined as the economics of Ricardo as it pertains to Say's Law, and of those who followed in this belief: J. S. Mill, Marshall, Edgeworth, and Pigou.

Although the single most important aspect of Keynes the economist was his policy orientation, his most important work, *The General Theory,* in spite of its policy overtones, is essentially a theoretical book whose major audience was to be found among professional economists. Keynes wrote, "This book is chiefly addressed to my fellow economists. I hope it will be intelligible to others. But its main purpose is to deal with difficult questions of theory, and only in the second place with the application of this theory to practice."[8]

We can reconcile this seeming contradiction by understanding the way in which Keynes used theory. Many economic theories are what might be called noncontextual; that is, developed in an institutional void. Such theories are best understood by deductive logic; they begin with first principles from which conclusions

---

[6] Paul Samuelson, "The General Theory: 1946," in *Keynes's General Theory: Reports of Three Decades,* ed. Robert Lekachman (New York: St. Martins Press, 1964), p. 315.

[7] R. F. Harrod, *The Life of John Maynard Keynes* (New York: Harcourt Brace, 1952), p. 121.

[8] J. M. Keynes, *The General Theory of Employment, Interest, and Money* (London: Macmillan and Co., 1936), p. 3.

are deduced on the basis of carefully stated assumptions. In making these assumptions, one does not take reality into account but tries instead to understand the inherent logic of the interactions among the assumptions. Such theories might be called analytic theories. General equilibrium analysis, done correctly, is an *analytic theory*. Because the assumptions are inevitably far removed from reality, drawing policy conclusions from broad-ranging analytic theories is extremely complicated.

Keynes used a different kind of theory, one that might be called "realytic," because it is a compromise between a realistic and an analytic approach. A *realytic theory* is contextual; it blends inductive information about the economy with deductive logic. Reality guides the choice of assumptions. Realytic theories are less inherently satisfying; but because they correspond closely to reality, it is easier to draw policy conclusions from them. Keynes did not start from first principles in *The General Theory* but instead used reality to guide his choice of assumptions. Thus, although he concentrated on theory, he never lost sight of its policy implications.

An example might make the distinction between realytic and analytic theories more clear. Keynes assumed prices and wages to be relatively constant without attempting to justify those assumptions. Although he briefly discussed in *The General Theory* the implications of flexible prices, arguing that they do not solve the unemployment problem, a thorough consideration of their implications was of little concern to him; for the problem at hand—what to do about unemployment— it was reasonable to assume fixed wages and prices. He could do this by using his realytic approach, whereas a truly analytic model would not have permitted such assumptions. Keynes left it to others to provide an analytic basis for his theory. Much of the subsequent development of macroeconomic thinking has been an attempt to provide an analytic base for macroeconomics.

Keynes began working on *The General Theory* immediately after completing his two-volume *Treatise on Money,* which made use of the quantity theory of money to discuss cyclical fluctuations. In *The General Theory* Keynes abandoned this approach, much to the chagrin of his colleague Dennis Robertson, with whom he had previously worked closely. He adopted instead the simple, new approach that became the core of undergraduate macroeconomics and remains so today. To provide himself with a heftier target, Keynes lumped together the neoclassical disequilibrium monetary approach and the earlier classical approach, exaggerated their beliefs, and called them collectively "classical theory." In so doing he created a caricature of classical thought that emphasized its differences from his new approach but concealed many of its subtleties.

The Demand for Output as a Whole

One of the best ways to appreciate Keynes's contribution is to look at him through the eyes of one of his early converts, Abba Lerner:

> We had heard that some very strange things were happening in Cambridge. We couldn't quite make out what it was, something about the elasticity of demand for

output as a whole, and we knew that was nonsense, because we were brought up properly on Marshall, and we knew all about elasticity and demand curves. We knew that if you drew a demand curve you had to assume all the other prices were fixed; otherwise you wouldn't know what the demand curve for this item was. If you were to draw a demand curve for another item (for example, say you wanted to look at the consumer surplus which you could enjoy from being able to buy some item for less than you would have been willing to pay), it was your duty to wipe out the first demand curve because the first one was allowing the price to vary. You had to have the prices fixed for everything else if you were going to draw a demand curve. Knowing this, we knew that demand curves, demand and elasticity, referred only to partial analysis, and, yet, somehow in Cambridge they must have known that and still, very perversely, they were talking about elasticity of demand for output as a whole.

Well, Joan Robinson started explaining it to us, but we didn't understand her, and so we arranged to have a weekend meeting symbolically at a place called Bishop's Stortford, halfway between London and Cambridge. There was a London contingent and a Cambridge contingent, and we spent a whole weekend trying to find out what they were doing. Joan Robinson was in charge. She was aided by a few other people from Cambridge and Oxford. Her husband [Austin Robinson] dropped in for a while; R. F. Kahn came once, James Meade was also there. I think there were one or two others but I've forgotten now who they were. Mainly, however, it was Joan Robinson in charge, and as we would try to understand, she'd say, "Yes, that's right; now you're getting the idea. . . . No, no; now you've gone backwards." When the weekend was over we still didn't know what they were talking about. However, we were sufficiently impressed to publish an article by Joan Robinson, which we didn't understand, on the demand for output as a whole. This was the first we saw of the Cambridge idea.

The weekend meeting had not been too successful; we still couldn't understand each other—at least we couldn't understand them. They were confident that we were either just very stupid or backward—and we thought they were crazy, obviously doing something that didn't make any sense, but we couldn't quite put our finger on what was wrong.[9]

Why was it so difficult for good Marshallian economists to understand Keynes's argument? To see the problem, consider Figure 16.1, in which we draw a normal demand and supply curve. Because it is partial equilibrium analysis, the price on the vertical axis is a relative price (relative to the general price level). Quantity of good per-unit time is on the horizontal axis. Partial equilibrium supply and demand curves are drawn on the assumption that all other prices and income (as well as everything else) remain constant. If that assumption does not hold, the partial disequilibrium adjustment mechanism and the analysis breaks down. Let us say, for example, that price is P_o, quantity demand is Q_d, and quantity supplied

[9] This statement is from an unpublished transcript of a recording of a Boston University seminar (April 24, 1972) in which Alvin Hansen and Abba Lerner were discussing their roles in the Keynesian revolution.

Figure 16.1   Partial Equilibrium Adjustment to Equilibrium

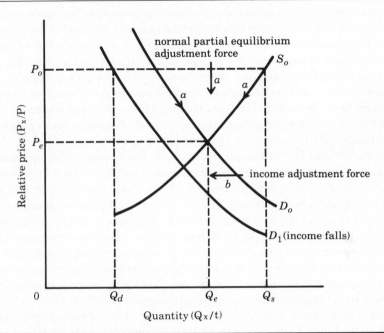

is Q_s. The standard adjustment mechanism is the following: because quantity supplied is greater than quality demanded, the relative price of good X falls. The process continues until equilibrium price, P_e, and quantity, Q_e, are reached.

Now consider what happens if all other things do not remain equal. Specifically, let us say that a decrease in quantity supplied lowers income. Because demand depends upon income as well as price, this means that as quantity supplied falls, the demand curve shifts back to, say, D_1. Now there are two disequilibrium adjustment forces, the price adjustment force (*a*) and the income adjustment force (*b*). As you can see, these forces are pushing in opposite directions. The relative price effect (the movement down along the demand curve) brings us closer to equilibrium, but the income effect shifts the demand curve to the left, moving us further from equilibrium. Without knowing the relative magnitudes of the shift, we cannot say whether an equilibrium will be achieved. Moreover, even if an equilibrium will be achieved, supply-and-demand analysis does not tell us what it will be, because the final equilibrium will not be at P_e and Q_e but at the intersection of the shifted demand curve and the supply curve.

What happens if we use supply-and-demand analysis to discuss the aggregate economy? Because the analysis is of the aggregate economy, there is no relative price effect (unless one assumes prices flexible and wages constant, which Keynes did not assume in his simple model). There is only a general price level, so it is unclear what the aggregate equivalent to the partial equilibrium supply and demand curves will be. One way to shed light on the assumed nature of the aggregate equilibrium would be to ask the same questions that are asked in the partial equilibrium case: what will happen to quantity supplied if the price level rises? The classicals' answer is that nothing will change, assuming as they did that there is a dichotomy between the real and nominal sectors. Thus, the supply curve will be perfectly inelastic. If we now invoke Say's Law (supply creates its own demand), we can also draw an aggregate demand curve coincidental with the aggregate supply curve. The two curves are not only perfectly inelastic, they are also coincidental at the full employment level of income, as in panel (a) of Figure 16.2.

Because the two curves are coincidental, the price level is indeterminate; but that indeterminacy is consistent with classical thought, in which the price level was determined by the quantity theory of money. Panel (b) of Figure 16.2 shows how the price level is determined. The price level is on the vertical axis, and the money supply is on the horizontal axis. Panel (b) graphs the relationship between money and prices as it exists in the quantity theory, assuming a constant velocity. When the money supply increases, the price level increases. Figure 16.2 is the classical analysis in a nutshell. The aggregate real economy is always in equilibrium. The price level is determined by the quantity of money, and Say's Law ensures that real equilibrium is at full employment.

Good Marshallians understood this argument. That is why Lerner and his cohorts knew it was foolish to think about a demand curve for aggregate output.

Figure 16.2   Classical Aggregate Equilibrium

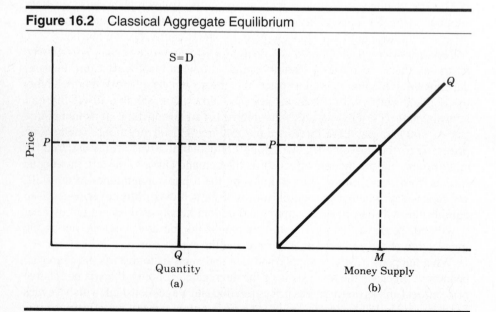

Keynes and Joan Robinson also knew this argument, but the demand curve for output as a whole that they were talking about was no ordinary partial equilibrium demand curve relating relative price and quantity. It is based on the consumption, investment, and government spending functions.

To understand how Keynes's aggregate demand analysis differs from a partial equilibrium demand analysis, it is helpful to consider Keynes's objection to classical analysis. Keynes's argument with the classicals can be understood by asking what would happen if for some reason planned demand did not equal planned supply. In this scenario the economy would be in a position such as that represented in Figure 16.3, rather than in panel (a) of Figure 16.2. What might bring about an equilibrium between aggregate supply and aggregate demand? In this case, as you can see in Figure 16.3, a fall in the price level, which could be brought about only by a change in the money supply, would have no effect in bringing about an aggregate equilibrium. The dichotomy assumption prevented it. Keynes argued that assuming an *initial* equilibrium, the economy *stayed* in equilibrium, given the classical assumptions (in particular, the dichotomy assumption); but if the economy was in disequilibrium, it had no way to achieve equilibrium.

Keynes continued his argument by stating that when there was aggregate disequilibrium, an infinitely falling price level luckily was not an economy's fate. Wages and prices were not perfectly flexible; they were institutionally fixed. And because they were fixed, aggregate disequilibrium adjustment did not occur through wage and price adjustments; it occurred in a different way. *Keynes's model was designed to focus on that alternative path of adjustment of the aggregate economy.*

Figure 16.3   Keynesian Aggregate Demand

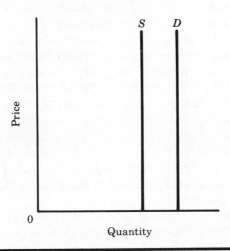

To understand Keynes's aggregate adjustment analysis, think back to the problem of determining the final equilibrium in the case in which supply and demand were interconnected. What prevented us from determining the equilibrium in that example was not knowing how much the demand curve would shift when the quantity supplied shifted. If we had known that, we could have determined whether there would be an ultimate equilibrium, and if so, what that equilibrium would be.

Marshallian analysis of equilibrium prices and quantities for individual micro markets solves the problem of the interrelatedness of the supply and demand curves by using partial equilibrium analysis. In short, the interrelatedness is ignored. Theoretical perfection is sacrificed in order to make headway in practical analysis. This approach is quite reasonable for understanding individual micro markets but unsatisfactory when applied at the level of aggregate supply and demand. Keynes recognized that ignoring the interconnection of aggregate supply and demand made it impossible to understand forces determining the level of income and employment. He therefore assumed an explicit connection between aggregate supply and demand by postulating a relationship between the income and consumption of an economy. Income (supply) and consumption (demand) had a stable relationship, so that as income fell, one could determine the position of the aggregate demand function. The relationship between income and consumption was called the *consumption function,* and the coefficient relating changes in demand spending (consumption) to changes in supply (income) was the *marginal propensity to consume.*

Keynes argued that the marginal propensity to consume was less than one, so that the difference between income and consumption decreased as income fell. For example, if income (supply) decreases by $1,000 but individuals have been saving 20 percent of their income, consumption (demand) will fall by only $800. As income continues to fall, any gap between aggregate supply and aggregate demand will continue to decrease, and eventually the two will meet at equilibrium. In Keynes's simple model, prices were fixed and changes in income provided all the adjustment. The assumption that the marginal propensity to consume is less than one is the key to explaining why income stops falling. If the marginal propensity to consume is equal to one, stable equilibrium is not possible.

Because this process "multiplies" an initial shock, Keynes used the term *multiplier* to relate how much income must change in response to an exogenous shock. The size of the multiplier depended upon the marginal propensity to consume. For example, if the marginal propensity to consume ($\Delta C/\Delta Y$) is 0.75 and the marginal propensity to save ($\Delta S/\Delta Y$) is 0.25, the multiplier is 4. From national income data for the United States, Keynes estimated the multiplier to have a value of about 2.5. Keynes's theory demonstrated that the total shift in demand and supply would be a multiple of the initial gap; hence the multiplier became a key element of Keynes's analysis.

The multiplier analysis is shown graphically in Figure 16.4, where $b = \Delta C/\Delta Y$. In it we draw a standard consumption function (with slope equal to a marginal

Figure 16.4   Keynesian Expenditure Function Analysis

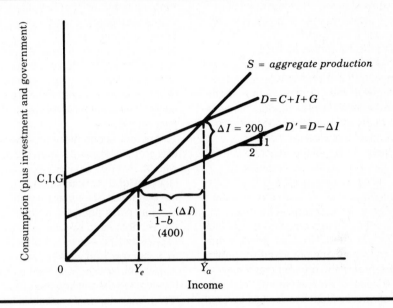

propensity to consume of 0.5) and add to it investment and government expenditures, which for simplicity we assume to be independent of income. This gives us the aggregate (income) expenditure function. Aggregate production or supply corresponds to total production and is represented by the 45-degree line. Initially the economy is in equilibrium at Y_a. Suppose investment falls by ΔI, or 200. If Y_a equals \$1,000, the economy is now in disequilibrium, with production at \$1,000 and spending at \$800. Because production is greater than spending, income falls as producers decide to produce less, decreasing both the quantity supplied and the quantity demanded. As income falls, production and spending become closer (the quantity demanded decreases by less than the quantity supplied) until finally, at income Y_e, aggregate supply and demand are equal. The distance between the initial income, Y_a, and the new equilibrium, Y_e, is two times the initial gap ($2\Delta I$), or 400.

With his theory Keynes provided an explanation for the Great Depression. He argued that investment spending was highly unstable and dependent upon expectations. As it fluctuated, it created a gap between aggregate production and expenditure. In response, firms would change production, which would lead to a multiplied effect on income. Keynes also provided a way out of the Depression: increase spending by a portion of the gap and rely on the multiplier to increase income by the remainder.

Precedents for Keynes's Analysis

In explaining why the level of income was volatile, Keynes stressed the role of investment spending. In this he followed the reasoning of Tugan-Baranowsky, who had argued that a change in investment spending would lead to changes in income of a greater magnitude than the original change in investment spending. Most economists did not accept this view, and before Keynes, no formal theoretical explanation of this process was developed.

The Great Depression of the 1930s changed all that. With 25 percent unemployment, the self-regulating nature of the market system could no longer simply be assumed. Noneconomists were advancing various proposals for public works programs, arguing that these would increase employment, and a number of neoclassical economists favored such proposals even though they conflicted with neoclassical theory.

In 1931 R. F. Kahn , a colleague of Keynes at Cambridge, provided a formal basis for these proposals with his employment-multiplier analysis.* Kahn argued as follows: suppose N is total employment and N_1 is employment in public works. A change in employment in the public works sector will increase income. As workers spend this income, other employers will find that they need more employees, and they too will increase employment. For example, if the employment multiplier is 3, then a public works project employing 1,000 more laborers will increase total employment by 3,000. Kahn called the coefficient that relates these changes the employment multiplier. Although it was expressed in terms of employment rather than income, it was the basis of Keynes's multiplier analysis.

Another economist who advanced many of the same ideas as did Keynes was Michal Kalecki (1899–1970).** Kalecki, a Polish economist, addressed the dynamics of capitalism within a Marxian class analysis. Kalecki divided the economy into two classes of people: capitalists who earn profit and save all their income, and workers who earn wages and spend or consume all they receive. He then asked the question, "What will happen if capitalists increase their profit rate, lowering wages?" and showed how their attempt to do so would lead to a multiplied fall in income. His model is often summed up in the phrase "Workers spend what they get and capitalists get what they spend."

*R. F. Kahn, "The Relation of Home Investment to Unemployment," *Economic Journal,* 51 (June 1931).
**Kalecki presented his ideas in the early 1930s before Keynes published *The General Theory* (1936), but they were not known to English-speaking economists until the late 1930s.

What Keynes Really Meant

In the 1930s and 1940s Keynes's arguments were extremely controversial, but because most economists were focusing their attention on the problems of war production, war finance, and postwar reconstruction, they did little work on macroeconomic theory. That changed in the late 1940s; the war ended and economists began working in earnest on Keynes's theory and on relating it to policy.

Because there were many strands of reasoning in Keynes's theory and many interconnected arguments, it was not at all clear what he really meant. He himself provided little assistance in clarifying his meaning. Thus, we should point out that the presentation of his ideas given here is not the one found in most introductory or intermediate macro textbooks. It is one of many interpretations of Keynes's model; we present it here because it is a helpful way to contrast micro- and macroeconomics and to provide insight into some modern developments in macroeconomics. Before considering those modern developments, however, we will present the prevailing interpretation of Keynes's model from the 1940s to the present.

The Rise of the Keynesian Expenditure Function Model: 1940–1960

Keynes's model was not initially interpreted as a disequilibrium adjustment model of the aggregate economy. Initially the focus was on the consumption function and the multiplier. In the 1940s and 1950s, economists explored this multiplier model, developing it in excruciating detail. It was expanded to include international effects, various types of government expenditure, and different types of individual spending. Terms such as the balanced budget multiplier became standard parts of economic terminology, and every economics student had to learn Keynes's model.

This now-standard consumption function model and the monetary and fiscal policies that were and are generally called Keynesian are not to be found in Keynes's book. There is not a single diagram in *The General Theory,* nor any discussion of the use of monetary and fiscal policy. How, then, did the consumption function model (done algebraically and geometrically) become the focal point of the macroeconomic debates of the 1950s? Part of the reason is that it seemed to provide a better description of current reality than did the alternatives. But other factors were also at work. The initial policy debates about the validity of Keynesian economics focused on fiscal policy (government deficits during the war had apparently pulled the Western world out of the Depression). Because the consumption function model nicely captured the effects of fiscal policy, it tended to become the Keynesian model. We suspect that sociological reasons also played a role in both the initial adoption and long-term acceptance of the model. The need for truth, which we discussed in Chapter 1, is often tempered by other needs of the profession—specifically, teaching requirements and the necessity of publishing journal articles. The consumption function model fit those needs beautifully.

It was in the United States that the consumption function analysis caught on; Paul Samuelson and Alvin Hansen (1887–1975) developed it into the primary Keynesian model. Samuelson's textbook introduced it into pedagogy, other books copied Samuelson's, and soon the consumption function model was Keynesian economics. The consumption function analysis had many pedagogical advantages: it was easy to teach and learn. It allowed macroeconomics to develop as a separate field by providing a core analytical structure for the course, just as supply-and-demand analysis had for microeconomics.

Simultaneously, Keynesian policy came to mean fine-tuning through monetary and fiscal policy. Abba Lerner (1903–1982) was an influential force in directing Keynesian analysis toward fine-tuning through monetary and fiscal policy. In his *Economics of Control* (1944) Lerner advocated that government should not follow a policy of *sound finance* (always balance the budget); it should instead follow a policy of *functional finance,* which considered only the results of policies, not the policies themselves. Functional finance allowed the government to "drive" the economy; in an oft-repeated metaphor, monetary and fiscal policy were portrayed as government's steering wheel. Lerner contended that fiscal and monetary policy were the tools government should use to achieve its macroeconomic goals: high employment, price stability, and high growth. The size of the deficit was totally irrelevant: if there was unemployment, the government should increase the deficit and the money supply; if there was inflation, the government should do the opposite.

Lerner's blunt statement of the "Keynesian" argument offended the sensibilities of many Keynesians and provoked considerable discussion, even causing Keynes to disavow Keynesianism.[10] Evsey Domar, a well-known Keynesian at the time, said, "Even Keynesians, upon hearing Lerner's argument that the size of the deficit did not matter, recoiled and said, no he had it wrong, in no uncertain terms."[11] But Keynes soon changed his mind and agreed with Lerner, as did much of the economics profession, and it was not long before Keynesian economic policy became synonymous with functional finance.

Monetary and fiscal policies were, moreover, politically palatable. Many economists and others believed the Depression proved that the government had to assume a much larger role in directing the economy. The use of monetary and fiscal policy kept that role to a minimum. Markets could be left free to operate as before. The government would not directly determine the level of investment; it could simply affect total income indirectly by running a budget deficit or surplus. For many, the legitimization of deficits had a second desirable characteristic: it allowed government to spend without taxing.

Keynes's Philosophical Approach to Policy

Policy combines theory with normative judgments. Understanding the Keynesian revolution, therefore, requires a consideration of the general philosophical views of economists at the time, and of Keynes in particular. Keynes was not a radical, although he was so accused after publishing *The General Theory.* We would hardly expect a person of his background, education, and experience to argue for drastic changes in the institutional structure of his society. Keynes was basically conservative in his views about altering the structure of society, generally advocating only such changes as would preserve the essential elements of capitalism. His view

[10] David Colander, "Was Keynes a Keynesian or a Lernerian?" *Journal of Economic Literature,* 22 (December 1984), p. 1572.

[11] The quotation is from an unpublished interview held with Evsey Domar by the authors.

was that if the worst defects of the system were not removed, individuals would discard the capitalistic system and lose much more than they gained. His rejection of Marxism reflects both a criticism of Marx's economics and a recognition that a Marxian social system would destroy the social class of which Keynes himself was very much a part:

> How can I accept a doctrine which sets up as its bible, above and beyond criticism, an obsolete economic textbook which I know to be not only scientifically erroneous but without interest or application for the modern world? How can I adopt a creed which, preferring the mud to the fish, exalts the boorish proletariat above the bourgeois and the intelligentsia who, with whatever faults, are the quality in life and surely carry the seeds of all human achievement?[12]

Keynes was dismayed by the growth of totalitarian government and dictatorship in Germany, Italy, and Russia. He was willing to admit that these changes in social organization might solve some economic problems, but such a solution, he felt, would be purchased only at the cost of individualism and its economic and political advantages. The economic advantages of individualism, stemming from the use of self-interest to achieve greater efficiency and innovation, are well known to economists:

> But, above all, individualism, if it can be purged of its defects and its abuses, is the best safeguard of personal liberty in the sense that, compared with any other system, it greatly widens the field for the exercise of personal choice. It is also the best safeguard of the variety of life, which emerges precisely from this extended field of personal choice, and the loss of which is the greatest of all losses of the homogeneous or totalitarian state.[13]

Keynes's broad philosophical views on the structure of the good society led to attacks from two sides: those to the left of him considered him an apologist for capitalism and for his own class, and those to the right regarded him as a wild-eyed reformer-socialist seeking to dismantle the capitalistic system. We have already seen his response to the Marxist approach. His response to criticism from the right was at least more conciliatory. He wrote, "While, therefore, the enlargement of the functions of government . . . would seem . . . to be a terrific encroachment on individualism, I defend it, on the contrary, both as the only practicable means of avoiding the destruction of existing economic forms in their entirety and as the condition of the successful functioning of individual initiative."[14] Keynes found one of the chief benefits of capitalism to be the free play it gives individualism. What abuses do come from individualism, he believed, could be corrected without destroying capitalism. The chief defects or faults of capitalism, he said, "are its

---

[12] J. M. Keynes, "A Short View of Russia," in *Essays in Persuasion* (New York: Harcourt, Brace, 1932), p. 300.

[13] Keynes, *General Theory,* p. 380.

[14] *Ibid.*

failure to provide for full employment and its arbitrary and inequitable distribution of wealth and incomes."[15]

The Depression of the 1930s convinced many economists that the failure to provide full employment was a major fault of capitalism. An important question faced by postwar economists was this: what policies can we use to preserve the best of capitalism and simultaneously prevent major depressions? Keynes's views on policy seemed at first too liberal for many people in the United States. Monetary and fiscal policy suggested by the Keynesians were finally embraced by U.S. economists, because they required little direct government intervention in the economy. Those policies, however, were attacked by some who considered Keynesians socialists. Lorie Tarshis, who wrote the first Keynesian introductory textbook, discovered this when a conservative group led a drive to stop alumni from giving to any school that used his book and to have him fired from Stanford University, where he taught. Tarshis's introductory textbook was not commercially successful; but it was followed by Samuelson's text, which was extremely successful and widely imitated, in part because it cloaked Keynesian economics in a scientific mantle, thereby avoiding the ideological attacks leveled against Tarshis.

There was a great deal of debate about the consequences of deficits created by expansionary fiscal policies, but these concerns were, for the most part, dispelled by the Keynesian argument that internally held government debt was no burden on future generations. In all these debates about policy it was not Keynes but Keynesians who led the way in reformulating policy, particularly concerning the proper role of government in the economy.

From the Consumption Function to IS-LM Analysis: 1960–1975

The consumption function model had proved to be inadequate for some theoretical debates because it did not include an analysis of the interconnection between the financial and real sectors. For the policy debates in the early 1950s, which had focused on fiscal policy, this had not mattered; but as soon as the debates began to include monetary policy, it did, and a new model was needed. Sir John Hicks's *IS-LM analysis* filled this need, superseding the consumption function model by the late 1950s and becoming the mainstream Keynesian model. It still forms the basis of most intermediate macroeconomic textbooks.

The IS-LM model was devised by Hicks in 1937 as a method of elucidating the difference between the Keynesian and classical theories of income determination. It was able to integrate the money market with the goods market, which the simple consumption function model did not do. To grasp the significance of this integrative effect, consider the aggregate adjustment process underlying Keynes's consumption function. The highly simplified analysis presented in Figures 16.3 and 16.4 assumes a complete dichotomy between the real and nominal sectors: by assumption, when the price level falls, the money supply falls by the same amount. Because of that assumption, price-level changes fail to bring about equilibrium in the model, because the aggregate demand curve is perfectly price inelastic. The

[15] *Ibid.*, p. 372.

simple Keynesian consumption function model avoided addressing this issue by assuming fixed prices. However, Keynes's book, the full title of which is *The General Theory of Employment, Interest, and Money,* included a long discussion of the role of money and interest rates. Thus, the simple Keynesian model was obviously an incomplete exposition of Keynes's analysis.

When Keynes analyzed what would happen if the price level fell but the nominal money supply remained constant, he determined that because the real money supply is the nominal money supply divided by the price level, a fall in the price level would increase the real money supply, and that increase would lower interest rates, thereby increasing investment and income. Thus, the price level was a factor in determining equilibrium income. In terms of an aggregate supply-and-demand model, this price level effect means that the aggregate demand curve would not be perfectly price inelastic but downward-sloping. The reason for this is different from the reason that the partial equilibrium demand curve is downward sloping. The aggregate demand curve slopes down because a fall in the price level increases the real money supply and the real money supply affects aggregate demand. Thus, Keynes provided a price adjustment mechanism so that price level fluctuations can bring about an aggregate equilibrium. Keynes felt, however, that because this effect was relatively weak and because in reality prices did not fluctuate enough for this to be a useful policy, it was much easier to change the *real* money supply by changing the *nominal* money supply, and not by waiting for prices to change.

This alternative mechanism for bringing about an aggregate equilibrium has become known as the *Keynes Effect.* It establishes a link between the real and nominal sectors via price levels, money supplies, interest rates, and investment spending. A decrease in the money supply raises interest rates, which decreases investment; an increase in the money supply causes a fall in interest rates, which increases investment. The change in investment, in turn, affects income through the multiplier effects of the simple consumption function model. The flow of causation is

$$\Delta P \longrightarrow \Delta M \longrightarrow \Delta i \longrightarrow \Delta I \longrightarrow \Delta Y$$

With the Keynes Effect the dichotomy assumption is discarded and price level fluctuations can bring about equilibrium between aggregate supply and demand by increasing the real money supply, which in turn increases the aggregate quantity demanded.

Pigou and others contended in debates with Keynesians that at least in theory, a fall in the price level did not have to work through a change in interest rates to effect a classical equilibrium. It could work directly on aggregate demand. Pigou reasoned that a fall in the price level makes the holders of money wealthier, and because they are wealthier they will spend more, thereby increasing aggregate demand.[16] The effect of price level changes on aggregate demand

---

[16] Pigou agreed that whereas, in reality, this effect would be minuscule, it preserved a classical aggregate adjustment mechanism without resorting to the Keynes Effect.

is therefore called the Wealth Effect, or the *Pigou Effect*. Debate about these issues and the relative roles of monetary and fiscal policy filled the journals in the 1960s.

The consumption function model does not allow for the Keynes Effect or the Pigou Effect; if we were to try to include them, the diagrams would become enormously complicated. Thus, it was natural that economists would turn to a model more suitable to the issues being debated. IS-LM analysis afforded such a model; it provided a neat geometric method of capturing the interrelationships between the real and nominal sectors. IS-LM analysis combined Keynes's analysis of the money market with his analysis of the goods market and demonstrated how equilibrium would be achieved through forces in both these markets. The inter-connection between the goods market and the money market occurs because the interest rate also affects investment, which is part of aggregate demand. Lower interest rates make borrowing cheaper, thereby increasing investment; higher interest rates decrease investment. Because investment is a part of aggregate demand, any change in investment has a multiplied effect on income via the multiplier.

The problem addressed by Hicks's IS-LM analysis was how to combine Keynes's analysis of the money market with the savings and investment market. Because there are feedback loops between the two markets, it is not a trivial

Figure 16.5   Monetary and Fiscal Policy

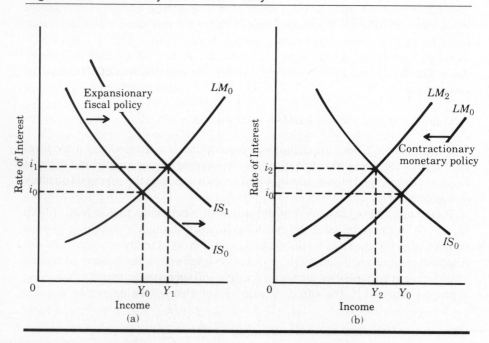

problem. An increase in investment, for example, will increase income, which will increase the demand for money, shifting the demand for money curve upward. As it does so it increases the explicit interest rates in the money market. That rise in the interest rate will offset some of the initial rise in investment, which in turn will offset some of the effect on income. The smaller effect on income means that the demand for money will not change so much, which means that determining the ultimate equilibrium is no inconsiderable exercise.

The IS-LM model reduces the discussion to a simple, two-dimensional diagram. In IS-LM analysis, the money market is represented by an LM curve, which graphs the combination of interest rates and income levels at which the money market is in equilibrium; that is, when the amount of money desired for liquidity purposes equals the quantity of money. Similarly, the goods market is represented by the IS curve, which graphs the combination of interest rates and income levels for which the goods market is in equilibrium, defined as equality between the desire to invest and the desire to save.

IS-LM analysis is shown in Figure 16.5. Aggregate equilibrium is at (i_0, Y_0), where the IS curve intersects the LM curve. The IS-LM curves neatly show the effect of expansionary or contractionary monetary and fiscal policy. In panel (a) of Figure 16.5, expansionary fiscal policy shifts the IS curve to the right (IS_0 to IS_1), increasing income (Y_0 to Y_1) and interest rates (i_0 to i_1). In panel (b) of Figure 16.5, contractionary monetary policy shifts the LM curve to the left, decreasing income (Y_0 to Y_2) and increasing interest rates (i_0 to i_2).

TOPICS IN MODERN MACROECONOMICS

Monetarists

In the 1950s and 1960s, the primary foil to the Keynesians was the *monetarists*. Under the leadership of Milton Friedman, they provided an effective opposition to Keynesian policy and theory. The consumption function model used by Keynesians in the 1950s had no role for money, nor did it consider prices or the price level. This initial lack of concern about money supply and prices manifested itself in policy based on Keynesian analysis. In an agreement with the Treasury that developed during World War II, the Federal Reserve Bank agreed to buy whatever bonds were necessary to maintain the interest rate at a fixed level. In so doing, the Fed relinquished all control of the money supply. Monetarists argued that the money supply played an important role in the economy and should not be limited to a role of holding the interest rate constant. Thus, the rallying cry for early monetarists was that money mattered.

Keynesians were soon willing to concur with the monetarists that money mattered, but they felt that the monetarists differed from them in believing that only money mattered. The debate was resolved by means of the IS-LM Keynesian-neoclassical synthesis, in which the monetarists assumed a highly inelastic LM curve and Keynesians assumed a highly elastic LM curve. Thus, at least in terms of the textbook presentation, monetarist and Keynesian analyses came together in the general IS-LM model, about which they differed slightly on some parameters.

The textbook treatment does not do justice to monetarists who objected to framing their analysis in a rigid IS-LM framework because it lost too many dimensions of the problem. Thus, the differences between monetarists and text-book Keynesians (who had come to be known as neo-Keynesians) was methodo-logical as much as it was empirical. Ironically, many of the policy ideas of the monetarists show up in the policy ideas of the new classicals (discussed in a subsequent section), even though methodologically they are poles apart.

Since the 1970s the state of macroeconomics has become much more confused and unsettled; in the 1990s various groups advocate many different approaches and there is no standard, core textbook model. The majority of textbooks continue to structure macroeconomics around the IS-LM model and short-run fluctuations. A few focus more on what is essentially a classical model and concentrate on long-run growth, leaving Keynesian-type questions of short-run fluctuation of income as side issues to be addressed at some later date. In exploring these issues, let us first consider some of the problems with IS-LM analysis that led economists to move away from it as an organizing model.

Problems with IS-LM Analysis

IS-LM analysis remains part of most macroeconomists' toolbox; it provides the framework most economists initially use in tackling macroeconomic analysis. By the 1960s, however, it had been well explored in the literature and found wanting in several ways. First, it forced the analysis into a comparative static equilibrium framework. In the view of many economists, Keynes's analysis concerned—or should have concerned—speeds of adjustment. They believed that Keynes was arguing that the income adjustment mechanism (the multiplier) occurred faster than the price or interest rate adjustment mechanisms. Comparative static analysis lost that aspect of Keynes.

Second, in IS-LM analysis the interrelationship between the real and nominal sectors had to occur through the interest rate and could not occur through other channels. Monetarists were unhappy with this because they thought money could affect the economy through several channels. Many Keynesians were unhappy with the framework because it shed little light on the problem of inflation, which in the 1960s was beginning to be seen as a serious economic problem. Third, the demand for money analysis used to derive the LM curve was not based on a general equilibrium model; instead, it was assumed in a rather ad hoc fashion. It had not truly integrated the nominal and real sectors. Because it did not capture the true role of money and the financial sector, it trivialized their function. It made it seem as if a fall in the price level could bring about an equilibrium, when in fact most economists believed that a falling price level would make matters worse, not better. Nonetheless, the IS-LM model was adopted. It was neat, it served its pedagogical function well, it was a rough and ready tool, it provided generally correct insight into the economy, and it was the best model available.

Dissatisfaction with existing analysis, however, led many macroeconomists to turn to other models in their research. This led to a dichotomy. While IS-LM analysis remained the key undergraduate model in the 1970s and 1980s, graduate research started to focus on quite different issues. By the early 1990s the change in focus was filtering down to undergraduate courses. Modern theoretical debates in macroeconomics have little to do with the shapes of the IS-LM curves. Instead, they approach macro issues from a microeconomic perspective, and they deal with issues such as the speeds of quantity and price adjustment. In a sense, many macro researchers in the 1970s and 1980s argued that we should skip the Keynesian IS-LM interval and return to the macroeconomic debate as it existed in the 1930s, when issues were framed in microeconomic terms.

The Microfoundations of Macroeconomics

The *microfoundations of macroeconomics* literature developed as economists attempted to grapple with the problem of inflation and integrate it into the Keynesian model. One of the first tasks economists undertook was to explain the underlying theory of the *Phillips curve*, an apparent empirical relationship between inflation and unemployment that had been discovered in 1958 by A. W. Phillips (1914–1975). This discovery opened up a number of theoretical questions. Why does inflation occur? Why is the relationship between inflation and unemployment stable? Will this stable relationship continue?

Its novelty of approach, as much as the profundity of its answers, distinguished the microfoundations literature. It established new ways of looking at unemployment. Whereas Keynesian analysis pictured unemployment as an equilibrium phenomenon in which individuals could not find jobs, the microfoundations literature pictured unemployment as a temporary phenomenon—the result of the interaction of a flow of workers leaving work and new workers entering. It argued that intersectoral flows were an important cause of unemployment and that these flows were the natural result of dynamic economic processes. For the new microfoundations approach to macroeconomics, unemployment was a micro, not a macro, issue.

Microfoundations economists argued that to understand unemployment and inflation economists must look at individuals' and firms' microeconomic decisions and relate those decisions to macroeconomic phenomena. *Search theory,* the study of an individual's optimal choice under uncertainty, became a central topic of macroeconomics, as did a variety of new dynamic adjustment models. As researchers began focusing more and more on these models, they focused less and less on IS-LM models. The initial microfoundations models had been partial equilibrium models, but once the microfoundations box was opened, economists needed to derive some method of combining the various markets. The obvious choice was to use general equilibrium models. Thus, general equilibrium analysis, which we saw in Chapter 15 had become the central model of microeconomics, was ushered into macroeconomics along with microfoundations literature.

Microfoundations literature was cemented into the profession's consciousness in the early 1970s by its accurate prediction about inflation. Advocates of the microfoundations approach argued on theoretical grounds that the Phillips curve— a curve showing tradeoff between inflation and unemployment—was only a short-term phenomenon and that once the inflation became built into expectations, the unemployment-inflation tradeoff would disappear. The long-run Phillips curve would be close to vertical and the economy would gravitate toward a *natural rate of unemployment*.

The policy implications of the new microfoundations approach were relatively strong. Its analyses removed the potential for government to affect the natural rate of long-run unemployment through expansionary monetary and fiscal policy. Attempts to do so would work in the short run by temporarily fooling workers, but expansionary policy would simply cause inflation in the long run. According to the new microeconomics, government's attempt to reduce unemployment below its natural rate was the cause of inflation in the late 1970s.

Keynesian monetary and fiscal policies were not, however, completely ruled out; in theory, at least, they could still be used temporarily to smooth out cycles. Thus, in the early 1970s a compromise arose between Keynesians and the advocates of a microfoundations approach to macroeconomics economics: in the long run the classical model is correct; the economy will gravitate to its natural rate. In the short run, however, because individuals are assumed to adjust their expectations slowly, Keynesian policies can have some effect.

The Rise of New Classical Economics

In the mid-1970s the term *rational expectations* first appeared on the macroeconomic horizon. The rational expectations hypothesis was a byproduct of the microeconomic analysis of Charles C. Holt (1921–   ), Franco Modigliani (1918–   ), John Muth (1930–   ), and Herbert Simon (1916–   ), who were trying to explain why many people did not seem to optimize in the way that neoclassical economics assumed they would. Their work was meant to explain by means of dynamic models what Simon called "satisficing" behavior (discussed in the last chapter); that is, why firms' behavior did not correspond to microeconomic models. John Muth turned that work on its head, writing as follows:

> It is sometimes argued that the assumption of rationality in economics leads to theories inconsistent with, or inadequate to explain, observed phenomena, especially changes over time. . . . Our hypothesis is based on exactly the opposite point of view: that dynamic economic models do not assume enough rationality.[17]

[17] John Muth, "Rational Expectations and the Theory of Price Movements," *Econometrica*, 29 (July 1961), 316.

Muth maintained that in modeling it is reasonable to assume that because expectations are informed predictors of future events, they would be essentially consistent with the relevant economic theory. As Simon wrote, "[Muth] would cut the Gordian knot. Instead of dealing with uncertainty by elaborating the model of the decision process, he would once and for all—if his hypothesis were correct— make process irrelevant."[18]

With his assumption of a "dynamic rationality," Muth turned disequilibrium into equilibrium. Just as neoclassical writers used rationality to ensure static individual optimality or to ensure that the individual moves to a tangency of his or her budget line and indifference curve, Muth used it to express "dynamic" individual optimality—to set the individual on his or her intertemporal indifference curve. As long as the private actors in the economy are optimally adjusting to the available information (and there is no good reason to assume the contrary), they will always be on the optimal adjustment path.

Although Muth wrote his article in 1961, the rational expectations assumption did not play an important role in economics until it was adopted by Robert Lucas into macroeconomics and combined with the work being done in microfoundations of macroeconomics. The rational expectations hypothesis struck at the heart of the compromise between microfoundations economists and Keynesians, because it held that people did not adjust their expectations toward equilibrium in stages. They can discover the underlying economic model and adjust immediately, and it would be beneficial for them to do so. Assuming that people have rational expectations, anything that will happen in the long run will happen in the short run. Because in the microfoundations-Keynesian compromise the effectiveness of monetary and fiscal policy depended upon incorrect expectations, the rational expectations hypothesis was devastating. In the new view, if Keynesian policy is ineffective in the long run it is ineffective in the short run.

In the mid-1970s rational expectations caught on in macroeconomics, and there were significant discussions of policy ineffectiveness and the unworkability of Keynesian-type monetary and fiscal policy. This developing work in rational expectations soon came to be known as *new classical economics,* because its policy conclusions were similar to earlier classical views. By the late 1970s it seemed to many that the future of macroeconomics lay in new classical thinking and that Keynesian economics was dead.

One of the lasting influences of the new classicals on macroeconomics was their contribution to the theory of macroeconomic modeling. As will be discussed in Chapter 17, Keynesians had developed macroeconomic models to a high level of sophistication in the work of economists such as Jan Tinbergen (1903–   ) and Lawrence Klein (1920–   ). In the 1960s and 1970s many of these econometric models were not good predictors of future movements in the economy, and many economists were beginning to lose faith in them. Robert Lucas, a

[18] Herbert Simon, "Rational Decision Making in Business Organizations," *American Economic Review,* 69 (March 1979), 505.

Table 16.1   New Keynesian Economics in Perspective

	Macroeconomic	
	No Prefix	
	Classical	Keynesian
Modeling Techniques	Informal; based on Quantity Theory and Say's Law	Informal; based on simple income expenditures model
Institutional Backdrop	Informal; contextual	Informal; contextual
Monetary Theory	Quantity Theory; dichotomy between real and nominal sectors	No monetary sector
Explanation of Unemployment	Wage rigidities	Cyclical fluctuations; shortfall or demand

leader of the new classicals, specified why these models were poor predictors in an argument that became known as the *Lucas critique* of econometric models. He argued that individuals' actions depend upon expected policies; therefore, the structure of the model will change as a policy is used. But if the underlying structure of the model changes, the appropriate policy will change and the model will no longer be the appropriate one. Thus, it is inappropriate to use econometric models to predict effects of future policy.

Recent new classical work has focused on issues of long-run growth and real business cycles in which fluctuations in income reflect individuals' desires.

Schools

Neo		New	
Classical	**Keynesian**	**Classical**	**Keynesian**
Semiformal; focused on IS-LM model	Semiformal; focused on IS-LM model	Formal; based on general equilibrium, Say's Law, Quantity Theory, rational expectations and market clearing	Formal; based on general equilibrium with macro externalities, rational expectations and multiple equilibria
Semiformal; semicontextual	Semiformal; semicontextual	Noncontextual; analytic	Noncontextual, analytic, although it employed the importance of context in deciding which equilibria will be arrived at
Formal money market analysis with LM curve rather inelastic; Quantity Theory dichotomy broken by Pigou effect	LM curve rather elastic; dichotomy broken by Keynes effect	Quantity Theory; dichotomy between real and nominal sectors; no formal analysis of money	Money is part of production function; dichotomy inherently broken
Wage rigidities	Wage rigidities combined with shortfall of demand	Model precludes unemployment; wage rigidities would cause unemployment	Initial model focuses on aggregate inefficiency, not unemployment

Keynesian Responses to the New Classicals

The spread of the rational expectations hypothesis to macroeconomics led to a number of Keynesian responses and a division of Keynesians into various sub-schools of thought. Thus, in the 1990s there are no longer just Keynesians. There are neo-Keynesians, who essentially accept the IS-LM model as a fair representation of Keynes's ideas. There are (no prefix) Keynesians, often called post-Keynesians, who argue that the IS-LM models do not do justice to Keynesian ideas and that we need to reread *The General Theory*. There are New Keynesians, who argue that the new classical abstract approach is the right one but that when we make reasonable assumptions about the macro institutional structure, Keynesian results follow. For each group of Keynesian economists there is a corresponding group of classical economists. Table 16.1 summarizes the thought of the three groups of Keynesians and their classical counterparts.

Notice that the groups differ along various dimensions. These include a methodological dimension as demonstrated in different modeling techniques, different institutional backdrops, and in their theoretical explanations of how the macroeconomy works. Because the neo-Keynesian model is the standard textbook model and the (no prefix) Keynesians are discussed in Chapter 14 on heterodox economists, we will focus on New Keynesian ideas, which can be divided into two groups. One subgroup focuses on providing microfoundations for macroeconomics, explaining why nominal prices were fixed with explanations such as menu costs (it costs money to change prices) or institutional fixities of wages or prices. They then show how the Keynesian conclusions follow, given these institutional realities.

The other subgroup of New Keynesians takes a much more radical position; they focus on the *macrofoundations of microeconomics*. They are quite willing to accept the new classical criticism of the neo-Keynesian model, but they argue that there is nothing inherently contradictory between Keynesian economics and rational expectations. This leads them to believe that the appropriate response to the new classicals should not be to derive a more institutionally realistic microfoundation to macro. Instead, they argue that the key to understanding Keynesian macro is to recognize the need for a macrofoundation to micro. One cannot analyze the choices of a representative agent independent of the macro context within which those choices are made. The aggregate production function cannot be derived from firm production functions, and output can shift around substantially for a variety of reasons, all concerning coordination failures. They argue that individual decisions are made contingent on others' expected decisions and that economies are likely to fall into expectation conundrums.

Hence a society of rational individuals can find itself in an expectational conundrum in which all individuals are making rational decisions but the net result of those individually rational decisions is socially irrational. According to the New Keynesians, the rational expectations assumption leads to the new classical conclusion that monetary and fiscal policy are ineffective only if it is combined with an assumption that all markets clear at the collectively desired level of output. But, they argue, that is an ad hoc assumption, not something that logically follows from the analysis.

For example, individuals collectively may expect that demand will be low and collectively produce little because of that expectation: supply is low because expected demand is low. Unless a coordinating system for expectations existed so that when one person lowered his or her expectations of demand, some mechanism existed to offset the effect of that lowering of expectations on the individual's supply decision, supply would be too low because demand was expected to be too low. It is this assumption, that the economy will inevitably equilibrate at the collectively desired equilibrium, not the rational expectations assumption, that these New Keynesians cannot accept.

Most New Keynesian work is highly abstract and theoretical, starting with abstract game-theoretic models and demonstrating that multiple equilibria are possible.[19] For the most part these abstract models have not filtered down to introductory and intermediate textbooks, but they should do so during the 1990s.

The revival of theoretical interest in Keynesian economics does not mean that what were known as Keynesian economic policies have regained their former status. In the 1970s there was growing concern about whether monetary and fiscal policy were politically effective tools, even if they were theoretically effective. Many Keynesians argued that monetary and fiscal policy were politically impossible to utilize and that politics, not sound economic principles, was determining the size of the deficit and the growth of the money supply.

The arguments between New Keynesians and new classicals quickly become complicated. It is not appropriate for a course on the history of thought to examine them. What is important to point out is that most modern macroeconomic research and most graduate training in macroeconomics consist of acquiring the technical background necessary to understand the modern debate.

SUMMARY

Although economists from the mercantilist era to the present have been interested in macroeconomic theory, there was a long period from roughly 1830 to 1930 when orthodox economic theory concentrated almost exclusively on analyzing the micro aspects of the economy. From 1870 to the 1930s, the major macro concern of orthodox theory was to explain the forces determining the general level of prices, whereas the macro issues of the forces determining the level of economic activity and the rate of growth were largely ignored. Although many mercantilists had emphasized the quantity of money as an important determinant of the level of activity, the rate of growth, and the general level of prices, from the time of Adam Smith until the 1930s one of the strong threads running throughout orthodox economic theory was that real forces determined the level of economic activity and the rate of growth of that activity. At that time orthodox theory held that the quantity of money had almost no effect on the level of output and the rate of growth of that output, its influence being wholly directed toward the general level of prices. Coupled with this lack of concern with the macro issue of stability and growth was the prevailing preconception of orthodox theory that market forces automatically led to desirable micro and macro results. Orthodox theory held that

---

[19] Examples are found in the sunspot model of Michael Woodford (1991) and game-theoretic macro models such as the work of John Bryant (1983).

an unregulated market economy with the government following a policy of laissez faire would automatically result in full utilization of resources and optimum rates of economic growth.

J. M. Keynes was reared in the orthodox tradition with its acceptance of Say's Law, its view that the quantity of money influenced only the general level of prices, and its predisposition toward laissez faire. Under the force of many influences, he and some of his contemporaries began to move away from this orthodox tradition; in the mid–1930s, Keynes offered a new analytical framework to explain the forces determining the level of economic activity. Keynes not only found capitalism inherently unstable but concluded that the usual outcome of the automatic working of the market was to produce equilibrium at less than full employment. Following the leads of Marx, Tugan-Baranowsky, Wicksell, and others, he focused on the role of investment spending in determining the level of economic activity.

Keynes's *General Theory* became the immediate starting point for modern macroeconomic theory and policy. A great deal of literature followed, which not only extended and improved the original Keynesian formulation but also threw into sharper perspective the contrasts and similarities between the Keynesian and pre-Keynesian models. The Keynesian concepts were in a form that invited mathematical model building and empirical testing. The theoretical revolution was followed shortly by a policy revolution as the major industrialized economies began programs and constructed agencies designed to foster full employment.

The Keynesianization of macroeconomics developed in a rather curious manner: it took the form of consumption function models advanced by leading Keynesians such as Alvin Hansen and Paul Samuelson. The close association of the development of Keynesian macro theory with the use of fiscal policy as a compensatory action available by government to promote full employment probably accounts for this focus on the consumption function model. In response to internal inconsistencies in the pure Keynesian formulation and to issues raised by monetarists concerning the role of money, the IS-LM model became the dominant macro model by 1960.

With the formalization of the debate around 1975, however, this model was found to be unsatisfactory for economic research. Inflation, as well as unemployment, seemed an important economic topic. A new literature appeared that tried to uncover the microfoundations of macroeconomics and in so doing blurred the one aspect of Keynesianism that had divided economics into micro and macro spheres. With the rise of the microfoundations literature, the debates and theoretical developments returned closer to the framework of the early 1930s. The only exception was that general equilibrium analysis was increasingly replacing partial equilibrium analysis. Initially, macroeconomics was closely associated with econometrics and the development of large-scale models of the economy. Although numerous such models exist, their early promise has not been realized. Thus, in the 1980s there was a movement away from such models and a focus on purely theoretical issues.

Modern macroeconomics in the 1990s is in a period of transition; scholars are carrying on a wide range of research programs addressing many different questions. The resulting confusion and diversity of approaches are not necessarily undesirable; the previously accepted Keynesian theory had a number of unresolved theoretical questions that economists swept under the rug. Uncovering them was bound to create confusion, but if doing so helps to provide better answers, the confusion will have been worthwhile.

Key Terms

underconsumption arguments
quantity theory of money
analytic theory
realytic theory
consumption function
marginal propensity to consume
multiplier
sound finance
functional finance
IS-LM analysis
Keynes Effect

Pigou Effect
monetarists
microfoundations of macro
Phillips Curve
search theory
natural rate of unemployment
rational expectations
new classical economics
Lucas critique
macrofoundations of micro

Questions for Review, Discussion, and Research

1. What is the relationship between mercantilist theory and Keynesian theory?
2. How does the income version of the quantity theory differ from the transaction version?
3. Why would an economist like A. C. Pigou advocate a public works program?
4. Was Keynesian theory contextual or noncontextual? Why is it important to know which it was?
5. Why did classical economists find the concept of "demand for output as a whole" problematic?
6. Keynes said that the economy was lucky that wages and prices were not highly flexible. What did he mean?
7. Describe the relationship of the multiplier to the marginal propensity to consume.
8. Distinguish between sound finance and functional finance.
9. What are some problems with IS-LM analysis?
10. Why would a new classical be likely to argue against a need for a macrofoundation to micro?
11. In a speech she will be giving, your employer wants to cite Keynes's famous quotation about practical men being "slaves of some defunct economist." Your assignment is to find the quotation.

Suggested Readings

Bryant, John. "A Simple Rational Expectations Keynes-Type Model." *Quarterly Journal of Economics,* 98 (August 1983).

Clower, Robert. "The Keynesian Counter-Revolution: A Theoretical Appraisal." In *The Theory of Interest Rates.* Eds. F. H. Hahn and F. Brechling. London: Macmillan, 1965.

Colander, David. *Macroeconomic Theory and Policy.* Glenview, Ill.: Scott Foresman and Co., 1986.

Fisher, Franklin M. *Disequilibrium Foundations of Equilibrium Economics.* New York: Cambridge University Press, 1983.

Harrod, R. F. *The Life of John Maynard Keynes.* New York: Harcourt Brace Jovanovich, 1962.

Hicks, John R. *The Crisis in Economic Theory.* New York: Basic Books, 1974.

————. "Mr. Keynes and The 'Classics': A Suggested Interpretation." In *Readings in the Theory of Income Distribution.* Philadelphia: Blakeston, 1949.

Hsieh, Ching-Yao, and Stephen L. Mangum. *A Search for a Synthesis in Economic Theory.* Armonk, N.Y.: Sharpe, 1986.

Keynes, John Maynard. *The General Theory of Employment, Interest, and Money.* London: Macmillan, 1936.

Klamer, Arjo. *Conversations with Economists.* Totowa, N.J.: Rowman and Allanheld, 1984.

Leijonhufvud, Axel. *On Keynesian Economics and the Economics of Keynes.* New York: Oxford University Press, 1968.

Lucas, Robert. *Studies in Business Cycle Theory.* Cambridge: Cambridge University Press, 1981.

Mankiw, Gregory, and David Romer, eds. *New Keynesian Economics,* 2 vols. Cambridge, Mass: MIT Press, 1991.

Skidelsky, Robert. *John Maynard Keynes.* London: Macmillan, 1983.

Weintraub, Roy. *Microfoundations: The Compatibility of Microeconomics and Macroeconomics.* New York: Cambridge University Press, 1979.

Woodford, Michael. "Self-Fulfilling Expectations and Fluctuations in Aggregate Demand." In *New Keynesian Economics.* Eds. G. Mankiw and D. Romer. Cambridge, Mass.: MIT Press, 1991.

17 The Development of Econometrics and Empirical Methods in Economics*

"What are you going to believe—your computer printout or what you see with your own eyes?"

—A former MIT professor at a student's Ph.D. oral

IMPORTANT WRITERS

WILLIAM PETTY	*Political Arithmetic* 1690
CHARLES DAVENANT	*An Essay upon the Probable Methods of Making a People Gainers in the Balance of Trade* 1699
CLEMENT JUGLAR	*Des crises commerciales et de leur rétour périodique en France, en Angleterre et aux États-Unis* 1862
W. S. JEVONS	"The Solar Period and the Price of Corn" 1875
HENRY L. MOORE	*Laws of Wages* 1911
W. C. MITCHELL	*Business Cycles* 1913
IRVING FISHER	*The Making of Index Numbers* 1922
E. J. WORKING	"What Do Statistical Demand Curves Show?" 1927
HENRY SCHULTZ	*Statistical Laws of Demand and Supply* 1928
RAGNAR FRISCH	*Statistical Confluence Analysis by Means of Complete Regression Systems* 1934
JAN TINBERGEN	*Statistical Testing of Business Cycle Theories* 1939

*This chapter draws heavily from three recent works: R. J. Epstein, *A History of Econometrics* (Chicago: University of Illinois at Chicago Press, 1987); Mary Morgan, *A History of Econometric Ideas* (Cambridge: Cambridge University Press, 1990); and Ronald Bodkin, Lawrence Klein, and Kanta Marwah, *A History of Macroeconometric Model Building* (Edward Elgar, 1991). We have, however, added our own perspective to the history they present.

489

WASSILY LEONTIEF   *The Structure of the American Economy,*
                         1919–1929 1941
TRYGVE HAAVELMO   "The Probability Approach to Econometrics" 1944
ROBERT W. FOGEL   *Railroads and American Economic Growth:*
                         Essays in Econometric History 1964

E conomics is about events in the real world. Thus, it is not surprising that much of the debate about whether we should accept one economic theory rather than another has concerned empirical methods of relating the theoretical ideas about economic processes to observation of the real world. Questions abound. Is there any way to relate theory to reality? If there is a way, is there more than one way? Will observation of the real world provide a meaningful test of a theory? How much should direct and purposeful observation of economic phenomena, as opposed to informal heuristic sensibility, drive our understanding of economic events? Given the ambiguity of data, is formal theorizing simply game-playing? Should economics focus more on direct observation and common sense? In this chapter we briefly consider economists' struggles with questions such as these. Their struggles began with simple observation, then moved to statistics, and next moved to econometrics.

The debate about empirical methods in economics has had both a microeconomic and a macroeconomic front. The microeconomic front has, for the most part, been concerned with empirically estimating production functions and supply-and-demand curves; the macroeconomic front has generally been concerned with the empirical estimation of macroeconomic relationships and their connections to individual behavior. The macroeconomic estimation problems include all the microeconomic problems plus many more, so it is not surprising that empirical work in macroeconomics is far more in debate than empirical work in microeconomics.

We begin our consideration with a general statement of four empirical approaches used by various economists. Then we consider economists' early attempts at integrating statistical work with informal observations. Next, we see how reasonable yet ad hoc decisions were made about the problems regarding the statistical treatment of data, leading to the development of a subdiscipline of economics—econometrics. Finally, we consider how those earlier ad hoc decisions have led to cynicism on the part of some economists about econometric work and the unsettled state of empirical economics today.

EMPIRICAL ECONOMICS

Almost all economists believe that economics must ultimately be an empirical discipline, that their theories of how the economy works must be related to (and, if possible, tested against) real-world events and data. But economists differ enormously on how one does this and what implications can be drawn afterward. We will distinguish four different approaches to relating theories to the real world: commonsense empiricism, statistical analysis, classical econometric analysis, and Bayesian econometric analysis.

Commonsense empiricism is an approach that relates theory to reality through direct observation of real world events with a minimum of statistical aids. You look at the world around you and determine if it matches your theoretical notions. It is the way in which most economists approached economic issues until the late nineteenth century; before then, most economists were not highly trained in statistical methods, the data necessary to undertake statistical methods did not exist, many standard statistical methods that we now take for granted had not yet been developed, and computational capabilities were limited.

Commonsense empiricism is sometimes disparagingly called armchair empiricism. The derogatory term conveys a sense of someone sitting at a desk, developing a theory, and then selectively choosing data and events to support that theory. Supporters of commonsense empiricism would object to that characterization because the approach can involve careful observation, extensive field work, case studies, and direct contact with the economic events and institutions being studied. Supporters of commonsense empiricism argue that individuals can be trained to be open to a wide range of real world events; individuals can objectively assess whether their theories match those events. The commonsense approach requires that economists constantly observe economic phenomena, with trained eyes, thereby seeing things that other people would miss. It has no precise line of demarcation to ultimately determine whether a theory should or should not be accepted, but it does have an imprecise line. If you expected one result and another occurred, you should question the theory. The researcher's honesty with himself or herself provides the line of demarcation.

The *statistical analysis* approach also requires one to look at reality but emphasizes aspects of events that can be quantified and thereby be subject to statistical measure and analysis. A focus is often given to statistically classifying, measuring, and describing economic phenomena. This approach is sometimes derisively called *measurement without theory.* Supporters of the approach object to that characterization, arguing that it is simply an approach that allows for the possibility of many theories and permits the researcher to choose the most relevant theory; they claim it is an approach that prevents preconsidered theoretical notions from shaping the interpretation of the data.

The statistical analysis approach is very similar to commonsense empiricism; but unlike that approach, the statistical approach uses whatever statistical tools and techniques are available to squeeze every last bit of understanding from a data set. It does not attempt to relate the data to a theory; instead, it lets the data (or the computer analyzing the data) do the talking. As the computer has increased researchers' capabilities of statistically analyzing data, the approaches of commonsense empiricism and statistical analysis have diverged.

The *classical econometric* approach is a method of empirical analysis that directly relates theory and data. The commonsense sensibility of the researcher, or his or her understanding of the phenomena, plays little role in the empirical analysis; the classical econometrician is simply a technician who allows the data to do the testing of the theory. This approach makes use of classical statistical methods to formally test the validity of a theory. The econometric approach developed in the 1930s, and in the 1990s it is the approach most typically taught in modern economics departments. Its history is the primary focus of this chapter.

The Bayesian approach[1] directly relates theory and data, but in the interpretation of any statistical test it takes the position that the test is not definitive. It is based on the Bayesian approach to statistics that seeks probability laws not as objective laws but as subjective degrees of belief. In Bayesian analysis, statistical analysis cannot be used to determine objective truth; it can be used only as an aid in coming to a subjective judgment. Thus, researchers must simply use the statistical tests to modify their subjective opinions. *Bayesian econometrics* is a technical extension of commonsense empiricism. In it, data and data analysis do not answer questions; they are simply tools to assist the researcher's common sense.

These approaches are not all mutually exclusive. For example, one can use commonsense empiricism in the initial development of a theory and then use econometrics to test the theory. Similarly, Bayesian analysis requires that researchers arrive at their own prior belief through some alternative manner, such as commonsense empiricism. However, the Bayesian and the classical interpretations of statistics are mutually exclusive, and ultimately each researcher must choose one or the other.

Mathematical Economics, Statistics, and Econometrics

Before we consider the development of econometrics, it is worthwhile to briefly consider the distinctions among mathematical economics, statistics, and econometrics. They are often grouped together, even though they should not be.

The term *mathematical economics* refers only to the application of mathematical techniques to the formulation of hypotheses. It is formal, abstract analysis used to develop hypotheses and clarify their implications. The term *statistics* refers to a collection of numerical observations, and statistical analysis refers to the use of statistical tests derived from probability theory to gain insight into those numerical observations. *Econometrics* combines mathematical economics, which is used to formulate hypotheses, and statistical analysis, which is used to formally test hypotheses. The combination is not symmetrical; one can do mathematical economics without doing econometrics, but one cannot do econometrics without first

---

[1] History can be kind, unkind, and strange. Thomas Bayes (1701–1761) was a minister who published nothing during his life. A paper, "An Essay Toward Solving a Problem in the Doctrine of Chances," was read in 1763 (after his death) to the Royal Society and was published in 1764. Bayes's ideas had little impact on the early development of classical statistics, but he is honored today because of his seminal insight.

Testable and Untestable Theories: Malthus's Population Theory

Malthus's statement of the population theory is a good example of an untestable theory. In the first edition of his *Essay on Population,* Malthus presented the hypothesis that in the long run, population tends to grow at a faster rate than the food supply. The hypothesis is thus potentially capable of being statistically refuted.

In the second and subsequent editions of his *Essay on Population,* however, Malthus stated the population thesis in such a way that it cannot be tested empirically; he added an unmeasurable check on population, the "growth of moral restraint," by which he meant postponement of marriage and abstinence from premarital sexual activity. When moral restraint as a check on birth rates is added to the theory, an observed population increase may be combined with a rising, falling, or constant per capita income and still be compatible with the theory. Thus, this version of Malthusian population theory becomes impossible to test empirically.

doing mathematical economics. Only mathematical economics gives one a theory specific enough that one has something to test formally.

The separation of mathematical economics from statistics can be seen in history. In the late nineteenth century, economists who most strongly opposed the mathematical formalization of economic thinking were the German historical school and the forerunners of the U.S. institutionalist school. These groups included some strong advocates of data collecting and statistical analysis—they argued that one had to know what real-world phenomena one was talking about before it made any sense to talk about theoretical generalizations. On the other hand, many formal theorists during that time were hesitant about using statistical analysis. For example, both Marshall and Edgeworth were hesitant about the ability to statistically measure a demand curve, believing that the *ceteris paribus* assumptions used to analytically derive the curves made them difficult to quantify. Edgeworth wrote in his discussion of demand curves in Palgraves (1910 edition): "It may be doubted whether Jevons's hope of constructing demand curves by statistics is capable of realization."

What economists hoped to gain from mathematical economics was a precision of hypothesis testing that would make it possible to reduce the ambiguity of tests. For example, instead of relying on common sense and a general heuristic understanding that demand curves slope downward, they wanted to be able to prove empirically that demand curves slope downward. Prior to the mathematical formalization of economic theory, economists employed words to state economic theories and hypotheses. Testing of general hypotheses was done in relation to current circumstances or in relation to historical events, but in either case the use of statistics was minimal. This essentially heuristic approach did not permit hypotheses to be tested in a manner acceptable to modern neoclassical economists.

The 1960s and 1970s saw enormous advances in formal statistical testing and in an understanding of econometric methods. Advances in computer technology made it possible to conduct extremely complicated empirical work. Statistical tests that earlier would have taken days now could be done in seconds. During that period the hopes for econometrics were high. Some believed that econometrics would make economics a science in which all theories could be tested. During this time, logical positivism and Popperian falsificationism were the reigning methodologies, and it was believed that the errors of the past—formulating theories in such a way as to render them untestable—could be avoided. Most of these initial hopes have not been realized.

Early Empirical Work

An early attempt to add empirical foundation to a demand relationship is the work of Gregory King (1648–1712), who restated some of the work of Charles Davenant (1656–1714). Davenant found a rough inverse relationship between price and quantity in *An Essay upon the Probable Methods of Making a People Gainers in the Balance of Trade* (1699), in which he proposed the following law:

> We take it, that a defect in the harvest may raise the price of corn in the following proportions:

Defect		Above the common rate
1 tenth		3 tenths
2 tenths	Raises	8 tenths
3 tenths	the	1.6 tenths
4 tenths	price	2.8 tenths
5 tenths		4.5 tenths

> So that when corn rises to treble the common rate, it may be presumed that we want above 1/3 of the common produce; and if we should want 5/10, or half the common produce, the price would rise to near five times the common rate.[2]

NEOCLASSICAL ECONOMICS AND EMPIRICAL ANALYSIS

Early attempts at empirical work were the exception, not the rule. In the late seventeenth century most classical economists followed the commonsense empiricism approach. They posited their laws about how the economy worked and supported those laws with examples. Because there was no accepted test of a theory, debates as to what theory was correct were ongoing.

[2] Charles Davenant, *The Political and Commercial Works of That Celebrated Writer Charles D'Avenant, Relating to the Trade and Revenue of England,* collected and revised by Sir Charles Whitworth in 5 volumes (London: Farnborough Gregg, 1967), II, pp. 224–225. Notice that the price elasticity of demand is falling from 0.33 to 0.11 as deviations from normal output increase.

With the beginning of neoclassical economics in the late 1800s, that approach was called into question. As we saw in Part III, neoclassical theories were becoming more formal and there was discussion of economics' becoming an exact science. That meant formalizing economists' approach to empirical work; and the approach that was most discussed was statistical analysis, which itself was undergoing a revolution.

Neoclassical economists followed many different approaches to statistical analysis. For example, Stanley Jevons saw statistics as a method of making economics into an exact science that could have exact laws. Léon Walras, on the other hand, had little place for empirical work; he continued to develop his theory independent of any chance of empirically testing it. Alfred Marshall believed in empirical work but did not conduct formal statistical analysis; he saw direct observation and commonsense empiricism as the most useful way to gather empirical information.

Jevons's Sunspot Theory

W. S. Jevons (1835–1882) was one of the pioneers in mathematical techniques and utility theory. For that work he was highly lauded. Although Jevons is now best known for his microeconomic contributions to neoclassical theory, it is his empirical attempts at measuring macroeconomic relationships that are best known in the history of econometrics. His was one of the early attempts at formal macroeconomic empirical work. Whereas his work in microeconomics was praised, his macroeconomic statistical work on economic cycles was not well received by the profession. In fact, it was often ridiculed.

Jevons was interested in discovering the cause of trade or business cycles that led to fluctuations in prices. Because cyclical behavior did not seem related to individual utility maximization behavior, he thought there must be a cause in nature—some natural phenomenon that led to fluctuations. Preliminary investigation led him to believe that the cause of fluctuations in economic activity probably had something to do with the weather. He focused on sunspots (fluctuations in the activity of the sun) as the probable cause.[3]

Jevons's specific hypothesis was that sunspot cycles occur with a periodicity of 11.1 years and these cycles lead to weather cycles that, in turn, lead to business cycles. To test his theory, Jevons looked at agricultural data, about fluctuations in the harvests, that were available from the thirteenth and fourteenth centuries. He

---

[3] The thought that economic fluctuations are caused by sunspots has a certain humorous ring. It is important to remember that the alternative explanation advanced earlier by J. S. Mill had to do with shifts in "commercial moods." There was no explanation of why moods shifted or why the shift seemed to have a certain regularlity. Given that, it was natural for economists interested in endogenizing the cycle to turn to physical phenomena such as sunspots. For an excellent discussion of Jevons's work on sunspots, see Sandra J. Peart, "Sunspots and Expectations: W. S. Jevons's Theory of Economic Fluctuations," *Journal of the History of Economic Theory,* 13, No. 2 (Fall 1991), 243–265.

then tried to relate those harvest fluctuations to nineteenth-century estimates of sunspot activity that suggested the 11.1 year periodicity. Making the assumption that the length of the sunspot cycle had not changed, he compared the two by laying out his data on a grid representing eleven years, eyeballing his data. He noticed a relatively good "fit"; the cycles seemed to match. He then looked at cycles in commercial credit during the nineteenth century and discovered an average cycle of 10.8 years. He concluded that the likely cause of the business cycle was sunspots.

Jevons's sunspot theory was not followed by economists in the nineteenth century, most of whom found it quite bizarre. It deserves mention primarily because it involves an attempt to use statistics to develop and test a macroeconomic theory and thereby establishes Jevons as a pioneer of econometric methods.

Henry L. Moore

In the late 1800s and early 1900s significant work was done in statistical methods and probability theory that led to their introduction into economics. One of the earliest advocates of the use of formal statistical methods in economics was Henry L. Moore (1869–1958). In the early 1900s Moore pioneered the use of many statistical approaches that would later become standard. Moore used the statistical work of Sir Francis Galton, Karl Pearson, and others. These statisticians had demonstrated that it was possible to formally determine inferences from statistical data in a controlled environment using multiple correlation and contingency tables. Moore was impressed with that work and decided that it was possible to apply these statistical methods to verify economic theories.

Rather than just "eyeballing" two graphs on the same grid, as Jevons did, Moore formally compared two series of data and developed statistics that gave him information about the relationships between the two. It is important to note, however, that in doing so he made a heroic jump from the work of Pearson, who analyzed work conducted in an environment in which other physical influences could be controlled. Moore did not have that luxury, because controlled experiments are usually impossible in economics; he was thus assuming that statistical methods developed for use with controlled experiments would work in an uncontrolled environment.

The theory he was specifically interested in testing was J. B. Clark's marginal productivity theory of wages, which predicted that individuals would be paid their marginal product. Toward that end Moore investigated the relationship between wages and marginal productivity, personal ability, strikes, and industrial concentration. Clark's theory implied that (1) higher-ability individuals would be paid more than low-ability individuals; (2) when like-ability individuals worked in monopolistic industries and competitive industries, those in monopolistic industries would be paid more; and (3) strikes for higher wages were more likely to be successful in concentrated than in unconcentrated industries.

Moore found a relationship between ability and wages, but there were significant problems with his analysis. In his tests Moore did not specify his theoretical structure very rigorously. For example, in one test he used average product rather than marginal product and tested not real wages but money wages. Moore also found a relationship between strikes and industrial concentration, but that relationship was based on limited data.

Moore's statistical work was also problematic because he was interested in more than simply scientifically testing Clark's theory. Moore had a strong interest in policy-related issues. He wanted to use his statistical analysis to argue against socialist policy proposals calling for more equality of income. He claimed that if marginal productivity theory could be proved true, then he could scientifically demonstrate to others that there were serious problems in moving to a socialist state bent on changing the distribution of income. Having an "axe to grind" does not necessarily invalidate results of theoretical or empirical work, but it does raise questions as to whether ambiguous results will be interpreted fairly. Discovering the motives of a theorist or econometrician is not a test of the validity of a hypothesis or theory. Research sometimes takes place in funded think tanks reflecting particular segments of the ideological spectrum; as long as the results become public property that can be examined by all, significant bias will likely be pointed out.

Moore's early work established him as a leader in integrating statistical methods with economics. His subsequent contributions, one on the empirical measurement of the demand curve and the other on the measurement of business cycles, are also important: the first forms the foundation for modern microeconomic econometrics, and the second forms the foundation for modern macroeconomic econometrics.

Moore's Demand Curve and the Identification Problem

Moore is probably best known for his work on the estimation of demand curves for agricultural goods and for pig iron. A careful analysis of his contribution is warranted, because it points out many of the problems with empirical estimation that play roles in later debates.

Consider the difficulty of empirically measuring a demand curve. Market observations are of combinations of prices and quantities at which trades take place. If the market is in equilibrium, the observed prices and quantities are points on both the supply and demand curves; if the market is not in equilibrium, the observed prices and quantities could be on the supply or demand curve or on neither curve. How can the researcher know which is the case? If the researcher could do a controlled experiment and hold everything else equal, as in the equations

$$Q_D = f(P_Q, \text{price of all other goods, tastes, income, } \ldots)$$
$$Q_S = g(P_Q, \text{prices of factors of production, technology, } \ldots)$$
$$Q_e = h(f, g)$$

where everything but the price and quantity is being held constant, then one could measure the true relationship between price and quantity. But where that cannot

Figure 17.1   The Equilibrium Assumption

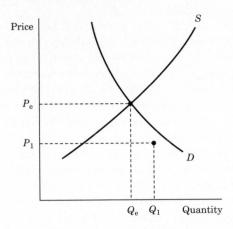

be done (and with economic statistics it cannot be done), the researcher must somehow relate the observed data on prices and quantities to the theory. Therein lies the heart of the econometric problem: relating observed data from uncontrolled experiments to theory.

In his analysis of agricultural markets, Moore was willing to accept that the markets would move to equilibrium, so that the observed prices and quantities could be assumed to be equilibrium prices and quantities, P_e and Q_e, and that they would be points on both the supply and demand curves. This assumption can be seen in Figure 17.1. It lets us assume that the observed point is a point such as (P_e, Q_e) rather than a point (P_1, Q_1) where the market is in disequilibrium in the process of adjusting to equilibrium.

Moore was also willing to assume that for agricultural commodities, supply was determined exogenously by summer rainfall and therefore would be unaffected by price in the current harvest period. He further implicitly assumed that past events had no effect on supply and demand and that changing expectations played no role in determining the actual data. These assumptions changed the graph of the model to one represented by Figure 17.2. Because quantity supplied is assumed to be determined exogenously, the estimated points (P_1, Q_1) and (P_2, Q_2) must be points on the demand curve.

In carrying out his analysis, Moore expressed the data as percentage changes around a trend and derived his demand relationship in terms of percentage changes. He proposed both a linear and a cubic equation for his demand curve. A linear demand curve would have the general form of $P = a - bQ$, where P is price, a is the price intercept of the demand curve, b is the slope of the demand curve, and Q is quantity. The negative sign for the b coefficient indicates a downward-sloping

Figure 17.2 Moore's Assumption about Exogenous Supply

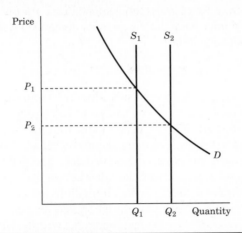

demand curve. Moore estimated two different curves with the following coefficients:

$$\Delta P/P_{t-1} = 7.8 - 0.89 \Delta Q/Q_{t-1}$$
$$R^2 = 0.61, \ s = 16$$

and

$$\Delta P/P_{t-1} = 1.6 - 1.1 \Delta Q/Q_{t-1} + 0.02(\Delta Q/Q_{t-1})^2 - 0.0002(\Delta Q/Q_{t-1})^3$$
$$R^2 = 0.71, \ s = 14$$

Notice that in both cases the demand curve has the negative sign predicted by theory (it is downward sloping) and that there is a fairly high coefficient of determination.

Moore's estimated demand curve did not bring him immediate acclaim; many did not understand his accomplishment, and others (such as Edgeworth) who did understand asserted that the empirical demand analysis was far too simple, given the complexity of the underlying theory. Edgeworth maintained that the many untested assumptions that underlay the conclusions were so great that the formality of the estimate gave little benefits. These criticisms, although substantial, are still leveled in various degrees against econometric work and should not demean Moore's contribution. He was one of the first economists to measure a demand curve statistically, although, as Nancy Wulwick points out,[4] it is not clear that Moore intended to estimate a traditional demand curve.

[4] Nancy Wulwick, "The Folklore of H. L. Moore on the Demand for Pig Iron," *Journal of the History of Economic Thought,* 14, No. 2 (Fall 1992), 168–188.

The cool reception of Moore's estimate of an agricultural demand curve was equivalent to positive adulation compared to the frosty reception of his estimate of demand for pig iron. He claimed the demand curve for pig iron to be positive sloping so that when price went up, the quantity demanded went up. He proposed the following demand equation:

$$\Delta P/P_{t-1} = 4.48 + .5211\,\Delta Q/Q_{t-1}$$

Moore's claim of having discovered a positively sloping demand curve went directly against microeconomic theory and provoked strong critical responses.

Given Moore's sophistication as an economic theorist, it is now suggested by Wulwick that Moore's positively sloping demand curve was not the result of error or failure to understand the *identification problem* (the need to hold supply or demand constant in order to estimate the other curve). According to Wulwick, it represented an attempt to address the data limitations and allow those limitations to direct his analysis, rather than letting the theoretical analysis direct his empirical work. This view is supported by the fact that in his writing, Moore was clear that his demand curve was not a typical demand curve that followed from Marshallian theory but was, instead, a dynamic demand curve that related empirical regularities involving many interactive changes.

A number of interrelationships could make his dynamic demand curves consistent with static demand theory. For example, when the price of pig iron went up, aggregate income and economic activity were likely to increase, which would be associated with an increase in demand. Because it was impossible to exogenously specify the supply of pig iron, as would be necessary to estimate a static demand curve, Moore contended that his dynamic demand curve, which captured an empirical regularity, was the closest one could come to theory and would be a useful tool in making predictions about the economy.

Moore argued that even though one could not exogenously specify supply, one could nonetheless estimate a curve that incorporates normal reactions to interrelated shifts in supply that can be measured. These normal reactions can include shifting the static demand curve in a time-consistent manner; they can make the measured dynamic demand curve incorporating these interdependencies upward sloping. If these later relationships are true, then whenever we see the supply of major industrial goods exogenously increasing, we should expect the price of these industrial goods to rise, not fall. That was Moore's conclusion. Moore felt little need to relate this dynamic demand curve to underlying static theory, because doing so would only be an exercise and would not be convincing. He wrote:

According to the statical method, the method of *caeteris paribus,* the proper course to follow in the explanation of the phenomenon is to investigate in turn, theoretically, the effect upon price of each factor, *caeteris paribus,* and then finally to make a synthesis! But if in case of the relation of each factor to price the assumption *caeteris paribus* involves large and at least questionable hypotheses, does one not completely lose himself in a maze of implicit hypotheses when he speaks of a final synthesis of the several effects? We shall not adopt this bewilder-

ing method, but shall follow the opposite course and attack the problem of the relation of prices and supply in its full concreteness.

The fruitfulness of the statistical theory of correlation stands in significant contrast to the vast barrenness of the method that has just been described, and the
two methods follow opposed courses in dealing with the problem of multiple effects. Take, for example, the question of the effects of weather upon crops. What
a useless bit of speculation it would be to try to solve, in a hypothetical way, the
question as to the effect of rainfall upon the crops, other unenumerated elements
of the weather remaining constant? The question as to the effect of temperature,
caeteris paribus? How, finally, would a synthesis be made of the several individual effects? The statistical method of multiple correlation formulates no such vain
questions. It inquires, directly, what is the relation between crop and rainfall, not
caeteris paribus, but other things changing according to their natural order.[5]

The problems addressed by Moore's justification of his work relate to some
still unresolved issues in econometrics. They provide perspective on the empirical
approach of the institutionalist school, which argued that the data should direct the
theoretical analysis rather than theory's directing the empirical work. Recent
justification for Moore's work has developed in an atmosphere in which the
profession is much more aware of the limitations of static analysis and relating
that analysis to empirical observation. Such justification was not forthcoming in
Moore's time or in the mid-1900s. Moore was attacked from both sides—from
those against formal theoretical and empirical work, who felt his statistical
methods were too complicated, and those in favor of formal theoretical and
empirical work, who felt he did not pay enough attention to theory.

The ridicule he endured about his upward-sloping demand curve ultimately led
him to abandon his econometric work, although not without having left his mark
on the profession. It remained for his students to carry forward the empirical
revolution. Of these students, the most famous was Henry Schultz, whose *Statistical Laws of Demand and Supply* (1928) and *Theory and Measurement of Demand*
(1938) would play major roles in the development of modern microeconometrics.

Henry Schultz and Independent and Dependent Variables

Henry Schultz's (1893–1938) contribution came as a derivative of his analysis of
tariffs, which required him to estimate a demand curve. As Schultz was attempting
to do so, he made an interesting discovery: one could obtain quite different
elasticities by regressing quantity on price rather than price on quantity, as Moore
had done. In discussing these issues, Schultz argued that if one had a prior belief
about which is the correct one to regress, which variable is dependent and which
independent, that would determine the correct choice. If, however, one did not
have a prior belief, there was no way of choosing between the two; he argued that

[5] Henry L. Moore, *Economic Cycles: Their Law and Causes* (New York: Macmillan, 1914),
pp. 66–67.

The Identification Problem in Modern Micro Theory

The identification problem with which Henry Moore wrestled is still with us today. Observed data give us information. What is the significance of that information? Can one identify how the data observed were generated in the economy, so that the observed data can be placed in the context of a theory?

An example of considerable theoretical interest will illustrate some of the problems of identifying observed data. In some industries (e.g., computers, digital watches, and color TVs) price and quantities sold have been inversely related over time: prices have fallen and quantities sold have increased. Is this an empirical manifestation that long-run supply curves for these industries are downward sloping (decreasing cost industries)? One possibility is that the observed data are generated by increasing demand and a downward-sloping long-run supply curve.

But the data could be generated in other ways. A new product is introduced by a firm or firms with monopoly power

and priced accordingly. Over time, new firms enter the industry because of excess profits and drive down price. A downward-sloping demand curve and outward-shifting supply curves resulting from increased competition generate the observed data.

Another possibility is that the industries observed have high rates of technological development. The data are generated by a downward-sloping demand curve with outward-shifting, long-run upward-sloping supply curves—improved technology shifts supply curves outward.

Panels (a) and (b) of Figure 17.3 illustrate the three possible ways of generating the data represented by price and quantity points H, I, and J. Panel (a) indicates that the industry has a downward-sloping long-run supply curve. Panel (b) indicates both the increased competition and improved technology explanations of falling prices over time. The data, unfortunately, cannot tell us how they were generated.

Figure 17.3   An Example of the Identification Problem

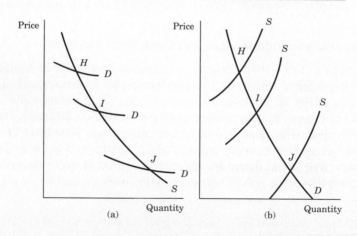

it was best to choose the regression that had the better fit as determined by a Pearson chi-squared test.

Schultz's insight was an important one; it means that statistical measurement cannot be considered independently of theory. What you see is partly determined by what you believe. This insight led to the current practice in econometrics that requires researchers to carefully distinguish independent from dependent variables.

Of course, to say that statistical measurement changes in relation to theory is not to say that measurement is totally dependent upon theory. It does not say that theory is determinant; it simply provides a limited range of interpretation that one can draw from statistics.

MACROECONOMICS AND EMPIRICAL ANALYSIS

Moore's Contributions to Macroeconometrics

The trade cycle has been an enduring economic phenomenon, and it is not surprising that Moore's contributions to estimating the demand for crops were supplemented by a macroeconomic contribution. In macroeconometrics, Moore's main contribution was to provide both a theory of the trade cycle and an attempt to measure it statistically. In analyzing the trade cycle, *Moore's dynamic demand curve* had even more justification. Whereas a static theory of demand existed, no similar theory of the trade cycle existed. Moore argued that *a priori* and *ceteris paribus* reasoning would be useless in explaining such fluctuations.

Like Jevons, Moore chose weather cycles as the exogenous cause of economic fluctuations. He integrated this view with his finding of an upward-sloping demand for pig iron as an explanation of the trade cycle. His five-part argument went as follows:

1. Rain increases and crop yields rise.
2. Balance of trade rises.
3. Demand, price, and the quantity of producers' goods rise.
4. Employment rises, so demand for crops rises.
5. General prices rise.

When rain decreased, the process would be reversed. Moore used statistical analysis to support this argument.

Moore's initial analysis was criticized by Philip Wright, who in a 1915 article adjusted the measure of rainfall to what was relevant for growing rather than the total yearly amount of rainfall; Wright showed that the statistical relationship breaks down. Wright's argument effectively undermined Moore's statistical analysis, which led Moore to expand his coverage to more countries. In his expanded analysis Moore found a persistence of eight-year cycles; in 1923 he wrote a second, more careful book on the subject in which he used weather as only one of many economic and social causes.

Clement Juglar

Whereas Jevons and Moore approached the analysis of trade cycles in essentially a statistical way, looking for a periodic cause of a periodic event (the trade cycle), Clement Juglar (1819–1905) approached the issue in essentially a historical way. Although Juglar made extensive use of statistics, he employed both qualitative and quantitative data to examine each cycle in an attempt to find peculiarities among cycles. This approach did not require an outside explanation and relied on sensible economic reasoning combined with careful analysis of the history and institutions of the time. Thus, whereas Jevons and Moore were forerunners of modern econometrics, Clement Juglar was a forerunner of the institutional or reasoned statistical approach to economic data. This approach placed a much lower emphasis on theory and much stronger emphasis on sensibility than does modern econometric analysis.

The broadening of the theory to include multiple causes found sympathetic support, but his deeper analysis of weather cycles in which he emphasized that Venus comes between the earth and the sun in eight-year intervals led to the designation of his theory as "the Venus Theory of trade cycles." Moore's particular approach to trade cycles was not pursued by others, but it provided some basis for later econometric work and set the stage for the institutional economists' analysis.

Wesley C. Mitchell: Heterodox Empiricist

One of the early institutionalists, Wesley C. Mitchell, differed significantly from orthodox neoclassical economists on issues of empirical work. Moore's work provides a useful focal point from which to consider Mitchell's approach to empirical work, which developed during the first half of the twentieth century and was the initial approach of the National Bureau of Economic Research (NBER). One of the reasons why Mitchell's approach gained favor was that there were problems with Moore's more formal statistical approach.

Mitchell's view of the appropriate relationship between theory and factual analysis was laid out in his early work on business cycles:

> One seeking to understand the recurrent ebb and flow of economic activity characteristic of the present day finds these numerous explanations [of business cycles] both suggestive and perplexing. All are plausible, but which is valid? None necessarily excludes all the others, but which is the most important? Each may account for certain phenomena; does any one account for all the phenomena? Or can these rival explanations be combined in such a fashion as to make a consistent theory which is wholly adequate?
>
> There is slight hope of getting answers to these questions by a logical process of proving and criticizing the theories. For whatever merits of ingenuity and

consistency they may possess, these theories have slight value except as they give keener insights into the phenomena of business cycles. It is by study of the facts which they purport to interpret that the theories must be tested.

But the perspective of the investigation would be disturbed if we set out to test each theory in turn by collecting evidence to confirm or to refute it. For the point of interest is not the validity of any writer's views, but clear comprehension of the facts. To observe, analyze, and systematize the phenomena of prosperity, crisis, and depression is the chief task. And there is better prospect of rendering service if we attack this task directly, than if we take the round about way of considering the phenomena with reference to the theories.

This plan of attacking the facts directly by no means precludes free use of the results achieved by others. On the contrary, their conclusions suggest certain facts to be looked for, certain analyses to be made, certain arrangements to be tried. Indeed, the whole investigation would be crude and superficial if we did not seek help from all quarters. But the help wanted is help in making a fresh examination into the facts.[6]

Mitchell's approach was pragmatic; it did not see a significant role for actually testing theories but instead saw theories as a backdrop useful in interpreting empirical observation. Consistent with this view, Mitchell did not see economics as a science but as an art to aid in policy formation. Ultimately, for Mitchell there was no unchanging theory that could be specified in a neat model; the economy was far too complicated and was undergoing continual structural change. Given such complicated changes, creating general theories was game-playing; the only acceptable theory was educated common sense, and the economy could be understood only through careful integration of common sense and statistical analysis.

Although data were, in a formal scientific sense, inappropriate to test theories, data were appropriate to test various hypotheses about the behavior of cycles. In a later book, *Measuring Business Cycles* (Burns and Mitchell, 1946), Mitchell tested Schumpeter's hypothesis about the relationship among different cycles and rejected it. He also tested his own hypothesis that there was a long-term secular change in cyclical behavior, which he and his co-author also rejected. They did find changes, but they were irregular and random. Thus, they were able to "test" hypotheses informally through a combination of formal statistical tests such as correlation tests and F-tests of significance, and judgment based on knowledge of institutions and of the data. Whereas in the scientific approach the formal tests determine the validity or falsity of a theory, for Mitchell such tests were merely aids to common sense and subjective judgment. Mitchell's approach to data and economic empirical analysis was used by the mainstream macroeconomists in the United States during the 1930s.

---

[6] W. C. Mitchell, *Business Cycles and Their Causes*, Vol. 3 (Berkeley: California University Memoirs, 1913), pp. 19–20.

Measurement and Data Collection

Some data, such as the price of coal, can be simply collected and used. Often data that fit theoretical constructs must be constructed. Quantifiable concepts must be determined and then data must be collected. That work is often difficult and demanding. Let's consider some examples.

Economists use a concept of the general level of prices, but there is no such measure of all prices in the economy. Since the 1940s increases in the general level of prices (inflation) have received a good deal of attention. Before inflation could be measured, a considerable amount of work had to be done on the construction of measures of the general level of prices. In *The Making of Index Numbers* (1922), Irving Fisher (1867–1947) examined some of the problems encountered in constructing index numbers designed to measure prices and economic activity. It was hoped that by eliminating intermediate goods and appropriately weighting final goods, one could construct an index that measured changes in the general level of prices. With such a measure it would be possible to add greater precision to the concept of inflation and to test hypotheses about the relationships between changes in the money supply and changes in prices. It should be noted that the money supply does not exist as simple data to be collected and analyzed; measures of the money supply must be constructed. There are many economists who have spent much of their lives working in the areas of measurement and data collection.

Other economists have made major contributions in the area of national income accounting. Keynesian theory cried out for measures of national income, consumption, spending, savings, and investment spending. These macro-theoretical concepts required the resolution of tremendously difficult conceptual issues before quantitative work could be done in data collection. Richard Stone (1913–   ) and James Meade (1907–   ), who received a Nobel Prize in economics for his work in international trade theory, developed national income accounts for Britain that fit the Keynesian theoretical mold.

In the United States national income accounting was studied by Simon Kuznets (1901–1985), a Nobel Prize winner, who wrote his Ph.D. dissertation under Wesley Mitchell and went on to work under Mitchell at the National Bureau of Economic Research. Kuznets's major contributions were the construction of measures of national income for the United States and the use of statistics to measure and compare growth patterns in different countries. The national income accounts Kuznets helped to create were an important ingredient in the post-Keynesian macroeconometric models.

Wassily Leontief also played a major role in organizing the collection of data; he designed input-output analysis, a practical planning tool for handling interrelationships in the economy. Leontief has been strongly critical of modern mainstream economic model building, which is devoid of empirical content. He advocates concentrating on the practical application of economics and working with data rather than building sophisticated mathematical models. His paper, "Theoretical Assumptions and Nonobserved Facts" (1971), is one of the best criticisms of ivory-tower model building one can find.

Two other economists who made contributions in data collection were Abram Bergson (1914–   ) and Alexander Gerschenkron (1904–1978). Bergson was an able theorist who wrote a classical paper in welfare economics at the age of twenty-four while he was a graduate student. He became the dean of American Sovietologists and did seminal work in the measurement of economic activity in the Soviet Union. It was often alleged before the breakup of the Soviet Union that Soviet planners used measures of their economy's activity that were generated in the United States because they were more reliable than their own statistics. Bergson was instrumental in building the Russian Center at Harvard University into a major research center for the study of Soviet society.

Gerschenkron was born in Russia, like Kuznets, but received his economic training in Vienna during the 1920s. He was a colleague of Kuznets and Bergson at Harvard. Although the volume of his written work is small, he was a professor's professor who had a command of many languages and published critical essays on Pasternak and on Nabokov's translation of Pushkin's *Eugene Onegin*. Gerschenkron did important work on the measurement of growth, particularly in the Soviet Union, and was able to show how the selection of the base year used for an index of industrial production influenced the growth rates shown by that index. His research disclosed that Soviet growth was not as rapid as Soviet planners indicated because their measurements were biased.

THE RISE OF ECONOMETRICS

By the 1960s Mitchell's approach to empirical analysis for the macro economy was a minority approach and was supplanted by the econometric approach in both micro and macro. There were a number of reasons why the mainstream turned away from Mitchell's methodology and toward econometrics: (1) the further development of statistical and econometric methods, which avoided some of Moore's problems; (2) the strong desire on the part of the profession and the society for precision in implementing and testing theories; (3) the development of mathematical economics; (4) the hope that econometrics would turn economics into an exact science; and (5) brilliant and strong-willed advocates of the econometric methods who proselytized for this approach.

E. J. Working and the Identification Problem

One of the developments that pushed forward the econometric approach in microeconomics was E. J. Working's (1900–1968) approach to the identification problem. A simple correlation between price and quantity that provides a "good fit" of the data has little meaning, because economic theory states that price and quantity are determined by an interaction of supply and demand. Has one found a supply curve or a demand curve?

Working showed that if one could independently specify supply so that one precisely knew the supply relationship and how it would shift, the derived points would estimate a demand curve. Alternatively, if one independently specified the demand relationship, one could estimate a supply curve. If one could not independently specify either, then one could not estimate either a supply or a demand curve without additional information.

This "solution" to the identification problem made it possible, in principle at least, to specify empirically static relationships even if *ceteris paribus* conditions did not hold. It was believed that as calculating technology improved (which it has done with computers), better relationships between static theory and empirical theory and empirical measurement would be forthcoming.

Keynesian Theory and Macroeconometrics

It was not developments in microeconomics that primarily propelled econometrics forward in the 1930s; it was developments in macroeconometrics. The Great Depression turned economists' thoughts to macroeconomics. By the late 1930s Keynesian theory was sweeping the field, and there were strong efforts to provide satisfactory explanations for, and policies to address, the Depression. Thus, the history of econometrics in the 1930s through the 1960s focuses on macroeconometrics.

The interest in macro modeling in the 1930s was logical. During this time macroeconomics was enormously influenced by Keynesian macroeconomics, and there were attempts to find empirical counterparts to the Keynesian theory. A number of estimates of the multiplier were derived. Colin Clark estimated the multiplier as somewhere between 1.5 and 2.1; Kalecki estimated it at about 2.25.

Of course, the multiplier made sense only if Keynesian theory made sense, so there was a strong push to determine empirically whether Keynesian theory was correct. There were many attempts to measure the relationship between consumption and income, what Keynes had called the consumption function. During this period there was also a loss of faith in the automatic tendency of economic forces to push the economy toward full employment and a corresponding increased interest in central planning. Such central planning required one to estimate relationships in the economy. Thus, it is not surprising that important work took place in institutes like the Netherlands Central Planning Bureau.

Ragnar Frisch, Jan Tinbergen, and the Development of Large Macro Models

One of the most influential econometricians of the late 1920s and early 1930s was the Norwegian economist Ragnar Frisch (1895–1973). Frisch was a highly trained mathematician who made contributions to both macro- and microeconometrics and played an important role in redirecting empirical economics away from the institutional approach and toward an econometric approach. In fact, it was he who coined the term *econometrics*. Although Frisch made some important discoveries in microeconometrics (he carried out a conclusive mathematical treatment of Working's identification problem and showed that the ordinary least squares estimator was biased), it was his contribution to macroeconometrics that accounts for his importance. Together with Jan Tinbergen, he played an important role in creating the field of macroeconometrics by developing a macroeconometric model of the economy. Frisch's primary work is found in his book *Statistical Confluence Analysis by Means of Complete Regression Systems* (1934). Here he argued that most economic variables were simultaneously interconnected in "confluent systems" in which no variable could be varied independently; he worked out a variety of methods to handle these problems.

Jan Tinbergen (1903–   ), a friend of Frisch, was recruited by the League of Nations in 1936 to undertake statistical tests of business cycle theories. His report was published in 1939 under the title *Statistical Testing of Business Cycle Theories*. This work focused on developing dynamic macro theories from the data and testing them. Tinbergen developed a theory of the business cycle, or model of the macroeconomy, that exhibited cyclical tendencies.

Econometricians such as Frisch and Tinbergen recognized that econometric work in macroeconomics was conceptually far more difficult than econometric work in microeconomics. In microeconomics one was worried about identification with two separate structural equations, supply and demand; in macroeconomics, theory suggested that there was a large system of interdependent equations that underlay macro forces. Somehow, the researcher had to extend the micro analysis almost ad infinitum for large numbers of equations, specify a system of structural equations, and test those equations.

It was to this task that Frisch and Tinbergen directed their analysis, and both won Nobel prizes for their contributions. Like Moore's, their purpose was more than simply testing the validity of a theory; they were interested in policy. They believed that if they could specify a structural set of equations describing the economy, they could thereafter determine a set of policies to change the structure of those equations and through those policies achieve desirable results in the economy.

Tinbergen's work evoked serious criticism from both John Maynard Keynes and Milton Friedman, who objected to the entire process and the implications drawn from it. They argued that Tinbergen's estimation procedures made use of the same data to derive the model that was used to test among possible competing theories, which would make the normal tests of statistical significance irrelevant. Their views represented the conviction that econometrics cannot replace educated common sense. Significant questions were raised about macroeconometrics even at its initial stages.

Trygve Haavelmo and the Probabilistic Revolution in Econometrics

Trygve Haavelmo (1911–   ), a Norwegian economist who studied with Frisch, has been credited with introducing the *probabilistic approach* to econometrics and to economic theory.[7] Before the introduction of the probabilistic approach, economists assumed that the underlying economic theories they were trying to measure were exact. If one could in fact hold everything else constant, one would have an exact relationship. Haavelmo argued against that assumption. He argued that we should treat economic theories as probabilistic theories that do not describe exact relationships but, instead, describe probabilistic relationships.

Before the publication of Haavelmo's paper "The Probability Approach to Econometrics" (1944, but widely circulated in manuscript form before 1941), econometricians used statistical methods but believed either implicitly or explicitly that probability theory had little to offer and that the underlying laws they were trying to find were exact laws. Haavelmo argued that because probability theory was the body of theory behind statistical methods, it was inappropriate to use statistical methods without accepting that one is searching for probabilistic laws. Acceptance of the probabilistic nature of economic laws allows the formal use of many statistical techniques and tests that previously were used without formal foundation; it lies at the heart of the modern approach to econometrics. Haavelmo received the Nobel Prize in economics in 1989.

The Cowles Commission and the Cowles Commission Method

Haavelmo's probabilistic approach was accepted by researchers in the Cowles Commission for Research in Economics, which was founded in 1932 by Alfred Cowles III, a wealthy investment adviser. Cowles assembled a group of very bright economists, including Irving Fisher, Harold Hotelling (1895–1973), and Ragnar Frisch, and set them to work on applying mathematical and statistical methods to the study of economic issues. The Cowles Commission was initially housed in Colorado Springs; in 1937 it moved to Chicago, where it remained until it moved to its current home, Yale, in the 1950s.

Much of what is now considered standard econometric work was done by the Cowles Commission. This work included estimating whether the ordinary least squares estimator would be biased downward (which it was found to be by as much as 25 percent); developing the Monte Carlo approach to small data sets; and working on issues of asymptotic convergence and unbiasedness of estimators.

During this time, it should be remembered, computational difficulties were enormous, because the computer as we currently know it did not exist. One did not simply type into the computer "Find OLS estimate" or "Find maximum likelihood estimate" to determine a result. One performed the work manually. The Cowles Commission followed Haavelmo in assuming that the best approach to econometrics was the probabilistic approach in which the structural equations had

---

[7] Econometrics is so young that its history has only recently been under consideration. It is not unusual to find disagreement over which economists were most significant. For example, Mary Morgan asserts that Haavelmo introduced the probabilistic approach into econometrics and economics, but Philip Mirowski argues that it was others, such as the Nobel Prize winner T. J. Koopmans (1910–1984).

Cliometrics and Robert W. Fogel

One of the interesting and controversial offshoots of the development of quantitative methods has been the application of econometrics to history. This new field has been termed new quantitative history, or *cliometrics* (in Greek mythology Clio was the muse of history). The most prominent of the new historians is Robert W. Fogel (1926–   ), who published *Railroads and American Economic Growth: Essays in Econometric History* in 1964. In this study Fogel merged neoclassical economics with statistical inference and cast doubt on many conclusions that literary historians had drawn from their studies of the relationships between railroads and American economic growth.

Other economists began to practice cliometrics, and much literature was produced. There was also a good deal of discussion about the legitimacy of the new methodology. A. H. Conrad and J. R. Meyer had published a controversial article in 1958, "The Economics of Slavery in the Ante-Bellum South," in which they rejected the conclusion that slavery was not a profitable institution. Fogel and S. L. Engerman (1936–   ) published *Time on the Cross: The Economics of American Negro Slavery* (1974) in which they accepted and extended the Conrad-Meyer thesis with massive amounts of data and research. This new application of neoclassical economics and econometrics to history has generated considerable controversy within the field of history and is another example of the encroachment of economics into other disciplines.

---

an assumed distribution of error terms. This probabilistic approach became known as the Cowles Commission method. One of the most famous econometric models coming from the Cowles Commission was the Klein-Goldberger macro model (an improvement of earlier Klein models), which was the first empirical representation of the broad Keynesian system. It contained 63 variables, many of which were endogenous, and 43 predetermined. Of those 43 predetermined variables, 19 were exogenous and 24 were lagged.

THE FALL FROM SCIENTIFIC GRACE OF MACROECONOMETRICS

During the 1960s, many Keynesian-type macroeconometric models were developed, all with a certain air of "scientific-ness." These included the Data Research Institute (DRI) model, the Wharton model, and various Federal Reserve models. As predictors of the economy, these macro models remained popular through the early 1970s, but by the mid-1970s this work was losing support. In his discussion of these models, Roy Epstein writes:

> The confidence of applied econometricians did not last long into the 1970s. The economic shocks of the decade began to invalidate the forecasts from the large structural macro models and drove researchers to constant re-specifications and

re-estimation of their systems. This work was accompanied by a growing number of studies that compared the forecasting qualities of large models to a new generation of univariate time series naive models. These comparisons still often showed that the structural models predicted no better than the naive models, an apparent confirmation of Friedman's predictions made in 1949.[8]

The reasons for the criticism of the macroeconometric models were similar to the reasons economists objected to earlier work. First, the validity of classical statistical tests depends upon the theory being developed *independently* of the data. In reality, however, most empirical economic researchers "mine the data," looking for the "best fit"—that is, the formulation of the theory that achieves the best r^2, t, and F statistics (statistics that measure the likelihood that the theory is correct). *Data mining* erodes the validity of the statistical tests. Second, even where statistical tests are conducted appropriately, the limited availability of data makes it necessary to designate proxies, which may or may not be appropriate. Thus, the validity of the tests depends upon the appropriateness of the proxy, but there is no statistical measure of the appropriateness of a proxy. Third, almost all economic theories include some immeasurable variables that can be, and often are, relied upon to explain statistical results that do not conform to the theory. Fourth, replication of econometric tests generally is impossible, because economists can seldom (if ever) conduct a controlled experiment. This makes any result's reliability unknown and dependent upon subjective judgment.

Robert Solow, a Nobel Prize–winning macroeconomist, captured the concern of much of the profession with the formal macroeconometric models when he wrote:

> I do not think that it is possible to settle these arguments econometrically. I do not think that econometrics is a powerful or usable enough tool with macroeconomic time series. And so one is reduced to a species of judgment about the structure of the economy. You can always provide models to support your position econometrically, but that is too easy for both sides. One was never able to find common empirical ground.[9]

Cynicism toward econometric testing has led many researchers to take a cavalier attitude toward their statistical work.[10] The result is that many studies

---

[8] Roy J. Epstein, *A History of Econometrics* (Chicago: University of Illinois at Chicago Press, 1987), p. 205.

[9] Robert Solow, in *Conversations with Economists,* ed. Arjo Klamer (Totowa, N.J.: Rowman and Allanheld, 1984), p. 137.

[10] Some sense of the current state of econometrics can be seen in a survey conducted by Thomas Mayer in an unpublished paper. He focused on the question of selective reporting of results, and asked how that affected the credence economists gave to empirical results in journals. Twenty-six percent said it made them quite skeptical; 54 percent said it made them somewhat skeptical; 9 percent said they distrusted all econometric results, so selective reporting was not a problem; and 8 percent said it was only a minor problem. Those results seem representative of the profession.

Modern Criticisms of Macro Models

One of the criticisms of macro models that has received much support is called the Lucas critique, because it was put forward by Robert Lucas, a macroeconomist who has been a leader in the new classical macroeconomic revolution.* Lucas argued that individuals' actions depend upon expected policies; therefore, the structure of the model will change as a policy is used. But if the underlying structure of the model changes, the appropriate policy will change and the model will no longer be the appropriate one. Thus, it is inappropriate to use econometric models to predict effects of future policy.

Other modern critics of modern macroeconometric models include David Hendry, who argues that macroeconometricians should use the latest techniques and heavy testing to get a fit of the data; that is, discovered statistical relationships should take precedence over theory. A third critic is Christopher Sims, whose argument is somewhat similar to Hendry's. He claims that current models impose too much theoretical structure on the data and that it would be better to impose no structure, essentially treating all variables as endogenous and using statistical techniques to reveal the relationships. He favors the use of vector autoregression, or ARIMA-type methods. These methods simply take all the numbers that one puts in and, without structure, find the best estimate of what those numbers would be in the future if the time structural relationship continued. Only the computer knows that underlying structure.

The vector autoregression approach is a modern reincarnation of the Mitchell approach, which focused on data with a minimum of theory. Traditional macroeconometricians point out that these new methods do not make use of any theoretical insights into the economy. Vector autoregression advocates respond, as did earlier critics of econometric theory, that the traditional macro models and structural models were based on such limited theory that it is better to have no theory.

*As with many insights, economists before Lucas were aware of these problems. It was discussed by the Cowles Commission in the late 1940s and can be found in the work of Jacob Marschak (1898–1977), Koopmans, and A. W. H. Phillips from the 1950s and 1960s. The influence of the critique, however, derives from Lucas's work.

cannot be duplicated, much less replicated, and that mistakes in published empirical articles are commonplace. Edward Leamer, an econometrician at UCLA, summarizes this view. He writes:

> the econometric modeling was done in the basement of the building and the econometric theory courses were taught on the top floor (the third). I was perplexed by the fact that the same language was used in both places. Even more amazing was the transmogrification of particular individuals who wantonly sinned in the basement and metamorphosed into the highest of high priests as they ascended to the third floor.[11]

[11] E. Leamer, *Specification Searches* (New York: Wiley, 1978), preface.

He suggests that one way out of the dilemma is to use Bayesian econometrics, in which a researcher's degree of belief is taken into account in any statistical test; but the process of doing this is so complicated that most researchers simply continue to do what they do. It is this difficulty of empirical testing that has spawned the rhetorical and sociological methodologies we described in Chapter 1.

BAYESIAN ECONOMETRICS

The Bayesian approach is a fundamentally different interpretation of the meaning of statistics. It proposes a subjective interpretation of statistics as opposed to an objective interpretation. Bayesians propose dropping the classical interpretation and, therefore, dropping traditional classical econometrics. Needless to say, there is significant controversy among statisticians about the Bayesian versus the classical method. An understanding of this difference is fundamental to an understanding of many of the confusions that surround econometric testing.

To see the distinction, suppose that we want to estimate the value of a parameter. In classical statistics, one arrives at a point estimate of the parameter that satisfies certain characteristics, such as *BLUE criteria* (best, linear, unbiased, estimator); in addition, it must have desirable asymptotic properties so that when large amounts of data are available, the estimate will converge to the true value of the parameter. The total focus in classical analysis is on the estimator and the statistics that characterize it.

In Bayesian analysis the interpretation of an estimator is quite different. Instead of producing a point estimate of data, Bayesian analysis produces a density function for data, which is called a posterior density function. The density function is not a sampling distribution. It can be interpreted only in reference to a prior conviction about what one believed. It is normally discussed as the odds a researcher would give when taking bets on the true value of data. It is a subjective notion of probability rather than an objective or frequentist notion of probability, as is the classical approach.

Thus, in the Bayesian approach one must specify one's initial degree of belief and use empirical evidence as a means of changing that degree of belief. One has both a prior density function and a posterior density function. In the Bayesian analysis one is simply using empirical data to modify one's prior beliefs, whereas in the classical approach one is continually attempting to establish the true nature of the model.

For the most part, economists have not used Bayesian methods. The reasons for this are not so much that they object to the underlying philosophical nature of subjectivist probability; instead, they are practical reasons: (1) formalizing prior beliefs into a formal distribution is difficult; (2) the mechanics of finding the posterior distribution are difficult; and (3) convincing others of the validity of Bayesian results is difficult because they are definitely contaminated or can only be interpreted by personal beliefs. These practical problems notwithstanding, a number of econometricians are seriously committed to Bayesian econometrics.

SUMMARY

It is difficult to evaluate recent developments in econometrics. Its history is one of unfulfilled hopes and expectations. These unfulfilled hopes are greater in macroeconometrics than in microeconometrics. We should, however, warn the reader that our view of the recent history of macroeconometric model building may be too pessimistic. The individuals who have been building these models feel as though progress has been made. Lawrence Klein and his colleagues have concluded:

> We find that many interesting lessons have been absorbed in the course of over a half century of macroeconomic model-building. Of course this is not to imply that progress in macroeconomic model-building has been linear or even monotonic or continuous. Some setbacks have occurred and with the wisdom of hindsight many things might have been done differently. But progress has been made and we feel that our knowledge of the real-world macroeconomy is considerably greater than it was a half century ago.[12]

This view, not ours, is probably the mainstream view. It would not be the view of the critics of traditional macroeconometrics, who argue that (1) mainstream structural models do not make clear what is being estimated and what is being tested, and (2) advocates claim far more for the models than is reasonable. It is not empirical work that critics question; it is the appropriate type of empirical work. There are attacks on both sides. Institutionalists want much more attention paid to qualitative data. Others want the computer to work on the data, unimpeded by theory. Still others want more complicated tests than those currently used.

Because microeconometrics focuses on partial equilibrium issues, it presents less severe methodological problems. Nonetheless, it has problems and critics. Specifically, critics charge that even microeconometrics requires information beyond what is available in economics, and that without controlled experiments, classical statistical tests do not mean what they purport to mean. As with macroeconometrics, the critics follow two quite different lines of argument: institutionalists claim that economists should focus more on educated, commonsense empiricism that better integrates institutional and historical knowledge; and Bayesian critics argue that we need more technical tests that capture the subjective nature of statistics.

It is difficult to evaluate recent developments in econometrics. Epstein, in his study of the history of econometrics, captures the sentiments of many of its critics.

[12] Ronald Bodkin, Lawrence Klein, and Kanta Marwah, *A History of Macroeconometric Model Building* (Edward Elgar, 1991), pp. 553–554.

Econometrics is possibly unique among the sciences for aspiring to great quantitative precision without benefit of controlled experiments or large samples from uniform, stable populations. Experience to date suggests that even the largest models have precise but simplistic structures which represent actual phenomena to a very low number of significant digits. The research program of the American Institutionalists . . . by contrast was quantitatively imprecise but stressed a complex, disaggregated, historical approach to economic structure. Their policies were most successful when the problems under attack were rather specific and allowed experimentation in the form of "learning by doing," e.g., design of an unemployment insurance program, implementation of a labor mediation board, or administration of a ration program. A further key factor was a detailed understanding of the diverse circumstances and motives of the different economic groups affected by these measures. By contrast, there is some justice to Vining's (1949) observation that the econometricians seem to be concerned with nothing less than the "pathology of entire civilizations." This study would suggest that the imprecision of many econometric models is an inevitable result of greatly simplified explanations of economic phenomena. It may be most fruitful for econometric analyses to be conducted on a new level where institutional constraints and individual behavior are more clearly discernible.[13]

Key Terms

commonsense empiricism
statistical analysis
measurement without theory
classical econometrics
Bayesian econometrics
mathematical economics
econometrics

Jevons's sunspot theory
identification problem
Moore's dynamic demand curve
probabilistic approach
cliometrics
data mining
BLUE criteria

Questions for Review, Discussion, and Research

1. How might supporters of commonsense empiricism defend themselves from the criticism that they are simply unable to understand the technical issues that econometrics resolves?
2. Is "measurement without theory" a fair summary of the institutionalist approach to empirical work?
3. Distinguish econometrics from mathematical economics.
4. How can Moore's upward-sloping demand for pig iron be justified?
5. How would you explain obtaining different elasticity estimates, depending on whether you regressed price on quantity or quantity on price?
6. What is the identification problem? How did Working solve it?
7. What is the probabilistic approach to econometrics? Why is it important?

[13] R. J. Epstein, *A History of Econometrics* (Chicago: University of Illinois at Chicago Press, 1987), pp. 217–218.

8. Why does data mining undermine the classical econometric approach?
9. What do you think W. C. Mitchell might have thought about Christopher Sims's vector autoregression approach to macroeconometrics?
10. Distinguish between the classical and the Bayesian approaches to econometrics.
11. This time, that absent-minded professor is doing an article on empirical methods in economics. She remembers that somewhere in an article, or more likely a published comment, Keynes attacked Tinbergen's econometric approach. She liked one of Keynes's comments in that article so much that she jotted it down, but as is her way, she forgot to jot down the citation. The quotation is:

> It will be remembered that the seventy translators of the Septuagint were shut up in seventy separate rooms with the Hebrew text and brought out with them, when they emerged, seventy identical translations. Would the same miracle be vouchsafed if seventy multiple correlators were shut up with the same statistical material?

Your assignment is to find the citation for the article.

Suggested Readings

Basmann, Robert, and Nancy Wulwick. "Reflections on the History of Econometrics." *Methodus* (June 1992), 154–165.

Bodkin, Ronald, Lawrence Klein, and Kanta Marwah. *A History of Macroeconometric Model Building*. Brookfield, Vt.: Edward Elgar, 1991.

Burns, Arthur, and W. C. Mitchell. *Measuring Business Cycles*. New York: National Bureau of Economic Research, 1946.

Colander, David, and Reuven Brenner. *Educating Economists*. Ann Arbor: University of Michigan Press, 1992.

Epstein, Roy J. *A History of Econometrics*. Chicago: University of Illinois at Chicago Press, 1987.

Fogel, Robert William. *Without Consent or Contract: The Rise and Fall of American Slavery*. New York: W. W. Norton, 1989.

Leamer, E. "Let's Take the Con Out of Econometrics." *American Economic Review*, 73 (March 1978), 31–43.

———. *Specification Searches*. New York: Wiley, 1978.

Morgan, Mary S. *The History of Econometric Ideas*. Cambridge: Cambridge University Press, 1990.

Stigler, George. "Henry L. Moore and Statistical Economics" and "The Early History of Empirical Studies of Consumer Behavior." In *Essays in the History of Economics*. Chicago: University of Chicago Press, 1965.

Stigler, Stephen M. *The History of Statistics*. Cambridge, Mass.: Belknap Press of Harvard University Press, 1986.

Index

Absolute value
  and J. S. Mill, 164
  Ricardo on, 117
Absolutist approach, 4
  and Whigs, 4
abstinence interest theory
  Senior on, 152–153
Abstraction
  and preclassical theory, 25–26
  and St. Thomas Aquinas, 25–26, 32–33
Adams, John, 382
Affluent society
  Galbraith on, 397–398, 400
Akerlof, George, 432
Alchian, Armen, 435
Alienation
  Marx on, 178–179
Allais, Maurice, 418
Allen, R. G. D.
  and indifference curves, 439
American economics
  and German historical school, 325
Analytic theory
  defined, 463
Anderson, James
  and diminishing returns, 110
Applebaum, Eileen
  on radical economics, 386–388
Aquinas, St. Thomas, 29–32
  and abstraction, 25–26
  and Aristotle, 27
  as abstract thinker, 32–33
  on just price, 30–32
  on private property, 30
Aristotle, 27–28
  and socialists, 28
  and St. Thomas Aquinas, 27
  and utopians, 28
  on needs and desires, 27
Arrow, Kenneth, 418
  and general equilibrium, 278
  and general equilibrium theory, 424
  and state preference theory, 442

  and welfare economics, 445
Art of economics
  and methodology, 132
  and Ricardo, 104–105, 132
  and Smith, 70–71
  J. N. Keynes on, 287–288
Ashley, William, 328
Austrian economics
  and entrepreneurship, 406–407
  and Hayek, 406–407
  and Mises, 406–407
  in twentieth century, 406–407
Austrians
  second generation, 228–230
Ayres, Clarence, 389–390
  and John Dewey, 390
  and University of Texas, 389, 346
Bagehot, Walter, 328
  and Marshall, 286
Banking School, 169
Baran, Paul
  and radical economics, 384–386
Barone, Enrico, 364
  and product exhaustion, 244
  Samuelson on, 364
Baumol, W. J.
  and transformation problem, 191
Bayes, Thomas, 492 fn
Bayesian econometrics, 492, 514–515
Becker, Gary, 418, 442
  and modern microeconomics, 435–436
Bell Clive, 461
Bentham, Jeremy
  and hedonism, 439
  and J. S. Mill, 144, 156–157
Bergson, Abram
  and income accounting, 507
  and welfare economics, 445
  on debate on socialism, 369
  on Mises and Hayek, 367–369
Berlin, Isaiah
  on Marx, 177

DATE DUE

APR 1 6 2002			
FE 20 '06			
APR 1 0 2011			

GAYLORD | | | PRINTED IN U.S.A

IMPORTANT PUBLICATIONS IN ECONOMICS (cont.)

DATE	AUTHOR	PUBLICATION	COMMENT
1922	Irving Fisher	*The Making of Index Numbers*	quantitative methods
1926	Piero Sraffa	"Laws of Returns Under Competitive Conditions"	market structures
1927	E. J. Working	"Statistical Demand Curves"	early econometrics
1928	Henry Schultz	*Statistical Laws of Demand and Supply*	empirical method
1930	Gunnar Myrdal	*Political Element in the Development of Theory*	methodology
1931	F. A. von Hayek	*Prices and Production*	business cycle theory
1931	Jacob Viner	"Cost Curves and Supply Curves"	microtheory
1932	Gustav Cassel	*Theory of Social Economy*	general equilibrium theory
1933	E. H. Chamberlin	*Theory of Monopolistic Competition*	market structures
1933	Joan Robinson	*Economics of Imperfect Competition*	market structures
1933	Michal Kalecki	*Essays on Business Cycles*	macro model some consider superior to Keynesian
1934	Ragnar Frisch	*Statistical Confluence Analysis*	econometrics
1934	John R. Commons	*Institutional Economics*	Wisconsin school of institutionalism
1935	F. A. von Hayek	*Collectivist Economic Planning*	allocation under socialism
1936	John Maynard Keynes	*The General Theory*	start of Keynesian revolution
1936	Oscar Lange	*Economic Theory of Socialism*	allocation under socialism
1937	Maurice Dobb	*Political Economy and Capitalism*	Marxist critic of orthodox theory
1937	F. A. von Hayek	"Economics and Knowledge"	market as a discovery process
1939	John R. Hicks	*Value and Capital*	general equilibrium theory, indifference curves
1939	Jan Tinbergen	*Statistical Testing of Business Cycle Theories*	econometrics
1940	Ludwig von Mises	*Human Action*	Austrian economics
1941	Wassily Leontief	*Structure of the American Economy*	input-output model
1942	Paul Sweezy	*Theory of Capitalist Development*	modern interpretation of Marx